Louis Rukeyser's Business Almanac

LOUIS RUKEYSER
Editor-in-Chief

JOHN COONEY
Managing Editor

GEORGE WINSLOW
Chief Researcher

SIMON AND SCHUSTER
New York   London   Toronto   Sydney   Tokyo

Published by Simon and Schuster
A Division of Simon & Schuster Inc.
Simon & Schuster Building
Rockefeller Center
1230 Avenue of the Americas
New York, NY 10020

SIMON AND SCHUSTER and colophon are registered trademarks
of Simon & Schuster Inc.

Designed by Irving Perkins Associates
Manufactured in the United States of America

10 9 8 7 6 5 4 3 2 1

LIBRARY OF CONGRESS
Library of Congress Cataloging-in-Publication Data

Louis Rukeyser's business almanac / Louis Rukeyser, editor-in-chief;
    John Cooney, managing editor; George Winslow, chief researcher.

    p.   cm.
    Includes index.
    ISBN 0-671-61892-X
    1. United States—Economic conditions—1981– 2. Industry and
state—United States. 3. United States—Industries. 4. Finance—
United States. I. Rukeyser, Louis. II. Cooney, John.
III. Winslow, George.   IV. Title: Business almanac.
HC106.8.L67 1988   88-3089
330.973'0927—dc19   CIP

ACKNOWLEDGMENTS

Foremost, we wish to thank Fred Hills, our editor who from the outset understood why there should be this book and whose advice and editing were invaluable. We also wish to thank Alex Kamaroff of the Irene Goodman Literary Agency, who first believed in the *Business Almanac*.

Putting together a book of this magnitude requires the help of a great many people. We would like to thank James Winslow and Frank D'Angelo for their painstaking research and fact checking. We also owe a debt of gratitude to Steve Messina for his extremely thorough copy editing and Jenny Cox for her editorial work.

Others we should thank right away include Ivan Boesky, who showed that arbitrageurs can lead lives as exciting and shady as Mississippi riverboat gamblers; T. Boone Pickens, who managed to scare half of corporate America to death with his takeover raids on companies, and USX Corporation for coming up with one of the dumbest and least imaginative corporate names ever, replacing "Steel" with an "X," as it tried to weasel out of the fact that it bore a lot of responsibility for how lousy America's steel industry has become.

In addition, there were hundreds of people at companies, government agencies, trade associations, and elsewhere who assisted us by providing facts and figures. We are indebted to them all and we appreciate their generosity. We also wish to thank the Standard & Poor's analysts, financial experts, *Wall Street Journal* writers and editors, and others who were kind enough to read sections of the book to determine whether our work contained any glaring omissions or blunders.

In particular, we would like to thank the following people:

James L. Loper, Academy of Television Arts and Sciences
AFL-CIO
Andrew J. Sobel, Airport Operators Council International
David Cohen, American Bankers Association
Charles Antin, American Booksellers Association
American Business Women's Association

M. Jane Moss, American Car Rental Association
William E. Kingsley, American Council of Life Insurance
John Hatch, American Electronics Association
Douglas G. Pinkham, American Gas Association
Steven E. Trombetti, American Hotel and Motel Association
Samuel C. Hoyt, American Institute of Certified Public Accountants
James Hughes, American Iron and Steel Institute
Thomas R. Horton, American Management Association
Wayne A. Lemburg, American Marketing Association
Cyndee Miller, American Marketing Association
Jens Knutson, American Meat Institute
John A. Knebel, American Mining Congress
Joseph J. Lorfano, American Newspaper Publishers Association
Linda Rogers, American Petroleum Institute
Charlotte Scroggins, American Productivity Center
C. A. Siegfried, Jr., American Rental Association
Catherine D. Bower, American Society for Personnel Administration
Helen Frank Bensimon, American Society for Training and Development
Bob Schabazian, American Stock Exchange
James A. Morrissey, American Textile Manufacturers Institute
Linda Rothbart, American Trucking Associations
William W. Carpenter, Amusement and Music Operators Association
Associated General Contractors of America
Association of Bank Holding Companies
Marsha D. Lewin, Association of Management Consultants
J. Christopher Svare, Bank Administration Institute
Philip C. Katz, Beer Institute
Charles L. Smith III, *Black Enterprise* magazine
Barbara A. Schwartz, Chicago Board of Trade
Ann Richardson, Club Managers Association of America
J. Dudley Waldner, Comic Magazine Association of America Inc.
George N. Christie, Credit Research Foundation
Jim Williams, Credit Union National Association
Bill Daniels, Daniels & Associates
Colette M. Urban, Data Processing Management Association
Karen Wysocki, Direct Marketing Association
Mark V. Rosenker, Electronic Industries Association
Frank B. McArdle, Employee Benefit Research Institute
Lance A. Selfa, Farm and Industrial Equipment Institute
Fertilizer Institute
Robert Van Riper, Financial Accounting Foundation
Barbara L. McBride, Food Marketing Institute
Annette Green, Fragrance Foundation
Vincent L. Turzo, Gulfstream Financial Associates Inc.
George W. Wells, Health Insurance Association of America
Matthew D. Ubben, Helicopter Association International

Raymond C. Ellis, Jr., The Hospitality, Lodging & Travel Research Foundation Inc.
Independent Bankers Association of America
Cathryn E. Kittell, The Institute of Chartered Financial Analysts
Carol Fraser, Insurance Information Institute
Hubert L. Harris, International Association for Financial Planning
International Association of Amusement Parks and Attractions
John Chapman, International Council of Shopping Centers
Scott F. Gray, International Exhibitors Association
William B. Cherkasky, International Franchise Association
Marvin Gropp, Magazine Publishers Association
Bruce Butterfield, Manufactured Housing Institute
Joyce Healy, Manufacturers Hanover Trust
Susan Boucher, Manufacturing Jewelers & Silversmiths of America
Jeffrey R. Waddle, Meeting Planners International
Warren Lasko, Mortgage Bankers Association of America
Teri Brouwer, Motorcycle Industry Council
National Association of Accountants
Walter W. Wurfel, National Association of Broadcasters
Enno Hobbing, National Association of Securities Dealers
Louise Gates, National Association of Temporary Services
National Association of Wholesaler-Distributors
Richard Lampl, National Business Aircraft Association
Lynn E. McReynolds, National Cable Television Association
Corey Rosen, National Center for Employee Ownership
Laura M. Oatney, National Futures Association
James A. Gray, National Machine Tool Builders' Association
Ann Walker Smalley, National Restaurant Association
Julie P. McCahill, National Soft Drink Association
James Dunaway, Newspaper Advertising Bureau, Inc.
Profit Sharing Council of America
P. Robert Farley, Publishers Information Bureau
Daniel S. Flamberg, Radio Advertising Bureau
Mary Walker Fleischmann, Real Estate Securities and Syndication Institute
Alan Gottesman, L. F. Rothschild & Co.
Linda Rohr Weber, Salomon Brothers
Evan Cooper, Securities Industry Association
H. Ted Olson, Specialty Advertising Association, International
Adele Archer, Standard & Poor's
Mark Bachmann, Standard & Poor's
Michael Crehan, Standard & Poor's
Daniel DiSenso, Standard & Poor's
Denise Gleason, Standard & Poor's
Heather Goodchild, Standard & Poor's
John Hardy, Standard & Poor's

Gerald Hirschberg, Standard & Poor's
Andrew Hornick, Standard & Poor's
Thomas Hyland, Standard & Poor's
Joseph Hynes, Standard & Poor's
Michael Kaplan, Standard & Poor's
Byron Klapper, Standard & Poor's
Thomas Mockler, Standard & Poor's
Robert Nelson, Standard & Poor's
Norman Schindler, Standard & Poor's
Richard Siderman, Standard & Poor's
Scott Sprinzen, Standard & Poor's
Edward Tyburczy, Standard & Poor's
Angela Uttaro, Standard & Poor's
William Wetreich, Standard & Poor's
William Wong, Standard & Poor's
Marci Shapiro, Standard & Poor's
Mauri Edwards, The Sunglass Association of America
Robert M. Grebe, Television Bureau of Advertising
James B. Poteat, Television Information Office
Douglas Thomson, Toy Manufacturers of America
William W. Mee, Trade Show Bureau
Kathy Baumann, United States Telephone Association
Douglas Frechtling, U.S. Travel Data Center
William Carley, *The Wall Street Journal*
Sandy Jacobs, *The Wall Street Journal*
Dan Machalaba, *The Wall Street Journal*
Alfred L. Malabre, Jr., *The Wall Street Journal*
Tim Metz, *The Wall Street Journal*
Stanley Penn, *The Wall Street Journal*
Roger Ricklefs, *The Wall Street Journal*
Jeff Tannenbaum, *The Wall Street Journal*
Hank Gilman, *The Boston Globe*

CONTENTS

PREFACE

With the possible exceptions of sex and baseball, no subject in America is the object of so much uninformed bombast as the state of business and the economy. And why not? As Talcott Williams, first director of the Columbia University Graduate School of Journalism, remarked in 1913, "All men have opinions; few men think." It's plainly a more reliable source of emotional release, not to mention much more fun, to vent one's spleen against enemies real or imagined than to engage in the painful process of confronting reality. Wallowing in prejudice and paranoia can be a marvelous substitute for mastering facts, provided only that you view life as your personal psychiatrist's couch. If, on the other hand, you are actually concerned with learning something and/or getting ahead, you may want to try a different tack. And that's where this book comes in.

The most astounding thing about this tome is that it wasn't done long ago. Anyone who, like myself, has gone looking for some specific piece of information on the economic scene and then spent hours tracking down a source that properly should have been right at hand will appreciate the value of having a single volume covering so much of interest and importance about American business. For this, all manner of credit is due to the Herculean efforts of Managing Editor John Cooney and Chief Researcher George Winslow, who by now are surely capable of putting themselves to sleep by reciting employment statistics and trade trends, and therefore will have no further need in this lifetime for the conventional counting of sheep. What they have produced, boiling away the nonessential and shaping the fascinating, has already been of immense use to me, as I hope it will be to you.

Change is the theme of this book, as it is the theme of life. Understanding the relationship between the past and the present is a prerequisite for mastering the future. Tomorrow's winners are unlikely to be those people who say, like the character in the old joke, "My mind's made up; don't confuse me with facts." The successes of the last decade of the twentieth century are far more likely to be built on the words of Francis Bacon, who declared in 1597, "Knowledge is power." The prolific English essayist, philosopher, and statesman, a tremendously busy man even if he didn't write Shakespeare's plays, delivered his insight centuries before the information explosions from computers, opinion polls, and magazines specifically designed for red-haired carpenter-skiers. But it is still the way to bring home the bacon today.

Our concern here is to go beyond the mere reporting of numbers and to give you a sense of what they may mean to you. Hence, for example, we tell you the facts on the aging of America and then report both the favorable and unfavorable implications of this phenomenon. (My own bias, incidentally, is unreservedly in favor of continued aging. The alternative, as I understand it, is worse.) This kind of knowledge is essential to an understanding of the future prospects in this country of everything from selling pizzas to funding Social Security. And in addition to their obvious utility on the job and in financial matters, such data can make terrific family dinner-table conversation. We learn, for instance, that the median age of the population today is roughly twice what it was in 1820, when the average American was less than 17 years old. Don't despair, though; he probably thought his parents were squares, too.

None of us, of course, is truly average. Did you drink your assigned 24 gallons of beer last year? And if you did, how did you possibly find room for your 238 pounds of milk and cream as well? (One possible answer, we learn, is that 62 percent of Americans are overweight. Those 8 million bagels we eat every day probably don't help.) I haven't got around to measuring yet, so I can't tell you whether I personally am producing the typical citizen's allotted 3.43 daily pounds of garbage, but if you count all the Wall Street reports I have to read each week, I suspect that is a distinct underestimate in my case. Garbage in, garbage out.

While we're being personal, I suspect that each of us will at least subconsciously be superimposing his or her own job history on the account of the changing patterns of employment in America. In less than a century, the majority of American workers have gone from overalls to blue collars to pinstripes. Women now account for two out of three net new workers, changing the lives and the minds of every American. Columbia's Talcott Williams, were he commenting today, three quarters of a century later, would undoubtedly be pressured to substitute "persons" for "men" in his memorable quote about thinking (though, in truth, many women may find the original version more telling). We report both the passing problems and the ultimate hope of moving toward a society that uses the full economic and human potential of all its citizens.

Some of the findings are unexpectedly happy. The right to bellyache about the boss is part of the Constitution, and one of the most frequently exercised portions thereof, but we find that an overwhelming majority of major lottery winners decide to keep on punching the same old time clock. Could it be that most Americans are less miserable than some of our weepier literature suggests?

I am reminded of a couple of visits I made to Iowa State University in the 1970s, at a time when farmland prices were soaring as unrestrainedly as they later tumbled. After my second speech in Ames, while chatting with some members of the faculty, I said: "Look, I've never claimed to be an expert on agricultural economics, but I can add. I know the average price of Iowa farmland today; I know the average size of an Iowa farm, and I have some idea of the capital costs involved in farming. Put all those numbers together, and the clear conclusion is that the average Iowa farmer today is a paper millionaire. Now, I know all the counterarguments: he doesn't live like a millionaire, he doesn't have the cash flow of a millionaire. But assuming that the paper calculations are right, why don't more Iowa farmers sell out and move to Scottsdale?"

The reply was illuminating. "Well, some do," I was told, "but you have to remember that the average farmer likes to farm. We like to tell the story around here of the Iowa farmer who hit the lottery for two million dollars. A reporter asked him, 'Henry, what are you going to do with all that money?' And Henry answered, 'I guess I'll just keep on farming till it's gone.' "

So it is with many of us: we just plain like what we're doing. But like Henry himself, who at times in the eighties may have regretted his earlier resistance to change, we are likely to wind up wealthier and wiser if we improve our information and understanding. This book tries to help both with the broad issues of American business and with the practical details, from investing and personal finance to the worlds of culture and entertainment, that may enable you to plow your personal plot with deeper delight and more fertile profit in the years ahead. Please look on this book as a collaboration that very much includes you: if an error has crept in, or if there's something not here that you'd like to see in a future edition, please do let us know. It's your almanac, too, and here's hoping that all your business turns out to be just great.

Louis Rukeyser

Louis Rukeyser

HOW TO USE THIS BOOK

Why a business almanac?

The answer is simple. Until now, there hasn't been one around and there should be. Over the years we could have saved an awful lot of time looking up the potpourri of business and economic information we have compiled here. What makes the almanac unique is that it tells us as much about ourselves as about our corporate society. How we earn our money. How we spend our money. Who woos our money. Who steals our money. Who has most of the money. Who doesn't.

The list goes on. Who, for instance, are the richest men and women in America? The highest paid executives? Which are the biggest companies in the nation? Which are the most secretive? What's the background of this T. Boone Pickens character? And what kind of a businessman is Ralph Lauren?

Just what is the International Monetary Fund? Who were the robber barons and what did they do? Who are the biggest crooks around today? How about arms dealers? What have been the biggest-grossing movies, books, record albums, videotapes?

You'll find the answers to these questions and hundreds more right here, organized in such a way that they can be found individually or read in conjunction with related facts and information—the big picture as well as the fascinating details of our economic history and our everyday business life.

Although, of course, we couldn't put *everything* in these pages, we've tried to make the almanac comprehensive. And we hope it is a compendium that entertains as well as informs. Thus, there is plenty for everyone: little-known facts for the trivia buffs, basic information for those who are unfamiliar with business, and a lot of useful information for everyone, no matter what his or her level of business or financial sophistication.

The gamut of information runs from small businesses to big businesses, from advertising to unions, from ingenious inventors and entrepreneurs to the corporate heavy hitters. We sought out the successes and the screwups, the visionaries and the scallywags. And the book is thoroughly indexed. You can easily turn to sections for information that interests you the most and the facts you need the most, all compiled from the most authoritative and up-to-date sources.

Here's how the book is put together:

We lead off with "The Economy: What's Going On Here?" The U.S. economy is in a state of transition with a lot of factors working on it for good and ill. If you number among the folks who find it baffling, don't despair. Throughout the rest of the book you'll find the facts and figures, the trends and statistics that will bring it all into focus.

Part I deals with "People in Business." That's us, the people who work (and, unfortunately, those of us who aren't working if we want to be) and what we're like—the jobs we hold, the money we make, and what the work world holds if we are men, women, minorities, and union members.

Part II is called "The Haves." Just what is money and who are the folks who have most of it? Here are the old family money and the nouveau billionaires, how they got it and how they keep it—or lose it.

Part III concerns "The Heavy Hand." This section is about the government's role in our economy—how it works and how it got the way it is. We also look at the power brokers who shape the laws that govern corporate America: the lobbyists, the regulators, and the taxmen.

Part IV deals with "The Business of Business." It discusses the businesses that are expanding and those that are contracting—our booming services and our eroding manufacturing. Here are also the small businesses that come and go, providing so much of our economic vitality.

Part V is about "The Money Game"—the markets for stocks and bonds, futures and mutual funds. There's an explanation of each of those markets and how they have been acting in the 1980s. Here, too, you can find out about insurance and pensions, Social Security and real estate.

Part VI details the nation's "Widget Makers." Here's a breakdown of scores of businesses and industries and what's going on in them. We've included descriptions of how each industry is doing as well as profiles of many important people and companies, tables that show trends, and the trivia, which often reveals more about an industry than any table possibly can.

Finally, we give a rundown of "The Heavy Hitters: America's Biggest Companies." Here are financial profiles of the leading utilities as well as industrial, transportation, retailing, and financial companies, the money they've made, and their return to investors.

Overall, the book is a look at business in America, what we have created and how it shapes our lives. Here are the facts and figures, stories behind successes and flops, and a wealth of business lore that hasn't been compiled in any other book.

We hope you enjoy it. Perhaps more than that, we hope you find it useful.

The Economy: An Overview

THE ECONOMY

The U.S. economy has slogged into an era that can be called the Great Time of Doubt. After breathlessly extolling the wonders of an economically strong America during the booming 1960s, economists wrung their hands and beat their breasts in the 1970s and 1980s as they saw signs of fiscal doom everywhere. Now the economic soothsayers are hedging their bets.

The Cassandras of yore had reason to be teary—actually, a lot of reasons. In the 1970s, inflation and double-digit interest rates were growing faster than a 13-year-old boy. The ranks of the jobless were swelling at a terrible pace. Debt was weighing down both consumers and business like Mafia-style cement shoes. And trade was showing a nagging deficit, which would have been fine if the nag hadn't turned into a scold in the 1980s.

Surely even our politicians could see something was wrong. Surely they wanted to do something about it. Well, they did. At least they said they did. But being politicians, they were better at promising than delivering panaceas for our economic ills. The one lesson our presidents consistently teach us is that their economic elixirs are never all they're cracked up to be. Often they just muck things up even more. Maybe we should be grateful their cures aren't fatal.

Not so strangely, though, they all find economists who tout whatever is the muddled presidential economic message of the moment as the right one. After all, why should a president hear what he doesn't want to hear? Wouldn't it be refreshing for a president or presidential candidate to answer the question, "What's going to happen with the economy?" with "Who knows?" Because nobody really does.

That's especially true because the Great Time of Doubt persisted until 1988. From one month to the next, the economy baffled just about everybody. Sometimes it seemed as if we were headed into a recession. Other times it seemed as if we were poised for an expansion. After the stock market crash of October 1987, a recession appeared almost inevitable. Then it didn't. Then it did.

1

So what have we got here? The answer is an economy still reeling from the harsh monetary and fiscal policies of the decade. Such policies loaded more than $1 trillion onto the federal debt while bashing inflation down from double-digit levels to 4.4% by 1987. For its part, the dollar was like an erratic cruise missile—soaring in the early to mid-1980s and then nose-diving and then jiggling.

The economy has been shaken by the phenomenon described by the 1980s buzzword *disinflation,* the process of bringing inflation down. The Federal Reserve Board's vigorous monetary policy from 1979 to 1982 actually ended double-digit inflation, but there's always a price to be paid for anything good. The fallout included having product prices tumble for certain key sectors of the economy: farming, manufacturing, and oil production.

And the policy also helped bring on our horrendous trade problems. It's not too hard to figure out how. Where did the nation turn to finance big budget deficits and spur expansion when the Fed got stringent about money? Overseas, of course. A swollen river of foreign capital roared into the U.S. That sent the dollar heading toward the moon. As a result, imports got cheap. Thus, the trade deficit headed toward the moon too.

So what do you do when the dollar goes up like a helium balloon that a child accidentally let go of? Try to grab the string and pull it back down. In 1985, Treasury Secretary James Baker began trying to pull the dollar down. Meanwhile, the trade deficit ballooned to $171.2 billion in 1987, and in 1988 the size of the deficit gasped in and out, contracting a little, expanding a little. The lesson: dollars that go up easily don't necessarily come down easily. And when they come down, they can come down too far.

And in the midst of all this, there have been those mixed economic signals—some good, some bad.

First the good news. Unemployment, inflation, and interest rates fell well below what they were. Until the market meltdown in October 1987, the stock market was on one of its best rolls ever. So wealth, at least in terms of portfolios, was greater than ever, which helped the economy for quite a while.

Statistics and generalities, of course, mask how individuals are making out. Most investment bankers, at least those who aren't worried about going to jail for insider trading, would tend to agree that the economy was better in 1987 than it was 10 or 15 years earlier. But try to tell a farmer or an oilman in the late 1980s that business has been great.

Most pharmaceutical executives should be pleased with the way business boomed, but there are a lot of long faces in the steel mills. And thanks to improved benefits, today's new retirees, for the most part, are better off than people who retired 30 years ago, but today's college graduates probably have a tougher time getting the kinds of jobs they want than did graduates 20 years ago. They are all experiencing the mix of good and bad in the economy.

As for the bad, there's plenty of it. The most spectacular came in October 1987 when the market made everybody uneasy by going into those wild gyrations that saw it plunge 508 points in just one day, October 19, the worst drop on record, which ended the best run-up on record. More than $500 billion in asset value was erased overnight, bringing total losses for a two-month period to more than $1 trillion. And that made *caution* the new buzzword, which, of course, has a negative connotation for the economy.

But stock prices are a less than perfect indicator of what's ahead for business. Stock market declines signaled the eight post-World War II recessions, but stocks fell by more than 10% on no fewer than 19 other occasions during this period. In other words, to modernize an observation made years ago by economist Paul Samuelson, the stock market predicted 27 of the last eight recessions.

So the Wall Street debacle doesn't necessarily mean that the economy has to fall through the floor and that the troubling market movements were echoes of the crash of 1929. But worried shareholders often think twice or thrice about what they will buy, and that worry can squeeze the economy. Few economists saw a rerun of the Great Depression but they all went scrambling back to their drawing boards to revise downward their figures on how the economy would fare.

Even so, there seemed to have been a silver lining to the crash. Long-term interest rates dropped by more than a percentage point right after the crash and lower rates usually give a boost to the economy. Also, the White House began rousing itself to confront the problems it had been sleeping on for years. The Reagan administration and Congress were shoved into almost serious negotiations on cutting the budget deficit. But neither side seemed willing to put any significant sacred cows on the chopping block.

What the market skid did was simply point out some of the horrors that were mounting for years, especially the bleak U.S. trade and deficit figures. Budget deficits have been around an awe-inspiring $200 billion in recent years. The Reagan administration also gets the dubious achievement award for attaining what once would have seemed ludicrous: the U.S. has the distinction, for the first time since the First World War, of owing foreigners more than they owe us. And the lower dollar and the trade retaliation nonsense in 1987 haven't dramatically improved the trade picture.

Moreover, American manufacturing almost became something people talk about in the past tense, as the productivity gains of American workers continued to disappoint. Also, we'll have to see how the tax overhaul shakes out. Cross your fingers.

Through it all, the administration has said—over and over—that a boom is just around the corner; well, maybe the next corner. Just be patient. Meanwhile, the ranks of the administration's cheerleaders thinned quite a bit and the Cassandras revved up for a good blast of gloom and doom.

If you look at the record, the law of averages was on the side of the Cassandras. The economic expansion of the 1980s is traceable to late 1982. The fact that it lasted with a few fits and starts until 1987 was remarkable if only because the five previous peacetime growth periods lasted only an average of 33 months. By that measure, simply avoiding a recession as long as we did was a big deal.

So with nothing fitting previous patterns, who can blame economists (artists or scientists or whatever they claim to be) if they aren't too sure which prediction to hang themselves by today? After all, nobody has ever before witnessed such behavior in the modern economic world.

Even though the forces at work on the economy and the economy itself are different from what we have ever experienced, there are some ways to get a better idea of what kind of shape the economy is in in the late 1980s. That means stepping back a bit and seeing what the economy did previously.

We can start with that ingenious barometer known as the misery index, the creation of Arthur Okun, chairman of President Johnson's Council of Economic Advisers. Arriving at the index is so simple, you don't even have to say, "Economic mumbo jumbo." Just add the annual inflation rate to the unemployment rate. Presto! You now know whether the mood of the nation is upbeat or downbeat.

Okun contended that when the combination hit 9%, the nation toppled into unhappiness. If it hit 20% or higher, the nation was miserable. In 1987, with a jobless rate of 6.2% and inflation having gone up 4.4%, we were an uneasy 10.6%.

Although the misery index sounds too simple to be accurate, Okun may have had something here. In 1976, when Jimmy Carter was president, unemployment stood at 7.6% and inflation had gone up to 5.8%, for an unhappy 13.4%; the year Carter was voted out of office, the index reached a miserable 20.6%. In prosperous and presumably happy, if not ecstatic, 1966, unemployment was a low 3.7% while inflation grew 2.9% for a benign 6.6%. And people who get nostalgic for the Eisenhower era may have their memories influenced by a 4% unemployment rate coupled with an annual inflation rate increase of only 1.5% for a seemingly serene 5.5% in 1956.

OUR CHANGED ECONOMY

Economies are always in a state of flux, but until we actually examine our own it's frequently hard to see just how dramatic the change can be. The change affects everything from how much we earn to the jobs we hold, the balance of political power domestically, and our foreign relations. Sometimes it's startling to note.

The once-mighty steel companies and their politically powerful unions, for instance, are mere troubled shadows of their former glorious selves. The industry was devastated by a combination of management's not investing in badly needed plants and equipment, unreasonable labor demands, ham-handed government regulatory and tax policies, and cheaper imports. And the combination of woes reflects, to a large degree, what has been happening to the manufacturing sector of our economy.

The biggest structural change in the economy has been the switch over to a service economy from a goods-producing economy. Service-producing businesses such as real estate, insurance, finance, retailing, and health care accounted for 75% of jobs by 1987, up from 46% in 1955. Meanwhile, our goods producers, the manufacturing, construction, and mining sectors, accounted for only 24.5% of all civilian nonagricultural jobs, down from 41% in 1955. (The drop in farm jobs as a percentage of civilian employment has been even more dramatic. Today, only 2.9% of jobs are held by farm workers, down from 21% in 1940.)

There's no reason to believe the service economy won't keep gaining ground. A Conference Board study, for instance, concludes that just about all U.S. job growth through the rest of the century will be in the service area. The report sees the biggest job jumps in the goods-distribution chain, such as in retailing and wholesaling; in people-tending industries such as health care; and, because we are a nation of slobs producing nearly 150 million tons of garbage a year, in "cleaner-upper" jobs, because "a litter-prone society requires plenty of manpower to handle its mess."

There has been change in income as well. Employee compensation, including wages, salaries, and benefits, has climbed steadily over the past 30 years to about 75% of total income from about 67%. Interest income has climbed to more than 10% in the 1980s from less than 2% in the 1950s. But the share of income from corporate profits has dwindled to about 8% in the 1980s from 14% in the 1950s. And rental income is now less than 1%, down from 4% of all income 30 years ago.

But while wages have climbed, productivity hasn't kept pace. Lagging productivity has become one of the nation's biggest problems. A factory worker who gets $1 an hour more has to produce $1 worth of goods more just for his output to remain the same. In the 1980s, average hourly wages have risen 3.9% a year, but output has only risen by one-third that amount. Just how bad things have gotten was revealed in a Labor Department study of average yearly productivity gains from 1973 to 1984 for eight industrial nations: U.S. performance was the worst: Belgium, 6.2%; Japan, 5.9%; France, 6.4%; the Netherlands, 4.6%; Italy, 3.8%; West Germany, 3.4%; Great Britain, 2.3%; the U.S., 2.1%.

Part of the productivity problem comes from the shift to a service economy. It's usually a lot harder to show productivity gains in service jobs. As more and more jobs wind up in that category, the problem becomes greater. But another factor is the failure of U.S. companies, compared to those in other countries, to plow money back into plants and equipment that will prod productivity. The wreckage of the once-mighty U.S. steel industry is a constant reminder of that.

Some aspects of the economy don't change all that much. Consumer spending, for instance, is about two thirds of the gross national product (GNP), about the same as it has been for the past 30 years. Business spending on capital equipment, however, fluctuates somewhat: 12% or more of the GNP in recent years; 9% in the 1960s; 11% in the 1950s. Likewise, defense spending is now around 7% of the GNP, up from 5% in the late 1970s but down from 14% in the 1950s.

One big and worrisome change in the economy is the increase in federal, consumer, and corporate debt in the mid- and late 1980s, which has topped

$1.6 trillion and should continue to rise rapidly if whopping federal deficits continue. For a peacetime economy, former Federal Reserve Board chairman Paul A. Volcker said, the buildup may reflect a "fragility in the financial system." Such debt represents about 40% of the GNP, up from 25% in 1980.

Of course, that 40% is well below the 60% in the mid-1950s, but that big number reflected a debt hangover from the heavy borrowing to finance the Second World War, when federal debt actually exceeded the GNP. Now Congress and the White House have tentatively nicked the federal budget, but nobody realistically expects the Gramm-Rudman law's target deficit in 1988 of $108 billion to be within reach. The reason, naturally, is that it's too politically perilous to make the needed spending cuts. (Optimists hoped that the stock market's gyrations would finally force Congress and the administration to toe the line of fiscal responsibility.) The problem with not squeezing the budget hard during an economic expansion is that, when a recession comes, the choice will be between foregoing the usual response of deficit spending—or letting the red ink flow totally out of control.

In addition, consumer debt is growing faster than incomes. Installment debt, for instance, is about 17% of personal income, up from 12% in the 1970s and almost twice what it was in the 1950s. Corporate debt is more troubling because of its ramifications. And corporate liquid assets (cash and anything that can readily be turned into cash) are only about 7.5% of the GNP, or half what they were in the 1950s. The big problem with corporate debt is that it often stymies new investment, as spare cash is used to pay off interest on borrowed money.

Such debt only serves to point out another problem—the number of companies going out of business. The rate has mushroomed during the decade. In 1985, the failure rate hit 114 per 10,000 companies, up from 35 in 1976. That represented $33.4 billion in liabilities, up from $3 billion in 1976. (The highest failure rate ever was in the Depression year 1932 when the rate was 154 per 10,000.)

But if you think that's something, look at our trade debt today. In 1976, the U.S. had a $4.2 billion trade surplus. The past few years have each suffered from $100 billion–plus trade deficits. The decline of the dollar began to help a little in 1987, but then became a major problem when it sank too low. The effects are often slow in coming, and import prices haven't risen as much as expected. Besides, a growing segment of our economy is dependent upon imports for businesses and jobs, and these can only be hurt by tumbling dollars and jingoistic tariffs.

Meanwhile, the Reagan administration repeatedly badgered countries that have big trade surpluses with the U.S.—West Germany, Taiwan, and Japan, especially Japan—to expand their economies as a way of helping to bring down the U.S. trade deficit. But how can Japan and West Germany cure America's bleak trade picture? The most they could possibly lop off the U.S. deficit is $15 billion or so. While that's more than a drop in the deficit bucket, it still isn't much more than a ladle's worth.

It doesn't appear that inflation will come roaring back. Creeping back is more like it. The more we pay for imports, the more inflation we get. Monetary policy remains a question mark. Congress keeps spending. And what happens if oil prices rebound strongly?

In the interim, the U.S. has become a debtor nation, something that at one time would have been considered preposterous. Until mid-1985, the value of U.S. assets in other nations exceeded that of U.S. assets held by foreigners, a situation that had held true since 1914. Then the balance tipped the other way. Now we're on the downside, and the prospects for what that means aren't so hot. We've wound up in a damned-if-we-do-damned-if-we-don't bind. If the situation continues, increased payments to foreigners on their U.S. investments will lower the standard of living for Americans. Yet, if such investments were withdrawn from the U.S., the result could be a credit-market squeeze that would drive up interest rates and set the stage for another recession.

But what all this obscures to some degree is the fundamental issue of the marked decline in U.S. competitiveness. Although there were signs of a manufacturing rebound in 1987 and early 1988, the sickness of American manufacturing alone more than accounts for the entire decline of U.S. trade. While it's great that the service industry has come on strong, we still need manufacturing if we want our economy to become truly vigorous. That means we have to compete with foreigners, not simply raise trade barriers against them. To compete, we need unions that deal responsibly with management, including recognizing the need for increased automation if any manufacturing jobs are to survive in America. We also need management that puts badly needed money into automation, even when that means postponing short-term profitability for the sake of long-term gains. Unfortunately, what we need and what we get are often two different animals.

If that sounds a tad cynical, it's just that the past is all too often an indicator of the future, at least where politicians are concerned. Let's hope the market scare has scared them enough to keep plugging away at our problems.

On a more upbeat note, you'll be able to judge from the following pages that things have been worse. Until the stock market panic of October 1987, we hadn't had a panic in this country for quite a while (see page 8). And we sidestepped a recession for a good long time, the longest period since they started keeping records in the last century (see page 8). Our GNP is up (see Table 1 below). Corporate profits rose steadily each year between 1982 and 1987 (see Table 2), but then so did our trade deficit (see Table 3).

So what does that mean to the future? We wish we could tell you but we can't.

Here we are, revved up for another presidential election. The Reaganomics that was to cure our ailing economy has turned out to be a lot less startling—and coherent—than either its proponents or its detractors once claimed. Once again, a newcomer will set foot in the Oval Office and have the opportunity to shape an economic policy. Let's hope the next one works. Perhaps it's too much to hope for, but maybe the next president, whoever he or she may be, will come up with a realistic program that includes tough calls on trimming the federal budget while avoiding recklessly reinflating the economy. That isn't too much to hope for. Is it?

DEPRESSIONS AND RECESSIONS

Depressions and recessions are economic bad news. When the economy retracts, there's a long-term decline in output, income, trade, and the number of people working. Depending on how long it goes on and how deep it is, we call one of these nasties a recession or a depression. Between 1920 and now, there have been more than a dozen of them.

Fortunately, just about all of them lasted only about a year. Only one lasted long enough and was deep enough to be a depression, but that was the Great Depression, the 43-month contraction between 1929 and 1933. By 1933, unemployment was about 25% compared to 6% to 9% for the six recessions between 1948 and 1975. Depressions hurt a great deal. Families suffer because of reduced income and prices, profits, interest rates, capital investment, income and buying power, and other parts of the economy are hard hit.

PANICS

Financial panics are more than forgetting to mail a check to the mortgage company. They are economic nightmares and they used to be almost a way of life in the U.S. Between 1790 and 1907, there were 21 panics— that's one every five or six years.

What happened? There were runs on banks, a lot of defaults on loans, big companies going belly-up, and stock prices going through the floor. (By comparison, the stock market panic on October 19, 1987, when stocks fell 508 points, doesn't look so bad.)

They usually came about when there was some horrific failure that shook people's belief in the economy. That's what happened in 1857 when the Ohio Life Insurance Company of Cincinnati failed. Another panic came about in 1873 when a lot of big companies failed. When the Reading Railroad and the National Cordage Company failed within months of each other in 1893, that sparked a stock-market panic.

After a panic in 1907, Congress passed the Aldrich-Vreeland Act (1908) to initiate bank reforms and to provide for the issuance of emergency bank currency. Ultimately, an investigation into the panic resulted in the establishment of the Federal Reserve System in 1913.

There weren't any more panics until the stock-market crash of 1929 and the subsequent host of bank failures—more than 9,000 between 1929 and 1933. In 1933, President Roosevelt temporarily shut down the nation's banks and created an insurance mechanism, the Federal Deposit Insurance Corporation (see the profile on page 177), to avert panics. The FDIC eased depositors' anxieties because it meant that if a bank failed, depositors wouldn't necessarily lose money. Thus, it headed off the widespread withdrawals and reduction in bank credit that had taken place in the past.

Table 1   Gross National Product, 1929 to 1987

(billions of dollars, except as noted; quarterly data at seasonally adjusted annual rates)

Year	Gross national product	Personal consumption expenditures Total	Durable goods	Non-durable goods	Services	Gross private domestic investment Total	Fixed investment Total	Nonresidential Total	Structures	Producers' durable equipment	Residential	Change in business inventories
1929	103.9	77.3	9.2	37.7	30.4	16.7	14.9	11.0	5.5	5.5	4.0	1.7
1933	56.0	45.8	3.5	22.3	20.1	1.6	3.1	2.5	1.1	1.4	.6	-1.6
1939	91.3	67.0	6.7	35.1	25.2	9.5	9.1	6.1	2.2	3.9	3.0	.4
1940	100.4	71.0	7.8	37.0	26.2	13.4	11.2	7.7	2.6	5.2	3.5	2.2
1941	125.5	80.8	9.7	42.9	28.3	18.3	13.8	9.7	3.3	6.4	4.1	4.5
1942	159.0	88.6	6.9	50.8	31.0	10.3	8.5	6.3	2.2	4.1	2.2	1.8
1943	192.7	99.5	6.5	58.6	34.3	6.2	6.9	5.4	1.8	3.7	1.4	-.6
1944	211.4	108.2	6.7	64.3	37.2	7.7	8.7	7.4	2.4	5.0	1.4	-1.0
1945	213.4	119.6	8.0	71.9	39.7	11.3	12.3	10.6	3.3	7.3	1.7	-1.0
1946	212.4	143.9	15.8	82.7	45.4	31.5	25.1	17.3	7.4	9.9	7.8	6.4
1947	235.2	161.9	20.4	90.9	50.6	35.0	35.5	23.5	8.1	15.3	12.1	-.5
1948	261.6	174.9	22.9	96.6	55.5	47.1	42.4	26.8	9.5	17.3	15.6	4.7
1949	260.4	178.3	25.0	94.9	58.4	36.5	39.5	24.9	9.2	15.7	14.6	-3.1
1950	288.3	192.1	30.8	98.2	63.2	55.1	48.3	27.8	10.0	17.8	20.5	6.8
1951	333.4	208.1	29.9	109.2	69.0	60.5	50.2	31.8	11.9	19.9	18.4	10.2
1952	351.6	219.1	29.3	114.7	75.1	53.5	50.5	31.9	12.2	19.7	18.6	3.1
1953	371.6	232.6	32.7	117.8	82.1	54.9	54.5	35.1	13.6	21.5	19.4	.4
1954	372.5	239.8	32.1	119.7	88.0	54.1	55.7	34.7	13.9	20.8	21.1	-1.6
1955	405.9	257.9	38.9	124.7	94.3	69.7	64.0	39.0	15.2	23.9	25.0	5.7
1956	428.2	270.6	38.2	130.8	101.6	72.7	68.0	44.5	18.2	26.3	23.5	4.6
1957	451.0	285.3	39.7	137.1	108.5	71.1	69.7	47.5	18.9	28.6	22.2	1.4
1958	456.8	294.6	37.2	141.7	115.7	63.6	65.1	42.4	17.5	24.9	22.7	-1.5
1959	495.8	316.3	42.8	148.5	125.0	80.2	74.4	46.3	18.0	28.3	28.1	5.8
1960	515.3	330.7	43.5	153.2	134.0	78.2	75.1	48.8	19.2	29.7	26.3	3.1
1961	533.8	341.1	41.9	157.4	141.8	77.1	74.7	48.3	19.4	28.9	26.4	2.4
1962	574.6	361.9	47.0	163.8	151.1	87.6	81.5	52.5	20.5	32.1	29.0	6.1
1963	606.9	381.7	51.8	169.4	160.6	93.1	87.3	55.2	20.8	34.4	32.1	5.8
1964	649.8	409.3	56.8	179.7	172.8	99.6	94.2	61.4	22.7	38.7	32.8	5.4
1965	705.1	440.7	63.5	191.9	185.4	116.2	106.2	73.1	27.4	45.8	33.1	9.9
1966	772.0	477.3	68.5	208.5	200.3	128.6	114.4	83.5	30.5	53.0	30.9	14.2
1967	816.4	503.6	70.6	216.9	216.0	125.7	115.4	84.4	30.7	53.7	31.1	10.3
1968	892.7	552.5	81.0	235.0	236.4	137.0	129.1	91.4	32.9	58.5	37.7	7.9
1969	963.9	597.9	86.2	252.2	259.4	153.2	143.4	102.3	37.1	65.2	41.2	9.8
1970	1,015.5	640.0	85.7	270.3	284.0	148.8	145.7	105.2	39.2	66.1	40.5	3.1
1971	1,102.7	691.6	97.6	283.3	310.7	172.5	164.7	109.6	40.9	68.7	55.1	7.8
1972	1,212.8	757.6	111.2	305.1	341.3	202.0	191.5	123.0	44.5	78.5	68.6	10.5
1973	1,359.3	837.2	124.7	339.6	373.0	238.8	219.2	145.9	51.4	94.5	73.3	19.6
1974	1,472.8	916.5	123.8	380.9	411.9	240.8	225.4	160.6	57.0	103.6	64.8	15.4
1975	1,598.4	1,012.8	135.4	416.2	461.2	219.6	225.2	162.9	56.3	106.6	62.3	-5.6
1976	1,782.8	1,129.3	161.5	452.0	515.9	277.7	261.7	180.0	60.1	119.9	81.7	16.0
1977	1,990.5	1,257.2	184.5	490.4	582.3	344.1	322.8	214.2	66.7	147.4	108.6	21.3
1978	2,249.7	1,403.5	205.6	541.8	656.1	416.8	388.2	259.0	81.0	178.0	129.2	28.6
1979	2,508.2	1,566.8	219.0	613.2	734.6	454.8	441.9	302.8	99.5	203.3	139.1	13.0
1980	2,732.0	1,732.6	219.3	681.4	831.9	437.0	445.3	322.8	113.9	208.9	122.5	-8.3
1981	3,052.6	1,915.1	239.9	740.6	934.7	515.5	491.5	369.2	138.5	230.7	122.3	24.0
1982	3,166.0	2,050.7	252.7	771.0	1,027.0	447.3	471.8	366.7	143.3	223.4	105.1	-24.5
1983	3,405.7	2,234.5	289.1	816.7	1,128.7	502.3	509.4	356.9	124.0	232.8	152.5	-7.1
1984	3,772.2	2,430.5	335.5	867.3	1,227.6	664.8	597.1	416.0	141.1	274.9	181.1	67.7
1985	4,010.3	2,629.4	368.7	913.1	1,347.51	641.6	631.6	442.6	152.5	290.1	189.0	10.0
1986	4,235.0	2,799.8	402.4	939.4	1,458.0	671.0	655.2	436.9	137.4	299.5	218.3	15.7
1987*	4,486.2	2,966.0	413.9	980.4	1,571.6	716.4	670.6	442.1	134.1	308.0	228.5	45.7
1987I	4,377.7	2,893.8	396.1	969.9	1,527.7	699.9	648.2	422.8	128.7	294.1	225.4	51.6
1987II	4,445.1	2,943.7	409.0	982.1	1,552.6	702.6	662.3	434.6	129.7	304.9	227.7	40.3
1987III	4,524.0	3,011.3	436.8	986.4	1,588.1	707.4	684.5	456.6	137.1	319.5	227.9	22.9
1987IV*	4,598.0	3,015.1	413.8	983.4	1,618.0	755.6	687.4	454.3	140.7	313.6	233.1	68.1

*Preliminary.

9

Table 1 Gross National Product, 1929 to 1987 (continued)

Year	Net exports of goods and services			Government purchases of goods and services					Final sales	Percent change from preceding period	
				Total	Federal			State and local		Gross national product	Final sales
	Net exports	Exports	Imports		Total	National defense	Non-defense				
1929	1.1	7.1	5.9	8.9	1.5			7.4	102.2		
1933	.4	2.4	2.1	8.3	2.2			6.1	57.6	−4.2	−5.5
1939	1.2	4.6	3.4	13.6	5.2	1.3	3.9	8.3	90.9	7.0	5.4
1940	1.8	5.4	3.7	14.2	6.1	2.3	3.9	8.1	98.3	10.0	8.1
1941	1.5	6.1	4.7	25.0	17.0	13.8	3.2	8.0	121.0	25.0	23.2
1942	.2	5.0	4.8	59.9	52.0	49.4	2.6	7.8	157.2	26.6	29.9
1943	−1.9	4.6	6.5	88.9	81.4	79.8	1.6	7.5	193.4	21.2	23.0
1944	−1.7	5.5	7.2	97.1	89.4	87.5	2.0	7.6	212.3	9.7	9.8
1945	−.5	7.4	7.9	83.0	74.8	73.7	1.1	8.2	214.4	.9	1.0
1946	7.8	15.2	7.3	29.1	19.2	16.4	2.8	9.9	206.0	−.5	−3.9
1947	11.9	20.3	8.3	26.4	13.6	10.0	3.6	12.8	235.7	10.8	14.4
1948	7.0	17.5	10.6	32.6	17.3	11.3	6.0	15.3	256.9	11.2	9.0
1949	6.5	16.4	9.8	39.0	21.1	13.9	7.2	18.0	263.4	−.5	2.5
1950	2.2	14.5	12.3	38.8	19.1	14.3	4.7	19.8	281.4	10.7	6.8
1951	4.5	19.8	15.3	60.4	38.6	33.8	4.8	21.8	323.2	15.7	14.8
1952	3.2	19.2	16.0	75.8	52.7	46.2	6.5	23.1	348.6	5.5	7.9
1953	1.3	18.1	16.8	82.8	57.9	49.0	8.9	24.8	371.1	5.7	6.5
1954	2.6	18.8	16.3	76.0	48.4	41.6	6.8	27.7	374.1	.2	.8
1955	3.0	21.1	18.1	75.3	44.9	39.0	6.0	30.3	400.2	9.0	7.0
1956	5.3	25.2	19.9	79.7	46.4	40.7	5.7	33.3	423.6	5.5	5.8
1957	7.3	28.2	20.9	87.3	50.5	44.6	5.9	36.9	449.6	5.3	6.1
1958	3.3	24.4	21.1	95.4	54.5	46.3	8.3	40.8	458.3	1.3	1.9
1959	1.5	25.0	23.5	97.9	54.6	46.4	8.2	43.3	490.0	8.5	6.9
1960	5.9	29.9	24.0	100.6	54.4	45.3	9.2	46.1	512.3	3.9	4.6
1961	7.2	31.1	23.9	108.4	58.2	47.9	10.2	50.2	531.4	3.6	3.7
1962	6.9	33.1	26.2	118.2	64.6	52.1	12.6	53.5	568.5	7.6	7.0
1963	8.2	35.7	27.5	123.8	65.7	51.5	14.2	58.1	601.1	5.6	5.7
1964	10.9	40.5	29.6	130.0	66.4	50.4	16.0	63.5	644.4	7.1	7.2
1965	9.7	42.9	33.2	138.6	68.7	51.0	17.7	69.9	695.2	8.5	7.9
1966	7.5	46.6	39.1	158.6	80.4	62.0	18.3	78.2	757.8	9.5	9.0
1967	7.4	49.5	42.1	179.7	92.7	73.4	19.3	87.0	806.1	5.8	6.4
1968	5.5	54.8	49.3	197.7	100.1	79.1	21.0	97.6	884.8	9.3	9.8
1969	5.6	60.4	54.7	207.3	100.0	78.9	21.1	107.2	954.1	8.0	7.8
1970	8.5	68.9	60.5	218.2	98.8	76.8	22.0	119.4	1,012.3	5.4	6.1
1971	6.3	72.4	66.1	232.4	99.8	74.1	25.8	132.5	1,094.9	8.6	8.2
1972	3.2	81.4	78.2	250.0	105.8	77.4	28.4	144.2	1,202.3	10.0	9.8
1973	16.8	114.1	97.3	266.5	106.4	77.5	28.9	160.1	1,339.7	12.1	11.4
1974	16.3	151.5	135.2	299.1	116.2	82.6	33.6	182.9	1,457.4	8.3	8.8
1975	31.1	161.3	130.3	335.0	129.2	89.6	39.6	205.9	1,604.1	8.5	10.1
1976	18.8	177.7	158.9	356.9	136.3	93.4	42.9	220.6	1,766.8	11.5	10.1
1977	1.9	191.6	189.7	387.3	151.1	100.9	50.3	236.2	1,969.2	11.7	11.5
1978	4.1	227.5	223.4	425.2	161.8	108.9	52.9	263.4	2,221.0	13.0	12.8
1979	18.8	291.2	272.5	467.8	178.0	121.9	56.1	289.9	2,495.2	11.5	12.3
1980	32.1	351.0	318.9	530.3	208.1	142.7	65.4	322.2	2,740.3	8.9	9.8
1981	33.9	382.8	348.9	588.1	242.2	167.5	74.8	345.9	3,028.6	11.7	10.5
1982	26.3	361.9	335.6	641.7	272.7	193.8	78.9	369.0	3,190.5	3.7	5.3
1983	−6.1	352.5	358.7	675.0	283.5	214.4	69.1	391.5	3,412.8	7.6	7.0
1984	−58.9	383.5	442.4	735.9	310.5	234.3	76.2	425.3	3,704.5	10.8	8.5
1985	−79.2	369.9	449.2	818.6	353.9	259.3	94.6	464.7	4,000.3	6.3	8.0
1986	−105.5	376.2	481.7	869.7	366.2	277.8	88.4	503.5	4,219.3	5.6	5.5
1987*	−119.9	426.7	546.7	923.8	380.6	295.2	85.3	543.2	4,440.4	5.9	5.2
1987I	−112.2	397.3	509.5	896.2	366.9	287.5	79.4	529.3	4,326.0	8.6	3.0
1987II	−118.4	416.5	534.8	917.1	379.6	294.5	85.1	537.6	4,404.8	6.3	7.5
1987III	−123.7	439.2	562.9	929.0	382.1	299.0	83.0	546.9	4,501.1	7.3	9.0
1987IV*	−125.5	453.9	579.4	952.8	393.7	300.0	93.7	559.1	4,529.9	6.7	2.6

*Preliminary.
Source: U.S. Bureau of Economic Analysis.

10

Table 2　Corporate Profits by Industry, 1929 to 1987
(billions of dollars)

Corporate profits with inventory valuation adjustment and without capital consumption adjustment

Year	Total	Domestic industries Total	Financial Total	Financial Federal Reserve banks	Financial Other	Nonfinancial Total	Manufacturing	Transportation and public utilities	Wholesale and retail trade	Other	Rest of the world
1929	10.5	10.2	1.3	0.0	1.3	8.9	5.2	1.8	1.0	0.9	0.2
1933	− 1.2	− 1.2	.3	.0	.3	− 1.5	− .4	.0	− .5	− .7	.0
1939	6.5	6.1	.8	.0	.8	5.3	3.3	1.0	.7	.3	.3
1940	9.8	9.6	1.0	.0	.9	8.6	5.5	1.3	1.2	.6	.3
1941	15.4	15.0	1.1	.0	1.0	14.0	9.5	2.0	1.4	1.1	.4
1942	20.5	20.1	1.2	.0	1.2	18.9	11.8	3.4	2.2	1.5	.4
1943	24.5	24.1	1.3	.0	1.3	22.8	13.8	4.4	3.0	1.6	.4
1944	24.0	23.5	1.6	.1	1.6	21.9	13.2	3.9	3.2	1.6	.4
1945	19.3	18.9	1.7	.1	1.6	17.3	9.7	2.7	3.3	1.5	.3
1946	19.6	18.9	2.1	.1	2.0	16.8	9.0	1.8	3.8	2.1	.7
1947	25.9	24.9	1.7	.1	1.6	23.2	13.6	2.2	4.6	2.9	1.0
1948	33.4	32.2	2.6	.2	2.3	29.6	17.6	3.0	5.5	3.6	1.3
1949	31.1	29.9	3.1	.2	2.9	26.8	16.2	3.0	4.5	3.1	1.1
1950	37.9	36.7	3.1	.2	3.0	33.5	20.9	4.0	5.0	3.6	1.3
1951	43.3	41.5	3.6	.3	3.3	37.9	24.6	4.6	5.0	3.7	1.7
1952	40.6	38.7	4.0	.4	3.7	34.7	21.7	4.9	4.8	3.3	1.9
1953	40.2	38.4	4.5	.4	4.1	33.9	22.0	5.0	3.8	3.1	1.8
1954	38.4	36.4	4.6	.3	4.3	31.8	19.9	4.7	3.8	3.4	2.0
1955	47.5	45.1	4.8	.3	4.5	40.3	26.0	5.6	5.0	3.6	2.4
1956	46.9	44.1	5.0	.5	4.5	39.1	24.7	5.9	4.5	4.1	2.8
1957	46.6	43.5	5.2	.6	4.6	38.3	24.0	5.8	4.4	4.0	3.1
1958	41.6	39.1	5.7	.6	5.1	33.5	19.4	5.9	4.6	3.6	2.5
1959	52.3	49.6	6.8	.7	6.0	42.9	26.4	7.0	5.9	3.6	2.7
1960	49.8	46.7	7.2	1.0	6.2	39.5	23.6	7.4	4.9	3.6	3.1
1961	50.1	46.8	7.0	.8	6.3	39.8	23.3	7.8	5.0	3.7	3.3
1962	55.2	51.5	7.3	.9	6.4	44.2	26.0	8.4	5.8	3.9	3.7
1963	59.8	55.8	6.8	1.0	5.8	49.0	29.3	9.3	5.9	4.4	4.0
1964	66.2	61.8	6.9	1.1	5.8	54.9	32.3	10.0	7.5	5.1	4.4
1965	76.2	71.5	7.5	1.4	6.2	64.0	39.3	11.0	8.1	5.6	4.6
1966	81.2	76.7	8.5	1.7	6.8	68.2	41.9	11.8	8.2	6.3	4.4
1967	78.6	73.9	9.0	2.0	7.0	64.9	38.6	10.7	9.1	6.5	4.7
1968	85.4	79.9	10.4	2.5	7.9	69.5	41.4	10.8	10.4	6.9	5.5
1969	81.4	74.8	11.2	3.1	8.1	63.7	36.7	10.3	10.5	6.1	6.5
1970	69.5	62.6	12.2	3.6	8.6	50.4	26.7	8.2	9.6	5.9	6.9
1971	82.7	75.1	14.1	3.3	10.7	61.0	34.3	8.5	11.7	6.5	7.6
1972	94.9	85.5	15.4	3.4	12.0	70.2	40.8	9.0	13.4	6.9	9.3
1973	107.1	92.6	15.8	4.5	11.2	76.8	46.2	8.5	13.9	8.2	14.5
1974	99.4	82.4	14.7	5.7	8.9	67.8	39.8	6.7	12.9	8.3	17.0
1975	123.9	109.5	11.2	5.7	5.5	98.3	53.6	10.3	22.2	12.2	14.4
1976	155.3	139.3	15.9	6.0	9.9	123.4	70.9	14.8	23.0	14.7	16.0
1977	183.8	165.5	21.6	6.2	15.4	143.9	80.6	17.9	27.5	17.8	18.3
1978	208.2	186.0	29.1	7.7	21.4	156.8	88.7	20.9	27.3	20.0	22.2
1979	214.1	180.4	27.8	9.6	18.2	152.6	87.5	15.2	28.7	21.1	33.7
1980	194.0	159.6	21.0	11.9	9.0	138.6	77.1	17.6	21.6	22.4	34.4
1981	202.3	173.8	16.5	14.5	1.9	157.3	88.5	19.5	32.5	16.8	28.5
1982	159.2	131.2	11.8	15.4	− 3.6	119.4	58.0	19.3	34.6	7.5	28.0
1983	196.7	166.6	18.1	14.8	3.3	148.5	70.1	28.5	38.9	10.9	30.2
1984	234.2	203.3	13.0	16.7	− 3.7	190.3	88.8	38.5	51.2	11.8	30.9
1985	224.1	193.6	18.4	16.8	1.6	175.2	72.2	37.5	51.4	14.1	30.5
1986	238.4	207.2	26.1	16.0	10.1	181.1	69.4	42.4	52.1	17.2	31.2
1987*	257.2	225.0	27.5	16.0	11.4	197.5	90.2	37.9	52.0	17.5	32.2

*Preliminary.
Source: U.S. Bureau of Economic Analysis.

11

Table 3   U.S.-International Transactions
(millions of dollars; quarterly data seasonally adjusted, except as noted)

Year	Merchandise			Investment Income			Net military transactions	Net travel and transportation receipts	Other services, net	Balance on goods and services	Remittances, pensions, and other unilateral transfers	Balance on current account
	Exports	Imports	Net	Receipts	Payments	Net						
1946	11,764	− 5,067	6,697	772	− 212	560	− 493	733	310	7,807	− 2,922	4,885
1947	16,097	− 5,973	10,124	1,102	− 245	857	− 455	946	145	11,617	− 2,625	8,992
1948	13,265	− 7,557	5,708	1,921	− 437	1,484	− 799	374	175	6,942	− 4,525	2,417
1949	12,213	− 6,874	5,339	1,831	− 476	1,355	− 621	230	208	6,511	− 5,638	873
1950	10,203	− 9,081	1,122	2,068	− 559	1,509	− 576	− 120	242	2,177	− 4,017	− 1,840
1951	14,243	− 11,176	3,067	2,633	− 583	2,050	− 1,270	298	254	4,399	− 3,515	884
1952	13,449	− 10,838	2,611	2,751	− 555	2,196	− 2,054	83	309	3,145	− 2,531	614
1953	12,412	− 10,975	1,437	2,736	− 624	2,112	− 2,423	− 238	307	1,195	− 2,481	− 1,286
1954	12,929	− 10,353	2,576	2,929	− 582	2,347	− 2,460	− 269	305	2,499	− 2,280	219
1955	14,424	− 11,527	2,897	3,406	− 676	2,730	− 2,701	− 297	299	2,928	− 2,498	430
1956	17,556	− 12,803	4,753	3,837	− 735	3,102	− 2,788	− 361	447	5,153	− 2,423	2,730
1957	19,562	− 13,291	6,271	4,180	− 796	3,384	− 2,841	− 189	482	7,107	− 2,345	4,762
1958	16,414	− 12,952	3,462	3,790	− 825	2,965	− 3,135	− 633	486	3,145	− 2,361	784
1959	16,458	− 15,310	1,148	4,132	− 1,061	3,071	− 2,805	− 821	573	1,166	− 2,448	− 1,282
1960	19,650	− 14,758	4,892	4,616	− 1,237	3,379	− 2,752	− 964	638	5,191	− 2,367	2,824
1961	20,108	− 14,537	5,571	4,999	− 1,245	3,754	− 2,596	− 978	732	6,484	− 2,662	3,822
1962	20,781	− 16,260	4,521	5,618	− 1,324	4,294	− 2,449	− 1,152	911	6,127	− 2,740	3,387
1963	22,272	− 17,048	5,224	6,157	− 1,561	4,596	− 2,304	− 1,309	1,037	7,244	− 2,831	4,414
1964	25,501	− 18,700	6,801	6,824	− 1,784	5,040	− 2,133	− 1,146	1,161	9,724	− 2,901	6,823
1965	26,461	− 21,510	4,951	7,437	− 2,088	5,349	− 2,122	− 1,280	1,480	8,378	− 2,948	5,431
1966	29,310	− 25,493	3,817	7,528	− 2,481	5,047	− 2,935	− 1,331	1,496	6,095	− 3,064	3,031
1967	30,666	− 26,866	3,800	8,020	− 2,747	5,273	− 3,226	− 1,750	1,742	5,838	− 3,255	2,583
1968	33,626	− 32,991	635	9,368	− 3,378	5,990	− 3,143	− 1,548	1,759	3,693	− 3,082	611
1969	36,414	− 35,807	607	10,912	− 4,869	6,043	− 3,328	− 1,763	1,964	3,524	− 3,125	399
1970	42,469	− 39,866	2,603	11,747	− 5,516	6,231	− 3,354	− 2,038	2,329	5,773	− 3,443	2,331
1971	43,319	− 45,579	− 2,260	12,707	− 5,436	7,271	− 2,893	− 2,345	2,649	2,423	− 3,856	− 1,433
1972	49,381	− 55,797	− 6,416	14,764	− 6,572	8,192	− 3,420	− 3,063	2,965	− 1,742	− 4,052	− 5,795
1973	71,410	− 70,499	911	21,808	− 9,655	12,153	− 2,070	− 3,158	3,406	11,244	− 4,103	7,140
1974	98,306	− 103,811	− 5,505	27,587	− 12,084	15,503	− 1,653	− 3,184	4,231	9,392	− 7,431	1,962
1975	107,088	− 98,185	8,903	25,351	− 12,564	12,787	− 746	− 2,812	4,853	22,984	− 4,868	18,116
1976	114,745	− 124,228	− 9,483	29,286	− 13,311	15,975	559	− 2,558	5,027	9,521	− 5,314	4,207
1977	120,816	− 151,907	− 31,091	32,179	− 14,217	17,962	1,528	− 3,565	5,679	− 9,488	− 5,023	− 14,511
1978	142,054	− 176,001	− 33,947	42,245	− 21,680	20,565	621	− 3,573	6,459	− 9,875	− 5,552	− 15,427
1979	184,473	− 212,009	− 27,536	64,132	− 32,960	31,172	− 1,778	− 2,935	6,214	5,138	− 6,128	− 991
1980	224,269	− 249,749	− 25,480	72,506	− 42,120	30,386	− 2,237	− 997	7,793	9,466	− 7,593	1,873
1981	237,085	− 265,063	− 27,978	86,411	− 52,329	34,082	− 1,183	144	8,699	13,764	− 7,425	6,339
1982	211,198	− 247,642	− 36,444	83,549	− 54,883	28,666	− 274	− 992	8,829	− 214	− 8,917	− 9,131
1983	201,820	− 268,900	− 67,080	77,251	− 52,410	24,841	− 369	− 4,227	9,711	− 37,123	− 9,481	− 46,604
1984	219,900	− 332,422	− 112,522	86,221	− 67,469	18,752	− 1,827	− 8,593	9,881	− 94,308	− 12,157	− 106,466
1985	215,935	− 338,083	− 122,148	88,299	− 62,901	25,398	− 3,339	− 10,866	9,861	− 101,093	− 15,301	− 116,393
1986	224,361	− 368,700	− 144,339	88,209	− 67,365	20,844	− 3,662	− 9,903	11,368	− 125,694	− 15,658	− 141,352

Table 3 U.S.-International Transactions (continued)

| Year | U.S. assets abroad, net [increase/capital outflow (−)] | | | | Foreign assets in the U.S., net [increase/capital inflow (+)] | | | Allocations of special drawing rights (SDRs) | Statistical discrepancy | |
	Total	U.S. official reserve assets[1]	Other U.S. government assets	U.S. private assets	Total	Foreign official assets	Other foreign assets		Total (sum of the items with sign reversed)	Of which: seasonal adjustment discrepancy
1946		−623								
1947		−3,315								
1948		−1,736								
1949		−266								
1950		1,758								
1951		−33								
1952		−415								
1953		1,256								
1954		480								
1955		182								
1956		−869								
1957		−1,165								
1958		2,292								
1959		1,035								
1960	−4,099	2,145	−1,100	−5,144	2,294	1,473	821		−1,019	
1961	−5,538	607	−910	−5,235	2,705	765	1,939		−989	
1962	−4,174	1,535	−1,085	−4,623	1,911	1,270	641		−1,124	
1963	−7,270	378	−1,662	−5,986	3,217	1,986	1,231		−360	
1964	−9,560	171	−1,680	−8,050	3,643	1,660	1,983		−907	
1965	−5,716	1,225	−1,605	−5,336	742	134	607		−457	
1966	−7,321	570	−1,543	−6,347	3,661	−672	4,333		629	
1967	−9,757	53	−2,423	−7,386	7,379	3,451	3,928		−205	
1968	−10,977	−870	−2,274	−7,833	9,928	−774	10,703		438	
1969	−11,585	−1,179	−2,200	−8,206	12,702	−1,301	14,002		−1,516	
1970	−9,337	2,481	−1,589	−10,229	6,359	6,908	−550	867	−219	
1971	−12,475	2,349	−1,884	−12,940	22,970	26,879	−3,909	717	−9,779	
1972	−14,497	−4	−1,568	−12,925	21,461	10,475	10,986	710	−1,879	
1973	−22,874	158	−2,644	−20,388	18,388	6,026	12,362		−2,654	
1974	−34,745	−1,467	366	−33,643	34,241	10,546	23,696		−1,458	
1975	−39,703	−849	−3,474	−35,380	15,670	7,027	8,643		5,917	
1976	−51,269	−2,558	−4,214	−44,498	36,518	17,693	18,826		10,544	
1977	−34,785	−375	−3,693	−30,717	51,319	36,816	14,503		−2,023	
1978	−61,130	732	−4,660	−57,202	64,036	33,678	30,358		12,521	
1979	−64,331	−1,133	−3,746	−59,453	38,752	−13,665	52,416	1,139	25,431	
1980	−86,118	−8,155	−5,162	−72,802	58,112	15,497	42,615	1,152	24,982	
1981	−111,031	−5,175	−5,097	−100,758	83,322	4,960	78,362	1,093	20,276	
1982	−121,273	−4,965	−6,131	−110,177	94,078	3,593	90,486		36,325	
1983	−50,022	−1,196	−5,005	−43,821	85,496	5,968	79,527		11,130	
1984	−23,639	−3,131	−5,523	−14,986	102,767	3,037	99,730		27,338	
1985	−32,436	−3,858	−2,824	−25,754	127,106	−1,324	128,430		23,006	
1986	−95,982	312	−1,920	−94,374	213,386	34,698	178,689		23,947	

[1]Consists of gold, special drawing rights, convertible currencies, and the U.S. reserve position in the International Monetary Fund (IMF).
Sources: Department of Commerce, Bureau of Economic Analysis, and Department of the Treasury.

13

PART I

People in Business

Chapter One
THE AVERAGE AMERICAN

Although few people would like to admit that they are "just average," finding the elusive average American is a big business. Statisticians, demographers, and marketing researchers track the lives and times of Americans from cradle to grave, collecting statistics about their jobs, their eating habits, their vacations, and even what goes on in their bedrooms. The everyman and everywoman who emerge from these data might be nobody in particular—no one, after all, has 1.8 children and has sex with 4.5 men during a lifetime. But that hardly matters. About $2 billion is spent every year collecting statistics on American life—how we spend our money, where we live, and what we want—simply because these facts are worth tens of billions of dollars to corporate planners marketing new products or government officials planning economic policy.

POPULATION

There are some 247.5 million Americans in 1988, just waiting to be surveyed. That represents a dramatic increase from the beginning of this century, when there were 76 million Americans, or from 1790, when there were a mere 3.9 million Americans.

When the first census was taken in 1790, America was a nation of rural pioneers—95% of the population lived in rural areas or in towns with fewer than 2,500 people. It wasn't until 1920 that over half the population lived in towns with more than 2,500 people, but since then America has become a country of city slickers. Today, about three quarters of the population live in urban areas.

And despite the country's well-deserved reputation for pioneering the hinterlands, living near the beach remains popular. In 1985, 95.4 million Americans (39.8%) lived within 50 miles of the ocean.

POPULATION FORECASTS

Even if there are more Americans than ever before, parents are having fewer Americans, average or otherwise. Only half of the 63 million families in the 1980s had a child under 18, and the average American woman has only produced 1.8 kids during her lifetime, down from 3.7 children in the late 1950s—the height of the baby boom. A birth rate of 2.1 is necessary to sustain zero population growth if the country has no immigration.

As a result, the population of the United States increased only 11.4% between 1970 and the 1980 census, the second-smallest increase in American history. (The smallest came during the Second World War.) In contrast, during the baby-boom decade of the 1950s the population rose 18.5%, and throughout the first half of the 19th century the population exploded at a rate of more than 30% a decade—faster than some third-world countries are growing today.

This means that if the average woman decides to produce 1.9 children during her life and the average American lives to be 79.6 years old, as government forecasters believe they will, then there will be nearly 268 million Americans in the year 2000. At that time, the country will be 13.3% black, 9.4% Hispanic, 3.6% other, and 74.2% white non-Hispanic. (The percentages add to over 100 because people of Spanish origin may be of any race—black, white, or Asian.) Some time in the year 2025 the population should top the 300 million mark.

By the year 2080 the face of America will have changed dramatically. The number of white non-Hispanics will fall from 192 million in 1990 to only 176 million in 2080, while the number of Hispanics will increase from 19.9 million to 59.6 million. The number of black Americans will grow from 31.4 million in 1990 to 55.7 million in 2080 while the number of members of other races will increase from 7.5 million to 23.4 million. In 2080, only about 56% of the country will be white non-Hispanic. About one fifth of the population will be Hispanic, followed by almost 18% black, and about 7.5% will be other races, including Asian.

THE AGING OF AMERICA

The average American is getting along in years. In 1820 the median age of the population was only 16.7, and by 1940 only 4.1% of the population was over 65. Today, however, 11.9% of the population is over 65 and the median age is 31.5, up from 27.9 in 1970. In the year 2000, when the baby-boom generation hits middle age, the government estimates that 35.8% of the population will be over 45 and 13.4% will be over 65. And in 2080, 73.1 million Americans, 23.5% of the population, will be over 65 and nearly half the population (47.3%) will be over 45. The number of people over 85 will hit 18.2 million in 2080, 5.9% of the population. Today only about 1.1% of the population is over 85.

But an older population isn't necessarily bad for business. If you think of the elderly as doddering old folks living on meager pensions, then you're at least 15 years out of date. Americans over 50 consume $800 billion worth of goods and services each year. They control one third of the country's net worth, even though they account for only one sixth of the population, and hold about 40% of all financial assets. The poverty rate of Americans over 65 has declined from 33% in 1959 to 12.4% in 1986. The over-65 set has the largest disposable income of any age group, and as their numbers grow, the markets catering to those over 50 will boom.

The aging of America will also be good for those growing up and entering the job market in the last years of the 20th century. With fewer younger workers to provide goods and services for an aging population, economists expect wages and salaries to rise. Unlike many members of the baby-boom generation, who had to fight for scarce jobs and accept lower standards of living than their parents, the members of the baby-bust generation will have more career opportunities and disposable income.

The bad news is the cost of caring for an older America. With fewer and fewer workers bearing the tax burden of supporting social programs for the elderly, Social Security and pension funds are headed toward financial trouble. The Congressional Budget Office has estimated that the Hospital Insurance Trust Fund of Medicare alone could have a deficit of $310 billion by 1995. And as medical science manages to keep people alive longer and longer, the cost of health care will skyrocket. One study estimates that, in order to house the baby-boom generation during their last years, a 100-bed nursing home will have to open *every day, 365 days a year*, between now and the year 2000.

INCOME

The economic slowdown of the 1970s and early 1980s hit the average American squarely in the pocketbook. With adjustment for inflation, the median income of the average household actually declined between 1969 and 1983, falling from $27,336 in 1970 to $26,116 in 1982. White families saw their income slide from an average of $30,489 in 1973 to only $27,420 in 1982, while black families saw their paychecks dwindle from an average of $17,395 in 1970 to only $15,155 in 1982. Since then, however, an economic rebound has improved incomes. Median incomes for all families reached $29,458 in 1986, up 4.2% from 1985, with white families earning $30,809, blacks $17,604, and Hispanics $19,995.

But when it comes to income, not everyone's hurting. About 2% of all families, or about 1.3 million families, have a net worth of $1 million or more according to a recent study by the Federal Reserve. In terms of constant 1982 dollars, the number of people making more than $41,456 a year increased by 112% between 1969 and 1983. By 1986, 20.7% of all families earned more than $50,000 a year and 6.8% made more than $75,000.

As the rich have been getting richer, the poor have been getting poorer—or, at least, officially more numerous. By the government's count, only 11.1% of the population lived in poverty in 1973, but 15.2% did by 1983. The most drastic increase in poverty has been among whites, not minorities. In 1973, 15.1 million whites lived in poverty (8.4%); by 1983 there were 24 million whites, about 12.1%, below the poverty line. But over time Americans have made progress in the war against poverty. In 1960, 22.2% of the population lived in poverty. And in the last few years the poverty rate has dropped again, to 13.6% (32.4 million people) in 1986. That year 22.2 million whites (11.0% of all whites) and 9 million blacks (31.1%) lived in poverty. About 5.1 million Hispanics (27%), who may be of any race, had incomes below the poverty line, which was $11,203 for a family of four in 1986.

Especially hard hit by stagnant personal income is the baby-boom generation, who are not living up to the Madison Avenue stereotype of young, BMW-driving, madly acquisitive yuppies. About 19.1% of all households headed by someone under 35 had zero or negative net worth. Approximately three fifths (59%) were worth under $10,000. Nearly a third of all households headed by someone between 25 and 34 has no discretionary income whatsoever.

PERSONAL CONSUMPTION

With personal income stagnant, consumers have turned to their credit cards to keep up with the Joneses. Consumer debt topped $600 billion in late 1987 for the first time ever, and Americans now own over 700 million credit cards. Installment debt was a whopping 19% of disposable personal income. That left consumers very little at the end of the month. Savings dropped to just 3.2% in the second quarter of 1987, down from 7.5% of disposable income in 1981.

When it comes time to spend income, the average American pays 22% right off the top for taxes. After that, the average urban household spent its money as shown in Table 5 (below).

All of that spending adds up over the course of a year. The average American eats some 88.2 pounds of fresh fruit, 81 pounds of fresh vegetables, 153 pounds of red meat, 596 pounds of dairy products, and 169 pounds of sweeteners every year. He or she drinks 24.1 gallons of beer, 2.4 gallons of wine, 44.8 gallons of soft drinks, 11.2 gallons of juice, 26 gallons of coffee, and 27 gallons of milk. Not surprisingly, about 62% of all Americans are overweight, more than in 1983, despite a booming market for health clubs. They eat 8 million bagels a day, buy 7 billion greeting cards a year, spend $100 billion on summer vacations and $1.9 billion on waterbeds and accessories, and between 1981 and 1985 they bought 70 million color TVs and 123 million portable audio sets.

Personal consumption also adds up to a lot of garbage. Americans produce 148.1 million tons of garbage a year. That is about 3.43 pounds of garbage every day of the year for every man, woman, and child, up from 2.5 pounds in 1960. At that rate, the average American would produce over 90,000 pounds of garbage during his or her lifetime.

THE FAMILY

There are now about 88.5 million households in America, but the American family is no longer the happy, close-knit unit portrayed on *Father Knows Best,* with a pipe-smoking suburban commuter as the chief wage

Table 4   Income in America, 1985

This chart provides a snapshot of the finances of American households by showing the income distribution among various kinds of households. On the left are listed the kinds of households: how old the head of the household is; where the household is located; its size; whether or not the head of the household is married, divorced, or single; and that person's education. On the far right, the chart lists the median income of each group. For example, the median income of all households in 1985 was $23,618 while a black household made only $14,819 and a household headed by someone with a college degree made $39,506. In the middle of the chart is shown the income distribution of the various households. It shows, for example, that 14.8% of all households made more than $50,000 a year, while only 1.9% of all households headed by someone with fewer than eight years of schooling made that much.

Characteristic	Total house-holds (thousands)	Percent distribution of households by income level (in dollars)								Median income (dollars)
		Under 5,000	5,000–9,999	10,000–14,999	15,000–19,999	20,000–24,999	25,000–34,999	35,000–49,999	50,000 and over	
Total¹	88,458	7.7	12.4	11.5	10.9	10.0	17.0	15.8	14.8	23,618
Age of householder:										
15–24 years	5,503	15.5	16.3	18.0	15.2	12.4	13.8	6.2	2.7	15,049
25–34 years	20,410	5.9	8.7	10.8	12.5	11.9	21.7	17.7	10.9	25,085
35–44 years	17,997	4.6	6.5	7.7	8.7	9.9	20.0	21.6	21.1	31,066
45–54 years	13,099	5.3	6.6	7.4	7.8	8.5	17.1	21.0	26.3	33,223
55–64 years	12,852	7.7	10.9	10.9	10.2	9.4	15.8	16.4	18.8	25,557
65 years and over	18,596	12.0	26.2	17.2	12.9	8.7	10.6	6.8	5.6	13,254
White	76,576	6.4	11.7	11.2	10.8	10.1	17.5	16.5	15.8	24,908
Black	9,797	17.6	18.8	14.0	12.4	8.5	12.9	9.9	5.8	14,819
Spanish origin²	5,213	10.8	17.9	14.7	12.2	10.8	15.2	11.0	7.3	17,465
Northeast	18,562	7.0	12.0	10.7	10.1	9.3	16.7	17.1	17.1	25,485
Midwest	21,847	7.4	12.6	11.3	10.9	10.5	17.9	16.0	13.4	23,551
South	30,311	9.5	13.1	12.7	11.6	10.0	16.2	14.1	12.8	21,397
West	17,738	5.6	11.7	10.5	10.7	10.0	17.3	16.9	17.3	25,782
Size of household:										
One person	21,178	17.7	25.5	15.9	12.3	9.0	11.3	5.3	3.0	11,884
Two persons	27,732	4.9	10.4	12.9	12.9	11.3	17.7	15.6	14.3	23,868
Three persons	16,088	5.1	7.2	9.1	9.0	10.3	19.3	19.9	20.1	29,658
Four persons	13,774	3.6	6.3	6.9	8.3	9.4	19.6	23.4	22.6	32,703
Five persons	6,276	3.9	6.6	7.5	9.3	8.6	20.6	22.1	21.4	31,758
Six persons	2,138	3.7	6.6	8.7	10.2	9.4	18.1	20.7	22.6	31,092
Seven persons or more	1,272	3.1	10.1	11.9	8.4	10.6	18.0	17.3	20.4	28,260
Marital status:										
Male householder	61,038	3.8	7.7	10.0	10.5	10.3	19.4	19.3	19.0	28,668
Married, wife present	47,976	2.2	5.8	9.2	9.9	10.2	20.0	21.3	21.6	31,216
Married, wife absent	1,533	11.5	17.1	13.2	12.2	10.3	16.4	10.7	8.6	18,346
Widowed	1,664	12.4	26.7	15.6	12.4	8.9	10.6	7.7	5.6	13,181
Divorced	3,839	7.1	11.5	12.8	12.1	12.3	18.3	14.2	11.5	22,138
Single (never married)	6,026	10.0	13.3	12.7	13.5	10.9	18.5	12.1	9.0	20,193
Female householder	27,420	16.4	22.9	14.7	11.9	9.2	11.5	7.9	5.4	13,471
Married, husband present	2,957	2.4	7.6	9.2	10.0	10.8	18.3	19.7	22.0	30,137
Married, husband absent	2,551	29.0	22.9	14.7	11.5	7.5	7.4	4.6	2.4	9,506
Widowed	9,699	18.5	34.3	15.8	9.7	6.3	7.9	4.8	2.8	9,466
Divorced	6,430	13.5	17.8	16.4	14.2	12.0	14.4	8.0	3.7	15,815
Single (never married)	5,782	17.6	17.5	13.9	14.0	11.1	12.8	8.5	4.5	15,348
Education attainment of householder:										
Elementary school	12,335	17.8	27.0	17.4	11.5	7.9	9.8	6.0	2.6	11,309
Less than 8 years	6,618	20.5	29.0	17.9	11.1	7.0	8.2	4.5	1.9	10,124
8 years	5,717	14.7	24.7	16.9	11.9	8.9	11.7	7.7	3.5	12,970
High school	42,338	8.5	13.5	13.2	12.5	10.9	17.8	14.8	8.7	20,934
1–3 years	11,067	13.9	19.3	16.3	13.2	9.7	12.9	9.7	5.0	15,171
4 years	31,271	6.6	11.5	12.2	12.2	11.3	19.6	16.7	10.0	23,134
College	33,785	2.9	5.7	7.1	8.8	9.7	18.5	20.5	26.8	33,250
1–3 years	15,300	4.3	8.7	9.4	10.6	11.4	20.4	19.5	15.8	27,337
4 years or more	18,485	1.7	3.3	5.2	7.3	8.2	16.9	21.3	35.9	39,506
Tenure										
Owner occupied	56,408	4.6	9.2	9.5	9.6	9.6	18.4	19.2	20.1	29,001
Renter occupied	30,516	12.8	18.0	14.9	13.3	11.0	14.5	9.9	5.6	16,518
Occupier paid no cash rent	1,534	18.1	22.5	16.9	12.3	8.7	12.5	6.3	2.7	12,615

¹Includes other races not shown separately.
²Persons of Spanish origin may be of any race.
Source: U.S. Bureau of the Census, *Current Population Reports*, Series P-60, No. 154.

Table 5 Spending in America—Average Income and Expenditures

This chart shows what the average urban household spends on various kinds of products every year. It also breaks expenditures down for various kinds of consumers by age, region, and income. What is called a consumer unit here could be a single person, a family, or a group of unrelated people. The data are for 1984.

Item	Income before taxes[1]	Total expenditures	Food	Alcoholic beverages	Housing Total	Shelter	Fuel, utilities, and public services	Household operations	House furnishings	Apparel and services	Transportation Gasoline and motor oil	Transportation All other transportation[2]	Health care	Other expenditures[3]	Life insurance	Retirement, pensions, Social Security	Personal taxes
All consumer units	$24,578	$21,788	$3,391	$299	$6,626	$3,747	$1,679	$333	$868	$1,192	$1,047	$3,337	$899	$2,973	$302	$1,721	$2,670
Age of reference person:																	
Under 25 years	12,579	13,178	2,030	364	3,740	2,386	722	118	513	787	759	2,543	305	1,836	57	757	1,943
25–34 years	24,652	21,506	3,063	353	7,107	4,289	1,483	432	903	1,186	1,011	3,630	626	2,521	226	1,784	2,964
35–44 years	32,058	27,702	4,342	344	8,698	5,142	1,977	408	1,171	1,646	1,272	3,870	795	4,009	362	2,363	3,210
45–54 years	32,285	28,623	4,337	339	7,878	4,189	2,156	331	1,201	1,620	1,490	4,622	1,061	4,114	477	2,686	3,633
55–64 years	26,989	23,000	3,747	272	6,451	3,403	1,946	262	840	1,224	1,117	3,360	1,060	3,152	498	2,121	3,099
65–74 years	16,815	15,873	2,831	179	4,848	2,386	1,644	269	549	715	764	2,277	1,340	2,140	220	558	1,088
75 years and over	12,442	11,196	1,912	90	3,972	2,014	1,311	356	291	346	354	1,096	1,487	1,711	86	142	950
Region of residence:																	
Northeast	24,887	21,138	3,614	326	6,369	3,571	1,802	275	721	1,245	872	3,121	890	2,864	245	1,589	2,239
Midwest	23,688	21,073	3,280	276	6,312	3,380	1,781	299	852	1,133	1,052	3,142	869	3,023	300	1,685	2,584
South	23,978	21,712	3,248	270	6,602	3,601	1,701	362	939	1,206	1,146	3,363	942	2,856	325	1,753	2,587
West	26,335	23,613	3,509	347	7,379	4,670	1,364	401	943	1,188	1,085	3,807	884	3,209	332	1,873	3,368
Size of consumer unit:																	
One person	14,740	13,220	1,916	311	4,252	2,669	977	147	460	722	559	1,868	547	2,021	147	878	1,812
Two persons	24,947	21,351	3,172	307	6,628	3,744	1,662	300	923	1,064	983	3,308	1,110	2,758	295	1,725	3,172
Three persons	28,660	25,955	3,924	301	7,624	4,180	1,951	445	1,049	1,429	1,282	4,252	908	3,669	413	2,153	2,829
Four persons	31,370	28,421	4,526	271	8,754	4,877	2,137	538	1,202	1,587	1,399	4,263	1,035	3,760	397	2,428	3,300
Five persons	33,194	29,546	5,125	305	8,575	4,632	2,390	486	1,068	1,810	1,563	4,377	1,027	4,077	452	2,236	2,522
Six persons or more	30,933	28,032	5,476	259	7,444	3,642	2,501	359	941	1,762	1,649	4,583	1,064	3,286	343	2,167	2,312
Income before taxes[1]	24,578	22,149	3,384	304	6,638	3,747	1,670	337	884	1,210	1,059	3,400	906	3,049	312	1,885	2,670
Quintiles of income:																	
Lowest 20 percent	3,577	11,347	2,130	166	3,916	2,219	1,114	155	428	612	537	1,411	571	1,566	211	224	39
Second 20 percent	10,828	13,864	2,448	209	4,447	2,449	1,340	185	473	670	756	2,003	842	1,784	132	572	661
Third 20 percent	19,297	18,981	3,119	277	5,866	3,296	1,618	244	708	988	1,016	2,986	902	2,324	214	1,291	1,797
Fourth 20 percent	30,370	25,525	3,843	347	7,367	4,171	1,821	388	987	1,272	1,319	3,978	919	3,528	361	2,590	3,144
Highest 20 percent	58,639	40,935	5,371	519	11,570	6,588	2,454	712	1,817	2,503	1,665	6,605	1,293	6,029	643	4,735	7,682
Incomplete reporting of income		18,513	3,447	260	6,515	3,740	1,754	299	722	1,026	940	2,770	838	2,271	208	237	(¹)

[1] Income values are derived from "complete income reporters" only. Represents the combined income of all consumer unit members 14 years or over during the 12 months preceding the interview. A complete reporter is a consumer unit who provided values for at least one of the major sources of income.
[2] Includes other private transportation and public transportation.
[3] Entertainment, personal care, reading, education, tobacco and smoking supplies, cash contributions, and miscellaneous expenditures.
Source: U.S. Bureau of Labor Statistics, Consumer Expenditure Survey: Interview Survey, 1984, Bulletin 2267, 1986.

earner and a contented housewife who works, without pay, to raise her three children. Rising divorce rates, working mothers, fewer children, and a changing economy have all changed the way many families live. Since the family is the basic consumer unit, these changes are sending shock waves through the economy.

Rising divorce rates have changed the composition of many American families. Women who were married in the late 1970s were twice as likely to see their marriages break up as those who were married between 1960 and 1964. One survey found that 20% of those who were married in the late 1970s were no longer married, compared to only 10% in the earlier period.

Broken marriages mean that more and more children are growing up in single-parent homes. Only 6.1% of all married couples live in poverty, while over one third (34.6%) of all households headed by a woman are impoverished. Because single-parent homes headed by women usually are poorer, 21.2% of all kids under the age of 15 were living in poverty in 1986. While the median income for a married couple with children is $32,805, the income for a single-parent family headed by a woman is only $13,647.

Another revolution going on in the American family is the massive migration of women from unpaid household work into the labor market. Over half of all women are now in the labor force, and unlike women of earlier generations, many of these women have young children. Half of all mothers with children under the age of 1 year are in the labor force and by the 1990s over 10 million children under the age of 6 will have working mothers. Yet of the 6 million U.S. employers, only an estimated 1,800 offer child-care benefits, according to the Employee Benefit Research Institute. Even that paltry percentage is three times higher than 1982.

Families are also more willing to postpone having children. To prevent any surprises, 36.7% of American women use some form of contraceptive, the most popular method being the pill, followed by a condom. And when birth control fails, women increasingly turn to abortions. There are now 419 abortions for every 1,000 live births. Thanks to birth control and declining fertility rates, 26% of the population growth in 1985 came from immigration.

There is a reason why many women are using contraceptives: half of all married women have sex at least one year before they are married. Only 30% of all married women were virgins in the month they were married; nearly 73.3% of all single women between 20 and 24 have had sex.

Even though it's been said that Americans are becoming a country of family planners, government studies show that many Americans still arrive unexpectedly. Exactly 28% of all children are "mistimed" according to one study and another 9.6% are "unwanted." About 21% of all children are now born to unmarried women: 13.4% of all white children, 9.6% of all Asian children, 28.3% of all Hispanic children, and 59.2% of all black children are born out of wedlock.

However, many of those who are having kids are waiting until they're older and more financially secure. In 1970 only 19% of all women had their first child after the age of 25; by the 1980s 36% were having kids for the first time after 25.

Parents who wait longer to have children often have more money to spend on kids. The $12 billion to $14 billion market in children's products is one of the fastest-growing parts of retailing and is expected to grow to $20 billion by the end of the decade, according to Packaged Facts, a New York research firm.

All of these trends have changed the face of the average home. The birth of fewer children and an aging population have shrunk the size of the average American household. In 1985, there were only 2.76 people in the average household, down from 3.14 in 1970. Almost one quarter of all households (23.7%) were made up of a single person, up from 9.1% in 1950. In contrast, only 27.9% consisted of a married couple with children under the age of 18, down from 45.1% in 1950. About 30.1% of all households included a married son or daughter without a child, down from 32.9% in 1950, while households composed of unrelated people grew from 1.8% in 1950 to 4% in 1985. Households with a single parent and other relatives hit 14.2% in 1985, up from 11.1% in 1950.

Yet despite all the strains that have been pulling many families apart, most Americans are still staying close to home. When asked how far they live from their parents, 71% of all adults said they lived within 100 miles, and 44% lived within 10 miles, according to a survey by Ethan Allen, Inc.

Table 6 U.S. Population and Projections
(In thousands, except as indicated. Includes Armed Forces abroad.)

Year	Total	Under 5	5–13	14–17	18–24	25–34	35–44	45–64	65 and over	85 and over
Total:										
1985	238,631	18,453	29,654	14,731	28,739	41,788	32,004	44,652	28,608	2,696
1990	249,657	19,198	32,189	12,950	25,794	43,529	37,847	46,453	31,697	3,313
2000	267,955	17,626	34,382	15,381	24,601	36,415	43,743	60,886	34,921	4,926
2080	310,762	17,202	31,650	14,316	25,296	37,237	38,222	73,748	73,090	18,227
Spanish origin:										
1985	17,286	1,999	2,997	1,282	2,349	3,254	2,129	2,391	885	67
1990	19,887	2,282	3,472	1,353	2,386	3,629	2,788	2,851	1,126	95
2000	25,225	2,496	4,382	1,825	2,766	3,804	3,803	4,430	1,719	168
2080	59,571	3,436	6,311	2,868	5,114	7,510	7,735	14,427	12,170	2,616
White non-Hispanic										
1985	186,791	12,930	21,390	10,940	21,603	32,253	25,611	37,024	25,039	2,414
1990	192,040	13,243	22,705	9,266	18,919	32,874	29,664	37,836	25,531	2,928
2000	198,918	11,496	23,235	10,595	17,200	26,011	32,783	48,097	29,502	4,286
2080	175,996	9,430	17,430	7,866	13,863	20,473	21,020	41,415	44,526	11,841
Black:										
1985	29,074	3,057	4,448	2,149	4,138	5,212	3,404	4,339	2,329	189
1990	31,412	3,215	5,098	1,944	3,798	5,860	4,295	4,624	2,579	257
2000	35,753	3,079	5,776	2,545	3,773	5,316	5,811	6,479	2,975	412
2080	55,698	3,181	5,842	2,652	4,676	6,773	6,981	13,337	12,255	2,834
Other races:										
1985	6,444	583	982	431	784	1,254	980	1,025	403	29
1990	7,456	593	1,112	461	826	1,381	1,261	1,298	522	38
2000	9,548	704	1,250	525	1,022	1,509	1,577	2,142	818	69
2080	23,439	1,385	2,514	1,120	1,982	2,982	3,003	5,522	4,931	1,101

Percent distribution

All races	Total	Under 5	5–13	14–17	18–24	25–34	35–44	45–64	65+	85+
1985	100	7.7	12.4	6.2	12.0	17.5	13.4	18.7	12.0	1.1
1990	100	7.7	12.9	5.2	10.3	17.4	15.2	18.6	12.7	1.3
2000	100	6.6	12.8	5.7	9.2	13.6	16.3	22.7	13.0	1.8
2080	100	5.5	10.2	4.6	8.1	12.0	12.3	23.7	23.5	5.9

	All races*	Spanish origin	White non-Hispanic	Black	Other
1985	100	7.2	78.3	12.2	2.7
1990	100	8.0	76.9	12.6	3.0
2000	100	9.4	74.2	13.3	3.6
2080	100	19.2	56.6	17.9	7.5

*Subtotals do not add to 100% because people of Spanish origin may be of any race.
Source: U.S. Bureau of the Census, *Current Population Reports,* series P-25, No. 995

Chapter Two
AMERICA AT WORK

HIGHLIGHTS AND TRENDS

• In 1870, approximately half of all American workers (53%) could be found down on the farm. But by 1920 more Americans (11.2 million) were employed in manufacturing than agriculture (10.8 million). And over the last forty years the labor force has changed its appearance once again, exchanging its blue collars for white and pink collars. Today about three quarters of all nonagricultural workers are employed in service-producing industries.

• And the trend toward service jobs will continue, with virtually all the 21.4 million new job openings between 1986 and 2000 being created in service-producing industries.

• Major changes will hit the labor force during the rest of the century. As population growth slows, the labor force is expected to grow at a slower rate than it did during the 1970s. But it will still increase by 1.2% a year, faster than the population, which will grow about 0.8% a year through 2000.

• Minorities, immigrants, and women will make up more and more of the labor force. Women will account for 60% of the increase in the labor force between now and 2000, while immigrants will account for about 25% of the growth in the labor force and blacks 17%, Hispanics 29%, and Asians 11%.

GETTING A JOB

There's good news and bad news at the employment office. The good news is demographic. In contrast to the 1970s and early and mid-1980s, when the baby-boom generation hit the labor market, producing keen competition for scarce jobs, the employment outlook for the late 1980s and 1990s is much brighter. Between now and 1995, the labor force is expected to grow about 1.5% a year, faster than the population, which will grow only about half as fast, 0.9% a year.

That means better pay and lower unemployment for many workers, trends that will put money in the bank for many younger workers. If the baby-boom generation continues to produce smaller families, fewer younger workers will be entering the labor force. With less competition for jobs, the sons and daughters of the baby boomers will be able to command better salaries, face less competition for career advancement, and see shorter lines at the unemployment office.

The bad news is that some of the new jobs won't pay as well as many jobs—like unionized blue-collar jobs—that once made up the backbone of the labor force. Service industries will produce 20.1 million new jobs, virtually all of the 21.4 million jobs created between now and 2000, and the 25 occupations showing the largest job growth are all service jobs. For example, there will be more new jobs created between now and 2000 for salespersons (1.2 million) than any other occupation. Yet, sales workers earned only $215 a week in 1986, compared to the average paycheck of $358. Seven of the ten largest job-producing occupations, salesworkers, waiters, janitors, cashiers, clerks, nurse's aides and food-counter workers all pay less than the average wage.

But don't buy the argument that the economy is only producing low-paying jobs. A field where employees earn $460 a week, registered nursing, will produce the third-highest job growth. And about 604,000 new jobs will be created for general managers and top executives and 525,000 for truck drivers, both high-paying occupations.

But the availability of fewer younger workers will be hard on some industries. By 2080 only 8.1% of the population will be between the ages of 18 and 24, down from 9.2% in the year 2000 and 13.1% in 1982. That will cut the number of people in college, will decrease the amount of money spent for education, and will probably cut the number of jobs available. Employers who are already having a hard time filling low-paying service jobs behind the cash register or the restaurant counter will undoubtedly be forced to up the ante. But the hardest-hit employer could be the Armed Forces. Since the Pentagon is still the largest employer of young people, the business of war is likely to get increasingly expensive and high-tech.

THE JOBS OF THE FUTURE

Overall, employment is expected to grow 19.2% to 133 million by 2000, according to Labor Department projections. The service economy will create more jobs than any other part of the economy (20.1 million) as service-industry employment grows 27% or about 1.7% a year to 94.5 million in the year 2000. About 890,000 construction jobs will be created as the number of construction workers grows 18.1% to 5.8 million at the start of the 21st century. The entrepreneurial spirit of the 1980s will continue through the rest of the century as the number of self-employed non-farmworkers increases by 1.66 million (20.5%) to 10.3 million.

But mining, manufacturing, and agriculture will not fare so well. The number of manufacturing jobs will drop 4.4% from 19 million in 1986 to 18.2 million in 2000, with 513,000 jobs lost in the durable goods sector of manufacturing and 321,000 lost in nondurable goods. Mining will see employment drop 7.5% to 724,000, and woes in the farm belt will cut the number of agricultural jobs by 335,000 to only 2.9 million, a 10.3% plunge. As a result, the number of people employed in agriculture, mining, and manufacturing will be way below their 1979 levels of 3.4 million, 958,000, and 21.0 million respectively.

Between 1986 and 2000, Labor Department forecasters believe that government employment will grow by 1.6 million to 18.3 million. Since problems with the federal deficit are expected to keep the number of federal employees virtually constant, almost all that growth will occur at the state and local level.

WORKING IN AMERICA

An economic rebound has improved civilian employment, bringing the number of Americans with jobs up to 114.5 million in September 1987, up from 107.2 million in 1985 and 99.3 million in 1980. And the job market continues to reflect the long-term growth of the service economy. Between 1946 and 1987, as many Americans exchanged a blue collar for a white or pink collar, service-producing industries grew from 58.6% to 75.7% of nonagricultural employment.

Yet during the same period, employment in goods-producing industries—construction, mining, and manufacturing—declined from 41.4% to only 24.3%. Agricultural employment also declined, falling to only 3.1 million—down from 8.3 million in 1946. Manufacturing now accounts for only 18.7% of all civilian nonagricultural jobs, down from 35.3% in 1946 and 27.3% in 1970.

Government employment in an age of fiscal austerity has remained virtually stagnant, growing from 16.2 million in 1980 to 17 million in 1987. In contrast, over 11.2 million jobs were created in the private nonagricultural sector during that period. (See Part III, "The Heavy Hand," for a discussion of government, and also see the chapters "Services," "Manufacturing," and "Agriculture.")

These employment trends are likely to continue into the 21st century. By the year 2000, manufacturing, mining, and construction will account for 20.7% of nonagricultural jobs, down from 32.2% in 1972. Meanwhile, services will account for nearly four fifths of all jobs (79.3%), up from 67.8% in 1972. Manufacturing will employ only 15.2% of all nonagricultural workers, down from 26.1% in 1972, and government's share of the job market will drop from 18.1% to only 15.4%. Even so, the U.S. will enter the 21st century with more government bureaucrats (18.3 million) than manufacturing workers (18.2 million) for the first time in the republic's history.

Women workers are one of the fastest-growing sectors of the economy, up 18.7% between 1980 and 1987. About 55.8% of all women were in the labor force—either looking for work or employed—in 1987, up from 33.9% in 1950 and 51.5% in 1980. In contrast, the percentage of men working or looking for a job is actually declining. The labor-force participation rate for men dropped from 86.7% in 1950 to 76.6% in 1987. (See the chapter "Working Women.")

Not everyone has been helped by the economic recovery of the past five years. But unemployment has declined from a postwar high of 10.6% at the end of 1982 to 5.8% in the first quarter of 1988; 1979 was the last year when unemployment was below 6%.

Unemployment rates for minorities in the mid-1980s remained disturbingly high: 12.3% for blacks in 1987 (down from 18.9% in 1982) and 8.2% for Hispanics (down from 15.3% in 1982).

In 1987, nonagricultural workers put in 191 billion hours at work every week, up from 182 billion in 1985. But over the long term the average American has been putting in less and less hours at his or her job. In 1987, the average nonsupervisory production workers worked about 34.7 hours per week, about five hours less than the average working week in 1947.

This trend toward a shorter and shorter workweek can be traced to the rise of retail and service industries, areas of the economy with larger numbers of part-time workers. In 1987, 19.5 million Americans worked part-time. About 5.2 million of those workers said they worked part-time because there wasn't enough work at their job or they couldn't find full-time work. But most (14.3 million) said they wanted to work part-time. An additional 700,000 jobs a year are filled by temporary workers.

By the 21st century these demographic trends will play a major role in reshaping the labor force. An older America will mean an older labor force, with the median age of the American worker rising to 38.9 years. That's up from 34.7 years in 1979 but still slightly less than 1962, when the typical age was 40.5 years. The proportion of young workers aged 16 to 24 will also drop from 20% in 1986 to only 16% in 2000.

Women will continue to enter the labor force in record numbers. They will account for about 60% of the labor force growth through the end of the century and by the year 2000 will account for nearly half of the labor force (47.3%), up from (38.5%) in 1972 and 42.1% in 1979.

The American workplace in the 21st century will also have more minorities than ever before. By the year 2000, Hispanics will account for 10.2% of the labor force, up from 5% in 1979 and 6.9% in 1986. Asians will hold 4.1% of all jobs, up from 2.3% in 1979 and 2.8% in 1986. The proportion of blacks will grow more slowly, hitting 11.8% in 2000, up from 10.2% in 1979 and 10.8% in 1986.

Lottery Winners

People grouse about their jobs, but how many people would up and quit if they came into a windfall? Not many if you judge by lottery winners. Within a year of hitting the jackpot, only 24% of state lottery winners stopped working, and that included 13% who were of an age to retire. Only 9% of those who won between $500,000 and $1,000,000 dropped out of the rat race.

Table 7   The Fastest-growing Jobs in America

This chart shows the fastest-growing and fastest-declining occupations in America through the end of the century. There are several ways of looking at job growth. The top part of the table lists those occupations that will have produced the most jobs between 1986 and 2000. The middle of the table shows those jobs that will have shown the fastest percentage increase, though not necessarily the largest increase in jobs. The bottom part of the chart shows the fastest-declining jobs in percentage terms. The Labor Department study produces high, middle, and low projections for the growth of various jobs. We have only listed the moderate or middle-range projections.

Occupation	Employment		Change in employment, 1986–2000	
	1986	Projected, 2000	Number	Percent
Total	111,623	133,030	21,407	19.2
Largest job growth				
Salespersons, retail	3,579	4,780	1,201	33.5
Waiters and waitresses	1,702	2,454	752	44.2
Registered nurses	1,406	2,018	612	43.6
Janitors and cleaners, including maids and housekeeping cleaners	2,676	3,280	604	22.6
General managers and top executives	2,383	2,965	582	24.4
Cashiers	2,165	2,740	575	26.5
Truck drivers, light and heavy	2,211	2,736	525	23.8
General office clerks	2,361	2,824	462	19.6
Food counter, fountain, and related workers	1,500	1,949	449	29.9
Nursing aides, orderlies, and attendants	1,224	1,658	433	35.4
Secretaries	3,234	3,658	424	13.1
Guards	794	1,177	383	48.3
Accountants and auditors	945	1,322	376	39.8
Computer programmers	479	813	335	69.9
Food preparation workers	949	1,273	324	34.2
Teachers, kindergarten and elementary	1,527	1,826	299	19.6
Receptionists and information clerks	682	964	282	41.4
Computer systems analysts, electronic data processing	331	582	251	75.6
Cooks, restaurant	520	759	240	46.2
Licensed practical nurses	631	869	238	37.7
Gardeners and groundskeepers, except farm	767	1,005	238	31.1

Table 7 The Fastest-growing Jobs in America (continued)

Occupation	Employment		Change in employment, 1986–2000	
	1986	Projected, 2000	Number	Percent
Maintenance repairers, general utility	1,039	1,270	232	22.3
Stock clerks, sales floor	1,087	1,312	225	20.7
First-line supervisors and managers	956	1,161	205	21.4
Dining room and cafeteria attendants and barroom helpers	433	631	197	45.6
Electrical and electronics engineers	401	592	192	47.8
Lawyers	527	718	191	36.3
Fastest-growing				
Paralegal personnel	61	125	64	103.7
Medical assistants	132	251	119	90.4
Physical therapists	61	115	53	87.5
Physical and corrective therapy assistants and aides	36	65	29	81.6
Data processing equipment repairers	69	125	56	80.4
Home health aides	138	249	111	80.1
Podiatrists	13	23	10	77.2
Computer systems analysts, electronic data processing	331	582	251	75.6
Medical records technicians	40	70	30	75.0
Employment interviewers, private or public employment service	75	129	54	71.2
Computer programmers	479	813	335	69.9
Radiologic technologists and technicians	115	190	75	64.7
Dental hygienists	87	141	54	62.6
Dental assistants	155	244	88	57.0
Physician assistants	26	41	15	56.7
Operations and systems researchers	38	59	21	54.1
Occupational therapists	29	45	15	52.2
Peripheral electronic data processing equipment operators	46	70	24	50.8
Data entry keyers, composing	29	43	15	50.8
Optometrists	37	55	18	49.2
Fastest-declining				
Electrical and electronic assemblers	249	116	133	−53.7
Electronic semiconductor processors	29	14	15	−51.1
Railroad conductors and yardmasters	29	17	12	−40.9
Railroad brake, signal, and switch operators	42	25	17	−39.9
Gas and petroleum plant and system occupations	31	20	9	−34.3
Industrial truck and tractor operators	426	283	143	−33.6
Shoe sewing machine operators and tenders	27	18	9	−32.1
Station installers and repairers, telephone	58	40	18	−31.8
Chemical equipment controllers, operators and tenders	73	52	21	−29.7
Chemical plant and system operators	33	23	10	−29.6

Source: U.S. Department of Labor, *Monthly Labor Review*, September 1987.

Table 8 Working in America

This chart shows the working-age population, the labor force, employment, unemployment, and the labor-force participation rate. Remember that the labor force includes people who are working and those who are looking for work. Employment includes part-time workers. The labor-force participation rate shows the percentage of working-age people who are employed or looking for work. The labor-force participation rate for women shows, for example, that more and more women are employed or looking for work.

Year	Civilian noninstitutional population	Resident Armed Forces	Labor force including resident Armed Forces	Employment including resident Armed Forces	Civilian labor force Total	Employment Total	Employment Agricultural	Employment Nonagricultural	Unemployment	Unemployment rate, Civilian workers (percent)	Participation Total	Participation Males	Participation Females	Participation Both sexes 16–19 years	Participation White	Participation Black and other	Participation Black
Thousands of persons 14 years of age and over																	
1929					49,180	47,630	10,450	37,180	1,550	3.2							
1933					51,590	38,760	10,090	28,670	12,830	24.9							
1939					55,230	45,750	9,610	36,140	9,480	17.2							
1940	99,840				55,640	47,520	9,540	37,980	8,120	14.6							
1941	99,900				55,910	50,350	9,100	41,250	5,560	9.9							
1942	98,640				56,410	53,750	9,250	44,500	2,660	4.7							
1943	94,640				55,540	54,470	9,080	45,390	1,070	1.9							
1944	93,220				54,630	53,960	8,950	45,010	670	1.2							
1945	94,090				53,860	52,820	8,580	44,240	1,040	1.9							
1946	103,070				57,520	55,250	8,320	46,930	2,270	3.9							
1947	106,018				60,168	57,812	8,256	49,557	2,356	3.9							
Thousands of persons 16 years of age and over																	
1947	101,827				59,350	57,038	7,890	49,148	2,311	3.9							
1948	103,068				60,621	58,343	7,629	50,714	2,276	3.8	58.8	86.6	32.7	52.5			
1949	103,994				61,286	57,651	7,658	49,993	3,637	5.9	58.9	86.4	33.1	52.2			
1950	104,995	1,169	63,377	60,087	62,208	58,918	7,160	51,758	3,288	5.3	59.2	86.4	33.9	51.8			
1951	104,621	2,143	64,160	62,104	62,017	59,961	6,726	53,235	2,055	3.3	59.2	86.3	34.6	52.2			
1952	105,231	2,386	64,524	62,636	62,138	60,250	6,500	53,749	1,883	3.0	59.0	86.3	34.7	51.3			
1953	107,056	2,231	65,246	63,410	63,015	61,179	6,260	54,919	1,834	2.9	58.9	86.0	34.4	50.2			

Year																	
1954	108,321	2,142	65,785	62,251	63,643	60,109	6,205	53,904	3,532	5.5	58.8	85.5	34.6	48.3	58.2	64.0	
1955	109,683	2,064	67,087	64,234	65,023	62,170	6,450	55,722	2,852	4.4	59.3	85.4	35.7	48.9	58.7	64.2	
1956	110,954	1,965	68,517	65,764	66,552	63,799	6,283	57,514	2,750	4.1	60.0	85.5	36.9	50.9	59.4	64.9	
1957	112,265	1,948	68,877	66,019	66,929	64,071	5,947	58,123	2,859	4.3	59.6	84.8	36.9	49.6	59.1	64.4	
1958	113,727	1,847	69,486	64,883	67,639	63,036	5,586	57,450	4,602	6.8	59.5	84.2	37.1	47.4	58.9	64.8	
1959	115,329	1,788	70,157	66,418	68,369	64,630	5,565	59,065	3,740	5.5	59.3	83.7	37.1	46.7	58.7	64.3	
1960	117,245	1,861	71,489	67,639	69,628	65,778	5,458	60,318	3,852	5.5	59.4	83.3	37.7	47.5	58.8	64.5	
1961	118,771	1,900	72,359	67,646	70,459	65,746	5,200	60,546	4,714	6.7	59.3	82.9	38.1	46.9	58.8	64.1	
1962	120,153	2,061	72,675	68,763	70,614	66,702	4,944	61,759	3,911	5.5	58.8	82.0	37.9	46.1	58.3	63.2	
1963	122,416	2,006	73,839	69,768	71,833	67,762	4,687	63,076	3,786	5.7	58.7	81.4	38.3	45.2	58.2	63.0	
1964	124,485	2,018	75,109	71,323	73,091	69,305	4,523	64,782	4,070	5.2	58.7	81.0	38.7	45.7	58.2	63.1	
1965	126,513	1,946	76,401	73,034	74,455	71,088	4,361	66,726	3,786	4.5	58.9	80.7	39.3	45.7	58.4	62.9	
1966	128,058	2,122	77,892	75,017	75,770	72,895	3,979	68,915	2,875	3.8	59.2	80.4	40.3	48.2	58.7	63.0	
1967	129,874	2,218	79,565	76,590	77,347	74,372	3,844	70,527	2,975	3.8	59.6	80.4	41.1	48.4	59.2	62.8	
1968	132,028	2,253	80,990	78,173	78,737	75,920	3,817	72,103	2,817	3.6	59.6	80.1	41.6	48.3	59.3	62.2	
1969	134,335	2,238	82,972	80,140	80,734	77,902	3,606	74,296	2,832	3.5	60.1	79.8	42.7	49.4	59.9	62.1	
1970	137,085	2,118	84,889	80,796	82,771	78,678	3,463	75,215	4,093	4.9	60.4	79.7	43.3	49.9	60.2	61.8	59.9
1971	140,216	1,973	86,355	81,340	84,382	79,367	3,394	75,972	5,016	5.9	60.2	79.1	43.4	49.7	60.1	60.9	60.2
1972	144,126	1,813	88,847	83,966	87,034	82,153	3,484	78,669	4,882	5.6	60.4	78.9	43.9	51.9	60.4	60.2	59.8
1973	147,096	1,774	91,203	86,838	89,429	85,064	3,470	81,594	4,365	4.9	60.8	78.8	44.7	53.7	60.8	60.5	58.8
1974	150,120	1,721	93,670	88,515	91,949	86,794	3,515	83,279	5,156	5.6	61.3	78.7	45.7	54.8	61.4	60.3	58.8
1975	153,153	1,678	95,453	87,524	93,775	85,846	3,408	82,438	7,929	8.5	61.2	77.9	46.3	54.0	61.8	59.6	58.0
1976	156,150	1,668	97,826	90,420	96,158	88,752	3,331	85,421	7,406	7.7	61.6	77.5	47.3	54.5	61.8	59.8	59.8
1977	159,033	1,656	100,665	93,673	99,009	92,017	3,283	88,734	6,991	7.1	62.3	77.7	48.4	56.0	62.5	60.4	59.8
1978	161,910	1,631	100,882	97,679	102,251	96,048	3,387	92,661	6,202	6.1	63.2	77.9	50.0	57.8	63.3	62.2	61.5
1979	164,863	1,597	106,559	100,421	104,962	98,824	3,347	95,477	6,137	5.8	63.7	77.8	50.9	57.9	63.9	62.2	61.4
1980	167,745	1,604	108,544	100,907	106,940	99,303	3,364	95,938	7,637	7.1	63.8	77.4	51.5	56.7	64.1	61.7	61.0
1981	170,130	1,645	110,315	102,042	108,670	100,397	3,368	97,030	8,273	7.6	63.9	77.0	52.1	55.4	64.3	61.3	60.8
1982	172,271	1,668	111,872	101,194	110,204	99,526	3,401	96,125	10,678	9.7	64.0	76.6	52.6	54.1	64.3	61.6	61.0
1983	174,215	1,676	113,226	102,510	111,550	100,834	3,383	97,450	10,717	9.6	64.0	76.4	52.9	53.5	64.6	62.1	61.5
1984	176,383	1,697	115,241	106,702	113,544	105,005	3,321	101,685	8,539	7.5	64.4	76.4	53.6	53.9	65.0	62.6	62.2
1985	178,206	1,706	117,167	108,856	115,461	107,150	3,179	103,971	8,312	7.2	64.8	76.3	54.5	54.5	65.5	62.9	62.9
1986	180,587	1,706	119,540	111,303	117,834	109,597	3,163	106,434	8,237	7.0	65.3	76.3	55.3	54.7	65.5	63.7	63.3
1987*	184,904	1,743	121,604	114,515	119,861	112,772	3,170	109,602	7,089	5.8	65.4	76.0	56.7	54.2	65.7	NA	63.8

*September 1987
Source: U.S. Bureau of Labor Statistics.

31

Table 9　The Work and Earnings of America

This chart shows the number of workers in various nonagricultural industries from 1960 to 1985. The next part of the chart lists a percentage breakdown for each industry. That breakdown shows a long-term trend away from manufacturing and toward services.

Item and year	Total	Mining	Construction	Manufacturing	Transportation and public utilities	Wholesale trade	Retail trade	Finance, insurance, and real estate	Services	Government	Goods-related	Service-related and all other
Employees (thousands)												
1960	54,189	712	2,926	16,796	4,004	3,143	8,248	2,629	7,378	8,353	20,434	33,755
1965	60,765	632	3,232	18,062	4,036	3,466	9,250	2,977	9,036	10,074	21,926	38,839
1970	70,880	623	3,588	19,367	4,515	3,993	11,047	3,645	11,548	12,554	23,578	47,302
1975	76,945	752	3,525	18,323	4,542	4,415	12,645	4,165	13,892	14,686	22,600	54,345
1980	90,406	1,027	4,346	20,285	5,146	5,275	15,035	5,160	17,890	16,241	25,658	64,748
1981	91,156	1,139	4,188	20,170	5,165	5,358	15,189	5,298	18,619	16,031	25,497	65,659
1982	89,566	1,128	3,905	18,781	5,082	5,278	15,179	5,341	19,036	15,837	23,813	65,752
1983	90,200	952	3,948	18,434	4,954	5,268	15,613	5,468	19,694	15,870	23,334	66,866
1984	94,496	966	4,383	19,378	5,159	5,555	16,545	5,689	20,797	16,024	24,727	69,769
1985	97,519	926	4,673	19,260	5,238	5,717	17,353	5,955	22,000	16,394	24,859	72,660
1986	99,610	783	4,904	18,994	5,244	5,735	17,845	6,297	23,099	16,711	24,681	74,930
1987*	102,396	758	4,978	19,174	5,406	5,813	18,319	6,626	24,274	17,048	24,910	77,486
Percent distribution												
1960	100.0	1.3	5.4	31.0	7.4	5.8	15.2	4.9	13.6	15.4	37.7	62.3
1965	100.0	1.0	5.3	29.7	6.7	5.7	15.2	4.9	14.9	16.6	36.1	63.9
1970	100.0	.9	5.1	27.3	6.4	5.6	15.6	5.1	16.3	17.7	33.3	66.7
1975	100.0	1.0	4.6	23.8	5.9	5.7	16.4	5.4	18.0	19.1	29.4	70.6
1980	100.0	1.1	4.8	22.4	5.7	5.8	16.6	5.7	19.8	18.0	28.4	71.6
1981	100.0	1.3	4.6	22.1	5.7	5.9	16.7	5.8	20.4	17.4	28.0	72.0
1982	100.0	1.3	4.4	21.0	5.7	5.9	16.9	6.0	21.3	17.7	26.6	73.4
1983	100.0	1.1	4.4	20.4	5.5	5.8	17.3	6.1	21.8	17.6	25.9	74.1
1984	100.0	1.0	4.6	20.5	5.5	5.9	17.5	6.0	22.0	17.0	26.2	73.8
1985	100.0	0.9	4.8	19.7	5.4	5.9	17.8	6.1	22.6	16.8	25.5	74.5
1986	100.0	0.8	4.9	19.1	5.3	5.8	17.9	6.3	23.2	16.8	24.8	75.2
1987*	100.0	0.7	4.9	18.7	5.3	5.7	17.9	6.5	23.7	16.6	24.3	75.7
Average weekly hours												
1960	38.6	40.4	36.7	39.7	(NA)	40.5	38.0	37.2	(NA)			
1965	38.8	42.3	37.4	41.2	41.3	40.8	36.6	37.2	35.9			
1970	37.1	42.7	37.3	39.8	40.5	39.9	33.8	36.7	34.4			
1975	36.1	41.9	36.4	39.5	39.7	38.7	32.4	36.5	33.5			
1980	35.3	43.3	37.0	39.7	39.6	38.5	30.2	36.2	33.5			
1981	35.2	43.7	36.9	39.8	39.4	38.5	30.1	36.3	32.6	(NA)	(NA)	(NA)
1982	34.8	42.7	36.7	38.9	39.0	38.3	29.9	36.2	32.6			
1983	35.0	42.5	37.1	40.1	39.0	38.5	29.8	36.2	32.7			
1984	35.2	43.3	37.8	40.7	39.4	38.5	29.8	36.5	32.6			
1985	34.9	43.4	37.7	40.5	39.5	38.4	29.4	36.4	32.5			
1986	34.8	42.2	37.4	40.7	39.2	38.4	29.2	36.4	32.5			
1987*	34.6	NA	NA	40.4	38.9	38.1	29.6	NA	32.5			
Average weekly earnings												
1960	$ 81	$105	$113	$90	(NA)	$91	$58	$75	(NA)			
1965	95	124	139	108	$125	106	67	89	$74			
1970	120	164	195	133	156	137	82	113	97			
1975	164	249	266	191	233	183	109	148	135			
1980	235	397	368	289	351	268	147	210	191			
1981	255	439	399	318	382	291	158	229	209	(NA)	(NA)	(NA)
1982	267	460	427	330	402	310	164	245	226			
1983	281	279	443	354	421	329	171	264	239			
1984	293	504	459	374	438	342	174	279	247			
1985	299	520	464	386	450	352	175	289	256			
1986	305	523	466	396	459	359	176	304	265			
1987**	314	524	465	406	468	370	184	317	277			
Average hourly earnings												
1960	$2.09	$2.60	$3.07	$2.26	(NA)	$2.24	$1.52	$2.02	(NA)			
1965	2.46	2.92	3.70	2.61	$3.03	2.61	1.82	2.39	$2.05			
1970	3.23	3.85	5.24	3.35	3.85	3.44	2.44	3.07	2.81			
1975	4.53	5.95	7.31	4.83	5.88	4.73	3.36	4.06	4.02			
1980	6.66	9.17	9.94	7.27	8.87	6.96	4.88	5.79	5.85			
1981	7.25	10.04	10.82	7.99	9.70	7.56	5.25	6.31	6.41	(NA)	(NA)	(NA)
1982	7.68	10.77	11.63	8.49	10.32	8.09	5.48	6.78	6.92			
1983	8.02	11.28	11.94	8.83	10.79	8.55	5.74	7.29	7.31			
1984	8.32	11.63	12.13	9.19	11.12	8.89	5.85	7.63	7.59			
1985	8.57	11.98	12.32	9.54	11.40	9.16	5.94	7.94	7.90			
1986	8.76	12.44	12.47	9.73	11.70	9.35	6.03	8.35	8.16			
1987*	9.08	NA	12.67	10.02	12.00	9.70	6.16	8.83	8.60			

(NA) Not available.
*June.
Source: U.S. Bureau of the Census, Employment and Earnings.
*September, seasonally adjusted except where noted.
**September, not seasonally adjusted.
NA = Not available

Table 10   U.S. Unemployment

Year	All civilian workers	White Total	White Males 16–19 years	White Males 20 years and over	White Females 16–19 years	White Females 20 years and over	Black Total	Black Males 16–19 years	Black Males 20 years and over	Black Females 16–19 years	Black Females 20 years and over
1948	3.8	3.5									
1949	5.9	5.6									
1950	5.3	4.9									
1951	3.3	3.1									
1952	3.0	2.8									
1953	2.9	2.7									
1954	5.5	5.0	13.4	4.4	10.4	5.1					
1955	4.4	3.9	11.3	3.3	9.1	3.9					
1956	4.1	3.6	10.5	3.0	9.7	3.7					
1957	4.3	3.8	11.5	3.2	9.5	3.8					
1958	6.8	6.1	15.7	5.5	12.7	5.6					
1959	5.5	4.8	14.0	4.1	12.0	4.7					
1960	5.5	5.0	14.0	4.2	12.7	4.6					
1961	6.7	6.0	15.7	5.1	14.8	5.7					
1962	5.5	4.9	13.7	4.0	12.8	4.7					
1963	5.7	5.0	15.9	3.9	15.1	4.8					
1964	5.2	4.6	14.7	3.4	14.9	4.6					
1965	4.5	4.1	12.9	2.9	14.0	4.0					
1966	3.8	3.4	10.5	2.2	12.1	3.3					
1967	3.8	3.4	10.7	2.1	11.5	3.8					
1968	3.6	3.2	10.1	2.0	12.1	3.4					
1969	3.5	3.1	10.0	1.9	11.5	3.4					
1970	4.9	4.5	13.7	3.2	13.4	4.4					
1971	5.9	5.4	15.1	4.0	15.1	5.3					
1972	5.6	5.1	14.2	3.6	14.2	4.9	10.4	31.7	7.0	40.5	9.0
1973	4.9	4.3	12.3	3.0	13.0	4.3	9.4	27.8	6.0	36.1	8.6
1974	5.6	5.0	13.5	3.5	14.5	5.1	10.5	33.1	7.4	37.4	8.8
1975	8.5	7.8	18.3	6.2	17.4	7.5	14.8	38.1	12.5	41.0	12.2
1976	7.7	7.0	17.3	5.4	16.4	6.8	14.0	37.5	11.4	41.6	11.7
1977	7.1	6.2	15.0	4.7	15.9	6.2	14.0	39.2	10.7	43.4	12.3
1978	6.1	5.2	13.5	3.7	14.4	5.2	12.8	36.7	9.3	40.8	11.2
1979	5.8	5.1	13.9	3.6	14.0	5.0	12.3	34.2	9.3	39.1	10.9
1980	7.1	6.3	16.2	5.3	14.8	5.6	14.3	37.5	12.4	39.8	11.9
1981	7.6	6.7	17.9	5.6	16.6	5.9	15.6	40.7	13.5	42.2	13.4
1982	9.7	8.6	21.7	7.8	19.0	7.3	18.9	48.9	17.8	47.1	15.4
1983	9.6	8.4	20.2	7.9	18.3	6.9	19.5	48.8	18.1	48.2	16.5
1984	7.5	6.5	16.8	5.7	15.2	5.8	15.9	42.7	14.3	42.6	13.5
1985	7.2	6.2	16.5	5.4	14.8	5.7	15.1	41.0	13.2	39.2	13.1
1986	7.0	6.0	16.3	5.3	14.9	5.4	14.5	39.3	12.9	39.2	12.4
1987	6.2	5.3	15.5	4.8	13.4	4.6	13.0	34.4	11.1	34.9	11.6

Source: U.S. Department of Labor.

Table 11   The Top Ten Corporate Employers, 1987

Big businesses, such as General Motors, remain the largest employers, but they are producing few jobs. Eight of the ten largest employers listed below cut employment in 1986. General Motors and IBM, the only two that increased employment in 1986, have since cut their work forces.

1.	General Motors	811,000
2.	Sears, Roebuck	485,500
3.	IBM	405,500
4.	Ford Motor	369,300
5.	AT&T	337,600
6.	K mart	320,000
7.	General Electric	304,000
8.	ITT	232,000
9.	United Technologies	184,000
10.	GTE	160,000

Table 12   Jobs and Money: Pay and Employment in Various Occupations, 1986

This chart shows how many people are employed in various occupations and their median weekly earnings. On the far right it shows what percentage of all managers and other workers are women. Another column shows the ratio of female to male earnings. For example, the median earnings for all women workers are 69.2% of men's, while women managers earn 68.1% of the median male manager's weekly paycheck. The data are for occupations employing over 50,000 workers and for full-time workers. The table lists employment in thousands.

Occupation	Both sexes Number of workers (thousands)	Both sexes Median weekly earnings (dollars)	Men Number of workers (thousands)	Men Median weekly earnings (dollars)	Women Number of workers (thousands)	Women Median weekly earnings (dollars)	Ratio female/male earnings times 100	Percent female workers
Total	78,727	358	46,233	419	32,494	290	69.2	41.3
Managerial and professional specialty occupations	20,095	505	11,333	608	8,762	414	68.1	43.6
Executive, administrative, and managerial occupations	9,777	511	5,980	620	3,797	395	63.7	38.8
Administrators and officials, public administration	434	513	259	617	176	414	67.1	40.6
Financial managers	396	584	245	703	150	458	65.1	37.9
Personnel and labor relations managers	109	621	57	759	52	474	62.5	47.7
Purchasing managers	101	633	67	741	33	(1)	(1)	32.7
Managers, marketing, advertising, and public relations	421	680	320	751	101	470	62.6	24.0
Administrators, education and related fields	440	610	255	691	185	495	71.6	42.0
Managers, medicine and health	113	503	45	(1)	67	463	(1)	59.3
Managers, properties and real estate	233	375	109	407	124	343	84.3	53.2
Management-related occupations	3,004	474	1,592	565	1,412	390	69.0	47.0
Accountants and auditors	1,083	478	589	554	493	398	71.8	45.5
Underwriters, and other financial officers	600	500	321	617	279	394	63.9	46.5
Management analysts	102	567	63	673	40	(1)	(1)	39.2
Personnel, training, and labor relations specialists	327	485	148	606	179	411	67.8	54.7
Buyers, wholesale and retail trade, except farm products	177	397	79	501	98	314	62.7	55.4
Inspectors and compliance officers, except construction	181	485	146	508	36	(1)	(1)	19.9
Professional specialty occupations	10,317	500	5,353	599	4,965	428	71.5	48.1
Engineers, architects, and surveyors	1,751	676	1,636	685	115	551	80.4	6.6
Architects	87	577	77	592	10	(1)	(1)	11.5
Engineers	1,644	682	1,540	691	104	580	83.9	6.3
Aerospace engineers	95	708	91	722	4	(1)	(1)	4.2
Chemical engineers	55	721	49	(1)	6	(1)	(1)	10.9
Civil engineers	209	618	202	620	7	(1)	(1)	3.3
Electrical and electronic engineers	511	704	471	715	40	(1)	(1)	7.8
Industrial engineers	191	628	173	647	19	(1)	(1)	9.9
Mechanical engineers	283	687	272	695	11	(1)	(1)	3.9
Mathematical and computer scientists	588	628	375	696	213	521	74.9	36.2
Computer systems analysts and scientists	337	631	219	687	118	537	78.2	35.0
Operations and systems researchers and analysts	203	617	127	695	77	511	73.5	37.9
Natural scientists	339	570	265	603	74	471	78.1	21.8
Chemists, except biochemists	116	601	92	624	24	(1)	(1)	20.7
Biological and life scientists	59	503	37	(1)	22	(1)	(1)	37.3
Health diagnosing occupations	254	653	188	722	66	499	69.1	26.0
Physicians	219	653	160	728	59	505	69.4	26.9
Health assessment and treating occupations	1,464	456	243	497	1,220	449	90.3	83.3
Registered nurses	1,068	460	84	490	984	458	93.5	92.1
Pharmacists	109	607	71	613	38	(1)	(1)	34.9
Dietitians	53	336	3	(1)	50	342	(1)	94.3
Therapists	195	404	58	415	136	400	96.4	69.7
Inhalation therapists	64	386	28	(1)	36	(1)	(1)	56.3
Teachers, college and university	443	600	322	656	122	479	73.0	27.5
Teachers, except college and university	2,884	437	836	501	2,048	411	82.0	71.0
Teachers, prekindergarten and kindergarten	240	274	4	(1)	236	279	(1)	98.3
Teachers, elementary school	1,173	422	172	490	1,001	415	84.7	85.3
Teachers, secondary school	1,076	481	518	508	558	443	87.2	51.9
Teachers, special education	198	424	29	(1)	169	417	(1)	85.4
Counselors, educational and vocational	146	494	72	535	74	471	88.0	50.7
Librarians, archivists, and curators	150	425	27	(1)	123	410	(1)	82.0
Librarians	139	423	21	(1)	118	408	(1)	84.9
Social scientists and urban planners	229	569	131	683	98	470	68.8	42.8
Economists	96	704	59	794	37	(1)	(1)	38.5
Psychologists	100	491	51	581	49	(1)	(1)	49.0
Social, recreation, and religious workers	750	389	413	420	337	350	83.3	44.9
Social workers	423	399	163	451	260	369	81.8	61.5
Recreation workers	60	232	23	(1)	37	(1)	(1)	61.7
Clergy	226	396	210	400	16	(1)	(1)	7.1
Lawyers and judges	342	767	256	812	85	609	75.0	24.9
Lawyers	314	767	234	806	79	624	77.4	25.2
Writers, artists, entertainers, and athletes	979	455	589	504	390	374	74.2	39.8
Designers	292	490	182	574	110	350	61.0	37.7
Actors and directors	55	423	32	(1)	23	(1)	(1)	41.8
Painters, sculptors, craft artists, and artist printmakers	86	385	49	(1)	36	(1)	(1)	41.9
Photographers	59	392	42	(1)	17	(1)	(1)	28.8
Editors and reporters	199	425	107	480	92	373	77.7	46.2
Public relations specialists	130	518	67	698	63	440	63.0	48.5

34

Table 12 Jobs and Money: Pay and Employment in Various Occupations, 1986 (continued)

	Both sexes		Men		Women			
Occupation	Number of workers (thousands)	Median weekly earnings (dollars)	Number of workers (thousands)	Median weekly earnings (dollars)	Number of workers (thousands)	Median weekly earnings (dollars)	Ratio female/male earnings times 100	Percent female workers
Technical, sales, and administrative support occupations	24,060	320	8,977	437	15,083	282	64.5	62.7
Technicians and related support occupations	2,821	416	1,597	490	1,224	343	70.0	43.4
Health technologists and technicians	852	328	167	405	685	317	78.3	80.4
Clinical laboratory technologists and technicians	239	388	68	436	170	371	85.1	71.1
Radiologic technicians	94	383	32	(1)	62	367	(1)	66.0
Licensed practical nurses	281	300	9	(1)	272	299	(1)	96.8
Engineering and related technologists and technicians	843	447	699	471	144	356	75.6	17.1
Electrical and electronic technicians	303	477	265	493	38	(1)	(1)	12.5
Drafting occupations	248	412	198	431	50	351	81.4	20.2
Surveying and mapping technicians	74	381	67	375	6	(1)	(1)	8.1
Science technicians	178	423	133	479	45	(1)	(1)	25.3
Chemical technicians	72	459	57	486	16	(1)	(1)	22.2
Technicians, except health, engineering, and science	949	499	598	548	351	424	77.4	37.0
Airplane pilots and navigators	54	754	53	760	1	(1)	(1)	1.9
Computer programmers	503	519	332	559	172	477	85.3	34.2
Legal assistants	145	372	34	(1)	111	361	(1)	76.6
Sales occupations	7,395	351	4,373	447	3,021	239	53.5	40.9
Supervisors	2,103	392	1,436	460	667	282	61.3	31.7
Sales representatives, finance and business services	1,388	453	789	519	599	360	69.4	43.2
Insurance sales	358	418	225	500	133	352	70.4	37.2
Real estate sales	326	457	145	518	181	389	75.1	55.5
Securities and financial services sales	215	608	164	740	52	423	57.2	24.2
Advertising and related sales	107	454	52	502	54	373	74.3	50.5
Sales occupations, other business services	382	397	203	487	178	315	64.7	46.6
Sales representatives, commodities, except retail, including sales engineers	1,226	492	1,017	508	209	382	75.2	17.0
Salesworkers, retail and personal services	2,660	215	1,122	301	1,538	183	60.8	57.8
Salesworkers, motor vehicle and boats	237	424	220	439	17	(1)	(1)	7.2
Salesworkers, apparel	166	192	40	(1)	126	174	(1)	75.9
Salesworkers, furniture and home furnishings	112	302	65	318	47	(1)	(1)	42.0
Salesworkers, radio, television, hi-fi, and appliances	107	304	84	313	24	(1)	(1)	22.4
Salesworkers, hardware and building supplies	135	267	105	292	30	(1)	(1)	22.2
Salesworkers, parts	155	274	140	286	14	(1)	(1)	9.0
Sales counter clerks	76	193	22	(1)	54	170	(1)	71.1
Cashiers	957	181	197	209	760	174	83.3	79.4
Street and door-to-door salesworkers	72	343	32	(1)	40	(1)	(1)	55.6
Administrative support occupations, including clerical	13,844	300	3,006	403	10,838	284	70.5	78.3
Supervisors, administrative support	709	424	296	521	413	385	73.9	58.3
Supervisors, general office	416	404	139	515	278	373	72.4	66.8
Supervisors, financial records processing	91	472	24	(1)	67	413	(1)	73.6
Supervisors, distribution, scheduling, and adjusting clerks	153	447	105	471	48	(1)	(1)	31.4
Computer equipment operators	722	318	236	396	486	296	74.7	67.3
Computer operators	716	318	234	396	482	296	74.7	67.3
Secretaries, stenographers, and typists	3,893	287	65	322	3,828	286	88.8	98.3
Secretaries	3,210	288	34	(1)	3,176	287	(1)	98.9
Typists	651	276	28	(1)	623	276	(1)	95.7
Information clerks	856	255	91	347	766	250	72.0	89.5
Interviewers	123	274	16	(1)	107	266	(1)	87.0
Hotel clerks	60	214	18	(1)	42	(1)	(1)	70.0
Transportation ticket and reservation agents	99	420	29	(1)	70	366	(1)	70.7
Receptionists	459	242	9	(1)	450	242	(1)	98.0
Records processing occupations, except financial	611	288	118	342	492	279	81.6	80.5
Order clerks	174	366	51	404	123	348	86.1	70.7
Personnel clerks, except payroll and timekeeping	53	317	5	(1)	48	(1)	(1)	90.6
Library clerks	54	248	8	(1)	46	(1)	(1)	85.2
File clerks	211	239	32	(1)	179	237	(1)	84.8
Records clerks	101	303	21	(1)	80	292	(1)	79.2
Financial records processing occupations	1,706	290	169	366	1,536	286	78.1	90.0
Bookkeepers, accounting and auditing clerks	1,319	287	127	343	1,193	283	82.5	90.4
Payroll and timekeeping clerks	149	316	14	(1)	135	313	(1)	90.6
Billing clerks	135	294	14	(1)	121	286	(1)	89.6
Cost and rate clerks	71	291	13	(1)	58	276	(1)	81.7
Duplicating, mail, and other office machine operators	60	266	28	(1)	33	(1)	(1)	55.0
Communications equipment operators	191	307	28	(1)	163	296	(1)	85.3
Telephone operators	181	315	25	(1)	157	304	(1)	86.7
Mail and message distributing occupations	754	445	520	465	234	405	87.1	31.0
Postal clerks, except mail carriers	274	479	164	484	110	467	96.5	40.1
Mail carriers, postal service	280	477	229	482	51	429	89.0	18.2
Mail clerks, except postal service	119	268	62	291	58	247	84.9	48.7
Messengers	81	271	65	279	16	(1)	(1)	19.8
Material recording, scheduling, and distributing clerks	1,455	322	908	359	547	285	79.4	37.6
Dispatchers	166	347	82	402	84	307	76.4	50.6
Production coordinators	178	458	100	506	78	346	68.4	43.8
Traffic, shipping, and receiving clerks	421	297	312	317	108	243	76.7	25.7
Stock and inventory clerks	479	315	299	347	180	285	82.1	37.6
Weighers, measurers, and checkers	65	279	39	(1)	26	(1)	(1)	40.0
Expediters	91	318	37	(1)	54	283	(1)	59.3

Table 12 Jobs and Money: Pay and Employment in Various Occupations, 1986 (continued)

Occupation	Both sexes Number of workers (thousands)	Both sexes Median weekly earnings (dollars)	Men Number of workers (thousands)	Men Median weekly earnings (dollars)	Women Number of workers (thousands)	Women Median weekly earnings (dollars)	Ratio female/male earnings times 100	Percent female workers
Adjusters and investigators	743	321	203	460	540	299	65.0	72.7
Insurance adjusters, examiners, and investigators	238	356	75	487	163	308	63.2	68.5
Investigators and adjusters, except insurance	334	323	89	465	244	301	64.7	73.1
Eligibility clerks, social welfare	64	300	7	(1)	58	291	(1)	90.6
Bill and account collectors	107	284	32	(1)	75	281	(1)	70.1
Miscellaneous administrative support occupations	2,144	272	345	375	1,800	262	69.9	84.0
General office clerks	548	283	123	373	425	267	71.6	77.6
Bank tellers	363	231	34	(1)	329	228	(1)	90.6
Data-entry keyers	290	277	21	(1)	269	273	(1)	92.8
Statistical clerks	88	343	19	(1)	69	327	(1)	78.4
Teachers aides	180	198	9	(1)	171	197	(1)	95.0
Service occupations	8,061	223	3,987	284	4,074	191	67.3	50.5
Private household occupations	334	121	14	(1)	320	119	(1)	95.8
Child care workers, private household	148	91	2	(1)	146	90	(1)	98.6
Private household cleaners and servants	157	147	9	(1)	149	146	(1)	94.9
Protective service occupations	1,589	392	1,433	402	156	292	72.6	9.8
Supervisors, protective service occupations	165	516	158	528	8	(1)	(1)	4.8
Supervisors, police and detectives	89	558	83	575	5	(1)	(1)	5.6
Firefighting and fire prevention occupations	222	455	217	461	4	(1)	(1)	1.8
Firefighting occupations	209	464	205	469	4	(1)	(1)	1.9
Police and detectives	648	431	579	443	69	350	79.0	10.6
Police and detectives, public service	392	478	367	481	24	(1)	(1)	6.1
Sheriffs, bailiffs, and other law enforcement officers	80	401	71	410	10	(1)	(1)	12.5
Correctional institution officers	176	362	142	370	34	(1)	(1)	19.3
Guards	554	266	479	272	75	231	84.9	13.5
Guards and police, except public services	516	272	456	275	59	254	92.4	11.4
Service occupations, except protective and household	6,138	209	2,540	239	3,598	195	81.6	58.6
Food preparation and service occupations	2,288	186	973	205	1,315	173	84.4	57.5
Supervisors, food preparation and service	177	238	68	294	109	212	72.1	61.6
Bartenders	184	214	100	245	84	184	75.1	45.7
Waiters and waitresses	576	172	103	209	472	168	80.4	81.9
Cooks, except short order	817	196	447	212	370	174	82.1	45.3
Food counter, fountain and related occupations	78	152	16	(1)	62	149	(1)	79.5
Kitchen workers, food preparation	64	166	15	(1)	49	(1)	(1)	76.6
Waiters'/waitresses' assistants	95	164	65	162	29	(1)	(1)	30.5
Health service occupations	1,277	216	145	252	1,132	213	84.5	88.6
Dental assistants	112	243	0	(1)	112	243	(1)	100.0
Health aides, except nursing	254	242	43	(1)	212	241	(1)	83.5
Nursing aides, orderlies, and attendants	910	206	102	253	808	202	79.8	88.8
Cleaning and building service occupations, except household	1,883	238	1,236	266	647	197	74.1	34.4
Supervisors, cleaning and building service workers	130	313	89	348	42	(1)	(1)	32.3
Maids and housemen	363	189	71	229	292	178	77.7	80.4
Janitors and cleaners	1,338	247	1,029	261	309	207	79.3	23.1
Personal service occupations	691	212	187	255	504	203	79.6	72.9
Hairdressers and cosmetologists	274	208	40	(1)	234	205	(1)	85.4
Attendants, amusement and recreation facilities	63	234	36	(1)	27	(1)	(1)	42.9
Child care workers, except private household	143	182	11	(1)	132	177	(1)	92.3
Precision production, craft, and repair occupations	10,851	408	9,973	418	878	277	66.3	8.1
Mechanics and repairers	3,723	414	3,588	413	136	431	104.4	3.7
Supervisors, mechanics and repairers	219	524	199	523	20	(1)	(1)	9.1
Mechanics and repairers, except supervisors	3,504	408	3,388	408	116	420	102.9	3.3
Vehicle and mobile equipment mechanics and repairers	1,444	375	1,426	375	19	(1)	(1)	1.3
Automobile mechanics	658	324	647	326	10	(1)	(1)	1.5
Bus, truck, and stationary engine mechanics	310	402	307	402	3	(1)	(1)	1.0
Aircraft engine mechanics	96	505	94	508	3	(1)	(1)	3.1
Small engine repairers	52	301	52	301	0	(1)	(1)	.0
Automobile body and related repairers	130	354	129	355	0	(1)	(1)	.0
Heavy equipment mechanics	157	438	156	437	1	(1)	(1)	.6
Industrial machinery repairers	515	415	502	417	13	(1)	(1)	2.5
Electrical and electronic equipment repairers	642	511	584	514	58	486	94.6	9.0
Electronic repairers, communications and industrial equipment	131	450	121	447	9	(1)	(1)	6.9
Data processing equipment repairers	127	514	115	531	11	(1)	(1)	8.7
Telephone line installers and repairers	64	549	60	547	4	(1)	(1)	6.3
Telephone installers and repairers	220	568	191	571	29	(1)	(1)	13.2
Heating, air conditioning, and refrigeration mechanics	214	390	213	389	1	(1)	(1)	.5
Miscellaneous mechanics and repairers	655	403	631	404	23	(1)	(1)	3.5
Office machine repairers	54	376	54	376	0	(1)	(1)	.0
Millwrights	93	501	91	501	2	(1)	(1)	2.2
Construction trades	3,469	401	3,413	401	56	333	83.0	1.6
Supervisors, construction occupations	420	500	413	500	6	(1)	(1)	1.4
Construction trades, except supervisors	3,049	389	2,999	389	50	315	81.0	1.6
Brickmasons and stonemasons	114	412	113	411	0	(1)	(1)	.0

36

Table 12   Jobs and Money: Pay and Employment in Various Occupations, 1986 (continued)

Occupation	Both sexes		Men		Women		Ratio female/male earnings times 100	Percent female workers
	Number of workers (thousands)	Median weekly earnings (dollars)	Number of workers (thousands)	Median weekly earnings (dollars)	Number of workers (thousands)	Median weekly earnings (dollars)		
Carpet installers	53	331	52	328	0	(1)	(1)	.0
Carpenters	855	348	846	349	9	(1)	(1)	1.1
Drywall installers	101	374	99	375	2	(1)	(1)	2.0
Electricians	562	473	551	475	12	(1)	(1)	2.1
Electrical power installers and repairers	106	514	104	515	2	(1)	(1)	1.9
Painters, construction and maintenance	267	299	257	301	10	(1)	(1)	3.7
Plumbers, pipefitters, steamfitters, and apprentices	376	470	374	470	2	(1)	(1)	.5
Concrete and terrazzo finishers	68	343	67	341	1	(1)	(1)	1.5
Insulation workers	53	369	52	363	1	(1)	(1)	1.9
Roofers	120	303	118	303	2	(1)	(1)	1.7
Structural metalworkers	65	467	65	467	0	(1)	(1)	.0
Extractive occupations	155	520	152	517	2	(1)	(1)	1.3
Precision production occupations	3,504	403	2,821	445	684	258	58.0	19.5
Supervisors, production occupations	1,308	474	1,127	495	181	297	60.0	13.8
Precision metalworking occupations	862	432	814	441	48	(1)	(1)	5.6
Tool and die makers	151	506	149	508	2	(1)	(1)	1.3
Machinists	468	419	450	422	18	(1)	(1)	3.8
Sheet metal workers	128	408	120	410	8	(1)	(1)	6.3
Precision woodworking occupations	67	285	55	299	11	(1)	(1)	16.4
Precision textile, apparel, and furnishings machine workers	134	242	73	268	61	211	78.7	45.5
Precision workers, assorted materials	471	284	194	329	277	259	78.7	58.8
Electrical and electronic equipment assemblers	311	271	98	305	213	255	83.6	68.5
Precision food production occupations	336	293	254	327	82	208	63.6	24.4
Butchers and meatcutters	241	299	192	338	49	(1)	(1)	20.3
Bakers	69	292	51	316	18	(1)	(1)	26.1
Precision inspectors, testers, and related workers	104	463	86	481	18	(1)	(1)	17.3
Inspectors, testers, and graders	99	468	82	483	17	(1)	(1)	17.2
Plant and system operators	223	493	218	493	5	(1)	(1)	2.2
Stationary engineers	103	493	102	493	1	(1)	(1)	1.0
Operators, fabricators, and laborers	14,342	301	10,784	332	3,558	225	67.8	24.8
Machine operators, assemblers, and inspectors	7,254	293	4,401	354	2,853	223	63.0	39.3
Machine operators and tenders, except precision	4,815	278	2,873	341	1,942	211	61.9	40.3
Metalworking and plastic working machine operators	476	361	392	379	84	271	71.5	17.6
Lathe and turning machine operators	61	383	57	388	4	(1)	(1)	6.6
Punching and stamping press machine operators	140	327	95	352	45	(1)	(1)	32.1
Grinding, abrading, buffing, and polishing machine operators	142	366	124	376	18	(1)	(1)	12.7
Metal and plastic processing machine operators	167	324	126	365	40	(1)	(1)	24.0
Molding and casting machine operators	99	305	67	354	32	(1)	(1)	32.3
Woodworking machine operators	137	258	114	263	22	(1)	(1)	16.1
Sawing machine operators	90	260	77	264	12	(1)	(1)	13.3
Printing machine operators	404	354	303	394	101	282	71.6	25.0
Printing machine operators	274	366	240	381	34	(1)	(1)	12.4
Typesetters and compositors	57	323	17	(1)	40	(1)	(1)	70.2
Textile, apparel, and furnishings machine operators	1,155	195	225	247	930	186	75.3	80.5
Winding and twisting machine operators	82	237	19	(1)	64	220	(1)	78.0
Textile sewing machine operators	676	179	69	205	607	177	86.3	89.8
Pressing machine operators	108	199	33	(1)	75	182	(1)	69.4
Laundering and dry cleaning machine operators	137	194	43	(1)	94	175	(1)	68.6
Machine operators, assorted materials	2,450	305	1,696	343	754	239	69.7	30.8
Packaging and filling machine operators	367	253	141	324	227	230	71.0	61.9
Mixing and blending machine operators	87	342	81	345	6	(1)	(1)	6.9
Separating, filtering, and clarifying machine operators	61	431	53	446	8	(1)	(1)	13.1
Painting and paint spraying machine operators	174	310	141	328	33	(1)	(1)	19.0
Furnace, kiln, and oven operators, except food	109	421	106	425	4	(1)	(1)	3.7
Crushing and grinding machine operators	54	243	42	(1)	12	(1)	(1)	22.2
Slicing and cutting machine operators	216	270	165	288	51	209	72.6	23.6
Photographic process machine operators	60	253	28	(1)	32	(1)	(1)	53.3
Fabricators, assemblers, and hand working occupations	1,659	319	1,131	365	527	251	68.8	31.8
Welders and cutters	534	376	499	382	34	(1)	(1)	6.4
Assemblers	1,001	299	567	350	434	254	72.6	43.4
Production inspectors, testers, samplers, and weighers	780	323	396	421	384	260	61.8	49.2
Production inspectors, checkers, and examiners	653	334	321	438	332	266	60.7	50.8
Production testers	51	420	39	(1)	12	(1)	(1)	23.5
Graders and sorters, except agricultural	70	230	33	(1)	37	(1)	(1)	52.9
Transportation and material moving occupations	3,684	366	3,494	372	190	287	77.2	5.2
Motor vehicle operators	2,577	346	2,426	353	151	275	77.9	5.9
Supervisors, motor vehicle operators	57	462	47	(1)	10	(1)	(1)	17.5
Truckdrivers, heavy	1,539	371	1,516	371	23	(1)	(1)	1.5
Truckdrivers, light	459	281	432	287	27	(1)	(1)	5.9
Drivers-salesworkers	188	395	179	400	9	(1)	(1)	4.8
Bus drivers	201	327	129	389	71	285	73.3	35.3
Taxicab drivers and chauffeurs	107	272	97	274	10	(1)	(1)	9.3
Transportation occupations, except motor vehicles	185	580	181	583	4	(1)	(1)	2.2
Rail transportation occupations	133	589	130	593	3	(1)	(1)	2.3

Table 12 Jobs and Money: Pay and Employment in Various Occupations, 1986 (continued)

Occupation	Both sexes		Men		Women		Ratio female/male earnings times 100	Percent female workers
	Number of workers (thousands)	Median weekly earnings (dollars)	Number of workers (thousands)	Median weekly earnings (dollars)	Number of workers (thousands)	Median weekly earnings (dollars)		
Locomotive operating occupations	57	625	57	630	1	(1)	(1)	1.8
Water transportation occupations	51	547	51	545	1	(1)	(1)	2.0
Material moving equipment operators	922	375	887	377	36	(1)	(1)	3.9
Operating engineers	155	410	154	410	1	(1)	(1)	.6
Crane and tower operators	85	459	84	458	1	(1)	(1)	1.2
Excavating and loading machine operators	81	368	80	366	1	(1)	(1)	1.2
Grader, dozer, and scraper operators	90	351	87	345	3	(1)	(1)	3.3
Industrial truck and tractor equipment operators	381	325	361	327	20	(1)	(1)	5.2
Handlers, equipment cleaners, helpers, and laborers	3,404	263	2,890	271	515	226	83.4	15.1
Helpers, construction and extractive occupations	161	240	158	237	4	(1)	(1)	2.5
Helpers, construction trades	143	236	139	233	4	(1)	(1)	2.8
Construction laborers	642	287	624	288	18	(1)	(1)	2.8
Production helpers	59	271	44	(1)	15	(1)	(1)	25.4
Freight, stock, and material handlers	1,020	263	870	272	150	221	81.3	14.7
Garbage collectors	51	286	50	285	1	(1)	(1)	2.0
Stock handlers and baggers	363	214	288	218	75	199	91.3	20.7
Machine feeders and offbearers	86	266	57	282	30	(1)	(1)	34.9
Garage and service station related occupations	185	200	178	202	7	(1)	(1)	3.8
Vehicle washers and equipment cleaners	139	215	116	214	24	(1)	(1)	17.3
Hand packers and packagers	238	233	90	257	149	222	86.4	62.6
Laborers, except construction	921	283	772	291	149	232	79.7	16.2
Farming, forestry, and fishing occupations	1,318	217	1,178	220	140	187	85.0	10.6
Farm operators and managers	67	321	59	325	9	(1)	(1)	13.4
Farm managers	60	329	54	333	7	(1)	(1)	11.7
Other agricultural and related occupations	1,162	211	1,034	215	128	184	85.6	11.0
Farm occupations, except managerial	620	195	552	199	69	167	83.9	11.1
Farm workers	575	192	519	195	57	165	84.6	9.9
Related agricultural occupations	542	235	482	242	59	205	84.7	10.9
Supervisors, related agricultural occupations	94	345	87	360	7	(1)	(1)	7.4
Groundskeepers and gardeners, except farm	396	222	379	223	17	(1)	(1)	4.3
Forestry and logging occupations	65	286	62	290	3	(1)	(1)	4.6

[1]Data not shown where base is less than 50,000.
Source: U.S. Department of Labor, Monthly Labor Review, June 1987.

Chapter Three

WORKING WOMEN: THE STRIDES AND STUMBLES

HIGHLIGHTS AND TRENDS

- Over half of all women (56.0%) were in the labor force in 1987, employed or looking for work.
- The number of women in the labor force increased by 173% (from 16.7 million to 45.6 million) between 1947 and 1980. Since then, it has grown even more, to 53.9 million in 1987. About 50.6 million women were employed and 3.3 million were unemployed and looking for work in 1987.
- Today, women make up 44.3% of the labor force. By the start of the 21st century they will make up nearly half (47.3%).
- As women have moved into the labor force they've decided to have fewer children; the fertility rate for American women is now 1.8, compared to 3.7 in the late 1950s at the height of the baby boom.
- About half of all women (49%) with children under the age of 1 are working.
- Today, women-owned businesses are the fastest-growing segment of small business. Estimates of the number of women-owned firms range from 2.8 million to 4.3 million. A study of 2.8 million firms owned by women found that they had sales of $98.2 billion and employed 1.3 million people with an annual payroll of $11.2 billion. Most of these firms, about 2.5 million, had no employees.
- Even though more women are working, more women are living in poverty. About 25 million mothers and their children now live in poverty.
- Women earned only 69.2 cents for every dollar men made in 1986, indicating that the wage gap between men and women has improved somewhat since 1955, when women made 65 cents for every dollar men did.
- Only 11% of all women fit the stereotype of a housewife—a married woman, not in the labor force, with children at home.
- Women are an increasingly important market for financial services: 57% of all new stock buyers were women; 62.5% of all working women have credit cards; 19.8% own securities.

39

- Women enrolled in college-level business programs increased by 626% between 1966 and the 1980s; women now account for nearly half of all business students.
- Over 38.8% of all managerial, executive, and administrative workers were women in 1986. There are about 3.8 million women managers, executives, and administrators, up from 2.2 million in 1972, when women were 27.5% of the total.
- Yet the single most common occupation for women is still secretary.

WOMEN AT WORK

In the past few decades, women have been muscling in on the labor market. Between 1947 and 1987, the number of women in the labor force more than tripled, from 16.7 million to 53.9 million. In contrast, the number of men increased only 52% (from 44.3 million to 67.7 million).

By September of 1987, 50.6 million women held jobs and another 3.3 million were unemployed but looking for work. And contrary to popular stereotypes, most of these new workers are not aging housewives, looking for something to do now that their children are off at college. The greatest increase has been among those of childbearing age, forever altering the nature of the American family. During the 1970s the increase for women under 45 was more than twice the overall increase, and today even women with young children are entering the labor market in record numbers. About 49.4% of all women with children less than a year old worked outside the home in 1985, up from 39% in 1970; 79% of all single mothers with children less than 3 years old worked. By 1985 about 25 million children lived in families in which the mother was away from home part of the working day, a fact that has been good for child-care centers and hard on their parents' pocketbooks. A recent study estimates that out-of-the-home child-care services cost an average of $3,000 a year per child.

The U.S. economy might be reeling from the effects of foreign competition, but when it comes to women workers the United States is holding its own. Only one country, Sweden, where 80% of all women are working or looking for work, has a higher labor-force participation rate. In Japan, the labor-force participation rate for women is 57.2%; in West Germany, the U.S.'s other major foreign competitor, about half of all women (50.4%) are employed or looking for work.

Nor is there any evidence that these trends represent a passing flirtation with the labor market. Nearly half of all working women (47%) regard their jobs as careers, according to a recent poll, up from 30% in 1970. The poll indicates that women are almost as career-oriented as men—only 57% of all men consider their work a career.

But, judging from the jobs women hold, many of their careers are in lower-paying service jobs. In 1986 women continued to be overrepresented in certain fields—for example, as domestics in private households (94.9% were women), dental assistants (100%), waiters and waitresses (81.9%), receptionists (98.0%), secretaries (98.9%), bank tellers (93%), nurses (92.1%), librarians (84.9%) and cashiers (79.4%). They also continued to be underrepresented in traditional male occupations—for example, as engineers (6.3%), lawyers (25.2%), police officers (10.6%), auto mechanics (1.5%), construction workers, (1.6%), clergy (7.1%), and truck drivers (1.5%).

Besides changing the nature of the work force, women have also altered the nature of the American family. For most working women, the job now shares center stage with marriage and motherhood. Less than 11% of all women fit the traditional stereotype of a housewife—a married woman, not in the labor force, with children at home.

The need to balance a job with a family has given rise to "superwomen" who must do it all. Only one third of all women who work full-time hire household help. And most men are still not much use around the house, despite all the rhetoric about growing male sensitivity. Only about 14% of all husbands do half the housework—71% of married women have to do over three quarters of the work.

No wonder women are having fewer children. The average woman is now having only 1.8 children, down from 3.7 children during the baby boom of late 1950s. And those having children are waiting longer than ever before. In 1985, 28.7% of all women aged 25 to 29 who had ever been married were childless; in 1960, only 12.6% were.

The stress of women working outside the home and rapidly changing sex roles also put new strains on family life. Although about 90% of all women will marry at least once, more marriages than ever before are ending in divorce. About half of all marriages that occurred in the late 1970s will end in divorce. The typical American marriage now lasts about seven years.

And when a marriage breaks up, women suffer more than men, at least in economic terms. Currently about 34.6% of all households headed by women are living in poverty. That state of affairs is one major reason why 20.5% of all Americans under the age of 18, 44.5% of all black children, and 37.7% of Hispanic children are growing up in poverty.

INCOME

A woman on the job helped many families with the job of paying the bills. The typical family with a woman working earns $36,431; families in which the wife does not work earn only $24,556.

Women are investing and becoming a major market for financial services. More than 24 million women now own stock in public companies, and 57% of the 6.8 million new investors who entered the market in the last two years were women, spending $8.5 billion. That means that one in three women owns stock. One out of every five owns real estate. Another 1.6 million women invested in gold and 3.8 million in silver. About half of all stocks are owned by women and about half of women have credit cards. One out of every three women who makes more than $60,000 uses a financial planner; one out of every five who earns more than $30,000 uses a financial planner.

Yet the wage gap remains. Women earned only 69.2 cents for every dollar men made in 1986, indicating that the wage gap between men and women has improved only slightly since 1955, when women made 65 cents for every dollar men made.

Women, though, are slowly catching up. The gap between men's and women's wages widened in the 1970s when large numbers of women entered the labor market. Since then women's pay has been increasing, with younger women making the biggest gains. Women aged 25–34 average 73.5% of what men make, up from 69% in 1980 and 65% in 1972.

The wage disparity has spawned a movement to equalize men's and women's pay for comparable jobs. Advocates argue that women in traditionally female-dominated occupations, such as nursing, are often paid less than men in male-dominated occupations, even though the jobs may require similar levels of education, skill, knowledge, and responsibility. To correct that problem, they have introduced legislation and brought suits against employers, trying to force them to equalize the pay of men and women for comparable jobs. Britain and Australia already have comparable-worth laws. And unions have also made comparable worth an important issue. Unions won at least 65 bargaining victories on this issue by 1985. Opponents argue that deciding "comparable worth" is a task beyond the reach of law, and that the real net effect of the movement will be the institution of government wage control.

Large business groups such as the National Association of Manufacturers and the Chamber of Commerce have been among those fighting the idea, saying that it would create a bureaucratic nightmare and cost businesses the right to set their own pay schedules. Their view is supported by the Reagan administration, and no federal legislation mandating comparable worth is likely to pass in the near future.

Despite all the rhetoric about the "new woman," it should be remembered that some of the gains women have made over the last twenty years were simply a matter of recapturing ground that was lost during the 1950s, when women left the labor market for the home. For example, in 1947–1948, 1 in 10 medical degrees was awarded to a woman; that percentage fell to 1 in 20 about 10 years later. It wasn't until the mid-1970s that women were again earning as many medical degrees as in 1947–1948.

It would also be wrong to assume that women have traditionally stayed at home or survived only with the help of men. Many poorer, single, and minority women have always worked, with 39.7% of all black women working in 1890, compared with 16.3% of white women.

So what's ahead for women? More and more will undoubtedly move into management ranks, especially younger women with M.B.A.'s. But the prospects for women getting the very top jobs still aren't so hot. By 1985, only 2% of the nation's top executives were female as were only 3% to 4% of corporate directors. Studies indicate that women still face sexual discrimination and men, usually older men, are still uncomfortable working around women. Dr. Rosabeth Moss Kanter, author of *Men and Women of the Corporation* and a teacher at the Harvard Graduate School of Business Administration, also finds that the new thrust towards entrepreneurism within companies works against women. Women who have patiently worked their way up through the ranks now confront a new star system of rewards. So do men, of course, but then the stars who get picked are usually men.

THE RICHEST WOMEN IN THE U.S.

Even the richest women have something in common with their more plebian counterparts—they are not as rich as the equivalent men. Only 55 women made the 1987 *Forbes* list of the 400 wealthiest Americans. The 5 wealthiest women were collectively worth a mere $6.85 billion, compared to the $19.62 billion of the 5 wealthiest men. And all of the 5 wealthiest women inherited their money, unlike the top 5 men, who built their fortunes from scratch. But, with business empires of at least $1 billion, the 5 wealthiest women in America don't have much to complain about:

1. and 2. Barbara Cox Anthony and Anne Cox Chambers

The two sisters own Cox Enterprises, which is worth over $3.6 billion, according to *Forbes,* simply because they are the daughters of James Cox, a former governor of Ohio who built a vast media empire. Cox Enterprises now owns 20 newspapers, eight TV stations, a cable system with 1.3 million subscribers, and 11 radio stations. Barbara's son James will become chairman of Cox Enterprises in 1988. Anne became the first woman bank director in Atlanta in 1973 and has served as U.S. ambassador to Belgium.

3. Jacqueline Mars Vogel

Jacqueline Mars Vogel shares the $4.6 billion Mars candy empire with three other family members. She serves on the board of directors.

4. Margaret Hunt Hill

The heiress of H. L. Hunt's fabulous Texas oil fortune managed to avoid her brothers' disastrous attempt to corner the world's silver market—a move that cost the Hunt brothers billions and eventually forced them into bankruptcy. She is suing to stay out of the brothers' Chapter 11 filings and has withdrawn her shares from the family's oil trusts. Margaret Hunt Hill controls assets, including her brother Hassie's trust, worth $1.1 billion.

5. Joan Beverly Kroc

The widow of Ray Kroc, founder of the McDonald's fast food empire, is worth $1 billion.

WOMEN IN BUSINESS

Twenty-five years ago, many parents sent their daughters to college to find husbands. Instead, the daughters found careers, becoming managers, executives, or entrepreneurs. Today, women-owned businesses are the fastest-growing segment of small business. Estimates of the number of women-owned firms range from 2.8 million to 4.3 million. A study of 2.8 million firms owned by women found that they had sales of $98.2 billion and employed 1.3 million people with an annual payroll of $11.2 billion. Most of these firms, about 2.5 million, had no employees.

The service industry, retail trade, finance, real estate and insurance, and other services account for 91% of all women-owned businesses. And although many women have translated traditional skills, such as fashion, into multimillion-dollar enterprises, the fastest-growing area for women-owned businesses is in traditionally male-dominated fields such as security brokerage, general building contracting, and legal services.

Better education has also helped women move into boardrooms and executive suites. Women increased their share of doctorates from 9.6% in 1950 to 13.3% in 1970 and to over 33% in 1984. They increased their percentage of M.D.'s from 5.5% in 1960 to 30.4% in 1985, law degrees from 2.5% in 1960 to 34.8% in 1985, and engineering degrees from 0.4% in 1960 to 10.2% in 1985. Finally, women enrolled in business programs in college have increased by a whopping 626% since 1966 and now account for 49.4% of all business students. In 1987, women accounted for 33% of the nation's 70,000 M.B.A. graduates, up from 24% 10 years ago and 4% in 1972.

WOMEN MANAGERS

Women are moving into the corporate world in record numbers. The nation's 3.8 million female managerial, executive, and administrative workers accounted for 38.8% of all managers in 1986, a dramatic increase over 1972, when there were 2.2 million women managers, 27.5% of the total. And more women than ever before are preparing for careers in business. Between 1970 and 1985, the number of doctorates in business increased from 10,000 (5.5% of the total) to 148,000 (17.1%); the number of masters in computers increased from 164,000 (3.6%) to 2,037,000 (31.0%), and the number of masters in communications from 642,000 (34.6%) to 2,093,000 (57%).

Women are no longer an anomaly in the boardrooms of American corporations. By 1985, 41% of 1,350 major corporations had women on the board, compared to 13% a decade earlier. But only 3% to 4% of all directorships are held by women, despite the increasing number of women workers, and only 25% of major companies have more than one woman on the board.

Though women now fill almost two fifths of all management positions, most have not reached top executive positions. Just one woman heads a

Table 13 Top Women-owned Businesses

Rank 1986	Rank 1985	Company Location Executive Industry	Fiscal year 1985 revenues (in millions of dollars)	Revenue growth (percentage)	Employees
1	1	Estée Lauder New York, New York Estée Lauder, chairman Cosmetics	1,200	0	10,000
2	2	The Washington Post Company Washington, D.C. Katharine Graham, chairman Publishing, broadcasting	1,100	12	7,000
3	3	Wells, Rich, Greene New York, New York Mary Wells Lawrence, chairman, CEO Advertising	640	2	900
4	4	Home Interiors and Gifts Dallas, Texas Mary C. Crowley, president, CEO Home furnishings	350	17	40,000
5	10	The Copley Press La Jolla, California Helen Copley, chairman, CEO Publishing	350	52	4,000
6	6	Christian Dior—New York New York, New York Colombe M. Nicholas, president Product licensing	320	6	20
7	9	Jockey International Kenosha, Wisconsin Donna Wolf Steigerwaldt, chairman, CEO Apparel manufacturing	300	9	3,200
8	7	Diane von Furstenberg New York, New York Diane von Furstenberg, president Furnishings, fashion	300	0	30
9	8	Mary Kay Cosmetics Dallas, Texas Mary Kay Ash, chairman Cosmetics	250	−10	1,200
10	11	Tatham-Laird & Kudner Chicago, Illinois Charlotte Beers, managing partner Advertising	235	5	350

Source: *Savvy*.

Fortune 500 company—Katharine Graham of The Washington Post Company—and she got the job because her father owned the paper. Only 2% of the country's top executives surveyed by Korn/Ferry International in 1985 were women.

Moreover, few women have broken into factory management. Chrysler and Ford have no women plant managers, nor do du Pont, Goodyear, and Hewlett-Packard. General Motors only hired its first woman plant manager in 1982.

Black women have fared worse than white women. Despite increasing numbers of black women earning M.B.A.'s, they still only account for 2% of all corporate managers. Another survey of the largest 1,000 corporations indicates that there are only 20 black women corporate officers.

One reason for the scarcity of top women executives is that the large numbers of women who got M.B.A.'s in the 1970s and early 1980s haven't had time to work their way up the corporate ladder. Yet part of the problem is still sex discrimination. A 1985 survey by the *Harvard Business Review* indicated that more than half of all men felt uncomfortable working with women. One in five also thought women were temperamentally unfit for management. Perhaps because of these attitudes, half of those surveyed felt that women would never be wholly accepted in business.

Their pay, probably more than anything else, shows where women are. Only 2% of all women managers earn over $50,000 a year compared with 14% of all men. In 1986, women in executive, administrative, and managerial jobs had median weekly earnings of $395 a week, 63.7% of the $620 weekly salaries of men.

Table 14 Women in Management

(1985 figures for U.S. only)

	Management jobs held by women (percentage)	Women in company (percentage)
Industrial companies		
du Pont	7	22
Exxon*	8	27
General Motors*	8	19
Goodyear Tire and Rubber	6	14
UAL	25	39
Technology		
AT&T*	32	48
General Electric	6	26
IBM	16	28
Xerox	23	38
Consumer Products		
Johnson & Johnson*	18	47
PepsiCo	28	46
Philip Morris		
(excluding General Foods)	14	31
Procter & Gamble	17	28
Retailing and trade		
Federated Department Stores	61	72
Kroger	16	47
Marriott	32	51
McDonald's	46	57
Sears, Roebuck*	36	55
Media		
ABC (excluding Capital Cities)	36	43
Time	46	54
Times Mirror	27	37
Financial Services		
American Express	37	57
BankAmerica	64	72
Chemical Bank	34	57
Prudential Life Insurance*	32	53
Wells Fargo Bank	58	71
Average for companies with more than 100 employees	24	44

*1984 figures.
Source: *The Wall Street Journal.*

Table 15   The Academic Revolution

Degree	1973		1985	
	Total awarded	Percent awarded to women	Total awarded	Percent awarded to women
Accounting				
Bachelor's	27,947	11.6	47,692*	47.0*
Master's	1,621	8.7	3,297*	36.6*
Advertising				
Bachelor's	1,047	30.9	2,360*	64.0*
Master's	54	22.2	127*	58.3*
Banking and finance				
Bachelor's	6,213	3.8	17,576*	33.9*
Master's	1,741	3.3	4,433*	28.4*
Business and management				
Bachelor's	126,830	10.6	233,351	45.1
Master's	31,166	4.9	67,527	31.0
Computer and information sciences				
Bachelor's	4,304	14.9	38,878	36.8
Master's	2,113	10.6	7,101	28.7
Data processing				
Bachelor's	556	13.1	882*	39.1*
Master's	144	4.9	52*	15.4*
Engineering				
Bachelor's	51,265	1.2	96,105	13.2
Master's	16,619	1.7	21,557	10.7
Journalism				
Bachelor's	6,360	45.2	9,795*	62.5*
Master's	976	35.1	1,141*	56.1*
Law	27,205	8.0	37,491	38.5
Personnel management				
Bachelor's	1,189	9.4	1,822*	52.3*
Master's	352	7.1	327*	34.3*
Pharmacy				
Bachelor's	4,964	24.0	5,480*	49.4*
Master's	167	21.6	333*	35.4*

* 1984 data.
Source: U.S. Department of Education, 1987.

Table 16 Women as Consumers

	Professional/ managerial women (percentage)	Other working women (percentage)	Non- working women (percentage)
Financial			
Own money market fund	13.0	6.3	10.3
Own mutual fund	5.8	2.8	4.3
Own securities (excluding U.S. savings bonds)	29.3	18.0	19.6
Have IRA	31.5	18.4	12.1
Use an accountant or accounting service	29.7	21.1	17.1
Carry auto insurance	83.1	77.2	62.4
Lifestyle			
Member of health club	9.3	5.7	4.0
Have credit cards	78.3	62.0	49.7
Went to movies in past three months	48.9	38.0	24.3
Took foreign vacation in past three years	19.9	11.0	9.3
Took domestic vacation in past year	60.0	47.4	39.2
Belong to book club	16.7	11.4	8.5
Bought from catalog in past year	62.5	51.1	42.0
Consumer preference			
Smoke cigarettes	25.8	35.9	27.0
Drink domestic table wine	47.0	30.6	24.8
Drink diet cola	57.4	51.5	41.7
Use "cents-off" coupons	66.8	63.3	66.0
Shopped at convenience store in past four weeks	52.5	53.8	37.7
Use baby food	4.0	5.5	7.1
Use denture adhesives/fixatives	4.6	8.1	13.6
Items owned			
Foreign car bought new	20.8	9.1	5.5
U.S. car bought new	44.7	35.8	32.4
Answering machine	10.6	5.3	2.8
Home/personal computer	17.0	10.2	7.3
Body-building equipment	7.6	6.3	3.4
Items purchased in the past year			
Clothing for a man	63.8	58.8	44.1
Microwave oven	13.1	16.8	12.4
Cordless telephone	4.2	3.3	2.6
35mm camera	9.0	6.3	3.5
Food processor	1.7	2.0	1.4
Prerecorded videocassette	7.9	3.9	2.6
Jewelry and gems	49.6	46.1	29.4

Source: Simmons Market Research Bureau, 1986. Study of Media & Markets.

Table 17   Women-owned Businesses

This chart provides a snapshot of women-owned business in 1982, the most recent year for which data are available. It provides a breakdown of women-owned businesses by industry, employment, payroll, and sales.

| | | Women-owned firms | | | | | | | |
| | | All firms | | | | With paid employees | | | |
Industry	All firms	Total	Per-cent distri-bution	Sales and receipts (millions of dollars)	Per-cent distri-bution	Total	Employees for pay period including March 12	Annual payroll (millions of dollars)	Sales and receipts (millions of dollars)
All Industries[2]	12,059,950	2,884,450	100.0	98,292	100.0	311,662	1,354,588	11,156	65,347
Agricultural services[3]	(NA)	21,344	.7	686	.7	2,843	8,998	77	408
Mining	(NA)	22,753	.8	2,221	2.3	1,335	11,632	209	1,323
Construction[4]	1,324,793	61,665	2.1	4,565	4.6	13,321	56,211	805	3,305
Special trade contractors	(NA)	47,219	1.6	2,497	2.5	8,891	36,425	522	1,812
Manufacturing[4]	314,219	49,727	1.7	5,303	5.4	10,239	93,470	1,126	4,759
Transportation public utilities[4]	499,656	40,596	1.4	3,229	3.3	8,431	38,699	464	2,501
Trucking and warehousing	(NA)	16,517	.6	1,342	1.4	3,676	15,698	216	929
Transportation services	(NA)	14,692	.5	1,282	1.3	2,913	10,186	118	1,103
Wholesale trade	} 2,886,187	34,252	1.2	9,190	9.3	8,704	49,673	688	8,241
Retail trade[4]		727,688	25.2	35,861	36.5	119,453	541,463	3,289	26,770
Food stores	(NA)	37,635	1.3	6,047	6.2	13,647	62,953	410	4,691
Auto dealers, service stations	(NA)	14,353	.5	4,754	4.8	6,205	27,936	281	4,045
Apparel accessory stores	(NA)	29,130	1.0	2,446	2.5	11,499	39,067	232	1,933
Eating and drinking places	(NA)	66,811	2.3	6,684	6.8	38,028	254,054	1,231	5,766
Finance, insurance, real estate[4]	1,703,321	263,734	9.1	6,370	6.5	16,483	49,126	532	2,830
Banking	(NA)	2,260	.1	204	.2	245	2,957	41	174
Credit agencies[5]	(NA)	352	(Z)	96	.1	176	1,257	18	90
Insurance carriers	(NA)	181	(Z)	16	(Z)	83	257	3	14
Insurance agents, brokers	(NA)	32,617	1.1	882	.9	3,998	8,291	101	461
Real estate	(NA)	225,551	7.8	4,733	4.8	11,459	34,279	331	1,909
Selected services[4]	4,723,771	1,401,776	48.6	26,278	26.7	122,002	490,744	3,804	14,149
Hotels and other lodging places	(NA)	17,771	.6	1,671	1.7	5,713	45,012	313	1,352
Personal services	(NA)	419,113	14.5	5,500	5.6	44,009	136,034	889	2,799
Auto repair, services, and garages	(NA)	11,322	.4	929	.9	4,050	15,511	175	753
Amusement, recreation, service	(NA)	51,694	1.8	1,132	1.2	3,579	21,200	161	699
Health services	(NA)	128,389	4.5	3,989	4.1	13,669	78,535	684	2,381
Legal services	(NA)	24,700	.9	853	.9	4,806	9,178	116	546
Social services	(NA)	2,330	.1	229	.2	2,180	14,931	84	225

(NA) Not available.
(X) Not applicable.
(Z) Less than .05 percent.
[1]Standard Industrial Classification.
[2]Includes industries not classified.
[3]Includes forestry and fishing.
[4]Includes industries not shown separately.
[5]Other than banks.
Source: U.S. Bureau of the Census, *1982 Survey of Women-Owned Businesses,* series WB82-1.

Chapter Four

MINORITIES: INCORPORATING THE AMERICAN DREAM

HIGHLIGHTS AND TRENDS

• After minority joblessness reached new heights in the 1982 recession, the job outlook for minorities improved. By 1987, black unemployment had dropped to 13.0% from 20.2% in November of 1982. The 1987 unemployment rate for Hispanics fell to 9.2%, down from a high of 16.3% in 1983.

• Between 1977 and 1983, the number of minorities who were self-employed or who owned businesses grew dramatically, reaching 503,000 in 1983, up from 332,000 in 1972.

• Generally, minorities continue to lag behind whites. For example, if blacks earned as much as other Americans, they would have had $318.9 billion worth of income in 1985. Yet actual black income was only $192.4, resulting in an income gap of over $127 million. The average net worth of a household was only $3,397 for blacks and $4,913 for Hispanics, as opposed to $38,135 for whites.

• Black-owned businesses continue to be overshadowed by large corporations. In 1985, the top 100 black-owned corporations had combined sales of $3.27 billion, about 3% of the sales of General Motors, the largest company, and only $628 million dollars more than Wang Laboratories, the largest Asian-owned business. The combined sales of the 100 largest black companies would have put them 124th in the *Fortune* 500.

• The 500 largest Hispanic companies had sales of only $8.7 billion and employed 65,389 people in 1985, according to *Hispanic Business*. The combined sales of all 500 companies would have ranked them only 40th on the *Fortune* 500.

MINORITIES IN AMERICA

America has always been a country of minorities, a nation of immigrants and refugees. In 1920, when there were 105 million Americans, 14 million were foreign born and 10.5 million were black. Only a little more than half of the population was white and had American-born parents.

Today, the country is still a kaleidoscope of races, religious minorities, and ethnic groups. Of the 226,546,000 Americans counted in the 1980 census, there were 26,683,000 blacks (11.8%), and 14,609,000 Hispanics (6.4%). There were also some 806,000 Chinese (0.36%), 774,700 Filipinos (0.34%), 701,000 Japanese (0.31%), 361,500 Asian Indians (0.16%), 354,600 Koreans (0.16%), 261,700 Vietnamese (0.12%), and nearly 7,000,000 people who belonged to various other races (3.1%).

In the year 2000, when there will be nearly 268 million Americans, the country will be 13.3% black, 9.4% Hispanic, 3.6% other, and 74.2% white non-Hispanic. The percentages do not add up to 100% because people of Spanish origin may be of any race, white, black, or Asian.

By the year 2080, the face of America will have changed dramatically. The number of white non-Hispanics will have fallen from 192 million in 1990 to only 176 million in 2080, while the number of Hispanics will have increased from 19.9 million to 59.6 million. The number of black Americans will grow from 31.4 million in 1990 to 55.7 million in 2080 while the number of members of other races will increase from 7.5 million to 23.4 million. In 2080, only 56.6% of the country will be white non-Hispanic. About one fifth of the population (19.2%) will be Hispanic, followed by 17.9% black, and 7.5% will be other races, including Asian.

A hundred years after the building of the Statue of Liberty, immigration is once again on the rise. During the 1970s the U.S. saw a new wave of immigration as more than 4.5 million people legally immigrated to the United States, the highest number since the 1910s, and the third-highest number for any decade in the nation's history. By 1980, 14 million Americans, 6.2% of the population, were foreign-born and 23 million people lived in households where a language other than English was spoken. Another 2.9 million legal immigrants arrived between 1981 and 1985. Others arrived illegally. The U.S. Census Bureau estimates that there are about 3 million to 4 million illegal aliens living in the United States.

But, as might be expected in a country of immigrants, only a small minority can trace its history far back into America's past. Only about 2 million people, under 1% of the population, can say they are real indigenous Americans—American Indians.

As minorities and immigrants increase their share of the population, they will play an increasingly important role in the American economy and workplace. By the year 2000, Hispanics will account for 10.2% of the labor force, up from 5% in 1979 and 6.9% in 1986. Asians will hold 4.1% of all jobs, up from 2.3% in 1979 and 2.8% in 1986. The proportion of blacks will grow more slowly, hitting 11.8% in 2000, up from 10.2% in 1979 and 10.8% in 1986. Immigrants will account for about 25% of the growth in the labor force between now and the end of the century; blacks will produce 17% of the growth, Hispanics 29%, and Asians 11%.

MINORITY-OWNED BUSINESSES

Like the rest of America, minorities are being bitten by the entrepreneurial bug. The number of nonwhite self-employed persons increased by 51.5%

Table 18   Minorities in America: Social and Economic Status

This chart shows the social and economic characteristics of black and Hispanic Americans, listing their median incomes, educational levels, labor force status, and types of families.

| Characteristic | Number (thousands) | | | | | | Percent distribution | | | | | |
| | Total popula-tion | White | Black | Spanish origin[1] | | | Total popula-tion | White | Black | Spanish origin[1] | | |
				Total	Mexi-can	Puerto Rican				Total[1]	Mexi-can	Puerto Rican
Total persons, 1985	234,066	199,117	28,151	16,940	10,269	2,562	100.0	100.0	100.0	100.0	100.0	100.0
Under 5 years old	17,958	14,610	2,699	1,809	1,205	271	7.7	7.3	9.6	10.7	11.7	10.6
5–14 years old	33,792	27,417	5,218	3,355	2,249	516	14.4	13.8	18.5	19.8	21.9	20.1
15–44 years old	110,948	93,852	13,590	8,550	5,160	1,333	47.4	47.1	48.3	50.5	50.3	52.0
45–64 years old	44,549	39,033	4,406	2,407	1,227	372	19.0	19.6	15.7	14.2	12.0	14.6
65 years old and over	26,818	24,205	2,238	819	428	68	11.5	12.2	7.9	4.8	4.2	2.7
Years of school completed, 1985												
Persons 25 years old and over	143,524	124,905	14,820	8,455	4,755	1,241	100.0	100.0	100.0	100.0	100.0	100.0
Elementary: 0–8 years	19,893	16,224	3,113	3,192	2,062	417	13.9	13.0	21.0	37.7	43.4	33.7
High school: 1–3 years	17,553	14,365	2,851	1,210	700	248	12.2	11.5	19.2	14.3	14.7	20.0
4 years	54,866	48,728	5,027	2,402	1,243	347	38.2	39.0	33.9	28.4	26.1	28.0
College: 1–3 years	23,405	20,652	2,188	932	486	141	16.3	16.5	14.8	11.0	10.2	11.4
4 years or more	27,808	24,935	1,640	718	264	87	19.4	20.0	11.1	8.5	5.5	7.0
Labor force status, 1985												
Civilian 16 years old and over	178,206	153,679	19,664	11,528	6,670	1,594	100.0	100.0	100.0	100.0	100.0	100.0
Civilian labor force	115,461	99,926	12,364	7,448	4,469	835	64.8	65.0	62.9	64.6	67.0	52.4
Employed	107,150	93,736	10,501	6,664	3,983	719	60.1	61.0	53.4	57.8	59.7	45.1
Unemployed	8,312	6,191	1,864	785	487	116	4.7	4.0	9.5	6.8	7.3	7.3
Unemployment rate	7.2	6.2	15.1	10.5	10.9	13.9	(X)	(X)	(X)	(X)	(X)	(X)
Not in labor force	62,744	53,753	7,299	4,080	2,201	759	35.2	35.0	37.1	35.4	33.0	47.6
Family type, 1985												
Total families	62,706	54,400	6,778	3,939	2,251	621	100.0	100.0	100.0	100.0	100.0	100.0
With own children[2]	31,112	26,232	3,890	2,602	1,543	447	49.6	48.2	57.4	66.1	68.5	72.1
Married couple	50,350	45,643	3,469	2,824	1,703	323	80.3	83.9	51.2	71.7	75.7	52.0
With own children[2]	24,210	21,565	1,822	1,892	1,207	218	38.6	39.6	26.9	48.0	53.6	35.1
Female householder, no spouse present	10,129	6,941	2,964	905	418	273	16.2	12.8	43.7	23.0	18.6	44.0
With own children[2]	6,006	3,922	1,942	642	302	213	9.6	7.2	28.7	16.3	13.4	34.3
Male householder, no spouse present	2,228	1,816	344	210	130	25	3.6	3.3	5.1	5.3	5.8	4.0
With own children[2]	896	744	126	68	34	16	1.4	1.4	1.9	1.7	1.5	2.6
Family income, 1984												
Total families	62,706	54,400	6,778	3,939	2,251	621	100.0	100.0	100.0	100.0	100.0	100.0
Less than $5,000	3,144	2,057	999	383	173	128	5.0	3.8	14.7	9.7	7.6	20.6
$5,000–$9,999	5,894	4,433	1,300	618	350	143	9.4	8.1	19.2	15.7	15.6	22.9
$10,000–$14,999	6,780	5,607	1,014	591	377	83	10.8	10.3	15.0	15.0	16.8	13.4
$15,000–$24,999	13,520	11,775	1,472	937	559	118	21.6	21.6	21.7	23.7	24.8	19.1
$25,000–$49,999	23,481	21,324	1,597	1,145	658	129	37.4	39.2	23.6	29.0	29.2	20.7
$50,000 or more	9,889	9,207	396	263	136	20	15.8	16.9	5.8	6.6	6.0	3.3
Median income (dollars)	26,433	27,686	15,432	18,833	19,184	12,371	(X)	(X)	(X)	(X)	(X)	(X)
Persons below poverty level	33,700	22,955	9,490	4,806	2,904	1,106	14.4	11.5	33.8	28.4	28.3	43.2
Housing tenure, 1985												
Total occupied units	86,789	75,328	9,480	4,883	(NA)	(NA)	100.0	100.0	100.0	100.0	(NA)	(NA)
Owner-occupied	55,845	50,661	4,185	2,007	(NA)	(NA)	64.3	67.3	44.1	41.1	(NA)	(NA)
Renter-occupied	30,943	24,667	5,295	2,876	(NA)	(NA)	35.7	32.7	55.9	58.9	(NA)	(NA)

(NA) Not available.
(X) Not applicable.
[1]Persons of Spanish origin may be of any race.
[2]Children under 18 years old.
Source: U.S. Bureau of the Census, *Current Population Reports*, P-60, Nos. 149, 151, 152, and P-20, No. 403. Labor force data are published by U.S. Bureau of Labor Statistics, *Employment and Earnings*, January 1986.

between 1972 and 1983, faster than white self-employment, which grew by 40.5% during the same period.

Yet minority-owned businesses continued lagging behind white businesses. In general, minority businesses are headed by younger and less affluent bosses. In 1980, the last year such figures were available, the average minority business was headed by someone 38 years old, compared to 43 years old for whites. And minority self-employed persons made less: their average income was only $7,208, only 77% of the $9,398 that the average white self-employed person made.

Minorities also have a long way to go before they are free at last to exert real power in the marketplace. In 1985, blacks, for example, earned an estimated $200 billion, yet they spent only $12.3 billion, about 6.6%, in the black community.

In 1986 *Black Enterprise*'s top 100 black-owned companies increased sales by a whopping 11.2%, outstripping the GNP's growth of 2.5%. But these companies still had combined revenues of only $3.27 billion, up from $2.562 billion in 1984. All well and good, but those sales were only 3% of what General Motors, the largest company in the United States, sold in 1986 and the combined sales of the top 100 black companies would have only ranked them 124th on the *Fortune* 500.

At the same time, the 39 black-owned banks had assets of only $1.61 billion, the 35 black-owned insurance companies had $809 million in assets, and the 33 black-owned savings and loans associations had assets of $1.4 billion. In contrast, Citicorp had assets of $196.1 billion (over 121 times the assets of all black-owned banks) and Prudential of America had assets of $103.7 billion (over 128 times the assets of all black-owned insurance companies). Moreover, 53 of the 100 largest black-owned companies were auto dealers, 8 were in construction, and 4 others were in the petroleum business—all companies that face highly volatile and uncertain markets.

Similarly, the 500 largest Hispanic companies had sales of only $8.7 billion and employed 65,389 people in 1985, according to *Hispanic Business*. The combined sales of all 500 companies would have ranked them only 40th on the *Fortune* 500.

Yet there are many bright spots. During the 1980s, black entrepreneurs made increasing inroads into the entertainment and media businesses. Led by long-established black-owned firms such as Motown (records) and Johnson Publishing (*Ebony* magazine), 7 of the top 100 black companies were in media or entertainment in 1986.

Black advertising agencies also flexed their economic muscles. Collectively, the top 6 black-owned ad agencies had $155 million worth of billings in 1985, up 70% from the year before. And black entrepreneurs in recent years also put together increasingly large deals. In 1987 TLC Group L.P. chairman Reginald F. Lewis put together a $985 million leveraged buyout of Beatrice International Food Companies. In 1985, a syndicate of 10 black businessmen or companies, including Michael Jackson and his brothers, O. J. Simpson, J. Bruce Llewellyn, Julius Erving, and Essence Communications (publisher of *Essence* magazine), put together a $65 million deal to buy one of the TV stations Capital Cities was forced to sell when it acquired ABC.

BUSINESS AND POLITICAL POWER

Government remains a major factor in the success of many minority businesses. Executive orders requiring increased employment of minorities and women by government contractors have helped many minorities break into occupations from construction to investment banking. A number of federal laws and regulations also require that a certain amount of

Table 19 Black-owned Businesses

This chart provides a snapshot of black-owned business in 1982, the most recent year for which data are available. It provides a breakdown of black-owned businesses by industry, employment, payroll, and sales.

	1977 All firms		1982 All firms — Sales and receipts			1982 Firms with paid employees			
Industry	Total	Sales and receipts (millions of dollars)	Total	Total (millions of dollars)	Percent change 1977–1982	Total	Employees	Annual payroll (millions of dollars)	Sales and receipts (millions of dollars)
All Industries[1]	231,203	8,645	339,239	12,444	43.9	38,631	165,765	1,531	8,529
Construction[2]	21,101	758	23,061	995	31.3	4,129	14,470	162	657
Special trade contractors	17,126	497	18,399	578	16.4	2,997	9,773	99	356
Manufacturing	4,243	614	4,171	988	61.0	1,159	15,186	193	943
Transportation, public utilities[2]	23,061	509	24,397	795	56.1	2,256	6,813	78	325
Trucking and warehousing	11,552	353	13,029	530	50.1	1,406	3,463	42	182
Wholesale trade	2,212	664	3,651	859	29.3	626	4,391	65	807
Retail trade[2]	55,428	3,352	84,053	4,119	22.9	10,237	43,140	296	3,034
Food stores	10,679	786	9,187	883	12.3	1,832	6,916	52	567
Auto dealers, service stations	5,002	1,108	3,448	1,307	18.0	1,431	6,641	70	1,164
Eating and drinking places	13,008	572	11,629	675	18.0	3,384	19,232	97	493
Finance, insurance, real estate[2]	9,805	641	14,829	748	16.6	1,165	13,454	149	615
Insurance carriers	58	249	51	254	2.1	44	6,954	75	254
Selected services[2]	101,739	1,890	147,263	3,249	71.9	16,858	64,355	547	1,933
Personal services	35,035	399	40,394	561	40.5	3,605	9,170	61	233
Health services	14,560	433	17,195	595	37.5	3,263	9,909	84	406

[1]Includes industries not classified.
[2]Includes industries not shown separately.
Source: U.S. Bureau of the Census, *1982 Survey of Minority-Owned Business Enterprises,* series MB82-1.

Table 20 Top Black-owned Businesses, 1986

Rank	Company	Staff	Type of business	1986 sales (in millions of dollars)
1.	Johnson Publishing Company, Inc. CEO: John H. Johnson Location: Chicago	1,826	Publishing/ cosmetics/ broadcasting (owns *Ebony*)	173.5
2.	Motown Industries CEO: Berry Gordy Location: Los Angeles	237	Entertainment	152.4
3.	H.J. Russell Construction, Inc. CEO: H.J. Russell Location: Atlanta	600	Construction/ development/ communication	132.0
4.	Philadelphia Coca-Cola Bottling Company CEO: J. Bruce Llewellyn Location: Chicago	875	Soft-drink bottling	110.0
5.	Soft Sheen Products CEO: Edward Gardner Location: Chicago	850	Hair-care product manufacture	85.0

Source: *Black Enterprise,* June 1987.

Table 21   Top Black-owned Banks, 1986

Rank	Bank	Assets	Deposits	Loans
		(in millions of dollars)		
1.	Seaway National Bank of Chicago CEO: Walter E. Grady Location: Chicago Founded: 1965 Staff: 157	137.3	120.6	41.2
2.	Freedom National Bank of New York CEO: Louis Prezeau Location: New York Founded: 1964 Staff: 119	104.6	83.8	43.6
3.	Independence Bank of Chicago CEO: Alvin J. Boute Location: Chicago Founded: 1964 Staff: 108	102.3	89.5	38.7
4.	City National Bank of New Jersey CEO: Charles L. Whigham Location: Newark Founded: 1973 Staff: 31	96.3	91.7	13.8
5.	Citizen Trust Bank CEO: I. Owen Funderburg Location: Atlanta Founded: 1921 Staff: 100	88.9	78.9	33.3

Source: *Black Enterprise,* June 1987. The Earl G. Graves Publishing Co.

Table 22   Largest Hispanic Companies

Rank	Company Type of business	Sales in 1985 (in millions of dollars)
1.	Bacardi Imports, Inc. Rum importing	475.0
2.	Banco Popular de Puerto Rico Banking services	382.0
3.	International Medical Centers Health care/hospitals	370.0
4.	V. Suarez & Co. Beer, wine, liquor distribution	260.0
5.	Goya Foods, Inc. Foods	250.0
6.	Bacardi Corporation Distilling/bottling rum, spirits	221.0
7.	Banco de Ponce Banking services	215.0
8.	The Vanir Group Diversified company (real estate/communications)	150.0
9.	E. & G. Trading, Inc. Wholesale meats/seafood	146.0
10.	Sedano's Supermarkets Supermarket chain	135.6

Source: *Hispanic Business,* June 1986.

Table 23   The Top Five Hispanic Banks in the U.S. and Puerto Rico

(in millions)

Rank	Bank	Sales*	Assets	Deposits
1.	Banco Popular de Puerto Rico San Juan, Puerto Rico	$381.96	$4,100.00	$3,365.00
2.	Banco de Ponce San Juan, Puerto Rico	215.60	1,959.05	1,905.97
3.	First Federal Savings Bank of Puerto Rico Santurce, Puerto Rico	126.81	1,327.00	862.00
4.	Republic Banking Corporation of Florida Miami, Florida (A holding company for Republic National Bank, Miami, Florida)	97.14	887.52	743.94
5.	Ponce Federal Savings Bank Ponce, Puerto Rico	73.08	716.86	371.78

*Hispanic Business defines "sales" as the sum of a bank's interest and noninterest income.
Source: Hispanic Business Data for 1985.

business be given to minority companies. Under such requirements, more than $5 billion dollars of government contracts went to minorities in 1985.

Increased black political clout, following three decades of marching and lobbying, also has encouraged the growth of minority-owned businesses. Although there was only one black in 1985 who held a statewide office, the number of black public officials has increased dramatically. Fueled in part by Jesse Jackson's controversial campaign, the number of black officeholders rose to 6,056 in 1985, up from 5,700 at the beginning of 1984. Even so, blacks hold only 1.2% of the nation's 490,800 elective offices.

Between 1984 and 1985, the number of black mayors grew to 286, an increase of 31. In the 1985 Congress, seven blacks in Congress headed up committees, including the powerful Representative William Gray (D-Pa.), who heads the House Budget Committee.

Increased political power is likely to translate into further help for black-owned business, especially on a local level. Like mayors in the 19th and early 20th centuries who were protective of their immigrant constituencies, black mayors are likely to be more sensitive to the desires of minority businesses. Cities with black mayors have 31 of the 100 largest black-owned businesses. And black mayors increasingly turn to black-owned firms for city contracts. This, for example, has helped some black-owned investment banking firms to break into the list of firms that dominate financing of city projects. In 1984, during Chicago Mayor Harold Washington's first year in power, four black-owned firms participated as co-managers in a $112 million mortgage revenue bond issue.

MINORITY MANAGERS

In the past decade, minorities have slowly moved into positions of corporate power. In 1987, there were over 1.6 million black managers, about

6.1% of all managerial, administrative, and executive employees, up from 2.4% in 1972. About 3.5% of all managers were Hispanic in 1985, up from 2.8% in 1983.

Despite the increase in minority managers, their numbers still are disproportionately small. Fewer than 20 black women are corporate officers in the United States and black women represent only about 8% of all women managers.

Although Cuban-born Roberto C. Goizueta is the CEO of Coca-Cola, the nation's 20th-largest company, no black headed a *Fortune* 500 company at the start of 1988. A 1985 survey of the 1,000 largest corporations showed that only about 26% had minority board members. *Black Enterprise* estimates that only 2% of all corporate board members are minorities, with about 300 blacks serving on boards. These minority board members are highly sought after: another survey shows that every minority board member serves on an average of 3.8 boards.

The difficulties faced by blacks and other minorities in the corporate world has also hurt their morale. A National Urban League study indicates that many black managers are getting fed up with the lack of corporate opportunities. Only 13% of the managers surveyed felt that they had a "high" potential for advancement; an alarming 42%, on the other hand, felt they had a "low" potential.

TOP MINORITY ENTREPRENEURS

An Wang America's wealthiest minority entrepreneur to be listed among *Forbes*'s 400 richest Americans is An Wang, a refugee from Communist China who built his computer firm, Wang Laboratories, into one of the country's largest firms. In 1948 he revolutionized computer technology by inventing the magnetic memory core, and in 1951 he founded his own company. Sales were only $15,000 during the first year but grew at the astonishing rate of 40% a year for the next three decades. By 1983, with 40% ownership in Wang Laboratories, Dr. Wang and his family were worth $1.6 billion, making him one of America's five wealthiest individuals.

Since then, the company has been hit by the general malaise affecting the computer industry and by the introduction of personal computers that were more versatile than Wang's word processors. In the fiscal year 1985, the company netted only $15.5 million on sales of $2.35 billion, showing a loss of $109 million for the last quarter. And, with the stock's trading price dropping from an all-time high of $42.50, the Wang family lost $1 billion. This decline prompted the 65-year-old Dr. Wang to return to active management of his company. Since then he has embarked on a drastic cost-cutting program, has started crisscrossing the country to visit employees and boost morale, and has introduced new IBM-compatible products. The verdict is still out, but sales did improve 12% in 1986 to $2.6 billion and profits jumped 228% to $50.0

million. In the summer of 1987, *U.S. News & World Report* estimated that the Wang family was worth about $621 million.

John H. Johnson   After founding Johnson Publishing Company in 1942, John Johnson built it into the largest black-owned company in the United States, with sales of $173.5 million in 1986, up 12.1% from the year before. The flagship of his empire is *Ebony* magazine, with circulation of 1.7 million. Johnson's publications, which also include *Jet,* grossed a total of $42.8 million in advertising in 1984. His business is not limited to publishing. The company's Fashion Fair Cosmetics have been selling well; it also has a book division and owns several radio stations.

Johnson created his media empire Horatio Alger–style. He and his mother moved north when he was 15 because there was no high school in his hometown in Arkansas. After working for a black-owned insurance company, he founded his first magazine, *Negro Digest.* Despite problems from white distributors who refused to carry the magazine, circulation quickly took off, reaching over 150,000 after Johnson convinced Eleanor Roosevelt to write an article called, "If I Were a Negro."

Johnson's next project was *Ebony,* founded in 1945. The magazine was designed for returning black servicemen to meet the rising expectations of postwar blacks. The magazine has always emphasized articles about accomplished blacks, a fabulously successful editorial formula. By the 1980s the combined circulation of Johnson's magazines equaled half the number of black adults in America. Johnson also is the first black publisher to crack the white advertising market. Johnson is worth over $180 million.

Berry Gordy   Today Motown Industries is located in Los Angeles, but in the late 1950s and 1960s Berry Gordy's Motown Record Corporation revolutionized the record business, rocking the whole country with the Motor City sound of Detroit. Back then, Gordy made money with the sound of the Supremes, the Marvelettes, and Marvin Gaye. More recently, top-selling musicians such as Lionel Richie boosted sales to $152.4 million in 1986. Gordy himself is still singing all the way to the bank, with a net worth of $150 million to $180 million.

Chapter Five

UNIONS: MORE LOSERS THAN WINNERS

HIGHLIGHTS AND TRENDS

• Stagnant incomes, a declining manufacturing sector, foreign competition, high unemployment, deregulation, a changing work force, and a high-tech workplace have all meant trouble in the union hall.

• In 1960 one third of American workers belonged to unions; by 1986 only 17.5% of the workforce, about 17 million people, carried union cards.

• Faced with foreign competition and financial troubles in its traditional power base—manufacturing and mining—organized labor is on the defensive. Strikes have declined dramatically, making the period between 1975 and 1987 the most peaceful in American labor history since 1945. More union workers have been forced to take lower wages and lesser benefits than nonunion workers every year since 1984. Wages for union members rose only 2.6% in 1986 compared to 3.5% for nonunion workers. Collective bargaining agreements negotiated in 1986 provided for the lowest wage hikes on record.

• This decline in unions' longstanding political and social power has forced them to conduct costly organizing drives and adopt new strategies. Even so, unions face a difficult future: wage increases for union employees are expected to average less than those for nonunion workers through the end of the decade.

• By the year 2000, as older union members retire, some forecasters say that only about 13% of the labor force will belong to unions, the lowest rate since 1930.

In short, organized labor is probably in the worst shape it's been in since the 1920s, thanks to a rapidly changing U.S. economy. Young people, part-time workers, women, service employees, and college-educated workers have historically not been part of unions, yet they are fastest-growing segments of the labor force. Unions represent only 8.4% of all part-time workers, 15.9% of all service workers, and 15.5% of all women employees.

Manufacturing and construction, which have always been the backbone of union membership, now employ a smaller share of the labor force, while service jobs are increasing. Service workers, women, and professional and technical workers, many of whom work in offices or smaller businesses, have also been harder to organize than workers in the large industrial factories that once provided the bulk of union membership.

At the same time, foreign competition and deregulation have hurt union bargaining power. Airlines, faced with stiff competition following deregulation, and steel makers, faced with tough foreign competition, have successfully demanded reduced benefits and salaries from their employees. Costly work rules have also been abolished, increasing productivity and cutting union power on the factory floor. Many unionized firms in the trucking and construction industry have gone bankrupt or turned to nonunion labor, and as a result the number of unionized workers in those industries has been cut. In the trucking industry, for example, nearly 200,000 union jobs have been lost in the last decade. In the railroad industry 100,000 jobs were lost following deregulation.

Management has also developed increasingly sophisticated techniques for reducing the cost of union contracts. Some companies have terminated their pension funds and used the proceeds to diversify; others have used Chapter 11 bankruptcy proceedings to get rid of unions altogether.

Moreover, financial troubles in its traditional power base—manufacturing, construction, and mining—have put organized labor on the defensive. The United Auto Workers (UAW) lost 27% of its membership while the AFL-CIO lost over 1.3 million members between 1974 and 1987. Strikes have also declined dramatically, making the period between 1975 and 1987 the most peaceful in American labor history since 1945.

And even since the 1981–1982 recession ended, unions have been forced to settle for less at the bargaining table. In 1984, 1985, and 1986, wage increases for union members were lower than for nonunion members. In 1986 wages for union members grew only 2.6%. The average new union contract in 1986 hiked wages only 1.2% in the first year and 1.8% over the life of the contract, not enough to keep up with inflation, or with nonunion wages, which rose 3.5%. Between 1984 and the end of 1986, union wages grew only 5.9%, while nonunion wages grew 8.2%.

Simultaneously, a second industrial revolution in the workplace is bringing increased automation to the factory and office, reducing the number of jobs available and forcing unions into the difficult position of bargaining over technological development. Already some unions have made job security one of their top priorities. In 1984, for example, the United Auto Workers' contract with General Motors established a $1 billion job security fund for workers who had been laid off because of technological change, transfer of work to outside suppliers, or changes in the work force. Contract negotiations in 1987 also focused on the issue of job security and guaranteed lifetime employment.

To keep unions out, management has also been more willing to improve wages and working conditions of nonunion employees. And as the courts have made it harder for employers to fire workers, unions also have a harder time arguing they are the only institutions that can protect worker's rights.

The most notable growth area for an otherwise declining union movement is the trend towards unionizing government employees. By 1974, following a series of tough strikes and favorable legal decisions, there were 2.9 million government employees in unions, up from only 0.9 million in 1956. Of this total, 1.5 million worked for state and local governments; 1.4 million were federal employees. Then, once the momentum began to build, union membership skyrocketed, hitting over 5.7 million by 1985. Public employees now account for 26% of the AFL-CIO membership, up from 15% a decade ago.

But even this trend is unlikely to reverse the declining fortunes of organized labor. In an era of fiscal austerity, government employment has increased more slowly and the percentage of unionized government employees has declined in the last few years from 36.7% in 1983 to 35.8% in 1986.

Finally, management has begun involving workers in the process of running businesses, putting unions in a new and often awkward position. A 1984 law provided for sweeping tax incentives for employee stock ownership plans. In other cases, where workers haven't become entrepreneurs, they've been brought into the management process through productivity committees. About one third of all companies with over 500 employees have participatory management programs and about 31% of all companies with more than 100 employees have profit-sharing plans. As unions become more involved in management, they may be forced to give up some of their antimanagement posturing, a development that could improve productivity.

Table 24 Union Membership, 1930 to 1987

Total In All Unions

Year	Membership (thousands)	Year	Membership (thousands)
1930*	3,401	1959	17,117
1931	3,310	1960	17,049
1932	3,050	1961	16,303
1933	2,689	1962	16,586
1934	3,088	1963	16,524
1935	3,584	1964	16,841
1936	3,989	1965	17,299
1937	7,001	1966	17,940
1938	8,034	1967	18,362
1939	8,763	1968**	20,721
1940	8,717	1969	20,776
1941	10,201	1970	21,248
1942	10,380	1971	21,327
1943	13,213	1972	21,657
1944	14,146	1973	22,276
1945	14,322	1974	22,809
1946	14,395	1975	22,361
1947	14,787	1976	22,662
1948	14,319	1977	22,456
1949	14,282	1978	22,880
1950	14,267	1979	22,618
1951	14,946	1980***	20,095
1952	15,892	1981	NA
1953	16,948	1982	NA
1954	17,022	1983	17,717
1955	16,802	1984	17,340
1956	17,490	1985	16,996
1957	17,369	1986	16,975
1958	17,029	1987	16,913

*1930–1980, Dues paying members, employed and unemployed.
**1968–1987, Includes union members and employee associations.
***1980–1987, From Current Population Survey, employed dues paying members of unions and employee associations.
Source: Bureau of Labor Statistics, U.S. Department of Labor.

NEW STRATEGIES FOR THE 1980s AND BEYOND

Faced with some of the toughest challenges in its history, organized labor has turned to new strategies. Realizing that service workers and office workers will have to be the rank and file of the future, unions have waged long and ultimately successful campaigns to organize office workers at such universities as Columbia, Yale, and the University of Cincinnati.

The Service Employees International Union (SEIU) has made organizing the service industry its primary goal. Already it counts 850,000 members, a 37% growth in the last five years, and in 1986 it began an ambitious attempt to organize 98,000 Blue Cross and Blue Shield workers across the country. Another union, the American Federation of State, County and Municipal Employees, has increased membership by 100,000 in two years by recruiting service workers in the public sector.

The Blue Cross organizing drive indicates labor's willingness to discard some of the feuds that have traditionally divided unions. The SEIU is leading seven other unions, with each union keeping the members that it organizes.

In other cases, merger mania has hit the union halls. There were 38 union mergers between 1975 and 1984, the most in any period of American labor. The most visible example of that trend was a 1987 vote by the United Mine Workers of America (UMW) to study the prospect of merging with another union. The UMW has been an independent union for nearly a century and was once one of the country's most powerful unions. But because it is faced with declining membership, a merger with another union may be the only way it can preserve what's left of its clout.

Unions are also following management's footsteps by bringing in outside consultants to wage sophisticated public-relations and organizing campaigns. One consulting group, Corporate Campaign, has built up a reputation as a union defender with slick PR campaigns designed to pressure companies into improving relations with unions.

For example, in the bitter battle over organizing the J. P. Stevens textile plants, Corporate Campaign got community and church groups to put pressure on directors of the company. These directors, who headed banks, insurance companies, and other large corporations, suddenly realized that the adverse publicity hurt their own corporate images. These outside directors forced J. P. Stevens to settle with the union.

Despite new tactics and strategies, unions still face an uphill battle. The public still worries about union bureaucrats, union democracy, an aging union leadership, and the influence of organized crime in a few unions. (See the chapter "Crime.") Moreover, drives to organize service workers have proved to be costly and difficult. The battle to organize workers at Columbia University, for example, dragged out over 10 years.

Unions are also finding it increasingly tough convincing workers they can deliver on bread-and-butter issues. Wage increases through 1988 are expected to be even lower than those for nonunion workers. By the year 2000, as older union members retire, some forecasters say that only about 13% of the labor force will belong to unions, the lowest rate since 1930.

Table 25 Highest-paid Union Presidents

Rank	Union President	Total salary and allowances (dollars)	Membership
1.	International Brotherhood of Teamsters, Chauffeurs, Warehousemen and Helpers of America Jackie Presser	571,960	1,700,000
2.	Seafarers' International Union of North America Frank Drozak	246,615	80,000
3.	Air Line Pilots Association Henry A. Duffy	243,382	34,000
4.	United Food and Commercial Workers International Union William H. Wynn	200,000	1,300,000
5.	Hotel Employees and Restaurant Employees International Union Edward T. Hanley	174,207	325,000
6.	United Transportation Union Fred A. Hardin	165,845	125,000
7.	American Federation of Labor and Congress of Industrial Organizations Lane Kirkland	150,000	13,100,000
8.	Laborers' International Union of North America Angelo Fosco	146,110	430,000
9.	American Federation of State, County and Municipal Employees Gerald W. McEntee	142,425	1,200,000
10.	United Association of Journeymen and Apprentices of the Plumbing and Pipe Fitting Industry of the United States and Canada Marvin J. Boede	141,200	350,000

Source: *Business Week.*

Table 26 Union Members: Who They Are, What They Earn

This chart presents the social and economic characteristics of America's union members and compares them to nonunion workers. It shows what percentages of various groups belong to unions and the median weekly earnings of union and nonunion workers, as well as union membership in various occupations for 1983 to 1985.

(Annual averages of monthly data. Covers employed wage and salary workers 16 years old and over. Excludes self-employed workers whose businesses are incorporated although they technically qualify as wage and salary workers. Based on Current Population Survey.)

	Employed wage and salary workers									Median usual weekly earnings (dollars)								
	Total (thousands)			Union members[1] (thousands)			Percent union members			Total (thousands)			Represented by unions			Not represented by unions		
Characteristic	1983	1985	1986	1983	1985	1986	1983	1985	1986	1983	1985	1986	1983	1985	1986	1983	1985	1986
Total	88,290	94,521	96,903	17,717	16,996	16,975	20.1	18.0	17.5	313	343	358	383	419	439	288	315	325
16–24 years	19,305	19,746	19,663	1,749	1,440	1,385	9.1	7.3	7.0	210	223	231	275	291	305	203	218	224
25–34 years	25,978	28,387	29,357	5,097	4,745	4,674	19.6	16.7	15.9	321	349	360	376	407	417	304	329	339
35–44 years	18,722	21,243	22,306	4,648	4,833	4,966	24.8	22.7	22.3	369	405	418	407	455	475	339	382	396
45–54 years	13,150	13,858	14,287	3,554	3,484	3,531	27.0	25.1	24.7	366	400	415	402	447	479	335	373	385
55–64 years	9,201	9,382	9,339	2,474	2,330	2,245	26.9	24.8	24.0	346	380	396	390	419	444	316	352	370
65 years and over	1,934	1,904	1,950	196	165	174	10.1	8.7	8.9	260	296	298	330	394	376	238	272	278
Men	47,856	51,015	51,952	11,809	11,264	11,173	24.7	22.1	21.5	378	406	419	414	463	481	349	383	394
Women	40,433	43,506	44,961	5,908	5,732	5,802	14.6	13.2	12.9	252	277	290	307	347	367	237	262	274
White	77,046	81,862	83,745	14,844	14,124	14,061	19.3	17.3	16.8	319	355	370	391	433	452	295	323	338
Men	42,168	44,680	45,334	10,134	9,623	9,505	24.0	21.5	21.0	387	417	433	421	475	488	362	395	407
Women	34,877	37,182	38,410	4,710	4,501	4,557	13.5	12.1	11.9	254	281	294	313	356	374	240	267	279
Black	8,979	10,073	10,380	2,440	2,445	2,436	27.2	24.3	23.5	261	277	291	324	352	383	222	246	255
Men	4,477	4,967	5,124	1,420	1,387	1,395	31.7	27.9	27.2	293	304	318	360	381	413	244	266	275
Women	4,502	5,106	5,257	1,020	1,058	1,040	22.7	20.7	19.8	231	252	263	287	316	335	209	228	236

Hispanic origin	(NA)	6,218	6,693	(NA)	(NA)	1,193	(NA)	(NA)	17.8	(NA)	269	277	(NA)	379	379	245	236	252
Men	(NA)	3,757	4,046	(NA)	842	826	(NA)	22.4	20.4	(NA)	295	299	(NA)	391	409	(NA)	265	268
Women	(NA)	2,460	2,648	(NA)	333	367	(NA)	13.5	13.9	(NA)	229)	241	(NA)	285	308	(NA)	218	227
Full-time workers	70,976	77,002	78,727	16,271	15,717	15,698	22.9	20.4	19.9	313	343	358	383	419	439	288	315	325
Part-time workers	17,314	17,518	18,176	1,446	1,280	1,277	8.4	7.3	7.0	(X)	(X)	(X)	(X)	(X)	(X)	(X)	(X)	(X)
Occupations																		
Managerial and professional specialty	19,657	21,688	22,492	3,354	3,307	3,328	17.1	15.2	14.8	437	488	505	421	481	497	446	490	507
Technical sales, and administrative support	28,024	30,082	31,046	3,377	3,243	3,340	12.1	10.8	10.8	281	307	320	341	380	397	270	297	309
Service occupations	12,875	13,325	13,609	1,971	1,922	1,920	15.3	14.4	14.1	205	216	223	299	322	350	182	195	201
Precision, production, craft, and repair	10,542	11,482	11,455	3,466	3,272	3,268	32.9	28.5	28.5	377	397	408	450	495	508	322	349	361
Operators, fabricators, and laborers	15,416	16,207	16,554	5,452	5,157	5,012	35.4	31.8	30.3	275	295	301	361	395	409	226	249	256
Farming, forestry, and fishing	1,775	1,736	1,747	98	95	109	5.5	5.5	6.2	196	212	217	287	334	350	189	206	209
Industries																		
Agricultural wage and salary workers	1,446	1,427	1,437	49	30	35	3.4	2.1	2.5	198	211	216	(B)	(B)	(NA)	195	210	213
Private nonagricultural wage and salary workers	71,225	77,044	79,091	11,933	11,227	11,051	16.8	14.6	14.0	307	332	347	385	418	437	286	312	322
Mining	869	881	822	180	153	144	20.7	17.3	17.5	481	501	510	470	507	513	488	499	509
Construction	4,109	4,716	4,959	1,131	1,051	1,092	27.5	22.3	22.0	348	369	380	510	556	581	296	315	327
Manufacturing	19,066	20,120	20,296	5,303	4,996	4,869	27.8	24.8	24.0	335	368	380	368	401	417	315	347	359
Transportation and public utilities	5,142	5,725	5,715	2,182	2,118	2,023	42.4	37.0	35.4	417	458	477	445	492	508	386	414	430
Wholesale and retail trade, total	18,081	19,402	19,839	1,568	1,400	1,425	8.7	7.2	7.2	252	270	280	348	373	381	242	262	272
Finance, insurance, and real estate	5,559	6,032	6,424	160	177	168	2.9	2.9	2.6	296	234	352	285	340	357	297	333	352
Services	18,400	20,167	21,036	1,410	1,331	1,329	7.7	6.6	6.3	272	298	310	303	327	350	268	294	306
Government	15,618	16,050	16,374	5,735	5,740	5,888	36.7	35.8	36.0	351	394	409	381	409	442	316	360	375

(B) Data not shown where base is less than 50,000.
(NA) Not available.
(X) Not applicable.
[1] Members of a labor union or an employee association similar to a labor union.
Source: U.S. Bureau of Labor Statistics, *Employment and Earnings*, annual.

Table 27　Work Stoppages Involving 1,000 Workers or More, 1947 to 1987

Year	Number of stoppages	Workers involved (thousands)	Days idle (thousands)
1947	270	1,629	25,720
1948	245	1,435	26,127
1949	262	2,537	43,420
1950	424	1,698	30,390
1951	415	1,462	15,070
1952	470	2,746	48,820
1953	437	1,623	18,130
1954	265	1,075	16,630
1955	363	2,055	21,180
1956	287	1,370	26,840
1957	279	887	10,340
1958	332	1,587	17,900
1959	245	1,381	60,850
1960	222	896	13,260
1961	195	1,031	10,140
1962	211	793	11,760
1963	181	512	10,020
1964	246	1,183	16,220
1965	268	999	15,140
1966	321	1,300	16,000
1967	381	2,192	31,320
1968	392	1,855	35,367
1969	412	1,576	29,397
1970	381	2,468	52,761
1971	298	2,516	35,538
1972	250	975	16,764
1973	317	1,400	16,260
1974	424	1,796	31,809
1975	235	965	17,563
1976	231	1,519	23,962
1977	298	1,212	21,258
1978	219	1,006	23,774
1979	235	1,021	20,409
1980	187	795	20,844
1981	145	729	16,908
1982	96	656	9,061
1983	81	909	17,461
1984	62	376	8,499
1985	54	324	7,079
1986	69	533	8,995
1987*	30	109.5	2,684

*Through August.

Source: Current Wage Developments, September 1987.

Table 28   Biggest Unions in the U.S.

Union	Address	Membership Locals
American Federation of Labor and Congress of Industrial Organizations Merged: 1955 President: Lane Kirkland	815 16th Street, N.W. Washington, D.C. 202-637-5000	13,100,000 89 Affiliates
National Education Association* Founded: 1857 President: Mary H. Futrell	1201 16th Street, N.W. Washington, D.C. 202-833-4000	1,900,000 12,500
International Brotherhood of Teamsters, Chauffeurs, Warehousemen and Helpers of America* Founded: 1903 President: Jackie Presser	25 Louisiana Avenue, N.W. Washington, D.C. 202-624-6800	1,700,000 694
United Food and Commercial Workers International Union Founded: 1979 President: William H. Wynn	1775 K Street, N.W. Washington, D.C. 202-223-3111	1,300,000 700
American Federation of State, County and Municipal Employees Founded: 1936 President: Gerald W. McEntee	1625 L Street, N.W. Washington, D.C. 202-452-4800	1,200,000 2,991
International Union, United Automotive, Aerospace and Agricultural Implement Workers of America (United Auto Workers) Founded: 1935 President: Owen Bieber	8000 Jefferson Avenue Detroit, Michigan 313-926-5000	1,000,000 1,400
International Brotherhood of Electrical Workers Founded: 1891 President: John J. Barry	1125 15th Street, N.W. Washington, D.C. 202-833-7000	900,000 1.417
Service Employees International Union Founded: 1921 President: John J. Sweeney	1313 L Street, N.W. Washington, D.C. 202-898-3200	850,000 300
United Steelworkers of America Founded: 1936 President: Lynn Williams	5 Gateway Center Pittsburgh, Pennsylvania 412-562-2400	778,000 4,000
United Brotherhood of Carpenters and Joiners of America Founded: 1881 President: Patrick J. Campbell	101 Constitution Avenue, N.W. Washington, D.C. 202-546-6206	600,000 1,800
Communications Workers of America Founded: 1938 President: Morton Bahr	1925 K Street, N.W. Washington, D.C. 202-728-2300	650,000 900
American Federation of Teachers Founded: 1916 President: Albert Shanker	555 New Jersey Avenue, N.W. Washington, D.C. 202-879-4400	660,000 2,000
International Association of Machinists and Aerospace Workers Founded: 1888 President: William W. Winpisinger	1300 Connecticut Avenue, N.W. Washington, D.C. 202-857-5200	567,000 1,530
Laborers' International Union of North America Founded: 1903 President: Angelo Fosco	905 16th Street, N.W. Washington, D.C. 202-737-8320	430,000 800
International Union of Operating Engineers Founded: 1896 President: Larry L. Dugan	1125 17th Street, N.W. Washington, D.C. 202-429-9100	375,000 203

Table 28 Biggest Unions in the U.S. (continued)

Union	Address	Membership Locals
United Association of Journeymen and Apprentices of the Plumbing and Pipe Fitting Industry of the United States and Canada Founded: 1889 President: Marvin J. Boede	901 Massachusetts Avenue, N.W. Washington, D.C. 202-628-5823	350,000 485
American Postal Workers Union Founded: 1971 President: Moe Biller	817 14th Street, N.W. Washington, D.C. 202-842-4200	330,000 2,500
Hotel Employees and Restaurant Employees International Union Founded: 1892 President: Edward T. Hanley	1219 28th Street, N.W. Washington, D.C. 202-393-4373	325,000 (seasonally adjusted) 191
National Association of Letter Carriers of the United States of America Founded: 1889 President: Vincent R. Sombrotto	100 Indiana Avenue, N.W. Washington, D.C. 202-393-4695	290,000 3,780
Amalgamated Clothing and Textile Workers Union Founded: 1914 President: Jack Sheinkman	15 Union Square West New York, New York 212-242-0700	281,000 1,351
United Paperworkers International Union Founded: 1884 President: Wayne E. Glenn	3340 Perimteter Hill Drive Nashville, Tennessee 615-834-8590	250,000 1,200
International Ladies' Garment Workers' Union Founded: 1900 President: Jay Mazur	275 7th Avenue New York, New York 212-741-6161	250,000 368
Retail, Wholesale and Department Store Union Founded: 1937 President: Lenore Miller	30 East 29th Street New York, New York 212-684-5300	250,000 315
American Federation of Government Employees Founded: 1932 President: Kenneth Blaylock	80 F Street, N.W. Washington, D.C. 202-737-8700	225,000 1,300
United Mine Workers of America* Founded: 1890 President: Richard Trumka	900 15th Street, N.W. Washington, D.C. 202-842-7200	220,000 750–800
American Federation of Musicians of the United States and Canada Founded: 1896 President: Jay Martin Emerson	1501 Broadway New York, New York 212-869-1330	200,000–250,000 500

*Independent unions. All other unions are members of the American Federation of Labor and Congress of Industrial Organizations.

Sources: U.S. Department of Labor and unions.

HIGHLIGHTS OF AMERICAN LABOR

1636 First labor dispute in America over money takes place in Maine, where fishermen strike over a proposal that would cost them a year in wages.

1648 The first American labor organization is formed by Boston shoe and barrel makers.

1734 New York maids form the first women's labor organization.

1786 Philadelphia printers hold the first authenticated strike in the United States. Their demand? A minimum wage of $6 a week.

1806 Members of the Philadelphia Journeymen Cordwainers strike to raise wages. As a result of that strike they become the first union to be tried and found guilty of a criminal conspiracy to raise wages.

1824 Women workers participate in a strike for the first time, one involving Pawtucket, Rhode Island, weavers.

1834 The first attempt to found a national labor federation in the U.S. is made when the National Trades Union is formed in New York City. The union, however, falls apart during the panic of 1837.

1847 The first state law limiting the workday to 10 hours is passed in New Hampshire.

1852 The first national organization of workers to endure to the present day, the National Typographical Union, is formed.

1863 New York mailmen form the first union for federal workers.

1868 An eight-hour workday for federal employees is declared.

1869 The Noble Order of the Knights of Labor is established. Unusual for the time is the fact that membership is open to both blacks and women. Knights, who have a socialist ideology, work in extreme secrecy until 1878 when they embark on a series of railroad strikes. By pushing for the eight-hour day, which is considered a revolutionary idea, they acquire 700,000 members by 1886, but decline thereafter because of the rise of the American Federation of Labor.

1869 The first black labor union, the Colored National Labor Union, is established.

1870 The first written contract between coal miners and operators is signed.

1874 The first use of the union label is introduced by Cigar Makers' International Union.

1875 American Express becomes the first private company to set up a pension plan.

1884 The Bureau of Labor is established in the Department of the Interior. It later becomes an independent agency without cabinet rank, is absorbed into the new Department of Commerce and Labor in 1903, and becomes, in 1913, the present Department of Labor, a cabinet-level position.

1886 The first convention of the American Federation of Labor takes place. Headed by Samuel Gompers, the union grows into the nation's largest, but is organized by crafts rather than by industry, making it difficult to organize some larger factories.

1886   On May 1, some 340,000 workers around the country go on strike
       for an eight-hour day, and in Chicago four strikers are killed. On
       May 4, a demonstration in Haymarket Square is held to protest
       their deaths and to support the eight-hour day. The rally is peaceful
       until police attempt to stop it; then a bomb explodes, killing seven
       policemen and four workers. The event becomes a labor cause
       célèbre and leads to the creation of May Day as a workers' holiday.
1888   The first federal labor relations law is passed, setting up arbitration
       and a presidential board of investigation for the railroad industry.
1890   The United Mine Workers union is formed. About a fifth of its
       early members are black.
1892   In one of the bloodiest strikes in U.S. history, workers at the
       Carnegie steel mills in Homestead, Pennsylvania, go on strike to
       protest wage cuts. During the six-month strike, four other Carnegie
       plants and several mills unrelated to the company are shut down.
       At one point Andrew Carnegie sends several boatloads of Pinkerton
       agents to retake the mill but they are attacked by the strikers,
       leaving four strikers and twelve Pinkerton guards dead. Eventually
       the strike fails and the union is ousted from most of the steel mills.
1900   The International Ladies' Garment Workers' Union is formed.
1905   The founding convention of the communist-oriented Industrial
       Workers of the World (the Wobblies) takes place. Under the lead-
       ership of Big Bill Haywood, the union picks up 100,000 members
       by 1917 (including the first mass unionization of migrant agricultural
       workers). The union is, however, effectively destroyed by the gov-
       ernment for its opposition to the First World War. The Wobblies
       are the last powerful union in the United States to advocate a
       socialist revolution. Since then, large unions restrict their demands
       to economic goals—higher wages and benefits.
1911   In one of the worst industrial accidents in the country's history, a
       fire at the Triangle Shirtwaist Company in New York kills 146
       workers. Most die because the garment-factory owners had locked
       the exits. The tragedy leads to the creation of the New York Fac-
       tory Investigating Commission and the passage of a number of laws
       designed to improve factory conditions.
1933   Frances Perkins becomes the first woman secretary of labor and
       the first woman named to a cabinet-level position. She is also the
       first secretary of labor who has had a college education and the
       first who has never been a union member.
1935   The National Labor Relations Act (the Wagner Act) guarantees
       workers the right to organize unions and have collective bargaining.
       This act, along with section 7A of the National Industrial Recovery
       Act (1933), marks a new deal for organized labor and leads to
       explosive union growth. The Wagner Act also establishes the Na-
       tional Labor Relations Board as a monitor for union organizing
       and collective bargaining.
1936   After the first large sit-down strike, the United Rubber Workers
       win recognition from the Goodyear Tire and Rubber Company.

1937 The United Auto Workers get a big break when General Motors recognizes the UAW as the bargaining agent for its workers.

1937 The United States Steel Corporation recognizes the Steel Workers Organizing Committee as the bargaining agent for its workers.

1937 In one of the bloodiest labor protests ever, 10 people are killed and 80 are wounded when police attack members of the Steel Workers Organizing Committee at the Republic Steel Corporation plant in South Chicago on Memorial Day.

1938 The Fair Labor Standards Act establishes the first minimum wage of 25 cents per hour. It also sets regulations on minimum work age and maximum work week and mandates time-and-a-half overtime pay for employees engaged in interstate commerce.

1941 The first union-shop agreement with a major auto company is signed between the United Auto Workers and Ford Motor Company after a 10-day strike.

1941 The AFL and the CIO issue a no-strike pledge effective for the duration of the war.

1941 Under pressure from black unionist A. Philip Randolph, who threatens a march on Washington to dramatize discrimination against black workers, President Roosevelt establishes a Fair Employment Practices Committee. Its mission is to ensure that workers employed in government or the defense industry are not discriminated against because of race, creed, color, or national origin.

1946 About 1.43% of all working time in the United States is lost because of strikes, the most in the country's history, as unions try to make up for the war years when they took no-strike pledges.

1947 The Labor Management Relations (Taft-Hartley) Act is passed over President Truman's veto. The act revises the Wagner Act and curbs the power of unions by prohibiting a list of unfair labor practices: the closed shop, secondary boycotts, and mass picketing. Taft-Hartley also encourages state right-to-work laws, establishes a cooling-off period before a strike can be called, requires unions to publish their finances, and allows employers to sue unions for broken contracts or damages inflicted during a strike.

1949 and 1950 Eleven unions charged with communist domination are expelled from the CIO.

1954 The longest major strike in the history of the United States begins on April 5 at the Wisconsin plumbing manufacturing plant of Kohler Company. The dispute is over whether employees can unionize and drags on until September 1, 1960. Eventually the company is cited for unfair labor practices. Almost all of the strikers are reinstated with $4.5 million back pay when the strike ends.

1955 The AFL and CIO settle their differences and agree to merge, forming the nation's largest union, with 16 million members and over 85% of all unionized workers.

1957 The AFL-CIO expels the Teamsters, the Bakery and Confectionery Workers and the Laundry, Dry Cleaning and Dye House Workers (a combined membership of 1.6 million) for union corruption.

1959   The longest strike ever in the steel industry begins on July 15 and
        ends on October 21, when a back-to-work injunction is invoked
        under the Taft-Hartley Act. In terms of employee time lost, the
        116-day strike, which idled hundreds of thousands, is the largest
        strike in the history of the United States. Workers return to their
        jobs for the 80-day cooling-off period as required under Taft-
        Hartley and a new contract is finally signed in January 1960.

1962   A major step in the unionization of federal employees takes place
        when an executive order gives unions the right to engage in col-
        lective bargaining with federal agencies.

1970   The first massive work stoppage by federal employees occurs when
        210,000 postal workers go on strike on March 18. An agreement
        is reached in two weeks after military units are summoned to handle
        the mail in New York City.

1970   Hawaii becomes the first state to grant state and local government
        employees the right to strike.

1972   A 35-year-long labor dispute, one of the longest in the history of
        labor relations, is settled by an agreement to phase out firemen's
        jobs on diesel freight locomotives gradually. The dispute between
        the United Transportation Union and major railroad companies
        began in 1937.

1974   Reflecting the increased importance of government employees in
        the labor movement, the AFL-CIO forms a new Public Employee
        Department. It includes 24 affiliated unions representing 2 million
        public workers, including Post Office employees.

1979   Lane Kirkland becomes president of the AFL-CIO, succeeding
        George Meany.

1980   Ronald Reagan becomes the first former union president to be
        elected president of the United States.

1980   After a 17-year-long battle, the Amalgamated Clothing and Textile
        Workers Union signs a collective bargaining agreement with J. P.
        Stevens & Co.

1981   President Reagan dismisses 8,590 members of the Professional Air
        Traffic Controllers Organization after they go on strike.

1982   A recession in smokestack industries hits the union movement
        hard. Economic troubles cost the AFL-CIO more than 400,000
        dues-paying members and forces some unions to lay off members
        of their staffs.

1984   Organized labor's declining political clout becomes apparent when
        the candidate of organized labor, Walter Mondale, is clobbered by
        President Reagan, despite heavy union support.

1986   Continuing the trend that began in 1983, nonunion workers earn
        higher wage increases than union workers. The average collective
        bargaining agreement provides for only a 1.2% wage hike in the
        first year and a 1.8% wage hike in the second year for union work-
        ers. Over 526,000 union workers accept contracts with no wage
        increases in the first year and 218,000 accept wage cuts averaging

−9.2%. Overall, union wages rise 2% in 1986, less than the wage increases of nonunion workers, who earn 3.5% wage hikes.

1987   Despite troubles in recent years, several polls indicate increased discontent in the workplace over wages and benefits. Labor leaders hope they can revive a flagging union movement by capitalizing on that discontent.

PART II

The Haves

Chapter Six

MONEY: FROM WAMPUM TO PLASTIC

Economists, who have a hard time explaining what constitutes money in a money economy, have an even harder time coming up with a definition that applies to the whole history of money. Generally, they admit defeat and say money is just about anything people say it is. Even bankers, who know a lot about money, aren't any more precise. The American Bankers Association says money is "anything that can be used to buy goods and services."

Money, in short, can act as money because people believe in it. Greenback dollars don't buy goods and services because paper is so expensive. They have value because people have faith in their value. That faith, as well as a certain vagueness about what constitutes money, allows gold, silver, dollars, and checks to function as money. It also allows notes printed by banks and governments that will eventually go bankrupt to circulate as money.

Of course, precious metals, usually gold and silver, have been the most common forms of money. But thanks to faith, most anything will work as money, as long as you believe in it. At various times, such commodities as tobacco, shells, and whiskey have served as mediums of exchange. Today, little pieces of paper in the form of checks and currency, plastic credit cards, and even electronic impulses used to credit and debit accounts can also be classified as mediums of exchange, that is, as money.

But faith can only take you so far, especially in the world of finance. Faith may explain why money has assumed so many different forms. It doesn't explain the history of money and how it has transformed our economy.

Money, banking, and our financial system were created and developed over time in response to a simple practical problem: the need to get the most out of one's goods, services, and capital.

The early development of money was a vast improvement over barter, allowing merchants to exchange money or precious metals rather than cumbersome products. For the state, money meant that taxes could be paid in coins, or, when taxes didn't cover its expenses, a sovereign could mint more money to finance wars, new palaces, and any other sort of nonsense.

At the same time, banking made the growth of a money economy possible. The earliest banks, as noted below, performed two vital functions: they exchanged foreign currency, thus facilitating international trade, and they provided short-term credit for merchants and tradesmen, increasing production and trade. In this way, both money and banking made the economy more liquid. They allowed producers and governments to take commodities, land, fixed assets, or even goodwill and turn them into liquid assets—money, credit, or other instruments that could be easily exchanged or used to buy goods and services.

Over time the evolution of banking and money has helped create increasingly efficient markets and economies. The development of land banks allowed landlords to monetarize an illiquid asset—real estate—and use the money to invest in other businesses and expand their operations. Short-term loans allowed businesses to expand their operations or tide themselves over seasonal shortages in cash.

But progress never moves in a straight line. Bankers, merchants, businesses, and especially governments occasionally display an alarming tendency to view money, banking, and finance as a kind of alchemy: a mysterious science that will somehow transpose future sales, not-yet-workable inventions, intangible hopes, vague schemes, visions of military might, soon-to-be-discovered El Dorados, rampant boosterism, and even revolutionary ardor into pure gold.

On this side of the history of money one finds government finance by the printing of paper money, speculation on Florida swamp land, the Tulip Bubble, and the 10,000 banks that failed in the early years of the Depression.

Such excesses help explain another basic theme running through the history of money, banking, and financial services: both banks and governments create money. Governments produce money by printing or coining money; banks accomplish the same feat either by issuing bank notes, as early American banks did, or by making loans and extending credit. Being in the business of manufacturing money, if you will, governments and banks have developed an uneasy but symbiotic relationship.

Speculative loans by banks have precipitated economic depressions, forcing governments to step in and regulate the financial industry. Similarly, and often with worse consequences, governments have discredited and delayed the development of key financial revolutions, such as paper money and central banks, by using them to finance disastrous spending sprees and harebrained economic policies. These excesses, in the public and private sector, go a long way toward explaining why the financial markets are the most heavily regulated sector of the American economy.

Here are a few key developments in the history of money and banking. (Key moments in the history of the stock exchanges can be found on page 295).

7000 B.C. Cattle are used as a medium of exchange. The relationship between money and cattle survives in our word *pecuniary,* which derives from the Latin word *pecus,* meaning "cow." In several other languages, the word for *money* is related to the word for *cattle* or some kind of domestic animal. Our word *fee* comes from the Anglo-Saxon *feoh,* meaning both money and cattle. Our words *capital, chattel,* and *cattle* are also all derived from the word *capitale.* During this period, grains such as wheat and barley are also used as mediums of exchange.

2000 B.C. Bronze ingots, often in the shape of cows, appear and are used as a medium of exchange. Though less cumbersome than actual commodities, the ingots still must be weighted, unlike modern coins. The Chinese are reported to have made coins as early as 2250 B.C.

1000 B.C. Purer metals such as gold and silver begin to replace bronze as mediums of exchange.

973 B.C. King Solomon's fleet trades in the Red Sea and begins mining gold in Africa and Arabia.

800 B.C. The forerunners of our modern coins appear. The Lydians of Asia Minor stamp ingots of electrum, a natural alloy of gold and silver, and each ingot bears a mark that shows its weight. This practice does away with the need for scales.

625 B.C. The first coins are introduced into Greece. They are stamped with the likeness of an ear of wheat, perhaps as a reminder that grains were once used as a medium of exchange.

540 B.C. Along with the creation of money come counterfeiters. On this date Polycrates of Samos cheats the Spartans with fake gold coins. Cheats also profit by raising the quantity of silver in relation to gold in coins.

4th century B.C. The Greeks invent the bill of exchange. It allows a merchant to deposit a sum of money with his banker, who gives him a letter. When the merchant presents this letter to another banker in another city, the banker pays the money. The forerunner of a bank check, the bill of exchange facilitates travel and trade by allowing people to journey from one place to another without the danger or inconvenience of taking large sums of gold or coins.

3rd century B.C. If money makes the economy more efficient by facilitating the exchange of goods and services, it also opens up even greater opportunities for fraud, inefficiency, and outright larceny. On a small scale, individuals and merchants often clip or shave small bits of gold off each coin before spending the money. But the biggest offenders are governments. As early as the Punic Wars, the Romans pioneer the idea of debased coinage by reducing the value of silver in their coins. The idea catches on and remains a common practice even today, when governments do the same thing with printing presses. In the short run, this technique allows kings to pay their debts by simply manufacturing money rather than by increasing taxes or curtailing spending. Over time, currency debasement causes inflation, since more money is chasing the same amount of goods. In extreme cases of hyperinflation or hyperdebasement, individuals and merchants stop accepting coins as payment.

6th to 11th centuries A.D.   The Dark Ages are bleak times for banking. Banking was widespread in the Mediterranean region during the Greek and Roman period, but it declines after the fall of the Roman Empire because of the decline of international trade, a radically reduced need to change foreign currencies, a decline of the money economy, and a falling demand for credit—that is, declines in the factors that led to the creation of banking in the first place. As trade revives, however, in the 11th century, banking reappears.

13th century   The Italians become Europe's bankers and banking houses play a major role in reviving European commerce and trade. Italian banking houses are prohibited from charging interest by church laws against usury but get around the rule by buying and selling bills of exchange at a discount. (The discount, or difference between the value of the bill of exchange and what the bank paid for it, produces a profit, just as a modern bank makes money by charging interest on loans.) But early banking is a perilous profession and many banking houses go broke in the highly profitable but risky business of loaning money to medieval princes. The Fugger family, for example, amasses a $50 million fortune but goes bankrupt with the fall of the Holy Roman Empire.

1492   Columbus discovers the New World. He doesn't make any money on his venture and dies poor. But Spain soon discovers vast treasures of silver and gold in Mexico and Latin America. Between 1500 and 1650 about 181 tons of gold and 16,000 tons of silver reach Europe from America. That capital helps finance Europe's growing dominance of the world's economy.

1558   Reflecting on the problem of creating a stable currency, Sir Thomas Gresham articulates a basic law of economics: bad money always drives out good. By this he means that debased money is spent while good money, with a higher value of gold and silver, is hoarded. Later, Gresham's law is applied to paper money. When governments print too much money, the paper often freely circulates, at reduced value, while precious metals and coins are hoarded.

17th century   Mints put serrated edges on coins so people can't shave bits of gold or silver off the sides of coins, thus reducing their weight. A common tactic is to put coins in a bag and shake them vigorously for several hours. The friction of the coins rubs off some gold dust, which is sold.

17th century   Lacking precious metals, the American colonists experiment with various commodities. In Massachusetts, corn and beaver skins are used as mediums of exchange. Indian currency of beads, or wampum, is made legal tender in 1637 by the Massachusetts Bay government, and in 1618 the Virginia colonists make tobacco legal tender. But these experiments run into problems. Wampum rapidly depreciates in value as the white man introduces one of his own inventions—counterfeit wampum. In Virginia, bumper crops of tobacco quickly depreciate the crop's value as money.

1652　The first colonial mint is established in the Massachusetts Bay Colony. The Crown is angered by colonists usurping the British monopoly on printing money, and royal decrees order the mints to close in the 1680s.

1658　The Riksbank of Stockholm becomes the first bank to issue bank notes.

1690　Failing with wampum, Massachusetts becomes the first colony to issue paper money. The experiment works until the colony prints far too much money, after which the currency declines dramatically in value. Other colonies make the same mistake, setting off high inflation. Worried about this fiscal mismanagement, Parliament prohibits paper money first in Massachusetts in 1751 and then in all the colonies in 1763. However, in Pennsylvania, where the money supply is controlled carefully, the experiment with paper money is successful.

1775　As one might expect in a country that started out as the result of a tax revolt, the first Continental Congress is opposed to financing the War of Independence with new taxes. The solution is to print money. As one delegate puts it, "Will I consent to load my constituents with taxes when we can send to our printer and get a wagon load of money, one quire of which will pay for the whole thing?" Obviously not. For the first two years, Congress restricts the amount of paper money issued, and the currency, known as continentals, holds its value. But after 1778, the printing presses move into high gear and by 1780 one dollar in specie is worth $80 in continentals. Eventually the U.S. government adopts a plan whereby all remaining continental currency is redeemed at the rate of $1 dollar in specie for $100 in paper.

1781　The first commercial bank is created when Congress gives Robert Morris, the superintendent of finance during the revolution, a charter to the Bank of North America. It is absorbed in the 1920s by the Pennsylvania Company.

1791　The issue of a central bank runs through American financial history. In the first battle over the creation of a central bank, James Madison and Alexander Hamilton debate the pros and cons. Madison, defending the idea of hard currency and attacking paper money as fiscally and economically irresponsible, argues that Congress doesn't have the power to charter a bank. He, like other opponents of the bank, believes that hard money is endangered by the speculative excesses of banks. But Congress is convinced by Hamilton's argument that banks increase productive capital by advancing credit, that banks help the government finance its programs, and that banks facilitate the payment of taxes. It charters the Bank of the United States as a central bank for twenty years with an authorized capital of $10 million, of which the federal government contributes $2 million. Investors snap up the stock when it goes on sale in July of 1791.

1792   As for most revolutionary governments, one of the first tasks of the new republic is to create its own money. In 1792 Congress sets up the first minting of U.S. coins and puts the U.S. on a bimetallic standard of gold and silver. Alexander Hamilton recommends the bimetallic standard to avoid the "evils of scanty circulation." But things don't work out the way Congress intends. The U.S. never functions on a bimetallic standard whereby both gold and silver circulate as money. Worse, U.S. coins or money are not widely circulated in the United States before the 1830s. During those years, foreign coins and paper money printed by private banks act as the country's money supply. Here's how Congress manages to accomplish exactly the opposite of what it intends: Worried about the states' past practices of printing worthless paper money, the Constitution of the United States gives the right to "coin Money" to the federal government and prohibits the states from issuing "bills of credit"—paper money. In 1792, when Congress gets around to setting up the money supply, it adopts the Spanish dollar as the unit of account, adopts a decimal system for smaller coins, decrees that gold or silver sold to the mint will be turned into coins, and puts the U.S. on a bimetallic standard with 15 ounces of silver equal to 1 ounce of gold. Congress also authorizes a ten-dollar gold eagle, a five-dollar gold piece, a two-dollar-and-fifty-cent piece, a gold dollar, a silver dollar, a half dollar, a quarter, a dime, a half dime, a cent, and a half cent. But the ratio overvalues silver. As a result, holders of gold sell gold only in the open market and only silver is brought to the mint to be coined. Since gold is not minted into coins and hence doesn't circulate, the U.S. operates on a de facto silver standard, like most of Europe. This state of affairs continues until 1834, when Congress changes the ratio. (See 1834.) Worse, very few American silver dollars circulate. The dollar minted in Philadelphia is slightly lighter than the Spanish silver dollar that is circulated in Latin America. But Spanish colonists discover that the U.S. dollar circulates just as well as the heavier and hence more valuable Spanish silver dollar. They bring Spanish silver dollars to the U.S., melt them down, and mint them into U.S. dollars for a profit. As a result the U.S. is forced to suspend coinage of silver dollars and foreign coins and paper money printed by private banks act as our currency.

19th century   The new country needs capital to develop frontier regions and banks appear almost as fast as saloons in frontier towns. Various state legislatures issue 29 bank charters by 1800, 90 by 1811, and 120 by 1816. These banks issue $100 million in notes in 1817, up from $45 million in 1812. Most play a major role in financing early development by proving needed capital. Some, however, simply print paper money. (See 1809.)

1804   The Farmers Bank of Maryland is the first bank to pay interest on bank deposits. Massachusetts banks begin paying interest on large deposits left in the 1810s, and in 1825 the country's central bank, the Bank of the United States, starts paying interest on specie deposits.

1809   The Farmers Exchange Bank of Gloucester, Rhode Island, earns the dubious distinction of becoming the first bank to fail in the United States. Founded in 1804, the bank began with only $3,000 in capital but issued hundreds of thousands of dollars worth of paper money. The owner had cashiers working overtime signing the bills the bank circulated as money and at another point the bank issued $648,000 in notes backed by only $86 in specie.

1811   After another debate between supporters of a central bank and hard-money proponents who oppose a central bank, Congress decides not to renew the charter of the Bank of the United States. Jefferson's party, the Democratic-Republicans, opposes the bank because it supports hard money and wants the government to accept only specie. In its view, the central bank encourages fiscal irresponsibility and the printing of paper money, which almost inevitably depreciates. Ending the bank's charter causes immediate economic and fiscal problems. When the War of 1812 starts, the U.S. no longer has a central bank to finance the war. Many state banks work their printing presses overtime and many bank notes circulate at a substantial discount. Banks also face temporary liquidity problems. Without a central bank they have no way of surviving temporary shortfalls that occur seasonally.

1816   The first savings banks, the Provident Institution for Savings in Boston and the Savings Fund Society in Philadelphia, are established. By the Civil War, traditional distinctions between American banks are well established. Savings banks encourage people to save and are required to hold a large portion of their assets as mortgages. National commercial banks are prohibited from making mortgages; their business is based on taking in demand deposits and making short-term business loans.

1816   Seeing the problems caused by unregulated state banks, the Democratic-Republicans reverse their earlier opposition to a central bank and Congress charters the Second Bank of the United States. With capital of $35 million it controls the money supply by collecting state bank notes and presenting them to the issuing bank for redemption in specie. That way it can loosen or tighten the money market. But political considerations force the bank to adopt a lenient policy and state banks continue on their merry way, printing money. This soon gets the central bank into trouble. By 1819 it has accumulated too many bank notes, and in order to avoid bankruptcy the Bank of the U.S. redeems the state bank notes for specie. This forces many banks into bankruptcy and throws the country into a depression. As a result of such actions, the bank irritates both the hard-money people, who feel it is too liberal, and the easy-money people, who think it is too conservative. These attacks grow after 1828, when Andrew Jackson is elected president. Jackson puts together a coalition of people who disagree on everything except their hatred of the central bank. With the backing of state banks (which favor easy money), hard-money supporters (who favor tight money policies and the return to specie), states'-rights proponents (who chafe at the idea of central power), free-market advocates (who call the bank a monopoly), and populist politicians (who view the bank as a rich man's tool), Jackson succeeds in preventing the bank's charter from being renewed in 1836 when it expires.

1834　Congress raises the coinage ratio to 16 ounces of silver for 1 ounce of gold. This and the California Gold Rush in 1849 push down the price of gold. As a result only gold is coined, effectively putting the U.S. on a gold standard. The change, however, does allow gold coins to circulate. But until the Civil War, the only paper money circulating in the United States is produced by private banks.

1836　The Specie Circular decrees that the government will only take gold and silver for public lands. This act, along with Jackson's destruction of the central bank, helps plunge the U.S. economy into a severe recession in 1837. Specie flows out of the U.S. to Britain, contracting the money supply, and there is no central bank to help banks and the economy make the transition.

1849　Gold is discovered in California; $450 million worth is mined during the next seven years.

1853　The New York Clearing House starts operations. The clearinghouse allows banks to balance their accounts with each other when checks are drawn on one bank and deposited with another.

1853　When the U.S. changes the ratio of gold and silver in coins in 1834, U.S. coins go into mass circulation for the first time. But as gold drives silver out of circulation, smaller coins like the quarter are not widely circulated and the U.S. continues to exist without having small coins in mass circulation. To remedy this problem, which makes it hard to conduct business, the silver content of small coins is reduced in 1853. After that year, for the first time in American history, half dollars, quarters, and dimes circulate freely.

1857　Congress repeals the legal-tender status of foreign coins, ending the use of Spanish pieces of eight and other foreign coins as legal tender.

1862　Congress continues the American tradition of financing wars by printing money. It authorizes the issuance of $150 million in notes. By the end of the Civil War the North issues $430 million worth of greenbacks—which take their name from the green ink on the paper money. Inflation naturally follows. After the war, some of the money is withdrawn, leading to protests against the government for pursuing a hard-money policy. Eventually, Congress allows $346,681,016 worth of paper money to remain in circulation.

1864   Congress passes the National Bank Act, establishing nationally chartered banks and creating the office of the Comptroller of the Currency to regulate those banks. The act allows five or more people to obtain a banking charter from the Comptroller of the Currency. To end the abuses caused by state banks issuing too many bank notes, the act also levies a tax on paper money issued by state banks.

1873   The U.S. has been on a bimetallic standard of gold and silver in theory but in practice it has always been on either gold or silver. (See 1792 and 1834.) Recognizing this fact, Congress finally discontinues minting the silver dollar. However, large silver deposits are discovered at this time and the price of silver is dropping. Soon easy-money theorists push for a return to silver coinage, which would expand the money supply. It is in support of this crusade that the Democratic Party candidate for President, William Jennings Bryan, declares in an 1896 speech that "you shall not crucify mankind upon a cross of gold."

1876   The Supreme Court affirms the separation of commercial banking and investment banking by writing that "dealing in stocks is not expressly prohibited under the National Bank Act of 1864 but such a prohibition is implied from the failure to grant the power." Separation of commercial and investment banking conforms to the British theory that the two functions should be performed in separate financial institutions since investment banking is "risky" and commercial banking should involve the conservative use of "other people's money." But over the next forty years banks break down the separation. (See 1914.)

1900   The battle of gold versus silver is won by gold when the Congress passes the Gold Standard Act in 1900. It puts the U.S. officially on the gold standard instead of on a de facto gold standard. But what really kills the silver movement is the increasing importance of checking accounts and bank deposits. As they expand, the money supply doubles between 1900 and 1912, easing credit restrictions.

1913   After numerous financial panics, Congress finally consents to the creation of a central bank with the passage of the Federal Reserve Act of 1913. The final bill is a compromise between fiscal conservatives and agrarian populists who have long opposed a central bank. But the Federal Reserve System's supporters hope the bank will smooth out fluctuations in the money supply and prevent financial panics by making loans to banks through its Discount window. During the 1920s, the Federal Reserve learns that buying and selling government securities also affects the money supply. The banking acts of the 1930s strengthen the Federal Reserve by concentrating the power to buy and sell securities in the Federal Open Market Committee. (See the profile of Federal Reserve System, page 90.)

1914   By this time banks manage to break down most effective barriers between investment and commercial banking. Though the Supreme Court has affirmed the distinction for national banks, that is, banks chartered under the National Bank Act, states issue charters giving companies the authority to engage in both investment and commercial banking. When the Comptroller of the Currency rules that national banks should not underwrite securities, national banks form affiliates chartered under state law that act as investment bankers. Increasingly, investment bankers also accept deposits and expand their activities into commercial banking. (See 1927.)

1927   Congress passes the McFadden Act. Designed to make national banks more competitive with state banks, the law allows national banks to establish branches in the states where they are already located, providing that state law allows branch banking. It also allows real-estate loans and increases the amount of money that can be loaned to one borrower. This act formally gives national banks the power to underwrite "investment securities," something they have been doing for some time. (See 1876 and 1914.) Commercial banks capitalize on the new law by dominating the investment banking field and expanding their share of bond underwriting from 37% in 1927 to 61% in 1930.

1932   The Great Depression causes the money supply to shrink by over one third. The Depression also touches off a national debate between proponents of hard money and easy money. The Roosevelt administration works to ease the money supply.

1932   Senate Banking Committee hearings criticize the banking industry, blaming banks and Wall Street for the Great Depression. The Committee charges that banks encouraged rampant speculation by providing loans for buying stocks on margin and for dubious real-estate ventures. Moreover, the committee also attacks affiliates of commercial banks that sold and underwrote stocks, saying they tricked the public into buying some nearly worthless public offerings and "devoted themselves . . . to perilous underwriting operations, stock speculation, and maintaining a market for the banks' own stock, often largely with the resources of parent banks." These charges and the publicity surrounding the Banking Committee hearings help create a political consensus for a reform of the banking and capital markets that will shape the nature of financial services during the next forty years. (See 1933.)

1933   Attacks on the banking system culminate with the passage of the Glass-Steagall Act. This law contains the following major provisions: (1) it divorces commercial banking institutions from investment banking institutions; (2) to protect depositors, many of whom lost their life savings when 10,000 banks failed between 1929 and

1933, it authorizes the establishment of the Federal Deposit Insurance Corporation (FDIC); (3) to curb the speculation of the Roaring Twenties, it restricts the extension of bank credit for speculation; (4) it restricts branch banking and group banking; (5) it regulates the interest paid on deposits; (6) it allows savings and industrial banks to join the Federal Reserve; and (7) it extends the open-market activities of the Federal Reserve.

1934   President Roosevelt takes the U.S. off the gold standard and the Gold Reserve Act of 1934 devalues the dollar. By lowering the amount of gold in the dollar from what it had been since 1837, the act effectively raises the price of gold from $20 to $35. The act also nationalizes gold. All gold imported or produced in the U.S. has to be bought by the U.S. Treasury. Moreover, Federal Reserve Banks have to maintain 25% of their notes and deposits as gold certificates. These provisions are changed in the 1960s and 1970s. (See 1963, 1965, and 1971.)

1935   The Banking Act of 1935 revises the structure of the Federal Reserve, making it more independent from political pressure. The law also sets up the Open Market Committee at the Federal Reserve, allows the Fed to require higher reserves of member banks, requires state nonmember banks with deposits over $1 million to become members or forfeit their deposit insurance, and authorizes the Fed to make loans to member banks.

1944   The Bretton Woods Conference is held at Bretton Woods, New Hampshire, in July to deal with the economic problems of the world after World War II. Forty-four nations send representatives. They create the International Monetary Fund (IMF) and the International Bank For Reconstruction and Development (the World Bank). (See profile of IMF, page 94.)

1950   Ralph Scheider sets up Diners Club, allowing members to eat and pay later at 27 New York restaurants. It is the first credit-card company.

mid-1950s   To satisfy complaints by large corporate borrowers that they are not earning enough interest on their deposits, banks issue certificates of deposit (CDs). In 1961 National City Bank of New York (later Citibank) announces it will issue negotiable CDs and a secondary market is created. The popularity of bank CDs is also aided in 1973 when interest-rate ceilings for large negotiable CDs with terms over 90 days are lifted.

1956   The Bank Holding Company Act gives the Federal Reserve the power to approve or disapprove the formation of a bank holding company. The Fed also must approve the acquisition of more than 5% interest in a bank by an existing bank holding company.

1958   Bank of America issues the BankAmericard, the first bank credit card.

1960   The Bank Merger Act makes bank mergers subject to approval by various federal agencies.

1962   The United States, the United Kingdom, West Germany, France,

Belgium, the Netherlands, Italy, Sweden, Canada, and Japan meet and sign the General Arrangements to Borrow. This agreement makes $6.2 billion of additional credit available to the IMF. Following this agreement, the ten nations, which account for most of the world's trade, are called the Group of Ten. They still meet on a regular basis to solve problems of international finance and the Group of Ten often participates in IMF activities. The group is also called the Paris Club.

1963   Congress passes the first of a series of measures that will make silver less important for the nation's currency. In 1963, following a rise in the price of silver that threatens to cause the disappearance of silver coins, Congress eliminates the silver certificate and allows the Federal Reserve to issue one-dollar and two-dollar notes. In 1965, another step is taken when the silver dollar is eliminated. Half dollars are to be made out of an alloy of silver and copper; quarters and dimes will have no silver, only copper and nickel. In 1967, Congress passes a law stating that silver certificates cannot be redeemed in silver.

1965   Congress moves away from gold as a basis for banking and currency. It abolishes a requirement created by the Gold Reserve Act of 1934 that Federal Reserve deposits be backed by a 25% gold security. This helps solve the deficit in the balance of payments and allows gold to move out of the country. In 1968, Congress goes further and removes the gold cover from Federal Reserve notes. As a result of the legislation, which says that Federal Reserve notes will be supported by government bonds and commercial paper rather than by gold, gold is no longer a driving force in banking and in the U.S. monetary system. (See 1971.)

1970   Amendments to the Bank Holding Company Act allow banks to open and conduct nonbanking activities across state lines.

1971   President Nixon does away with the gold-dollar standard. The latter emerged from a 1944 agreement reached at Bretton Woods, New Hampshire, that tied all the world's currencies to the dollar and the dollar to gold. Under this system, the Treasury Department was committed to buying gold at $35 an ounce. For many years the agreement allowed the U.S. to inflate the money supply all it wanted while other countries had to take our dollars at artificially high exchange rates. But with a worsening balance of payments and rising government expenditures, foreigners demand gold. U.S. gold reserves drop and Nixon takes the country off the gold standard. Since gold no longer supports currency, in 1974 Congress allows Americans to freely buy and sell gold, ending the 1934 provision that nationalized gold.

1978   The International Banking Act provides for federal regulation of foreign banks in domestic financial markets.

1978   Banks and thrifts offer savings certificates tied to market interest rates.

1980   The Depository Institutions Deregulation and Monetary Control

Act of 1980 phases out interest-rate ceilings over the next six years, allows money-market accounts, gives savings and loans more lending powers in the areas of commercial and consumer finance, and permits payment of interest on demand deposits (such as checking accounts).

1982 The Depository Institutions Act authorizes money-market accounts with $2,500 minimum balances, expands thrift lending power and makes provisions for failing thrifts, and allows interest-rate differentials paid by banks and thrifts to be phased out by 1984.

1982 BankAmerica acquires Charles Schwab & Co., the brokerage. Subsequently about 1,000 banks acquire discount brokerages, start their own operations, or make other arrangements to provide discount brokerage services.

1982 A commercial bank acquires a failed thrift for the first time. This opens the way for more commercial banks to acquire thrifts and helps blur the distinctions between the two.

1983 The minimum balance on money-market accounts is reduced to $1,000.

1983 Facing a third-world debt crisis and worries about U.S. banks that have loaned billions to nearly bankrupt developing countries, the chairman of the Federal Reserve, Paul Volcker, asks Congress to increase its support of the IMF. Congress does but also passes the International Lending Supervision Act of 1983. The Federal Reserve and other regulatory agencies are given greater powers to supervise international lending by U.S. banks.

1984 The Supreme Court upholds the right of banks to buy discount brokerage firms.

1985 The Supreme Court rules that regional pacts that permit interstate banking are constitutional. The ruling breaks down barriers to interstate banking by allowing the development of large regional banks but is a setback for large New York City banks, such as Citibank, which brought the suit. The rise of interstate banking is expected to reduce the number of banks and produce some giant regional banks. Mergers in the midwest, New England, and other areas where states have signed regional pacts have already produced super regional banks like SunTrust Banks, First Wachovia, NCNB, the Bank of New England, Fleet Financial, and the Bank of Boston. Other large banks, such as Chemical, have acquired banks in Texas, and Citibank already owns thrifts in California. New York City banks will undoubtedly acquire commercial banks in California after such acquisitions become legal in 1990. The merger activity is driving up the stocks of many banks in some states in anticipation of outside takeovers.

1986 In April the last restrictions on savings deposit rates—which had been set by the regulators at 5.5%—end. This means commercial banks and thrift institutions can pay any rate they choose on millions of accounts amounting to nearly $305 billion.

1987 Worried about increased deregulation of the financial services industry (which includes both banks and securities firms) and Wall Street's growing insider-trading scandal, Congress passes legislation that puts a temporary moratorium on any further banking deregulation by the Federal Reserve and other regulatory agencies until March of 1988.

THE FEDERAL RESERVE SYSTEM

Ever since the 1790s, when Alexander Hamilton and James Madison debated the pros and cons of a central bank, no banking and financial issue has produced more political heat—or, it must be admitted, less economic sense.

The Federal Reserve System, created in 1913 as the nation's central bank, has in recent years been championed by Wall Street as the white knight that slew inflation. But the Federal Reserve's conservative approach to banking deregulation has caused some banks to attack this white knight for saddling the banking system with outmoded regulations. Other banks, of course, applaud the Federal Reserve's banking regulations as a way of keeping big New York City banks off Main Street, Peoria. And populist politicians and bankrupt farmers, repeating arguments that go back to William Jennings Bryan and his "cross of gold" speech, blame the Federal Reserve's tight-money policies for causing the 1982 recession.

Reality, it must be said, doesn't quite support all these claims. The Federal Reserve System's policies, which are supposed to keep the economy on an even keel, haven't solved or created all the world's problems.

But there is little doubt why the Federal Reserve System gets so much criticism and praise. The Fed is the nation's most important financial institution. It is the nation's central banking system and its most important responsibility is control over monetary policy. The Federal Reserve also handles government deposits and debt issues, supervises and regulates banks that belong to the system, acts as a clearinghouse for checks and other instruments, and loans banks money as a lender of last resort. Economic statistics collected by the Federal Reserve are a key indicator of the nation's economic health.

One of its most important and difficult tasks is using the money supply to control economic growth. The Fed's defenders claim its policies have moderated the well-known economic shortcomings of Congress and the White House. Its critics blame the Fed for every recession in the last 70 years.

History, however, shows a record of mixed results. Consider, for example, how the Federal Reserve's policies have affected the money supply and the economy:

It wasn't until the 1920s that the Federal Reserve System understood the power of open-market operations—that is, buying and selling government securities—to regulate the money supply. Its first sales, however, were uncoordinated and actually contributed to problems in the financial markets. Later, after the crash of 1929, the Fed did little to increase the money supply by open-market operations. In those years the Fed not only failed to keep the nation's money supply growing at a steady, moderate, predictable rate, it actually allowed the money supply to collapse, shrinking by an astounding 35%!

In the 1960s and 1970s, the Keynesians in the Federal Reserve targeted interest rates as the key to economic growth and stability. The theory was that changes in the money supply were unpredictable in their effects, depending on such factors as the public's desire to spend or save. Since low interest rates would encourage investments, the Fed focused its policy on targeting the Federal Funds rate, which is the interest rate on overnight borrowing between member banks to obtain required reserves. In practice, however, tinkering with interest rates managed to accentuate cyclical swings of the economy and in many cases didn't lower interest rates. For example, when the Fed increased the money supply to lower interest rates, it increased inflation. Investors recognized that more money meant more inflation so they demanded even higher interest rates than the rates the Fed was trying to lower.

Under former Federal Reserve chairman Paul Volcker, the Fed announced in 1979 that it would control the money supply rather than emphasizing interest rates. This decision, though actually never fully implemented, has often been viewed as a turn away from Keynesian economics toward a monetarist view. Volcker's overall effort to moderate the inflationary growth of money worked dramatically, and while earning him a reputation for creating a "tight money" policy, it got him reappointed to a new term in 1983 by President Reagan. Inflation during his tenure dropped from 13.3% in 1979 to only 1.9% in 1986.

But despite this success, the Fed's monetary policy has remained erratic. At times M1 (currency in circulation, commercial bank demand deposits such as checking, NOW accounts, automatic transfer from savings accounts, nonbank traveler's checks, credit union share drafts, and mutual savings bank demand deposits) fell dramatically while M2 (M1 plus overnight repurchase agreements issued by commercial banks, overnight Eurodollars, savings accounts, time deposits over $100,000, and money-market mutual-fund shares) grew sharply. At other times, a stop-go money policy shocked the economy. The erratic month-to-month implementation of the Fed's policy served to keep interest rates higher than they would have been and prolonged the 1981–1982 recession.

There is no reason to imagine that inflation could have been cured without some decline of economic activity. Still, the economic slowdown could have been mitigated and shortened if the Fed's policy had been clearer and more consistent in execution—two areas in which the Fed has faltered over the past 70 years.

In the mid-1980s, the Federal Reserve allowed the money supply to expand much faster than its own targets. In 1985, Volcker said the Fed would allow M1 to grow at a rate of 4% to 7%. Instead it grew 12%. Then in 1986, Volcker said M1 would expand 3% to 8%. It grew by 17%.

While the Fed was grappling with the problems of controlling the money supply, longtime chairman Paul Volcker was tiring of his job. In the summer of 1987 he submitted his resignation and President Reagan appointed economist Alan Greenspan to the job. A follower of the laissez-faire philosopher Ayn Rand and a staunch supporter of free markets, Greenspan served as head of Council of Economic Advisers under President Ford. He was known for his anti-inflation stance, his opposition to large government deficits, and his political acumen, three qualities he shared with Volcker.

Greenspan had little time to ease into his new post. Shortly after he was appointed, the stock market crash of October 19 raised fears that the economy might face its worst financial crisis since 1929. But by easing credit and making money available to the securities industry, the Fed helped avert a serious crisis. Greenspan's handling of the crisis was widely applauded, but over the next few years he'll have to tackle some even tougher issues. As a bank regulator, the Federal Reserve is one of several agencies that regulate the country's banks. Under Volcker, the Federal Reserve moved cautiously, but regulations were eased, allowing banks to underwrite some kinds of securities. Those moves have been attacked in Congress for breaking down the distinction between the securities industry and commercial banking, which was established by the Glass-Steagall Act. However, banks want less government regulation since they are more heavily regulated than many other parts of the financial services industry. Some banks have already threatened to leave the Federal Reserve System and give up commercial banking to specialize in the more profitable securities field unless deregulation continues. Greenspan, who is known for his enthusiasm for deregulation, will undoubtedly push for fewer restrictions on banking practices.

As a bank regulator, Greenspan will also have to face the problem of keeping banks solvent. U.S. banks still face huge loan losses on their third-world loans, farm loans, energy loans, and real-estate loans. As a central banker, Greenspan will have to balance his anti-inflation ideas with the need to produce enough economic growth in third-world countries so that they can pay off their loans.

Greenspan's most ticklish problem will be economic and monetary policy. He'll have to balance fears of renewed inflation with the desire by several of Reagan's appointees that the Federal Reserve keep interest rates low. Clamping the brakes on the growth of money supply would send interest rates up and slow down the economy—not a politically popular idea. On the other hand, allowing the money supply to grow as fast as it has could rekindle inflation. And Greenspan will have to watch the falling dollar to make certain that its free-fall doesn't disrupt international trade.

The Federal Reserve can affect short-term interest rates and the money supply in three ways: (1) In its open market operations, it can choose to buy or sell Government securities. When it sells such securities, it removes money from the private economy, thereby contracting the available supply of credit. When it buys such securities, it creates the funds out of thin air, thus in effect "printing money at will," and expanding the money supply. These open-market operations are the most important way the Fed affects economic growth and the money supply. (2) It can raise or lower the Discount rate at which it lends to the banks in its system, thus sending a loud and clear signal of its overall policy intentions. Raising the Discount rate would make it more expensive for banks to buy money and loan it out; lowering the Discount rate has the opposite effect. (3) It can change the reserve requirements governing the amount of money banks must keep in relation to their deposits; higher reserve requirements mean "tighter" money since the banks will then have less available for loans.

As chairman, Greenspan will be the most powerful man in the Federal Reserve System. But the power of the chairman is by no means absolute. His most important policies have to be approved by a majority of the Board of Governors of the Federal Reserve and have to be carried out through the structure of the Federal Reserve. Here's how the system is structured and works:

The Structure of the Federal Reserve

The Federal Reserve System consists of five parts: (1) the Board of Governors in Washington, (2) the 12 Federal Reserve Banks and their 25 branches and other facilities situated around the country, (3) the Federal Open Market Committee, (4) the Federal Advisory Council, and (5) the nation's financial institutions, including commercial banks, savings and loan associations, mutual savings banks, and credit unions.

(1) The Board of Governors

The most powerful part of the Federal Reserve System is the Board of Governors. It's made up of seven members appointed by the President and approved by the Senate. The board determines monetary and interest-rate policies, monitors credit conditions, enforces various consumer-protection laws such as the Truth in Lending Act, supervises Federal Reserve Banks, and regulates banks belonging to the system. Though the other members of the Board of Governors traditionally follow the lead of the chairman, Greenspan will have to forge a working majority on the Board of Governors to carry out his policies. The governors also sit on the Open Market Committee.

(2) The Federal Open Market Committee

One of the most important ways the Board of Governors influences credit conditions, monetary policy, and economic growth is through the Federal Open Market Committee. The committee is composed of the Board of Governors and the five presidents of the Reserve Banks. Greenspan, as chairman of the Board of Governors, heads the Open Market Committee. As noted above, the Open Market Committee buys and sells securities on the open market—hence its name—as a way of influencing credit conditions, controlling the money supply, and regulating economic growth. Selling securities takes money out of the economy, slows economic growth, and, by making money more scarce, raises interest rates. Buying has the opposite effect. Since the Federal Reserve is not funded by Congress, buying and selling securities also produces most of its income. Under the committee's direction, the Federal Reserve Bank of New York also buys and sells foreign currencies to help regulate the value of the dollar on foreign markets.

(3) The Federal Reserve Banks

There are Federal Reserve Banks in 12 cities and branches of these banks in 25. Each Reserve Bank has nine members on its Board of Directors. Under the supervision of the Board of Governors, the Reserve Banks set the interest rates for loans to banks that belong to Federal Reserve.

(4) The Federal Advisory Council

It confers with the Board of Governors and advises the board on general business conditions. The council is composed of 12 members, one from each Federal Reserve district. The council is required to meet in Washington at least four times a year but can meet more often if called by the Board of Governors.

(5) Member banks

The banks that belong to the system actually own it. They are required to subscribe 6% of its capital stock and in return receive a dividend of 6% a year on their investment. The Federal Reserve System regulates state-chartered banks that are members.

THE IMF

The International Monetary Fund was established in 1944 as a way of stabilizing the world's currency. But over the years it has become the closest thing to a worldwide central bank, acting as a creditor and regulator of third-world economies. How it got that way says a lot about the third-world debt crisis and economic relations between developed and developing nations.

In 1944, when representatives from 44 countries met at Bretton Woods, New Hampshire, the specter of worldwide depression and war was still fresh in their minds. During the early 1930s nationalistic trade barriers and currency devaluations had helped deepen the worldwide depression. Finding a way of stabilizing the world's currency and allowing countries to solve temporary balance-of-payments deficits without restoring trade barriers and currency devaluations would, they hoped, prevent the recurrence of another worldwide depression.

Out of the Bretton Woods conference came an agreement to create the International Monetary Fund and the International Bank for Reconstruction and Development, usually known as the World Bank. The IMF was given the responsibility for maintaining orderly currency prices in international trade, while the World Bank was given the task of creating long-term investments to improve the world's economy.

In the beginning, a member of the IMF could borrow foreign currency from the IMF in exchange for its own currency if it had a balance-of-payments deficit—that is, if its imports exceeded exports. The borrowing country then had to repurchase the currency in three to five years. That way, the borrower could take care of a balance-of-payments problem without having to unduly depress its own economy, put up trade barriers, or devalue its currency and thus disrupt world trade. When the temporary loans were made, the IMF also negotiated with the borrowing country so that changes in its economic policy would solve the underlying balance-of-payments deficit.

Since the IMF was never intended to be a major lending institution or an agency for economic development, it was overshadowed in its early years by the World Bank. Later, in 1973, it appeared that the IMF's influence would decline even further. When the major powers abandoned fixed exchange rates and allowed their currencies to float that year, the IMF stood to lose its power over exchange rates.

But several measures made the IMF a more important lender and provider of international credit. In 1969, the IMF created special drawing rights and in 1974, with the support of the Federal Reserve and the U.S. Treasury, the IMF decided to expand its long-term and short-term lending. On one hand it moved to help countries whose balance-of-payments deficits were hurt by OPEC's price hikes; on the other, as private lending institutions reached their limits, the IMF stepped in by providing more funds and by coordinating debt renegotiations between countries and private lenders.

Since its creation, the IMF has made loan commitments totaling $140 billion. But, considering that the third world has nearly $1 trillion in outstanding loans, that amount is really inconsequential. The IMF's real power comes from the fact that commercial banks will not extend new loans or renegotiate old ones until the country has reached an agreement with the IMF.

Increased lending and a greater say over the economies of debtor nations, however, have led to growing criticism of the Fund. In the early 1980s, as a condition for obtaining new loans, the IMF ordered debtor countries to improve their trade balances and pushed for freer markets. The idea was that, by increasing exports and cutting imports, the debtor nations would earn the foreign currency they needed.

In some ways the strategy worked, at least for a while. Ten of the largest debtor nations improved their trade balances from only $2.9 billion in 1981–1982 to $45 billion by 1984. But the policy also created heavy political costs. To improve their trade balances, governments had to undertake austerity measures such as cutting price supports for food, cutting government services, slashing wages, and devaluing currency. Even though the bitter medicine was necessary for a long-term solution to the problem, it resulted in the short run in reduced living standards and fewer goods. These conditions provoked riots in several countries.

Faced with the prospect that IMF austerity could provoke political unrest, some third-world governments have talked more openly of a debt moratorium or outright default. They argue that the western countries need to provide more help for their economies and that the IMF should grant them more lenient terms for renewed debt. Only if their economies are allowed to grow, they say, can they generate the goods and services they need to pay off their debts.

Third-world critics also charge that the IMF is controlled by large western powers, promoting their interests more than those of poor, less-developed countries. To some degree that charge is correct. While the IMF is governed by its 151 member countries, power over the Fund's policy is based on money. Each member is allowed a basic 250 votes and additional votes are allotted according to a country's payment into the Fund, which in turn is proportional to the country's share of the world economy. That means large industrial nations effectively control the Fund's policies. As of January 1988, the U.S. held just over 19% of the total votes, with Britain holding 7%, West Germany 6%, and Japan 4.5%. The vote of the U.S. gives it an effective veto over major Fund decisions that require an 85% majority.

The debate over austerity versus a more lenient policy towards debtor nations was played out in the 1986 selection of a new head of the IMF. One candidate was Dutch finance minister H. Onno Ruding; the other, Michel Camdessus, a former head of France's central bank. Ruding hit the campaign trail for the IMF job as a fiscal conservative enjoying the support of private banks that had loaned billions to third-world debtors. Camdessus was known to be more sympathetic to the debtors' problems. He favored a policy that would promote economic growth rather than austerity.

Camdessus's election, with U.S. support, indicates that the IMF plans to shift its tactics. Debtors will probably get more lenient terms from the IMF in the hopes that expanding third-world economies will allow the governments to repay their debts.

But a new policy is not likely to solve the problem. Even if third-world economies were efficiently managed and based on policies that encouraged investment and growth—which they aren't—most of them would still be facing major problems. High energy costs following the oil embargo of 1973 wreaked havoc on many third-world economies. Later, in the 1980s, reduced prices for commodities and stagnant western economies reduced the demand for third-world exports and made it impossible for them to finance their debts. Add to those basic structural problems harebrained development schemes, extravagant arms purchases by dictators on the right and the left, rampant government corruption that diverts aid money to Swiss bank accounts, and capital flight. In the last decade at least $198 billion worth of capital has fled from 18 debtor countries to the west, making it harder for them to pay their debts and finance new development.

As the debt crisis worsened again in 1986, when Brazil suspended payments on its debt, the IMF faced new criticism. After working for several years to promote more free markets in third-world economies, U.S. officials worried that Camdessus was too sympathetic to a large government role in third-world economies. But Camdessus's main preoccupation won't be ideology or a long-term solution to the debt crisis. Simply negotiating with debtors to reduce their obligations while avoiding the crisis that could ignite a destructive chain of defaults will take up all his time.

Table 29   Money Stock, Liquid Assets, and Debt, 1959 to 1987

(Averages of daily figures; billions of dollars, seasonally adjusted)

Year and month	M1: sum of currency, demand deposits, traveler's checks, and other checkable deposits (OCDs)	M2: M1 plus overnight RPs and Eurodollars, money-market mutual fund balances (general-purpose and broker/dealer), money-market deposit accounts, and savings and small time deposits	M3: M2 plus large time deposits, term repurchase agreements, term Eurodollars, and institution-only money-market mutual fund balances	L: M3 plus other liquid assets	Debt: debt of domestic nonfinancial sectors (monthly average)	M1	M2	M3	Debt
December: 1959	141.0	297.8	299.8	388.6	673.0				8.0
1960	141.8	312.3	315.3	403.6	708.2	0.6	4.9	5.2	5.2
1961	146.5	335.5	341.0	430.8	750.4	3.3	7.4	8.2	6.0
1962	149.2	362.7	371.4	466.1	802.8	1.8	8.1	8.9	7.0
1963	154.7	393.2	406.0	503.8	858.5	3.7	8.4	9.3	6.9
1964	161.9	424.8	442.5	540.4	921.6	4.7	8.0	9.0	7.4
1965	169.5	459.4	482.2	584.4	990.8	4.7	8.1	9.0	7.5
1966	173.7	480.0	505.1	614.8	1,058.2	2.5	4.5	4.7	6.8
1967	185.1	524.3	557.1	666.5	1,134.8	6.6	9.2	10.3	7.2
1968	199.4	566.3	606.2	728.9	1,230.1	7.7	8.0	8.8	8.4
1969	205.8	589.5	615.0	763.5	1,320.0	3.2	4.1	1.5	7.3
1970	216.6	628.2	677.5	816.3	1,410.6	5.2	6.6	10.2	6.9
1971	230.8	712.7	776.2	903.1	1,544.2	6.6	13.5	14.6	9.5
1972	252.0	805.1	886.0	1,023.0	1,700.5	9.2	13.0	14.1	10.1
1973	265.9	861.0	985.0	1,141.7	1,889.5	5.5	6.9	11.2	11.1
1974	277.5	908.4	1,070.4	1,249.2	2,062.7	4.4	5.5	8.7	9.2
1975	291.1	1,023.1	1,172.2	1,366.6	2,245.6	4.9	12.6	9.5	8.9
1976	310.4	1,163.6	1,311.8	1,515.9	2,485.8	6.6	13.7	11.9	10.7
1977	335.3	1,286.6	1,472.6	1,704.1	2,800.2	8.0	10.6	12.3	12.6
1978	363.0	1,389.2	1,647.1	1,911.2	3,158.6	8.3	8.0	11.8	13.4
1979	391.1	1,500.3	1,806.7	2,119.6	3,541.6	7.7	8.0	9.7	12.1
1980	416.6	1,633.1	1,990.9	2,327.6	3,880.9	6.5	8.9	10.2	9.6
1981	443.2	1,795.5	2,236.4	2,598.9	4,262.1	6.4	9.9	12.3	9.8
1982	481.3	1,953.8	2,443.1	2,853.0	4,645.5	8.6	8.8	9.2	9.0
1983	526.9	2,184.6	2,692.8	3,154.6	5,181.7	9.5	11.8	10.2	11.5
1984	557.5	2,369.1	2,985.4	3,528.1	5,932.6	5.8	8.4	10.9	14.5
1985	627.0	2,569.5	3,205.0	3,837.1	6,749.4	12.5	8.5	7.4	13.8
1986*	730.5	2,801.2	3,493.1	4,140.7	7,606.1	16.5	9.0	9.0	12.7
1987*	753.2	2,894.8	3,661.8	4,330.3	8,299.0	3.1	3.3	4.8	9.1

*Preliminary.
(NA) Not available.
Source: Board of Governors of the Federal Reserve System.

Table 30   Consumer Price Index

This chart shows the consumer price index for various major types of expenditures, such as transportation and medical care. Using 1967 as the base year, equal to 100, the index shows that the price of all items rose to 328.4 in 1986. That means it costs $3.28 to buy the same amount of goods and services you could buy in 1967 for $1. The figures are for all urban consumers.

(1967 = 100)

Year or month	All items	Food and beverages Total	Food	Housing Total	Shelter	Fuel and other utilities	House-hold furnish-ings and operation	Apparel and upkeep	Trans-portation	Medical care	Enter-tainment	Other goods and services	Energy
1946	58.5		58.1	60.6				67.5	50.3	44.4			
1947	66.9		70.6	65.2				78.2	55.5	48.1			
1948	72.1		76.6	69.8				83.3	61.8	51.1			
1949	71.4		73.5	70.9				80.1	66.4	52.7			
1950	72.1		74.5	72.8				79.0	68.2	53.7			
1951	77.8		82.8	77.2				86.1	72.5	56.3			
1952	79.5		84.3	78.7				85.3	77.3	59.3			
1953	80.1		83.0	80.8	76.5	83.0	91.3	84.6	79.5	61.4			
1954	80.5		82.8	81.7	78.2	83.5	90.9	84.5	78.3	63.4			
1955	80.2		81.6	82.3	79.1	85.1	89.9	84.1	77.4	64.8			
1956	81.4		82.2	83.6	80.4	87.3	89.9	85.8	78.8	67.2			
1957	84.3		84.9	86.2	83.4	89.9	91.9	87.3	83.3	69.9			90.1
1958	86.6		88.5	87.7	85.1	91.7	92.3	87.5	86.0	73.2			90.3
1959	87.3		87.1	88.6	86.0	93.8	93.1	88.2	89.6	76.4			91.8
1960	88.7		88.0	90.2	87.8	95.9	93.8	89.6	89.6	79.1			94.2
1961	89.6		89.1	90.9	88.5	97.1	93.7	90.4	90.6	81.4			94.4
1962	90.6		89.9	91.7	89.6	97.3	93.8	90.9	92.5	83.5			94.7
1963	91.7		91.2	92.7	90.7	98.2	94.6	91.9	93.0	85.6			95.0
1964	92.9		92.4	93.8	92.2	98.4	95.0	92.7	94.3	87.3			94.6
1965	94.5		94.4	94.9	93.8	98.3	95.3	93.7	95.9	89.5			96.3
1966	97.2		99.1	97.2	96.8	98.8	97.0	96.1	97.2	93.4			97.8
1967	100.0	100.0	100.0	100.0	100.0	100.0	100.0	100.0	100.0	100.0	100.0	100.0	100.0
1968	104.2	103.6	103.6	104.0	104.8	101.3	103.8	105.4	103.2	106.1	105.7	105.2	101.5
1969	109.8	108.8	108.9	110.4	113.3	103.6	107.7	111.5	107.2	113.4	111.0	110.4	104.2
1970	116.3	114.7	114.9	118.2	123.6	107.6	111.5	116.1	112.7	120.6	116.7	116.8	107.0
1971	121.3	118.3	118.4	123.4	128.8	115.0	115.7	119.8	118.6	128.4	122.9	122.4	111.2
1972	125.3	123.2	123.5	128.1	134.5	120.1	118.3	122.3	119.9	132.5	126.5	127.5	114.3
1973	133.1	139.5	141.4	133.7	140.7	126.9	121.6	126.8	123.8	137.7	130.0	132.5	123.5
1974	147.7	158.7	161.7	148.8	154.4	150.2	135.3	136.2	137.7	150.5	139.8	142.0	159.7
1975	161.2	172.1	175.4	164.5	169.7	167.8	151.0	142.3	150.6	168.6	152.2	153.9	176.6
1976	170.5	177.4	180.8	174.6	179.0	182.7	160.1	147.6	165.5	184.7	159.8	162.7	189.3
1977	181.5	188.0	192.2	186.5	191.1	202.2	167.5	154.2	177.2	202.4	167.7	172.2	207.3
1978	195.4	206.3	211.4	202.8	210.4	216.0	177.7	159.6	185.5	219.4	176.6	183.3	220.4
1979	217.4	228.5	234.5	227.6	239.7	239.3	190.3	166.6	212.0	239.7	188.5	196.7	275.9
1980	246.8	248.0	254.6	263.3	281.7	278.6	205.4	178.4	249.7	265.9	205.3	214.5	361.1
1981	272.4	267.3	274.6	293.5	314.7	319.2	221.3	186.9	280.0	294.5	221.4	235.7	410.0
1982	289.1	278.2	285.7	314.7	337.0	350.8	233.2	191.8	291.5	328.7	235.8	259.9	416.1
1983	298.4	284.4	291.7	323.1	344.8	370.3	238.5	196.5	298.4	357.3	246.0	288.3	419.3
1984	311.1	295.1	302.9	336.5	361.7	387.3	242.5	200.2	311.7	379.5	255.1	307.7	423.6
1985	322.2	302.0	309.8	349.9	382.0	393.6	247.2	206.0	319.9	403.1	265.0	326.6	426.5
1986	328.4	311.8	319.7	360.2	402.9	384.7	250.4	207.8	307.5	433.5	274.1	346.4	370.3
1987	340.4	324.5	333.0	371.0	421.8	380.7	254.9	216.9	316.8	462.2	283.2	366.5	371.7

(NA) Not available.
Source: U.S. Department of Labor, Bureau of Labor Statistics.

Table 31 The Rising Cost of Goods and Services

This chart shows changes in the consumer price indexes and lists the inflation or deflation rate for various types of goods and services. It shows, for example, that the cost of energy skyrocketed 30.9% in 1980 and then dropped 13.2% in 1986.

(percent changes in consumer price indexes, commodities and services, 1929–1986)

	All items		Commodities Total		Food		Commodities less food		Services Total		Medical care services		Energy[2]	
Year	December to December[1]	Year to year	December to December[1]	Year to year	December to December[1]	Year to year	December to December[1]	Year to year	December to December[1]	Year to year	December to December[1]	Year to year	December to December[1]	Year to year
1929	0.2	0			2.3	1.3								
1933	.5	-5.1			7.0	-2.9								
1939	-.5	-1.4	-1.0	-2.0	-2.5	-2.8	0.2	-1.6	0.2	0.2	0.3	0.3		
1940	1.0	1.0	1.2	1.0	2.6	1.7	.4	.6	.7	.2	0	0		
1941	9.7	5.0	13.5	6.7	16.4	9.1	10.8	5.0	2.5	1.4	1.5	.6		
1942	9.3	10.7	13.0	14.5	17.5	17.4	6.4	11.1	2.0	3.2	3.9	3.1		
1943	3.2	6.1	4.0	8.9	3.1	11.5	5.4	4.3	2.6	1.8	5.8	5.0		
1944	2.1	1.7	2.2	1.3	.2	-1.4	5.0	5.5	1.7	2.4	2.8	4.2		
1945	2.3	2.3	2.9	2.9	3.0	2.2	3.0	4.1	1.0	1.5	2.9	2.7		
1946	18.2	8.5	24.9	10.8	31.5	14.6	12.9	6.2	3.5	1.9	8.9	5.8		
1947	9.0	14.4	10.4	20.2	11.2	21.5	9.1	12.8	5.2	4.1	6.5	8.5		
1948	2.7	7.8	1.7	7.2	-.8	8.5	5.3	7.7	6.1	6.3	7.0	6.7		
1949	-1.8	-1.0	-4.1	-2.6	-3.7	-4.0	-4.8	-1.5	3.6	4.8	2.1	3.7		
1950	5.8	1.0	7.7	.6	9.6	1.4	5.7	-.1	3.6	3.2	3.3	2.3		
1951	5.9	7.9	5.9	9.0	7.4	11.1	4.6	7.5	5.2	5.3	5.8	5.1		
1952	.9	2.2	-.7	1.3	-1.1	1.8	-.5	.9	4.6	4.4	5.5	6.4		
1953	.6	.8	-.6	-.3	-1.3	-1.5	.2	.2	4.2	4.3	3.6	3.6		
1954	-.5	.5	-1.4	-.9	-1.6	-.2	-1.4	-1.1	1.9	3.3	2.6	3.0		
1955	.4	-.4	-.4	-.9	-.9	-1.4	0	-.7	2.3	2.0	3.2	2.9		
1956	2.9	1.5	2.6	.9	3.1	.7	2.5	1.0	3.1	2.5	4.1	4.0		
1957	3.0	3.6	2.6	3.1	2.8	3.3	2.2	3.1	4.5	4.0	4.5	4.3		
1958	1.8	2.7	1.3	2.3	2.2	4.2	.8	1.1	2.7	3.8	4.9	4.9	-0.7	0.2
1959	1.5	.8	.6	.1	-.8	-1.6	1.5	1.3	3.7	2.9	4.6	4.8	4.3	1.7
1960	1.5	1.6	1.1	.9	3.1	1.0	-.3	.4	2.7	3.3	3.8	4.0	1.5	2.6
1961	.7	1.0	0	.5	-.9	1.3	.6	.3	1.9	2.0	3.5	3.7	-1.1	.2
1962	1.2	1.1	1.0	.9	1.5	.9	.7	.7	1.7	1.9	3.0	3.2	2.1	.3
1963	1.6	1.2	1.4	.9	1.9	1.4	1.2	.7	2.3	2.0	2.6	3.0	-.8	.3
1964	1.2	1.3	.8	1.1	1.4	1.3	.4	.8	1.8	1.9	2.6	2.4	-.2	-.4
1965	1.9	1.7	1.6	1.2	3.4	2.2	.7	.6	2.6	2.2	3.5	3.2	2.0	1.8
1966	3.4	2.9	2.5	2.6	3.9	5.0	1.9	1.4	4.9	3.9	8.1	5.4	1.8	1.6
1967	3.0	2.9	2.5	1.8	1.2	.9	3.1	2.6	4.0	4.4	7.9	8.7	1.4	2.2
1968	4.7	4.2	3.8	3.7	4.3	3.6	3.7	3.7	6.1	5.2	7.4	7.3	1.7	1.5
1969	6.1	5.4	5.5	4.5	7.2	5.1	4.5	4.2	7.4	6.9	7.0	8.1	3.1	2.7
1970	5.5	5.9	4.0	4.7	2.2	5.5	4.8	4.1	8.2	8.1	8.3	7.1	4.5	2.7
1971	3.4	4.3	2.9	3.4	4.3	3.0	2.3	3.8	4.1	5.6	5.3	7.3	3.1	3.9
1972	3.4	3.3	3.4	3.0	4.7	4.3	2.5	2.2	3.6	3.8	3.8	3.7	2.8	2.8
1973	8.8	6.2	10.4	7.4	20.1	14.5	5.0	3.4	6.2	4.4	5.8	4.4	16.8	8.0
1974	12.2	11.0	12.7	12.0	12.2	14.4	13.2	10.6	11.3	9.3	13.3	10.3	21.6	29.3
1975	7.0	9.1	6.3	8.9	8.6	8.5	6.2	9.2	8.1	9.5	10.3	12.6	11.6	10.6
1976	4.8	5.8	3.3	4.3	.6	3.1	5.1	5.0	7.3	8.3	10.7	10.1	6.9	7.2
1977	6.8	6.5	6.1	5.8	8.0	6.3	4.9	5.4	7.9	7.7	9.0	9.9	7.2	9.5
1978	9.0	7.7	8.9	7.1	11.8	10.0	7.7	5.8	9.3	8.5	9.2	8.6	8.0	6.3
1979	13.3	11.3	13.0	11.4	10.2	10.9	14.3	11.7	13.7	11.0	10.6	9.7	37.4	25.2
1980	12.4	13.5	11.1	12.2	10.2	8.6	11.5	13.8	14.2	15.4	10.0	11.3	18.1	30.9
1981	8.9	10.4	6.0	8.4	4.3	7.9	6.7	8.6	13.0	13.1	12.7	10.7	11.9	13.5
1982	3.9	6.1	3.6	4.0	3.1	4.0	3.8	4.0	4.3	9.0	11.2	11.9	1.3	1.5
1983	3.8	3.2	2.9	2.9	2.6	2.1	3.1	3.2	4.8	3.5	6.1	8.7	-.5	.8
1984	4.0	4.3	2.6	3.4	3.8	3.8	2.0	3.1	5.4	5.2	5.8	6.0	.2	1.0
1985	3.8	3.6	2.5	2.1	2.7	2.3	2.4	2.1	5.1	5.1	6.8	6.0	1.8	.7
1986	1.1	1.9	-2.0	-1.0	3.8	3.2	-5.3	-3.3	4.4	5.0	7.9	7.7	-19.7	-13.2
1987	4.4	3.7	4.6	3.2	3.5	4.2	5.1	2.6	4.3	4.1	5.6	6.6	8.2	.4

[1]Changes from December to December are based on unadjusted indexes.
[2]Fuel oil, coal, and bottled gas; gas (piped) and electricity; and motor fuel. Motor oil, coolant, etc., also included through 1982.
Source: U.S. Department of Labor, Bureau of Labor Statistics.

Table 32 Consumer Installment Credit Outstanding, 1950 to 1987

[Amount outstanding (end of month); millions of dollars, seasonally adjusted]

Year and month	Installment credit				
	Total	Automobile	Revolving	Mobile home	Other
December:					
1950	15,166	6,035			9,131
1951	15,859	5,981			9,878
1952	20,121	7,651			12,470
1953	23,870	9,702			14,168
1954	24,470	9,755			14,715
1955	29,809	13,485			16,324
1956	32,660	14,499			18,161
1957	34,914	15,493			19,421
1958	34,736	14,267			20,469
1959	40,421	16,641			23,780
1960	44,335	18,108			26,227
1961	45,438	17,656			27,782
1962	50,375	20,001			30,374
1963	57,056	22,891			34,165
1964	64,674	25,865			38,809
1965	72,814	29,378			43,436
1966	78,162	31,024			47,138
1967	81,783	31,136			50,647
1968	90,112	34,352	2,022		53,738
1969	99,381	36,946	3,563		58,872
1970	103,905	36,348	4,900	2,433	60,224
1971	116,434	40,522	8,252	7,171	60,489
1972	131,258	47,835	9,391	9,468	64,564
1973	152,910	53,740	11,318	13,505	74,347
1974	162,203	54,241	13,232	14,582	80,148
1975	167,043	56,989	14,507	15,388	80,159
1976	187,782	66,821	16,595	15,738	88,628
1977	221,475	80,948	36,689	16,362	87,476
1978	261,976	98,739	45,202	16,921	101,114
1979	296,483	112,475	53,357	18,207	112,444
1980	297,667	112,255	54,894	19,119	111,399
1981	314,321	120,020	60,750	20,382	113,169
1982	327,173	125,369	66,007	20,998	114,799
1983	376,239	145,908	78,369	22,194	129,768
1984	453,580	173,122	98,514	24,184	157,760
1985	522,805	208,057	122,021	25,488	167,239
1986	577,784	245,055	134,938	25,710	172,081
1987*	612,571	261,654	145,940	25,612	179,365

*Preliminary.
(NA) Not available
Source: Board of Governors of the Federal Reserve System.

Table 33 The Rise and Fall of the Dollar: Exchange Rates for Major Currencies

(Cents per unit of foreign currency, except as noted)

Period	Belgian franc	Canadian dollar	French franc	German mark	Italian lira	Japanese yen
March 1973	2.5378	100.333	22.191	35.548	0.17604	0.38190
1967	2.0125	92.689	20.323	25.084	.16022	.27613
1968	2.0026	92.801	20.191	25.048	.16042	.27735
1969	1.9942	92.855	19.302	25.491	.15940	.27903
1970	2.0139	95.802	18.087	27.424	.15945	.27921
1971	2.0598	99.021	18.148	28.768	.16174	.28779
1972	2.2716	100.937	19.825	31.364	.17132	.32995
1973	2.5761	99.977	22.536	37.758	.17192	.36915
1974	2.5713	102.257	20.805	38.723	.15372	.34302
1975	2.7253	98.297	23.354	40.729	.15328	.33705
1976	2.5921	101.410	20.942	39.737	.12044	.33741
1977	2.7911	94.112	20.344	43.079	.11328	.37342
1978	3.1809	87.729	22.218	49.867	.11782	.47981
1979	3.4098	85.386	23.504	54.561	.12035	.45834
1980	3.4247	85.530	23.694	55.089	.11694	.44311
1981	2.7007	83.408	18.489	44.362	.08842	.45432
1982	2.1982	81.077	15.293	41.236	.07411	.40284
1983	1.9621	81.133	13.183	39.235	.06605	.42128
1984	1.7348	77.244	11.474	35.230	.05708	.42139
1985	1.6968	73.226	11.220	34.247	.05255	.42248
1986	2.2464	71.959	14.467	46.266	.06730	.59709
1987	37.357.	1.3259	6.0121	1.7981	1297.03	144.60

Period	Netherlands guilder	Swedish krona	Swiss franc	United Kingdom pound	Multilateral trade-weighted value of the U.S. dollar (March 1973 = 100) Nominal
March 1973	34.834	22.582	31.084	247.24	100.0
1967	27.759	19.373	23.104	275.04	120.0
1968	27.626	19.349	23.169	239.35	122.1
1969	27.592	19.342	23.186	239.01	122.4
1970	27.651	19.282	23.199	239.59	121.1
1971	28.650	19.592	24.325	244.42	117.8
1972	31.153	21.022	26.193	250.08	109.1
1973	35.977	22.970	31.700	245.10	99.1
1974	37.267	22.563	33.688	234.03	101.4
1975	39.632	24.141	38.743	222.16	98.5
1976	37.846	22.957	40.013	180.48	105.6
1977	40.752	22.383	41.714	174.49	103.3
1978	46.284	22.139	56.283	191.84	92.4
1979	49.843	23.323	60.121	212.24	88.1
1980	50.369	23.647	59.697	232.58	87.4
1981	40.191	19.860	51.025	202.43	102.9
1982	37.473	16.063	49.373	174.80	116.6
1983	35.120	13.044	47.660	151.59	125.3
1984	31.245	12.103	42.676	133.56	138.3
1985	30.370	11.672	41.058	129.56	143.2
1986	41.008	14.041	55.925	146.68	112.0
1987	2.0263	6.3468	1.4918	163.98	96.9

[1]Adjusted by changes in consumer prices.
Source: Board of Governors of the Federal Reserve System.

Table 34 Savings Around the World

This chart shows savings rates around the world. On the left is shown savings as a percentage of disposable personal income and on the right is shown gross domestic savings as a percentage of GDP—gross domestic product.

	1985 Savings as Percentage of Disposable Personal Income	1984 Gross Domestic Savings as Percentage of GDP
United States	4.6	16
France	12.4	19
West Germany	12.9	23
Italy	21.9*	18
Netherlands	N/A	23
United Kingdom	11.7	17
Japan	17.2	31
Canada	12.1	22

*1984 data
Sources: World Bank, Central Intelligence Agency.

Chapter Seven
MORE AND MORE: THE RICH IN AMERICA

HIGHLIGHTS AND TRENDS

• A recent Federal Reserve study of wealth, the first major government study of the rich in twenty years, found that "a surprisingly large percentage of all U.S. families [4%] were estimated to have a net worth of more than $500,000." The study found that almost 2% of all families (1,310,000) had a net worth of more than $1 million and that almost 0.5% of the families (320,000 households) had net financial assets (which exclude business, property, and housing assets) of at least $1 million.

• But becoming a millionaire is not the distinction it used to be. After adjusting for inflation, a million dollars in 1948 was worth only $619,900 in 1967; by 1987, it was down to a mere $219,500.

• America's millionaires control about $1 trillion in assets, about one third of the country's wealth. About $220 billion was controlled by the richest 400 Americans in September of 1987.

• Many of the wealthiest families—such as the du Ponts ($10 billion), the Mellons ($4+ billion) and the Rockefellers ($3.5 billion)—are dynasties that were founded in the 19th century. One hundred sixty-two members of the *Forbes* list of the 400 wealthiest Americans inherited their wealth.

• Large fortunes continue to be made. The three richest men in the United States are all self-made men; 214 of *Forbes*'s 400 wealthiest Americans created their own fortunes. One, William Gates, the founder of Microsoft, joined the ranks of America's billionaires early in 1987 at the age of 30.

THE LAST BILLIONAIRES?

In the mid-1970s there were only two billionaires alive—insurance magnate John D. MacArthur and shipping tycoon Daniel Ludwig—and many people wondered if they might be the last of their breed.

But like the fish in New York's East River, billionaires have staged a comeback. There are more than 40 of them in *Forbes*'s 1987 list of the 400 richest Americans (almost double their number a year earlier) and in *Fortune* magazine's 1987 list of billionaires. (The stock market decline in late 1987, however, may have reduced a lot of marginal billionaires to mere multi-millionaire status.) Though a billion dollars might not be worth what it was when John D. Rockefeller became the first American billionaire, there's little doubt that a billion (or a near billion) still leaves someone nicely off. Consider a list of America's billionaires compiled by *Fortune* magazine (see Table 35 below).

Table 35   The Billionaires

Sam Walton, founder of Wal-Mart. Worth $8.7 billion. (See the profile in the "Retail" section.)

Samuel 1. Newhouse, Jr. and Donald E., own advance Publications and Newhouse Broadcasting. (See the profile in the "Magazines" section.)

Lester Crown owns 23% of General Dynamics; real estate and sports teams. Worth $5.7 billion.

Forrest E. Mars, Sr., Forrest E., Jr., and John F. own Mars Inc., the candy company now run by Forrest E., Jr., and brother, John F. Worth $5 billion.

Sid Richardson Bass and brothers, Edward Perry, Robert Muse, and Lee Marshall, have investments in oil, real estate, Walt Disney Productions, American Medical International and more. Worth $4 billion.

Edgar F. Bronfman, Sr. of New York and his brother, *Charles R.* in Montreal own 33% of Seagram Inc., the world's largest distiller.

John Werner Kluge, who built up Metromedia and sold most of it off. Worth $3.1 billion.

Henry Lea Hillman, owns Hillman Co., real estate and venture capital bets in Silicon Valley. Worth $3 billion.

Charles Koch and brother David, own Koch Industries: oil, gas, coal, cattle ranches and more. Worth $3 billion.

David Packard, cofounder of Hewlett-Packard. Worth $3 billion.

Whitney MacMillan and brother Cargill, Jr., own 60% of Cargill. (See profile under "Agriculture" section.)

Anne Cox Chambers and Barbara Cox Anthony, own 97% of Cox Enterprises. Worth $2.5 billion.

Henry Ross Perot, founder of Electronic Data Systems. Worth $2.5 billion.

A. Alfred Taubman, owns real estate; 100% of Woodward & Lothrop and John Wanamaker department storechains, A&W restaurant company, and 60% of Sotheby's auction house. Worth $2.5 billion.

Leslie Wexner, owns 28% of The Limited retail clothing stores and real estate. Worth $2.4 billion.

Keith Rupert Murdoch, owns 47% of News Corp., an international media conglomerate. Worth $2.2 billion.

Warren Edward Buffet, owns 45% of Berkshire Hathaway, the vehicle for large investments in Capital Cities/ABC, Geico, Washington Post and others. Worth $2 billion.

William R. Hewlett, co-founder of Hewlett-Packard. Worth $2 billion.

Laurence Alan Tisch and brother Preston Robert, own 24% of Loews Corp., which owns Loews Hotels, 25% of CBS Inc., 80% of CNA Financial, 95% of Bulova and others. Worth $1.8 billion.

Margaret Hunt Hill and brother Harold "Hassie" Hunt III, have large investments in Hunt Petroleum Corp., real estate and other investments. Worth $1.6 billion.

Estee Lauder, owns Estee Lauder Inc. Worth $1.6 billion.

John T. Dorrance, Jr., owns 32% of Campbell Soup Co. Worth 1.5 billion.

William R. Hearst, Jr. and Randolph A. Hearst, own 40% of Hearst Corp. Worth $1.5 billion.

Table 35 The Billionaires (continued)

Jay Arthur Pritzker and Robert Alan Pritzker, financiers with major interest in Hyatt hotel chain. Worth $3.8 billion.

Milton Petrie, owns Petrie Stores Corp. Worth $1.1 billion.

Walter H. Annenberg, owns Triangle Publications, which owns *TV Guide* and the *Racing Form.* Worth $1 billion.

Philip Frederick Anschutz, owns Anschutz Corp., which invests in oil exploration, coal and uranium mining, real estate, railroads and stocks. Worth $1 billion.

Marvin Davis, owns Davis Oil Co. Worth $1 billion. (See profile in oil section.)

Donald G. Fisher, owns 41% of the Gap Inc., (Gap, GapKids, and Banana Republic clothing stores). Worth $1 billion.

Ernest Gallo and brother Julio, own E&J Gallo Winery. Worth $1 billion. (See profile in beverages section.)

Ray Hunt, owns Hunt Oil Co. Worth $1 billion.

Samuel Jayson Lefrak, a real estate mogul. Worth $1 billion.

Roger Milliken and brother Gerrish, own Milliken & Co., a textile manufacturer. Worth $1 billion.

John Richard Simplot, owns J.R. Simplot Co., the world's largest potato grower and processor. Worth $1 billion.

David Rockefeller and brother Laurance S., whose joint investments include $1.1 billion in a family trust as well as $350 million in stocks, bonds, real estate and venture deals. Worth $1.5 billion.

August Anheuser Busch, Jr., owns 13.2% of Anheuser-Busch Cos. Worth $1.3 billion.

Harry B. Helmsley, a real estate mogul. Worth $1.3 billion.

Ewing M. Kauffman, owns 23% of Marion Laboratories. Worth $1.3 billion.

John Thomas Lupton, derives wealth from Coca-Cola bottling. Worth $1.3 billion.

John Willard Marriott, Jr., brother Richard Edwin and mother, Alice, own 20% of Marriott Corp. Worth $1.3 billion.

Donald Bren, owns 92% of Irvine Ranch, with 65,200 largely undeveloped acres in Orange County, Calif. Worth $1.2 billion.

William K. Coors and brother Joseph, own 72% of Adolph-Coors Co. brewery. Worth $1.2 billion.

Michael Fribourg, owns 90% of Continental Grain. Worth $1.2 billion.

William H. Gates III, owns 40% of Microsoft computer software company. Worth $1.2 billion.

Gorden Peter Getty, has trusts, inheritance and investments. Worth $1.2 billion.

Katherine Meyer Graham and son Donald Edward, own 35% of Washington Post Co., which owns Newsweek and TV stations. Worth $1.1 billion.

THE MYSTERIES OF WEALTH

Studying the rich is a national pastime. In fact, you could say that glitz, glamour, and glitter are big business—all because the American public has a seemingly inexhaustible interest in the rich and famous. Our fascination with the rich sells magazines such as *People* and it boosts the ratings of TV shows such as *Dallas.* Without the rich, an army of journalists, publicists, and gossip columnists would be reduced to penury or, even worse, forced to cover subjects such as the national debt.

Considering the amount of effort spent studying the rich, it is not surprising that journalists have uncovered a few facts. Reporters have already exposed the mysteries of how multimillionaire celebrities such as Michael Jackson decorate their game rooms, as well as the constant divorces,

scandals, and drug deals that seem to afflict the rich. We even know a
thing or two about how a pair of overweight Texas billionaires lost their
shirts trying to buy all the silver in the world.

But for all that's said and written about the rich, it must be admitted
that most of what we know is relatively trivial—at least from an economic
standpoint. Even though the rich complain about constant press coverage,
they have done an expert job of hiding their wealth from public scrutiny.
In fact, any honest analysis of the rich must begin with the embarrassing
admission that no one quite knows how rich the rich really are—even
though this is a country where wealth is the most obvious sign of success.
Even when reasonable estimates of wealth are available, it's often impossible to cut through the morass of paper corporations, holding companies, and offshore banks to figure out the exact holdings of the rich and
superrich.

Lacking exact information, it's hard to know what to make of the rich.
Are they a new aristocracy? Or are the rich the real backbone of the
American economy, men and women transforming industries, creating
new companies, wealth, and jobs? Do the great American dynasties—the
Rockefellers, the du Ponts, the Fords, and the Hunts to name a few—
really run the country, controlling Wall Street and the White House? Or
are the rich an endangered species—a class threatened by an anonymous
army of mediocre middle managers, technocrats, and government regulators hell-bent on driving the great industrial fortunes out of existence?

Table 36   Billion-Dollar Dynasties

Here are America's richest families:

Family	Holdings	Value
du Pont	17.5% of E. I. du Pont de Nemours, (revenues $36 billion), etc.	$4.7–8.5 billion
Mellon	Mellon Bank, First Boston, oil, aluminum, foundations, etc; they no longer act together in investments	$4–5 billion
Bass	Four brothers have investments in Walt Disney, Taft Broadcasting, Alexanders, real estate, American Medical International	$4 billion
Rockefeller	Exxon (oil), real estate, Chase Manhattan, etc.	$3.5 billion
Getty	Four branches of the family that are not on good terms earned $3 billion from sale of Getty Oil to Texaco	$3 billion
Cargill, MacMillan	Cargill (grain trading)	$2.9 billion
Hearst	Hearst Corporation (media), real estate	$1.5 billion
Philpps	Steel, stocks, real estate	$1.8 billion

Sources: *Fortune* magazine and various press reports.

AMERICA'S MILLIONAIRES: WHO ARE THEY AND WHAT DO THEY OWN?

Although the rich are secretive about their holdings, tracking the life and times of America's millionaires is helped by the fact that the Internal Revenue Service has a long-standing obsession with discovering large and preferably taxable fortunes. Based on tax returns, the IRS estimated in 1982, the most recent year for which figures are available, that there were 407,700 Americans, about 1.7% of the population, who had net assets worth a million dollars.

But these figures are probably understated. A recent Federal Reserve survey of wealth, the first major government study of the rich in twenty years, found that "a surprisingly large percentage of all U.S. families [4% in 1983] were estimated to have a net worth of more than $500,000." The study, which was published in 1986, found that almost 2% of all families (1,310,000) had a net worth of over $1 million and that 0.5% of the families (320,000 households) had net financial assets (excluding business, property, and housing assets) of at least $1 million. About 14% of all families surveyed had a net worth of at least $163,800, up from 1962, when only 6% were that wealthy.

But joining the Millionaires' Club of America is no longer quite the distinction it used to be. In terms of assets, only 13,000 Americans—one in 11,287—were worth a million in 1948.

Inflation has also played havoc with the value of a million dollars. As we noted, a million dollars in terms of its 1948 buying power was worth only $619,900 in 1970; by 1987, it was down to a mere $219,500.

And keeping up with the Rockefellers is getting harder and harder for America's nouveaux riches. In fact, many of the de rigueur status symbols of the truly wealthy have increased in cost faster than most basic necessities. In the 19th century, the first act of any self-respecting millionaire was to put a mansion on Fifth Avenue in Manhattan. But over the years, that prestigious address has gotten more expensive: the cost of a Fifth Avenue townhouse has skyrocketed from $55,000 in 1940 to $10 million or so today. Similarly, since 1940 the price of a painting by Jan Brueghel has gone from $2,000 to $560,000, a flawless diamond from $3,000 to $75,000, and a tin of caviar from $15 to $300. A van Gogh that you could pick up at the end of the 19th century for nothing sold for $39.9 million in 1987, the most ever paid for a painting up to that time.

But then, most millionaires can't afford that kind of conspicuous consumption. When you get down to it, someone worth a mere million has only joined the peasantry of the rich. In 1987 a man or woman had to be worth $225 million to make the real aristocracy of American money, the *Forbes* list of the 400 richest Americans. The richest man, Sam Walton of Wal-Mart fame, was worth $8.5 billion; collectively the richest 400 Americans were worth $220 billion in 1987. In contrast, the 407,000 millionaires discovered by the IRS in 1982 controlled about $1 trillion dollars in net assets.

No one would deny that $220 billion is a lot of money. On March 20, 1987 it was enough to buy all of the common stock in General Motors, IBM, Exxon, du Pont, and Proctor & Gamble. It would pay for the $50 billion in illegal drugs Americans use every year for over four years running. With the $1 trillion owned by America's millionaires you could pay off a hefty chunk of the national debt or run the federal government for most of the year. But is $1 trillion enough to buy real political and economic power? Is it enough to control the economy?

Certainly not. Even a trillion dollars doesn't buy the kind of political and economic clout it used to. If the trillion dollars owned by American millionaires in 1982 was nationalized and distributed to the public, every American would only receive a little over $4,300, not even enough to buy a new car. And its even possible to lose a trillion dollars. The stock market dropped that much in value between its peak in August and the end of October 1987.

A PROFILE OF THE TOP EXECUTIVE

Throughout most of America's economic history, the surest way to the top of a major company was to start one, inherit one, or buy one. At the end of the 19th century there was little doubt that many big businesses were firmly controlled by a few powerful and often self-made entrepreneurs, men such as John D. Rockefeller and Andrew Carnegie.

Yet over the next half-century the path to corporate power changed dramatically. Stock ownership became more diffuse, making it harder for the great economic dynasties of the 19th century to hold onto their family fortunes. In established industries such as steel or, later on, the auto industry, entrepreneurs had little chance of raising the kind of capital they needed to start a new General Motors or U.S. Steel. And as the size of companies grew dramatically, huge corporate bureaucracies were created to run these firms.

The result was the rise of the modern manager. Unlike entrepreneurs such as Rockefeller or Carnegie, these men rarely owned large parts of the companies they ran. Their power was based on the separation of ownership and actual corporate power. Since the 1950s, most corporations have been run by professional managers. They set long-term strategies, plan acquisitions, and direct the companies' day-to-day operations, while the actual owners of the companies, the stockholders, have little power over the companies' direction. Nor are stockholders likely to interfere with the companies' management. Usually the chief executive officer (CEO) and top corporate executives of each company control the board of directors by appointing outside directors who are likely to do their bidding. Only in unusual cases do stockholders revolt and try to run their own slate of directors. Yet even then, management holds the upper hand in proxy fights because of its power to sway shareholders.

This is not to imply that professional managers are completely independent. Besides government regulators and unions, who often have the power to derail the best-laid plans, a company's creditors often are represented on the board of directors.

More importantly, Wall Street can signal its disapproval by cutting the price of the company's stock, making it harder for the company to secure new credit or financing. In the past few years, management's autonomy has been further eroded by corporate raiders. They've delivered a rude ultimatum to the management of many undervalued companies—either increase shareholder value or lose control of the company.

Yet even though American business bears little resemblance to the way companies were run in the 19th century, there are some similarities between the entrepreneurs who ran 19th-century corporations and today's professional managers. A survey of top CEOs by *Fortune* indicates that many of the values and characteristics of top executives of the past have survived and in fact thrived.

Like the proverbial 19th-century entrepreneurs who spent a lifetime building their companies, most American CEOs work long hours and spend most of their lives with one company. The majority (68%) work over 55 hours a week, and most (58%) take less than three weeks' vacation, about the same vacation time given to an assembly-line worker with seniority. About 33% have worked for only one company in their lives, and over half (57.6%) have only worked for two companies. Only 8.3% have worked for five or more companies.

And although family members have been replaced by managers in most large corporations, many of these managers have a large financial stake in the companies they run. Over half of all top CEOs (51.6%) own stock in their companies valued at over $1 million, 18% have stock valued at over $5 million, and 33% have stock valued at over $2.5 million.

Socially, America's captains of industry also have some resemblance to their 19th-century predecessors. America's top executives are still overwhelmingly male—only Katharine Graham of the Washington Post Company and Elizabeth Ortenberg of Liz Claiborne, Inc., run one of the 1,000 largest companies in America. And CEOs typically assumed their position at 50 years of age, about the same as in 1900, when they were 48.

But in other very important ways American managers are very different, reflecting the way business has changed. With top corporations becoming increasingly complex, American managers are better educated than ever before. Nearly 31% hold master's degrees, 12% have doctorates, and another 20.3% have spent some time in graduate school. Although most come from middle- or lower-middle-class backgrounds, many of them also attended elite schools. By 1980, Harvard could boast that its graduates made up 19% of the top three officers of *Fortune* 500 companies and that over 3,500 alumni headed U.S. corporations.

THE WITHERING AWAY OF INDIVIDUAL WEALTH?

No doubt the managerial revolution has profoundly transformed the nature of economic power. And, over time, the assets of most dynasties become widely dispersed, weakening their economic and political clout. But it would be wrong to conclude that the great industrial dynasties play only a minor role in the economy. A study in the late 1970s by Wharton School professor Edward Herman for the Twentieth Century Fund found that individual owners and families controlled 21% of the top 100 industrial corporations. About 16% of the largest 200 industrial corporations were controlled by individuals or families. Family- or owner-controlled corporations had assets of $95 billion, about 13.2% of the total assets of the top 200 corporations.

Today, a study of smaller public corporations or privately held companies would probably reveal that individual owners have even more power than owners of the largest corporations because it takes much less capital to control the companies. For example, privately owned companies make up about 98% of all companies, producing about one third of all the goods and services in the United States. The combined sales of the 400 largest privately held companies in 1987 was $449 billion, according to *Forbes*. Half of the country's billionaires get their wealth from privately owned companies, *Forbes* notes. These 400 largest private companies employ 2.8 million people.

Moreover, there is no sign that the richest and most powerful families will fade from the scene. While it's true that a few wealthy families no longer control smokestack companies such as U.S. Steel, many families still control powerful empires in newly emerging high-tech industries or in the media. In the media, for example, Rupert Murdoch, the Newhouses, the Grahams, and the Annenbergs all control far-flung empires. Table 37 (see page 111) lists the families and individuals who hold large stakes in major corporations, making them the nation's largest individual stockholders.

Table 37 The People Who Own Corporate America

Rank* (1986)	Family	Holdings	Value of holdings	% of company shares owned
1 (1)	Sam Walton and Family *Supersuccess in small-town, sun-belt retailing*	Wal-Mart Stores, Inc.	$6,268,548,800	38.6
2 (2)	Irenee, Edward du Pont and Family *Heirs to famed chemical empire*	E. I. du Pont de Nemours & Co.	$4,707,015,360	17.5
3 (5)	Bancroft Family *Relatives of Wall Street Journal founder*	Dow Jones & Co., Inc.	$2,805,504,363	53.9
4 (6)	Edgar, Charles Bronfman and Family *One of world's largest liquor firms*	Seagram Co., Ltd.	$2,742,233,869	38.3
5 (9)	Leslie Wexner *Wizard of women's wear*	The Limited	$2,566,134,767	32.1
6 (3)	John T. Dorrance, Jr., and Family *The real Campbell kids*	Campbell Soup Co.	$2,564,030,525	57.1
7 (4)	David Packard *The dean of Silicon Valley*	Hewlett-Packard Co.	$2,485,154,489	17.0
8 (7)	Bass Brothers and Family *Not just Mickey Mouse stuff*	Total value	$2,067,233,641	
		Walt Disney Co.	$1,382,769,974	17.0
		Taft Broadcasting	$363,400,000	24.7
		American Medical International	$189,857,181	11.4
			$108,381,800	5.6
		National Dist. & Chem.	$11,568,435	15.5
		Iomega	$9,397,666	32.7
		Drew Industries	$1,858,585	30.2
		Niki-Lu Industries		
9 (11)	Otis Chandler and Family *Los Angeles Times clan*	Times Mirror Co.	$1,875,908,254	34.9
10 (8)	Warren Buffett *Billionaire bargain hunter*	Berkshire Hathaway, Inc.	$1,687,752,000	41.8
11 (13)	Henry, William Ford and Family *Riding the comeback road*	Ford Motor Co.	$1,605,572,008	7.3
12 (10)	Laurence and Preston R. Tisch *They head CBS and U.S. Postal Service*	Loews Corp.	$1,294,432,249	23.7
13 (14)	William Hewlett *First name in Hewlett-Packard*	Hewlett-Packard Co.	$1,241,650,186	8.5
14 (32)	Ewing M. Kauffman *Started rapidly growing drug business*	Marion Labs	$1,208,962,041	23.4
15 (16)	August A. Busch, Jr. *St. Louis brewmaster*	Anheuser-Busch Cos., Inc.	$1,179,450,992	13.2

111

Table 37 The People Who Own Corporate America (continued)

Rank* (1986)	Family	Holdings	Value of holdings	% of company shares owned
16 (56)	William H. Gates III *Young computer-software genius*	Microsoft Corp.	$1,056,408,896	41.8
17 (17)	J. W. Marriott, Jr., and Family *From root-beer stand to hotels*	Marriott Corp.	$1,029,143,170	20.7
18 (18)	Robert, Sigfried Weis and Family *Ringing up Northeastern sales*	Weis Markets	$950,902,805	71.4
19 (35)	Nordstrom Family *Western retailers head east*	Nordstrom Corp.	$918,965,336	41.4
20 (47)	Donald Fisher and Family *Trendy pacesetter in youth fashions*	The Gap, Inc.	$901,773,228	42.9
21 (19)	Milton Petrie *A women's-wear leader*	Petrie Stores	$867,703,625	59.4
22 (15)	Lester Crown and Family *Defense contracting plus*	Total value General Dynamics Vulcan Materials Chicago Pacific American Ship Building	$804,029,974 $664,067,837 $85,428,200 $49,223,216 $5,310,721	 21.4 5.9 10.5 9.6
23 (20)	Joan Kroc *First lady of the golden arches*	McDonald's Corp.	$797,082,790	7.9
24 (38)	Don Tyson and Family *Potentates of poultry*	Tyson Foods, Inc.	$785,794,028	54.7
25 (31)	Arthur Ochs Sulzberger and Family *A family for the* Times	New York Times Co.	$781,350,938	21.8
26 (23)	James E. Davis and Family *Purveyors to the South*	Winn-Dixie Stores, Inc.	$707,318,348	37.1
27 (27)	George Gund III and Family *A stake in Tony, the cornflakes tiger*	Total value Kellogg Co. AmeriTrust	$695,403,600 $633,542,000 $61,861,600	 8.7 6.0
28 (21)	Coors Family *The fifth-largest brewer*	Adolph Coors Co.	$672,186,854	70.0
29 (43)	Daniel Hillenbrand and Family *Casket makers to the nation*	Hillenbrand Industries, Inc.	$666,876,280	62.0
30 (26)	Roger Milliken and Family *They rule a giant textile firm*	Mercantile Stores Co., Inc.	$665,184,251	39.1
31 (36)	Katharine Graham and Family *Power on the Potomac*	Washington Post Co.	$662,298,359	27.9
32 (37)	Erivan Haub *German ruler of an old-line food firm*	Great A&P Tea Co., Inc.	$658,436,889	52.4

Table 37 The People Who Own Corporate America (continued)

Rank* (1986)	Family	Holdings	Value of holdings	% of company shares owned
33 (24)	Oakleigh B. Thorne and Family *A success story in business publishing*	Commerce Clearing House	$630,100,359	55.6
34 (12)	An Wang and Family *A computer innovator*	Wang Laboratories, Inc.	$621,946,788	26.4
35 (29)	Morton Mandel and Family *Founders of an electronics company*	Premier Industrial Corp.	$621,096,308	56.6
36 (34)	Harold McGraw, Jr., and Family *Books,* Business Week, *and more*	McGraw-Hill, Inc.	$620,728,005	19.0
37 (41)	Floyd and Bruce Gottwald and Family *Out of gasoline, into chemicals*	Ethyl Corp.	$617,925,780	16.8
38 (28)	Roy, Lillian Disney and Family *Profits from Walt's "Magic Kingdom"*	Walt Disney Co.	$602,783,804	7.4
39 (NL)	W. L. Lyons Brown, Jr., and Family *Whiskey Barons of Kentucky*	Brown-Forman, Inc.	$575,052,142	37.5
40 (22)	Gaylord Donnelley and Family *Yellow Pages galore*	R. R. Donnelley	$574,783,015	20.0
41 (33)	Richard A. Smith and Family *Pictures and popcorn, coast to coast*	General Cinema Corp.	$567,555,005	32.5
42 (NL)	Saul P. Steinberg *Onetime boy wonder goes public*	Reliance Group Holdings, Inc.	$552,031,605	77.5
43 (30)	Henry Singleton *Builder of defense, electronics business*	Total value Teledyne Argonaut Group, Inc. American Ecology Corp.	$547,519,950 $502,812,168 $40,800,060 $3,907,722	 13.3 13.3 7.8
44 (40)	J. H. Krehbiel and Family *Millions in electronic connectors*	Molex, Inc.	$543,354,604	49.1
45 (39)	Stanton W. Mead and Family *Plenty of paper and packaging*	Consolidated Papers, Inc.	$537,290,160	41.1
46 (49)	W. R. Kelly and T. E. Adderley *Leaders of the Kelly Girls— and boys*	Kelly Services	$537,114,150	59.6
47 (NL)	Paul G. Allen *Original partner with Bill Gates*	Microsoft Corp.	$517,300,772	20.5

Table 37 The People Who Own Corporate America (continued)

Rank* (1986)	Family	Holdings	Value of holdings	% of company shares owned
48 (25)	Harold Byron Smith, Jr., and Family *Supplier to industry*	Total value Illinois Tool Works Northern Trust	$494,871,126 $389,735,775 $105,135,351	 21.8 16.8
49 (42)	Robert W. Galvin *In his father's footsteps*	Motorola, Inc.	$484,466,712	7.0
50 (45)	John, Otto Haas and Family *Chemical company's second generation*	Rohm & Haas	$454,612,410	15.2
51 (44)	James L. Knight *Builder of news-and- broadcast empire*	Knight-Ridder, Inc.	$439,025,216	14.4
52 (67)	George P. Mitchell *Texan in energy and real estate*	Mitchell Energy & Development	$431,315,150	62.3
53 (46)	L. S. Skaggs *Founded vast grocery, drugstore operation*	American Stores Co.	$408,286,263	20.1
54 (54)	Alex and Richard Manoogian *They'll supply home fix-up needs*	Masco Corp.	$405,090,640	7.9
55 (50)	Roy H. Park *Upstate New York media owner*	Park Communications	$403,498,013	89.3
56 (83)	William O. Taylor and Family *Atop the* Boston Globe	Affiliated Publications, Inc.	$402,334,300	25.3
57 (70)	C. H. Murphy, Jr., and Family *Arkansans in the oil patch*	Murphy Oil Corp.	$388,094,520	35.0
58 (66)	R. T. Parfet, Jr., and Family *The Minoxidil man*	Upjohn Co.	$387,188,820	5.2
59 (51)	Louis Cabot and Family *Old money in chemicals and energy*	Cabot Corp.	$383,350,821	40.0
60 (53)	James Sherman and Family *Big business in business forms*	Standard Register Co.	$367,718,694	52.5
61 (59)	Ted Turner *Captain of CNN*	Turner Broadcasting System	$351,837,737	83.3
62 (52)	H. John Heinz III *57 varieties*	H. J. Heinz Co.	$351,321,856	5.6
63 (NL)	Joseph Pulitzer, Jr., and Family *A prize in newspapering*	Pulitzer Publishing Co.	$344,275,520	82.2
64 (82)	Gordon Earle Moore *Cofounder of a computer- chip maker*	Intel Corp.	$335,705,643	7.2
65 (69)	Russell Berrie *Founded firm that sells gift items*	Russ Berrie & Co., Inc.	$334,192,196	54.1

Table 37 The People Who Own Corporate America (continued)

Rank* (1986)	Family	Holdings	Value of holdings	% of company shares owned
66 (55)	John Hechinger and Family *Hardware for do-it-yourselfers*	Hechinger Co.	$329,214,930	49.1
67 (91)	Leon Hess *Built massive oil refiner*	Amerada Hess Corp.	$324,979,778	12.4
68 (NL)	Lloyd E. Cotsen *Natural cosmetics is the mainstay*	Neutrogena Corp.	$318,579,561	53.8
69 (NL)	Bob Magness and Family *Nation's largest cable-TV firm*	Tele-Communications, Inc.	$316,143,234	10.6
70 (62)	Sol Price and Family *Discount-club pioneer*	The Price Co.	$304,220,160	13.0
71 (48)	Amory, James Houghton and Family *A glass act*	Corning Glass Works	$303,026,860	11.0
72 (NL)	J. B. Hunt *Coast to coast by truck*	J. B. Hunt Transport Services	$302,736,616	42.3
73 (81)	William Wrigley *Third generation in chewing gum*	William Wrigley, Jr., Co.	$295,396,297	28.1
74 (86)	Sam J. Frankino *Phenom in discount car rentals*	Agency Rent-A-Car, Inc.	$294,845,563	59.5
75 (78)	Roger King and Family *Leader in TV distribution and syndication*	King World Productions	$293,511,330	45.3
76 (76)	Crandall Close Bowles and Family *The Springmaid sheets folks*	Springs Industries, Inc.	$292,489,200	58.4
77 (NL)	Robert and Bruce Toll *Home builders*	Toll Brothers, Inc.	$288,750,000	70.0
78 (68)	Lucille A. Carver and Family *New tread for old tires*	Bandag, Inc.	$287,779,184	30.0
79 (85)	J. A. Albertson *Selling groceries to the West*	Albertson's, Inc.	$287,477,400	16.4
80 (96)	P. H. Glatfelter III and Family *Printing for more than 100 years*	P. H. Glatfelter Co.	$282,166,487	33.1
81 (74)	Stephen H. Van Every and Family *Ruler of a snack-food empire*	Lance, Inc.	$280,051,571	41.7
82 (99)	James H. Ottaway, Jr., and Family *Dow Jones owns their newspaper chain*	Dow Jones & Co., Inc.	$277,512,646	5.3
83 (64)	Philip H. Knight *Stepping out with athletic gear*	Nike, Inc.	$270,501,395	39.4

115

Table 37 The People Who Own Corporate America (continued)

Rank* (1986)	Family	Holdings	Value of holdings	% of company shares owned
84 (61)	Frederick W. Smith *Father of overnight delivery*	Federal Express	$264,305,314	8.2
85 (65)	William Paley *Guiding light of TV giant*	CBS, Inc.	$259,693,891	7.2
86 (NL)	Paul Fireman *Sports shoes for yuppies*	Reebok International, Ltd.	$258,365,932	10.4
87 (NL)	A. C. Markkula, Jr., and Family *Polishing up the Macintosh computer*	Apple Computer, Inc.	$257,994,969	6.2
88 (77)	Stewart Bainum and Family *Lord of major nursing-home chain*	Manor Care	$253,589,550	33.8
89 (94)	Kenneth N. Pontikes *Leasing king of IBM computers*	Comdisco, Inc.	$246,410,048	22.3
90 (NL)	Gary C. Comer *Mail-order clothes for yuppies*	Land's End, Inc.	$245,305,200	64.4
91 (98)	Monroe Milstein and Family *And discount clothes for anyone*	Burlington Coat Factory	$243,795,500	63.9
92 (93)	Arnold Bernhard *A half-century of investment advice*	Value Line, Inc.	$238,232,050	80.6
93 (NL)	Robert A. Swanson *In on the birth of genetic engineering*	Genentech, Inc.	$234,788,433	5.3
94 (NL)	George L. Bunting, Jr., and Family *The sweet smell of cosmetics and shaving cream*	Noxell Corp.	$232,565,289	20.6
95 (80)	William G. Bennett *Ringmaster of a casino empire*	Circus Circus Enterprises	$232,557,625	25.9
95 (79)	William N. Pennington *Bennett's center-ring partner*	Circus Circus Enterprises	$232,557,625	25.9
97 (63)	Lew Wasserman *A movie mogul and more*	MCA, Inc.	$232,450,880	6.9
98 (NL)	F. M. Kirby and Family *Holdings in title insurance and metals*	Alleghany Corp.	$231,676,902	39.7
99 (90)	John P. Thompson and Family *7-Elevens come up winners*	Southland Corp.	$231,562,500	9.8
100 (NL)	Angelo J. Bruno and Family *Started Alabama supermarket chain*	Total value Bruno's, Inc. Big B, Inc.	$228,802,635 $215,637,847 $13,164,788	 27.7 12.9

*Source: *U.S. News & World Report,* July 6, 1987.

WHAT THE RICH OWN

The difficulties of finding out what the rich own were revealed in 1986 when the Joint Economic Committee of Congress rushed out a study under the headline "The Rich Get Richer." The study, based on Federal Reserve figures, concluded that 0.5% of the population owned 35% of the nation's wealth, up from only 25.4% in 1963, when the last Federal Reserve study was undertaken. Most of the public (90%) owned only 28.2% of the wealth, down from 35% in 1963.

But then it was discovered that a mistake had been made. Someone had recorded one man's wealth as $200 million when it should have been $2 million. Oops.

The revised data indicate that 0.5% of population, who had an average net worth of over $2.5 million, controlled 26.9% of the nation's wealth, up only slightly from 1963 when the richest Americans owned 25.4%. Ninety percent of the households, on the other hand, were worth less then $206,340.

Those results were consistent with studies of American wealth made since the 1920s, most of which have shown that the wealthiest 1% of the population has controlled about one third of the wealth, and the wealthiest 0.5% about 20% to 25% of the nation's wealth. A 1983 Federal Reserve survey found that the top 0.5% held 19% of all assets and 31% of all financial assets. Financial assets, according to the Federal Reserve, do not include assets in business, property, and housing and include such things as stocks and bonds.

Other government studies indicate that because of their large timber, agricultural, and farming interests, about 3% of the population own about 55% of the land, or 95% of the land that is privately owned. And the top 0.5% own about 56% of all municipal bonds and 43% of all stock.

IS THERE ROOM AT THE TOP?

Absolutely. Despite the difficulties of cracking many markets dominated by huge corporations, new American fortunes are still being created. The four wealthiest men in America—Wal-Mart founder Sam Walton, Metromedia owner John Kluge, computer entrepreneur H. Ross Perot, and Hewlett-Packard cofounder David Packard—are all self-made men. Perot started his first company, Electronic Data Systems, which was eventually bought out by General Motors, with only $1,000. Number three on the list of the superrich, David Packard, who once served as Nixon's deputy defense secretary, got started with even less, a mere $595. Moreover, most of the CEOs of the nation's 500 largest companies were not born into great wealth. These executives might not found economic dynasties the size of a Rockefeller's, but while they head companies such as Exxon they have much more economic power than many of the nation's richest families.

How do they do it? Being in the right place at the right time helps. Many of the fortunes profiled below were created in emerging and developing industries. John D. Rockefeller made a billion dollars in the early days of the oil industry while David Packard made his billion-dollar fortune as a pioneer in the electronics industry. In 1987, William Gates, the founder of the software firm Microsoft, became the first of the computer entrepreneurs who capitalized on the personal-computer revolution to become a billionaire. Gates was only 30.

More importantly, America's great entrepreneurs show a marked talent for shaping new industries in their own images. Rockefeller virtually invented big business with his Standard Oil Company, showing the importance of economies of scale. Henry Ford, Sr., wasn't the first auto manufacturer or even the most technically brilliant, but he was the first to mass-produce a car, thus lowering costs and allowing middle-class and working-class buyers to afford his Model T. Here's how they did it:

The Rockefellers   Around the world, the Rockefeller name is better known than the names of most American presidents, thanks to the $2 billion to $4 billion fortune that was established by John D. Rockefeller and his brother William during the last half of the 19th century. Born on a modest farm in upstate New York, John D. started out as a commodity merchant. He got into the oil business in the 1860s, in the early days of the world's first oil boom, and by 1878 his company, Standard Oil, had a virtual monopoly on the oil business.

In creating his oil empire, Rockefeller created the first trust, which got around state laws prohibiting corporations from doing business in more than one state. Later, when the Sherman Antitrust Act forced him to dissolve the trust, he pioneered the use of the holding company to control his vast holdings. The growth of monopolistic power brought profits into the Rockefeller empire. By 1883, after gaining control of the market, Rockefeller was worth $40 million. His fortune grew to $200 million by 1897, and by 1913 he had become the country's first billionaire.

However, Rockefeller came under attack because of Standard Oil's economic power and ruthless tactics—competitors' refineries had a nasty habit of blowing up. To polish his tarnished reputation, Rockefeller spent the last third of his life giving away money—$531 million in all. His son John gave away another $544 million and other Rockefellers gave away hundreds of millions more. One of the family's foundations, the Rockefeller Brothers Fund, had assets of $220 million in 1986, and the dynasty has remained active in public life, philanthropy, and social causes.

But like all dynasties, the Rockefellers have had their problems. While David Rockefeller, the former head of Chase Manhattan Bank, is worth about $1 billion, many of the 87 other living Rockefellers have not done so well. Recently they were upset that some family assets, such as Rockefeller Center, were not producing enough income. To improve the cash flow to less affluent heirs, the family sold 71.5% of Rockefeller Center for $1.3 billion in a worldwide public offering. Trust managers, reversing a long-standing policy of pursuing long-term capital gains, have invested the family's money in ventures likely to produce better short-term gains. The results should help the family avoid the kind of family feuds and costly litigation that have wrecked many other dynasties. But since David Rockefeller's retirement from Chase Manhattan, it's unlikely that any member of the family will emerge as a spokesman or spokeswoman for American business, ending a century-long tradition. The family is worth about $3.5 billion according to an 1986 estimate by *Fortune*.

The Vanderbilts   The Vanderbilts made the first great industrial fortune of the latter half of the 19th century. In 1860, when John D. Rockefeller was still an unknown commodity merchant, Cornelius Vanderbilt was already 60, a successful shipping magnate worth a million dollars. But, at an age when most men were thinking of retiring, Vanderbilt was looking for new worlds to conquer. During the next 15 years he became one of the country's most powerful railroad magnates and Wall Street operatives. By the time of his death, in 1877, he was worth nearly $100 million, with most of that money invested in railroads. In a mere seven years after his death, his son had doubled the family fortune to $200 million.

A former sailor who never lost his taste for unprintable language, Cornelius Vanderbilt was an able manager who improved the equipment of the railroad lines he owned—such as the New York Central—and was an accomplished speculator in railroad stocks, doing battle with the likes of Jay Gould. He spent heavily to improve his railroad holdings. His son William turned New York Central into a powerful railroad line and consolidated the family holdings. William and the third generation of the dynasty also followed a familiar pattern by gaining admittance into high society, something that would have been impossible for the hard-swearing family patriarch.

Family holdings in the New York Central Railroad dwindled in the 20th century, and by the time the line went bankrupt in 1970 the family had few or no holdings in it. One family member, however, heiress Gloria Vanderbilt, showed the old entrepreneurial spirit by cashing in on the highly profitable fad in designer jeans.

The Mellons   Family patriarch Judge Thomas Mellon grew wealthy in the mid-19th century from his law practice and real estate investments. In 1870 he founded the family bank, T. Mellon and Sons (later Mellon National Bank, now Mellon Bank), which financed much of Andrew Carnegie's growing steel empire, and his heirs played a major role in financing Pittsburgh's booming industrial economy. His youngest son Andrew invested in the aluminum industry, backing Alcoa as well as the Carborundum Company and Union Steel (sold for $30 million to

U.S. Steel in 1902). The Mellon National Bank's most profitable investment, however, was in an oil company that became Gulf Oil Corporation.

Today, several family members have remained in the public eye. Mellon heir Richard Scaife has become the nation's largest financier of conservative causes. Paul Mellon, who failed with such ventures as the In-N-Out hamburger restaurant, has since devoted his life to art, amassing one of the largest collections in the United States. His French Impressionist collection alone is valued at over $100 million. He and his sister Ailsa spent nearly $100 million to build the east wing of the National Gallery of Art. In the late 1970s he donated another $200 million worth of art to Yale University. Various members of the family are probably worth well over $5 billion altogether, but no one has been either willing or able to consolidate the family holdings so that all the various trusts and family members act together. And the Mellon Bank, no longer run by family members, has fallen onto hard times, with huge loan losses.

The Astors   In New York the Astor family has long been synonymous with high society. Family wealth was created by John Jacob Astor, a financier, fur trader, and real estate investor. He got his start by selling whiskey, illegally, to the Indians in exchange for pelts. By the time of his death in 1848, his $20 million fortune made him the richest man in America. His son William continued buying New York real estate, earning him the title "landlord of New York." By 1875, when William died, the family was worth $40 million. In the third generation the family established its rein over high society, causing one minister to report that "not to have received an invitation to an Astor ball" was equivalent to being banned from high society. The Astors were famous for their parties; it was at the Cliveden estate of the British Astors where call girl Christine Keeler cavorted with the English elite, setting off the notorious Profumo affair. Today, the family has sold off most of its New York real estate, valued at $125 million in the late 1950s, and established a $50 million foundation, the Vincent Astor Foundation. Vincent's widow, the aging Brooke Astor, still plays a major role in lavish New York charity balls.

The Cabots   The family that defined "Boston brahmin" was the Cabots. The family first arrived in Boston in 1700 and by the early part of the 18th century had built up a merchant empire in the not-so-genteel trade of rum, slaves, and opium (thanks largely to the efforts of shipbuilder, pirate, and U.S. Senator George Cabot). But wealth sanitizes all sins, and in the 19th century the family attempted to recreate a European aristocracy in Boston. Intermarrying with the Lowells, Higginsons, Jacksons, and other top Boston families, they established a line of senators, governors, and capitalists, setting up the first cotton mill and providing money for the early railroads, copper mines, and the telephone. By the early 1900s a wit could note, "And this is good old Boston, / The home of the bean and the cod, / Where the Lowells talk to the Cabots / And the Cabots talk only to God." Today, with a family fortune estimated at $350 million, Louis W. Cabot is a director and former chairman of the Cabot Corporation, the world's largest producer of carbon black (sales $1.31 billion). Other family members sit as trustees on prominent universities, run mutual funds, or work as investment bankers.

The Bronfmans   The family arrived in Canada as Russian immigrants in 1889 and made money in hotels and saloons. When Prohibition hit Canada in 1916, they sold liquor through a mail-order business from Quebec, which was still wet. Later they supplied U.S. bootleggers and bought Seagram's in 1928.

Today, one side of the family, Edgar and Charles Bronfman, owns 38.3% of Seagram Company Ltd., worth $2.7 billion in 1987. Edgar and Charles's control of Seagram's was assured in 1953, when their father, Samuel Bronfman, ousted his two nephews. Edgar and Charles took over the company in 1971. Edgar, Jr., is slated to be the next Bronfman to run the $2.9 billion liquor company. Seagram's also owns a 22.6% stake in du Pont, which was worth $6.6 billion in July of 1987. The du Pont stake was acquired as a result of the unsuccessful bid for Conoco by Seagram's in 1981.

After their ouster from Seagram's, nephews Edward and Peter moved to Toronto and started their own financial empire. Their Edper Investments Ltd. now controls over 100 companies with assets of $100 billion.

Though the family says it has no plans to sell its Seagram's holdings, it has decided to break up the family holding company, Cemp Investment Ltd. This move will avert squabbles between third-generation heirs and will allow them to invest their fortunes as they see fit. But the breakup will limit the family's ability to act together, the first step in a pattern that often dilutes the power of economic dynasties.

The Tisches   Laurence Tisch and his brother Preston Robert are two businessmen who have a reputation for having built up a $2.0 billion family fortune by purchasing distressed properties and turning them around. So in 1986, it was in character when they took charge of another pair of down-and-out businesses—CBS and the U.S. Postal Service. Laurence moved into the executive suites of Black Rock, as the CBS headquarters is known, as the CEO while Bob was named Postmaster General. No one has ever managed to turn the U.S. Mail into an efficient, well-run organization. Still, brother Bob may have gotten the easier job.

The Tisches entered Black Rock in 1985 as white knights, when CBS was fighting takeover threats by Ted Turner and several others. Their Loews Corporation agreed to buy up a substantial stake in CBS to protect the company from outside takeovers and Laurence was put on the board. But by the fall of 1986, they had boosted their share of CBS to 25% and had ousted the company's chairman.

Again they were hailed as white knights, this time by the CBS staff and the news division. Ex-CEO Thomas Wyman had angered the news department and founder William Paley by cutting the news staff and axing such corporate perks as the company jet. CBS was foundering in the ratings, hadn't produced a hit to match NBC's top rated *Cosby Show,* and its once-vaunted news division was in a three-way ratings war with NBC and ABC. Paley, the news division, and board member Walter Cronkite all asserted that Tisch would restore the network to its former splendor.

But within months the white knight had his armor tarnished. The cost cutting that Wyman began continued under Tisch. Hundreds of employees, from pages and security guards to top managers, were fired. CBS Technology Center, an influential 50-year-old laboratory where the long-playing record and a prototype of color TV were developed, was shut down. And the news division, which believed it would be spared further cuts, was ordered to shave $30 million off its $300 million budget, forcing staff layoffs of 200 people, about 15% of its payroll.

But cost cutting was simply what the Tisches had always done. The brothers bought a New Jersey resort in 1946 and built it up to a 12-hotel chain by 1955. In 1960 they gained control over Loews Corporation and over the years turned it into a profitable conglomerate with $8.6 billion in 1986 revenues.

Laurence Tisch's cost-cutting philosophy may in fact be the best for CBS in the short run. Paley ran a company that never worried about costs, and in fact never needed to as long as network advertising kept rising and CBS remained head and shoulders above its rivals in the entertainment and news ratings wars. With network ad revenues not even keeping up with inflation, the networks are keeping a sharper eye on budgets. Still, network TV is an industry where a hit such as *The Cosby Show* can produce high ratings and huge profits. Tisch's cost cutting won't be worth much if the network fails to revive its programming.

The Basses   This is one of the few families that has made the transition from Texas oil to Wall Street. The second-generation Bass brothers—Sid, Edward, Robert, Perry, and Lee—have built a $50 million oil fortune into a financial empire valued at least $4 billion.

The first Bass family millions were created by Sid Williams Richardson. He built up a $105 million fortune in the Texas oil fields during the Depression. Nephew Perry Bass was Richardson's partner, but when Richardson died, Perry was left with only a $12 million stake in their company. The bulk of Richardson's fortune went to the Sid W. Richardson Foundation.

So the Bass family started all over. They consolidated their assets in 1960 into Bass Brothers Enterprises, and in 1970 Sid Rainwater joined Bass Brothers Enterprises as an investment adviser. A former Yale classmate of Sid Bass, Rainwater helped the Basses put together hundreds of profitable deals.

One of their most profitable deals came in 1984 when they bought up a major stake in The Walt Disney Company, saving Disney from raiders who wanted to sell off the company's assets. When the new management brought in by the Basses turned the company around, the Disney investment earned the family over $850 million. In other cases they earned a reputation as shrewd corporate raiders. Rainwater and the Basses, for example, bought up a 10% stake in Texaco after its Getty Oil takeover deal was announced. Fearing a Bass takeover, Texaco bought their shares for $1.2 billion, leaving the Basses with a $450 million profit.

Over the years, family wealth has ballooned to more than $4 billion, while Rainwater has also amassed a $175 million personal fortune. In 1985 the brothers finally liquidated Bass Brothers Enterprises, their main investment company, and split the profits. Recently they have not been as active on Wall Street but have held major stakes in several companies—Taft Broadcasting, Walt Disney, and American Medical International—as well as holdings in technology, real estate, retailing, fast foods, services, technology, and manufacturing.

The Gettys   Unlike many of the other wildcatters who struck it rich in oil, Jean Paul Getty was well educated, having studied economics at Oxford. He joined his father George's successful Minnehoma Oil Company in 1914. With his father's backing he bought and sold leases, determined to make his first million in two years. By 1916, only one year behind schedule, Getty was a millionaire, and during the 1920s his fortune grew to $3 million, including a one-third interest in a company that would evolve into Getty Oil. However when his father died, Getty got only half a million dollars out of his father's $10 million estate because of his loose living. (Young Getty was already on his third of five wives by this point.)

Nonetheless, Getty, who got along no better with his own children, recovered from this setback and prospered during the Depression, buying new companies and real estate, including the $2.3 million Pierre Hotel in New York. His most profitable venture was in 1949. He purchased the right to an oil field between Saudi Arabia and Kuwait for $9.5 million. After investing $30 million, he hit an oil field that would eventually make him a billionaire. In 1967, Getty merged the Tidewater Oil Company and the Missouri Oil Company into the Getty Oil Company, which then had a value of $3 billion.

But wealth did not bring domestic bliss. One son committed suicide. Another became a drug addict. Son Gordon left the company in 1966 and sued his father to increase the dividends from Getty Oil. So when Jean Paul died, he left most of his money to the J. Paul Getty Museum.

Without a trust set up by his mother, Sarah, Jean Paul Getty's five sons would have been left with little.

Gordon became the sole trustee of the family's trust in 1982, but the current generation has been unable to patch up the family feuds. Gordon decided Getty Oil was not producing enough revenues, and as head of the family trust he attempted to sell Getty Oil to an outsider, Pennzoil. But family members sued, opening the way for a much higher bid by Texaco. That put more money in the Getty family trust, but produced a legal nightmare. Getty family members sued each other for control of the family's $3.5 billion trust and Pennzoil won a $10.2 billion suit against Texaco. At that point, Texaco backed out of its agreement to protect the Gettys from any lawsuits surrounding the sale of Getty Oil. Further lawsuits could cost millions in legal fees and could even threaten the family fortune.

LOSING A BILLION

Being rich is not as simple as making money. The trick is keeping it. In recent years, some of America's richest men have found that it's also possible to lose a billion dollars.

The Hunts and the Silver Crash

The Hunt brothers first became interested in silver in 1970 when silver was at a historic low, selling for only $1.50 an ounce. After a few initial purchases, they made a tidy profit when the metal went up to $3. As double-digit inflation hit, the Hunts saw silver as a hedge against both inflation and economic disaster. By 1973, the Hunts had taken delivery on 55 million ounces in silver, worth $160 million. But it wasn't until the late 1970s that they began their silver play in earnest. With Arab backers they bought 130 million ounces of silver and held silver contracts for 90 million ounces. Some traders believed it was possible to corner the silver market with only 200 million ounces, and naturally the price of silver began to rise, hitting $34.45 at the end of 1979 and climbing to $50 in January 1980. By this point, the Hunts had nearly $4.5 billion in silver, giving them a profit of $3.5 billion. But they didn't cash in their chips, and government regulators limited futures buying in an attempt to stabilize the market. Soon the price dropped, hitting $21 by March. With their margin calls at $10 million a day, the Hunts were in trouble, and they were eventually forced to announce that they wouldn't be able to meet their margin calls. To keep the market from crashing, Federal Reserve chairman Paul Volcker gave his approval to a $1.1 billion loan to bail out the Hunts.

The Hunts' losses from failing to sell at the right time were enormous. Their silver holdings had declined $4 billion from their peak in 1980, and the Hunts' silver play left them $1.5 billion in debt. Still, Bunker Hunt's only comment was, "A billion dollars isn't what it used to be."

The brothers finally sold their last silver holdings in 1985 for a $1 billion loss. By that time, everyone was saying the Hunts' billions weren't what they used to be. For several years the Hunts managed to pay their loans, but a dramatic drop in the price of oil soon threatened the very existence of the Hunt dynasty. For example, their speculative oil leases, once valued at over $2.27 billion, were rendered almost worthless by 1982. Placid Oil's assets had lost $1.35 billion in value in the 1980s and the value of their offshore oil rigs fell dramatically.

So, hounded by their creditors, the Hunts defaulted on their Penrod and Placid Oil loans in the spring of 1986. Efforts to restructure payments failed and the Hunts filed for protection under Chapter 11.

If one adds their silver losses ($1.5 billion) to the losses they've sustained in the oil business, the Hunts have lost an estimated $7.15 billion in less than six years. Chapter 11 may protect them from their creditors, but if a judge orders them to liquidate their holdings, the Hunt brothers will be left with only a few hundred million dollars in private holdings, largely in real estate. That would be one of the largest transfers of personal wealth since the Czar was overthrown.

Taking big risks is in the family tradition. H. L. Hunt, the founder of the family fortune, was the quintessential Texas wildcatter. After making and losing a fortune speculating in cotton and timberland, he moved to the oil fields of El Dorado, Arkansas. There he used his photographic memory to become a professional gambler, making a tidy profit at the gaming tables of the tough boomtown. But in 1921, the local Ku Klux Klan labeled him a "moral degenerate" and threatened to burn down his saloon. So Hunt took up an even riskier profession—speculating in oil leases. His luck at the gaming tables stayed with him. By 1924 he was able to sell a 50% interest in his oil wells for $600,000, and during the 1930s he capitalized on the financial difficulties of another oilman to buy an East Texas field that became the site of the greatest oil discovery up to that time. Over the next 50 years, this field produced more than 4 billion barrels of oil.

After that discovery, Hunt built up his company, Hunt Oil, into the largest independent oil producer in the United States, and in the 1970s, before his death, he was worth $2 billion or $3 billion. His oil properties pumped out an income of over $1 million a week into the pockets of the old gambler.

Like many gamblers, Hunt was always a character, reminiscent of many other empire builders. He sired 15 children by three wives. Although he built a replica of George Washington's Mount Vernon mansion, he carried his lunch to work every day in a brown paper bag. H. L. Hunt also tried his hand as a novelist. His self-published novel *Alpaca* included the obligatory love story. But its real purpose was to describe Hunt's vision of a utopia—a mythical country where votes and political power are based on the amount of taxes a person pays.

126   THE HAVES

Table 38   The Largest Privately Held Companies in America

To preserve family control over companies, many corporations have remained private. Private firms comprise 98% of all American businesses and account for about one third of the country's production. Some of these privately held corporations are run by outside managers but in many cases they are still run by entrepreneurs, families, owner-managers, or, in a few cases, by the employees. Buying out the stockholders and taking the company private has also been a way for families to preserve their control over companies. Firms that have gone private in the last five years through leveraged buyouts are marked with asterisks.

Rank	Company/business	Sales (in millions of dollars)	Employees
1.	Cargill/grain trading	32,000	46,000
2.	Safeway Stores/grocery stores	20,311(e)	150,000
3.	Continental Grain/grain trading	13,500(e)	12,000
4.	Koch Industries/petroleum and natural gas	13,000	7,000
5.	Apex Oil/oil trading	9,000(e)	10,000
6.	United Parcel Service/package delivery	8,620	170,000
7.	Mars/candy	7,700	22,000
8.	Bechtel Group/engineering	6,572	28,000
9.	Supermarkets General/grocery stores	5,508	56,000
10.	R. H. Macy/department stores	5,210	56,000

Source: "The Largest Private Companies in the U.S.," *Forbes,* December 14, 1987.
(e) Estimate. Does not include 1987 divestitures.

Henry Ross Perot

In just three short months Perot, the founder and chairman of Electronic Data Systems of Dallas, managed to lose $1.2 billion, losing $450 million in just one day, April 22, 1970.

This disaster began auspiciously enough in 1968, when Perot took EDS public. The stock soared to an all-time high of $162 a share in March of 1970, making Perot the richest man in America, worth an estimated $1.5 billion. But then the stock dropped drastically, to $85 in April, and tumbled to only $29 in May, leaving Perot worth a mere $270 million.

Since then he has bounced back nicely. In 1984, he sold his 46% of EDS to General Motors for $1 billion and received 11.3 million shares of class-E GM stock. In 1986 GM bought him out, and today he is worth an estimated $2.5 billion. Looking back, he dismisses the $1 billion paper loss: "That was Mickey Mouse." (See the profile of Perot in the "Electronics" section.)

Daniel Ludwig

By the late 1960s this reclusive entrepreneur, who had only an eighth-grade education, built up a $2–3 billion fortune in shipping, real estate, and oil refining. Known for his conservative management, Ludwig, however, then embarked on one of the riskiest and most grandiose business

Table 39   The Corporate Rich: The Highest-paid Executives in the U.S., 1986

Top executives are making more money than ever before. The salaries for *Fortune* 500 CEOs rose over 160% between 1975 and 1985, to $543,000. *Business Week* found that CEOs averaged $1.2 million in 1986 (including stocks, salary, and bonuses), up 29% from 1985. The two highest-paid executives in each of the companies surveyed by *Business Week* averaged $1,019,226 in 1986, up 26% from 1985.

Those figures confirm a Federal Reserve survey of wealth in the United States that found the wealthiest Americans were in business professions. That study found that banking, insurance, and real estate employed only about 2% of all family heads, but accounted for 31% of the richest families, the one half of one percent of all families that earned over $280,000 a year.

Executive pay is increasing much faster than the pay of the rest of the population, though top executives are not as well paid as people in many other high-paying professions. No CEO pulled in the $27 million Bill Cosby made in 1986 or the $57 million he earned in 1987. Many earned no more than the salary of the average professional baseball player, $371,000. Here are the highest-paid executives:

(thousands of dollars)

Rank	Executive and position	Company	1986 salary and bonus	Long-term compensation	Total
1.	Lee A. Iacocca, chairman	Chrysler	10,984	9,558	20,542
2.	Paul Fireman, chairman	Reebok International	13,063	—	13,063
3.	Victor Posner, chairman	DWG	8,400	—	8,400
4.	John J. Nevin, chairman	Firestone	785	5,570	6,355
5.	Charles E. Exley, Jr., chairman	NCR	938	5,357	6,295
6.	Sidney J. Sheinberg, president	MCA	559	5,520	6,079
7.	Maurice R. Greenberg, president	American International Group	823	3,780	4,603
8.	Donald Petersen, chairman	Ford	1,961	2,375	4,336
9.	Rand V. Araskog, chairman	ITT	1,665	2,590	4,255
10.	Alan Greenberg, chairman	Bear, Stearns	4,078	—	4,078

Source: *Business Week,* May 4, 1987.

ventures in the last 50 years—the development of a tract of land in the Amazon jungle that is larger than the state of Connecticut.

Ludwig bought 6,000 square miles of Amazon forest in 1968 for only $3 million. Over the next 15 years, he poured about $1.1 billion into his quixotic dream of developing the Amazon.

Like everything else Ludwig has done, the project, in the Jari Valley, was shrouded in secrecy. That secrecy fueled rumors of Indians held as slaves in his compounds, of a vast smuggling operation in gold and silver,

Table 40 What the Rich Own

This table lists the net worth and assets of America's rich, defined here by the IRS as anyone with gross assets of over $500,000. The left side of the table shows how many wealthy Americans there are and how many own various types of assets. For example, there are 1,965,100 Americans with gross assets over $500,000; 254,900 Americans with over $500,000 in gross assets have a net worth of under $250,000; and 368,100 wealthy Americans who have a net worth of over $1 million own corporate stocks. The right side shows how much net worth they derive from various assets. For example, millionaires have an aggregate net worth of $1,122 billion; their aggregate net worth in corporate stocks is $350 million. In contrast, those Americans who have over $500,000 in gross assets but under $250,000 in net worth hold only $11 billion worth of corporate stocks. The figures are for 1982, the most recent year for which data are available.

(All figures are estimates based on a sample of estate tax returns)

| | Number (thousands) | | | | | Amount (billions of dollars) | | | | |
| | | Net worth | | | | | | Net worth | | |
Type of asset	Total	Under $250,000[1]	$250,000–$500,000	$500,000–$1,000,000	$1,000,000 or more	Total	Under $250,000[1]	$250,000–$500,000	$500,000–$1,000,000	$1,000,000 or more
Total	1,965.1	254.9	434.5	868.0	407.7	2,140	122	244	651	1,122
Real estate	1,740.3	237.3	371.8	771.7	359.4	675	63	105	242	265
Corporate stock	1,555.3	169.3	307.4	710.5	368.1	531	11	35	135	350
Noncorporate business assets	829.7	112.6	176.6	325.9	214.6	181	15	21	35	111
Cash	1,911.1	236.7	422.7	851.4	400.3	167	5	16	78	67
Bonds	755.2	43.7	96.7	398.5	216.3	128	1	4	36	88
State and local government	411.3	8.9	37.0	212.6	152.9	62	(Z)	1	14	46
Federal savings	204.5	19.2	30.7	108.4	46.2	6	(Z)	(Z)	3	3
Other Federal	219.9	11.8	27.1	112.7	68.3	46	(Z)	1	13	32
Corporate and foreign	328.2	13.1	40.5	191.5	83.1	14	(Z)	1	6	7
Notes and mortgages	922.8	60.6	198.3	430.0	233.9	97	6	10	30	51
Life insurance equity	1,450.1	245.9	370.2	564.0	270.0	26	5	7	7	7
Other assets	1,903.0	245.2	427.2	835.8	394.9	336	16	48	89	184
Debts and mortgages	1,813.5	251.3	419.3	770.2	372.6	375	115	69	70	121
Net worth	(X)	(X)	(X)	(X)	(X)	1,765	8	175	582	1,001

(X) Not applicable.
(Z) Less than $500 million.
[1]Includes those wealthholders with negative net worth.
Source: U.S. Internal Revenue Service, *Statistics of Income Bulletin*, winter 1984–1985.

and of a plan to turn the area into an American enclave that would eventually secede from Brazil.

The reality wasn't quite as strange, but certainly more grandiose. In vast stretches of jungle he built airstrips, thousands of miles of roads, a private railroad, hospitals, and a city for 35,000 people.

The plan was to build a lumber and paper business to provide these products during what Ludwig believed would soon be a worldwide shortage. But here he ran into trouble. He planted a Southeast Asian tree that grows about a foot a year, but it wouldn't grow in the thin Amazon soil. Then he had trouble with the Brazilian government, which refused to confirm his title to his land. That made it hard for him to get additional financing. In 1982, he finally threw in the towel. After selling the project for $280 million, he was left with an $820 million loss. Since then, he has given about $1.5 billion to the Swiss foundation he created to study cancer. Today, Ludwig is worth a mere $500 million. Still, that's not bad for someone who dropped out of junior high school and got started in business with only a $5,000 loan.

Table 41 Where America's Millionaires Live

If you're looking for a millionaire, this chart will help you out. It shows where the wealthiest Americans live. It shows the number of top wealth holders (defined as people with gross assets of $300,000 or more) for various regions and states and how much their net assets are worth. [California leads the pack (64,500 millionaires), followed by Florida, and Texas.] The data are for 1982, the most recent available. The IRS probably underestimates the number of millionaires in the U.S.

(All figures are estimates based on estate tax return samples. Net worth equals assets minus debts and mortgages.)

Region, division, and state	Number of top wealth-holders (thousands)	Total assets (billions of dollars)	Net worth (billions of dollars)	Millionaires as defined by net worth Number (thousands)	Millionaires as defined by net worth Amount (billions of dollars)
Total	4,377.9	2,897.2	2,423.1	407.7	1,001.3
Regions:					
Northeast	805.3	526.3	468.6	86.3	210.5
Midwest	1,137.0	686.5	549.6	83.3	178.9
South	1,413.4	937.6	793.0	135.0	351.5
West	1,012.7	740.3	605.6	101.5	257.7
New England	195.3	135.1	118.0	21.4	52.0
Maine	10.8	8.6	4.6	.1	1.8
New Hampshire	14.5	8.5	7.9	2.1	3.1
Vermont	7.5	4.9	4.0	.7	1.8
Massachusetts	78.9	49.8	43.5	7.6	18.3
Rhode Island	7.8	4.3	3.5	.8	1.4
Connecticut	75.8	59.0	54.5	9.4	25.6
Middle Atlantic	610.0	391.2	350.6	64.9	158.5
New York	306.0	209.5	189.3	30.9	98.1
New Jersey	144.8	79.8	73.3	8.3	22.7
Pennsylvania	159.2	101.9	88.0	25.7	37.8
East north central	664.0	372.3	311.8	43.2	96.4
Ohio	158.5	86.1	75.6	12.6	25.6
Indiana	60.6	32.5	28.1	4.5	9.2
Illinois	241.0	147.0	116.4	14.5	34.4
Michigan	118.1	64.2	56.7	7.3	17.2
Wisconsin	85.8	42.5	35.0	4.3	10.0
West north central	473.0	314.2	237.8	40.1	82.5
Minnesota	91.0	102.4	62.4	17.6	37.7
Iowa	115.5	56.9	44.6	3.3	4.9
Missouri	72.7	48.6	41.0	7.7	15.6
North Dakota	51.1	23.7	20.2	3.8	4.5
South Dakota	15.4	8.5	6.6	1.2	2.1
Nebraska	66.5	36.5	29.8	3.3	7.3
Kansas	60.8	37.7	33.2	3.2	10.4
South Atlantic	678.2	465.6	396.1	67.3	189.1
Delaware	8.0	5.0	4.0	.7	1.5
South Atlantic—continued					
Maryland	98.0	67.9	60.2	8.9	33.3
Virginia	99.2	43.8	38.5	4.9	14.8
West Virginia	8.4	7.7	4.7	.6	1.5
North Carolina	70.1	36.4	29.6	3.6	8.0
South Carolina	42.1	18.9	16.3	2.2	4.0
Georgia	72.9	46.8	37.4	5.8	14.4
Florida	279.5	239.2	205.4	40.6	111.8
East south central	153.2	90.0	73.8	14.9	30.2
Kentucky	42.2	23.8	18.5	3.5	7.4
Tennessee	47.9	28.8	23.1	5.3	10.0
Alabama	33.9	21.3	19.0	4.1	8.9
Mississippi	29.2	16.1	13.2	2.0	3.8
West south central	582.0	382.0	323.1	52.8	132.2
Arkansas	36.2	20.6	15.8	2.6	5.1
Louisiana	59.9	40.2	32.8	6.2	15.4
Oklahoma	68.4	40.2	31.9	4.5	10.5
Texas	417.5	281.0	242.6	39.5	101.2
Mountain	251.5	172.6	138.3	22.5	55.8
Montana	23.0	13.1	9.1	.9	2.1
Idaho	14.5	10.8	7.7	1.0	2.5
Wyoming	13.3	10.1	8.4	1.3	2.8
Colorado	72.9	52.9	42.0	6.9	19.3
New Mexico	13.6	9.1	7.0	1.1	2.8
Arizona	66.0	42.5	35.7	5.5	12.9
Utah	22.2	18.3	15.5	4.3	9.7
Nevada	26.0	15.8	12.8	1.5	3.8
Pacific	761.2	567.7	467.4	79.0	201.9
Washington	65.4	56.2	49.6	10.4	26.5
Oregon	48.5	27.2	23.3	2.1	4.1
California	617.0	467.2	383.4	64.5	166.7
Alaska	16.1	8.2	6.8	1.2	2.9
Hawaii	14.2	8.8	4.3	.8	1.7
Other areas	9.8	6.5	6.2	1.5	2.7

Source: U.S. Internal Revenue Service, *Statistics of Income Bulletin*, winter 1984–1985.

Table 42 The Wealth of America: What We Own and How Much We're Worth

This table shows what percentages of various kinds of households own certain types of assets and what the median values of those assets are. On the left, the chart lists various kinds of households by race, education, and other characteristics. The middle of the chart shows what percentages of those households own various kinds of assets. It shows, for example, that 22% of all white households own stock compared to only 5.4% of all black households. The right part of the chart lists the median values of those assets. It lists the median net worth of black, white, and other households. It also shows the median values of various assets. For example, the white family that owns a home has a median $41,999 worth of equity in its home. The data are for 1984.

Characteristic	Number of house-holds (thousands)	Percent owning											Median value of holdings for asset owner (dollars)						
		Interest-earning assets[1]	Other interest-earning assets[2]	Regular checking accounts[3]	Stocks and mutual fund shares	Own business or profession	Motor vehicles	Own home	Rental property	Other real estate	U.S. savings bonds	IRA or KEOGH accounts	Net worth	Interest-earning deposits[1]	Other interest-earning assets[2]	Regular checking accounts[3]	Stocks and mutual fund shares	Equity in own home	IRA and KEOGH accounts
Total	86,790	71.8	8.5	53.9	20.0	12.9	85.8	64.3	9.8	10.0	15.0	19.5	32,667	3,066	9,471	449	3,892	40,597	4,805
Age of householder:																			
Less than 35 years old	25,730	64.5	4.8	50.6	13.1	10.3	87.5	40.3	3.8	5.2	13.0	10.3	5,764	901	2,318	327	1,218	17,586	2,484
35 to 44 years old	17,393	72.4	7.9	59.0	22.9	18.3	91.7	69.3	10.0	10.4	17.8	21.6	35,581	1,894	5,260	410	3,197	37,268	4,438
45 to 54 years old	12,596	72.9	9.1	60.0	23.1	19.7	91.6	77.7	14.3	15.4	17.5	31.4	56,791	3,387	7,766	538	4,048	48,172	5,351
55 to 64 years old	12,920	76.0	11.5	55.4	25.5	15.1	89.1	80.2	15.4	15.9	18.3	38.9	73,664	7,340	13,559	568	5,662	54,059	6,390
65 years old and over	18,151	77.5	11.6	48.5	21.1	5.1	71.4	73.0	10.8	8.4	11.3	8.5	60,266	13,255	18,144	651	6,882	46,192	6,369
Race of householder:																			
White	75,343	75.4	9.4	56.9	22.0	14.0	88.5	67.3	10.1	10.9	16.1	21.4	39,135	3,457	9,826	457	3,908	41,999	4,922
Black	9,509	43.8	2.1	32.0	5.4	4.0	65.0	43.8	6.6	3.3	7.4	5.1	3,397	739	(B)	318	2,777	24,077	2,450
Spanish origin[4]	4,162	50.8	2.0	36.6	7.5	9.6	74.6	39.9	6.6	5.8	6.1	9.1	4,913	1,178	(B)	359	2,488	38,867	3,257
Region:																			
Northeast	18,533	77.4	8.7	50.7	22.2	10.7	78.5	61.0	9.1	7.3	19.9	23.8	37,734	3,923	9,101	424	3,872	49,213	4,914
Midwest	22,141	74.6	8.9	54.2	20.6	13.4	88.2	68.1	10.4	10.6	17.0	20.5	35,707	2,964	8,784	374	2,959	37,139	4,672
South	29,430	64.5	7.4	55.0	17.5	13.0	87.0	66.6	8.6	11.1	12.3	15.0	27,296	2,774	9,570	501	4,166	34,129	4,878
West	16,686	74.4	9.6	55.3	21.3	14.5	88.6	59.0	11.7	10.3	11.8	21.6	33,525	2,962	10,017	496	4,103	52,062	4,781
Type of household:																			
Married-couple households	50,606	78.2	9.6	59.5	24.4	17.6	95.9	77.2	11.8	13.3	18.9	25.1	50,116	3,336	9,150	477	3,488	42,634	5,499
Male householder	12,588	65.0	8.1	46.7	15.4	10.4	81.9	41.5	7.4	6.9	10.3	14.4	9,883	2,091	8,368	481	4,098	30,238	4,262
Female householder	23,596	61.5	6.2	45.9	13.1	4.0	66.1	48.8	6.6	4.6	9.2	10.3	13,885	2,941	10,083	358	4,277	38,009	3,976
Education of householder:																			
Less than 12 years	24,736	57.6	3.6	41.9	8.5	8.6	73.5	62.1	7.6	6.5	9.0	8.6	23,477	3,888	9,972	392	2,959	34,905	4,692
High school: 4 years	27,454	70.9	6.2	56.4	16.6	11.7	88.9	65.1	8.8	9.5	15.7	18.1	31,892	2,563	7,434	391	3,187	39,890	4,487
College: 1 to 3 years	17,171	77.3	8.7	60.1	23.4	14.2	91.3	61.1	9.0	10.6	16.4	20.6	29,121	2,049	8,077	433	3,416	41,114	4,442
4 or more years	17,430	87.7	18.7	60.9	38.4	19.7	92.9	69.4	15.1	15.0	21.2	36.2	60,417	4,296	9,890	677	4,848	51,188	5,520
Tenure:																			
Owner	55,820	80.2	10.8	59.8	26.0	16.0	92.7	100.0	13.6	13.0	18.4	25.7	63,253	4,333	10,051	508	4,116	40,597	5,265
Renter	30,970	56.5	4.3	43.3	9.2	7.3	73.3	(X)	2.8	4.6	9.0	8.5	1,921	1,182	5,056	342	2,745	(X)	3,205

(B) Base figure too small to meet statistical standards for reliability of derived figure.
(X) Not applicable.
[1] At financial institutions. Includes passbook savings accounts, money market deposit accounts, certificates of deposit, and interest-earning checking accounts.
[2] Includes money-market funds, U.S. Government securities, municipal and corporate bonds, and other interest-earning assets.
[3] Excludes interest-earning checking.
[4] Persons of Spanish origin may be of any race.
Source: U.S. Bureau of the Census, Current Population Reports, series P-70, No. 7.

Table 43   Household Net Worth—Percentage Distribution

This chart provides a percentage distribution of the net worth of various kinds of households. It shows that 19.1% of all households headed by someone under 35 have zero or negative net worth and that 12.6% of all households headed by some with four years of college education are worth over $250,000. The far right column shows the median net worth of various kinds of households.

Characteristic	Number of households (thousands)	Percent distribution of households by net worth								Median (dollars)
		Zero or negative	$1 to $4,999	$5,000 to $9,999	$10,000 to $24,999	$25,000 to $49,999	$50,000 to $99,999	$100,000 to $249,999	$250,000 and over	
Total	86,790	11.0	15.3	6.4	12.4	14.5	19.3	15.3	5.9	32,667
Age of householder:										
Under 35 years old	25,730	19.1	28.9	11.0	17.2	11.9	8.2	2.9	.9	5,764
35–44 years old	17,393	9.7	12.5	6.1	13.4	18.3	21.4	13.7	4.7	35,581
45–54 years old	12,596	8.2	8.5	4.1	10.6	14.1	24.9	21.0	8.7	56,791
55–64 years old	12,920	5.3	7.7	3.3	7.8	13.3	25.3	25.7	11.6	73,664
65 years old and over	18,151	6.7	8.7	4.0	9.1	15.5	24.7	23.1	8.2	60,266
Race of householder:										
White	75,343	8.4	14.0	6.3	12.2	15.0	20.7	16.9	6.5	39,135
Black	9,509	30.5	23.9	6.8	14.0	11.7	9.3	3.3	3.1	3,397
Spanish origin[1]	4,162	23.9	26.3	7.6	11.4	9.5	13.1	5.1	3.1	4,913
Region:										
Northeast	18,533	12.4	13.7	6.2	10.5	13.6	21.2	17.0	5.6	37,734
Midwest	22,141	9.7	14.4	5.7	12.4	16.7	21.0	14.5	5.7	35,707
South	29,430	10.6	16.2	7.1	14.5	15.5	17.8	13.4	4.9	27,296
West	16,686	11.9	16.7	6.4	10.6	10.7	17.4	17.9	8.5	33,525
Type of household:										
Married-couple	50,606	6.0	10.5	5.6	12.2	15.6	22.7	19.5	8.0	50,116
Male householder	12,588	15.5	25.1	9.7	13.3	11.6	13.0	8.0	4.0	9,883
Female householder	23,596	19.3	20.3	6.4	12.2	13.5	15.3	10.3	2.6	13,885
Education of householder:										
Less than 12 years	24,736	15.1	17.2	6.6	12.4	15.9	18.6	11.3	2.9	23,447
High school, 4 years	27,454	10.1	17.0	6.3	12.7	14.6	19.9	14.8	4.6	31,892
College: 1–3 years	17,171	10.2	16.7	7.2	13.0	13.8	19.3	14.4	5.5	29,121
4 years	17,430	7.4	8.5	5.6	11.3	12.8	19.1	22.7	12.6	60,417
Tenure:										
Owner-occupied	55,820	1.4	2.9	3.9	13.1	19.6	28.0	22.5	8.7	63,253
Renter-occupied	30,970	28.3	37.6	11.0	11.1	5.2	3.6	2.3	.9	1,921

[1]Persons of Spanish origin may be of any race.
Source: U.S. Bureau of the Census, *Current Population Reports*, series P-70, No. 7.

Table 44   The Biggest Money-Makers on Wall Street

Rank	Person	Company	Earnings (millions of dollars)
1.	Michel David-Weill	Lazard Frères	125
2.	George Soros	Soros Fund Management	90 to 100
3.	Richard Dennis	C&D Commodities	80
4.	Michael Milken	Drexel Burnham Lambert	up to 80
5.	J. Morton Davis	D. H. Blair	60 to 65
6.	Jerome Kohlberg	Kohlberg Kravis Roberts	50
	Henry Kravis	Kohlberg Kravis Roberts	50
	George Roberts	Kohlberg Kravis Roberts	50
9.	Raymond Chambers	Wesray Capital Corporation	45 to 50
	William Simon	Wesray Capital Corporation	45 to 50
11.	Michael Steinhardt	Steinhardt Partners	40
12.	Edward Johnson III	FMR Corporation	35
13.	Jeffrey Tarr	Junction Partners	30
14.	Asher Edelman	Plaza Securities, Arbitrage Securities	25 to 30
15.	Frederick R. Adler	Adler & Shaykin	20
	Theodore Forstmann	Forstmann Little	20
	Leon Levy	Odyssey Partners	20
	Jack Nash	Odyssey Partners	20
19.	Donald Carter	The Carter Organization	16
20.	John Weinberg	Goldman, Sachs	15.8

Source: *Financial World,* July 14, 1987.

PART III

The Heavy Hand

Chapter Eight

GOVERNMENT: FOR GOOD OR BAD

HIGHLIGHTS AND TRENDS

• Federal, state, and local governments spent $1,515 trillion in 1986, an amount equal to more than one third of the GNP (36%). The same year federal government also passed a landmark of sorts, managing to spend over $1 trillion for the first time ($1004.6 billion).

• Per capita, federal government expenditures have increased from $280 in 1950 to $3,506 today, while state and local governments spend $2,779 on every person in the U.S., up from $184 in 1950.

• Federal, state, and local governments are the country's largest landlord, owning 39.1% of all land in the U.S., about 885 million acres.

• Federal, state, and local governments own equipment and buildings valued at $3.858 trillion, including the world's largest office building, the Pentagon.

• If federal, state, and local governments seceded from the Union and formed their own country with a GNP the size of today's government expenditures ($1,515 billion), that country's government would have the third-largest GNP in the world.

• Between 1950 and 1987, outstanding debts of the federal government increased from $257 billion to $2,355.3 billion. They could rise to $2,825.3 billion by 1989.

• Per capita, the debt of all government agencies has increased from $1,856 in 1950 for each man, woman, and child in America to $11,565 in 1986.

• To pay the interest on a $2.1 trillion debt, U.S. taxpayers forked over $190 billion in gross interest payments and $136 billion in net interest payments in 1986.

• By 1988 net interest payments on the nation's debt will be large enough to pay for all the money the federal government spent on Medicare, health, and international affairs combined!

• If you've ever doubted the fact that big government hurts the competitiveness of American business consider this: the interest on the national debt is $42 billion more than the $142 billion U.S. manufacturers spent on new plant and equipment in 1986.

THE STATE'S BUSINESS

The U.S. government can't quite boast, as one monarch once did, that it is "the only merchant in town." There's little doubt, however, that government is the country's largest business. Government expenditures equal 36% of the GNP. Put together, government agencies spend more money, employ more people, and own more land than any company or individual in the U.S. That makes big government the biggest business in America.

The sheer size of these expenditures and activities can boggle the mind. Unlike individual finances, which are counted in dollars, or corporate finances, which are counted in thousands or millions of dollars, government finances work on the level of billions and trillions of dollars—sums of money so monumental they become almost absurd. As one U.S. senator once quipped about the way Congress spends money, "A billion here, a billion there, and pretty soon you're talking about real money."

Because a billion dollars—let alone the idea of a two-trillion-dollar government debt—has almost no meaning to most people, this chapter, the first of four chapters on government and the business of power, is devoted to translating those figures into terms that can be understood. That we've devoted so much space to government indicates the magnitude of government power over the economy.

GOVERNMENT: WHAT IT OWNS

Land

Federal, state, and local governments are the country's largest landlord, owning 39.1% of all land in the U.S., about 885 million acres. Most of this, about 726.6 million acres, or 32.2% of all land, is owned by the federal government. The feds own 60% of the land in the Western part of the U.S., only 0.5% of the land in Connecticut but 85% of the land in Nevada, 47.9% of the land in California, half of Oregon, and 61.4% of Utah, as well as the 400,000 caribou, 152,000 moose, and 64,000 wild horses and burros that live on these lands.

Federal-owned land would fill up an area the size of Delaware, Maryland, the District of Columbia, Virginia, West Virginia, North Carolina, South Carolina, Georgia, Florida Kentucky, Tennessee, Alabama, Mississippi, Arkansas, Louisiana, Oklahoma, Texas, Maine, New Hampshire, Vermont, Massachusetts, Rhode Island, Connecticut, New York, New Jersey, Pennsylvania, Ohio, and Illinois.

If turned into a separate country, federal lands would constitute the sixth-largest country in the world.

Moreover, the federal government leases another 1.8 million acres, as well as 203 million square feet of office space at a cost of $1.5 billion a year.

If you divide up all the 885 million acres owned by federal, state, and local governments, every man, woman, and child in the U.S. would get about 3.6 acres.

And, as you might expect from an enterprise that's primarily devoted to producing and pushing paper, the federal government owns a lot of trees. About 10 billion board feet of timber are cut every year on federal lands. The federal government owns 20 million acres of forest land in Idaho (39% of the state), 16 million acres in Oregon (27%), 20 million acres in California (20%), and 17 million acres in Montana (18%).

Precious Metals and Resources

The federal government owns some of the country's most valuable mineral and environmental resources: 80% of the shale reserves, a third of the coal, a third of its uranium, and large reserves of gold, silver, oil, copper, and molybdenum (an element used to strengthen and harden steel).

Equipment and Buildings

Federal, state, and local governments own equipment and buildings valued at $3,858.6 billion; state and local government own about $2,616 billion of this figure. If all the equipment and buildings owned by the federal, state, and local governments were sold off, every American would get about $15,700.

Among these holdings is the world's largest office building, the Pentagon. This 6.5-million-square-foot building houses 29,000 workers. The Pentagon receives 280,000 telephone calls a day on 44,000 telephones. Staffers walk down 17 miles of corridors, look out 7,748 windows, and eat at 2 restaurants, 6 cafeterias, and 10 snack bars.

Food

You could say that the government is the world's largest supermarket and commodities broker all rolled into one. To stabilize and support the price of farm goods, the Commodity Credit Corporation (owned by the federal government) buys various agricultural products, such as wheat, corn, and cheese. In 1985 it bought $4.3 billion worth of food and by the end of the year it owned $6.9 billion dollars worth of food: 882 million pounds of cheese, 1,328 pounds of dried milk, 305 million pounds of butter and butter oil, 194,000 bales of cotton, 557 million bushels of wheat, 124 million bushels of soybeans, 161 million bushels of sorghum, and 477 million bushels of corn.

There is no end in sight to the amount of food piling up in government warehouses. On June 1, 1986, the government owned 1.2 billion bushels of wheat and corn (about 11% of all the wheat and corn produced in the

U.S.), up 70% in only three years. With storage bins bursting at the seams, government officials are forced to allow warehouse companies to store all this surplus grain in temporary buildings, railroad cars, and even barges.

Nuclear Weapons

The U.S. government owns over 10,398 strategic or long-range nuclear weapons. If the U.S. government had a fire sale on its nuclear arsenal and distributed these weapons to American counties, every county government would get 3 strategic long-range nuclear weapons.

These 10,398 strategic weapons have an explosive power of 2,649 megatons or about 5.3 billion pounds of TNT. If these nuclear weapons were dismantled and replaced with the equivalent amount of TNT, the U.S. government could distribute 21,624 pounds of TNT to every man, woman, and child in the U.S. That would give every American enough TNT to destroy a city the size of Nagasaki.

WHAT THE GOVERNMENT DOES

Spend Money

Primarily the government collects money, lots of it, and then spends even more of it. Federal, state, and local governments spent $1,515 billion in 1986, with the federal government managing to spend over $1 trillion for the first time ($1,030 billion). Per-capita federal government expenditures have increased from $280 in 1950 to $3,506 today, while state and local governments spend $2,779 on every person in the U.S., up from $184 in 1950.

Spending by government agencies increased over 21.6 times between 1950 and 1986. In contrast, during this period the population increased by 59% and the number of employed people paying taxes to finance all this increased only 85%. The GNP increased 14.5 times, and the median family income increased only 8.4 times.

If federal, state, and local governments seceded from the Union and formed a country with a GNP the size of today's government expenditures, that government would have the third-largest GNP in the world—only the private sector of the U.S. and the whole Soviet Union would have a larger GNP.

Stay in Debt

As for most big spenders, the revenues of government agencies have not kept up with ever-growing expenditures. Between 1950 and 1987, outstanding debts of the federal government increased from $257 billion to $2,355.3 billion. It could rise to $2,825.3 billion by 1989.

The national debt increased from $1,856 in 1950 for each man, woman, and child in America to $11,565 in 1986. To pay the interest on a $2.1

trillion debt, U.S. taxpayers, as we have noted, forked over $190 billion in 1986, $136 billion in net interest payments. In 1988, net interest payments will be enough to pay for all the federal government spending on Medicare, health, and international affairs combined! Net interest payments would fund nearly half of our Defense Department budget and over two fifths of all Social Security expenses. The net interest on the national debt is almost as much as the $142 billion U.S. manufacturers spent on new plant and equipment in 1986.

In 1985, the last year for which comparable statistics were available, the government was certainly the nation's biggest debtor, with $2.4 trillion in outstanding debts. The federal government owed $1.82 trillion and state and local governments owed $569 billion. In contrast, total consumer debt in the U.S. was $668.2 billion and mortgage debt stood at $2.2 trillion. Farm debt was $866.8 billion.

Employ People

One of the things governments do best is create bureaucracies. In 1987 the federal government was by far the nation's largest employer, employing 2.98 million civilians. The largest private employer, General Motors, employs less than a third as many people, a mere 811,000 workers. State governments employed 3.98 million while local governments employed 10.11 million.

Overall, federal, state, and local governments employ 17 million people, about 16.6% of the nonagricultural labor force. Altogether, government employees form the 44th-largest country in the world. There are more government employees than the entire population of Australia. The number of government employees is larger than the combined populations of Maine, New Hampshire, Vermont, Massachusetts, Rhode Island, Connecticut, and Oklahoma.

But government bureaucracies aren't growing as fast as everyone imagines. Federal employment grew 28.7% between 1960 and 1987, less than total nonagricultural employment (80.9%) and the population (57.2%). But total government employment grew 103.9% between 1960 and 1987, from 8.8 million to 17 million, largely because state and local employment grew 132%. By 1987, state and local bureaucrats numbered 14.1 million, up from 6.1 million in 1960.

And the life of a government bureaucrat isn't as easy as most people imagine. Some 6,888 federal employees were bitten by dogs in 1984 alone, proving the point that taxpayers aren't the only ones who get irritated with bureaucrats. But that wasn't the most common way federal employees hurt themselves on the job: "falls" (24,949 accidents), accidents while "handling materials" (24,608); "slipping, twisting and tripping" (18,781), and "striking against objects" (13,640) led the list. "Flying particles" (5,244 accidents), "vehicles" (4,173), "dust and gases" (3,667) "bites by other animals [not including dogs] and insects" (2,642) and "violence" (1,992) rounded off the list of the top ten hazards faced by federal employees. Strangely enough, the most hazardous duty in government is not at the CIA, the Pentagon, or the FBI, but at an obscure agency known as the Architect of the Capitol that includes the carpenters, electricians, and gardeners in the capital and the botanic gardens. Following that were the Panama Canal Commission, the Postal Service (bedeviled by 5,200 dog bites), and the Government Printing Office.

But all of these injuries are no joke, at least in terms of balancing the budget. The cost of workers' compensation claims for federal employees runs around $964 million a year.

Provide Social Services

Besides spending money and employing people, the government provides a bewildering array of social services, many of which involve giving away money. About 37.1 million people (only a little less than the population of Poland) collect Social Security, 10.9 million people (more than the population of Hungary) get Aid to Families with Dependent Children, 19.2 million people (more than the population of East Germany) get food stamps, and 21.8 million people (more than the population of North Korea) get Medicaid. And who says that communist countries are the only countries with big government?

Per capita, government programs on the federal, state, and local levels spent $2,801 on various social-welfare programs in 1984. That figure included $1,424 on social insurance, $635 on education, $376 on public aid, $158 on health and medical care, and $108 on veterans' benefits.

Unlike defense spending, which has declined as a percentage of GNP and total government spending, social-welfare programs have increased. For all levels of government, social-welfare expenditures increased as a percentage of the total budget from 38.4% in 1960 to 52.8% by the mid-1980s. Most of this increase occurred at the federal level, where 50% of the budget went to social-welfare programs, up from 28.1% in 1960, and down from 54.6% in 1979. The percentage of local and state government money spent on social-welfare programs has actually dropped from 60.1% in 1960 to 58.9%. As a percentage of GNP, social-welfare spending stands at 18.2%, up from 10.3% in 1960. Again, the federal government accounted for most of the increase as social-welfare spending hit 11.3% of the GNP, up from 4.9% in 1960.

The highest welfare benefits are to be found in Alaska, where the maximum monthly payment for a family of four in 1987 was $833. Still, that's only 23% of the median family income for a family of four. But someone working 40 hours a week at the minimum wage would only earn $536 a month. The next-best state for welfare payments is California ($734 a month), followed by New York ($706), Connecticut ($688), and Wisconsin ($649).

The state with the lowest welfare benefits for a family of four is Mississippi, where state bureaucrats expect you to get along on a paltry $144 a month—about 7.3% of the median family income. Other states to avoid if you plan to support a family on welfare payments are Alabama ($147), Tennessee ($189), Texas ($221), and Arkansas ($224).

Another major social program is Social Security. For the time being, the system is quite solvent. As the baby-boom generation moves into its peak earning years, the system will do something government agencies rarely do—rack up huge surpluses. The projected surplus will hit $40 billion in 1990, over $70 billion in 1996, and then soar to well over $150 billion in the first decade of the 21st century. But then the Social Security system will face problems. The system may start running a deficit in the second decade and by 2025 could be losing over $350 billion a year.

Thanks to all the money the federal government gives away, Washington is the biggest check writer in the U.S. Every year the federal government issues 650 million checks. Since there is no limit on how long you can hold a federal government check, not everyone cashes them right away. In 1986, the Treasury disbursed $32,221.40 for checks that were more than 30 years old.

Other government agencies make certain you can drive to the bank to cash your government check. Government is responsible for building, repairing, and maintaining the 3.8 million miles of roads in the U.S. at a cost of $60.6 billion a year. Local and state police have to regulate cars that drive about 1.8 trillion miles each year and investigate the 18.8 million traffic accidents that occur each year. Add the 170 million motor-vehicle registrations that exist in the U.S., all of which have to be renewed every few years, and you have a monumental bureaucratic gridlock.

Government agencies also spend about $12.1 billion on the unsavory service of public sewer systems. A total of $12.3 billion is spent on pollution abatement. The job of picking up the nearly 150 million tons of garbage produced every year is so massive that no one even seems to know how much government money is spent on this problem. State and local governments, however, spend $16.2 billion on sewage and sanitation. New York City spent $1 million just cleaning up the trash produced by the celebration held on the 100th birthday of the Statue of Liberty. And that celebration didn't even rank as the biggest trash-producing day in the city's history. The sanitation department cleaned up a record 5,438 tons of garbage on the V-J Day celebration in 1945, 3,474 tons for a parade for John Glenn in 1962, and 3,249 tons in 1951 for General Douglas MacArthur. Not surprisingly, New York City's largest export is not clothes from its famous garment district, but recycled wastepaper.

And then there is the Postal Service, everyone's nominee for the least efficient government agency. It ships 140 billion pieces of mail each year, about 585 for every man, woman, and child.

Create Paperwork

Some government agencies don't ship paper, they create it. It's been estimated that small businesses fill out 850 million pages of government forms to comply with various federal edicts. Laid end to end, the paperwork would circle the earth nearly 6 times; stacked up in a federal office, it would rise 67 miles into the atmosphere.

Estimates of the cost of government paperwork vary but all of them are alarming. The Commission on Federal Paperwork found that in 1977 the cost of filling out a mountain of federal paperwork was $25 billion to $32 billion for private industry. In 1986 dollars, that estimate would mean private industry spent $52.3 billion to $67 billion to fill out paperwork, state and local governments spent $10.5 billion to $18.8 billion, individuals other than farmers spent $18.2 billion, and farmers spent $732.4 million. Overall, the cost of government paperwork amounted to about $1,046 for each American.

In 1987, the Office of Management and Budget estimated that the American public spent 1.7 billion hours filling out government forms. Depending on how one values the time spent on filling out government forms, the total costs could range from $17 billion to $34 billion and more.

Pay Politicians

Large sums of money are spent each year keeping America's political leaders fed and clothed. In the private and public sector an estimated $1.8 billion a year is spent on party politics and the electoral process.

It cost $3.2 billion to run the 100th Congress. Included in that cost is the pay for 11,604 staff members in the House of Representatives and 7,200 Senate employees. In 1987, the House members spent $176,853,600 for staff and $64,380,000 for offices; the Senate spent $104,030,000 for staff and $6,100,000 for offices. This, of course, was a big change from the first Congress, for which there were only 7 employees in the House and 6 employees in the Senate. Senators and congressmen were paid $6 a day plus a travel allowance of $6 for every 20 miles. It only cost $378,853 to run the first Congress—the 100th Congress spent over $8.7 million a day, 365 days a year.

But like many of the members of the first Congress, many political leaders today are wealthy men. Some of the wealthiest men in the Senate are Senator John Heinz (R-Pa., with assets of $9.3 million to $12.1 million), Senator John C. Danforth (R-Mo., with assets of at least $7.2 million), Senator John D. Rockefeller IV (D-W. Va., with assets of at least $3.7 million), Senator Dennis DeConcini (D-Ariz., with assets of $6.5 million to more than $8.9 million), Senator Lowell P. Weicker (R-Conn., with assets of nearly $5.8 million), Senator Bob Graham (D-Fla., with assets of $3.3 million to $6.3 million), and Senator John W. Warner (R-Va., with assets of $3.1 million to $3.5 million). Forbes says Senator Edward Kennedy (D-Mass.) and the Kennedy clan are worth $286 million.

Fight Crime

Government agencies are charged with solving the 19,000 murders, 87,300 rapes, 498,000 robberies, 3 million burglaries, and 1.1 million car thefts committed each year. To pay for all this protection, the taxpayers coughed up $39.8 billion. And when criminals are caught it costs the taxpayers more money. By 1985, there were half a million Americans behind bars, a 53% increase since 1980. At that rate, there will be nearly 1.7 million Americans behind bars by the year 2000, 12.8 million by 2025. Already the tide is overflowing U.S. prisons. In 1985, prisons were forced to grant 18,617 prisoners early releases because they lacked the space.

Fight War

One of the main pastimes of governments has always been war. The total cost of American wars, from the American Revolution to the Vietnam conflict, assumed by the government has been $723,374 million. The cost of wars since 1940 has been $664,481 million, or about $2,700 for every living American. James Clayton of the University of Utah estimates that the cost of the Vietnam War reached $161.2 billion by 1985, the Korean War cost $64.7 billion, and spending for World War II hit $438.6 billion. In contrast, earlier American wars were strictly low-budget affairs. The American Revolution cost $170 million, the War of 1812 cost $120 million, and the Mexican War set back taxpayers only $120 million. The Civil War, which many military historians view as the first modern war, was also the first American war to cost over a billion dollars. Union spending was $6.8 billion. The Spanish-American War cost $2.4 billion, while total costs of World War I hit $58.2 billion, only enough money to keep the Pentagon running for a few months today. These figures include veterans' benefits and interest payments on war loans as well as the direct cost of buying weapons and supplies.

Preparing for a war can be even more expensive than actually waging one. The government spent $1.9 trillion between 1978 and 1988, when the country was at peace, about 2.6 times what was spent in all the wars in American history up to that time.

Keeping the military going is also big business. Every day the military signs 52,000 contracts—the Air Force alone entered into 5 million contracts in 1985.

Military procurement remains one of the most complex systems known to man—which may explain why a lot of expensive weapons systems never work. Defense firms typically face over 44,000 specifications for a weapons system. The instructions on procurement runs to 32 volumes and take up six feet of shelf space. One Pentagon study found that regulations accounted for one third of procurement costs.

Play Big Brother

With all of its resources, the government is busy collecting information on all of us. Scattered throughout its massive bureaucracy are some 11,000 computers, which have access to over 4,000 data systems. These systems contain almost 4 billion records on individuals—20 dossiers for every

American. But given the skill of your typical bureaucrat, many of these records may be inaccurate. As of 1986, the IRS estimates its employees enter about 20% of the information from tax returns incorrectly into computers. In the late 1970s, Congress's Office of Technology Assessment found that about 20% of the arrest records stored at the FBI's National Crime Information Center were inaccurate.

Table 45   Government Spending, Revenue, and Debt
(for fiscal years shown)

Item and year	All governments (billions of dollars)	Federal Total (billions of dollars)	Federal Percent of total	State and local (billions of dollars) Total	State	Local	Annual percent change[1] Federal	State	Local	Per capita[2] (dollars) Total	Federal	State and local
Revenue from own sources:												
1960	153	100	65.2	53	26	27	6.8	9.4	8.8	851	554	296
1965	203	126	62.1	77	39	38	4.8	8.1	7.0	1,045	649	396
1970	334	206	61.6	128	69	60	3.0	12.3	9.3	1,642	1,011	631
1973	432	254	58.8	178	97	81	7.2	12.0	10.5	2,044	1,200	844
1974	484	288	59.5	196	108	88	13.4	11.3	8.6	2,289	1,367	927
1975	519	302	58.2	217	119	98	5.0	10.7	10.6	2,436	1,418	1,018
1976	571	324	56.6	248	139	109	7.0	16.7	11.1	2,661	1,507	1,154
1977	658	383	58.1	275	156	120	18.1	12.0	10.2	3,039	1,766	1,272
1978	732	430	58.7	302	172	130	12.3	10.1	9.1	3,356	1,971	1,385
1979	829	500	60.3	330	190	140	16.3	10.7	7.2	3,768	2,270	1,498
1980	932	564	60.5	369	213	156	12.8	12.0	11.5	4,116	2,489	1,627
1981	1,075	659	61.3	416	240	176	16.9	12.9	13.2	4,747	2,909	1,838
1982	1,146	686	59.8	460	262	199	4.1	9.0	12.6	5,060	3,027	2,032
1983	1,181	678	57.4	503	285	218	− 1.2	8.9	10.0	5,049	2,897	2,151
1984	1,307	752	57.5	555	315	239	11.0	10.8	9.6	5,536	3,186	2,350
1985	1,419	805	56.7	614	350	264	7.0	10.7	10.4	5,943	3,371	2,571
1986	1,515	845	55.8	670	383	287	5.0	9.5	8.7	6,286	3,506	2,776
Direct expenditure:												
1960	151	90	59.7	61	22	39	5.2	9.0	8.4	841	502	339
1965	206	119	57.9	87	31	55	5.7	7.3	7.3	1,061	614	447
1970	333	185	55.5	148	56	92	4.5	12.3	10.7	1,638	910	728
1973	437	231	52.9	205	78	127	7.8	11.7	11.3	2,067	1,095	972
1974	478	253	52.8	226	86	139	9.5	10.3	9.5	2,263	1,195	1,069
1975	560	292	52.1	268	107	161	15.5	24.0	15.7	2,628	1,370	1,259
1976	625	322	51.5	303	123	180	10.3	15.1	11.6	2,912	1,500	1,417
1977	682	359	52.8	323	129	194	11.5	4.6	8.0	3,154	1,661	1,494
1978	745	400	53.7	345	137	209	11.5	6.0	7.4	3,418	1,835	1,584
1979	832	452	54.3	380	149	232	13.0	8.9	11.0	3,782	2,054	1,728
1980	959	526	54.8	432	173	259	16.4	16.6	11.8	4,232	2,324	1,909
1981	1,110	625	56.3	485	198	287	18.7	14.4	10.7	4,899	2,757	2,142
1982	1,233	710	57.6	523	212	311	13.7	6.7	8.6	5,445	3,136	2,309
1983	1,351	786	58.2	565	233	332	10.6	10.0	6.6	5,773	3,358	2,415
1984	1,428	829	58.1	599	243	355	5.5	4.3	7.1	6,047	3,511	2,537
1985	1,581	925	58.5	656	269	387	11.5	10.7	8.7	6,622	3,874	2,748
1986	1,697	981	57.8	716	292	424	6.0	8.6	9.6	7,039	4,068	2,971
Debt outstanding:[3]												
1960	356	286	80.4	70	19	51	.9	10.6	9.2	1,979	1,591	389
1965	417	317	76.1	100	27	72	2.1	7.8	7.1	2,150	1,637	513
1970	514	371	72.1	144	42	102	4.8	9.2	7.0	2,531	1,825	706
1973	657	468	71.2	188	59	129	8.1	12.0	8.1	3,108	2,216	892
1974	693	486	70.2	207	65	141	3.8	10.2	9.3	3,278	2,300	977
1975	764	544	71.1	220	72	148	11.9	10.5	4.6	3,591	2,553	1,038
1976	872	631	72.4	241	85	156	16.0	17.6	5.4	4,061	2,941	1,121
1977	969	709	73.2	260	90	169	12.3	6.4	6.4	4,477	3,278	1,200
1978	1,061	780	73.5	280	103	178	10.0	13.7	5.0	4,865	3,579	1,286
1979	1,138	834	73.3	304	112	192	6.9	8.9	8.2	5,170	3,788	1,382
1980	1,250	914	73.1	336	122	214	9.6	9.1	11.1	5,518	4,037	1,482
1981	1,368	1,004	73.4	364	135	229	9.8	10.6	7.2	6,038	4,431	1,606
1982	1,552	1,147	73.9	405	147	257	14.2	9.4	12.3	6,849	5,063	1,786
1983	1,836	1,382	75.3	455	167	287	20.5	13.4	11.7	7,848	5,906	1,942
1984	2,082	1,577	75.7	505	186	319	14.1	11.4	10.9	8,815	6,677	2,139
1985	2,396	1,827	76.3	569	212	357	15.9	13.7	11.9	10,036	7,655	2,382
1986	2,788	2,130	76.4	659	248	411	16.5	16.9	15.3	11,565	8,833	2,733

[1]Represents average for period of intervals shown; for 1960, change from 1955. Minus sign (−) indicates decrease.
[2]Based on estimated resident population as of July 1; except 1970 based on resident population enumerated as of April 1, 1970, and 1980 to 1982 based on resident population enumerated as of April 1, 1980. Excludes intergovernmental amounts.
[3]As of end of fiscal year.
Sources: U.S. Bureau of the Census, *Census of Governments: 1982*, vol. 4, no. 5, *Compendium of Government Finances* (GC 82(4)-5), and vol. 6, no. 4, *Historical Statistics on Governmental Finances and Employment* (GC 82(6)-4); and *Governmental Finances*, series GF no. 5, annual.

Table 46 State and Local Governments with the Most Outstanding Debt, Per Capita, By State, 1986

Rank	State	State and local debt (in millions of dollars)	Per-capita debt (dollars)
1.	Alaska	11,866	22,221
2.	Delaware	3,553	5,612
3.	Utah	8,770	5,268
4.	Wyoming	2,318	4,572
5.	Washington	18,985	4,254

States with the Least Outstanding Debt, Per Capita, 1986

Rank	State	State and local debt (in millions of dollars)	Per-capita debt (dollars)
50.	Idaho	1,245	1,241
49.	Indiana	7,251	1,241
48.	Mississippi	3,521	1,341
47.	Missouri	7,701	1,520
46.	Arkansas	3,781	1,594

Source: U.S. Bureau of the Census.

Table 47 How Washington Spends Your Tax Dollar

This chart shows revenues, expenditures, and debt of the federal government. The middle of the chart shows the national debt. One of the most significant measures of the impact of government spending is its relationship to the GNP. The right side shows how federal spending is eating up an ever-larger share of the GNP.

Year	Total receipts[1]	Total outlays[1]	Total surplus or deficit (−)[1]	Outstanding gross debt[2]	Average annual percent change — Receipts	Average annual percent change — Total outlays	Average annual percent change — Outstanding gross debt	Percent of GNP[3] — Outlays Total	Percent of GNP[3] — Outlays Human resources	Percent of GNP[3] — Outlays National defense	Percent of GNP[3] — Outstanding gross debt	Percent of GNP[3] — Outlays, off-budget
1940	6.5	9.5	−2.9	50.7	(X)	(X)	5.1	9.9	4.3	1.7	52.9	(−Z)
1945	45.2	92.7	−47.6	260.1	47.1	57.8	38.7	43.6	.9	39.1	122.5	.1
1950	39.4	42.6	−3.1	256.9	−2.7	−14.4	−.3	15.9	5.3	5.1	96.2	.5
1955	65.5	68.4	−3.0	274.4	10.7	10.0	1.3	17.7	3.8	11.0	70.8	4.0
1960	92.5	92.2	.3	290.9	7.2	6.1	1.2	18.2	5.2	9.5	57.3	10.9
1961	94.4	97.7	−3.3	292.9	2.0	6.0	.7	18.8	5.7	9.6	56.4	11.7
1962	99.7	106.8	−7.1	303.3	5.6	9.3	3.6	19.2	5.7	9.4	54.5	13.5
1963	106.6	111.3	−4.8	310.8	6.9	4.2	2.5	18.9	5.7	9.1	52.8	15.0
1964	112.6	118.5	−5.9	316.8	5.7	6.5	1.9	18.8	5.6	8.7	50.3	15.7
1965	116.8	118.2	−1.4	323.2	3.7	−.3	2.0	17.6	5.4	7.5	48.0	16.5
1966	130.8	134.5	−3.7	329.5	12.0	13.8	2.0	18.2	5.8	7.8	44.5	19.7
1967	148.8	157.5	−8.6	341.3	13.7	17.0	3.6	19.8	6.5	9.0	43.0	20.4
1968	153.0	178.1	−25.2	369.8	2.8	13.1	8.3	20.9	7.0	9.6	43.4	22.3
1969	186.9	183.6	3.2	367.1	22.2	3.1	−.7	19.8	7.1	8.9	39.5	25.2
1970	192.8	195.6	−2.8	382.6	3.2	6.5	4.2	19.8	7.6	8.2	38.6	27.6
1971	187.1	210.2	−23.0	409.5	−2.9	7.4	7.0	19.9	8.7	7.5	38.7	32.8
1972	207.3	230.7	−23.4	437.3	10.8	9.8	6.8	20.0	9.3	6.9	38.0	36.9
1973	230.8	245.7	−14.9	468.4	11.3	6.5	7.1	19.1	9.3	6.0	36.4	45.6
1974	263.2	269.4	−6.1	486.2	14.0	9.6	3.8	19.0	9.6	5.6	34.3	52.1
1975	279.1	332.3	−53.2	544.1	6.0	23.4	11.9	21.8	11.4	5.7	35.7	60.4
1976	298.1	371.8	−73.7	631.9	6.8	11.9	16.1	21.9	12.0	5.3	37.2	69.6
1976, transition quarter	81.2	96.0	−14.7	646.4	(X)	(X)	(X)	21.4	11.6	5.0	36.0	19.4
1977	355.6	409.2	−53.6	709.1	19.3	10.1	12.2	21.1	11.5	5.0	36.6	80.7
1978	399.6	458.7	−59.2	780.4	12.4	12.1	10.1	21.1	11.1	4.8	35.9	89.7
1979	463.3	503.5	−40.2	833.8	16.0	9.8	6.8	20.5	10.9	4.7	34.0	100.0
1980	517.1	590.9	−73.8	914.3	11.6	17.4	9.7	22.2	11.7	5.0	34.3	114.3
1981	599.3	678.2	−78.9	1,003.9	15.9	14.8	9.8	22.7	12.1	5.3	33.6	135.2
1982	617.8	745.7	−127.9	1,147.0	3.1	10.0	14.3	23.7	12.4	5.9	36.5	151.4
1983	600.6	808.3	−207.8	1,381.9	−2.8	8.4	20.5	24.3	12.8	6.3	41.6	147.1
1984	666.5	851.8	−185.3	1,576.7	11.0	5.4	14.1	23.1	11.7	6.2	42.7	165.8
1985	734.1	946.3	−212.3	1,827.5	10.1	11.1	15.9	24.0	12.0	6.4	46.4	176.8
1986	769.1	990.3	−221.2	2,130.0	4.8	4.6	16.6	23.6	11.5	6.5	50.8	183.5
1987	854.1	1,004.6	−150.4	2,355.3	11.1	1.4	10.6	22.8	11.4	6.4	53.4	193.8
1988	909.2	1,055.9	−146.7	2,581.6	6.5	5.1	9.6	22.4	11.3	6.1	54.9	203.1

(X) Not applicable.
(Z) Less than $50 million.
[1] Includes off-budget receipts, outlays, and interfund transactions.
[2] End of fiscal year.
[3] Gross national product as of fiscal year.
Source: U.S. Office of Management and Budget, *Historical Tables, Budget of the United States Government, 1987.*

Chapter Nine
POWER BROKERS

THE BUSINESS OF POWER

In 1868, when railroader speculator Jay Gould was in the middle of his battle with shipping magnate Cornelius Vanderbilt for control of the Erie Railroad, he and his partners decided that they needed help from the New York state legislature. So Gould packed his suitcases, carefully filling one of them with $500,000 in cash, and sneaked up to Albany, New York. There he set up his lobbying headquarters in a luxury hotel suite and began passing money to legislators in exchange for their support of a bill that would prevent Vanderbilt from taking over the railroad. A million dollars later, Gould won out.

"In a Republican district, I was a Republican," he told an investigating committee when asked to explain his tactics and his actions; "in a Democratic district, I was a Democrat; in a doubtful district I was doubtful; but I was always for Erie [the railroad he wanted to control]."

Today, doing business with government is a lot more complicated. Gould's pliant legislators have been replaced with vast bureaucracies and strict laws governing how politicians earn their money. But even though the rules have changed, the stakes haven't. Government regulators and legislators routinely make decisions that can save or ruin entire industries. In recent years, some industries, such as the chemical and auto industries, have seen a drastic growth in environmental regulations that have added billions to the cost of doing business. Other industries, such as the railroads and airlines, which grew fat under the protection of government regulations, have seen their industries deregulated, forcing them to deal with increased competition and lower rates.

As a result, the growth of big government in the last fifty years has created another big business—the business of influencing political decisions. About $1.8 billion is spent every year on party politics and the electoral process. There are somewhere between 2,000 and 5,000 political consulting firms that earn about $100 million a year. Political advertising on television alone cost $160 million in 1986, up from $90 million in 1980, and it could hit $350 million in 1988. In 1984, Ronald Reagan spent $66.6 million to be reelected president; his opponent, Walter Mondale, spent even more, $67.4 million, to be clobbered. Candidates for the U.S. Senate in 1986 spent $211.1 million, with the average winner spending $3.1 million. Candidates for the House spent $200 million, with the average winner paying $340,000 to convince voters he or she was the best person for the job. In 1987 there were 4,567 political action committees (PACs). They provided 28% of all the campaign financing for House and Senate seats and an even larger share of the campaign contributions received by winners. PACs provided 41.9% of the $149 million spent by winners in races for House of Representative seats and 27% of the $101.5 million spent by winning Senators.

Once elected, politicians are hounded by a small army of lobbyists. In Washington, D.C., alone, there are more than 20,000 people employed as lobbyists, making lobbying the fourth-largest business in the nation's capital, after government, printing, and tourism. In 1986, over $60.8 million was spent by registered lobbyists, up 25% from 1985 and 45% from 1984. There are over 800 trade associations that keep headquarters in the city and there are innumerable public-relations people working around the clock to make certain the press prints nice stories about their particular causes or special interests. Even the government itself employs 19,000 PR people.

But these figures don't quite describe the size of the enterprise that is solely devoted to manipulating and influencing politics. There are the think tanks, ranging from such well-known policy setters as the American Enterprise Institute to lesser-known but influential institutes such as Georgetown University's Center for Strategic and International Studies. And don't forget the lawyers (Washington has one lawyer for every 40 people, the most anywhere), the political consultants, the direct mailers (some political junk mailers have computerized lists of over 20 million people), the academics, and the large political contributors who lobby, mold opinions, set the tone of political campaigns, and help set policy. This, of course, only covers the political world of the nation's capital, Washington, D.C. Out in the hinterlands, lining the corridors of statehouses, city halls, and county courthouses, there is another army of influence peddlers, too vast to be enumerated.

THE POWERHOUSES: THE MOST POWERFUL INSTITUTIONS IN AMERICA

In a city governed by vast, impersonal bureaucracies, it's not surprising that some of the most important centers of political power in Washington are institutions, not individuals. Regulatory agencies control how businesses do business; international banks like the World Bank and the International Monetary Fund help determine the economic health of the entire world. At home, the Federal Reserve uses its control of the money supply to manipulate the economy. Prestigious institutions like the Council on Foreign Relations issue policy statements that affect the international business climate; large foundations and organizations like the American Enterprise Institute produce studies that become the basis of economic policy. Think tanks prove the old adage that knowledge is power. Other groups like the Business Roundtable protect the power of business in Congress, lobbying for legislation or funding grass-roots campaigns to influence the public. Finally, private clubs provide a place where business leaders and power brokers can meet to exchange ideas, get to know each other, and establish contacts that will later be useful in setting policy. What follows is a list of institutions that help mold the direction of the economy, creating or destroying profits.

The Regulators

The federal government employs 118,000 permanent full-time workers in its 54 regulatory agencies. The regulatory agencies, which are perhaps the most powerful institutions in the American economy, control virtually every aspect of American business, from how products are labeled to how factories are built. The budgets of federal regulatory agencies soared from $1.6 billion in 1970 to $10.5 billion in 1988. Government regulation was costing business $120 billion by the early 1980s.

Estimates of the cost of government paperwork vary but all of them are alarming. The Commission on Federal Paperwork found that in 1977 the cost of filling out a mountain of federal paperwork was $25 billion to $32 billion for private industry. In 1986 dollars, that estimate would mean private industry spent $52.3 billion to $67 billion to fill out paperwork, state and local governments spent $10.5 billion to $18.8 billion, individuals other than farmers spent $18.2 billion, and farmers spent $732.4 million. Overall, the cost of government paperwork amounted to about $1,046 for each American.

In 1987, the Office of Management and Budget estimated that the American public spent 1.7 billion hours filling out government forms. Depending on how one values the time spent on filing out government forms, the total costs could range from $17 billion to $34 billion and more.

And the cost of regulation is growing. Congress is already moving away from deregulation and passing new laws imposing huge costs. For example, the badly named Tax Reform Act of 1986 will increase the amount of time the American people have to spend filling out government forms by 105 million hours. In the area of environmental regulation, new regulations on the Superfund for toxic waste cleanup will add 10 million hours of new paperwork. Even though the Reagan administration has cut agency budgets and cracked down on some of the most costly regulations, few long-term changes have been made. Look for the regulators to continue their relentless rise to power in 1988 under either a Republican or Democratic administration. (See the chapter "Regulation and Deregulation.")

The Bankers

Several international and national agencies help set the course of the world's economy. Falling on the shoulders of the World Bank and International Monetary Fund are the problems of third-world economic development, the third-world debt crisis, balances of payments that threaten the solvency of many countries, and regulation of currencies. How these problems are dealt with determines the solvency of major banks as well as the course of third-world development. Closer to home, the Federal Reserve, with its regulatory power over the banks and its ability to control the money supply, exerts tremendous power over the economy. (See profiles of the IMF and Federal Reserve, pages 90 and 94.)

The Judges

A forty-year surge in judicial activism may have been temporarily tempered by Reagan's widespread appointments to the federal bench. But during that period the judiciary has played an important rule in rewriting the nation's laws, often in ways that have cost business money: in employment law, judges have all but dispensed with the long-held doctrine of employment at will (which allows companies to hire and fire any nonunion employee for any reason, as long as the firing is not based on discrimination); in tort law, defendants with only 5% share of blame can be required to pay 100% of damages; in product liability, courts have ruled against companies that had only an indirect responsibility for a problem, in contrast to the traditional theory that requires the plaintiff to prove direct "causation"; in real estate law, landlords are even being held responsible for burglars entering buildings.

In the next few years some of this activism should change. By the fall of 1986, Reagan had appointed 288 federal judges, about 39% of the total, and he is expected to have appointed over half by the time he retires. With the opportunity for three Reagan appointees on the Supreme Court, the judiciary should start hewing to the President's philosophy of judicial restraint. (See the "Law" section.)

The Foundations

There are 5,148 foundations in the U.S. that each have over $1 million in assets or distribute $100,000 a year in grants. In total, these foundations control $89.9 billion in assets, a large part of which is used for studies that play an important role in determining public policy. When the Ford Foundation (the country's largest foundation with assets of $4.8 billion) or the Rockefeller Foundation (the seventh-largest foundation) releases one of the studies it's commissioned, policymakers listen.

The Brookings Institution

The Brookings Institution became the model for the modern policy-setting think tank when it was founded in 1916, under the name of the Institute for Government Research. In its early days the institution, which assumed its current name in 1927, was a haven of conservative ideas, opposing the New Deal, but the group moved to the left in the 1950s, establishing its reputation as the center of liberal policy ideas. Brookings Institution studies were the basis of most of the Great Society programs of the 1960s, the tax-reform efforts of the 1960s and 1970s, as well as the Kennedy Administration's wage and price controls. After Nixon's 1968 election, it became a center for former Kennedy- and Johnson-administration intellectuals, and, in the 1970s, a Brookings study helped kill the B-1 bomber. Since 1980, however, the Institution has chafed at efforts to pigeonhole it as an elite liberal group. Brookings Institution studies since the late 1970s have been calling for budget cutting and timely tax cuts (that means tax cuts that aren't going to cause inflation). Though the Institution is out of favor in the current Republican administration, the next generation of Democratic leaders will certainly call on Brookings scholars to help set policy. In 1986 it had a budget of $14.7 million.

The Council on Foreign Relations

The most prestigious of all foreign-policy think tanks is without a doubt the Council on Foreign Relations (CFR). It has been helping politicians set foreign policy and creating the climate for international business since it was founded in 1921 with grants from the Rockefeller and Carnegie Foundations. A list of ideas proposed by the CFR would read like a history of American foreign policy: it developed the Kellogg-Briand Pact of the 1920s; opposed Japanese expansion in the 1930s; put forward large parts of the U.N. charter; published in its journal the writings of State Department official George F. Kennan in which he first put forward the idea of containing Soviet expansion; devised the Marshall Plan; supported NATO; originally supported the Vietnam war and later worked out parts of the U.S. negotiating positions; pushed Carter's human rights campaign; and since 1979 has been tilting to the right, supporting a tougher stance against the Soviets.

Though many conservatives have complained about CFR's supposed "liberal" orientation, forcing George Bush to resign from the Council and its sister organization the Trilateral Commission during the 1980 campaign, CFR is very well represented in the Reagan administration. CFR members have included Reagan's first Secretary of State, Alexander Haig; Defense Secretary Caspar Weinberger; former Treasury Secretary and chief of staff Donald Regan; and former CIA Director William Casey.

The Committee on the Present Danger

The Committee on the Present Danger (CPD) is occasionally portrayed as an upstart, attempting to rival the CFR's clout in setting foreign policy. In fact, the CPD is an elite establishment group that recruited such Cold War liberals and neoconservatives as Eugene Rostow, Dean Rusk, and

Lane Kirkland as well as conservative Nixon appointees David Packard and Richard Allen when it was founded in 1976. All were strong supporters of the Vietnam War who felt that, as the 1970s progressed, the U.S. was losing the will to oppose Soviet expansionism. Carter didn't buy their argument for a tough stance against the Soviets but, in 1980, Reagan, a CPD member himself, put leading members of the group in power, appointing 32 of them, including Richard Allen as national security adviser, Jeane Kirkpatrick as UN ambassador, William Casey as CIA director, and CPD chairman Eugene Rostow as the head of the Arms Control and Disarmament Agency. Their get-tough-with-the-Soviets philosophy has pushed forward a huge defense buildup and, contrary to those who imagine that ideas have little impact on business, helped revive a flagging arms industry.

The American Enterprise Institute for Public Policy Research

The Brookings Institution of the right, the American Enterprise Institute for Public Policy Research (AEI), has become the most influential conservative think tank in the 1980s, having already established itself as a prestigious peddler of free-market ideals, respected among conservative and liberal opinion makers. Founded in 1943, the AEI at first closely followed the line of the corporations that backed it and, as a result, gained little academic respect or political clout. It was revitalized by Bill Baroody, whose father had previously headed the group. In 1976, like the Brookings Institution, which provided places for out-of-favor Democratic Party ideologues, the AEI provided haven for more than 20 members of the Ford administration. This greatly increased its prestige, and in 1980, when the Republicans returned to power, it quickly became one of the most important policy organs in the Reagan administration. More than 20 fellows and scholars left the AEI to join the Reagan administration, including UN ambassador Jeane Kirkpatrick; Arthur Burns, ambassador to West Germany; Federal Trade Commission head James Miller III; and Council of Economic Advisers chairman Murray Weidenbaum. However, success has caused problems at the AEI. The loss of prominent scholars to the Reagan administration hurt the AEI budget, forcing cutbacks. Some donors also grew dissatisfied with Baroody's policy of moving the institute toward the political center. In 1986 Baroody was forced out and Willard C. Butcher, chairman of Chase Manhattan, became the new part-time chairman. The new president, Christopher C. DeMuth, says the institute was "weeks away from Chapter 11." He cut $1.5 million out of the $10 million budget and trimmed staff. Former UN ambassador Jeane Kirkpatrick was brought in as one of three new research directors to attract new talent and grant money. With 650 corporate donors, the AEI has provided and will continue to provide ideas for Reagan's attempts to curb federal regulations, cut social welfare, and increase defense spending. Despite the AEI's money problems, its 1986 budget of $12.4 million was way up from its budget of only $1 million in the early 1970s.

The Heritage Foundation

The AEI's rival on the right for funds is the Heritage Foundation. Founded in 1973 with a quarter-million-dollar grant from right-wing brewer Joseph Coors, the Heritage Foundation had a 1986 budget of $11.5 million. Sometimes the group is described as an unofficial government agency because of its close ties to the Reagan administration. A 3,000-page report issued by the foundation in 1980 became a Reagan administration wish list. Among its proposals were $60 billion cuts in domestic spending and a $53 billion dollar defense-spending hike by 1982; abolishing the Energy Department; scaling back the powers of the Environmental Protection Agency; and free-enterprise zones. Subsequent reports have had the same clout, though getting its ideas past Congress has proved to be more difficult.

The Business Roundtable

Made up of the chief executive officers of the nation's 200 largest corporations who each pay up to $50,000 to join, the Business Roundtable was founded in 1972. It achieved its greatest successes in the 1970s during the Carter administration. Carter, who had little contact with the business community before taking office, worked closely with the Business Roundtable in order to establish a closer relationship with major corporations. This helped produce such results as halting labor-law "reform," building congressional support for deregulation, delaying antitrust legislation, diluting one of the Clean Air Acts, and defeating a proposed Consumer Protection Agency. Business also won major tax breaks and increased the number of business deductions by tenfold during the 1970s, according to Senator Bill Bradley of New Jersey, a leading proponent of "tax reform." One chat between Carter and Irving Shapiro, chairman of the Roundtable and of du Pont, convinced the president that his staff's proposals for antitrust legislation were all wrong.

With the advent of the Reagan administration, the Roundtable took the unusual step of issuing an unqualified statement of support for his program—in the past the organization had always worked on policy issue by issue. The organization continues to push for deregulation, budget cuts, and other ideas close to the president's heart, but relations between the Roundtable and the administration have not been as cordial as they were under Carter. Some members of the Business Roundtable have advocated more trade protection and a weaker dollar. And while the Roundtable supported the final "tax reform" bill, it was not happy with the president's idea of doing away with the investment tax credit or the fact that "reform" meant increasing business taxes by about $100 billion. The Roundtable has also declined in power—as have other mainstream business organizations such as the National Association of Manufacturers and the Chamber of Commerce—because heavy industry is less economically powerful. Like other major business organizations it played a relatively minor role in the development of the most important business legislation of the 1980s—the Tax Reform Act of 1986.

THE LOBBYISTS

Until recently there was a well-defined business establishment in Washington. When the National Association of Manufacturers, the Council on Economic Development, the Business Council, or the Business Roundtable spoke up on issues, most members of Congress knew that they were listening to the voice of American business. They might disagree with these organizations, but no one doubted their power.

Since 1980, however, changing political winds, the retirement of the old political power brokers, and the emergence of a new breed of business leaders has begun to change how business protects its interests in Washington.

The change began in the late 1970s and early 1980s when prominent business power brokers like David Rockefeller (chairman of Chase Manhattan and of the Council on Foreign Relations), Irving Shapiro (chairman of du Pont and founder of the Business Roundtable), Reginald Jones (head of General Electric), John deButts (head of AT&T), Thomas Murphy (head of General Motors), and Henry Ford II (head of the Ford Motor Company) retired from their positions. Although these men never achieved the celebrity status that Ted Turner, Steven Jobs, or Lee Iacocca obtained, they were far more powerful in Congress. They were the business leaders who pioneered a period of postwar cooperation between business and government, and their retirement left a power vacuum.

At the same time, long-term political and economic changes hurt the political and economic power of the old business establishment. As manufacturing and oil struggled through hard times, new entrepreneurs who were creating high-tech industries or executives who were revitalizing decaying manufacturing companies became more powerful. Many of these business leaders were from the West or the Sunbelt and had been long-time Reagan supporters. They opposed the kind of government intervention that the old guard had accepted. But unlike their predecessors, none of the new entrepreneurs or executives had the political experience of a David Rockefeller or an Irving Shapiro. As a result, the political power of business became more diffuse and decentralized at a time, ironically, when some business leaders were becoming household names and media celebrities.

Perhaps for that reason, professional lobbyists are becoming even more important in the power politics of the nation's capital. The number of lobbyists registered with the Secretary of the Senate increased from 5,662 in 1981 to 20,400 in 1986. In 1986, over $60.8 million was spent by registered lobbyists, up 25% from 1985, 45% from 1984, and more than double the amount spent on lobbying in 1975. But a more accurate figure of how much is spent on influencing politicians and government officials might be as high as $1.5 billion, including campaign contributions.

But numbers alone don't tell the power of Washington's lobbyists. As noted above, many of them are former government appointees or elected officials who have access to their former colleagues. As a result, lobbyists are playing an increasingly powerful role in the legislative process. Major

Table 48   The Biggest-spending Lobbyists, 1986

1. Citizens for Sensible Control of Acid Rain	$3,028,235
2. National Committee to Preserve Social Security and Medicare	3,011,412
3. Common Cause	2,074,807
4. National Association of Letter Carriers of the United States of America	1,633,716
5. Fiber, Fabric and Apparel Coalition for Trade	1,482,349
6. Committee to Protect the Family	1,469,866
7. American Council of Life Insurance	1,119,881
8. Sierra Club	1,059,721
9. Handgun Control, Inc.	1,002,522
10. Gun Owners of America	981,500
11. American Petroleum Institute	917,515
12. National Rifle Association of America	904,895
13. Communications Management, Inc. (for Philip Morris)	883,842
14. Association for a Better New York	785,574
15. Free the Eagle	783,234
Total spent by registered lobbyists	60,689,183

Source: Associated Press.

legislation, including the Chrysler bailout bill, has been written in lobbyists' offices. Lobbyists have played a major role in getting committee assignments and subcommittee chairmanships for friendly members of Congress. Increasingly, lobbyists control political action committees or act as political consultants, making members of Congress more beholden to them. And, as in everything else that gets done in Washington, power and money take precedence over ideology. Many of Reagan's former employees worked hard for companies that wanted to defeat his tax plan or foreign governments that disagree with their former boss's trade policies.

No list of Washington power brokers and lobbyists could touch on all the power brokers for hire, but here are a few of the biggest names and most important special-interest groups.

Democrats for Hire

Many former Washington politicians or bureaucrats stick around the capital city long after the voters have turned them out of office, working as lobbyists or setting policy at various think tanks. Its been estimated that over 200 former members of Congress have stayed in the city as lobbyists to try to get special favors from their former colleagues. And just because a party has been turned out of the White House, it doesn't mean it's lost a place in the business of power.

Take the Democrats. In the late 1960s the Brookings Institution became a nest of former Johnson- and Kennedy-administration officials who were waiting around for the next Democratic president. In 1980 some liberal senators (like Frank Church, Birch Bayh, and John Culver) ousted by the recent turn to the right stayed on in Washington as lawyers. Gaylord Nelson, author of much of the nation's major environmental-protection legislation, stayed on as chairman of the Wilderness Society, lobbying for conservation; George McGovern set up Americans for Common Sense, an anti–New Right group that gave $1 million to Democratic candidates in 1982. In 1984, key figures in the Mondale campaign stayed on in Washington to collect large salaries as lobbyists. Robert Beckel, Mondale's campaign manager, and Timothy Finchem, Mondale's finance director, set up their own firm, National Strategies. As an illustration of how the business of power cuts across ideological lines, Beckel and Finchem worked in 1986 on a $700,000 lobbying campaign with two long-time political opponents from the Reagan campaign who are now lobbyists—James Lake and Roger Stone. Their purpose is to stop a tax bill that would end the tax-exempt status of state and municipal bonds. Both describe themselves as political liberals, but their other clients include a toxic-waste disposal company and insurance companies that want to limit their liabilities by means of toxic-waste legislation before Congress.

Other top Democrats with lots of clout in Washington include the former Democratic National Committee chairman, Robert Strauss. His law firm, Akin, Gump, Strauss, Hauer & Feld, is one of the city's most important lobbying groups.

Another long-time Democratic power broker who has done well as one of Washington's lawyer-lobbyists is Joseph Califano. After working in the Kennedy and Johnson administrations, where he helped create the Transportation Department and steered most of the Great Society legislation through Congress, Califano became Carter's Secretary of Health, Education, and Welfare. In between he worked as ranking partner and manager of Williams, Connolly and Califano. His long-time knowledge of the ins and outs of the federal bureaucracies, many of which he helped create, has made him one of Washington's most prestigious and sought-after lawyers.

Republicans for Hire

For most of the 1980s, the hottest former government officials cashing in on their political connections have been former Reagan appointees. By applying their former boss's free-market philosophies to the marketplace of political power, several have done quite well. Former governmental or campaign aides with close ties to President Reagan who have earned large fees representing dozens of blue-chip domestic and foreign clients include Richard V. Allen, former national security adviser, who was turned out of office after "forgetting" to report a gift from Japanese journalists; former White House chief of staff Michael Deaver, who was convicted of perjury in connection with his lobbying activities; Joseph Canzeri, who was Mr. Deaver's assistant; Lyn Nofziger, who was indicted for his lobbying on behalf of the defense contractor Wedtech; Edward J. Rollins, former assistant for political affairs; Kenneth Duberstein, White House deputy chief of staff; and Lee Atwater, former White House aide. Deaver, who has been described as like a son to the president, used his clout to get $2,475,000 worth of contracts with foreign governments, but his indictment has virtually destroyed his business. Several other aides formerly closely involved with trade policy have also received six-figure fees from foreign governments.

The Gun Lobby

Led by the National Rifle Association ($904,895 in lobbying expenses in 1986), the Gun Owners of America (now Gun Owners Incorporated; $981,500) and the Citizens Committee for the Right to Keep and Bear Arms ($417,625) the gun lobby leads the fight against handgun restrictions. Following increased street crime and Martin Luther King's assassination in the 1960s, the NRA was unable to stop some handgun legislation, but has beaten back any further attempts to increase restrictions. Ironically enough, the NRA has received strong support from President Reagan, who himself was the victim of handgun violence. In 1986, it managed to stop handgun restrictions and passed legislation, over the objections of police groups around the country, to ease restrictions on gun sales.

The Oil Lobby

In the fight to protect the sacred oil depletion allowance the oil lobby has for decades been an unassailable power on Capitol Hill. In Washington the oil lobby maintains several organizations, the largest of which, the American Petroleum Institute, has a staff of 350 people and an annual budget of $50 million. It spent $917,515 in 1986 as a registered lobbying group. Texas oil money has played a major role in financing friendly political candidates, especially Democrats, helping, for example, to promote Lyndon Johnson into the White House and spending over $800,000 a year in political contributions by the middle 1970s. Thanks to this clout, the oil depletion allowance saved the oil industry about $5 billion a year until Congress ended it in the mid-1970s for major oil companies. Independent oil companies were, however, still allowed to use it and saved $1.5 billion through this device in 1985, according to the Treasury Department. More recently, the industry has lobbied for an oil import tax that would raise the price of oil and improve the industry's slumping profits.

The Defense Lobby

Led by McDonnell Douglas ($7.7 billion in defense contracts), Rockwell International ($6.2 billion), General Dynamics ($6 billion), Lockheed ($5 billion), Boeing ($4.6 billion), General Electric ($4.5 billion), Raytheon ($3.1 billion), and other top contractors, the defense lobby is undoubtedly the most powerful in Congress, where a coalition of Southern Democrats and Republicans has protected it from every onslaught in the last 40 years. But a widening deficit threatens the military buildup and defense contractors' biggest hope for the future is Star Wars, which the defense lobby will bring out its big guns to protect.

The Environmental Lobby

Led by such groups as the Sierra Club (the nation's eighth-largest registered lobbying group in 1986 with spending of $1,059,721), various environmental and conservationist groups continue to push for new environmental legislation. Their major victories came in the 1970s, when they pushed through the legislation that created the Environmental Protection Agency and several major bills regulating the environment, toxic substances, and the workplace. But even in the 1980s their political clout has defeated Reagan-backed initiatives to curb increased regulation. In recent years the budget of the EPA has once again resumed its inexorable growth.

The Union Lobby

Gone are the days when organized labor could count on the undivided support of major Democratic-party politicians and at least some influence on moderate Northeastern Republicans. Despite the fact that union PACs spent $24.8 million in 1983 and 1984 for presidential, congressional, state, and local races, their most heavily funded candidate, Walter Mondale, never had a chance and was in fact hurt by his close identification with organized labor. Still, union PACs remain among the biggest-spending campaign contributors. Striving to revive the political fortunes of organized labor is Robert M. McGlotten, chief lobbyist of the AFL-CIO. He has seven staff members and nominal command over the more than 60 labor lobbyists attached to the affiliates of the AFL-CIO. With such powerful political fundraisers as the United Auto Workers PAC (spent $2.1 million in 1983–1984) and the National Education Association PAC (another $2.1 million in 1983–1984), unions will provide massive support for Democratic Party candidates in 1988.

PACS

One of the most controversial and important changes in the business of power has been the development of PACs—political action committees. In 1987 there were 4,567 PACs. They provided 28% of all the campaign financing for House and Senate seats and an even larger share of the campaign contributions received by winners. PACs provided 41.9% of the $149 million spent by winners in races for House of Representative seats, and 27% of the $101.5 million spent by winning Senators. Overall, PACs spent at least $126 million in House and Senate races in 1986, up from only $55.2 million in the 1979–1980 election campaign.

The growth of PACs has helped fuel a trend toward more expensive campaigns. In 1984, Ronald Reagan spent $66.6 million to be reelected president; his opponent, Walter Mondale, spent even more, $67.4 million, to be defeated. Candidates for the U.S. Senate in 1986 spent $211.1 million, with the average winner spending $3.1 million, five times more than was spent in 1976. Candidates for the House spent $200 million, with the average winner paying $340,000 to convince voters he or she was the best person for the job. That was four times more than a decade earlier.

The growth of political action committees, so attacked these days by campaign-law reformers, was ironically a result of campaign reform. In 1971 Congress passed the first campaign reform law since the 1920s; organized labor, which invented political action committees, pushed through an exemption for its PACs. Following Watergate, when Congress limited individual contributions, PACs became a major way for high rollers to continue to contribute large sums of money.

The result was something that organized labor and campaign reformers have complained about ever since: the growth of corporate political action committees. Corporate PACs are increasing at a far faster rate than union PACs or PACs affiliated with trade and health organizations. From 1974 through the end of 1984, the number of business PACs grew from 89 to 1,682, while union PACs went from 318 to 698. Spending has also been skyrocketing, with funding for corporate PACs growing to $43.3 million in 1982, up from $5.8 million in 1976, much faster than funding for union PACs, which increased to $34.8 million, up from $17.5 million. As these figures suggest, however, business has only been catching up with organized labor's long-time domination of the PAC business. After all, the CIO founded the first modern PAC in 1943, the Congress of Industrial Organizations' Political Action Committee.

Chapter Ten
REGULATION AND DEREGULATION: CHANGING THE RULES

HIGHLIGHTS AND TRENDS

• Government regulation has grown dramatically. The *Federal Register,* which publishes all proposed and final regulations, skyrocketed from 9,562 pages in 1960 to 87,012 pages in 1980, the size of a small encyclopedia. Since then a move towards deregulation has cut it 45%, to 47,418 pages.

• Federal departments and agencies send out more than 9,800 different types of forms and receive 556 million responses each year.

• In the late 1960s and 1970s, regulatory agencies grew faster than during the New Deal. Despite a trend toward deregulation in the 1980s, there are now 118,000 permanent full-time employees in the 54 federal government regulatory agencies. Those agencies will spend $10.5 billion in 1988 up from $1.6 billion in 1970.

• Government regulations cost business $120 billion a year by the early 1980s, according to the Reagan administration.

• Congress deregulated certain industries—such as telecommunications, transportation, and banking—in the late 1970s and early 1980s.

• Deregulation creates new businesses. A 1987 study by the Small Business Administration found that the number of new businesses in the deregulated industries of financial services and transportation grew 12.3%. By contrast, the number of new businesses in the whole economy increased 8.2%. Most of the new businesses in deregulated industries were small entrepreneurial firms, according to the Small Business Administration, and most of the new jobs were in such firms. Small businesses with fewer than 20 employees created 495,246 jobs in deregulated industries, 68% of all the jobs created in those industries.

• Deregulation produces new jobs. Almost one fourth, or 24.1%, of the 12 million new jobs created in the U.S. between 1976 and 1982 were in deregulated industries. Another study found that one fifth of all new jobs between 1980 and 1984 were created in deregulated industries.

• Deregulation allows American businesses to move faster in the development of new goods and services. In transportation and communications, deregulation permitted more rapid marketing of innovative products and services such as satellite communications networks, cellular phones, and innovative truck redesigns.

• And deregulation faces a tough future. Most legislation creating deregulation was passed in the late 1970s and early 1980s. President Reagan has not been able to continue that momentum in Congress. Although his appointees to regulatory agencies have loosened government control over the economy, he will probably not leave behind a legislative mandate for further deregulation. As a result, it will be easier for future administrations to reverse the policies of his appointees and move towards further regulation.

• Government paperwork already imposes huge costs on the economy. Estimates of the cost of government paperwork vary but all of them are alarming. The Commission on Federal Paperwork found that in 1977 the cost of filling out the mountain of federal paperwork was $25 billion to $32 billion for private industry. In 1986 dollars that estimate would mean that private industry spent $52.3 billion to $67 billion to fill out paperwork, state and local governments spent $10.5 billion to $18.8 billion, individuals other than farmers spent $18.2 billion, and farmers spent $732.4 million. Overall, the cost of government paperwork amounted to about $1,046 for each American. In 1987, the Office of Management and Budget estimated that the American public spent 1.7 billion hours filling out government forms. Depending on how one values the time spent on filling out government forms, the total costs could range from $17 billion to $34 billion and more.

• The regulatory burden caused by several recent laws indicates that the economy would be hurt by the failure of deregulation. For example, the badly named Tax Reform Act of 1986 will increase the amount of time the American people have to spend filling out government forms by 105 million hours. In the area of environmental regulation, new regulations on the Superfund for toxic waste cleanup will add 10 million hours of new paperwork.

REGULATING THE REGULATORS

Government is not only big business, it also has a big impact on how business can be done. Today, government is involved in nearly everything business does. Government regulations determine how our homes are built, how we do our jobs, the ingredients that go into the food we eat, how our products are transported to market, how our banks take care of our money, what kind of television we watch, the drugs we take, and even the number of maggots allowed in canned mushrooms. (By government decree, there can be no more than 20 maggots in 100 grams of canned mushrooms.)

There is little doubt that many of these regulations improve our health and safety by making sure companies sell safe products, avoid environmental pollution, and properly advertise their services. But there is also little doubt that regulations cost money. And often they cost more money than they're worth.

The Costs of Regulation

In the late 1970s, government regulators increased their control over the economy by tightening regulatory standards. But these new standards often imposed high costs on business for what may have been only relatively minor benefits. For instance, it cost the pulp and paper industry about $3 billion in the 1970s to comply with federal orders to reduce water pollution by 95%. Then, the Environmental Protection Agency proposed new standards that would cost the industry another $4.8 billion and only achieve a 3% improvement in water quality.

During the 1960s and 1970s, government regulations grew dramatically. The *Federal Register,* which publishes all proposed and final regulations, skyrocketed from 9,562 pages in 1960 to 87,012 pages in 1980, the size of a small encyclopedia. Since then a move towards deregulation has cut it 45%, to 47,418 pages.

Government paperwork alone imposes huge costs on the economy. One survey found that federal departments and agencies send out more than 9,800 different types of forms and receive 556 million responses each year. Estimates of the cost of filling out this mountain of paperwork vary but all of them are alarming.

The Commission on Federal Paperwork found that in 1977 the cost of filling out the mountain of federal paperwork was $25 billion to $32 billion for private industry. In 1986 dollars, that estimate would mean that private industry spent $52.3 billion to $67 billion to fill out paperwork, state and local governments spent $10.5 billion to $18.8 billion, individuals other than farmers spent $18.2 billion, and farmers spent $732.4 million. Overall, the cost of government paperwork amounted to about $1,046 for each American. In 1987, the Office of Management and Budget estimated that the American public spent 1.7 billion hours filling out government forms. Depending on how one values the time spent on filling out government forms, the total costs could range from $17 billion to $34 billion and more. About 61% of the 1.1 billion hours was imposed on businesses and other institutions, followed by 27% on individuals and households, 10% on state and local governments, and 2% on farms.

Many of these regulations do nothing more than waste the paper they're printed on. In Omaha, Nebraska, a barber who shaves the hairy chest of a customer can lose his license. In Brooklyn, New York, you can't let your pet go to sleep in the bathtub. In Garfield County, Montana, it's against the law to draw cartoons on window shades, even in your own home.

Other regulations and laws have more serious consequences. Taking a new drug from conception to market can take 10 years and cost $100 million. The paperwork required by the Food and Drug Administration can exceed 100,000 pages of documentation. A 1984 Supreme Court ruling noted that Monsanto spent $23.6 million to compile the health, safety, and environmental data required by the Environmental Protection Agency for its pesticide roundup.

One of the worst offenders is probably the Pentagon. Every day, the military signs 52,000 contracts—the Air Force alone entered into 5 million contracts in 1985. Military procurement remains one of the most complex systems known to man—which may explain why so many of our expensive weapons systems never work. Defense firms typically face over 44,000 specifications for a weapons system. The instruction book on procurement runs 32 volumes and takes up six feet of shelf space. One Pentagon study found that regulations accounted for one third of procurement costs.

As the budgets of federal regulators increased 50% just between 1974 and 1981, private industry became more concerned about the cost of government regulation. A number of studies undertaken in the late 1970s also pointed out the high costs of regulation.

The Business Roundtable Study

This study found that six federal agencies cost 48 major corporations in 20 industries a total of $2.6 billion. That amounted to over 15% of the after-tax income of those companies, 43% of the money they spent on research and development. Worse, about two thirds of these costs were operating, administration, and product costs that will occur year after year. The EPA accounted for $2 billion of the costs, and most of the cost ($2.3 billion) fell on the manufacturing companies, especially primary metals companies facing hard times. For consumers, the costs of regulation increased prices by 1.1% in a period when the economy was buffeted by high inflation and low-priced foreign goods. Naturally, the companies argued most of these costs were wasteful.

Murray L. Weidenbaum's Study

"Government regulation of business is one of the growth areas of the economy," economist Weidenbaum tartly observes. His controversial 1978 study of regulatory costs for the Subcommittee on Economic Growth and Stabilization of Congress's Joint Economic Committee is probably the most influential look at regulatory costs made in the last decade. He found that business spent about $65.5 billion in 1976, or about $307 for every man, woman, and child, to comply with government regulations. The "direct and indirect compliance costs of Federal regulation . . . [are] about twenty times the administrative costs of $3 billion for regulatory agencies," Weidenbaum wrote more recently. In 1976, Weidenbaum found, paperwork alone cost businesses $18 billion; regulations requiring the inclusion of catalytic converters in cars to reduce air pollution added $666 to the cost of each car and increased fuel consumption by $3 billion (at a time when the economy was hurt by foreign cars and a fuel crisis); a myriad of zoning, land-use, building-code, and other government regulations on housing boosted the costs of new houses by $2,000 apiece (at a time when young couples were finding it increasingly difficult to afford the price of a home); regulations forced some business to close facilities and lay off workers (at a time when unemployment was edging toward new heights); and government equipment regulations forced companies to spend $10 billion on capital (at a time when this capital investment could have been used to boost declining productivity).

More recently, Weidenbaum, while serving as Reagan's Chairman of the Council of Economic Advisers, estimated that if regulatory agencies impose costs of about 20 times their budgets (as they did in the 1970s) then government regulation was costing business $120 billion by the 1980s, with the cost of filling out the mountain of federal paperwork costing business over $25 billion.

Because of this expense, President Reagan issued a 1981 executive order mandating that regulatory agencies institute a cost-benefit analysis of any new regulation: "The Federal Government should not regulate unless there is adequate information concerning the need for and the consequences of proposed regulatory action. . . . The Federal Government should be sure that the benefits of a given regulatory action exceed the costs."

Armed with Weidenbaum's influential study, politicians and government officials pushed for less regulation. In the late 1970s, a Democratic Congress under President Carter passed landmark legislation deregulating several key areas of the economy, including transportation, telecommunications, and banking. Then President Reagan began a palace revolution. Many of his appointees had spent years criticizing the very regulations that they were now supposed to enforce. In some cases whole agencies, such as the Civilian Aeronautics Board, were deregulated out of existence. In other cases the excesses of appointees such as James Watt in the Interior Department and Rita Lavelle in the Environmental Protection Agency backfired, creating increased pressure for new regulations. But in every case, members of the Reagan administration were determined to reverse a century-long trend toward increased government regulation.

The Rise of the Regulators

The history of regulation is the history of economic crises—a history of problems that seemed to contemporary observers to have eluded the hidden regulator of Adam Smith's benevolent marketplace. In every case of increased government regulation during the past 150 years, the government has stepped in to protect the so-called "public interest" from alleged abuses—such as monopolies or "cutthroat" competition—that were thought to be disrupting the marketplace. The problem, which runs through the history of government regulation, is how industry and government ended up defining such a vague concept as "public interest." Quite often the result had little to offer the public.

The first attempts at government regulation were aimed at the railroads. Like later targets of government regulation, the railroad industry created problems that seemed to elude the mechanism of free-market competition. Because they were expensive to build, it made little sense to run two competing railroad lines through the same area, so railroad companies usually operated as monopolies, controlling the transportation costs of a certain region. As monopolies, 19th-century rail lines had the power to charge high rates or offer secret rebates to favored customers. These rebates gave some companies, such as Standard Oil, an edge in the market and allowed favored customers to destroy their rivals.

To control an industry that threatened to do away with a competitive marketplace, state legislatures began setting up railroad commissions. The Massachusetts Board of Railroad Commissioners, the first modern regulatory agency with a paid staff, was created in 1869. During the next few years, farmers and other customers who were angry about excessive rates forced the creation of other regulatory agencies. But the agencies soon ran into a problem that would bedevil attempts at regulation during the next century: either the agencies were hampered by court rulings that limited their powers or a lack of staff to carry out their mandates, or, more often, they quickly developed close relations with the very industries they were supposed to regulate.

Legislators recognized those problems, but strangely enough, the failure of one agency or set of regulations did not result in a reexamination of government regulation. Rather, legislators typically followed the most fundamental law of government intervention: if one regulation doesn't work, add another one, and if that doesn't work, create a new agency.

After it became obvious to everyone that the state railroad commissions had failed, Congress created the first federal regulatory agency in 1887—the Interstate Commerce Commission (ICC). Its mission was to set "just and reasonable rates" and to stop abuses such as rebates, pools, and rate discrimination.

The ICC was in principle a more promising way of regulating the railroads. In contrast to the crazy-quilt pattern of state commissions, each governing a section of a nationwide network, the ICC would be able to deal with the whole railroad system, not just a part of it. This obviously made more sense for both business—which wanted some form of regulation—and the public.

Unfortunately, the ICC soon became a prime example of how regulatory agencies thrive on an atmosphere of dull inefficiency. By the late 1890s the ICC's powers were gutted by Supreme Court rulings that reduced it to a mere information-gathering agency. Congress responded with a series of acts between 1903 and 1940 that were designed to give the agency some real power. These laws, however, satisfied no one. On one hand, industry continued attacking the agency for restricting its management prerogatives and for usurping the power to set rates. Consumers, on the other hand, attacked the agency for protecting the railroads at the expense of the public. Both, of course, were right. The commission set rates at levels that hurt the public and benefited industry. At the same time, its regulatory control over the industry prevented the railroads from vigorously responding to alternative forms of transportation such as trucking.

Given its track record, one would imagine that the ICC would have quickly disappeared. But instead of being disbanded as a bureaucratic failure, a menace to the consumer and industry, the ICC continued to grow and expand its powers. By the end of the Second World War it had control over not just railroads, but all interstate surface transportation—trains, trucks, buses, inland ships, freight forwarders, transportation brokers, and even a coal slurry line.

The fact that neither the public nor business liked the kind of regulation it was getting from the country's first regulatory agency should have set off alarm bells in Congress, but it didn't. The ICC became the model for a whole slew of regulatory agencies. The Federal Trade Commission was set up in 1914 to deal with the problem of growing monopolies that were threatening to do away with market competition. The Federal Power Commission (now called the Federal Energy Regulatory Commission) was created in 1920 to curb the monopolistic power of the utilities. The Radio Act of 1927 created the Federal Radio Commission; in 1934 the Federal Communications Commission replaced that agency and was also given the job of regulating the telecommunications industry, a job it inherited from the ICC.

The Great Depression set off another spurt in government regulation in the 1930s. As government agencies and Congress groped for ways to end the Great Depression and to eliminate some of the problems that had caused the stock-market crash, new regulatory agencies sprouted like weeds. Congress set up the Securities and Exchange Commission in 1934 to regulate Wall Street, the Federal Deposit Insurance Corporation in 1933, the Federal Home Loan Bank Board in 1934, the Farm Credit Administration in 1933 to regulate the cooperative Farm Credit System, the Civil Aeronautics Board in 1938, and the National Labor Relations Board in 1935 to regulate collective bargaining, to name a few. The power of the Federal Reserve System, which had been regulating the banking industry since 1913, was also increased.

Only a few agencies were set up in the two decades following the New Deal—the Atomic Energy Commission (1946) and the Federal Aviation Agency (1958), now called the Federal Aviation Administration, were the two most important.

In 1960, looking back over the first 90 years of government regulation, it would have been safe to say that most government regulation had been economic. That is, it had been concerned with regulating the marketplace, for example, by setting rates for railroads or utilities.

However, a new era of government activism in the 1960s touched off a new alphabet soup of government regulators and a different type of government regulation. The Equal Employment Opportunity Commission was created to administer the Civil Rights Act of 1964. Following the passage of auto safety legislation in 1966, Congress created the National Highway Traffic Safety Administration as part of the Transportation Department to set auto safety and fuel efficiency standards. Also created was the Consumer Product Safety Commission (1972), as well as a number of landmark consumer laws, which were administered by already existing agencies.

During the same period, a growing environmental protection movement led to the establishment of the Environmental Protection Agency in 1970; the Occupational Safety and Health Administration in 1970 to regulate health and safety standards in the workplace; the Mining Enforcement and Safety Administration in 1973 (today the Mine Safety and Health Administration) to regulate mine safety and health; the Nuclear Regulatory Commission in 1974 to take over the regulatory functions of the Atomic Energy Commission, which was abolished; the Materials Transportation Bureau in 1975 to regulate the movement of hazardous material; and the Office of Surface Mining, Reclamation, and Enforcement in 1977 to regulate strip mining, just to name a few.

These new agencies represented a new turn in government regulation. Many of these agencies had social rather than strictly economic goals. Reflecting the social activism of American society and the federal government during the 1960s and 1970s, these agencies pursued social agendas such as ending racial discrimination or providing consumer education. Unlike earlier regulatory agencies that had been set up to protect the marketplace from monopolies and other forces that were threatening to destroy it, these new agencies were not so much concerned with preserving an orderly marketplace as they were in imposing moral and political values—clean air, small cars that produced less air pollution, truth in lending—on the workings of the marketplace.

As might be expected, the shift from economic regulation to social regulation also entailed widespread interference in the workings of the market and a dramatic growth in the cost of government regulation. Nearly every government regulatory agency, however, has followed the predictable and alarming patterns first established by the ICC. The regulators have been continually criticized by business, especially smaller businesses that do not have the resources to deal with the paperwork of the regulatory process. And, equally importantly, they haven't satisfied the critics who argue that many of these agencies soon developed very close ties with the industries they were supposed to regulate.

The biggest loser has been the economy. From the standpoint of long-term economic growth, regulatory agencies have enshrined some of the most inefficient economic practices ever created. In its regulation of the transportation industry, for example, the ICC inhibited economic forces that could have selected the best and cheapest ways of moving freight. Rates were kept artificially high, producing a moribund railroad industry that didn't have to compete with other forms of transportation. As a result, railroads didn't have to make the changes that could have revitalized the industry and kept it competitive with other forms of transportation. How many billions in higher freight bills the ICC cost the public is hard to determine, but it is known that after deregulation the nation's freight bill dropped from 7.7% of GNP in 1980 to only 6.7% in 1986.

Yet, despite the low marks they have received from business and the public, regulatory agencies slowly managed to enlarge their powers at least until the middle of the 1970s. By that time, the pendulum was beginning to swing in the other direction. An ailing economy and a decline in the reforming zeal of the 1960s forced policymakers to reassess the role of government regulators. Their solution was deregulation.

For a time everyone liked the idea, even if they didn't agree on what deregulation meant. Republicans were for it. Democrats were for it. Conservatives were for it. Neoconservatives were for it. Neoliberals were for it. Jimmy Carter was for it. Ronald Reagan was for it. Unfortunately, as with most buzzwords, no one agreed on what deregulation entails—a factor that clouds the future of deregulation.

Deregulation

In what might be called the first wave of deregulation, Congress began passing a series of landmark laws deregulating the transportation, financial services, and aviation industries in the late 1970s. And then, after Ronald Reagan's 1980 election, he initiated another wave of deregulation by appointing officials who promised to get government out of the business of regulation whenever possible.

The results were even better than expected. In the industries deregulated by Congress, many benefits, in the form of new jobs, better products, service innovations, lower prices, and new businesses, can already be seen. For example, deregulation in the transportation industry produced lower air faires and dramatically increased the number of passengers.

Deregulation revived some industries that had developed a case of terminal stagnation by introducing a breath of increased competition. Railroad deregulation allowed railroads some freedom in rate setting and led the ICC to exempt railroads from regulated rates for transporting fruits and vegetables. The resulting price competition increased the railroads' share of the perishables market from 11% in 1978 to 15% in 1980.

Deregulation also helped many small businesses. Traditionally, regulation hit small businesses hardest. They rarely had the staff or the expertise to deal with government paperwork and their smaller market shares made it harder for them to pass on the costs to consumers. In some industries, such as trucking, regulators set up barriers that made it extremely difficult for small businesses to enter the industry.

After deregulation, business starts in deregulated industries rose much faster than the rest of the economy. The number of new businesses increased by 12.3% in the deregulated industries of transportation and financial services, compared to 8.2% for the whole economy. That meant new jobs. Almost one fourth, or 24.1%, of the 12 million new jobs created in the U.S. between 1976 and 1982 were in deregulated industries. More recently, one fifth of all new jobs between 1980 and 1984 were created in deregulated industries.

And deregulation has allowed American businesses to move faster in the development of new goods and services. In transportation and communications, deregulation permitted more rapid marketing of innovative products and services such as satellite communications networks, cellular phones, and innovative truck redesigns.

But the impact of deregulation has not been altogether measurable or, from the point of view of some powerful interest groups, positive. Deregulation in the airlines industry and telecommunications has been hard on long-established unions, forcing wage cuts, reducing benefits, and leading to layoffs and the hiring of more nonunion workers in those industries. As businesses shop around for bargains on their freight bills, they also discover that some of the new, deregulated shippers are providing cheaper but bare-bones services, causing many complaints. Critics of telephone deregulation have noted that while long-distance charges have been cut—reducing business costs—local companies have increased the cost of local calls, making it more difficult for lower-income people to own phones. Afraid of being driven out of business, smaller state banks are against any deregulation that will allow nationwide banks to compete on their home turf. Deregulated banks have started charging customers for the cost of providing financial services that were once subsidized. The results are increased fees for checking and savings accounts.

The forces behind deregulation have also been widely misinterpreted. Widespread attacks on big government and President Reagan's popular "get the government off our backs" policies have led many commentators to argue that deregulation reflects an underlying commitment by policy-makers, politicians, regulatory agencies, and, most importantly, the American public to reduce the government's interference in the economy.

In fact, the forces behind deregulation are more complex. Americans have a schizophrenic attitude toward government regulation. Most Americans have a knee-jerk reaction against big government, yet some of the same people support strong environmental and health regulations. The most successful attempts at deregulation have occurred in industries such as transportation and telecommunications in which long-term technological changes have transformed the way the industries work. In these industries, deregulation began during the 1960s and 1970s and had little or nothing to do with a general political commitment to free-market policies. In contrast, deregulation has faced an uphill battle in the areas of environmental and antitrust policies, about which the public is politically divided and in which powerful interest groups have managed to protect regulatory agencies. This diverse band of critics—ranging from small state banks to environmentalists—represents a powerful political bloc that could derail deregulation.

Moreover, deregulation has not gotten rid of government regulation, thereby creating a freer marketplace. Some industries such as the airlines have, of course, been dramatically changed; others have been relatively unaffected. As a result, it's one thing to tout the virtues of deregulation; it's quite another to see how deregulation has been carried out. Here's a quick tour of the effects of deregulation:

Banking

In April of 1986, the last restrictions on savings deposit rates—which had been set by the regulators at 5.5%—were ended. That meant that the country's commercial banks and thrift institutions could pay any rate they chose on millions of accounts. But the ceiling on interest rates banks could offer for saving accounts is only one of the banking practices that have been changed during the past few years. As a result of banking deregulation, banks are permitted to pay interest on demand accounts, offer money-market accounts, and establish separate discount brokerage units (which are limited to executing orders for securities and can offer no investment advice). (See the "Banking" section for more details on the changes in what services banks offer.)

These changes marked the end of some fundamental restrictions that were created in the 1930s as a result of the banking crisis of the Great Depression. But like regulation, deregulation seems to have pleased no one.

Many bankers don't feel that deregulation has gone far enough. Commercial bankers believe that deregulation allows other companies, such as Sears and Merrill Lynch, to offer services that banks once monopolized. At the same time, banks remain more heavily regulated, making it difficult for them to compete.

But the financial services industry is divided on how to proceed. Larger banks want an end to barriers that prevent them from setting up nationwide banking systems; smaller state banks would fight for such barriers. Securities companies like deregulation when it allows them to offer commercial banking services; they oppose deregulation when it allows banks to underwrite securities.

With the financial services industry divided over further deregulation, critics of deregulation are becoming more vocal. Like bankers, they agree that deregulation has not been perfect. Record numbers of bank failures, growing problems in the savings and loan industry, and huge losses on third-world loans cause critics to argue for more, not less, regulation. With the Reagan administration leaving office and the Democrats in control of the Congress, deregulation in the banking industry may be stalled. (See the "Banking" section.)

Broadcasting

No aspect of deregulation has touched the American public more directly than the deregulation of broadcasting. In recent years, the Federal Communications Commission (FCC) has dramatically altered its stance on media ownership. Individual owners are now allowed to own 12 stations, up from 7; transferring licenses has become easier and the old rule prohibiting a buyer from reselling a station within three years after purchase has been rescinded. A relaxed attitude toward concentration of individual ownership made the merger between Capital Cities Communications and ABC possible, as well as raising the once-unthinkable possibility of a hostile takeover of a major network.

At the same time, the FCC has moved to get out of the business of regulating programming. The Fairness Doctrine, which required broadcasters to air opposing viewpoints, has been abolished. The FCC has also changed rules to allow cartoons based on toys, ended the requirement that broadcasters show a certain amount of informative children's programming, and eliminated rules that regulated the time and frequency of TV commercials.

Of course, such moves are controversial. Not everyone likes the idea that viewers should be subjected to longer commercials and less informative children programs. But given the generally moronic level of network television programming, it's questionable whether things can get much worse. If stricter programming regulations during the 1960s and 1970s brought us shows like *Hogan's Heroes* and *The Beverly Hillbillies,* why not try deregulation?

More worrisome to some media critics is the idea that the FCC, by raising the number of stations an individual can own, is reducing market competition and creating increased media concentration. They would rather see the agency work for more diversity and competition on the public airways. If fact, the FCC's original proposal would have ended the limits on how many stations a company could own by 1990. That would have created even more media concentration, but the FCC's plan was derailed by Congress. (See the "Television and Cable" section.)

Transportation and Telecommunications

As noted above, the transportation and telecommunications industries are often cited as examples of the miracles wrought by deregulation. Certainly deregulation of these industries has increased competition and speeded up the introduction of new technologies. But it also must be admitted that deregulation of these industries is nothing new. Prodded by court rulings, a sluggish FCC began allowing private long-distance systems in the late 1960s. Also in the 1960s, at the height of a reform drive for increased government regulation, the ICC began deregulating the transportation industry.

In fact, the deregulation of these two industries has little to do with criticism of government regulation or polemics about the virtues of free-market competition. The real reason for deregulation in these two industries has been a long-term technological transformation that has made free-market competition possible.

When the government began regulating the railroads and phone utilities, hardly anyone envisioned a day when the laws of free-market competition could apply to such large-scale enterprises. They were simply too big; it was too costly and inefficient to set up competing phone and railroad lines. So the government opted for the next best thing. It accepted the monopolistic character of these giant corporations and attempted to regulate their activities to prevent monopolistic abuses.

Those technological conditions, of course, have changed. Companies like MCI have proved that they can compete with AT&T—especially if they can get giants like IBM to back them. The rise of the trucking industry has decentralized the transportation industry, making it possible for one man with a truck to become an independent carrier and compete efficiently with a railroad capitalized at a billion dollars.

Of course, the fact that it took the ICC 50 years to realize how the internal combustion engine was revolutionizing the transportation system is testimony to the kind of bureaucratic inertia that seems to afflict regulatory agencies.

Airlines

A fine example of how deregulation has spurred increased competition is the airline industry, where many new airlines have started operations since the beginning of deregulation in 1978. Competition has drastically reduced fares and increased the number of passengers to 425 million in 1987, up from 292 million in 1982. But introducing competition after years of government protection has also been hard on the industry. Price cutting has hurt profits. People Express and 33 other new airlines created since 1978 have gone out of business.

New passengers and a dramatic increase in the number of flights have also led to questions about the industry's safety. Complaints from passengers have increased dramatically, the number of delayed flights is up, and, most ominously, the number of near misses—incidents in which aircraft have almost collided—set a new record in 1987, hitting 1,063, up from 311 in 1982. Faced with record numbers of flights (a new one-day record of 111,152 flights was recently set), more airlines, and 125 million new passengers in the last four years alone, airports are also straining under the load of handling all this traffic. In the end, increased competition will be good for both the consumer and the industry. The former head of Eastern Airlines, Frank Borman, has noted that even though he once opposed deregulation, he now feels that "deregulation saved the industry. It turned it from what would have become a moribund, stagnant industry like the Europeans' into a vibrant, growing industry."

WHO OWNED WHOM

Nobody likes to give up business, yet sometimes the government forces the issue. And sometimes the result is companies spinning off other companies that become powerhouses in their own right. Here are some examples of government-created companies and the parents that grudgingly let them go:

Parent	*Offspring*
1. American Telephone & Telegraph	American Information Technologies
In 1984, the company divested itself of the 22 wholly-owned Bell operating companies. These companies were organized into seven regional holding companies.	Bell Atlantic BellSouth NYNEX Pacific Telesis Group Southwestern Bell U S WEST
2. CBS	Viacom International
In 1970, after the FCC barred major broadcasters from owning cable-TV companies, Viacom was spun off.	
3. United Aircraft (now UAL)	Boeing
In 1934, following government hearings and passage of a law prohibiting air-mail contractors from being associated with aviation manufacturing companies, United Aircraft was forced to split up into three companies, including United Airlines.	Pratt & Whitney
4. J.P. Morgan Company (now part of Morgan Guranty Trust Company of New York)	Morgan Stanley
The Glass-Steagall Act in 1933 erected a Chinese wall between the functions of investment and commercial banking. J. P. Morgan's investment house was spun off; others were divested.	

5. Standard Oil Company of New Jersey (now Exxon)

    In 1911, the U.S. Supreme Court sustained a lower court decision that the company was in violation of anti-trust laws, and it was broken up into 34 companies.

Anglo-American Oil
Atlantic Refining
Borne-Scrymser
Buckeye Pipe Line
Chesebrough Manufacturing
Colonial Oil
Continental Oil
Crescent Pipe Line
Cumberland Pipe Line
Eureka Pipe Line
Galena-Signal Oil
Indian Pipe Line
National Transit
New York Transit
Northern Pipe Line
Ohio Oil Company
Prairie Oil and Gas
Solar Refining
South Penn Oil
Southern Pipe Line
South Western Pennsylvania Pipelines
Standard Oil (California)
Standard Oil (Indiana)
Standard Oil (Kentucky)
Standard Oil (Nebraska)
Standard Oil (New York)
Standard Oil (Ohio)
Standard Oil (Kansas)
Swan and Finch
Union Tank Line
Vacuum Oil
Washington Oil
Waters-Pierce Oil

Antitrust

Antitrust is the only area in which Reagan appointees may have made a greater impact than the FCC has by its deregulation of broadcasting and telecommunications. They dropped the government's 13-year suit to break up IBM and inaugurated a program whereby the government could intervene on the side of corporations sued for violating antitrust laws. Their most important stand, however, has been on the issue of merger mania. With only a few exceptions, no actions have been taken against the megamergers sweeping Wall Street. Justice Department antitrust actions against a few key mergers would have stopped the movement and prevented the restructuring of several major industries.

Of course, there is little doubt that antitrust laws need to be revised to reflect modern business conditions and the importance of a worldwide market. For example, an American company can face antitrust violations by acquiring another company if the merger gives it too large a share of the U.S. market in, say, color TVs. But this same company might hold only a small share of the world market and its competitive strength on the world market would be weakened by U.S. antitrust laws prohibiting its expansion. New standards judging U.S. corporations on their shares of a world market and the competitiveness of that world market would improve the competitive position of U.S. companies. Businesses also need to be freed from the threat of triple damages for antitrust violations. Such damages punish businesses far beyond the cost of their antitrust violations.

But the Reagan administration's antitrust policy has fallen into a pattern that has plagued its fight for deregulation. Top administrators have eased government enforcement, but no major legislation has been passed. Some of the antitrust proposals offered by the Justice Department have been so controversial they have never been given to Congress. The Reagan administration's most recent legislation to reform antitrust laws, submitted in February of 1986, provoked opposition from business lobbies, consumer groups, and powerful members of Congress. Even before the legislative package was made public, the laws were pronounced dead on arrival by the largely sympathetic business press.

In the wake of Wall Street's insider-trading scandal, Congress moved quickly to propose new legislation governing mergers and acquisitions. As a result it seems possible that, in the area of antitrust, the most pro-business administration of the last 50 years will not have been able to accomplish anything of lasting value.

Environment

The same problem of great expectations and failed plans has also plagued the overhaul of environmental regulations. While some environmental regulations have helped clean up the environment, others have placed heavy costs on small businesses. For example, in the foundry industry, 80% of the 4,000 foundries in the U.S. employ fewer than 100 workers. When these small firms began to go out of business about a third of them blamed EPA regulations for their demise.

The Reagan appointees to the Environmental Protection Agency raised hopes among business leaders that such regulations might be changed. The EPA is the best example of Reagan's approach to regulation—do away with regulation by appointing long-time critics of government regulation to enforce those regulations. Rita Lavelle, appointed to head the EPA's Superfund to clean up toxic waste dumps, was a former public-relations employee for a subsidiary of Aerojet-General Corporation, a firm that environmentalists had attacked as one of California's biggest polluters. The chief of staff had been a lobbyist for paper companies and Manville Corporation, a company that went bankrupt because of asbestos-related lawsuits and the assistant administrator for air, noise, and radiation was a lobbyist for the paper company Crown Zellerbach Corporation, another company that had faced problems with environmental regulations. Heading up this band of anti-EPA regulators was Anne (Gorsuch) Burford, a Colorado colleague of James Watt. Burford helped cut the agency's budget and reduce the number of antipollution cases brought by the agency.

But then everything came apart. Like many of Reagan's appointees, the new EPA regulators misjudged the political climate and moved too far too fast in an effort to favor industry. In 1982 a scandal erupted over the agency's management of the Superfund program. Critics charged that the EPA had been lax in enforcing toxic-waste law, that it made secret deals with companies accused of pollution, that agency employees had profited from conflicts of interest, and that political hit lists were used to terminate dissidents within the agency.

None of these charges were prosecuted but Rita Lavelle, the head of the Superfund program, was jailed for perjury, and to quiet the controversy Burford was forced out in early 1983. Since then, under several new chiefs, the EPA has increased its budget and added new regulations, including a plan to reduce lead content in gas. While the agency has not returned to the activism of the Carter years, the political future for environmental deregulation is not bright.

Office of Management and Budget

Early on, the Reagan administration decided that there was no point in saddling business with expensive regulations that produced few if any cost benefits. A 1981 executive order mandated that government regulators weigh the benefits of a new regulation against its costs. As a result of this philosophy, the Office of Management and Budget (OMB) was given the power to review new regulations to make certain that they didn't impose undue costs. This review power quickly made the OMB a regulator of the regulators. For example, OMB, reviewing an Occupational Safety and Health Administration (OSHA) rule on exposure in the workplace to ethylene oxide, found that the rule would cost $42.2 million a year to implement ($2.1 billion over a 50-year period), but would only result in 871 fewer cancer cases over the next half-century. It objected to the rule.

However, like most of Reagan's plans to curb the power of regulatory agencies, the granting of review power to the OMB has come under increasing attack and no major legislation forcing regulations to be cost-effective has succeeded or is likely to succeed.

The Future

Coming into office, Reagan promised a major overhaul of government regulation. But when he leaves office in 1989, little will have been accomplished. The administration's greatest successes have been in transportation and telecommunications, but, as noted before, deregulation in those industries began much earlier. And deregulation in those industries had little to do with the realization that government regulation was harming the economy. Rather, in each case the underlying technology had changed, making the regulatory agency largely irrelevant.

Elsewhere, the Reagan administration has been able to staff regulatory agencies with competent people who are committed to reducing government's costly interference in business. That has at least temporarily halted a century-long trend toward more and more government regulations. No doubt a reprieve from government regulation and a lax attitude toward mergers helped fuel a bull market on Wall Street.

But in many cases the Reagan administration has confused substance with appearance. It has been unable to pass any major legislation that will permanently reduce government regulation. The outspoken ideological attacks on regulation by James Watt only strengthened the hands of the administration's opponents. The head of one major environmental group once quipped that James Watt was the best thing that ever happened to the environmental movement—every time he gave a speech the group could count on more contributions and members.

Watt, of course, scored points with Reagan's supporters and became one of the Republican party's biggest fund-raisers. But strong words, when not accompanied by any legislation, may produce little long-term impact. From 1980 to 1988, the budgets for 54 regulatory agencies continued to grow, jumping from $6.7 billion in 1980 to an estimated $10.5 billion in 1988, according to a study by the Center for the Study of American Business at Washington University. The number of bureaucrats in regulatory agencies dropped from 130,242 in 1980 to 111,103 in 1985 but jumped back up to 118,037 in 1988. As a result, Reagan's attack on regulation may go down in history as little more than a curious footnote—a palace revolution that briefly took control of the government bureaucracy without leaving a legislative mandate to stop the seemingly inexorable march of big government.

THE REGULATORS

Comptroller of the Currency
490 L'Enfant Plaza, S.W.
Washington, D.C. 20219
202-566-2000

Comptroller: Robert L. Clarke

An office in the Department of the Treasury, the office of the Comptroller of the Currency is one of the three federal regulatory agencies that oversee nationally chartered banks. (See also the profiles of the Federal Reserve System and the Federal Deposit Insurance Corporation, below). Created by the 1864 National Banking Act, the office was the first federal agency created to regulate financial institutions. It regulates some 4,900 national and District of Columbia banks. Approval of the Comptroller is required for the organization of new national banks, conversion of state-chartered banks into national banks, consolidations or mergers of banks in which the surviving institution is a national bank, and establishment of branches by national banks. Bank examiners from the office of the Comptroller periodically appraise the financial conditions of the banks, the soundness of their operations, the quality of their management, and their compliance with laws, rules, and regulations.

Commodity Futures Trading Commission
2033 K Street, N.W.
Washington, D.C. 20581
202-254-6387

Chairman: Susan Phillips

Established by the Commodity Futures Trading Commission Act of 1974, the Commission regulates trading on 11 U.S. futures exchanges, commodity exchange members, public brokerage houses, Commission-registered futures industry salespeople, commodity trading advisers, and commodity pool operations.

Consumer Product Safety Commission
1111 18th Street, N.W.
Washington, D.C. 20207
202-634-7740

Chairman: Terrence M. Scanlon

The Consumer Product Safety Commission is an independent federal regulatory agency established in 1972 by the Consumer Product Safety Act. It has power to enforce a number of laws designed to protect the public from unsafe products. The Commission can force manufacturers to correct products that are hazardous or ban consumer products. The Commission also collects information on injuries caused by consumer products, maintains a comprehensive National Injury Information Clearinghouse, conducts research on consumer product hazards, encourages the development of voluntary standards for consumer products, and establishes mandatory consumer product standards when necessary.

Environmental Protection Agency
401 M Street, S.W.
Washington, D.C. 20460
202-382-2090

Administrator: Lee M. Thomas

Established in 1970 under Reorganization Plan 3, the EPA took over the air-pollution, water-pollution, solid-waste, pesticide, radiation, and toxic-substances regulation that had been scattered among many federal agencies. Since then it has enforced a number of environmental laws and has worked with state and local governments to curb environmental pollution.

Equal Employment Opportunity Commission
2401 E Street, N.W.
Washington, D.C. 20507
202-634-1947

Chairman: Clarence Thomas

Created by Title VII of the Civil Rights Act of 1964, the Commission enforces federal statutes and executive orders prohibiting discrimination on the basis of race, sex, creed, age and national origin in hiring, promoting, firing, wages, testing, training, apprenticeship, and other aspects of employment. The Commission also promotes voluntary action programs for equal opportunity and enforces mandatory provisions for equal opportunity for federal employees and applicants.

Federal Communications Commission
1919 M Street, N.W.
Washington, D.C. 20554
202-632-7000

Chairman: Dennis R. Patrick

Created by the Communications Act of 1934, the Commission regulates and licenses radio and television broadcasting; telephone, telegraph, and cable television operation; two-way radio and radio operators; and satellite communications.

Federal Deposit Insurance Corporation
550 17th Street, N.W.
Washington, D.C. 20429
202-393-8400

Chairman: L. William Seidman

Created by section 12B of the Federal Reserve Act in 1933, the FDIC insures bank deposits and has various regulatory powers over banks that are not members of the Federal Reserve System. It can examine a bank to determine its condition for insurance purposes, approve or disapprove a merger, and approve or disapprove a bank's proposal to open new branches, move its main office, move branches, or retire its capital. It can also issue cease-and-desist orders for violations, suspend or remove bank personnel, regulate bank securities, require reports of changes of stock ownership, require reports of a bank's condition and income, regulate a bank's security against robbery, and regulate advertising.

Federal Home Loan Bank Board
Federal Savings and Loan Insurance Corporation
1700 G Street, N.W.
Washington, D.C. 20552
202-377-6000

Chairman: M. Danny Wall

The Federal Home Loan Bank Board (FHLB) was established in 1932 by the Federal Home Loan Bank Act as an independent agency to encourage savings and economical home ownership. The FHLB charters, regulates, and supervises federal savings and loan associations, which specialize in the financing of homes and home construction, and approves the establishment of new savings and loan associations. It also operates the Federal Home Loan Bank System and the Federal Savings and Loan Insurance Corporation (FSLIC).

The Federal Home Loan Bank System, to which federal savings and loan associations belong, operates as the Federal Reserve System does for banks. It provides reserve credit to member savings institutions so they can remain financially healthy and continue to be a source of economical financing for homes.

The FSLIC insures the savings of more than 84 million Americans who have savings accounts in FSLIC-insured savings and loan associations. It regulates savings and loan association holding companies; acts to prevent the default of insured institutions by making loans, purchasing assets, and making contributions; establishes reserve requirements for savings and loan associations; insures savings accounts up to $100,000 for members of the FHLB; and regulates savings and loans.

The FHLB also acts as the board of directors of the Federal Home Loan Mortgage Corporation, commonly known as Freddie Mac. The Federal Home Loan Mortgage Corporation provides a secondary market in residential mortgages by selling mortgage participation certificates and guaranteed mortgage certificates, thus providing an additional source of housing funds to home mortgage lenders.

By acting as a regulator, a creator of funds for home mortgages, a buyer and seller of mortgage loans, a licensing agency, and an insurer of savings accounts, the FHLB has wider powers than any other federal agency involved in regulating financial institutions.

Federal Maritime Commission
1100 L Street, N.W.
Washington, D.C. 20573
202-523-5773

Chairman: Edward V. Hickey, Jr.

Created by 1961 legislation that is called Reorganization Plan 7, the Commission regulates the foreign and domestic shipping of the U.S. It oversees agreements reached by a variety of rate-making conferences of ship carriers, makes certain that only rates on file with the commission are charged, ensures that adequate money is available to indemnify passengers, and guarantees equal treatment of shippers, carriers, and others regulated by shipping statutes.

Federal Reserve System
Board of Governors of the Federal Reserve System
20th Street and C Street, N.W.
Washington, D.C. 20551
202-452-3000

Chairman: Alan Greenspan

Established by the Federal Reserve Act of 1913, the Federal Reserve was created as the central bank of the U.S., charged with administering and making policy for the nation's credit and monetary affairs. As well as being the country's central bank, the Fed has also been given a number of supervisory and regulatory powers designed to keep the banking industry in sound condition. It is authorized to approve state banks and trust companies for membership in the Federal Reserve System and has the power to revoke that membership. It examines the affairs of all banks that are members of the Federal Reserve and approves bank mergers and new branches of member banks. (See page 90 for a more complete profile.)

Federal Trade Commission
Pennsylvania Avenue at Sixth Street, N.W.
Washington, D.C. 20580
202-326-2000

Chairman: Daniel Oliver

The Commission is charged with enforcing the Clayton Act and stopping "unfair methods of competition" and "unfair or deceptive acts or practices." It attempts to stop monopolistic activities, protects the consumer against unfair advertisements, regulates corporate mergers, and is supposed to protect consumers from misleading information.

Food and Drug Administration
5600 Fishers Lane
Rockville, Maryland 20857
301-443-1544

Commissioner: Frank E. Young

An agency in the Department of Health and Human Services, the FDA received its current name in 1931. The FDA focuses on protecting the public from impure and unsafe foods, drugs, and cosmetics and other hazards.

Interstate Commerce Commission
12th Street and Constitution Avenue, N.W.
Washington, D.C. 20423
202-275-7252

Chairman: Heather J. Gradison

The ICC was created as an independent agency by an 1887 act now known as the Interstate Commerce Act and over the years its authority has been strengthened by various laws. Traditionally the ICC regulates interstate surface transportation, including trains, trucks, buses, water carriers, freight forwarders, and transportation brokers. Regulatory functions involve certification of carriers seeking to provide transportation for the public and regulation of rates, adequacy of service, purchases, and mergers. However, the Railroad Revitalization and Regulatory Reform Act of 1976, the Motor Carrier Act of 1980, the Staggers Rail Act of 1980, the Household Goods Transportation Act of 1980, and the Bus Regulatory Reform Act of 1982 have reduced the agency's role in regulating the trucking, railroad, and bus industries.

National Labor Relations Board
1717 Pennsylvania Avenue, N.W.
Washington, D.C. 20570
202-632-4950

Chairman: Donald L. Dotson

Created by the Wagner Act (also known as the National Labor Relations Act) in 1935, the NLRB administers federal labor laws and regulates relations between labor and management. It has the power to make certain that employees have the opportunity to organize, to determine through elections whether workers want unions as their bargaining representatives, and to prevent and remedy unfair labor practices.

National Transportation Safety Board
800 Independence Avenue, S.W.
Washington, D.C. 20594
202-382-6600

Chairman: James E. Burnett

Created by the Independent Safety Board Act of 1974, the NTSB promotes safety in the transportation industry by investigating accidents, conducting studies, and making recommendations to government agencies, the transportation industry, and others on safety measures and practices.

Nuclear Regulatory Commission
1717 H Street, N.W.
Washington, D.C. 20555
301-492-7000

Chairman: Lando Zech

The successor to the Atomic Energy Commission, which was set up in 1946, the NRC was established as a result of the Energy Reorganization Act of 1974 and Executive Order 11834 of January 15, 1975. The NRC licenses and regulates the civilian use of nuclear energy, in order to project the public health and safety and environment. It has the power to license companies to build and operate nuclear reactors and to own and use nuclear materials. The NRC also has the power to inspect nuclear plants and to make certain safety rules established by the Commission are not violated.

Occupational Safety and Health Administration
200 Constitution Avenue, N.W.
Washington, D.C. 20210
202-523-8151

Assistant Secretary: John A. Pendergrass

Established as an agency in the Department of Labor by the Occupational Safety and Health Act of 1970, OSHA oversees occupational health and safety. It issues occupational safety and health rules, conducts investigations and inspections to make certain these regulations are followed, and issues citations and proposes penalties for violations.

Securities and Exchange Commission
450 Fifth Street, N.W.
Washington, D.C. 20549
202-272-2650

Chairman: David Ruder

Created by the Securities Exchange Act of 1934, the SEC regulates Wall Street and the securities markets. The SEC requires that issuers of securities make full and fair disclosure, regulates people working in the securities business, regulates mutual funds and other investment companies, regulates companies controlling electric or gas utilities, regulates investment counselors and advisers, takes part in reorganization and bankruptcy proceedings under Chapter 11, works with self-regulatory agencies such as the New York Stock Exchange, and enforces its rules and regulations.

SEC DISCLOSURE FORMS

Form 3 is for individuals considered insiders. The form is filed with the SEC and the pertinent stock exchange by holders of 10% or more of the stock of a public company and by all directors and officers, even if they don't hold shares. It details the number of shares owned as well as the number of warrants, rights, convertible bonds, and options to purchase common stock. Form 3 must be updated whenever such changes are reported.

Form 4 is an amendment updating Form 3, and must be filed within 10 days of the end of the month in which a major change in ownership takes place. Form 4 filings must be constantly updated during a takeover attempt when the acquirer buys more than 10% of a company's outstanding shares.

Form 8-K reports any material change that might affect a public company's financial position or stock value. The SEC determines "material" to include everything an average, prudent investor should be aware of before deciding whether to buy, sell, or hold a security. That ranges from merger activity to amendment of the company's bylaws. Form 8-K must be filed within a month of the activity. Timely disclosure rules usually require a corporation to issue a press release immediately about an event subsequently reported in the form.

Form 10-K is required of every issuer of a registered security, every exchange-listed company, and every company with 500 or more shareholders or $1 million or more in gross assets. It provides for disclosure of sales, revenues, and pretax operating income, as well as sales by separate classes of products for each of a company's lines of business in each of the last five years. Also required is a source-and-application-of-funds statement presented on a comparative basis for at least the past two years. This becomes public knowledge upon filing.

Form 10-Q is a quarterly report for listed companies. It's less comprehensive than a 10-K and doesn't need to be audited. It should contain comparative figures for the same period a year ago.

Chapter Eleven
TAXES: ONE OF THE INEVITABLES

HIGHLIGHTS AND TRENDS

• The current tax system is so complicated that over 15 million Americans are forced to turn to professionals to prepare their taxes. Many of these taxpayers are not wealthy individuals with complicated tax problems. At H. & R. Block the typical customer has a household income of $15,000 to $30,000; about 75% file the long form with itemized deductions.

• Taxes for all levels of government hit $845 billion for fiscal 1986. That's about 7.5 times higher than the tax revenues that federal, state, and local governments collected in 1960. During that period, local tax revenues jumped an average of 8.0 times from $18,081 million to $144,997 million, while state taxes jumped an average of 12.6 times from $18,036 million to $228,054 million. Those whopping tax hikes meant that every man, woman, and child in the U.S. paid an average of $3,504 in federal, state, and local taxes in 1986, up from an average of a mere $629 in 1960.

• Ever wonder why there were so many antitax measures in the late 1970s and the mid-1980s? Between 1967 and June of 1987, receipts from federal personal income taxes jumped 532%, Social Security and other social insurance taxes rocketed 898%, and corporate taxes grew 256%. Total federal tax receipts grew 504%, much faster than consumer prices (240%).

• Since the 1970s, federal tax revenues have remained nearly constant as a percentage of the GNP, accounting for 19.3% of the GNP in 1988, about the same as in 1970, when they accounted for 19.5%. But state and local taxes have risen so fast that the total share taken by government set a record in 1987.

• Budget cutbacks have curbed the power of the IRS to audit taxpayers; about 1.1 million Americans are audited, only 1% of all taxpayers.

TAXES: WHO CREATES THEM AND WHO PAYS THEM

Few people understand taxes, but almost everyone hates them, primarily because they keep going up and up. As federal, state, and local governments embarked on a period of proliferating expenses, ranging from increased social services payments to newer and better bombs, taxes rose dramatically. But figuring out exactly how much they've gone up is no easy matter. Over the last 50 years, federal, state, and local governments have increasingly moved some large programs "off budget," established programs that are funded by insurance trusts, created public authorities and set up quasi-government agencies that are not included in the budget. As a result, "off-budget receipts" for the federal government alone grew from only half a billion in 1939 to a projected $203.1 billion in 1988. And, some surveys of government income don't include revenue that might look like a tax to the average citizen. For example, the Bureau of the Census survey of federal, state, and local tax revenues cited in Table 49 doesn't include social insurance taxes such as Social Security or unemployment insurance. (That income is classified as "insurance trust revenues.") As previously noted, taxes for all levels of government hit $845 billion in 1986, producing a tax bill of $3,504 for each American. If one adds social insurance taxes for federal, state, and local government, the total tax bill averaged about $4,954 for every American.

As a result of mounting tax bills, a political firestorm developed in the late 1970s. In California, a tax revolt forced public officials to put a cap on property taxes—which had doubled and tripled in the booming California real-estate market of the 1970s. In 1980, Ronald Reagan was swept into the White House with a promise to cut taxes and get the government off the backs and out of the wallets of middle-class taxpayers.

But ever-growing tax bills weren't the only reason many Americans were fed up with the tax man. Part of the widespread anger resulted from the way government finances its revenues. In recent years, taxes that fall primarily on working, middle-income, and upper-middle-income families have increased the most dramatically. For example, property tax revenues collected by state and local governments increased from the $16,405 million in 1960 to $111,711 million for fiscal 1987. Sales tax revenues jumped from $11,849 million in 1960 to $134,971 million in 1987, and state and local personal income taxes grew from $2,463 million in 1960 to $74,417 million in 1986. By comparison, between 1960 and 1986, the population of the U.S. increased only 1.3 times and the cost of living increased 3.7 times.

Most of those increases have come since the late 1960s. Between 1967 and June 1987, total federal tax receipts, including social insurance taxes, jumped 504%. Personal income taxes collected by Washington grew 532%, and social insurance contributions increased a whopping 797%. Those tax increases were especially painful if you remember that the median income of the average family, adjusted for inflation and expressed in constant 1985 dollars, increased from $25,560 in 1967 to only $27,735 in 1985.

A sign of our heavy tax bills can be found on your calendar. May 4 was designated by the Washington-based nonprofit Tax Foundation as 1987's "Tax Freedom Day."

On that day, the average American finally got to keep some of the fruits of his or her labors. From January 1 through May 3, every penny of income was confiscated by federal, state, and local tax men—which is another way of saying that more than one third of U.S. annual earnings is grabbed by big government. For many Americans, of course, Tax Freedom Day comes much later.

If history is any guide, Tax Freedom Day will probably be celebrated even later in the year by 1990. In 1950, in the wake of the New Deal and in the midst of the Fair Deal, Tax Freedom Day could have been marked more than a month earlier than it is today. The average taxpayer's share of all government taxes was fully paid by April 3. Since then it has advanced through the calendar, reaching May 4 in 1981.

Reagan's tax cuts provided a temporary respite, and by 1983 Tax Freedom Day was celebrated on April 28. But that was the end of the good news. Every year since then tax receipts have gone up.

The growing tax burden has especially irritated middle-income voters. Some think that discontent can be traced to how the government finances its activities. The most popular federal program is undoubtedly Social Security. Unlike most other social-welfare programs, which are intended to benefit the poor, this program also benefits middle-class voters and their parents. Yet since Social Security is financed by a payroll tax, its burden falls heavily on small business and the average worker.

Locally, the situation is even more obvious. For the most part, middle-income families still depend on the public education system. Yet school districts primarily finance schools through the property taxes that fall mainly on middle-income homeowners or on renters, who pay property taxes indirectly as a part of their rent. Similarly, the state and local governments—which finance police and fire departments, education, garbage pickup, road repair, and other programs popular with middle-class taxpayers—still get two thirds of their revenues from either property taxes (which account for three quarters of local government tax revenue) or sales taxes (which account for nearly half of all state tax receipts and one seventh of all local taxes). Both taxes, levied at a fixed rate regardless of income, are felt immediately, directly, and painfully, by middle-income voters. Faced with rising tax bills on their homes or rising sales taxes at the stores, middle-class homeowners have become increasingly fed up with a system of government financing that costs more but seems to deliver less of the local sanitation, police, and educational services they need.

These problems have made taxes one of the most politically important issues of the 1980s, with both Republicans and Democrats vying for the hearts and minds of disgruntled taxpayers. But perhaps a more important problem, and, unfortunately, one that has been given less serious attention, is how taxes affect the economy. To understand that, it's worth taking a look at the development of government taxes.

TAXES: THE HISTORY OF A DISAGREEABLE INSTITUTION

Like the evolution of life, the evolution of taxation is a progression from the simple to the complex. However, unlike the evolution of people from the apes, there is little reason to believe that the social evolution of the tax system has followed a trajectory from a primitive, less intelligent system to a complex, more rational system.

In the relatively underdeveloped colonial economy of the U.S., the tax system was based on poll taxes, import and export duties, and faculty taxes on the income of various tradesmen. Following the revolution, Congress depended heavily on custom duties and on an internal revenue system based on excises on liquor, carriages, sugar, snuff, and other commodities. However, taxes on the sale of liquor and other commodities proved to be highly unpopular, leading to a bloody tax revolt known as the Whiskey Rebellion in 1794. (See "Tax Revolts" below.) Under political pressure, Congress abolished such taxes by 1817.

After 1817 and for most of the 19th century, Congress relied on customs duties and the sale of public lands. Only during the Civil War, when faced with the need for vast new revenues, did Congress turn to an income tax. This tax, which expired in 1872, brought in $310 million in 1866, the most collected until 1911, several years after a corporate income tax was established. An 1894 income tax law was declared unconstitutional in 1895.

The simplicity of the early tax system had its virtues and its drawbacks, illustrating the ironclad law that any tax policy, by transferring money from the private to the public sector, will affect the economy, benefiting some groups and hurting, at least temporarily, other groups. In the 18th and 19th centuries, the reliance on excise taxes and duties meant that most of the tax burden fell on the lower and middle classes, who paid out a higher proportion of their income in taxes than did the rich.

However, regressive tax systems, when coupled with a booming investment climate, encouraged capital spending by giving the wealthy more money to invest. Some economists believe that as much as $156 million was put into capital investment as a result of federal tax policies between 1790 and 1860. Moreover, such tax policies were possible only if government spending was kept to a bare minimum—it accounted for only 1% or 2% of the GNP before the Civil War and only 2% to 4% between 1866 and 1914. Today, government spending is over a third of the GNP.

The same income inequality that helped spur investment and a booming 19th-century development also created political pressure on government to devise a tax system that was not so biased against the lower and middle classes and to raise revenues to finance more social-welfare programs. In 1909, a Republican Congress put through the first corporate income tax system—a 1% tax on corporate profits. In 1913, a progressive income tax was established for individuals.

During the next half-century, three trends guided the development of the tax system. One was an ever-increasing tendency to raise the tax rates. For example, the tax rate for a single person with an income of $5,000 increased from 0.4% in 1913 to 16.7% in 1967, raising the tax bill from $20 in 1913 to $856 in 1967. Similarly, the tax rates for someone earning $1 million a year soared from 6% in 1930 to 90% in 1943 and then fell thereafter down to 70.2% by 1970.

The second trend had already become familiar under earlier tax systems: the desire of special interests to lobby for tax breaks. Just as various industries had lobbied, usually successfully, for favors under the tariff and excise taxes, special interests soon began feeding on the income tax code. Rates for various tax brackets increased and the IRS began taxing new types of income, but special interests also managed to get new tax deductions. The result was a kind of Rube Goldberg device that few people understood, forcing 15 million Americans each year to use professionals to prepare their taxes.

The complexity and seemingly unfair nature of the income tax system also touched off a third major aspect of postwar debates about taxes—political pressure for tax simplification and reduction. Every administration since Eisenhower's has discussed proposals to simplify taxes. Unfortunately, unlike the other two trends, this one led to little action. One result of the failure to reform and simplify the tax system was ever-growing complexity. A system of tax deductions means, however, that taxes and tax deductions have become a way for governments to regulate the economy.

TAXES: THE HIDDEN REGULATOR

As it developed in the 20th century, the tax system was not only a way of raising more and more money for social programs, it was also a way for government to intervene in the marketplace. By raising or lowering taxes through an increasingly Byzantine system of tax breaks and loopholes, the tax system became a hidden regulator of the economy—perhaps the most powerful regulator in Washington, determining which goods and services would be financed or subsidized partially by tax deductions.

Over time, almost every sector of America was given tax breaks. In an attempt to equalize income distribution, tax rates were raised for higher earners. For middle-class homeowners (and, of course, for the ever-powerful real estate industry), there were interest deductions on mortgages; for manufacturers, there were investment tax credits; for the timber industry, lower tax rates; for the oil patch, the oil depletion allowance; for multinationals, foreign tax credits; and so forth until Congress, in its attempt to regulate the economy through taxation, had created the most complicated system known to humanity.

In 1871, the tax code filled one page. Today IRS rulings on obscure subsections fill thousands of pages. As an illustration of how bad things have gotten, the so-called Tax Reform Law of 1986 covers 876 pages. The bill did simplify and reduce taxes for several million Americans, but overall this dismal excuse for tax reform is so complicated that Americans spent an estimated extra 10 million hours working on tax returns in 1987!

That's good news, of course, for accountants and tax lawyers, but bad news for the concept of tax reform. It also means the government is going to stay in the business of regulating the economy through tax policies.

Supporters of government regulation by tax deduction have long claimed that the tax system should reflect the social policy priorities of Congress and the White House. That sounds fine in theory. In practice the results have often been less than beneficial. Take, for example, the two most notorious tax shelters, the oil depletion allowance and accelerated depreciation for real estate.

Thanks to real estate tax shelters, many real estate deals were structured around tax write-offs, not cash flows or the market for commercial properties. Fueled by billions of dollars worth of tax-shelter money, real estate developers built a lot of office buildings. Unfortunately, no one was building office tenants, at least at the same rate or with quite as many tax deductions. The vacancy rate in many cities, such as Houston and Los Angeles, hit 25% in 1985. In 1986, when Congress cut off the flow of tax dollars to real estate shelters, there were problems, and the real estate industry faced the difficult prospect of withdrawing from decades of government subsidies.

The famous oil depletion allowance had the same effect before it was finally abolished. It encouraged oil production, but by keeping oil prices low it encouraged auto makers to make gas guzzlers. When OPEC finally turned off the spigot, the economy, drivers, and the auto industry faced the trauma of adjusting to higher energy costs.

The moral is not that real estate shelters or oil depletion allowances are unjustified. Both produced certain benefits, not only to the industry but to the whole economy. However, they did this at the cost of increasing government interference in the economy. Tax subsidies given by Congress allow an industry to pursue investment strategies that are very different from those that would have been allowed by the free market. Cheap oil, made possible by government tax deductions—which are really subsidies—prods industry into producing larger cars and works against the use of other energy sources. Accelerated depreciation schedules on real estate prompt developers to put up buildings that would not be profitable if no such subsidies existed. Money spent on these buildings is money that is not spent on factory modernization or in other sectors of the economy.

Faced with how the government tax system is changing the working of the economy, the Reagan administration moved to support tax reform and simplification. Unfortunately, what we got was neither.

TAX LAW HIGHLIGHTS

The confusing changes in the tax laws were supposed to simplify filings for everybody. The forms are so simple that H & R Block should double its business over the next few years as taxpayers go crazy trying to figure out what's going on. Anyway, here are the major elements of the tax bill signed into law on October 22, 1986:

Revenues

From 1987 to 1992, the total projected revenue is expected to be the same as the amount that would have been raised under the old law, although the figure varies a little more or a little less in different years. Corporate taxes will increase $120 million during that period, while individual taxes will go down by that amount.

Business Taxes

The top corporate tax rate was lowered to 34% after 1987, when it was 40%. The previous top rate was 46%. Investment tax credits were repealed, retroactive to January 1, 1986. Depreciation allowances were made more favorable for investments in machinery and other equipment and less favorable for real estate investments. A lot of special preferences were kept for certain industries but discontinued for others.

Individual Taxes

In 1987 there were five brackets, ranging from 11% to 38.5%. There are two brackets, 15% and 28%, in 1988, plus a 5% surtax on the income of couples earning between $71,900 and $149,250, unmarried parents earning between $61,650 and $123,790, and single people earning between $43,150 and $89,560. (Some 6 million poor people will be taken off the tax rolls.)

Capital Gains

Capital gains are taxed at the same rate as other income instead of being given preferential treatment.

Personal Exemptions

An exemption of $2,000 is allowed in 1989 to each taxpayer and each of his or her dependents. The exemption is being phased out for upper-income taxpayers.

Standard Deductions

For those who don't itemize, for 1988 the standard deduction is $3,000 for single people, $4,400 for heads of households, and $5,000 for couples. Those taking the standard deduction can no longer deduct charitable donations, which they could under the old law.

Personal Deductions

Taxpayers who itemize deductions can deduct interest payments on mortgages for up to two homes, charitable donations, and state and local income and property tax payments. (Interest other than on mortgages will no longer be deductible after a four-year phase-out period.) Medical expenses are deductible only if they exceed 7.5% of adjusted gross income. Business meals and entertainment expenses are 80% deductible.

Retirement

Individual retirement account (IRA) contributions up to $2,000 are deductible for workers not covered by employer-paid pension plans. But taxpayers who contribute to nondeductible IRAs may defer tax on the accumulating dividends and interest. The maximum contribution to 401(k) plans is $7,000. The schedule under which employees must be vested in private pension plans has been accelerated.

Tax-exempt Bonds

Bonds issued for public purposes, such as schools and highways, are tax-exempt. Limits are imposed on the amount of tax-exempt bonds that may be issued to finance private activities, such as commercial development, and the income is subject to the minimum tax.

Others

Most tax shelters are eliminated since taxpayers can no longer use paper losses from partnership investments to offset income from salaries, interest, and dividends. Shifting of income to children for tax purposes is curtailed. Unemployment compensation is taxable for couples with incomes over $18,000 and single people with incomes over $12,000. Some scholarships and fellowships are taxable. The alternative minimum tax is toughened. The tax break for two-earner couples is repealed.

THE INTERNAL REVENUE SERVICE

Easily the most hated government agency, the Internal Revenue Service is facing hard times of late. The number of returns increased to 196 million in 1986, up from 143 million in 1980, but the agency's full-time employment only inched ahead from 85,500 in 1980 to 96,395 in 1986. And the paperwork just keeps growing. About 223 million tax forms will be filed with the IRS by 1994.

To keep up with the work, the IRS recently decided to go high-tech. But, as in every other kind of tax reform the government has attempted, the results were disastrous. In 1985, a new computer system, installed to improve efficiency, caused unprecedented backlogs, forcing the government to pay $42.8 million more in interest on late refunds. In some IRS offices, workers simply threw away returns that couldn't be processed. Tapes containing $185 million in tax records disappeared for 11 days.

Now, even though the bugs are out of the computer system, the long-term outlook for the agency is far from rosy. Even though the IRS says it takes about three years to become effective on the job, only about 25% of its employees stay that long. As a result, IRS studies have found that about 20% of the information typed in the agency's records by keypunch operators is wrong. The number of returns audited has also fallen drastically, from 5% 20 years ago to 2.6% 10 years ago, and to about 1.1% in 1986. In 1986, only 1.09 million returns were audited, down from 2 million in 1975. But Congress now wants to beef up the IRS as a way of tackling the budget deficit through tougher enforcement.

To cope with the ever-growing pile of unprocessed tax returns, the IRS is banking on high technology, despite its problems in 1985 with a new computer system. Several years ago the IRS dreamed of a system that would abolish tax forms for as many as two thirds of all Americans. With this system IRS computers would automatically calculate taxpayers' bills based on W-2 and 1099 forms received from employers. Then each taxpayer would be mailed a printout. If everything checked out, the taxpayer could sign the form and pay the extra money owed or soon get a refund. However, the return-free program is not likely to be implemented in the near future, largely because tax reform turned out more complex than expected. The IRS has been more successful with a program that allows accountants and paid preparers to file forms electronically. This system is being tested in a few locations and could eventually lead to filing tax forms from a home computer.

The IRS Audit

With the number of audits declining, many taxpayers seem to believe that their problems with audits are over. Not so. First of all, the more you earn, the better chance you have of being audited. Only 1.1% of all forms were audited in 1986, but 4.7% of the 1.1 million taxpayers earning more than $100,000 were audited. And the IRS is increasingly turning to high tech in its war against tax fraud. Currently, IRS computers sort high-income taxpayers into two categories and apply a formula the IRS calls the "discriminant function," or DIF. This formula flags returns that have higher- or lower-than-average deductions, use of tax shelters, types of income, and other factors. The formula rates each return and assigns it a score for each factor; those returns with the highest scores get audited.

About 75% of all audited returns are selected this way, but another 15% are selected by computers that match documents. In these cases, a bank might say a person received $3,000 in interest payments, but the taxpayer failed to report it as income.

Knowing exactly how the DIF formula works would be a gold mine to anyone seeking to avoid audits. But the IRS isn't about to release the workings of this top-secret formula, which in the wrong hands would be a formula for tax fraud. Only 12 agency employees know the formula, which is kept in top-secret vaults. However, it is known that the IRS leans toward auditing forms with certain characteristics. The most common one is, perhaps, the extensive use of tax shelters. But the IRS also goes after returns that show higher-than-average charitable donations, medical costs, and business expenses; large numbers of adult dependents; apparent underreporting of business income; and deductions for hobbies, sideline businesses, home offices, and rental and vacation homes.

It's no surprise that the IRS succeeds with many of its audits. The agency demanded $19.1 billion in additional taxes in 1986, up 12% from 1985. But the IRS doesn't always win. The agency came up empty-handed in more than two out of five audits. The average extra levy was $10,854 for audits done at the taxpayer's home or office, $1,539 for audits done in the IRS's offices, and $496 for audits done by mail. In 70,000 cases, the IRS ended up paying a refund, averaging $2,257.

TAX FRAUD

As the tax system has grown more and more complex, taxpayers have increasingly resorted to tax fraud, threatening the integrity of the entire system. Tax fraud has grown from $29 billion in 1973 to $100 billion in 1986 and is expected to reach $160 billion by 1990. Only 81.6% of the taxes owed were collected in 1986. Here are some of the biggest tax-fraud cases:

The Markowitz Case

The largest tax fraud case ever prosecuted was masterminded by a financial promoter and part-owner of the Washington Capitals hockey team, Edward Markowitz. He tricked more than 100 investors into putting money in his tax-sheltered partnerships. The shelters supposedly involved legitimate buying and selling of government securities, but in fact Markowitz forged documents showing fictitious trades that made it seem as if his partnerships suffered enormous losses between 1979 and 1983. A number of celebrities, including Woody Allen, Bill Murray, Erica Jong, Peter Boyle, and Dick Cavett, put up a total of $20 million that netted them $445 million in false deductions. But the IRS, which has been stepping up its investigations of tax shelters, cracked down on the scam. In April of 1985, Markowitz was convicted, and the investors, who thought they were investing in a legal tax shelter, now owe nearly a half-billion dollars in back taxes and interest.

The Annenberg Case

The biggest individual tax-fraud case until the 1980s involved Moe Annenberg, an immigrant with ties to organized crime who had built up a multimillion-dollar newspaper empire. The linchpin of this empire was the Nationwide News Service, a telephone and telegraph wire service with a monopoly on horse-racing information that served bookies in 39 states. But it wasn't Annenberg's ties to illegal betting and organized crime that got him into trouble. President Roosevelt, angry with attacks on the New Deal by Annenberg-owned newspapers, unleashed a massive IRS investigation. In 1940, Annenberg was convicted of $9.6 million in income tax evasion. Despite this disaster, his son Walter managed to salvage his father's business, turning it into a billion-dollar media empire. (See the profile in the "Magazines" section.)

The Newhouse Case

In probably the largest estate tax case ever, the IRS wants $914 million from the Newhouse family for taxes and penalties from the estate of Samuel Newhouse, who died in 1979. About $305 million is for fraud penalties. The family claims it owes only $47 million. Losing this case could put a big dent in the $2.3 billion fortune of the sons of Samuel and Donald Newhouse.

TAX REVOLTS

As might be imagined in a country that can trace its origins to a successful tax revolt, America's history is full of tax protests. Some protests, like the Boston Tea Party and the Proposition 13 movement in California, have involved many people and shaped the very course of our history. Others, like Henry David Thoreau's tax protest against the Mexican War, have been private protests, matters of intellectual conviction.

Boston Tea Party

The British imposed a vast and heavy burden of taxes on American colonists, but thanks to a lax and fairly corrupt government bureaucracy few of these taxes and trading regulations were ever enforced. However, following the Seven Years' War (1756–1763), the British decided to get tough with the colonists and make them pay for some of the costs of running the empire. The Townshend Acts of 1767 imposed duties on vital colonial imports and in 1773, angered by the fact that the British East India Company was seeking a monopoly on tea sales to the colonies, 150 Boston radicals dressed as Indians dumped 342 cases of tea into the Boston Harbor. Cost of the lost tea was 18,000 pounds sterling, but the eventual result was the loss of the colonies.

The fact that the American Revolution began as a tax revolt, however, caused problems for the early revolutionary government. It managed to collect only $5.8 million from the colonies during the war and General George Washington was forced to spend a great deal of time requesting funds and supplies.

The Whiskey Rebellion

In 1794, President Washington sent in 13,000 troops when some 3,000 Pennsylvania farmers revolted instead of paying an excise tax on liquor. As a result, Congress gradually turned away from using excise taxes to finance the government, abolishing most of them in 1802 and the rest in 1817.

Proposition 13

California's famous tax revolt actually resulted from an earlier attempt to reform the property tax system. After a corrupt San Francisco property tax assessor was sent to jail for taking bribes from corporations in exchange for lower property taxes, the state legislature reformed the property tax code. The legislators believed that home owners were being overtaxed, and so the new law required that all properties be taxed at the same rate. In fact, however, the reverse was true. For political reasons, local governments had always kept taxes on homes low by undervaluing the homes. So, property taxes on homes skyrocketed. In the 1970s, Howard Jarvis, a long-time conservative activist, capitalized on the discontent by organizing one of the largest mass tax protests in recent years. He and Paul Gann collected 1 million signatures to get Proposition 13 on the ballot. Local politicians howled, saying mandated property tax cuts would cripple government and force it to eliminate essential services. No matter. The voters wanted lower taxes and Proposition 13 passed in 1978 by a two-to-one margin. The movement spread to other states, and popular sentiment for lower taxes helped push Congress toward reducing income taxes.

In the short run, Proposition 13 did not cause a fiscal crisis in California, as everyone predicted. Government budgets had been running a surplus—thanks to rising taxes. There were only minor cuts in services. But home owners never received much of a tax cut since the $6.15 billion tax relief created by Jarvis's formula rewarded business and corporate property owners first, wealthy home owners second, and poorer households last. Rental tenants got nothing. However, 10 years after it was passed political pressure was building to repeal Proposition 13 in order to increase social services and improve the educational system.

Table 49 Taxes Collected by Federal, State, and Local Governments

This chart shows how government finances its spending, how fast the average tax bill is growing, and per-capita collections of various types of taxes. The tax figures listed below do not include social insurance taxes such as Social Security and as a result do not agree with some of the figures in Table 50.

Source and year	All governments Total (millions of dollars)	All governments Per-cent of total	Federal[1] Total (millions of dollars)	Federal Percent of all governments' tax	State and local State (millions of dollars)	State and local Local (millions of dollars)	Per capita (dollars) Federal	Per capita (dollars) State and local
Total:								
1960	113,120	100.0	77,003	68.1	18,036	18,081	428	201
1965	144,963	100.0	93,710	64.6	26,126	25,116	483	264
1970	232,877	100.0	146,082	62.7	47,962	38,833	719	427
1975	331,435	100.0	189,970	57.3	80,155	61,310	892	664
1978	468,161	100.0	274,519	58.6	113,261	80,381	1,259	888
1979	524,446	100.0	318,932	60.8	124,908	80,606	1,449	934
1980	574,244	100.0	350,781	61.1	137,075	86,387	1,549	987
1981	650,228	100.0	405,714	62.4	149,738	94,776	1,791	1,079
1982	671,515	100.0	405,125	60.3	162,607	103,783	1,788	1,176
1983	665,615	100.0	381,179	57.3	171,440	112,996	1,629	1,216
1984	735,023	100.0	414,829	56.4	196,795	123,399	1,757	1,356
1985	808,404	100.0	454,037	56.4	215,893	134,473	1,902	1,468
1986	844,949	100.0	471,898	55.8	228,054	144,997	1,957	1,547
Individual income:								
1960	43,178	38.2	40,715	94.3	2,209	254[3]	226	14
1965	52,882	36.5	48,792	92.3	3,657	433[3]	252	21
1970	101,224	43.5	90,412	89.3	9,183	1,630[3]	445	53
1975	143,840	43.4	122,386	85.1	18,819	2,635[3]	574	101
1978	214,164	45.7	180,988	84.5	29,105	4,071[3]	830	152
1979	254,773	48.6	217,841	85.5	32,622	4,309[3]	990	168
1980	286,149	49.8	244,069	85.3	37,089	4,990[3]	1,078	186
1981	331,977	51.0	285,551	86.0	40,895	5,531[3]	1,260	205
1982	348,849	51.9	298,111	85.5	45,668	5,071	1,316	224
1983	344,067	51.7	288,938	84.0	49,789	5,340	1,235	236
1984	360,578	49.1	295,955	82.1	58,942	5,680	1,253	274
1985	401,279		330,918	82.5	63,908	6,453	1,386	294
1986	423,376		348,959	82.4	67,469	6,948	1,447	309
Corporation income:								
1960	22,674	20.0	21,494	94.8	1,180	(3)	119	7
1965	27,390	18.9	25,461	93.0	1,929	(3)	131	10
1970	36,567	15.7	32,829	89.8	3,738	(3)	162	18
1975	47,263	14.3	40,621	85.9	6,642	(3)	191	31
1978	70,690	15.1	59,952	84.8	10,738	(3)	275	49
1979	77,805	14.8	65,677	84.4	12,128	(3)	298	55
1980	77,921	13.6	64,600	82.9	13,321	(3)	285	59
1981	75,280	11.6	61,137	81.2	14,143	(3)	270	62
1982	64,235	9.6	49,207	76.6	14,002	1,027	217	66
1983	51,280	7.7	37,022	72.2	13,153	1,105	158	61
1984	73,940	10.1	56,893	76.9	15,511	1,535	241	72
1985	80,483		61,331	76.2	17,631	1,521	257	80
1986	83,094		63,143	76.0	18,363	1,588	262	83
Sales and gross receipts:[4]								
1960	24,452	21.6	12,603	51.5	10,510	1,339	70	66
1965	32,904	22.7	15,786	48.0	15,059	2,059	81	88
1970	48,619	20.9	18,297	37.6	27,254	3,068	90	149
1975	70,905	21.4	21,090	29.7	43,346	6,468	99	234
1978	93,049	19.9	25,453	27.4	58,270	9,326	117	310
1979	100,961	19.3	26,714	26.5	63,668	10,579	121	337
1980	111,961	19.5	32,034	28.6	67,855	12,072	141	353
1981	134,532	20.7	48,561	36.1	72,751	13,220	214	379
1982	139,288	20.7	45,675	32.8	78,789	14,824	202	413
1983	144,718	21.7	44,471	30.7	83,895	16,352	190	428
1984	163,556	22.3	49,459	30.2	95,801	18,296	209	483
1985	175,535		49,159	28.0	105,419	20,956	206	529
1986	182,017		47,046	25.8	112,343	22,628	195	560

194

Table 49 Taxes Collected by Federal, State, and Local Governments (continued)

Source and year	All governments Total (millions of dollars)	All governments Per-cent of total	Federal[1] Total (millions of dollars)	Federal[1] Percent of all govern- ments' tax	State and local State (millions of dollars)	State and local Local (millions of dollars)	Per capita (dollars) Federal	Per capita (dollars) State and local
Property:								
1960	16,405	14.5	(X)	(X)	607	15,798	(X)	91
1965	22,583	15.6	(X)	(X)	766	21,817	(X)	117
1970	34,054	14.6	(X)	(X)	1,092	32,963	(X)	168
1975	51,491	15.5	(X)	(X)	1,451	50,040	(X)	242
1978	66,422	14.1	(X)	(X)	2,364	64,058	(X)	305
1979	64,944	12.4	(X)	(X)	2,490	62,453	(X)	295
1980	68,499	11.9	(X)	(X)	2,892	65,607	(X)	302
1981	74,969	11.5	(X)	(X)	2,949	72,020	(X)	331
1982	82,067	12.2	(X)	(X)	3,116	78,952	(X)	362
1983	89,105	13.4	(X)	(X)	3,281	85,824	(X)	381
1984	96,457	13.1	(X)	(X)	3,862	92,595	(X)	408
1985	103,757	12.9	(X)	(X)	3,984	99,772	(X)	435
1986	111,711	13.2	(X)	(X)	4,355	107,356	(X)	463
Other taxes:[5]								
1960	6,411	5.7	2,191	34.2	3,530	692	12	23
1965	9,191	6.3	3,670	39.9	4,715	807	19	28
1970	12,413	5.3	4,544	36.6	6,695	1,173	22	39
1975	17,936	5.4	5,873	32.7	9,897	2,166	28	57
1978	23,835	5.1	8,126	34.1	12,784	2,925	37	72
1979	25,964	5.0	8,700	33.5	13,999	3,264	40	78
1980	29,714	5.2	10,078	33.9	15,917	3,718	44	87
1981	33,469	5.1	10,465	31.3	18,999	4,005	46	102
1982	37,075	5.5	12,132	32.7	21,034	3,909	54	110
1983	36,447	5.5	10,748	29.5	21,324	4,375	46	110
1984	40,492	5.5	12,522	30.9	22,679	5,291	53	118
1985	43,350	5.4	12,629		24,730	5,770	53	129
1986	44,751	5.3	12,750		25,525	6,477	53	133

(X) Not applicable.
[1]Corporation income taxes include excess profits tax, normal tax, and surtax.
[2]Represents average for period of intervals shown here; for 1960, change from 1955. Minus sign (—) indicates decrease.
[3]Corporation included with individual income.
[4]Federal taxes include customs.
[5]Includes licenses.
[6]Fiscal year, ending June 30
NA = Not available.
Sources: U.S. Bureau of the Census, *Census of Governments: 1982, Vol. 6, No. 4, Historical Statistics on Governmental Finances and Employment* (GC82(6)-4), and *Governmental Finances*, series GF No. 5, annual; and *Government Quarterly Report* GT87 No. 1, July, 1987.

Table 50   Your Rising Tax Bill

This chart uses an index of tax revenues to show how U.S. taxes have risen. Using 1967 as a base year, it shows that the federal government now collects 6.3 times more personal income taxes than in 1967.

(federal tax index and tax receipts by type of tax[a], calendar years 1970 to 1987)

Tax index, 1967 = 100

Year	All taxes	Personal income taxes	Corporate profit taxes	Indirect business taxes[b]	Social insurance contributions[c]	Estate and gift
1970	128.0	137.9	102.0	119.7	135.8	119.4
1971	132.8	133.1	111.7	125.7	150.7	148.4
1972	152.1	159.5	122.0	122.4	173.5	174.2
1973	173.1	170.0	144.3	131.6	218.8	164.5
1974	192.8	196.3	150.3	132.9	247.7	154.8
1975	193.2	187.6	145.3	146.1	262.6	158.1
1976	223.1	219.7	182.0	142.1	297.9	180.6
1977	252.1	252.3	205.3	151.3	331.0	232.3
1978	289.6	294.3	238.0	167.8	381.4	171.0
1979	331.1	349.7	248.0	171.1	442.7	177.4
1980	362.4	389.9	234.3	223.7	485.7	212.9
1981	418.5	453.0	219.0	330.9	569.5	225.8
1982	414.6	460.4	163.3	271.7	607.7	245.2
1983	430.7	447.4	204.3	295.4	656.8	190.3
1984	473.4	471.6	250.7	316.4	739.8	196.8
1985	514.1	527.2	253.7	308.6	806.9	209.7
1986	541.4	551.6	279.0	295.4	857.6	229.0
1987 I[c]	575.7	580.1	343.3	311.2	887.8	232.3
1987 II[c]	603.7	631.7	355.7	316.4	897.3	258.1

Tax Receipts (billions of dollars)

Year	All taxes	Personal income taxes	Corporate profit taxes	Indirect business taxes[b]	Social insurance contributions[c]	Estate and gift
1970	192.5	88.8	30.6	18.2	51.2	3.7
1971	199.7	85.7	33.5	19.1	56.8	4.6
1972	228.7	102.7	36.6	18.6	65.4	5.4
1973	260.4	109.5	43.3	20.0	82.5	5.1
1974	289.9	126.4	45.1	20.2	93.4	4.8
1975	290.5	120.8	43.6	22.2	99.0	4.9
1976	335.6	141.5	54.6	21.6	112.3	5.6
1977	379.1	162.5	61.6	23.0	124.8	7.2
1978	435.5	189.5	71.4	25.5	143.8	5.3
1979	498.0	225.2	74.4	26.0	166.9	5.5
1980	545.1	251.1	70.3	34.0	183.1	6.6
1981	629.4	291.7	65.7	50.3	214.7	7.0
1982	623.5	296.5	49.0	41.3	229.1	7.6
1983	647.8	288.1	61.3	44.9	247.6	5.9
1984	712.0	303.7	75.2	48.1	278.9	6.1
1985	773.2	339.5	76.1	46.9	304.2	6.5
1986	814.2	355.2	83.7	44.9	323.3	7.1
1987 I[c]	865.8	373.6	103.0	47.3	334.7	7.2
1987 II[c]	907.9	406.8	106.7	48.1	338.3	8.0

[a]Tax receipts, net of refunds, as shown in the national income accounts, generally on an accrual basis.
[b]Excise taxes and custom duties.
[c]Seasonally adjusted annual rates.
Source: Department of Commerce, Bureau of Economic Analysis; and Tax Foundation computations.

196

Table 51   The Most Heavily Taxed States

Highest state and local tax burden, 1986

Rank	State	Per-capita tax (dollars)
1.	Alaska	4,489
2.	Wyoming	2,628
3.	Washington, D.C.	2,743
4.	New York	2,539
5.	Connecticut	1,947
6.	Massachusetts	1,933
7.	New Jersey	1,868
8.	Hawaii	1,785
9.	Maryland	1,785
10.	Wisconsin	1,730

The Least Heavily Taxed States

Lowest state and local tax burden, 1986

Rank	State	Per-capita taxes (dollars)
51.	Mississippi	965
50.	Arkansas	1,011
49.	Alabama	1,022
48.	Idaho	1,054
47.	Tennessee	1,077

Source: U.S. Bureau of the Census.

Table 52   Government Finance Around the World

This table shows how the U.S. and other countries finance their governments. It shows that while the U.S. raises only 7.1% of its tax revenues from corporate taxes, Japan raises 21.1%.

(percent distribution of tax receipts by type of tax)

Country and year	Total[1]	Income and profits taxes[2] Total[3]	Individual	Corporate	Social Security contributions Total[4]	Employees	Employers	Taxes on goods and services[5] Total[3]	General consumption taxes[6]	Taxes on specific goods, services[7]
United States: 1984	100.0	42.4	35.3	7.1	29.1	11.2	17.1	18.2	7.3	8.5
Canada: 1984	100.0	43.4	33.9	8.8	12.8	4.4	8.2	32.7	12.1	14.4
France: 1984	100.0	17.5	13.3	4.1	43.5	12.2	28.3	28.7	19.9	8.1
Germany, Federal Republic: 1984	100.0	33.3	27.9	5.4	36.4	15.9	19.1	27.1	16.8	9.2
Italy: 1984	100.0	36.2	26.3	9.8	33.9	6.9	23.9	26.1	15.1	9.5
Japan: 1984	100.0	45.6	24.5	21.1	29.7	10.5	15.2	15.1	—	13.0
Netherlands: 1984	100.0	26.6	20.8	5.7	44.3	18.6	17.9	25.5	15.7	7.5
Sweden: 1984	100.0	42.1	38.4	3.7	26.2	—	25.1	25.1	13.4	10.6
United Kingdom: 1984	100.0	38.1	26.7	11.5	18.1	8.5	9.1	30.5	14.7	14.1

—Represents zero.
[1] Includes property taxes, employer payroll taxes other than Social Security contributions, and miscellaneous taxes, not shown separately.
[2] Includes taxes on capital gains.
[3] Includes other taxes, not shown separately.
[4] Includes contributions of self-employed, not shown separately.
[5] Taxes on the production, sales, transfer, leasing, and delivery of goods and services and rendering of services.
[6] Primarily value-added and sales taxes.
[7] For example, excise taxes on alcohol, tobacco, and gasoline.
Source: Organization for Economic Cooperation and Development, Paris, France, *Revenue Statistics of OECD Member Countries,* annual.

Table 53   A Tax Tour: The Tax Bill Around the World

This chart shows the tax revenues in other major countries. America's per-capita tax bill is higher than those of such countries as Finland and Japan but far lower than those of such countries as Norway and Sweden. As a percentage of gross domestic product (GDP), the U.S. tax bill is, however, lower than those of most countries. Only in Japan, Spain, and Portugal do taxes make up a lower percentage of GDP. In many other countries it is above 40%, compared to 29% in the U.S.

Country	Tax revenues, 1984 (billions of dollars)	Tax revenues per capita, 1984 (dollars)	Tax revenues as percent of GDP		
			1975	1980	1984
United States	1,030.9	4,356	29.6	30.4	29.0
Australia	57.4	3,697	28.5	29.8	31.2
Austria	27.0	3,581	38.6	41.2	42.0
Belgium	36.3	3,682	41.1	43.7	46.7
Canada	115.6	4,598	33.0	32.0	33.7
Denmark	26.0	5,079	41.4	45.5	48.0
Finland	18.5	3,783	35.3	33.3	36.0
France	222.9	4,057	37.4	42.5	45.5
Germany, Federal Republic	231.4	3,783	35.7	38.0	37.7
Greece	11.8	1,190	24.6	28.6	35.2
Italy	144.2	2,530	29.0	33.2	41.2
Japan	348.8	2,906	20.9	25.5	27.4
Netherlands	56.0	3,886	43.6	45.8	45.5
New Zealand	7.2	2,222	29.6	30.9	31.0
Norway	25.4	6,133	44.8	47.1	46.4
Portugal	6.2	609	24.7	28.7	32.0
Spain	45.7	1,190	19.6	24.1	28.4
Sweden	48.0	5,760	43.9	49.4	50.5
Switzerland	29.3	4,505	29.6	30.8	32.2
United Kingdom	163.0	2,886	35.5	35.3	38.5

Source: Organization for Economic Co-operation and Development, Paris, France, *Revenue Statistics of OECD Member Countries*, annual.

PART IV

The Business of Business

Chapter Twelve

SERVICES: PRODUCTS ARE PASSÉ

HIGHLIGHTS AND TRENDS

• Today over 75% of all American workers are employed in service-producing industries. That stands in sharp contrast to the beginning of the 20th century, when about 73% of the population worked in agriculture and blue-collar occupations.

• More than ever Americans are providing services instead of producing goods. Today, over three quarters of all nonagricultural workers are employed in service occupations, up from 58.6% in 1952. By the end of the century, manufacturing, mining, and construction will only account for 20.7% of nonagricultural jobs, down from 32.2% in 1972. Meanwhile, service jobs will comprise nearly four fifths of all jobs (79.3%), up from 67.8% in 1972.

• Services have been the only bright spot in America's ballooning trade deficit. Services ran a $22.3 billion trade surplus in 1986.

• The nonagricultural sector of the economy produced about 30.8 million jobs between 1970 and September of 1987—30.2 million of them in the service sector.

• The services boom is likely to continue. Most of the 21 million new jobs created between now and the year 2000 will be service jobs. The U.S. Department of Labor indicates that 20.1 million service jobs will be created between 1986 and 2000, with such jobs totaling 94.5 million at the turn of the century. Meanwhile, manufacturing jobs will drop 4.4% from 19 million in 1986 to 18.2 million in 2000.

• A lot of new service jobs won't pay as well as the blue-collar jobs that once made up the backbone of the economy. Take the new jobs expected to be created between now and 2000 for salespersons (1.2 million), more than any other occupation. But salesworkers earned only an average of $215 a week in 1986. Similarly, 7 out of the 10 largest job-producing occupations, salesworkers, waiters, janitors, cashiers, clerks, nurses aides, and food-counter workers pay less than the average wage.

• The economy, however, is producing well-paying jobs too. Some 604,000 new managerial and executive jobs will be created. Another 525,000 new jobs will open up for truck drivers. Both executing and truck driving are high-paying service occupations.

THE NEW SERVICE ECONOMY

A hundred years ago, only a lunatic might have imagined an economy in which over 75% of all workers were not involved in the production of food, housing, and manufactured products.

But that's exactly the kind of economy we have.

Even more surprising, this strange economy works, at least part of the time.

For the first time in history, most Americans don't produce the things we all need to survive. Few grow food, build homes and offices, mine raw materials, or manufacture goods. They produce services.

With over half of the labor force working in offices, we are accustomed to the idea that services are an important part of the economy. But to get an idea how unusual the service economy is, it's worth remembering that in 1900 about 73% of the population worked in agriculture and blue-collar occupations. Today, the figure is nearly reversed, with over 75% of all nonagricultural employees in service-producing industries. About 24.9 million Americans produce goods—working in manufacturing, construction, or mining. Over three times as many (77 million) work in service-producing industries. Only 3.3 million Americans have jobs in agriculture. And services will be even more important in the future. Just about all of the jobs expected to be created in America will be in the service sector.

Services Serve the Economy

If the service economy does not produce goods, what does it do? Unlike manufacturing, mining, construction, farming, and other goods-producing industries, service industries are hard to define. Indeed, service-producing industries are a mixed bag. Education is a service industry; so is banking. The esoteric business of dredging rivers to improve trout fishing is a service, as is the more mundane job of driving a truck. All government agencies, from the Central Intelligence Agency to the Parks Department, are part of the service sector, as are wholesale and retail trade, communications, public utilities, health care, education, repair and maintenance, transportation, insurance, banking, finance, advertising, consultants, lawyers, engineering firms, nonprofit organizations, hotels, barber shops, data processing, employment agencies, restaurants, bars, and headhunters.

Some sections of the service sector—such as prostitution—are among the world's oldest businesses. Others, such as data processing, are only possible in a modern industrial economy. Although it's tempting to dismiss the service economy as only producing paperwork, modern economies that rely on high technology and information would not be possible without service industries.

In fact, service industries make the production of goods possible. Services such as banking arrange complicated financing for multinational corporations that are wealthier than many countries. Service workers educate the people who run those corporations. Service workers do market research, helping companies to produce new products. Service workers transport these products to the market. Service workers create advertisements to show how these products will make you sexier, wealthier, and wiser.

That's not all. Service workers repair products when they break and file lawsuits if a product isn't all it's cracked up to be. Service workers even dispose of the trash produced by other service workers.

The growth of services is also a reflection of long-term social as well as economic changes. As more and more women enter the labor force, service industries care for their children and prepare meals for families too busy to cook at home. With the decline of the extended family, government and health services care for the elderly, the disabled, and the poor.

And service industries make the so-called consumer society possible. Increasingly affluent workers turn to a variety of financial services to invest their money and to other services, such as recreation and travel, when they want to spend their money. In fact, such services as advertising and retail sales create the very psychology of consumerism.

The State of the Service Industries

How the service economy affects the economic health of the American economy is the subject of a widespread and often confusing debate. Some pop economists say services will save the country from the decline of manufacturing; others argue, just as vehemently, that the rise of the service economy will produce a period of slower economic growth, declining productivity, and stagnant wages.

In fact, neither position makes much sense. Service industries are no panacea for a healthy manufacturing, construction, and farm economy. A declining manufacturing sector hurts the future of rapidly growing service industries dependent on manufacturing concerns.

Since some service occupations pay worse than many manufacturing or construction jobs, critics have charged that the continuing shift of jobs to the service sector could help drag down consumer incomes. As noted, seven of the 10 occupations expected to produce most of the jobs— salesworkers, waiters, janitors, cashiers, clerks, nurse's aides, and food-counter workers—are all service jobs that pay less than the average weekly wage.

Fortunately, the third-highest number of jobs will be created in registered nursing, an occupation where salaried employees earn $460 a week.

And the economy at least will need all those well paying executives and truck drivers as we have seen.

A more worrisome problem is productivity in the service sector. Companies have spent tens of billions of dollars on computers and other equipment to automate their offices, yet productivity in service-producing industries has shown virtually no improvement since 1979. That dismal showing held down productivity and, as a result, wages, for the entire economy. If no gains are made in service-sector productivity, some forecasters believe that the GNP will grow less than 3% a year between now and 1995, with per-capita income growing only 1.5%. (See the chapter "Trade, Productivity, and Staying Ahead" for a discussion of how low productivity is holding down our incomes.)

Also remember that service jobs are just as vulnerable to technological displacement and foreign competition as manufacturing jobs have been. For example, continuing automation in the office has caused the number of clerical workers to decline since 1980 by about 200,000.

Moreover, lower wages in other countries have caused employers to move some office jobs overseas. For example, newspaper articles contained in one computer database are keyed into the computer by Chinese workers who can't even read English. Likewise, a recent study of the Office of Technology Assessment of the U.S. Congress estimates that even more service companies will move overseas to find cheap wages. Data-entry clerks in the Caribbean earn weekly wages of only $15 to $60; clerks in China might earn only $2 a week. Indian workers, for example, enter data into computers for only 10% to 15% of what it would cost to do the job with American workers.

Such statistics contradict those who imagine services will ensure economic prosperity. However, it's also wrong to blame the economy's recent woes on services as others have done.

A popular myth that emerged from the tough 1981–1982 recession was that the decline of manufacturing and the rise of services are relatively recent phenomena. In fact, if you define a service economy as one in which more than half of the workers are employed in service-producing industries, then the U.S. has been a service economy since 1950. Yet the growth of the service economy didn't wreck the whole economy. Wages for both manufacturing and services grew rapidly during the 1950s and 1960s, when both service and manufacturing pay increased by about $9,500. Moreover, the gap between service and manufacturing pay is shrinking, indicating that the problems with the U.S. economy are not simply the fault of the service sector.

Services have also been growing faster than manufacturing for some time. Between 1960 and 1981, service employment grew 3.2% a year while manufacturing grew 1% a year. The service sector created 17 million of the 19 million new jobs produced in the 1970s.

The nonagricultural sector of the economy produced about 31.5 million jobs between 1970 and 1987—30.2 million of them were in the service sector.

THE CREATION OF THE MODERN OFFICE

2nd century A.D.   Becoming a paper pusher becomes possible when the Chinese invent paper, manufacturing it with some unknown type of plant fiber. The Arabs introduce paper to Europe in the 9th century. Paper made from wood pulp does not appear until the 14th century.

1564   The pencil is invented shortly after the discovery of graphite in England.

1750   The eraser is invented around this time by Magalhaens, a Portuguese physicist, making it possible for a paper pusher to erase his or her mistakes.

mid-18th century   The word *bureaucracy* is coined by Frenchman Vincent de Gournay. Derived from the Latin *burrus,* referring to the dark-brown cloth used to cover a writing desk or bureau, and from the Greek *kratein,* meaning "to rule," the new word means "government by desk." Gournay coins the word to refer to the novel phenomenon of clerks working in government or private offices at desks in contrast to the older system whereby aristocrats worked out of their estates. From the beginning, the word has a pejorative connotation. Gournay suggests these new bureaucrats suffer from excessive zeal, a disease he calls *bureaumania.*

1773   The first duplicating machine is invented by James Watt, the famous British inventor of the steam engine, so he can handle the paperwork at his factory.

1802   A Frenchman, Descroissilles, invents the coffeepot, making the coffee break possible. The first coffeehouses appeared in 1554 in Constantinople.

1806   An Englishman, R. Wedgewood, invents carbon paper.

1808   An Italian, Pellegrine Turri, builds the first typewriter for the Countess Caroline Frantoni, who is blind, so they can send each other letters. A Danish pastor, Malling Hansen, markets the first typewriter in 1870. The first electric typewriter is built by Dr. Thaddeus Cahill in 1901, but IBM popularizes electric typewriters by marketing the Electromatic in 1933.

1820   An Englishman named S. K. Brewer announces that he has invented the envelope. Though a few earlier envelopes have been found, most letters were folded and mailed without an envelope.

1875   The first want ads for typists appear. The pay is $10 to $20 a week, which is considered good pay at the time.

1875   The first commercial telephone is connected at the Cambridge, Massachusetts, Board of Waterworks. Employees can only call one other party—the Board's branch office. By the 1980s there are 151 million telephones in America.

1884   Fountain pens are reported as early as the 17th century. In 1884 Lewis Waterman founds the first fountain pen factory.

1900   The paper clip is invented by a Norwegian, Johann Waaler.

1911   An American, Willis Carrier, invents the air conditioner.

1913   The first U.S. crossword puzzle is published. It is written by journalist Arthur Wynne. The crossword puzzle soon becomes a favorite way of wasting time in offices.

1925   Scotch tape is invented by Dick Drew of the Minnesota Mining and Manufacturing Company (3M) as a masking tape for painting cars in two tones. The product gets its name because the original tape only has adhesive on the edges. Auto workers think the company is trying to save money by scrimping on adhesive so they call the tape "Scotch tape," after the frugal citizens of Scotland. The first clear or cellulose Scotch tape appears in 1930.

1938   Lazlo Biro, a Hungarian journalist, invents the ballpoint pen. Ballpoint pens first go on sale at Gimbel's at $12.50 apiece in 1945 and sell out on the first day. Banks, however, suggest that signatures made using the new ballpoint pen may not be legal.

1954   The first electronic computer used in business goes into service at J. Lyons & Co. in London. The same year the computer Univac I starts operations at the GE Appliance Park.

1959   Revolutionizing the art of creating paperwork, Xerox introduces its first office copier, the Xerox 914. It only makes six copies a minute. The Xerox machine, which was invented by Chester Carlson in 1938, was the first to use dry photocopying on untreated paper. Carlson had trouble finding someone to sell his invention but in 1947, after 20 companies refused to develop his patents, Haloid, a small company that eventually becomes Xerox, signed an agreement.

1959   Digital Equipment Corporation produces the first minicomputer, setting off a trend toward smaller and smaller computers that eventually opens up the market for small office computers.

1972   The first pocket calculator is developed by Texas Instruments.

1979   Apple introduces the first mass-market personal computer, touching off a revolution in office technology.

Chapter Thirteen

MANUFACTURING:
THE RUSTING OF AMERICA

HIGHLIGHTS AND TRENDS

• American manufacturing has entered a long-term decline. Only 18.7% of all nonagricultural workers were employed in manufacturing in 1987, down from 22.4% in 1980, 27.3% in 1970, and 35.2% in 1947. Manufacturing's share of the GNP has also been sagging, dropping from 28.1% in 1947 about 20% today.

• The decline of manufacturing is a major contributor to the ever-widening trade deficit of the United States. Americans imported $139.1 billion more manufactured goods in 1986 than they exported, with nearly half of that deficit ($67.9 billion) in goods from Japan. In contrast, the U.S. had a positive trade balance of $16.9 billion in 1980.

• Even with improvement in the economy, the country's factories face an uncertain future. Few economists believe that the auto industry will ever again produce the 9.6 million cars it did in 1973 or that the steel industry will ever again employ 602,000 workers, as it did in 1974.

• Declining American competitiveness has hurt the manufacturing sector. About 5.1 million experienced American workers lost their jobs because of plant closings or employment cutbacks between 1981 and 1986. About half of these jobs, 2.55 million, were lost in the manufacturing sector even though manufacturing employs about one fifth of all nonagricultural workers.

• About 18.2% of these experienced workers, who had held the same manufacturing job for at least three years before being laid off, remained unemployed; another 15.9% left the labor force.

• About 432,000 (30.6%) of the 1.4 million displaced manufacturing workers who eventually found full-time work suffered wage cuts of more than 20%. About half (52.5%) of all steelworkers who found new full-time jobs earned 20% less than before. Another 186,000 manufacturing workers were hit with earning cuts of 1% to 20% at their new jobs. About 162,000, or about 9.8% of the 1.657 million who found full-time or part-time work or started their own businesses, now work part-time. But not all displaced manufacturing workers were hurt by the layoffs. About 48.8% (689,000) of those who found full-time work were earning more at their new jobs.

• One explanation for employment problems in American manufacturing is simple: American companies are failing to match the productivity improvements of their toughest competitors. U.S. productivity in the manufacturing sector as measured by output per hour grew only 2.2% between 1973 and 1985, down from a 3.2% increase between 1960 and 1973. That was way below Japan's growth rate of 10.3% a year between 1960 and 1973 and 5.6% between 1973 and 1985. As a result, U.S. productivity growth between 1960 and 1985 lagged way behind the average 5.4% annual rate of increase in productivity of its 11 major industrial competitors. While U.S. manufacturing productivity grew only 2.7% a year between 1960 and 1985, productivity grew 8.0% in Japan, 5.5% in France, 3.4% in Canada, 4.8% in Germany, 5.4% in Italy, 3.5% in the United Kingdom, 6.5% in Belgium, 4.8% in Denmark, 6.2% in the Netherlands, 3.2% in Norway, and 4.7% in Sweden.

• Since then, however, U.S. manufacturers have been making a comeback in the productivity race. In 1986, U.S. manufacturing productivity grew by 3.5%, faster than Canada (−0.5%), Japan (2.7%), France (1.9%), Germany (1.9%), Italy (1.2%), and the United Kingdom (3.0%).

THE CRISIS IN AMERICAN MANUFACTURING

In 1870 more than half of all American workers (53%) could be found down on the farm. But by 1920 more Americans (11.2 million) were employed in manufacturing than in agriculture (10.8 million), and in the 1930s, as the Dust Bowl forced thousands of farmers into the cities, it finally became apparent that the U.S. was no longer a rural, agricultural nation. By 1960 there were 16.8 million Americans employed in manufacturing, more than three times the 5.5 million employed in agriculture. Manufacturing accounted for 28% of GNP compared to only 4% for agriculture.

But in the late 1970s and early 1980s disaster struck. During the recession of 1982, American manufacturing underwent its own Dust Bowl, a Rust Bowl that rocked the boardrooms of the old industrial giants. U.S. auto makers sold only 5.7 million cars in 1982, the worst slump since the 1950s, producing long lines at the unemployment office. In Michigan, unemployment hit 14.2% in 1982, and in some cities, such as Flint where 20,000 auto workers were laid off, nearly a quarter of the labor force was out of work.

Like the Dust Bowl 50 years earlier, the crisis of American manufacturing also supposedly heralded a new economic era—the rise of the service economy. Faced with the declining prospects at home, tens of thousands of laid-off blue-collar workers migrated from the old industrial heartland of the midwest and northeast into service jobs in the more prosperous western and southern states, just as the farmers put their possessions in Model T's and fled the Dust Bowl during the 1930s.

That migration marked more than an economic change; it was a major political change. Just as manufacturing made the midwest and northeast states dominant economic and political powers in the first half of the 20th century, the Rust Bowl sapped those states, shifting economic power toward the west and the Sunbelt. Not surprisingly, the last four presidents to be elected to office—Johnson, Nixon, Carter, and Reagan—were from the west or the south. In contrast, organized labor, with its traditional base in manufacturing, was weakened. Labor was unable to get the Mondale campaign off the ground, despite millions of dollars in contributions.

The spectacle of rusty steel mills, idle auto plants, and U.S. manufacturers moving their factories overseas touched off a long-overdue debate over the future of the American economy. Unfortunately, this debate, like most discussions of the American economy, produced more heat than light.

As the media descended on the industrial heartland, looking for the best disaster story since the eruption of Mount St. Helens, some of the most pessimistic pundits began predicting that the heyday of manufacturing was long gone. Soon, it was said, we'd have an economy whose principal products were fast food, unemployment checks, and paperwork.

A few went even further, having the temerity to suggest that this wasn't such a bad development, and that services, not manufacturing, were the wave of the future. Soon those unemployed blue-collar workers would find new service jobs and go back to work as white-collar workers. They could become data processors. After all, who needs a dirty, smelly factory when you can work in a nice clean office?

But, as usual, the economy confounded the forecasters. Contrary to the faddish belief that factories are disappearing in industrialized nations, manufacturing is alive and well in many parts of the world. For example, while employment in the manufacturing sector of the economy declined by 1.9 million in the U.S. between 1980 and 1984, it grew by 4.8 million in Japan.

Also, it would be a mistake to overemphasize the growth of the service economy. Some of the drastic growth in the service industry is simply because the cost of services has increased faster than the cost of goods. For example, half of all consumer spending (52.2%) in 1986 was for services, up from the 36.6% spent in 1955. But when you adjust for inflation in the service industry, the service economy's share of consumer spending has been virtually unchanged since 1979 and has grown only about 7 percentage points, rather than 16, since 1955.

Some economists would also argue that manufacturing has only declined in current dollars, not in real dollars—that is, not in dollars that are adjusted for inflation. In 1970, manufacturing accounted for 21% of GNP; by 1985, it still held at 21.7% in constant 1982 dollars.

Even those alarmed by manufacturing's declining share of GNP argue that the future of manufacturing remains vital to the American economy. Although manufacturing only employs 18.7% of all nonagricultural workers, it still calls the shots for most of the economy. Spending for durable and nondurable goods, for example, accounts for nearly half of all personal consumption. As a result, cyclical swings in the economy are still touched off by declines in the manufacturing sector. Moreover, the service sector, traditionally less affected by economic cycles of boom and bust, is now more closely tied to the profitability of manufacturing. If you imagine that GM's biggest supplier is a steel maker or a tire manufacturer, you're wrong. It's Blue Cross and Blue Shield. Also, two of the fastest-growing areas of the service economy are business services and health services. These industries would have a hard time if there were no manufacturing companies to buy their services.

Does this mean American manufacturing is in fine shape? No. After-tax profits of American manufacturers dropped 18% from $101.3 billion in 1981 to only $83.1 billion in 1986. About 1.1 million jobs were lost in the manufacturing sector between 1980 and September of 1987. Productivity gains in the manufacturing sector have been only half those of Japan. Making American manufacturers more competitive at home and in the international markets will dominate economic debates for the next decade.

The human effects of a declining manufacturing sector are readily apparent. A 1987 study by the Bureau of Labor Statistics found that about 10.8 million Americans lost their jobs because of plant closings or employment cutbacks between the start of 1981 and January of 1986. The Labor Department study focused on the 5.1 million displaced workers who had been on their jobs for over three years. About half of these experienced workers, 2.55 million, were in the manufacturing sector even though manufacturing employs less than one fifth of all nonagricultural workers.

Many of the experienced manufacturing workers did not find new work and their skills have been lost to the economy. About 18.2% of the workers who had held the same job for at least three years before being laid off remained unemployed; another 15.9% left the labor force.

And many of the workers who found work saw sharp cuts in their paychecks. About 432,000 (30.6%) of the 1.4 million displaced manufacturing workers who eventually found full-time work suffered wage cuts of more than 20%. About half (52.5%) of all steelworkers who found new full-time jobs earned 20% less than before. Another 186,000 manufacturing workers were hit with earning cuts of 1% to 20% at their new jobs. About 162,000, or about 9.8% of the 1.657 million who started their own businesses or found full-time or part-time work, now work part-time and presumably earn less than before.

But not all displaced manufacturing workers were hurt by the layoffs. About 48.8% (689,000) of those who found full-time work were earning more at their new jobs.

A simple explanation for the employment problems in American manufacturing can be found in American productivity. As previously noted, U.S. productivity in the manufacturing sector as measured by output per hour grew a mere 2.2% between 1973 and 1985, down from a 3.2% increase between 1960 and 1973. Meanwhile, Japan's growth rate was much higher, 10.3% and 5.6% for the respective periods, and productivity growth in the U.S. was falling behind that of all its major industrial competitors.

In recent years, U.S. manufacturers have gotten back in the race; in 1984, for instance, U.S. manufacturing productivity grew 4.1%, faster than half of its biggest competitors, and it jumped another 4.4% in 1985, outperforming 8 of 11 major competitors. U.S. manufacturing productivity slowed somewhat in 1986 to 3.5%, but still outdid Canada, Japan, France, Germany, Italy, and the United Kingdom.

Part of the improved productivity in American manufacturing can be traced to its responses to some of its wrenching problems. To hold down prices, companies have slashed corporate bureaucracies, shut down aging plants, and forced wage concessions from unions. Few economists believe the auto industry will ever again produce the 9.6 million cars it did during the early 1970s or that the steel industry will ever again employ 602,000 workers, but many manufacturers won't have to return to the good old days. Ford Motor Company, for example, cut costs and is now producing record profits in a stagnant auto market.

Thanks in part to that tough medicine, U.S. factories once again were showing signs of life in 1987. Aided by a falling dollar, rising exports, and a strong economy, some manufacturers were resuming U.S. production. U.S. factories were operating at 81.7% of capacity in October 1987, up from 70.3% in the dog days of 1982. Industrial production measured on an index where 1977 production equals 100 spurted to 130.9 in September 1987, a hefty 5.1% increase.

But the manufacturing sector may have a harder time keeping up the good work. While a falling dollar will continue to help exports, the stock market crash of 1987 raised doubts about the health of the economy in 1988. And even if the economy weathers the problems created by black and blue Monday, October 19, soaring manufacturing output could raise renewed fears of inflation, forcing the Fed to cut the growth of the money supply and cool off the economy.

To avoid another Rust Bowl, moreover, some long-term changes must be made. The tax system will have to become more supportive of capital investment; labor will have to make concessions on work rules and costs; management is going to have to learn that long-term investments in technology are the best way to increase profits for shareholders; the U.S. will have to increase pressure on foreign countries to open their markets to American goods. Perhaps most importantly, all of these solutions are going to take time. Lowering the taxes on capital gains or giving investment tax credits for three years and then taking them away because they don't solve all the world's problems are not the ways to promote long-term investment. (See the chapter "Trade, Productivity, and Staying Ahead" for a complete discussion of how American companies are fighting to improve their competitive position.)

Table 54   Value of Shipments in Selected Manufacturing Industries

The following table gives a sense of how individual industries have fared by showing the value of shipments for individual industries. It shows that many industries, particularly primary metals (which includes the steel industry) and farm machinery, have still not recovered from the crisis of 1981 and 1982 while other industries, such as office- and computing-machine manufacturers, (which includes computers) and electronic-component manufacturers, grew even during the worst recession since the 1930s.

(in billions of dollars)

Industry	1978	1980	1981	1982	1983	1984	1985	1986*	1987*
Shipments, total	1,522.9	1,852.2	2,017.5	1,908.3	2,045.3	2,274.9	2,341.2	2,273,298	2,408,593
Durable goods	814.2	930.6	1,006.5	920.3	1,019.4	1,182.0	1,243.8	1,201,704	1,263,875
Stone, clay, and glass products	41.7	46.1	48.0	44.0	49.1	55.0	57.3	56,787	60,997
Primary metals	118.1	133.9	141.9	107.0	117.9	131.2	125.8	101,733	111,465
Fabricated metal products	101.3	116.2	123.7	114.0	120.6	139.2	169.0	135,974	134,177
Machinery excluding electrical	143.2	180.7	201.5	180.6	178.3	210.2	212.6	205,804	212,631
Engines and turbines	12.4	13.7	15.3	12.8	12.2	14.9	15.1	14,770	15,077
Farm machinery and equipment	11.9	15.1	16.0	11.8	10.6	10.5	10.4	NA	NA
Construction, mining, and material handling equipment	28.9	33.6	39.0	34.5	28.4	32.6	33.6	26,589	26,242
Office and computing machines	21.0	32.4	37.8	40.4	46.0	55.4	55.5	56,230	56,269
Electrical machinery	100.5	128.6	140.2	141.1	156.0	182.5	185.5	205,613	224,482
Electrical transmission & distribution	17.9	21.3	23.4	21.9	21.9	24.8	24.9	25,374	26,969
Household appliances	11.5	12.9	13.1	12.1	14.9	17.4	17.1	17,090	18,583
Radio and TV	7.9	8.1	8.8	7.8	8.6	10.6	11.2	12,851	13,053
Communication equipment	17.9	27.6	30.4	31.3	35.3	44.9	62.5	69,725	74,055
Electronic components	17.9	27.6	30.4	31.3	35.3	44.9	38.9	44,006	50,223
Transportation equipment	188.8	186.5	205.2	195.1	240.5	268.3	313.4	314,081	323,400
Motor vehicles and parts	132.0	104.6	117.0	112.2	151.9	191.5	203.4	194,725	201,199
Aircraft, missiles, and parts	37.5	58.5	64.8	63.6	70.9	77.0	90.6	98,984	101,299
Instruments and related products	33.7	44.1	48.3	46.7	47.9	53.5	56.7	60,860	63,250
Scientific and engineering equipment	19.2	25.6	28.7	28.0	29.3	33.3	37.3	40,642	42,191
Photographic goods	11.5	15.9	16.9	16.6	16.3	17.9	17.2	18,035	19,058

Industry	1978	1980	1981	1982	1983	1984	1985	1986*	1987*
Nondurable goods	708.7	922.1	1,011.1	988.0	1,025.9	1,092.9	1,097.4		
Food and kindred products	216.0	256.2	272.1	277.3	286.6	291.1	296.1		
Meat products	55.6	63.0	65.9	66.2	66.8	70.1	67.6	NA	NA
Fat and oils	16.2	18.2	17.9	15.4	16.5	15.6	13.7	NA	NA
Beverages	26.6	33.0	36.1	40.3	41.7	43.1	45.2	43,853	43,404
Tobacco products	10.0	12.2	13.1	14.5	15.5	16.9	20.6	18,016	18,619
Textile mill products	42.3	47.3	50.3	47.2	52.2	55.1	52.6	54,607	56,547
Paper and allied products	57.0	72.8	80.2	79.0	85.1	95.9	97.6	103,834	118,882
Paper, pulp, paperboard, and mill products	24.0	31.8	35.1	33.5	36.3	41.5	41.8	43,990	51,547
Paperboard containers	14.5	17.2	19.0	18.4	19.1	21.7	21.4	22,414	25,674
Chemical & allied products	129.4	162.5	180.5	172.8	190.2	211.8	214.3	198,348	214,635
Industrial inorganic chemicals	44.8	57.3	62.7	55.8	59.2	68.7	71.6	56,492	62,704
Drugs, soaps, and toiletries	34.2	41.9	46.9	48.6	50.4	53.9	56.1	69,164	72,512
Petroleum and coal products	103.9	198.7	224.1	206.4	191.6	200.6	194.0	129,320	129,743
Rubber and plastic products	43.2	47.3	53.2	50.2	50.3	52.1	48.2	72,170	78,878

Source: U.S. Department of Commerce.
*Preliminary.

210

Table 55 Manufacturing Profits

(billions of dollars; quarterly data at seasonally adjusted annual rates)

Corporate profits with inventory valuation adjustment and without capital consumption adjustment

Year	Total manufac-turing	Durable goods							Nondurable goods				
		Total	Primary metal industries	Fabricated metal products	Machinery, except electrical	Electric and electronic equipment	Motor vehicles and equipment	Other	Total	Food and kindred products	Chemicals and allied products	Petroleum and coal products	Other
1929	5.2	2.6							2.6				
1933	−.4	−.4							.0				
1939	3.3	1.7							1.7				
1940	5.5	3.1							2.4				
1941	9.5	6.4							3.1				
1942	11.8	7.2							4.6				
1943	13.8	8.1							5.7				
1944	13.2	7.4							5.9				
1945	9.7	4.5							5.2				
1946	9.0	2.4							6.6				
1947	13.6	5.8							7.8				
1948	17.6	7.5	1.6	0.8	1.2	0.7	1.4	1.8	10.0	1.9	1.7	2.8	3.7
1949	16.2	8.1	1.5	.7	1.3	.8	2.1	1.7	8.1	1.6	1.8	1.9	2.8
1950	20.9	12.0	2.3	1.1	1.6	1.2	3.1	2.6	8.9	1.6	2.3	2.3	2.7
1951	24.6	13.2	3.1	1.3	2.3	1.3	2.4	2.8	11.4	1.4	2.8	2.7	4.4
1952	21.7	11.7	1.9	1.0	2.3	1.5	2.4	2.6	9.9	1.7	2.3	2.3	3.6
1953	22.0	11.9	2.5	1.0	1.9	1.4	2.6	2.6	10.1	1.8	2.2	2.8	3.3
1954	19.9	10.5	1.7	.9	1.7	1.2	2.1	2.9	9.4	1.6	2.2	2.7	2.9
1955	26.0	14.3	2.9	1.1	1.7	1.1	4.1	3.5	11.8	2.2	3.0	3.0	3.6
1956	24.7	12.8	3.0	1.1	2.1	1.2	2.2	3.2	11.9	1.8	2.8	3.3	4.1
1957	24.0	13.3	3.0	1.1	2.0	1.5	2.6	3.1	10.7	1.8	2.8	2.6	3.6
1958	19.4	9.3	1.9	.9	1.4	1.3	0.9	2.9	10.0	2.1	2.5	2.1	3.3
1959	26.4	13.7	2.3	1.1	2.1	1.7	3.0	3.5	12.7	2.4	3.5	2.5	4.3
1960	23.6	11.6	2.0	.8	1.8	1.3	3.0	2.7	12.0	2.2	3.1	2.5	4.2
1961	23.3	11.4	1.6	1.0	1.9	1.3	2.5	3.1	11.9	2.3	3.2	2.2	4.1
1962	26.0	14.0	1.6	1.1	2.3	1.5	4.0	3.5	12.0	2.3	3.2	2.2	4.3
1963	29.3	16.3	2.0	1.3	2.5	1.6	4.9	4.0	13.1	2.7	3.6	2.1	4.6
1964	32.3	17.9	2.5	1.4	3.3	1.7	4.7	4.4	14.4	2.7	4.0	2.4	5.3
1965	39.3	23.0	3.1	2.0	3.9	2.7	6.2	5.1	16.3	2.8	4.6	2.9	6.0
1966	41.9	23.8	3.6	2.4	4.5	3.0	5.1	5.2	18.1	3.2	4.9	3.2	6.8
1967	38.6	21.0	2.7	2.4	4.1	2.9	3.9	4.9	17.6	3.2	4.3	3.9	6.3
1968	41.4	22.2	1.9	2.3	4.1	2.8	5.5	5.7	19.1	3.2	5.2	3.7	7.0
1969	36.7	19.0	1.4	2.0	3.7	2.3	4.8	4.9	17.7	3.0	4.6	3.3	6.9
1970	26.7	10.2	0.8	1.1	3.0	1.2	1.2	2.9	16.5	3.2	3.9	3.5	5.9
1971	34.3	16.4	.7	1.5	2.9	1.9	5.1	4.3	17.9	3.5	4.5	3.6	6.4
1972	40.8	22.5	1.6	2.1	4.3	2.8	5.9	5.8	18.3	2.9	5.2	3.0	7.2
1973	46.2	24.7	2.3	2.6	4.7	3.0	5.8	6.2	21.6	2.5	6.0	5.2	7.9
1974	39.8	14.6	4.9	1.6	3.1	.3	0.7	4.0	25.2	2.5	5.1	10.7	7.0
1975	53.6	19.8	2.7	3.1	4.8	2.4	2.0	4.8	33.8	8.8	6.4	9.5	9.1
1976	70.9	31.3	2.0	3.9	6.7	3.7	7.2	7.9	39.6	7.1	8.2	13.1	11.2
1977	80.6	38.6	1.3	4.4	8.9	5.8	9.4	8.8	42.0	6.9	7.8	12.9	14.4
1978	88.7	44.6	3.5	4.9	9.6	6.7	8.9	10.9	44.0	6.2	8.2	14.7	14.9
1979	87.5	37.3	3.6	5.2	9.1	5.2	4.7	9.5	50.2	5.8	7.2	22.5	14.7
1980	77.1	21.3	2.5	4.3	7.7	4.7	−2.5	4.5	55.8	6.1	5.4	31.4	12.9
1981	88.5	21.0	3.1	4.4	8.6	4.1	.1	.7	67.5	8.7	8.2	36.5	14.1
1982	58.0	2.1	−4.9	2.4	4.1	1.7	−.8	−.4	55.9	7.0	5.2	29.1	14.5
1983	70.1	17.2	−4.9	3.0	3.1	3.7	5.1	7.2	53.0	7.2	6.7	21.4	17.7
1984	88.8	38.1	.6	4.7	6.2	5.5	9.0	13.3	50.7	6.7	8.0	17.2	18.8
1985	72.2	29.2	−2.5	4.0	4.2	4.5	6.5	12.6	43.0	7.0	4.2	13.7	18.0
1986	69.4	31.1	−1.8	4.1	3.9	4.3	5.9	14.7	38.4	8.7	6.7	5.4	17.6
1987	90.2	39.4	.6	4.8	5.6	5.0	5.7	17.8	50.8	9.2	9.1	11.7	20.8

Source: U.S. Department of Commerce, Bureau of Economic Analysis.

Table 56   Manufacturing Industries with Constant Patterns of Growth or Contraction, 1973–1986

The previous chart showed that not all manufacturing industries have reacted in the same way to the troubles of the 1980s—some of the industries have followed a pattern of long-term growth or contraction. The following chart highlights the industries that have been growing or declining year after year since 1973.

Growing industries	Years of growth	Declining industries	Years of decline
Computing equipment	16	Rubber/plastic footwear	13
Radio/TV communications equipment	16	Cigars	13
Optical devices/lenses	16	Textile machinery	12
Periodicals	15	Women's footwear	11
Surgical and medical equipment	15	Leather-lined clothing	11
Envelopes	15	Women's handbags/purses	11
Semiconductor devices	15	Turbine generator sets	11
Biological products	14	Musical instruments	11
Commercial printing	14	Men's footwear	10
Paper mills	14	Glass containers	10

Source: U.S. Department of Commerce.

Table 57 Fastest- and Slowest-Growing Manufacturing Industries, 1972–1987

The industries named in the previous chart have shown long-term patterns of growth or contraction. The following chart shows the fastest-growing and fastest-declining manufacturing industries. The industries are ranked by the average annual growth or decline of shipments between 1972 and 1987.

Fastest-growing industries	Annual rate (percent)	Slowest-growing industries	Annual rate (percent)
Semiconductor devices	+35.3	Steel mill products	−31.6
Radio/TV communications equipment	31.5	Iron and steel foundries	−5.7
Petroleum refining	29.4	Turbine generator sets	−5.4
Miscellaneous plastics products	25.3	Construction machinery	−3.7
Commercial printing	15.3	Farm machinery and equipment	−3.0
Aircraft	11.7	Tires and inner tubes	−2.8
Paper mills excluding building	11.6	Jewelry and precious metals	−2.3
Telephone apparatus	11.5	Glass containers	−1.7
Aircraft Equipment not elsewhere classified	11.4	Primary aluminum	−1.7
Vehicles and car bodies	10.7	Fabricated structural metal	−1.5

Source: U.S. Department of Commerce.

Table 58 Manufacturing Employment

One aspect of the crisis in the manufacturing sector has been widespread layoffs. As employment dropped in the steel industry from 644,000 in 1969 to 394,000 in 1982 and 284,000 auto workers were laid off between 1979 and 1982, the future for manufacturing jobs seemed bleak. The following chart shows the job picture for manufacturing jobs producing both durable and nondurable goods. It shows actual employment for years between 1959 and 1987 to give the reader a sense of how the employment picture has developed and it shows the projections for 1995 that were made by the Bureau of Labor Statistics.

(thousands; actual except as noted)

	1959	1969	1979	1982	1987*	2000
Manufacturing	16,675	20,167	21,040	18,781	19,182	18,160
Durable goods	9,373	11,895	12,760	11,039	11,279	10,731
Nondurable goods	7,303	8,272	8,280	7,741	7,903	7,429

*September.
**Projected.
Source: U.S. Department of Labor, Bureau of Labor Statistics.

Table 59 Displaced Workers

No issue illustrates the human cost of declining American competitiveness better than the problem of displaced workers. This chart shows the number of displaced workers in various industries in its left column. In its right columns it shows what percentages are now employed, unemployed, or no longer in the labor force. In this study, "displaced workers" refers to someone who held a job longer than three years and was laid off because of a plant or business closing between January of 1981 and January of 1986.

(in percent)

Industry and class of worker	Number (thousands)	Total	Employed	Unemployed	Not in the labor force
Total, 20 years and over	5,130	100.0	66.9	17.8	15.3
Nonagricultural private wage and salary workers	4,772	100.0	67.2	17.6	15.2
Mining	175	100.0	67.4	17.4	15.2
Construction	316	100.0	74.8	16.6	8.6
Manufacturing	2,550	100.0	65.9	18.2	15.9
Durable goods	1,691	100.0	66.7	18.9	14.4
Lumber and wood products	104	100.0	67.0	23.2	9.8
Furniture and fixtures	63	100.0	—	—	—
Stone, clay, and glass products	87	100.0	64.7	17.3	17.9
Primary metal industries	235	100.0	62.0	15.0	23.0
Fabricated metal products	187	100.0	64.1	24.8	11.0
Machinery, except electrical	361	100.0	71.9	18.6	9.5
Electrical machinery	255	100.0	54.9	23.2	21.9
Transportation equipment	260	100.0	74.3	16.7	8.9
Automobiles	148	100.0	70.2	21.1	8.7
Other transportation equipment	112	100.0	79.8	11.0	9.2
Professional and photographic equipment	73	100.0	—	—	—
Other durable goods industries	66	100.0	—	—	—
Nondurable goods	859	100.0	64.3	16.8	18.9
Food and kindred products	178	100.0	57.1	19.5	23.4
Textile mill products	123	100.0	71.2	9.9	19.0
Apparel and other finished textile products	171	100.0	51.9	18.0	30.1
Paper and allied products	39	100.0	—	—	—
Printing and publishing	94	100.0	69.8	14.8	15.4
Chemical and allied products	98	100.0	75.2	11.9	12.8
Rubber and miscellaneous plastics products	67	100.0	—	—	—
Other nondurable goods industries	88	100.0	62.8	25.9	11.3
Transportation and public utilities	386	100.0	66.9	20.0	13.1
Transportation	303	100.0	66.1	20.6	13.3
Communication and other public utilities	83	100.0	69.9	17.7	12.4
Wholesale and retail trade	689	100.0	66.3	12.4	21.3
Wholesale trade	294	100.0	74.4	12.5	13.1
Retail trade	395	100.0	60.3	12.4	27.4
Finance, insurance, and real estate	107	100.0	73.5	12.5	14.0
Services	540	100.0	68.4	21.4	10.2
Professional services	198	100.0	66.8	19.1	14.1
Other service industries	342	100.0	69.3	22.8	8.0
Agricultural wage and salary workers	141	100.0	66.0	20.9	13.1
Government workers	172	100.0	63.0	18.9	18.0
Self-employed and unpaid family workers	33	100.0	—	—	—

Source: *Monthly Labor Review*, June 1987.

214

BANKRUPTCY: USING CHAPTER 11 AS A TACTIC

Like people, companies usually file for bankruptcy when their bills outstrip their ability to pay them. But when Texaco Inc. became the biggest company ever to file under Chapter 11 for bankruptcy protection, the company was solvent. Texaco joined the growing ranks of troubled corporations that turn to bankruptcy as a tactic for everything from breaking union contracts to battling back in a litigious era when hefty penalties are imposed in what have become the equivalent of corporate whiplash cases.

Chapter 11, which deals with reorganization—the working out of a plan to return a company to financial health—provides that, unless the court rules otherwise, the debtor remains in possession and control of the business. It provides for a great deal of flexibility, the law in 1978 having relaxed the old rule that gave the creditor claims over ownership claims. It allows for the restructuring of debt, the working out of new payment schedules, and even the granting of loans by creditors to the debtor.

In Texaco's case, the company filed to protect itself from a $10.4 billion judgment it lost to Pennzoil Company in a legal tussle over Texaco's having displaced Pennzoil in 1984 as the buyer of the Getty Oil Company. While appealing the judgment, Texaco filed under Chapter 11, which essentially got the immediate pressure of Pennzoil's payment demands off its back. (In November 1987, the Texas Supreme Court let the judgment stand against Texaco, which then asked the U.S. Supreme Court to hear the case. Pennzoil eventually settled for $3 billion.)

Continental Airlines Corporation turned to Chapter 11 in 1983 to break labor contracts that helped transform its parent company, Texas Air Corporation, into the biggest noncommunist-nation airline. About two thirds of Continental's employees were axed and the carrier gained the enmity of labor. Manville Corporation used the tactic in 1982 when the company was faced with thousands of lawsuits alleging death or disease among workers exposed to Manville asbestos products. Likewise, the A. H. Robins Company did the same when confronting claims by women that its Dalkon Shield birth-control device caused various health problems, including sterility.

A much more traditional Chapter 11 bankruptcy filing was made by the once-mighty LTV Corporation in 1986. Once the nation's number-two steel maker, LTV was part of the rusting U.S. steel industry and unable to pay more than $2 billion in debt-service and pension obligations. The company doesn't expect a reorganization plan until 1989 at the earliest.

Table 60   Billion-Dollar Bankruptcies

Seven U.S. companies that have filed for bankruptcy protection under Chapter 11 all had assets of at least $1 billion.

Rank	Company	Assets (dollars)	Year of filing
1.	Texaco Inc.	35 billion	1987
2.	Penn Central Corporation	7 billion	1970
3.	LTV Corporation	6 billion	1986
4.	Manville Corporation	2 billion	1982
5.	Wickes Companies, Inc.	2 billion	1982
6.	Storage Technology Corporation	1 billion	1984
7.	Wheeling-Pittsburgh Steel Corporation	1 billion	1985

Chapter Fourteen

SMALL BUSINESS: WINGING IT

HIGHLIGHTS AND TRENDS

• The 1980s is the decade of the entrepreneur, with the number of self-employed Americans increasing by 50% since 1970. Until 1970, the number of self-employed Americans had been decreasing, largely due to the decline of the small farm.

• There are now some 17 million small businesses in America, most of which are sole proprietorships or partnerships. The nation's 10.7 million sole proprietorships had $465 billion in receipts in 1983.

• Another indication of a growing entrepreneurial spirit is the fact that more businesses than ever before are being started. The number of businesses incorporated every year has more than doubled since 1975. Dun & Bradstreet estimates that 702,601 new corporations were created in 1986, up from only 326,345 in 1975.

• These new businesses are one of the most dynamic sectors of the economy, producing more jobs and wealth. For example, small businesses that employ fewer than 100 people are creating jobs faster than larger businesses. These small businesses accounted for over half of all the jobs created between 1976 and 1982, about 6.24 million jobs. In contrast, larger firms that employ more than 500 people reduced their payrolls by about 900,000 jobs. More recently, employment in industries dominated by small businesses has grown much faster than in industries dominated by larger firms. In 1986, small business–dominated industries increased their employment by 2.9%, seven times faster than the paltry 0.4% increase in jobs in industries that were dominated by larger firms.

• The average net income of small businesses remains small, only $5,005 in 1982, down from over $5,876 in 1977.

• Presidents of small and medium-sized companies earn modest salaries and bonuses compared to the top executives in large companies. The average compensation for presidents of small businesses employing fewer than 250 employees is $75,650. The average compensation for presidents of companies with revenues under $1 million is $76,000; it is $102,000 for presidents of companies with $1 million to $2 million in revenues; $151,000 for presidents of companies in the $2 million to $5 million class; and $173,000 for presidents of companies earning $5 million to $10 million. In contrast, CEOs of companies with sales over $6 billion have an average annual compensation of over $1.2 million.

• For statistical purposes, the federal government defines a small business as one that employs fewer than 500 people. Most small businesses are partnerships or sole proprietorships, but they can also be corporations. Except where otherwise noted, we have followed the federal government's definition.

THE STATE OF SMALL BUSINESS

The 1980s has been the decade of the entrepreneur. Dun & Bradstreet estimates that 702,601 new businesses were incorporated in 1986, up from 662,047 in 1985, 533,520 in 1980, and 264,209 in 1970. Dun & Bradstreet also estimates that the number of businesses grew by a hefty 79% just between 1980 and 1985.

The economic record of the last 10 years also illustrates that bigger is not necessarily better, at least in terms of putting people to work. The number of self-employed Americans has been growing faster than wage- and salary-paying employment. Moreover, the Small Business Administration estimates that small businesses have been creating jobs faster than bigger companies. Between 1976 and 1982, firms employing fewer than 20 people created 38.5% of all new jobs, while firms employing fewer than 100 people created over half (52.6%) of all new jobs. During the economic slowdown between 1980 and 1982, small firms with fewer than 20 employees created over 2.3 million jobs, or about 232% of all the new jobs during those recession years! In contrast, firms with more than 500 employees lost 900,000 jobs!

More recently, a study by the Small Business Administration found that in 1985 and 1986 industries dominated by small business produced jobs at a faster rate than industries where large firms are the norm. In 1986, for example, industries dominated by large firms produced only 97,400 jobs, a paltry 0.4% increase while industries with large numbers of small businesses produced 1 million new jobs, a 2.9% growth in employment.

But if small businesses are becoming one of the most dynamic sectors of the economy, government statisticians don't pay them a lot of attention. The most recent data on small businesses date from 1982 and 1983 and even those data are often wildly inconsistent. In 1985, Dun & Bradstreet estimated that there were nearly 5 million business concerns, while the IRS estimated that it received 17.5 million tax returns for businesses in 1986. The same agency estimates that in 1986, there were about 3.6 million corporations, 1.8 million partnerships, and 12.1 million proprietorships. A majority of these firms (58%) had receipts of less than $25,000.

A 1987 study of small businesses done by Sheldon Haber, Enrique

Lamas, and Jules Lichtenstein estimates that there were 12.84 million business owners and some 13.53 million businesses in 1983. There were 8.77 million male entrepreneurs who owned 9.15 million businesses and 4.17 million women business owners who ran 4.38 million firms. Just to put those numbers in perspective: about 11.9% of all Americans working outside agriculture own a business. About 9.5% of all male workers operate a business full-time; 3.2% of all women have a full-time business.

About 65.3% of all male business owners operate their businesses full-time, compared to 37% of all female business owners. And, as you might guess from the large number of part-time businesses, the median earnings for small businesses are, well, small. In 1983, male business owners earned $14,787 and females earned $4,894. Men who ran their businesses as side operations to supplement income from other jobs had median earnings of $4,784 while male entrepreneurs who worked full-time at their businesses earned $15,600. The average man who worked full-time and had a business that was large enough to support a full-time employee earned even more, $20,039. In contrast, the average woman owner who was substantially engaged in running a business earned only $4,894 and the average woman owner who had a full-time employee earned $12,079.

Overall, about 28.5 million business owners, paid and unpaid family members, and paid employees work in privately held companies. That's about 36.6% of everyone who works in the private sector. Just as a point of comparison, the 500 largest industrial corporations employ about 14 million people.

But despite the resurgence of small business and its economic importance, there is little reason to believe that the U.S. economy is on its way back to the good old days of mom-and-pop stores and small factories. Nationwide statistics indicate that the business of America is still big business. IRS statistics indicate that smaller corporations with assets under $10 million dollars total 2,959,000, about 98.7% of the nation's 2,999,000 corporations; the nation's 3,000 larger corporations (those with more than $250 million in assets) account for only 0.1% of the total. Yet larger corporations bring in $3,658.7 billion, about 51.3% of the nation's $7,135 billion worth of corporate business receipts. Smaller corporations (those with assets under $10 million) bring in only $2,256.9 billion, about 31.6% of the total.

Similarly, in 1983, the most recent year for which comparable statistics are available, the *Fortune* 500 had $1.686 trillion in sales while the nation's 1.5 million partnerships had only $278.3 billion in sales. That same year, nonfarm sole proprietorships totaled 10.7 million, but they had $465 billion in business receipts, less than a third of the receipts of the 500 largest industrial corporations. All the partnerships in the U.S. had assets of $887 billion while the 500 largest corporations had $1,519 billion in assets.

More recently, in 1985, the nation's manufacturing corporations had $1.9 trillion in total assets. About 67% of those assets were controlled by corporations with more than $1 billion in assets; only 8% of all assets were controlled by smaller corporations with less than $10 million in assets. These smaller manufacturing corporations earned $8.6 billion in profits, about 9.6% of the $87.6 billion in profits earned by all manufacturing corporations. Corporations with $1 billion or more in assets earned $60.4 billion, 68.9% of all manufacturing profits.

Small-business owners also face huge risks. New businesses are opening at record rates, but they're also going out of business at an alarming rate. Business failures grew from 11,742 in 1980 to 57,067 in 1985 and 61,183 in 1986. The failure rate per 10,000 business has skyrocketed from 36 in 1973 to 120 in 1986. And these statistics understate the number of business failures. About 9 out of 10 businesses close their doors voluntarily without filing for bankruptcy and thus do not appear in Dun and Bradstreet's statistics of business failures. About half (53%) of all new businesses go bankrupt within the first five years of operation, two thirds by the end of the seventh year, according to Dun & Bradstreet.

Some states are worse than others when it comes to going broke. As you might expect, a high number of business failures were in the oil-producing states. The states of Texas, Arkansas, Louisiana, and Oklahoma had a total of 7,914 business failures in 1985. California (10,257) had the most business failures, followed by Texas (4,892), Illinois (3,388), Florida (2,792), Colorado (2,654), Ohio (2,447), New York (1,866), Pennsylvania (1,638), and Washington (1,634).

Studies indicate that about 90% of all businesses fail because of managerial inexperience or incompetence. Managerial problems result in inadequate sales in nearly 60% of failed businesses and in excessive operating expenses in another 30%. As these alarming statistics indicate, having a good idea isn't enough. You also need to know the basics of marketing, accounting, finance, and taxes to make your business survive over the long haul.

After all those dismal statistics on business failures, it's worth remembering that small businesses have done a remarkable job of adapting to a rapidly changing economy. In fact, they've responded faster to changes in the market than many larger firms. Take, for instance, deregulated industries such as the airlines, trucking, transportation, shipping, finance, and telecommunications, to name a few. In these industries, government regulations traditionally fixed rates, made it difficult for new firms to enter the industry, and generally restricted free-market competition. However, in the late 1970s and early 1980s Congress passed a series of laws that deregulated those industries and opened the way for renewed competition. Almost immediately, small businesses responded to the challenge and the opportunities of a competitive marketplace. In the deregulated industries of financial services and transportation, new business starts increased by 12.3% between 1980 and 1984, faster than the 8.2% increase for the whole economy. The Small Business Administration estimates that most of those new business (84%) were small, with fewer than 500 employees.

And despite the uncertain and volatile markets in many deregulated industries, small businesses have led the way in creating new jobs in those industries. About one fifth of all new jobs between 1980 and 1984 were created in the deregulated industries of financial services and transportation. Firms with fewer than 500 employees represented 48% of the employment in those industries but produced 58% of all new jobs.

Small businesses have also been on the cutting edge of developing new technology. Even though large companies spend most of the research and development money, small companies frequently offer the kind of entrepreneurial environment that allows them to produce more technological advances and innovations for their money, as a quick study of Silicon Valley would indicate. However, to quantify the ability of small and large companies to create technological advances, the SBA undertook a study of the various inventions that were marketed in 1982. To compare large and small companies, the SBA tallied the number of innovations made by firms employing fewer than 500 people and the innovations made by larger firms. The innovations rate (or the number of innovations for every million employees employed by small or larger businesses) was higher for small business. Small businesses produced 36.2 innovations for every million people employed; larger companies produced 31.0 innovations per million employees. That small business accounted for 16.8% more innovations is especially startling if you remember that larger firms spend 96% of the research and development money in the U.S.

All of which points up a fundamental truth. For all the problems facing small business, the entrepreneurial spirit plays an important role in the economy. Without small business producing more new technology and jobs than larger firms, the country's sluggish economic performance in the early 1980s would have been much worse.

Table 61   Earnings of Small-Business Owners

This chart shows the median earnings of business owners. For example, it shows the median income for male business owners was $14,787 in 1983, the most recent year for which statistics are available.

(in thousands)

Category	Men	Women
Business owners, including owners of a side business	$14,787	$ 4,894 [1]
Owners of a side business	4,784	
Business owners, excluding owners of a side business	15,600	4,894
Unincorporated business owners[2]	13,520	3,767
Sole proprietors	12,235	3,671
Partners[3]	20,216	[1]
Incorporated business owners[3]	24,012	9,302
Paid employees only	20,039	12,079

[1]Fewer than 50 observations.

[2]Excludes partners of noncasual businesses who could not be distinguished from incorporated owners of noncasual businesses.

[3]Excludes incorporated owners of noncasual businesses who could not be distinguished from partners of noncasual businesses.

Source: *Monthly Labor Review*, May 1987.

Table 62   Business Formation and Business Failure

This chart shows the country's rising entrepreneurial spirit, as well as the problems faced by many businesses. The chart lists the number of new business formations and the number of failures. The index on the left side of the chart shows that new businesses have recently been formed at record rates compared to earlier years. But the business failure rate per 10,000 businesses is also growing, skyrocketing from 27.8 businesses per 10,000 in 1979 to 114.0 in 1985.

				Business failures					
					Number of failures			Amount of current liabilities (millions of dollars)	
	Index of net business formation (1967 = 100)	New business incorporations (number)	Business failure rate		Liability size class			Liability size class	
Year				Total	Under $100,000	$100,000 and over	Total	Under $100,000	$100,000 and over
1945			4.2	809	759	50	30.2	11.4	18.8
1946		132,916	5.2	1,129	1,003	126	67.3	15.7	51.6
1947		112,897	14.3	3,474	3,103	371	204.6	63.7	140.9
1948	101.1	96,346	20.4	5,250	4,853	397	234.6	93.9	140.7
1949	83.7	85,640	34.4	9,246	8,708	538	308.1	161.4	146.7
1950	87.7	93,092	34.3	9,162	8,746	416	248.3	151.2	97.1
1951	86.7	83,778	30.7	8,058	7,626	432	259.5	131.6	128.0
1952	90.8	92,946	28.7	7,611	7,081	530	283.3	131.9	151.4
1953	89.7	102,706	33.2	8,862	8,075	787	394.2	167.5	226.6
1954	88.8	117,411	42.0	11,086	10,226	860	462.6	211.4	251.2
1955	96.6	139,915	41.6	10,969	10,113	856	449.4	206.4	243.0
1956	94.6	141,163	48.0	12,686	11,615	1,071	562.7	239.8	322.9
1957	90.3	137,112	51.7	13,739	12,547	1,192	615.3	267.1	348.2
1958	90.2	150,781	55.9	14,964	13,499	1,465	728.3	297.6	430.7
1959	97.9	193,067	51.8	14,053	12,707	1,346	692.8	278.9	413.9
1960	94.5	182,713	57.0	15,445	13,650	1,795	938.6	327.2	611.4
1961	90.8	181,535	64.4	17,075	15,006	2,069	1,090.1	370.1	720.0
1962	92.6	182,057	60.8	15,782	13,772	2,010	1,213.6	346.5	867.1
1963	94.4	186,404	56.3	14,374	12,192	2,182	1,352.6	321.0	1,031.6
1964	98.2	197,724	53.2	13,501	11,346	2,155	1,329.2	313.6	1,015.6
1965	99.8	203,897	53.3	13,514	11,340	2,174	1,321.7	321.7	1,000.0
1966	99.3	200,010	51.6	13,061	10,833	2,228	1,385.7	321.5	1,064.1
1967	100.0	206,569	49.0	12,364	10,144	2,220	1,265.2	297.9	967.3
1968	108.3	233,635	38.6	9,636	7,829	1,807	941.0	241.1	699.9
1969	115.8	274,267	37.3	9,154	7,192	1,962	1,142.1	231.3	910.8
1970	108.8	264,209	43.8	10,748	8,019	2,729	1,887.8	269.3	1,618.4
1971	111.1	287,577	41.7	10,326	7,611	2,715	1,916.9	271.3	1,645.6
1972	119.3	316,601	38.3	9,566	7,040	2,526	2,000.2	258.8	1,741.5
1973	119.1	329,358	36.4	9,345	6,627	2,718	2,298.6	235.6	2,063.0
1974	113.2	319,149	38.4	9,915	6,733	3,182	3,053.1	256.9	2,796.3
1975	109.9	326,345	42.6	11,432	7,504	3,928	4,380.2	298.6	4,081.6
1976	120.4	375,766	34.8	9,628	6,176	3,452	3,011.3	257.8	2,753.4
1977	130.8	436,170	28.4	7,919	4,861	3,058	3,095.3	208.3	2,887.0
1978	138.1	478,019	23.9	6,619	3,712	2,907	2,656.0	164.7	2,491.3
1979	138.3	524,565	27.8	7,564	3,930	3,634	2,667.4	179.9	2,487.5
1980	129.9	533,520	42.1	11,742	5,682	6,060	4,635.1	272.5	4,362.6
1981	124.8	581,242	61.3	16,794	8,233	8,561	6,955.2	405.8	6,549.3
1982	116.4	566,942	89.0	24,908	11,509	13,399	15,610.8	541.7	15,069.1
1983	117.5	600,400	110.0	31,334	15,509	15,825	16,072.9	635.1	15,437.8
1984	121.3	634,991	107.0	52,078	19,618	32,460	29,268.6	409.8	28,858.8
1985	120.9	662,047	115.0	57,253	36,551	20,702	36,808.8	790.8	36,018.0
1986	120.4	702,601	120.0	61,616	38,908	22,708	44,724.0	838.3	43,885.7
1987	121.4		102.0	61,209	39,091	22,118	36,337.1	756.7	35,580.4

Sources: Department of Commerce (Bureau of Economic Analysis) and The Dun & Bradstreet Corporation.

222

Table 63 Big Business and Small Business

The following chart shows the structure of the U.S. economy. It shows, for example, that large firms with over 500 employees account for only 0.2% of all businesses but earn 65.1% of all net incomes.

(percentages)

	Total	1–19	20–99	Under 100	100–499	Under 500	500 or more
Firms	100	88	10.5	98.5	1.3	99.8	0.2
Employees	100	21	20	41	12	53	47
Receipts	100	17	16	33	12	45	55
Assets	100	9	13	22	13	35	65
Net income	100	16.5	10.2	26.7	8.2	34.9	65.1

Source: U.S. Small Business Administration, *The State of Small Business: A Report of the President, 1986.*

223

Chapter Fifteen

CRIME: OFFERS SOME CAN'T REFUSE

HIGHLIGHTS AND TRENDS

• Crime squeezes taxpayers $39.6 billion a year just in costs for the criminal justice system. A half-million Americans are now in prison. To keep each prisoner in jail costs an average of $10,000 a year.

• Americans stand an 83% chance of being victims of a violent crime at some point in their lives; 52% will be victimized more than once, according to a 1987 Justice Department study. Over a lifetime, one in 133 Americans will be murdered; one in 30 black males will be murdered. About three quarters of all Americans (74%) will be victims of an assault or attempted assault, 40% will be injured by a robber or assailant, and 99% will be victims of a theft. One out of every 12 women will be the victim of a rape or attempted rape. Three out of every four houses will be burglarized during a 20-year period. One in five households will have its car stolen during a 20-year period. Not surprisingly, given these odds, Americans spend an additional $13.4 billion dollars on private security.

• A recent study by the Office of Technology Assessment of the U.S. Congress estimates that Americans spend about $50.6 billion a year on illegal drugs. About 20 million people use marijuana regularly; between 5 and 6 million people use cocaine regularly; a half-million are addicted to heroin. About 12 million Americans are addicted to the legal drug of choice, alcohol.

• Drug abuse on the job costs the economy about $60 billion. Various studies estimate that 10% to 25% of the work force abuses drugs on the job. But despite all the attention given to drug abuse, the biggest drug problem in America remains alcoholism. Health problems and lost productivity caused by alcoholism cost the economy $117 billion a year.

• Employee theft and shoplifting produce a sea of red ink. The U.S. Commerce Department estimates that employee theft costs American business about $40 billion a year, while the National Institute of Justice puts the loss at $5 billion to $10 billion. Shoplifting costs retailers around the world about $20 billion to $30 billion a year, or as much as 1% to 2%

224

of their sales. Surveys indicate that about 43% of lost inventory is due to employee theft, 30% to shoplifting, 23% to poor paperwork control, and 4% to vendor theft. These losses force retailers to spend about 0.42% of sales revenues on security.

• The so-called underground economy is made up of untaxed legal and illegal income. One estimate states that the value of the underground economy may be as high as $431.7 billion, about 15% of disposable income. Money from criminal activities accounts for about 1% to 7% of the GNP every year. But a larger amount, over $266 billion a year, or about 4% to 8% of the GNP, is legitimate income that is not reported to the IRS. This income includes unreported tips, profits, capital gains, and even state income tax refunds that are not declared.

• In contrast to the few hundred dollars a mugger might steal in a night of violence, organized crime pulls in about $50 billion a year, according to a 1986 study by the President's Commission on Organized Crime.

• About $5 billion to $15 billion of money used in the illegal drug trade is laundered through U.S. banks and financial institutions, according to the U.S. Justice Department. Money laundering, by moving cash to off-shore bank accounts, costs the IRS as much as $9 billion a year in lost tax revenues.

• Estimates of white-collar crime range from $40 billion a year to over $100 billion. One white-collar criminal, Ivan Boesky, earned $50 million to $100 million in illegal insider-trading profits between 1982 and 1986.

THE BUSINESS OF CRIME

The 19th-century French novelist Honoré de Balzac once claimed that behind every fortune there was a crime. And, although there is little evidence to suggest that most businesses or individuals are dangerously or systematically dishonest, crime has always been a very important, though poorly understood, part of the economy. As early as the 18th century, Americans considered smuggling and tax evasion to be legitimate enterprises, almost patriotic duties. This tradition continued in the 19th century, when American merchants profited from the booming Chinese opium trade, and on a more popular level in the 1920s, when millions ignored Prohibition. Today, in the Roaring '80s, some 10% to 25% of the population admit they use drugs on the job; another 25% cheat on their taxes.

All of this is part of the economy of crime, a booming underground marketplace whose dimensions and effects remain obscure. What follows is a survey of that business, from crime in the streets to crime in the suites.

Crime in the Streets

The odds of living a crime-free life are not good. Americans stand an 83% chance of being victims of a violent crime at some point in their lives;

52% will be victimized more than once, according to a 1987 Justice Department study. As noted, chances for Americans to be murdered are quite high: 1 in 133. About three quarters of all Americans (74%) will be victims of an assault or attempted assault, 40% will be injured by a robber or assailant, and 99% will be victims of a theft. Rapists will rape or try to rape one of every 12 women. Three out of every four houses will be burglarized during a 20-year period. One in five households will have its car stolen during a 20-year period.

Not surprisingly, given these odds, crime in the streets forces federal, state, and local governments to spend $39.6 billion a year on police protection and the criminal justice system, up from $22 billion in 1980. Increased spending and a trend toward tough sentences have increased the number of criminals behind bars to 483,053 in 1985, up from 196,429 in 1970. That increase has left jails bursting at the seams—the average American jail now operates at 113.9% of capacity.

But despite the crackdown on crime and a leveling off of violent crimes, private citizens and businesses spent $13.4 billion dollars on security in 1985, up from $7.5 billion in 1980. In 1990, Robert McCrie, editor of *Security Letter,* estimates that $21 billion will be spent on security.

Added to these costs are the traumatic effects of violent crime. No one can put a dollar-and-cent figure on the costs to the 498,000 people who were raped in 1985 or the 723,000 people who were assaulted, or a value on the 19,000 Americans murdered in 1985, 148 of whom were police officers. Overall, 12.4 million crimes were reported in 1985, down from 13.4 million in 1980.

And although crime terrorizes people of all classes, it falls especially hard on minorities and the poor. Violent crimes were the leading cause of death among young black men aged 15 to 24, accounting for one third of all the young blacks who die. A white female has 1 chance in 606 of being murdered and a white male 1 chance in 186, but a young black male has 1 chance in 30 of being murdered.

Drug Abuse

A major factor in the increase in crime has been drug abuse. The use of drugs such as marijuana, cocaine, and heroin has skyrocketed in the last 20 years. A 1987 study by the Office of Technology Assessment of the U.S. Congress estimates that Americans spent $50.6 billion on illegal drugs in 1985. About 20 million people use marijuana regularly; between 5 and 6 million people use cocaine regularly; a half-million are addicted to heroin. In addition, about 12 million people are addicted to alcohol, according to the National Institute on Alcohol Abuse and Alcoholism.

No figures are available on drug use among top executives. In 1985, the CEO of Iroquois Brands, which sells such products as Champale, Black Horse Ale, and Schiff vitamins, was arrested with 17 grams of cocaine. That arrest capped what some employees had described as a drug-induced reign of terror at the company that clearly hurt profits—earnings were only $19,000 on $125 million in sales. Counselors at hot-line numbers for people seeking help with cocaine addiction say that many of the callers are relatively affluent, holding well-paying jobs. About half of all callers to the 800-COCAINE hotline have jobs that pay over $25,000 a year.

Drug abuse among young people appears to be dropping. In 1985, about 42% of all college students had used marijuana (down from 51% in 1980), 12% had used amphetamines (22% in 1980), 2% had used opiates (5% in 1980), 2% had used LSD (6% in 1980), and 1% had used Quaaludes (7% in 1980), according to the Institute of Social Research at the University of Michigan. But cocaine abuse remained about the same, 17%. A whopping 92% had used alcohol.

Despite the evidence that drug use is declining, some 75% to 80% of all young adults have used an illegal drug by their mid-20s.

Drugs on the Job

The costs of drug use on the job have increased dramatically. Various studies estimate that 10% to 25% of the work force has abused drugs on the job. The most comprehensive study of the problem ever undertaken, a 1984 study by the Research Triangle Institute, found that drug abuse on the job cost the economy $60 billion in 1983, up 30% from $46 billion in 1979. About $30 billion worth of this damage was in lost employee productivity.

Drug abuse hurts everyone, users and nonusers. Health hazards are a major cost of drug abuse and some studies have shown that drug users are three times more likely to be injured on the job. Drug abuse has also been associated with some major accidents. Since 1975, about 50 train wrecks and accidents, which resulted in 37 deaths, 80 injuries, and $34 million in damage, have been attributable to drug or alcohol abuse.

In 1986, the President's Commission on Organized Crime recommended that all employers test their workers for drugs. When the Commission made that controversial recommendation, about 25% of the country's largest corporations already had instituted drug screening programs requiring urine tests before a person is hired. The percentage of drug screening programs among *Fortune* 500 companies was estimated to be 50% in 1987. But these programs have come under attack, often because of inaccurate drug tests. Critics note that in 1984 the Army admitted it had mishandled half of the 60,000 tests it had given; others attack the growth of drug tests as an unconstitutional invasion of privacy. "Trying to stop organized crime's multimillion-dollar drug business by creating a police state in federal office buildings would be virtually ineffective and would create one crime to stop another," Representative Charles Schumer of New York says.

But despite all that has been said and written about cocaine, crack, and heroin, alcoholism remains the most costly addiction in America. Health problems and lost productivity caused by alcoholism cost the economy $117 billion a year.

The Worldwide Drug Trade

By the mid-1980s, the U.S., Europe, and other developed countries were inundated with a flood of illegal drugs. There was heroin and opium from Afghanistan, Iran, Mexico, and the Golden Triangle (parts of Thailand, Burma, and Laos); cocaine from Colombia, Peru, and Bolivia; marijuana from the Caribbean, Mexico, Asia, and Africa. Worldwide, no one knows the exact value of this trade, but a 1987 study by the Office of Technology Assessment estimates that Americans spent $50.6 billion in 1985 on illegal drugs. That figure, the study points out, is equal to the sales of the nation's two largest retail companies, Sears and K mart. A study by THE WEFA GROUP, formerly Wharton Econometric Forecasting Associates, Inc., for the President's Commission on Organized Crime indicates that organized crime earned about $9.1 billion in gross receipts and $7.7 billion in profits from heroin, about $13 billion in receipts and $12.6 billion in profits from cocaine, and about $8.3 billion in gross marijuana sales and $7.3 billion in profits from the marijuana trade. That represents total drug sales of $30.4 billion and profits of $27.6 billion for organized crime.

Those involved don't always live up to the stereotypes of a street junkie or Mafia thug. In Bolivia, where 32,000 to 38,000 hectares are used to produce cocaine, the drug traffic is so lucrative that two military coups in the early 1980s have been indirectly traced to feuds over cocaine profits. In Afghanistan, one of the world's largest opium and heroin producers, the tribesmen are using the profits of their trade to fight the Soviet army. "We must grow and sell opium to fight our holy war against the Russian nonbelievers," the brother of a leading rebel commander and a major owner of opium fields told *The New York Times* in 1986. And here at home, the traffic has even corrupted some straitlaced bankers. Documents in one 1986 trial of a Mexican drug ring that brought $125 million of marijuana to the U.S. showed that the money was laundered through over 40 U.S. banks. (See the discussion of money laundering below.)

But even the drug trade can't escape the laws of the market. All of the world's production exists to supply a booming market. About 4,693.9 metric tons of marijuana and about 72.3 metric tons of cocaine were consumed in the U.S. in 1986. Worldwide production of cocaine is estimated at 251 to 373 metric tons. About 75% of the cocaine that reaches the U.S. comes from Colombia.

And with profit margins of over 90%, more and more renegade entrepreneurs have gotten into the act, flooding the market with illegal drugs. Yet drug use has remained stagnant, and U.S. law-enforcement officials say that the U.S. market for cocaine and other drugs is glutted, hurting profits and prices. As a result, the prices of drugs have been falling dramatically while their purity has increased. The average potency of commercial-grade marijuana increased from 2.94% in 1983 to 3.67% in 1986 while the price of a pound hardly rose, ranging from $350 to $600 a pound in 1983 to $350 to $700 a pound in 1986. The purity of cocaine at the retail level skyrocketed from 35% in 1983 to 55% to 65% in 1986 while the price of kilogram of cocaine dropped from $45,000 to $55,000 in 1983 to only $22,000 to $45,000 in 1986. The oversupply of cocaine is the major reason why more potent forms of the drug, such as crack, have become more popular in the last few years.

But drug dealers aren't going into Chapter 11. A drug smuggler can still increase the value of pound of heroin by 30 to 40 times simply by bringing it from a foreign country to the U.S. In 1986 transporting cocaine into the United States added $1.6 billion in profits to its value. The wholesale value of marijuana in the U.S. is 20 to 30 times the price in a foreign country.

Those profit margins are encouraging beleaguered American farmers and high-tech drug entrepreneurs to get into the act. U.S. marijuana farmers now produce 19% of the 10.8 million pounds of marijuana consumed each year—about 2 million pounds. In the early 1980s in California, the nation's agribusiness center, marijuana was the largest cash crop. In 1986, 4.7 million cultivated cannabis plants and over 125 million low-potency cannabis plants known as ditchweed were destroyed. About 5,537 pot farmers were arrested in 1986, up from 4,941 in 1984.

Drug factories are also popping up all over the country. Traditionally, illicit drugs such as cocaine and heroin were manufactured abroad because it was too difficult to smuggle the bulky raw materials into the country. It takes about 500 kilograms of dry coca leaf to produce one kilogram of cocaine HCl. But that way of doing business is changing as more drugs are grown in the U.S. and it becomes harder to smuggle drugs into the U.S. In 1985 police discovered one laboratory in upstate New York that was equipped to produce 1,000 pounds of cocaine a week, enough to supply about a third of the U.S. market. The police have also uncovered a $225-million-a-year heroin factory in Arizona, the first one ever found in the U.S. A sign of that trend is that the number of cocaine labs seized by federal authorities increased from 11 in 1983 to 33 in 1985 while the total number of illegal drug labs seized grew from 226 in 1983 to 545 in 1986.

Solutions to the problem are not easy. Even without high-level government corruption, Latin American and Asian countries would still have trouble stopping the drug trade. Because those countries are faced with huge foreign debts, crops such as opium, cocaine, and marijuana (in the case of Jamaica) play an important role in keeping them solvent on the international market and in paying for badly needed imports. Finally, on the lowest level of the international drug trade, far away from the powerful cocaine generals and the illicit drugs-for-arms deals, are the poor Asian and Latin American peasants who grow the crops. Opium and cocaine provide them with far more income than any other cash crop, especially on the currently depressed international market for commodities. Any plan to curb the international drug trade must provide them with an equally lucrative way of making a living.

Table 64 (below) provides a survey of this huge business, based upon information culled from several government agencies. It lists the leading producers of various kinds of drugs and their market share, revenues, profit margins, and profits, wherever such information is available.

Table 64   The Illegal Drug Market

TOTAL DRUG REVENUES 1985

Foreign wholesale	Domestic wholesale	Retail
$1,600,000,000	$10,000,000,000	$50,000,000,000

Profit Margins

Over 90%

The value of a pound of cocaine increases four to five times from the time it moves from the foreign wholesale market to the time it reaches the domestic wholesale market, adding $1.6 billion in value to the product.

The value of total marijuana production increases by about $6 billion as it moves from foreign to domestic wholesalers.

Heroin increases some 30 to 40 times in value as it moves from the foreign to the domestic wholesale market.

Cost of Fighting Drug Smuggling

$800 million in
U.S. government spending

Why It's So Hard to Stop Drug Smuggling

Each year 25 million passengers enter the U.S. on commercial airlines; 115 million people come into the U.S. from the Mexican border; 48,000 commercial vessels landed in U.S. ports; 100 million letters and parcels enter the U.S. from overseas.

THE MARIJUANA MARKET

Revenues from the Sale of Marijuana, 1985

Foreign wholesale	Domestic wholesale	Retail
$400,000,000	$6,300,000,000	$16,800,000,000

U.S. Marijuana Consumption (Pounds):

1982	1985
10,804,059	10,350,049 (−4%)

Americans Who Used Marijuana at Least Once in the Past Month

1982	1985
20.0 million	18.2 million

Marijuana Prices

	1983	1984	1985	1986
Commercial-grade				
Wholesale (pound)	$350–600	$400–600	$300–600	$300–700
Retail (ounce)	$40–65	$45–75	$50–100	$45–120
Sinsemilla				
Wholesale (pound)	$1,000–2,000	$1,200–2,500	$1,200–2,000	$800–2,000
Retail (ounce)	$100–150	$120–200	$120–200	$100–200

Table 64   The Illegal Drug Market (continued)

THE MARIJUANA MARKET

Marijuana Growers

	Quantity (metric tons)			Market share (percentage of total supply available for U.S. use)		
	1984	1985	1986	1984	1985	1986
Domestic growers	1,700	2,100	2,100	12	19	18
Mexico	2,500–3,000	3,000–4,000	3,000–4,000	20	32	30
Columbia	4,100–7,500	2,600–4,000	2,200–3,900	42	31	27
Jamaica	1,500–2,250	350–850	1,100–1,700	14	6	12
Belize	1,100	550	500	8	5	4
Other	500	800	800–1,100	4	7	8

Gross marijuana available 1986: 9,700–13,400 metric tons
Less U.S. seizures, seizures in transit, and losses: 3,000–4,000 metric tons
Net marijuana available: 6,700–9,400 metric tons

THE COCAINE MARKET

Revenues from the Sale of Cocaine, 1985

Foreign wholesale	Domestic wholesale	Retail
$1,200,000,000	$2,800,000,000	$20,000,000,000

U.S. Cocaine Consumption (Pounds)

1982	1985
68,355	159,422 (+133%)

Americans Who Used Cocaine at Least Once in the Past Month

1982	1985
4.2 million	5.8 million

Cocaine Prices

	1983	1984	1985	1986
Wholesale (kilogram)	$45,000–55,000	$40,000–50,000	$30,000–50,000	$22,000–45,000
Retail (gram)	$100–125	$100–120	$100	$80–120

Cocaine Growers

While Peru produced more of the coca leaf used to process cocaine in 1986, Colombia continued to dominate the final stage of cocaine production and supplied about 75% of the cocaine reaching the U.S. market, compared to 5% for Peru. It takes about 500 kilograms of dry leaf to produce one kilogram of cocaine.

Country	Land used to cultivate coca leaf (hectares), 1986	Coca leaf produced (metric tons), 1986	Market share in 1985 and 1986 (percentage of supply available for U.S. use)
Peru	95,000–120,000	95,000–120,000	5%
Bolivia	32,000–38,000	44,800–53,200	15%
Colombia	15,000–17,000	12,000–13,600	75%
Ecuador	1,000–2,000	1,000–2,000	NA

THE MARKET FOR HEROIN AND OPIATES

Revenues from the Sale of Heroin, 1985

Foreign wholesale	Domestic wholesale	Retail
—	$1,000,000,000	$13,800,000,000

231

Table 64   The Illegal Drug Market (continued)

THE MARKET FOR HEROIN AND OPIATES

Market Share in Heroin and Morphine

Region or country	1983	1984	1985	1986
Southwest Asia	48%	51%	47%	40%
Mexico	33%	32%	39%	41%
Southeast Asia	19%	17%	14%	19%

Heroin Prices (per Pure Milligram)

1983	1984	1985	1986
$2.15	$2.37	$2.30	$2.12

Foreign wholesale price (pound) 1985:	$4,500
Domestic wholesale price (pound), 1985:	$160,000
Domestic retail price (pound), 1985:	$2,300,000

Opium Production (Metric Tons)

Country	1983	1984	1985	1986
Afghanistan	400–575	140–180	400–500	500–800
Iran	400–600	400–600	200–400	200–400
Pakistan	45–60	40–50	40–70	140–160
Mexico	17	21	28.4	20–40
Burma	600	740	490	700–1,100
Thailand	35	45	35	20–25
Laos	35	30	100	100–290

Heroin and Opium Addicts, Here and in the Countries That Produce Opiates

U.S.	490,000 heroin addicts
Thailand	300,000–500,000 opium and heroin addicts
Pakistan	400,000–500,000 heroin addicts
India	500,000 heroin addicts
India	500,000 chronic opium users
Iran	100,000 heroin addicts and 500,000 opium users
Afghanistan	100,000–125,000 chronic opium users
Malaysia	250,000–350,000 heroin addicts
Hong Kong	50,000 heroin addicts

THE HASHISH MARKET

	Production in major source countries (metric tons)		Market share, 1985 and 1986
	1984	1986	
Lebanon	350–400	600	25–30%
Afghanistan	200–400	200–400	Pakistan/Afghanistan:
Pakistan	200	200	
			60–65%
Morocco	60–225	30–60	5%
Total	810–1,225	1,030–1,260	

Sources: National Institute on Drug Abuse, 1985 National Household Survey of Drug Abuse; National Narcotics Intelligence Consumers Committee, *The NNICC Report 1985–1986: The Supply of Illicit Drugs to the United States from Foreign and Domestic Sources in 1985 and 1986;* Drug Enforcement Administration; U.S. Congress, Office of Technology Assessment, *The Border War on Drugs;* U.S. Department of State, *International Narcotics Control Strategy Report.*

Employee Theft and Shoplifting

Few crimes hit retailers harder than employee theft and shoplifting. Employee theft and shoplifting produce a sea of red ink. The U.S. Commerce Department estimates that employee theft costs American business about $40 billion a year, while the National Institute of Justice puts the loss at $5 billion to $10 billion.

In 1980, shoplifting in the U.S. was already costing about $20 million a day, or $7.3 billion a year. Today, shoplifting costs retailers around the world about $20 billion to $30 billion a year, or as much as 1% to 2% of their sales according to E. Gray Glass III, an analyst for Kidder, Peabody & Co. To stop the losses, the retail industry spent about $200 million on security in 1986 and is expected to spend $500 million in 1990.

Put together, employee theft and shoplifting—which the industry so blandly calls "shrinkage"—cost retailers about 1.7% of their inventory, according to a 1985 Arthur Young survey of retail security and loss prevention. The study surveyed 78 mass merchants, 44 department stores, and 46 specialty stores that suffered $1.9 billion in losses. These retailers found that they were spending about 0.42% of their sales revenues on security. Surveys indicate that about 43% of lost inventory is due to employee theft, 30% to shoplifting, 23% to poor paperwork control, and 4% to vendor theft.

The Underground Economy

There is a vast economy that is not mentioned in government statistics—the underground economy. The very name sounds mysterious, like a secret criminal society, but a large part of the underground economy is really quite mundane. What economists mean by the underground economy is simply income that should be taxed but isn't. This income comes from two sources. Part of the underground economy is money from criminal activities such as drugs, loan-sharking, or numbers rackets and the rest is legitimate income such as wages and tips that isn't reported on tax returns.

James O'Leary at the U.S. Trust Co. believes that the underground economy is a growth industry. His self-described "guesstimates" of the underground economy suggest that it grew from about 5.7% of disposable income (about $52.5 billion) in the early 1970s to a whopping 21% of disposable income—about $558.4 billion in 1984. Since then it's dropped to only $431.7 billion, about 15% of disposable income.

The IRS comes up with different figures but agrees with O'Leary's contention that the underground economy is growing by leaps and bounds. Thanks to the underground economy, the IRS believes that the federal government lost $86.3 billion in taxes in 1982, up from only $15.5 billion in 1965. In 1981, the IRS estimates that Americans failed to report $260 billion in legitimate income.

Most studies suggest that the largest part of the underground economy is legitimate income that is hidden from the tax collector. This income comes from such mundane sources as unreported tips, profits, capital gains, and even state income tax refunds that were not reported to the government. But all of this tax fraud adds up. About $260 billion, or about 50% to 75% of the underground economy and about 4% to 8% of the GNP, is legitimate income that was not reported to the IRS. The illegal part of the underground economy—income from drugs, prostitution, illegal gambling, etc.—accounts for about 1% to 7% of the GNP every year.

Overall, tax fraud is the most popular crime in America, even more popular than drug abuse, and certainly more profitable. IRS surveys show that about 20% to 25% of all Americans admit they underreport their income for tax purposes. Even though the long arm of the IRS collects a major share of this money, the government still lost about $75 billion in revenue in 1981 and $86 billion in 1982, the last years for which such figures are available. Since the underground economy is largely a creation of high taxes or complicated reporting requirements, tax simplification could reduce or at least slow its growth.

Organized Crime

Just as big business took over many major industries in the early 20th century, organized crime has moved into the most lucrative areas of criminal activity—drug smuggling, gambling, racketeering, counterfeiting, and union corruption. Organized crime doesn't publish an annual report and estimates of its income vary widely, but it is believed to total about $50 billion.

Using profits from illegal activities and muscle from corrupt unions, organized crime figures have moved into legitimate business. For instance, prosecutors recently alleged that organized crime groups control New York City's $250-million-a-year moving and storage business by extorting more than $500,000 in kickbacks from employers. Mob-dominated construction unions allegedly have a grip on New York's construction and concrete industry, forcing contractors to pay kickbacks amounting to 2% of the value of all jobs and creating a system in which a group of mob-dominated firms bid on all concrete jobs valued at over $2 million. Kickbacks to organized crime families also allegedly added $1.4 million to the cost of 26 construction jobs in New York, including $184,000 to the cost of the $4.35 million Bank of America building in Manhattan.

The WEFA study of the cost of organized crime estimates that organized crime adds 2% to the cost of construction, warehousing, trucking, and waste hauling, about 1% to the price of garments, 0.5% to prices in the wholesale and retail trade, and 0.2% to the cost of banking services and real estate. These small percentage increases don't sound like much but they add up. As a result of higher price levels caused by organized crime and continued underpayment of taxes, the WEFA researchers estimated that U.S. output was reduced by $18.2 billion dollars, U.S. employment was cut by 414,000 jobs, consumer prices were 0.3% higher than was necessary, and per-capita personal income was reduced by $77.22. Because organized crime income is not taxed, U.S. citizens paid $6.5 billion in higher taxes.

Organized crime is also a big business. WEFA's study produced several estimates of organized crime income, each based on different data and assumptions. One WEFA estimate of $47 billion in income "in 1986 for organized crime equals 1.13 percent of U.S. gross national product," the WEFA study states. "At $47 billion, organized crime is about the same size as all the U.S. metal producers (iron, steel, aluminum, copper, etc.), is larger than the U.S. paper industry, is larger than the U.S. rubber and tire industry and is about the same size as the textile and apparel industry. Organized crime is estimated to employ at least 281,487 people as members and associates with the estimated number of crime related jobs ranging to over 520,000."

Profits from organized crime activities also come from a variety of other activities: gambling, prostitution, drugs, counterfeiting, etc. Table 65 (below) shows how WEFA estimates the breakdown of organized crime income.

Table 65 The Mob's Marketplace

The chart below estimates the income of organized crime. The data column on the left shows the market share of organized crime in various industries, such as prostitution. The center column contains midrange estimates of total criminal receipts from each industry and the right column shows estimates of net income. Profits are very high because the profit margins on many of the mob's products and services are very high.

	Organized crime's share	Total criminal gross receipts (midrange) (millions of dollars)	Total criminal net income (midrange) (millions of dollars)
Heroin	100%	9.066	7.706
Cocaine	100%	13.046	12.552
Marijuana	100%	8.536	7.305
Loan-sharking	100%	7.015	7.015
Illegal gambling	42%	2.348	1.878
Prostitution	20%	3.332	2.665
Household and personal theft	20%	1.713	0.895
Shoplifting and employee theft	50%	4.879	3.049
Trucking cargo theft	100%	0.874	0.607
Air cargo theft	100%	0.041	0.035
Railroad cargo theft	100%	0.035	0.024
Bank robbery	0%	0.000	0.000
Business robbery	0%	0.000	0.000
Nonresidential burglary	0%	0.000	0.000
Fraud arson	50%	0.253	0.202
Bank embezzlement	0%	0.000	0.000
Counterfeiting	30%	0.020	0.018
Cigarette smuggling	100%	0.290	0.232
Total		51.449	44.185

Sources: THE WEFA GROUP, formerly Wharton Econometric Forecasting Associates, Inc., and President's Commission on Organized Crime, 1986.

All of these profits have not escaped government notice. In 1984 alone, there were 3,118 indictments against organized crime figures, resulting in 2,194 convictions, with another 4,190 indictments in 1985 and 3,530 convictions or plea bargains. These cases resulted in $15 million worth of fines, and courts seized $387 million in contraband and assets.

This crackdown, which has put heads of crime families in New York, Kansas City, New Orleans, Milwaukee, and Cleveland behind bars, has hurt older families and will hasten a long-term shift in power from La Cosa Nostra and the Mafia to newer organized crime groups. One of the newest groups, Colombian drug dealers, has been linked to 113 murders between 1984 and 1987 in just one small area of Queens in New York City. Colombian drug dealers now import about $20 billion a year worth of drugs but they aren't the only new group to spread terror and crime in their wake. Prosecutors have also become concerned about Asian organized crime groups, motorcycle gangs like the Hell's Angels, and various other Latin American groups, including some members of the Cuban exile community.

Counterfeiting

Any mention of counterfeiting makes most people think of someone printing nice crisp currency. But counterfeit money is really small potatoes compared to the booming business of counterfeiting everything from Rubik's Cubes to bootleg Bruce Springsteen tapes. The cost of counterfeited products to the economy range from the 1983 House Energy and Commerce Committee's estimate of $20 billion year to the estimate of $60 billion by the Counterfeit Intelligence Bureau in London. The U.S. International Trade Commission and the U.S. Chamber of Commerce say that counterfeiting costs U.S. business about $8 billion to $20 billion a year, up from only $3 billion in 1978.

Products routinely counterfeited are chemicals, computers, drugs, fertilizers, pesticides, medical devices, military hardware, foods, Cabbage Patch Kids, tape cassettes, Gucci shoes, and expensive watches. The Recording Industry Association of America says the $4.3 billion U.S. music industry loses $300 million a year on illegal or counterfeit recordings, or about 7% of its sales. Organized crime operations earn nearly $750 million counterfeiting credit cards and have a major share of the $500-million-a-year industry in counterfeiting airline tickets.

Most counterfeit goods sold in the U.S. are produced overseas, especially in Asia; only about 20% of them are made in the U.S.A. Consumers who buy counterfeit goods often get stuck with shoddy goods, as anyone who has ever bought a bootleg album can tell you. In other cases counterfeit goods have posed a direct threat to the consumer's health. A million fake birth control pills hit the U.S. market in 1984, causing heavy bleeding in some women, and, in 1982, surgeons got a scare when a counterfeit and defective part was found in pumps used to keep hearts beating during open-heart surgery. In other cases, bogus parts have caused helicopter crashes, auto wrecks, and even construction accidents.

And just how much counterfeit money is floating around out there? No one knows. But about $90 million in counterfeit U.S. currency was seized around the world in 1986. In the U.S. about $46 million was captured by the Secret Service. Only about $6 million had gone into circulation.

In the counterfeit-money business, foreign producers are starting to beat out U.S. counterfeiters with better quality and better business methods. Just as the Japanese have earned a reputation for producing better cars, the Italians now produce the best bogus bills. Their technique is simple. To get around the problem of imitating the paper used in U.S. currency, counterfeiters in Milan take a $1 bill, bleach it, and then print a $100 bill over it. Presto. A $99 profit.

Overseas counterfeiters also have better distribution networks and printing techniques, thanks to their experience in counterfeiting European currency that is multicolored and hence harder to duplicate. Already the flood of foreign counterfeit money is causing problems. Even though the Treasury Department has changed the currency to make it harder to copy, some foreign banks will no longer change $100 bills. Government officials believe that U.S. crooks will fight back with a new generation of color photocopy machines. And if that fails? Well there's always protectionism and quotas. . . .

Credit-Card Fraud

A crime with a rosy future is credit-card fraud. As the economy shifts more and more towards a cashless society, credit-card fraud has skyrocketed. By the mid-1980s this crime was costing banks and consumers more than $700 million a year. Consumers, who hold some 731 million credit cards, are generally protected by a federal law that limits individual liability, but they eventually end up footing the bill through higher interest payments and annual credit-card fees.

But companies are also fighting back with technology. Visa and MasterCard have already put holograms on their cards, making them harder to counterfeit. That cut Visa's losses 53% to $14.7 million and MasterCard's losses 19% to $15.9 million. Stolen credit cards, however, still cost the industry $164 million.

Union Corruption

Union corruption illustrates how crime can tarnish the good name of an entire enterprise. Thanks to union corruption, a poll by the Conference Board found that only 12% of the American public thought unions were well managed—Congress and the Pentagon were the only two institutions to get lower ratings.

Of course, like most corporations, most unions are honest. Federal investigators estimate that organized crime influences only 400 of the 70,000 union locals in the U.S. But corrupt union leaders can earn big profits. The President's Commission on Organized Crime found that "organized crime can use unions in four principal ways: First, it can convert union resources—members' dues, union assets, or worker benefit funds—to its own use. Second, it can use unions to exact payoffs from businesses in the form of sweetheart contracts or strike insurance. Third, it can use the union as a way to influence an entire market. This last use may generate the kind of payoffs that come from the sweetheart deal or a strike insurance. Indeed, these rackets may be part of a general market corruption scheme. Finally, organized crime can use unions as a means of access to and protection from the political and governmental process.''

Union corruption is heavily concentrated in only a few mob-dominated unions. The dubious distinction of being the nation's most corrupt union falls to the Teamsters, one of the nation's most politically powerful unions with 1.7 million members. Close behind them in racketeering, if not in size, are the Laborers' International Union of North America; the Hotel Employees and Restaurant Employees International Union; and the International Longshoremen's Association. These unions, according to the FBI, are ''substantially influenced and/or controlled by organized crime.'' They accounted for 45% of the 930 indictments handed down against unions between 1980 and 1984 and about 33% of all convictions. About two thirds of the 400 mob-dominated locals belong to those unions. They control about $3 billion in multiemployer health and welfare funds and about 30% of the multiemployer plans nationwide that are under direct union control. In one of these unions, the Teamsters, every president between 1951 and 1981 was indicted and convicted for crimes committed while in office.

The current president of the Teamsters, Jackie Presser, has been indicted for allegedly bilking the union out of more than $700,000 by putting organized crime figures on the union payroll for no-show jobs. President Reagan, who appointed Presser to his transition team in 1981 and his inauguration committee in 1984 because the Teamsters were the only union to support him, recently came under strong attack from his own President's Commission on Organized Crime for associating with a union leader who has reported organized crime ties. Presser, the highest-paid union official in the U.S., earned about $571,960 in 1986. (See the profile of the Teamsters in the ''Trucking'' section.)

Union pension and benefit plans represent the biggest area of fraud. About $70 billion a year flows into union pension and profit-sharing plans, with another $100 billion going into health and welfare funds. Most of the health and welfare money is administered by companies like Blue Cross, but about $10 billion is overseen by the unions themselves in multiemployer plans.

Several reasons have been cited by many analysts for the rise of corruption and organized crime influence in unions. One of the most important is that once mobsters and corrupt officials establish themselves in the ranks of a union bureaucracy, they are difficult to remove unless the union has a strong tradition of union democracy. As a result, unions with a strong commitment to union democracy, such as the United Auto Workers, have been free from the taint of corruption and organized crime ties;

others, such as the Teamsters, with its history of corruption, keep a tight control over union members and allow little dissent. In the past, Teamsters dissidents have been beaten or threatened.

An equally important factor in union corruption and the influence of organized crime is simply the kind of marketplace in which a business or union operates. In trucking, restaurants, construction, shipping, and other industries dominated by small businesses, businesses and unions have been more vulnerable to racketeers. Unions have used racketeers to provide the muscle needed to control those anarchic industries while employers, being small and vulnerable, have been less able to resist the power of racketeers. Not surprisingly, the four most corrupt unions—the Teamsters, the International Longshoremen's Association, the Hotel Employees and Restaurant Employees International Union, and the Laborers' International Union (a construction-trades union)—are in those industries. In contrast, unions in large, established industries, such as the UAW and the Steel Workers, have been less vulnerable in part because of the size of the industries. Finally, unions in industries that rely on white-collar workers, such as the Air line Pilots, have more sophisticated members and have been less vulnerable to racketeering.

Business itself has played an important role in the rise of union corruption by agreeing to do business with mobsters. In some cases, businesses have worked with mob-run unions to keep wages and benefits low. In the 1970s, the Teamsters allegedly negotiated favorable contracts—so-called sweetheart contracts—with dozens of companies that kept down wages in return for kickbacks to union leaders. In some cases, though, there is a fine line between businesses' sanctioning agreements that hurt their employees and businesses' being blackmailed into agreements that help only a few union bosses. In 1980, for example, Douglas LaChance, the president of the Newspaper and Mail Deliverers Union, was convicted of taking $330,000 in illegal payments to ensure labor peace.

Money Laundering

Laundering money is perhaps the most important aspect of organized crime, simply because it allows criminals to use their money. The U.S. Justice Department estimates that $5 billion to $15 billion of money used in the illegal drug trade in the U.S. is laundered each year through the American and international financial system. In addition, embezzlers, swindlers, stockbrokers involved in insider trading, racketeers, dealers in counterfeit bonds and securities, and a host of other criminals launder many billions of dollars more. The IRS estimates that it loses as much as $9 billion a year in taxes because of laundering of illegal profits.

The actual process of laundering money typically involves a series of Byzantine financial transactions too complicated for any normal person to understand. But the basic idea behind money laundering is simple. A criminal wants to take his profits and make it impossible for government agents to trace the money to his illegal activities. To accomplish this end, he might take the $2 million he earned in a cocaine deal and, using a private plane, smuggle it out of the country to Panama or one of the other offshore banking areas in the Caribbean or Hong Kong. Then the money can be deposited under the name of a paper corporation set up for such purposes—easy enough because the Panamanian government doesn't impose regulations or taxes. This corporation can wire the money back to him in the Bahamas in the form of dividend payments. That way he can invest his dirty money in regular business—the "legitimate rackets," as Al Capone used to say—or use the cash to finance future drug deals.

This might sound like a lot of work. But failure to launder money properly can be catastrophic. Al Capone, Frank Costello, and most of the organized crime figures arrested before 1970 were arrested not for the violent crimes committed by them or their henchmen but for income tax evasion. More recently, several major drug cases have been broken by federal agents who were able to trace large movements of cash through the banks back to suspected smugglers.

The Bank Secrecy Act of 1970 required banks to file a Currency Transaction Report whenever more than $10,000 in cash was deposited. Before the passage of that law, law-enforcement agencies paid little attention to the problem of money laundering, but since the late 1970s a number of major banks have been prosecuted and forced to pay large fines for helping people launder money. By the start of 1986, 21 banks had been penalized for laundering money; another 41 were under investigation. Here are some of the major cases.

- Chemical Bank was the first bank prosecuted for laundering money. In 1977 the bank and three executives were charged with laundering $8.5 million for several narcotics dealers. The bank pleaded guilty to 200 misdemeanors and was fined a mere $200,000 plus court costs even though it had allowed a multimillion-dollar drug business to flourish.
- In the so-called pizza connection case, La Cosa Nostra members distributed heroin through New York pizza parlors and sent the cash (about $25 million in $5 to $20 denominations) overseas to Bermuda, Switzerland and Italy where, after being laundered, it was used to buy more heroin. The money was first deposited and wired overseas through an account at Merrill Lynch, but the brokerage firm soon became suspicious and stopped all deposits. Then the operation began depositing money at E. F. Hutton & Co., which was more cooperative. Ever anxious to please, E. F. Hutton executives arranged for large cash deposits at Bankers Trust and helped soothe the suspicions of bank employees. Finally, when Hutton officials were served with grand-jury subpoenas, they warned associates of Franco Della Torre, the man who made the deposits, even though government agents had asked Hutton officials not to contact him. After the warning the company that received the money in Switzerland was deregistered and Della Torre made no further deposits. E. F. Hutton was not charged with any wrongdoing.
- In the Great American Bank case, this Dade County, Florida, bank

laundered $94 million for three narcotics organizations. Even though the bank treated the drug smugglers as valuable customers and allowed them to process such large amounts of cash, it was only fined $500,000.
• In the Eduardo Orozco case, 11 different banks helped him launder $151 million for cocaine and heroin dealers. Of these, only one bank contacted law-enforcement officials about its suspicions. A major portion of this money—about $97 million—was deposited in cardboard boxes at Deak-Perera, a currency exchange based in New York.
• The largest criminal fines for money laundering came in 1986. The Bank of New England, the second-largest financial institution in the region, was fined $1.24 million for not reporting 31 cash transactions totaling $817,000. That same year the Bank of America received civil penalties of $4.7 million and Texas Commerce Bancshares was hit with $1.9 million in civil fines for not reporting cash transactions.

While money laundering has hit some of the country's largest banks, the center of activities remains abroad. Panama, the Caribbean, and Switzerland all have strict bank-secrecy laws that protect the identity of drug dealers. Lax corporate regulations in those countries allow dealers to create front companies. Of the $5 billion to $15 billion in U.S. drug money laundered each year, the Justice Department believes that about one third is moved overseas in currency—the other two thirds is deposited in U.S. banks. Once the money is moved overseas, the Justice Department believes that about two thirds of it passes through Colombia or the offshore banking centers of the Caribbean Basin, mainly Panama, the Bahamas, and the Cayman Islands.

Panama, they believe, is the banking center for cocaine; Hong Kong does the banking for the heroin business, handling the money coming in and out of the Golden Triangle in Southeast Asia, an area that may produce as much as 19% of the heroin that reaches the U.S.

Security Fraud

Merger mania has done more than restructure American management. It has also opened up new temptations for insider trading and stock fraud. No figures are available on the volume of insider trading. While there is little doubt that most firms and brokers are honest, the problem seems to be growing. In 1986 alone, the SEC prosecuted several of the biggest insider-trading cases in history.

The Dennis Levine Case

In the largest insider-trading case up to that time, Dennis Levine, managing director of Drexel Burnham Lambert, pleaded guilty in the summer of 1986 to making $12.6 million on inside trades. According to investigators, Levine conducted his trade through the Bahamian branch of Swiss-owned Bank Leu of the Bahamas. Officials of the bank allegedly profited from this information and participated in an elaborate cover-up to hide their role in the affair. But they weren't the only ones involved. Levine fingered several other investment bankers before receiving a two-year jail sentence.

The Ivan F. Boesky Case

Information provided by Dennis Levine soon led government investigators to Ivan Boesky. In November of 1986, Boesky agreed to give up $50 million in insider-trading profits and to pay fines of $50 million. He was required to dissolve his $1 billion fund, Ivan F. Boesky & Co., that speculated in takeover stocks, and he was barred from the securities industry for life. Boesky has also pleaded guilty to one felony charge for securities-law violations and was sentenced to three years in jail.

The Boesky case sent shockwaves through the investment community. Founder of his own firm in 1975 at the age of 29, Boesky was known as one of the nation's boldest arbitrageurs. More than anyone else he had legitimized the practice of risk arbitrage—which involves speculating on takeover stocks. In 1986, he set up a $1 billion arbitrage fund, Ivan F. Boesky & Co., to speculate on takeover stock. Worth $250 million by the summer of 1986, he made up to $150 million from his attempted takeover of CBS, $50 million on Texaco's takeover of Getty, $65 million when Chevron bought Gulf, and millions more when Holiday Inn offered to buy back its stock in 1985. But even with his 100 employees, a small army of paid tipsters, and illegal insider information, he was occasionally wrong. Boesky lost $40 to $70 million speculating in Phillips Petroleum stock during a failed takeover bid by T. Boone Pickens.

On November 14, 1986, when the Securities and Exchange Commission announced the largest insider-trading case ever, it became apparent that Boesky was not the wizard he seemed to be. The SEC's case against Boesky showed that Boesky had learned of upcoming takeovers from Dennis Levine and a network of Levine's tipsters. Levine provided the information in exchange for a share of the profits. Later, in a case against Kidder, Peabody executive Martin Siegel, the government showed that Boesky had also paid Siegel for tips on forthcoming mergers. The government said Boesky earned $50 million in insider profits but some reports argue that the actual figure may be as much as $100 million.

The Boesky case soon led to even larger investigations, here and overseas. Information provided by Boesky started a British investigation into the brewer Guinness PLC's 1986 takeover of Distiller's Company. That investigation is shaping up as Britain's worst corporate scandal in years. At home, Boesky provided investigators with information that led to cases against Kidder, Peabody executive Martin Siegel and Boyd Jefferies, the chairman of the Jefferies Group. Investigations were also being conducted into several top raiders, including Victor Posner, Carl Icahn, Drexel Burnham Lambert, and executives at Kidder, Peabody and Goldman, Sachs. Boesky's lawyer claims that Boesky provided government investigators with information about wrongdoing in five unidentified securities firms.

Kidder, Peabody & Co. became the first major Wall Street firm snared by the government investigation. In 1987, Kidder was forced to settle insider-trading and other securities violations with the SEC. Kidder agreed to cough up $25 million in fines and penalties for insider-trading and securities-law violations to settle a civil suit brought by the SEC but escaped criminal charges. The firm was also forced to make widespread changes in the way it does business. To make certain the company does not repeat the violations—such as insider trading, swapping of nonpublic information, and stock parking—alleged by the SEC, Kidder agreed to let outside consultants investigate how well it oversees its employees. Furthermore, Kidder agreed to liquidate its risk arbitrage positions and not to take up risk arbitrage trading until it has set up a workable system to detect insider trading by its employees.

Wall Street's reputation as the big loser and a renewed criticism of arbitrageurs like Boesky could prompt Congress to pass tough antitake-over legislation. But lawyers have been doing just fine. Within months after the SEC announced its insider-trading case, Boesky faced an ever-growing number of civil suits and was forced to set aside $5 million to handle his legal fees. Total legal fees for the insider-trading cases related to Ivan Boesky could top $20 million.

The Boyd Jefferies Case

The government's case against Ivan Boesky led prosecutors to another prominent figure, Boyd Jefferies, the chairman of the Jefferies Group. Jefferies had close ties to Drexel Burnham Lambert and other corporate raiders and was an innovator in the so-called third market. That is, his California securities firm acted as its own securities exchange, allowing investors to trade large blocks of stock during off hours when regular exchanges were closed or during periods when stock exchanges stopped trading on takeover stocks. The third market was important to corporate raiders because it allowed them to accumulate huge blocks of stock quickly and relatively anonymously. But Jefferies's involvement with Boesky and takeovers got him into trouble. After agreeing to cooperate with the government investigation, Jefferies pleaded guilty to charges of "parking stocks." According to government prosecutors, he held blocks of stock for Boesky's security firms under a secret agreement that allowed Boesky to avoid SEC rules on disclosing stock ownership and the capital require-ments of security firms. The Jefferies case was important because it could lead government investigators on to Drexel Burnham Lambert and be-cause it indicated the government's willingness to crack down on other types of securities violations used by corporate raiders.

Corporate Crime

Crime in the suites—white-collar and corporate crime—rarely has the immediate, devastating effects of a rape or a murder; nonetheless, the economic consequences are great. In perhaps the best study of the problem, the U.S. Chamber of Commerce estimated in 1974 that the cost of white-collar crime was over $40 billion a year. Corporate crime has also affected a wide segment of the business community. A 1982 survey by *U.S. News & World Report* found that "of America's 500 largest corporations, 115 have been convicted in the last decade of at least one major crime or have paid civil penalties for serious misbehavior. That finding confirmed earlier studies, such as a 1975 survey of federal court action that found that 60% of the largest corporations had at least one action brought against them in 1975 or 1976, with 42% facing multiple charges.

Getting an accurate tally of the total costs of corporate crime is difficult because it covers a number of areas that have never been fully studied. Price fixing adds billions to the cost of goods and services. Water pollution caused by U.S. corporations in violation of federal laws could cost the economy $10 billion a year. The Office of Technology Assessment believes it could cost as much as $100 billion to clean up the 32,000 toxic waste dumps in the U.S. A study by the Congressional Research Service estimates that discrimination costs minorities about $37.6 billion in lost jobs or inequitable salaries. About $30 billion to $50 billion might be lost in treating occupational diseases such as asbestosis. Wasteful car repairs cost about $9 billion a year while deceptive grocery labeling costs around $14 billion. In the late 1970s, the American Management Association estimated that commercial bribery and kickbacks ranged from $3.5 billion to $10 billion a year. Another billion dollars was spent in the 1970s by about 500 U.S. companies to bribe foreign officials.

Embezzling is another serious aspect of business crime. The U.S. Chamber of Commerce believes that about 30% of all business failures each year are caused by employee theft. About $4 billion a year is lost in securities thefts and frauds. Between 1950 and 1971, there were as many as 100 bank failures directly attributable to fraud or embezzlement; in the first half of 1975, commercial banks lost nearly five times as much money in fraud and embezzlements, usually by insiders, as they did from armed bank robberies. Here are some of the largest cases of corporate fraud:

The Robert Vesco Case

Son of an auto worker and a high school dropout, Vesco built up a financial empire in the 1960s by using other people's money to take over companies. Using his New Jersey–based company, International Controls Corporation (ICC), he set up an international shell game of offshore companies, highly leveraged deals, and shady finances to build ICC in only four years into the 688th largest company in the U.S. In 1970, he managed to take over the foundering Investors Overseas Services, Ltd., and over the next few years the SEC accused him of pilfering $224 million. However, the SEC had been watching him. Denver oilman John King filed a $1 billion suit against him for using illegal funds to gain control of U.S. companies, and, in 1971, Vesco was arrested in Switzerland. However, the CIA, under orders from the Nixon administration, had him released. Once released, Vesco bribed the governments of Costa Rica and later the Bahamas to prevent his extradition. Vesco became a major figure in the Watergate scandal when it was reported that he gave a $200,000 contribution to the Committee to Re-elect the President in an attempt to block the SEC investigation. Subsequently, narcotics agents linked him to international drug deals, and he was eventually thrown out of the Bahamas for his alleged involvement in drug smuggling. Currently Vesco's exact location is unknown, though he was spotted in Cuba by reporters for NBC, fueling speculation that he was either receiving medical treatment or operating his drug operations from Havana. Former Attorney General John Mitchell and former Secretary of Commerce Maurice Stans were acquitted in 1974 of attempting to block the SEC investigation of Vesco in exchange for the campaign contributions.

The Michele Sindona Case

After beginning his business career as a seller of art books, the Italian financier Michele Sindona applied the art of fraud to divert illegally as much as $225 million from his Italian holdings to overseas banks. By 1972, using his expertise as a tax lawyer and accountant, Sindona acquired the Franklin National Bank (the 19th largest bank in the U.S.) and built up an empire of banks and industries scattered around the world that was valued at $450 million. However, when the Franklin Bank collapsed in 1974, Sindona's empire came unglued. Losses from his illegal banking practices at the Franklin and other banks totaled several hundred million dollars. The powerful Vatican bank lost millions in its dealings with him. As Sindona's creditors filed lawsuits, the lawyer Giorgio Ambrosoli, appointed by the Italian courts to liquidate his holdings, was murdered on Sindona's orders, apparently because Ambrosoli discovered evidence of fraud. Subsequent investigations led to Sindona's conviction for the murder of Ambrosoli in a U.S. trial and a conviction by Italian courts for fraud. These trials also revealed that Sindona had a tangled web of associations with organized crime figures and P2, an Italian lodge whose illegal activities and links with top Italian politicians touched off the biggest political scandal in postwar Italian history. In 1986 Sindona was poisoned while in prison, touching off speculation that he was murdered to prevent other top political leaders from being hurt by the scandal. His last words were, "They have poisoned me."

The OPM Leasing Scandal

Myron Goodman and Mordecai Weissman started their computer leasing operation in a one-room office in Brooklyn and built it into one of the nation's largest computer leasing companies. Or at least that's what everyone thought. Somewhere along the way, these two entrepreneurs discovered that all was not well in the computer leasing business. Provisions in most contracts allowed customers to trade up to better computers. That forced OPM and other companies to buy new computer lines, increasing their debts and leaving them with old computers that could only be leased for lower rates. Many companies went belly-up but OPM survived by crime. Its founders forged contracts to show nonexistent leasing deals and then used the contracts to get financing from banks and other investors. Before the scam was finally exposed Weissman and Goodman made off with $200 million. OPM went into Chapter 11. In 1982 Goodman received a 12-year prison sentence and Weissman a 10-year sentence.

The Charles Ponzi Case

The famous Ponzi scheme began in 1919, when this former messenger placed an ad in the paper saying investors in his Securities Exchange Company would earn a 50% profit in only a month and a half. Guaranteed or your money back. That sounded pretty good to thousands of investors and within six months 20,000 investors had coughed up $10 million. Ponzi claimed he was earning investors huge profits by buying International Postal Reply Coupons and then selling them in countries with higher exchange rates, thus profiting from the fluctuating currency markets. A constant flow of new investment money allowed him to buy up the Hanover Trust Company and achieve national fame as a Horatio Alger figure. However, in 1920 it was revealed that none of the investors' money had been invested and Ponzi was shipped off to federal prison. Most investors never got any money back.

That, however, didn't quite end his investment career. He was later indicted for larceny in Massachusetts and for fraud for speculating in Florida swampland. After being deported to Italy he moved to Brazil. He failed at running a hot dog stand in Brazil, but managed to make a modest living giving language lessons—it is easy to see him explaining how to conjugate verbs like *steal* and *defraud*.

Chapter Sixteen

DEALS AND MERGERS:
BIGGER IS BETTER?

HIGHLIGHTS AND TRENDS

• So far the 1980s have been the decade of the deal. Mergers, acquisitions, divestments, and leveraged buyouts reached unprecedented levels in the last few years, totaling $857.7 billion between 1979 and 1987, with over two thirds of that figure (71%) spent between 1984 and 1987. About $190.5 billion worth of deals were made in 1986, a record according to *Mergers & Acquisitions Magazine.*

• Through most of 1987, the takeover game continued to be hot, with $133.5 billion worth deals before the October 19 crash. However, only $16.5 billion worth of mergers, leveraged buyouts, or divestitures were completed during the rest of the year, indicating that merger mania may at last be calming down.

• Merger mania produced some of the largest deals ever put together. Only 12 transactions worth more than $1 billion were completed between 1969 and 1980, but in 1985 alone 37 billion-dollar deals were put together. And that was just a prelude to 1986, when 39 billion-dollar mergers, acquisitions, leveraged buyouts, or initial public offerings were financed.

• But merger mania was only one part of a supermarket of corporate assets. In 1986, there were over 308 leveraged buyouts (LBOs) worth a total of $40.9 billion, up from 99 LBOs worth $3.1 billion in 1981. Between 1981 and 1987 there were a total of 1,548 leveraged buyouts worth $119.3 billion. Three quarters of those buyouts (75.1%) occurred between 1985 and 1987.

• Corporate America also sold off assets and subsidiaries at a record-breaking pace. In 1987 there were 1,049 divestitures totaling of $45.9 billion, down from the record year of 1986, when 1,316 divestitures sold for $65.2 billion.

• By 1987, merger mania had left its mark on big business. Nearly half of the 1,000 largest U.S. corporations have undergone some type of significant reorganization in the 1980s. Many of the mergers took place in the most troubled parts of the economy—oil, manufacturing, and mining.

Manufacturing and mining, for example, have accounted for 50% to 65% of all merger activity since 1980.

• Overall, merger mania boosted shareholder assets and helped fuel the great bull market of the 1980s. W. T. Grimm & Co. concluded that from 1981 to 1986 shareholder wealth increased $118.4 billion as a result of mergers, selloffs, leveraged buyouts, and takeover bids for companies. An SEC study found that the value of stock increased by $54 billion as a result of successful tender offers.

• But a growing government investigation of insider trading has cast a pall over the merger and acquisition industry. One of Wall Street's top corporate arbitrageurs, Ivan Boesky, was sentenced to three years in jail for securities violations and agreed to pay the Securities and Exchange Commission $100 million in fines and insider-trading profits.

• Congress and state governments have also moved to curb mergers and regulate corporate takeovers, often at the expense of shareholders. A 1987 SEC study of the effects of an Ohio antitakeover law concluded that the antitakeover regulation cost shareholders about 2% of the value of their stocks.

• A worse threat to merger mania comes from Wall Street itself. Several deals collapsed when the Dow fell more than 500 points on October 19, 1987, and some raiders and arbitrageurs suffered huge losses, making it harder for them to finance a new round of takeover speculation. Still, uncertainty on Wall Street is not necessarily bad for merger mania. Lower stock prices make many companies more attractive takeover targets and falling interest rates would make it easier to finance new deals. The end of the Reagan era could be good for the merger game in 1988. While the Reagan administration has rarely used antitrust statutes against mergers, fears that a new administration would take a hard line against takeovers and beef up antitrust enforcement could boost mergers in the short run. Few analysts, however, expect the takeover game in 1988 or 1989 to return to the heated years of the mid-1980s.

LET'S MAKE A DEAL

"Let's Make a Deal" became the theme song of the 1980s as American business took its assets to the market. Mergers, acquisitions, and leveraged buyouts reached unprecedented levels in the 1980s, totaling $857.7 billion between 1979 and 1985, with over two thirds of that figure (71%) spent between 1984 and 1987. In 1987, deals totaled $150 billion, down from 1986's record $190.5 billion.

In the feverish pace of merger mania, some of the biggest deals in the history of American business were put together. Only 12 transactions worth more than a $1 billion were completed between 1969 and 1980, but in 1985 alone, 37 billion-dollar deals were put together. In fact, in 1985, when General Electric announced its plan to swallow RCA in a $6.4 billion deal that would produce the sixth-largest industrial company in the U.S., a billion-dollar merger wasn't even enough to put you in the top 20 deals. And that was only the beginning. In 1986, 39 billion-dollar deals were completed. All of the 20 largest mergers in U.S. history have been completed since 1981. Seventeen of 26 were done between 1985 and 1987.

But the worst dementia of merger mania may be over. Through most of 1987, the merger game continued to be hot, with $133.5 billion worth deals before the October 19 crash. However, with Wall Street licking its wounds, only $16.5 billion worth of mergers, leveraged buyouts, or divestitures were completed during the rest of 1987. The comparatively meager number of post-crash deals indicated that merger mania was over, but a new spate started in early 1988.

In retrospect, it's worth wondering if it was worth all the trouble. Sprawling conglomerates like ITT that were put together in the 1960s promised shareholders the world and delivered only disappointing earnings. Will merger mania in the 1980s fare no better? Or will this shopping spree go down in history as the kind of eccentricity that historians eventually call success?

Merger Mania

The most recent urge to merge hit American business in 1980 and 1981 when oil prices hit the skids, dropping the price for stocks of oil companies to absurdly low levels—and making them attractive to takeover attempts. These companies had assets worth two and sometimes three times as much as the stock. Since many analysts believed oil prices would eventually recover, buying these low-priced stocks was much like buying oil at $5 a barrel.

Take Conoco: Savvy raiders noticed that Conoco had domestic reserves of 400 million barrels of oil, lots of North Sea oil, and a subsidiary that was the second-largest coal producer in the U.S. Yet while Conoco's assets were worth over $140 a share, its stock was only selling for about $50 on Wall Street.

That was the kind of bargain few cash-rich companies could resist. During 1980 and 1981, some of the country's largest corporations—Seagram, du Pont, and Mobil—began wooing Conoco shareholders in a multibillion-dollar takeover battle that touched off merger mania. Du Pont, which rode into the fray as a white knight, finally won the right to buy Conoco for $8 billion—the most expensive merger completed up to that time.

Other undervalued oil companies, such as Marathon (whose stock was trading at $68 despite assets of $210 a share in 1981) and Getty (with stock trading at $72 even though it had assets worth $250 a share), also fell to merger mania. U.S. Steel acquired Marathon for $6.6 billion and Texaco got Getty for $10.1 billion.

But the oil patch wasn't the only part of the economy affected. The total value of mergers and acquisitions grew from $33.0 billion in 1980 to $67.2 billion in 1981. After a leveling-off period in 1982 and 1983, the mergers doubled to $125.7 in 1984, increased to $144.3 billion in 1985 and went through the roof in 1986, when a record $190.5 billion worth of deals were completed, according to *Mergers & Acquisitions*. No industry was forgotten.

- In the food industry, R. J. Reynolds paid $4.9 billion to eat up Nabisco, and Philip Morris gobbled up General Foods for $5.6 billion.
- In retail, Safeway, the nation's largest supermarket chain, went private for $4.3 billion while Macy's managers took the department-store firm private for $3.6 billion.
- In electronics, General Electric plugged into RCA, producing an industrial, financial, and electronics powerhouse with $35.2 billion in revenue in 1986.
- In the health-care industry, Baxter Travenol bought American Hospital Supply for $3.7 billion and Monsanto bought Searle for $2.7 billion.
- In television, two of the major networks got new owners as Capital Cities took over ABC for $3.5 billion and General Electric took over NBC's parent company, RCA. Rupert Murdoch moved toward his goal of setting up a fourth network by buying Metromedia's television stations for $2 billion.
- Failing to buy a TV empire from CBS, Ted Turner went to the movies, buying MGM/UA for $1.5 billion.
- In telecommunications, Southwestern Bell spent $1.2 billion for Metromedia's cellular phone division and ITT sold off its telecommunications division for $1.5 billion.
- In chemicals, the West German company Hoechst paid $2.8 billion for Celanese.
- Banks such as SunTrust Banks, First Wachovia, NCNB, the Bank of New England, Fleet Financial, and the Bank of Boston created regional banking empires by buying up banks in other states. The takeover spree drove up bank stocks in some states in anticipation of outside takeovers.
- On Wall Street, General Electric bought Kidder, Peabody & Co. in 1986. In 1981 alone, Sears acquired Dean Witter, Prudential Insurance took over the Bache Group, American Express gobbled up Shearson Lehman, and Philbro bought up Salomon Brothers. Equitable Life took over Donaldson, Lufkin & Jenrette in 1984.
- Even aerospace went into orbit. In Detroit, General Motors spent $5.0 billion to take over Hughes Aircraft, a major defense contractor.

Armed with junk bonds (see the discussion of junk bonds, page 310) to finance a deal, you didn't even have to be an industrial giant like General Motors or General Electric to play merger mania. Pantry Pride managed to swallow Revlon, which was three times its size, for $2.7 billion. Similarly, Capital Cities Communications managed to pull off the unthinkable—taking over a major network, ABC, for a mere $3.5 billion.

There's little doubt merger mania has profoundly affected the economy. To finance their shopping sprees some companies, such as Ted Turner's Turner Broadcasting System, went deeply in debt, and found that most of their cash flow was going to service their debt. Others, such as CBS, assumed new debts to avoid hostile takeovers and then had to make massive layoffs to make ends meet.

But while mergers have forced companies to struggle to pay off billion-dollar IOUs, stockholders have benefited from high takeover bids. The stockholders of Gulf, Getty, and Conoco alone gained more than $17 billion. Fueled by merger profits, an unprecedented bull market took hold of Wall Street, pushing the Dow up past 2,700 in 1987. W. T. Grimm & Co. concluded that from 1981 to 1986 shareholder wealth increased $118.4 billion as a result of mergers, selloffs, leveraged buyouts, and takeover bids for companies. An SEC study found that the value of stock increased by $54 billion as a result of successful tender offers.

The biggest winners were a few raiders such as T. Boone Pickens, whose company, Mesa Limited Partnership (formerly Mesa Oil) made more than $1 billion in its corporate raids, and the lawyers and the financial advisers who put together these deals. For example, the financial advisers and lawyers involved in Pantry Pride's takeover of Revlon made $100 million, with Drexel Burnham taking a $60 million cut. Wall Street companies involved in 39 billion-dollar deals in 1986 made $615 million in advisory fees.

The Dealmakers

T. Boone Pickens

No man is more closely identified with merger mania or, for that matter, more closely represents the spirit of the corporate raiders. Thanks to his successful raids, Pickens claimed he was worth $106 million in the fall of 1986.

As chairman of Mesa Petroleum, Pickens turned it into the largest independent oil producer, but it was hardly an industrial giant. In fact, Pickens admits that he undertook some of his early raids to bolster profits that had been hurt by sagging oil revenues. But in the 1980s his raids have forced Gulf (the fifth-largest oil company), Cities Service and other companies into mergers.

Although the goal of some corporate raids is to gain 51% control of a company by buying a substantial block of stock and making an offer that will get enough shareholders to sell, Pickens almost never takes control of the company. Typically, the prospect of selling the company to Pickens frightens management into a friendly takeover by a white knight who makes an offer higher than Pickens's. The white knight takes over the company and buys Pickens's stocks, leaving the oilman with a substantial profit! For his aborted 1984 raid on Gulf Oil that eventually forced the company to sell out to Chevron for $13.2 billion, Pickens and his backers made about $760 million. Mesa made another $120 million on a failed bids to take over Unocal and Phillips.

Although Pickens made millions by boosting the price of stocks in his raids, he bristles at the idea that he and others are only interested in short-term speculative gains. He claims that merger mania forces stock prices up to their real levels, gets rid of inefficient managers, and makes companies more conscious of stockholders' interests. "Chief executives who themselves own few shares of their companies," he says, "have no more feeling for the average stockholder than they do for baboons in Africa."

Pickens has also launched a kind of populist crusade to sell his brand of merger mania to the masses. During 1984 alone he spoke to over 47,000 people, telling them that common people as well as major arbitrageurs have benefited from his corporate raids. Since then, he's pledged $1.7 million to set up his United Shareholders Association, a group that stands up for shareholder rights and, of course, the inalienable right to satisfy the urge to merge. Pickens estimates that three quarters of a billion shareholders have realized gains of about $12 billion as a result of his takeover battles. A political conservative, Pickens has raised over $7 million for political candidates even though he argues that big business has too much clout in Congress.

Pickens's critics point out that his own management is not above reproach. Before he turned Mesa into a master limited partnership in 1985, Pickens's salary was six times the oil industry average and the company had one of the lowest payout records in the industry.

But overall, shareholders probably have few complaints. Pickens turned Mesa into the country's largest independent oil producer. While many other companies have been flooded out of business by the worldwide oil glut, Mesa has pared down its debt with the money Pickens has made as a corporate raider.

Kohlberg Kravis Roberts & Co. (KKR)

Known on Wall Street as the kings of leveraged buyouts, Jerome Kohlberg, Jr., Henry R. Kravis, George R. Roberts, and Robert I. MacDonnell, the four partners of KKR, have built up enormous personal fortunes by acting as financial advisers for leveraged buyouts. Kohlberg, Kravis, and Roberts each made an estimated $50 million in 1986 (MacDonnell, who has a small stake, took in $15 million.) The company has a $5.6 billion buyout fund. In 1985 it put together the $2.4 billion deal to take Storer Communications private, as well as the $2 billion deal to take Union Texas Petroleum private. In all, these deals accounted for $6 billion of the record $16 billion in leveraged buyouts in 1985. In 1986 it managed the largest leveraged buyouts ever, a $6.2 billion deal to take the food concern Beatrice Companies private and a $5.3 billion leveraged buyout for Safeway Stores. For engineering the Beatrice deal, KKR earned $45 million, the largest single investment advisory fee ever. In 1987 it arranged a $3.6 billion leveraged buyout of Owens-Illinois. In all, it has put together three of the largest leveraged buyouts on record.

Saul Steinberg

He got his start leasing computers and, as a brash young man, attempted unsuccessfully to take over Chemical Bank. In 1968 his corporate leasing company Leasco bought Reliance Insurance Company and today his family's holdings in the Reliance Group ($3.1 billion in revenues and $103 million in profits in 1986) are worth about $650 million. He made $32 million in a battle for The Walt Disney Company and $10.5 million green-mailing Quaker State Oil Refining, and he survived a messy 1983 divorce during which his wife made unsubstantiated charges that he was taking drugs, bribing New York City officials, and diverting corporate funds. Living in a 34-room triplex once owned by John D. Rockefeller, Jr., he's proof that arbitrageurs are founding the financial empires of the 1980s.

Carl Icahn

In 1986, Carl Icahn emerged as the "victor" in a takeover battle for Trans World Airlines—*victor* in quotes because analysts wondered if taking control of the troubled airline was any kind of prize. TWA was a perennial money loser and critics said Icahn should have stuck with his usual *modus operandi:* offer to buy a company, watch the stock run up in the ensuing takeover speculation, and then sell his stake to the winner of the bidding war at a handsome profit.

Icahn's takeover of TWA was the riskiest move he has made in a long career of taking risks. A corporate raider since the late 1970s, Carl Icahn has made over $220 million on a dozen-plus raids. He made $20 million buying up Gulf + Western shares in 1983, $35 million in 1985 on his stake in Phillips Petroleum, and $80 million going after Union Carbide and Viacom in 1986. Nice work if you can get it.

His takeover of TWA in early 1986 put him on the edge of a $500 million gamble. Stuck with 73% of the company's stock, Icahn, who had never run an airline or much of anything else for that matter, thought he could quickly reduce costs. But a nasty strike by flight attendants hurt earnings and the company lost $256.6 million in the first half of 1986. His critics claimed there was no end in sight to the red ink and wondered if Icahn's tenure at TWA would disprove the hypothesis that corporate raiders were improving companies by restructuring their operations and finances.

Icahn confounded their predictions, at least temporarily. He cut $600 million in costs and the airline actually made a $100 million profit in the third quarter of 1986. By the middle of 1987, Icahn was sitting on a paper profit of $188 million on his original $412 million investment in TWA stock. To boost revenues, TWA is also starting to do what it did so successfully in earlier years—expand on-the-ground operations. The company opened stores to sell merchandise and has a cable TV channel designed to sell travel-related services to home viewers. Icahn hopes the new ventures will cost only $10 million to operate and can be spun off for as much as $300 million in a few years.

But the company is by no means flying into the sunset, profitable and ready to pay dividends happily ever after. TWA under Icahn has cut back on maintenance and buying new airplanes. That means an oil-price hike could leave the company with older, less fuel-efficient airplanes and higher costs. Worse, an October 1987 plunge in the stock market wiped out his paper profits in TWA stock and forced him to give up his plan to take the company private. Icahn may still succeed with his TWA turnaround. But with an airline that lost $106 million on $3.1 billion in revenues in 1986, he won't see the quick paper profits he's grown to expect.

There is also turbulence in the rest of Icahn's financial empire. He failed in his $8 billion bid to take over USX, tying up $650 million in a company that is struggling with a rusty steel market, and his bid to take over American Airlines in early 1987 never got off the ground. But he shows no signs of slowing down. He bought a hefty stake in Texaco after the October 1987 crash.

Michael Milken and Drexel Burnham Lambert Inc.

The king of the junk bonds, Drexel Burnham Lambert Inc., has its own kingmaker, Michael Milken, who has been aptly compared to J. P. Morgan. Like Morgan, who restructured American industry in the late 19th and early 20th centuries by putting together the financing for such industrial giants as U.S. Steel, Milken has used his ability to arrange junk bond financing to restructure corporate America. In the 1980s Milken's list of clients has read like a who's who of corporate raiders and entrepreneurs: T. Boone Pickens, Ivan F. Boesky, Ronald Perlman, Rupert Murdoch, Ted Turner, Victor Posner, Carl Icahn, and so on.

Milken is credited with earning $250 million of the $545.5 million in profits on $4 billion in revenue Drexel earned in 1986. With his 4% stake in Drexel and holdings in numerous private investment partnerships, Milken may have made as much as $125 million in 1986 alone. *Forbes* figures he might be worth as much as a half-billion dollars.

Milken accomplished most of this before the age of 40. In the late 1970s and early 1980s Drexel Burnham Lambert established a reputation as an outsider on Wall Street. Milken thrived in its freewheeling deal-making atmosphere that meshed well with corporate raiders such as T. Boone Pickens. Milken's success, however, relied on putting together a personal network of financiers and companies. Soon he and Drexel built up a reputation for being able to arrange the financing of corporate takeovers with high-yield, below-investment-grade bonds (junk bonds). Using Milken's network, Drexel was able to raise billions almost overnight for many of the largest corporate raids in the 1980s. Milken and Drexel, for example, arranged the financing for Pickens's raids on Gulf, Unocal, and Phillips Petroleum.

Junk bonds, thanks to Milken and Drexel, changed the way deals were done. Companies didn't have to have triple-A credit ratings—which in practice were given to only a few of the country's most profitable and largest corporations. By issuing junk bonds, a raider like Ronald Perelman could buy a huge company like Revlon and build up an empire without investing a cent of his own money.

That success catapulted junk bonds, Drexel Burnham Lambert, and Milken onto front pages and the nightly news. Cut in the mold of a reclusive financier, Milken refuses to have his picture taken and won't sit for media interviews. But reclusiveness hasn't ended the press attention, or for that matter government investigations. The SEC and U.S. Attorney Rudolph Giuliani have been investigating Milken and Drexel ever since one of their major clients, Ivan F. Boesky, settled a $100 million insider-trading case, the largest in history.

Milken and Drexel deny they've done anything wrong, and despite a year of speculation, no charges were filed by the start of 1988. But even if they survive government probes, they face stiff competition that may end their reign as the kings of junk bonds. Lured by the huge advisory and investment-banking fees Drexel has been earning in the junk-bond market, other Wall Street firms and even commercial banks have moved into the junk-bond market. Drexel's share of the junk-bond market fell from nearly 60% in 1984 to 51.6% in the first half of 1986 and only 32.3% in 1987. Uncertainty on Wall Street could also cool down the feverish pace of merger mania and cut into Drexel's huge investment banking fees. Drexel has had an explosive 58%-a-year growth rate over the last half-decade, but new competition suggests slower growth, at least over the next few years.

William E. Simon

After leaving the post of Treasury Secretary in the Ford administration, William E. Simon turned his energies to building his personal fortune. Wesray Capital Corporation, a company founded by Simon and his partner Raymond Chambers in 1981, specializes in leveraged buyouts.

Typically, Simon and Chambers put up very little of their own money and make lots more money in profits. For example, in 1982 they put up only $1 million for the $80.5 million leveraged buyout of Gibson Greetings but made $200 million on the deal. They also made big profits on a leveraged buyout of Permian Corporation: Wesray put up only $10 million but made $137 million when the company was sold to National Intergroup.

Those kinds of numbers helped Simon and Chambers become two of the highest-paid men on Wall Street, pulling down some $45 million to $50 million in earnings in 1986 alone. Simon had the high-powered contacts that made it easy for Wesray to finance its deals. Chambers handled the details as well as many of the important decisions and strategies.

After heated confrontations between the partners, Simon greatly reduced his presence at Wesray, leaving little more than his name on the door. He has turned toward the Pacific and the Asian rim, where he believes properties are still undervalued. In 1986 and 1987, he and other high-powered partners such as the former vice-chairman of the Federal Reserve Board, Preston Martin, bought up $4.4 billion in thrifts.

As usual, Simon is putting up very little of his own money. He and his partners, for example, put up only $17 million to $20 million to buy the troubled Honolulu Federal Savings and Loan Association, which has $1.6 billion in assets. So far, they have not been able to turn the thrifts around as fast as expected. But if Simon's gamble pays off and he can turn the money-losing thrifts into profitable businesses, the profits could exceed anything he earned in leveraged buyouts.

The Restructuring of American Business

Merger mania took place in a supermarket of corporate assets. As some companies fought vicious takeover battles to enlarge their corporate domains, others sold off the corporate fat. Through most of the 1980s, corporate America sold assets and subsidiaries at a record-breaking pace. In 1987 there were 1,049 divestitures of a total of $45.9 billion, down from the record year of 1986, when 1,316 divestitures sold for $65.2 billion. Even with the slowdown in 1987, that year's total was higher than the $40.8 billion worth of sales in 1985 and the $29.9 billion in 1984, according to *Mergers & Acquisitions*. And the 1984 figure was nearly twice as large as that for 1983.

Even companies such as ITT, long the leader of corporate expansion, were cutting fat. Since 1980, ITT has sold off more than 100 businesses, including its European telecommunications operations. But ITT wasn't alone. Gulf + Western, which once specialized in buying up everything in sight, agreed in 1985 to sell nearly half of its businesses to Wickes Companies for about $1 billion.

But selling off assets was in no way incompatible with pursuing a strategy of corporate mergers. General Electric, for example, was buying and selling companies at a frantic pace. In the 1980s it has bought 24 companies for $8.5 billion and sold off 22 for $4 billion.

Other companies went private in record numbers. Leveraged buyouts— a process in which a group, usually the management or a large shareholder, buys out the other stockholders or owners using borrowed funds—also hit record numbers. Frequently, the company's assets serve as security for the loans and quite often the new owners take the company private.

In 1986 there were 308 leveraged buyouts worth a total of $40.9 billion, up from 99 leveraged buyouts worth $3.1 billion in 1981. Between 1981 and 1987 there were a total of 1,548 leveraged buyouts worth $119.3 billion. Three quarters of those buyouts (75.1%) came between 1985 and 1987. In 1987, the LBO market slowed, with 243 buyouts worth $29.4 billion consummated.

Some management theorists acknowledge that these buyouts leave a company saddled with a mountain of debt, threatening its future with huge interest payments. But they claim this debt will force the new owners (often the old management) to make tough decisions to sell off inefficient assets, reduce costs, cut wages, and generally do the kinds of things that are avoided when things are going well. Eventually, so the theory goes, the company will emerge from the debt crisis leaner and meaner. Then the owners can sell the more efficient company or take it public again for huge profits.

Another reason for the upsurge in leveraged buyouts is the fact that they became a favorite tactic for owners and management worried about losing their power to corporate raiders. Revlon's management tried and failed to take the company private to avoid an outside takeover and other companies did it as a way of avoiding the likes of T. Boone Pickens. Going private, of course, also has the advantage of removing management and ownership from the glare of public disclosures. They can make decisions without having to release earnings, without having to satisfy the demands of short-term investors and speculators, and without having to file endless paperwork with the SEC.

And there is little doubt that some leveraged buyouts have resulted in quick profits for their new owners. Former Treasury Secretary William Simon, for example, led a group of investors in 1982 who bought Gibson Greetings, Inc., for $80 million, using only $1 million of their own money. Then, 18 months later, they took the company public. Over time, Simon's company, Wesray, has made about $200 million on the deal.

In another case, Metromedia owner John Kluge took the company private in 1984 for $1.1 billion. Since then he's been selling off the company's assets. Total profits could hit $3 billion by the time he's done.

What's going on here is simple: For one reason or another, a company's stock is trading below the value of its assets. Smart managers can sell off the company's dogs, cut costs to turn around previously unprofitable holdings, and presto—suddenly the company is worth much more than it once was.

Do These Deals Work?

The urge to merge is, of course, nothing new. At the turn of the century, the U.S. economy was hit with its first wave of merger mania, as the investment bankers of the period put together the megadeals that created such industrial giants as U.S. Steel, Anaconda Copper, du Pont, American Tobacco, Allis-Chalmers, and American Smelting and Refining. Between 1898 and 1902, over 2,653 companies disappeared in merger deals worth about $6.3 billion. Another period of merger mania hit the economy in the 1920s when the cost of mergers reached about two thirds of what was spent on capital and equipment in 1928 and 1929. In the late 1960s, go-go conglomerates like Ling-Temco-Vought assembled huge, and often ill-defined, corporate empires.

The jury is still out on the megadeals of the 1980s. Analysts point out that many industries, such as energy, mining, and financial services, needed to be restructured by mergers or leveraged buyouts. Economist Michael C. Jensen, for example, has written, "Shareholders and the economy would gain enormously if companies in industries . . . such as energy, airlines, broadcasting and cable TV, felt the pressure of potential hostile takeovers. Otherwise, managers are free to waste resources on marginal enterprises, rather than paying out excess cash to shareholders." He points out that shareholders benefited to the tune of $17 billion in the Gulf, Getty, and Conoco takeovers.

There is also little doubt that merger mania has helped fuel the great bull market of the 1980s. W. T. Grimm & Co. concluded that from 1981 to 1986 shareholder wealth increased $118.4 billion as a result of mergers, selloffs, leveraged buyouts, and takeover bids for companies. An SEC study found that the value of stock increased by $54 billion as a result of successful tender offers.

Proponents of junk bonds also deny the notion that the junk bonds used to finance merger mania are threatening the solvency of corporate America. "Corporate debt has grown," James Balog, vice chairman of Drexel Burnham Lambert, a major issuer of junk bonds, admits. But "corporate debt hasn't gone up that much. In fact, corporate debt today, corporate debt ratios, are lower than they were in 1974 and 1977. These are not high debt ratios even in our own historical terms and they are certainly not high in world terms." That view is confirmed by a December 1985 Federal Reserve staff memorandum that found corporations had a debt equity ratio of 71.4% in 1985, up from 35.3% in 1961, down from 91.1% in 1974 and about the same as in 1981, when merger mania was getting started.

Reshuffling assets has probably helped many businesses. Selling off dogs has allowed companies to get rid of subsidiaries they aren't equipped to manage and buy companies they can successfully run. Often the new owners can take a previously unprofitable business and turn it around. A study by Frederic M. Scherer, a Swarthmore College economist, indicates that 14 out of 15 subsidiaries sold between 1970 and 1982 did better on their own.

Finally, what's behind merger mania is a fundamental restructuring of the economy—not simply a speculative frenzy. Well over half of the 1,000 largest corporations in the U.S. have undergone some form of restructuring in the 1980s. And most of the mergers have taken place in the most troubled parts of the economy—oil, manufacturing, and mining. Manufacturing and mining, for example, have accounted for 50% to 65% of all merger activity since 1980.

Corporate raids have in many cases plunged companies into debt to fight off the raiders. To pay off those debts, managers have slashed costs, laid off middle management, closed unprofitable plants, and sold off unprofitable subsidiaries. No doubt the human costs are high, causing many commentators to argue that speculation on Wall Street is ruining the economies of Main Street. But viewed from another angle, mergers and acquisitions are the first step in making American business more competitive and productive.

The Future: The Legacy of Ivan Boesky

November 14, 1986, was an important day in the history of deals. That's when the SEC announced that Ivan Boesky had agreed to pay $100 million in fines and illegal insider-trading profits to settle a civil suit with the government. Boesky, who ran his own $1 billion fund that specialized in speculation on corporate takeovers, later was sentenced to three years in jail. (For details of the insider-trading cases see the chapter "Crime.")

As part of his deal with government prosecutors, Boesky also fingered a number of other Wall Street firms and executives, creating a public backlash against Wall Street and takeover artists. As a result, the real impact of the Boesky affair has not been the body count, which keeps rising, but the public and political fallout. Merger mania has never been popular on Capitol Hill or in statehouses around the country, so it was no surprise that Boesky's case gave new life to long-standing attempts to regulate merger activity. The Supreme Court gave increased regulation a shot in the arm in 1987 when it upheld an Indiana statute curbing hostile takeovers. Top congressional leaders have also introduced legislation that would further restrict mergers and acquisitions.

Less than a year later, the October 19, 1987, stock market crash touched off more doubts about the future of merger mania. Within weeks after the Dow fell 500 points in one day, several deals had collapsed and some raiders and arbitrageurs suffered huge losses. If stocks continue their freefall and the economy spins into a major recession Congress will certainly pass even tougher antitakeover legislation. A recession could also trigger some junk-bond defaults and make it harder for raiders to finance deals with junk bonds. After the fall, mergers slowed dramatically. Though $133.5 billion worth of deals were made before the October 19 crash, only $16.5 billion worth of mergers, leveraged buyouts, or divestitures were completed during the rest of 1987, indicating that merger mania may at last be calming down.

Even so, the merger game may not disappear. Every year since 1984, forecasters predicted the imminent demise of merger mania. Until the fall of the stock market in the fall of 1987, they've been wrong. The underlying cause of merger mania—the need to restructure corporate assets—remains valid. The value of many corporate assets could be perked up if unprofitable divisions are spun off or costs are cut. As long as smart investors see money to be made in buying cheap assets and increasing their value, merger mania will seem like a sensible way of making money. And uncertainty on Wall Street isn't necessarily bad for merger mania as long as the economy remains strong. Lower stock prices make many companies more attractive takeover targets and falling interest rates would make it easier to finance new deals.

Table 66 The Urge to Merge

This chart provides an idea of how rapidly the mergers and acquisitions field has grown. It shows the number of corporate mergers, acquisitions, leveraged buyouts, and divestitures that were valued at over $1 million. On the right are the dollar amounts of those deals.

Year	Number of corporate mergers and acquisitions completed or pending	Volume of mergers, acquisitions, leveraged buyouts, and divestitures (billions of dollars)
1976	1,145	NA
1977	1,209	NA
1978	1,452	NA
1979	1,529	34.2
1980	1,565	33.0
1981	2,326	67.2
1982	2,297	60.4
1983	2,385	52.5
1984	3,144	125.7
1985	3,397	144.3
1986	4,024	190.5
1987	3,469	149.9

(NA) Not available.
Source: *Mergers & Acquisitions,* various issues.

Table 67   The Largest Mergers, First Half of 1987 and Historical

First half 1987

Acquisitor/Acquired	Approximate value (millions of dollars)	Announce date*
British Petroleum/Standard Oil	7,900	March 20
Amoco/Dome Petroleum	3,870	April 20
Unilever N.V./Chesebrough-Pond's	3,100	January 2*
American Hoechst/Celanese Corporation	2,720	March 2*
Rorer Group/A. H. Robins	2,600	June 29
JMB Realty/Cadillac Fairview Corporation	2,000	May 8
USAir Group/Piedmont Aviation	1,590	March 9
Fleet Financial Group/Norstar Bancorp	1,300	March 19
Hughes Tool/Baker International	1,200	March 12*
Chrysler/American Motors	1,180	March 10
Wickes Companies/Collins and Aikman	1,160	January 15*
Security Pacific/Ranier Bancorp	1,100	February 25
Chemical New York/Texas Commerce Bancshares	1,040	May 1*
Tele-Communications/Heritage Communications	887	February 27
Delta Air/Western Airline	860	April 2*
Computer Association/UCCEL Corporation	780	June 2
PNC Financial Corporation/Citizens Fidelity Corporation	770	March 2*
Primerica/Smith Barney	750	June 22*
Sovran Financial Corporation/Commerce Union Corporation	605	April 27
American Brands/ACCO World	602	June 23
WPP Group PLC/JWT Group, Inc.	566	June 29
Dainippon Ink/Sun Chemical	550	May 26
RepublicBank Corporation/InterFirst Corporation	544	May 28*
Baxter Travenol/Caremark, Inc.	528	May 12
Banner Industries/Rexnord, Inc.	525	May 15*

Historical

Acquisitor/Acquired	Approximate value (millions of dollars)	Year
Chevron/Gulf Corporation	13,205	1984
Texaco/Getty Oil	10,128	1984
du Pont/Conoco	8,039	1981
British Petroleum/Standard Oil	7,900	1987
U.S. Steel/Marathon Oil	6,618	1981
General Electric/RCA Corporation	6,400	1986
Philip Morris/General Foods	5,627	1985
Mobil Corp/Superior Oil	5,725	1984
General Motors/Hughes Aircraft	5,025	1985
R. J. Reynolds/Nabisco Brands	4,906	1985
Burroughs/Sperry Corporation	4,780	1986
Allied Corp/Signal Companies	4,476	1985
Elf Aquitaine/Texasgulf	4,293	1981
Occidental Petroleum/Cities Service	4,115	1982
Amoco/Dome Petroleum	3,870	1987
Baxter Travenol/American Hospital Supply	3,702	1985
Shell Oil/Belridge Oil	3,653	1979
Campeau Corporation/Allied Stores	3,500	1986
Capital Cities Communications/American Broadcasting	3,500	1986
Unilever N.V./Chesebrough-Pond's	3,100	1987
Occidental Petroleum/MidCon Corporation	3,000	1986
U.S. Steel/Texas Oil and Gas	3,000	1986
Nestlé/Carnation	2,885	1984
American Hoechst/Celanese Corporation	2,720	1987
Kohlberg Kravis Roberts/Storer Communications	2,717	1985
Monsanto/G. D. Searle	2,717	1985

*Completion date.
Source: W. T. Grimm & Co. *Fortune*, Salomon Brothers Inc., and Securities Data Company.

Table 68 The Largest Divestitures

This chart shows the largest divestitures in the first half of 1987 and between 1981 and the first half of 1987. Amounts are in millions of dollars.

First half 1987

Acquisitor/Acquired	Approximate value (millions of dollars)	Announce date
Shearson Lehman Brothers/Standard Oil: industrial holding	1,800	May 27*
Grand Metropolitan PLC/RJR Nabisco: Heublein	1,200	January 16
Argyll Group PLC/Safeway Food Stores	1,040	March 4
Continental AG/GenCorp: General Tire	650	June 29*
Feruzzi/CPC International: European operations	630	April 1
Wesray Capital Corporation/Bally Mfg: Six Flags	600	May 20*
Loral Corporation/Goodyear Tire: aerospace unit	588	March 12
American Brands/National Distillers: spirits division	545	April 9
Cain Chemical/du Pont: polyethylene business	510	June 10
Freeport McMoRan Inc/Williams Companies: AGRICO Chemical	500	March 4*
Lasalle Energy/Occidental Petroleum: United Gas	500	April 21
Bally Manufacturing/Golden Nugget Corporation: casino operations	440	January 19
Lanesborough Corporation/Allied Signal: Ampex division	430	April 6
JBM Realty Corporation/Walt Disney: ARVIDA unit	400	January 20
Valley National Bank/Avco National Bank: miscellaneous assets	400	May 29
Getty Petroleum/Apex Holding: Clark Oil and Refining	400	June 11
CPC International/Ajinomoto: Far East operations	340	April 2
Greyhound Corporation/Carson Pine: food service lines	326	May 28
Walt Disney/GenCorp: KHJ-TV	320	March 10
Coca-Cola Enterprises/Coca-Cola Company: bottling operations	300	February 20
First Capital Holdings/E. F. Hutton: insurance unit	300	May 21
Kraft/General Host: American Gourmet	296	June 8
Lomas & Nettleton/Equitable Life Assurance: leasing unit	289	May 12
Conseco, Inc./Beneficial Corporation: insurance unit	275	March 16
Provident Life and Accident/Transamerica: Transamerica Occident Life Insurance	275	May 5*

1981 through first half of 1987

Acquisitor/Acquired	Approximate value (millions of dollars)	Year
Investors/British Gas	7,000	1983
General Motors/Hughes Aircraft (Hughes)	5,300	1985
Broken Hill Proprietary/General Electric: Utah International	2,400	1984
Rupert Murdoch/Metromedia: WNEW-TV	2,000	1986
News Corporation Ltd./Metromedia: TV stations	1,990	1986
Shearson Lehman Brothers/Standard Oil: industrial holding	1,800	1987
Phillips Petroleum/R. J. Reynolds: Aminoil	1,700	1984
Mfrs Hanover/RCA: CIT Financial	1,510	1984
Ralston Purina/Union Carbide: battery division	1,415	1986
Lorimar/Wometco/SCI Holdings: TV stations	1,410	1986
Coca-Cola/JTL Corporation: beverage assets	1,400	1986
ICH Corporation/Tenneco: insurance operations	1,340	1986
Compagnie Générale d'Electricité/ITT: telecommunications business	1,200	1986
JSC/MS Holdings/Mobil: Container Corporation	1,200	1986
Southwestern Bell/Metromedia: mobile telephone business	1,200	1986
Grand Metropolitan PLC/RJR Nabisco: Heublein, Inc.	1,200	1987
Wickes Companies/Gulf + Western: consumer group	1,090	1985
General Electric Credit/Texaco: Employers Reinsurance	1,080	1984
Wells Fargo/Midland Bank: Crocker National	1,070	1986
Argyll Group PLC/Safeway Stores: Safeway Food Stores	1,040	1987
Honeywell/Unisys Corporation: Sperry Aerospace	1,030	1986
BASF America/United Technologies: Inmont Corporation	1,000	1985
BCE Development/Oxford Industries: Oxford Properties	1,000	1986
Coca-Cola/Beatrice Foods: bottling operations	1,000	1986
Southland Corporation/Occidental Petroleum: CITGO	995	1983

*Completion date.
Source: Salomon Brothers Inc. and Securities Data Company.

Table 69 The Largest Leveraged Buyouts

The left side of this chart shows the largest leveraged buyouts in the first half of 1987; the right side shows the largest ones between 1980 and the first half of 1987. Amounts are in millions of dollars.

First half 1987			1980 through first half of 1987		
Acquisitor/Acquired	Approximate value (millions of dollars)	Announce date	Acquisitor/Acquired	Approximate value (millions of dollars)	Year
AV Acquisition Corporation/Borg-Warner	3,760	April 13	Kohlberg Kravis Roberts/Beatrice Companies	6,200	1986
Kohlberg Kravis Roberts/Owens-Illinois	3,640	February 11*	Kohlberg Kravis Roberts/Safeway Stores	5,300	1986
National Amusements, Inc./Viacom International	3,400	March 5*	AV Acquisition Corporation/Borg-Warner	3,760	1987
Morgan Stanley/Burlington Industries	2,160	June 24	Investors/R. H. Macy	3,700	1986
Forstmann Little/Lear-Siegler	2,100	January 26*	Kohlberg Kravis Roberts/Owens-Illinois	3,640	1987
Employee Group/Hospital Corporation of America	1,800	June 2	National Amusements Inc/Viacom International	3,400	1987
TFBA Limited Partnership/Taft Broadcasting	1,450	June 9*	Management/Viacom International	2,730	1986
MacAndrews & Forbes/Revlon	880	March 9*	SCI Holdings/Storer Communications	2,510	1985
Adler & Shaykin/Joy Manufacturing	620	January 2*	Morgan Stanley/Burlington Industries	2,160	1987
Citicorp Capital Investors/Leaseway Transportation	600	June 17*	Forstmann Little/Lear-Siegler	2,100	1987
Morgan & Lewis/Alleghany Beverage Corporation	500	April 23	Employee Group/Hospital Corporation of America	1,800	1987
LPL Investment Group/Allied-Signal	479	April 6	Management/Beverly Enterprises	1,730	1986
Hicks & Haas/Spectradyne	452	May 27	Management/National Gypsum	1,640	1986
Welsh Carson Anderson/Comdata Network	314	March 6	Kohlberg Kravis Roberts/Rheem Manufacturing	1,550	1984
Allen & Co/Cottrell, Inc.	293	June 9	JWK Acquisition Corporation/Metromedia	1,450	1984
			HHF Corp/Levi Strauss	1,450	1985
			TFBA Limited Partnership/Taft Broadcasting	1,450	1987

*Completion date.
Source: Salomon Brothers Inc. and Securities Data Company.

263

Chapter Seventeen

TRADE, PRODUCTIVITY, AND STAYING AHEAD: WORLD WAR III?

HIGHLIGHTS AND TRENDS

• Foreign trade is an increasingly important part of the U.S. economy, accounting for one quarter of our GNP in 1980, up from 13.1% in 1972 and only 6% in 1860.

• One out of every six manufacturing workers owed his or her job to foreign trade in 1984. More than 5.4 million Americans find work in jobs that produce goods for export.

• An ever-widening trade deficit hit $171.2 billion in 1987, up from a previous record of $148.5 billion in 1985.

• One reason the U.S. is losing the trade war is that it's losing the productivity war. U.S. productivity in the manufacturing sector as measured by output per hour grew only 2.2% between 1973 and 1985, down from a 3.2% increase between 1960 and 1973. That was way below Japan's growth rate of 10.3% a year between 1960 and 1973 and 5.6% between 1973 and 1985. As a result, U.S. productivity growth between 1960 and 1985 lagged way behind the 5.4% annual growth in productivity of 11 major foreign competitors. While U.S. manufacturing productivity grew only 2.7% a year between 1960 and 1985, productivity grew 8.0% in Japan, 5.5% in France, 3.4% in Canada, 4.8% in Germany, 5.4% in Italy, 3.5% in the United Kingdom, 6.5% in Belgium, 4.8% in Denmark, 6.2% in the Netherlands, 3.2% in Norway, and 4.7% in Sweden.

• Since then, however, U.S. manufacturers have been making a comeback in the productivity race. In 1986, U.S. manufacturing productivity grew by 3.5%, faster than Canada (− 0.5%), Japan (2.7%), France (1.9%), Germany (1.9%), Italy (1.2%), and the United Kingdom (3.0%).

• Congress has decided that protectionism is the best way of helping the economy. But protectionism will do more harm than good. Protectionist legislation is now costing U.S. consumers $65 billion a year, up from $33 billion in 1980. Export control on U.S. products cost American companies 188,000 jobs and $9.3 billion in sales. Moreover, Congress and

President Reagan's retreat from free-trade policies means that 20% of all imports are affected by some restrictions, up from 12% in 1981.

TRADING FOR DOLLARS: THE IMPORTANCE OF STAYING COMPETITIVE

Gone are the days when the U.S. could thumb its nose at the rest of the world, knowing that its economy was remarkably self-sufficient. Although foreign trade in 1860 accounted for only 6% of our GNP, it accounted for about one quarter of GNP in 1980, up from 13.1% in 1972. One out of every six manufacturing workers owed his or her job to foreign trade in 1984; about 5.4 million Americans hold jobs created by the export trade. Almost one fifth of our industrial production is exported; 70% of the goods we produce compete with merchandise from abroad.

As trade becomes more important to the economy, there is increasing debate over its effects. Huge trade deficits have already cost the economy about 1.1 million manufacturing jobs and could put a damper on future economic growth. For example, if the trade deficit continues at the level of the mid-1980s, the U.S. will rack up a foreign debt of $750 million to $1 trillion by 1990.

And although everyone keeps predicting that the worst is over, the trade deficit isn't going away. Between 1982 and 1985, the U.S. trade deficit rose from $42.6 billion to a record $148.5 billion. The trade deficit hit a new record in 1986 ($169.8 billion) and despite the plummeting dollar, records a deficit of $171.2 billion in 1987.

The problem has already created its own buzzword—*competitiveness*. Many manufacturing companies are in trouble but studying competitiveness, talking about competitiveness, and making political hay on competitiveness is a growth industry. Republicans and Democrats have formed a special Congressional Caucus on Competitiveness. Foundations of all political stripes are issuing reports on the subject. Every presidential candidate has his or her own surefire method of restoring competitiveness. But most of the discussion has produced more heat, in the form of political posturing, than enlightened solutions.

Congress, for example, debated the problem, studied the problem, and then came up with a solution that will make everything much worse—protectionism. With the true backbone of a politician, President Reagan acquiesced. In 1987, abandoning his long-standing commitment to free trade, he agreed to clamp draconian tariffs on some Japanese goods.

Meanwhile, foreign and U.S. companies prepared for the end of free trade. The Japanese, for instance, moved some of their manufacturing operations to the U.S., setting up auto factories, electronics manufacturing firms, and other operations. By the end of 1986, Japanese investment in manufacturing, real estate, and distribution facilities was up to $23.4 billion, tripling since 1980, and it is expected to grow at an annual rate of over 14% between now and the end of the century. This investment is expected to create 840,000 jobs.

But if Japanese investment created some jobs, Congress's faddish preoccupation with protection has little chance of helping the job market or solving America's economic woes. Why? Protectionist legislation ignores the real causes of the trade deficit.

THE TRADE DEFICIT THAT WON'T GO AWAY

After all that's been written about the growing trade deficit, it's easy to imagine that the problem has been with us for some time, like death and taxes. Despite the rising cost of foreign oil, the U.S. held a narrow surplus throughout most of the 1970s.

What ended all of that was a combination of events that taken together spelled disaster. The dollar rose to record highs, pricing many U.S. goods out of the world market.

But the dollar wasn't the only culprit. American manufacturers had survived a strong dollar during the 1950s; however, in the 1980s American leadership in technology and productivity was gone, making U.S. companies more vulnerable to foreign competition. At the same time, a strong economy helped worsen the trade deficit. In 1984 and 1985, as the economy emerged from the worst recession since the 1930s, consumers created a strong demand for foreign products, especially electronics, but the economies of our trading partners did not show the same growth, and demand for U.S. exports remained sluggish. On top of that, the seemingly unsolvable debt crisis of third-world countries continued to hurt the market for U.S. exports.

The result was a disaster. Consider some of the following numbers:

- The deficit in manufactured goods increased to about $139.1 billion in 1986, up from $107.6 billion in 1985, and a surplus of $16.9 billion in 1980.
- The trade outlook in agricultural goods, traditionally among the country's largest exports, worsened. In 1986, agricultural exports totaled only $29.6 billion, the lowest in 10 years. Between 1982 and 1986 the U.S. agricultural trade surplus declined from $19.7 billion to only $3.4 billion as exports fell 28% and imports grew 34%.
- In smokestack industries—motor vehicles, iron, steel, primary copper, aluminum, lead, zinc, industrial machinery, farm machinery, and machine tools—the trade deficit grew from $21.5 billion in 1980 to over $65 billion in 1985.
- The picture wasn't even bright in high-tech industries. The trade surplus in high-tech products declined from $26 billion in 1980 to only $7 billion in 1985.
- Between 1982 and 1986, U.S. exports of manufactured goods increased a paltry 12% while imports surged 95%.

Region by region, the outlook wasn't any better. In 1986, the U.S. managed to have a trade deficit with almost every major country and region of the world:

- In 1986 for the first time in a decade, the U.S. ran a trade deficit with developed industrialized nations ($113.4 billion), developing countries ($54.1 billion), and even communist countries ($2.5 billion.)
- Our trade deficit with Japan increased from $19 billion in 1982 to $58.6 billion in 1986. Japan bought 12.4% of our exports—making it the second-largest buyer of U.S. exports—but supplied 22.1% of our imports, more than any other nation in 1986. As a result, the U.S. ran a larger trade deficit with Japan than with any other country.
- The U.S. had a huge trade deficit of $26.4 billion with the 12 members of the European Economic Community, having had a surplus of $5.9 billion in 1982. Exports between 1982 and 1986 grew only 2% during that period while imports jumped 71%.
- The U.S. trade deficit with Canada jumped from $13.1 billion in 1982 to $23.3 billion in 1986. During that period, exports to our northern neighbor increased by 34% while imports gained 47%. Canada bought more U.S. exports than any other country, was this country's second-largest supplier of imports, and ran the second-largest trade deficit of any country.
- The U.S. trading deficits with the East Asian newly industrializing countries of Hong Kong, Singapore, South Korea, and Taiwan more than tripled from $8.2 billion in 1982 to $30.8 billion in 1986.
- Even communist countries were winning the trade war. Our trade balance with China dropped from a $410 surplus in 1982 to a $2.1 billion deficit in 1986. The U.S. trade surplus with the U.S.S.R. dropped from $2.3 billion in 1982 to only $642 in 1986, and our trade balance with Eastern European countries slipped from a $102 million surplus in 1982 to a deficit of $859 million in 1986.
- Despite the plunging price of oil, the U.S. trade balance with the Middle East dropped from a $3.5 billion surplus in 1982 to a $179 million deficit in 1986.

Evidence of declining competitiveness can be found in almost any department store. Many popular consumer goods are no longer produced in the U.S. For example, about half of all homes have VCRs—yet no VCRs are manufactured in the U.S. U.S. companies produce them overseas and simply put their corporate logos on them.

Another measure of America's losing battle with foreign competition is foreign companies' capturing significant shares of the domestic market. By 1986, imports supplied 13.5% of the U.S. market, up from 10.2% in only four years. Over one quarter of all new cars sold were imports (28.4%), compared to 15.3% in 1970. Since 1980 imports of textile products have nearly doubled, while the value of exports has fallen from $2.488 billion to only $1.751 billion. Imported steel has 16% of the market, up from 8% in 1973.

But those industries are only a few of those faced with an invasion of foreign goods. From jewelry (an industry in which imports had 40.8% of the market in 1987, up from 4.2% in 1972) and dolls (83.8%, up from 21.8%) to copper (24.2%, up from 7.8%) and primary zinc (67.1%, up from 28.4%) to radios and TV sets (62.0%, up from 34.9%) to luggage (59.9%, up from 15.4%) to telephone and telegraph equipment (12.6%, up from 2.1%) to photographic equipment and supplies (20.2%, up from 6.2%) to shoes (63.7%, up from 17.1%) and household furniture (17.8%, up from 2.8%), American manufacturers are losing their traditional share of the domestic market.

PROTECTIONISM

Protectionism seems at first glance to be such a simple solution to such a tough problem. With protectionism, beleaguered industries wouldn't have to reduce labor costs, spend money to modernize factories, improve productivity, or change shortsighted management policies. No national policy to promote industrial development by reducing taxes on capital gains or investments would be necessary. All you would need to do is simply raise tariffs and price foreign goods out of the market.

Sounds almost too good to be true, doesn't it? Well, it is. Protectionism has been tried before, with disastrous results. In the Great Depression, the attempt to cut foreign products out of the U.S. market touched off a trade war that reduced world trade, deepening the worldwide recession.

Today, the effects of protectionism would probably be even worse than in the 1930s. Currently the U.S. is more heavily dependent upon overseas trade. A recent U.S. Census Department study estimates that one out of every nine manufacturing jobs depends upon foreign trade. Moreover, many of the same industries facing tough foreign competition are also those that account for a large share of America's exports. In 1986, 9 out of the 25 largest import products were also among the 25 largest export products. Motor vehicles and car bodies, for example, were America's leading import *and* its fifth-largest export. As a result, any attempt to restrict imports to protect the auto industry and other industries would trigger a trade war that would only cut down our exports of products from these industries.

Moreover, many U.S. companies have huge overseas operations that would be hurt by protectionist legislation, which would force those companies to lay off U.S. workers. About 15% of our imports come from foreign affiliates of U.S. companies. Those affiliates import over $80 billion in goods each year that could be cut off by protectionist legislation. Many of those companies are also in industries that are already struggling with foreign competition and the loss of those imports would make it harder for them to raise capital to compete with foreign companies. For example, in the auto industry General Motors imported $7.2 billion (8% of U.S. sales), Ford imported $6.3 billion (13%), and Chrysler imported $4.5 billion (25%) worth of goods from foreign affiliates in 1986.

Protectionism also increases the profits of many foreign companies. For example, quotas on many popular products have boosted the prices of foreign imports and given foreign companies higher profits—money they can use to improve their factories and become even tougher competitors.

Foreign companies earned an extra $10 billion in profits in 1986 thanks to quotas, in such key industries as apparel ($3.5 billion), steel ($2.8 billion), automobiles ($2.5 billion), and machine tools ($320 million).

Finally, protectionism is no more than a tax on U.S. consumers. Quotas and protectionist legislation already cost consumers $49.9 billion a year, according to economists Gary Hufbauer and Howard Rosen. Protectionist legislation increases the cost of textiles and apparel by $27 billion, carbon steel by $6.8 billion, and autos by $5.8 billion. These higher prices, of course, decrease the amount of money saved by the American public and reduce the capital available for modernization of U.S. plants and companies.

Ultimately, there's very little point in looking for foreign scapegoats. Despite some recent signs of movement, there's little political chance that countries like Japan and Korea will make the kind of major changes in their trade policies that the U.S. would wish, at least in the near future. Besides, protectionism hasn't helped some of our big industrial losers anyway. The steel industry, for example, has enjoyed significant protection from imports in the last 15 years, yet its competitive position is weaker than ever. In 1984 President Reagan proposed even more protectionism with a measure that would limit imports to 18.5% of domestic consumption, but shortly after the program was passed a Federal Trade Commission study estimated the proposal would cost about $1.1 billion and save only 9,951 jobs, at a cost of about $185,000 a job! And even with this billion-dollar gift, employment in the steel industry continues to drop with no end in sight.

And protectionism is, at best, a short-term solution. Much of the blame— for the practices of American management, labor, and government—can be found on this side of any protectionist barrier.

PROBLEMS IN THE FACTORY: LABOR

Faced with massive layoffs in many manufacturing industries, American labor has launched a campaign against foreign competition. Demonstrating auto workers have smashed Japanese cars with sledgehammers and union leaders want legislation to restrict imports of foreign cars. Auto makers have put through rules that have forced employees driving foreign cars to take the least desirable parking spaces. Bob Hope and other stars have appeared on T.V. with appeals to "buy American."

Yet many economists and executives believe that American labor, not Japanese business, is the real villain. American labor, so the argument goes, has grown fat and arrogant, with increased wages and benefits pricing American goods out of the world market.

In some ways at least, it also seems that American workers are less motivated than their foreign counterparts. The average U.S. worker loses 3.5 days a year to absenteeism, compared to only 1.6 for the average Japanese worker. U.S. workers are also much more likely to change jobs then West Germans and Japanese. Labor and management in the U.S.

have traditionally adopted an adversarial stance, causing more time to be lost to strikes and disputes over work rules.

Wages have also increased faster than productivity. Between 1960 and 1985, output by U.S. workers increased by 2.3 times while unit labor costs grew 2.4 times. In contrast, output by Japanese workers increased over 9 times while unit labor costs increased only 2.4 times.

U.S. productivity in the manufacturing sector as measured by output an hour grew only 2.2% between 1973 and 1985, down from a 3.2% increase between 1960 and 1973. That was way below Japan's growth rate of 10.3% a year between 1960 and 1973 and 5.6% between 1973 and 1985. As a result, U.S. productivity growth between 1960 and 1985 lagged way behind the 5.4% annual growth in productivity of 11 major foreign competitors. While U.S. manufacturing productivity grew only 2.7% a year between 1960 and 1985, productivity grew 8.0% in Japan, 5.5% in France, 3.4% in Canada, 4.8% in Germany, 5.4% in Italy, 3.5% in the United Kingdom, 6.5% in Belgium, 4.8% in Denmark, 6.2% in the Netherlands, 3.2% in Norway, and 4.7% in Sweden.

Those are the depressing numbers. But what happens to productivity is more than an idle statistical game. If everything else remains the same, increased output from labor and capital means there is more money to pay workers and shareholders. To illustrate how productivity affects a country's standard of living, the American Productivity Center did a study comparing what would have happened to our standard of living if the U.S. had maintained its high levels of productivity growth. Let's assume labor productivity never slowed down, as it did after 1965. Instead, between 1965 and 1985, labor productivity continued growing at the 1948 to 1965 rate—3.2% a year for the whole economy. In that case the average worker would have produced $56,704 of goods and services in 1985, according to the American Productivity Center. Now, let's assume labor productivity only grew 0.9% a year during those 20 years, as it did between 1979 and 1985. Then the average worker would only have produced $33,728 in goods and services in 1985. In short, America's failure to sustain a high rate of productivity costs every worker $10,000 to $20,000 in higher living standards.

The notion that improved productivity will improve wages isn't just an academic theory. Increased productivity allowed Japanese wages to increase 11.9% a year between 1960 and 1985 while unit labor costs only grew 3.6%. In America, where productivity was not growing as fast, wages only increased 6.5%. Higher productivity also did wonders for Japanese shareholders. If, for example, you compare the performance of U.S. and Japanese stocks between the end of the 1960s and the mid-1980s, Japanese companies' stocks outperformed American stocks, producing much higher yields.

And decreased productivity has its human costs in layoffs, plant shutdowns, and unemployment. A 1987 study by the Bureau of Labor Statistics found that about 10.8 million Americans lost their jobs because of plant closings or employment cutbacks between the start of 1981 and

January of 1986. The Labor Department study focused on the 5.1 million displaced workers who had been on their jobs for over three years. About half of these experienced workers, 2.55 million, were in the manufacturing sector, even though manufacturing employs less than one fifth of all non-agricultural workers.

Many of the experienced manufacturing workers did not find new work and their skills have been lost to the economy. About 18.2% of the workers who had held the same job for at least three years before being laid off remained unemployed; another 15.9% left the labor force.

And many of the workers who found work saw sharp cuts in their paychecks. About 432,000 (30.6%) of the 1.4 million displaced manufacturing workers who eventually found full-time work suffered wage cuts of more than 20%. About half (52.5%) of all steelworkers who found new full-time jobs earned 20% less than before. Another 186,000 manufacturing workers were hit with earning cuts of 1% to 20% at their new jobs. About 162,000, or about 9.8% of the 1.657 million who found full-time or part-time work, now work part-time and presumably earn less than before.

Yet it would be a mistake to blame the decline of American manufacturing entirely on labor or imagine that simple solutions such as cutting wages will have much effect. Increased automation has made labor costs a smaller part of the cost of doing business. Also, if lowering wages were the only way for the U.S. to regain its edge, then the solution might be worse than the problem. American business has long known that its welfare ultimately depends on having workers who make enough to buy its products. Since relatively high wages in the postwar world have made a boom in consumer goods possible, a concerted attack on the income levels of American workers would be much like killing the goose that laid the golden egg. No solution to the problem of foreign competition can come without improved management and changes in the way America allocates its resources.

PROBLEMS IN THE FACTORY: MANAGEMENT

Management, for all its talk about regaining competitiveness in the international marketplace, isn't putting its money where its mouth is. Consider some of the following facts:

- U.S. manufacturers spent only $142.7 billion on new plant and equipment, billions less than the $190 billion they spent on mergers and acquisitions.
- Private research and development expenditures have fallen behind those of some of our keenest competitors. Both West Germany and Japan spend over 2.6% of their GNP on civilian research; the U.S. spends under 1.8%.
- The U.S. developed robot technology but today it has the worst record of any industrialized nation for applying new robot technology.

- Thanks to lack of investment in the American future, many factories are showing their age. The average age of a manufacturing plant is now 15 years, up from 13.8 years in 1980.

In the late 1970s, American management was also slow to adopt techniques that could cut costs. While Japanese managers cut costs by reducing inventories of parts, Americans kept their capital tied up in warehouses of parts and supplies.

American managers also deserve low marks for their quality control. For example, most American managers checked the quality of goods as they left the plant. However, by this time many goods had already been repaired or worked on several times, adding huge hidden costs. Japanese managers, however, worked to make certain the job was done right the first time. That not only cut costs, it improved quality.

Starting in the early 1980s, management scrambled to regain its competitive edge. Aging, unprofitable plants were closed. Layers of middle management were sent packing. Job classifications that required one worker to plug in a piece of equipment and another to run it were done away with. A million-plus manufacturing jobs were slashed.

The results were promising. In 1984, U.S. manufacturing productivity as measured by output per hour increased 4.1%, faster than France, Canada, and West Germany. It spurted another 4.4% in 1985, faster than 8 of the 11 major industrial competitors tracked by the U.S. Department of Labor. In 1986 manufacturing productivity growth slowed to 3.5%, but that rate was still higher than Canada (-0.5%), Japan (2.7%), France (1.9%), Germany (1.9%), Italy (1.2%), and the United Kingdom (3.0%).

Unfortunately, much remains to be done. Productivity has not improved in services despite a $150 billion investment in computers, telecommunications, and other high-tech equipment in the last few years. Recent Labor Department figures show that Canada has replaced the U.S. as the world's most productive nation. And closing plants, laying off workers, restructuring operations, and moving factories overseas may improve profits for a few years, but they are not long-term solutions.

PUTTING CAPITAL BACK TO WORK

No improvement in productivity can take place until businesses are able to afford new equipment and factories. But U.S. companies face much higher costs to finance new capital than many of our major competitors. The real cost of capital in Japan was only 2.5% in 1984, the latest data available. In the U.S. it was 7.5%.

Why is it so much more expensive to finance new investments in the U.S.? Huge federal deficits, which have kept interest rates high, are the main culprit. If Congress would forget about protectionist legislation and start worrying about the deficit it could dramatically improve the ability of American companies to finance new factories and capital.

Congress could also cut the cost of capital by reducing heavy-handed government regulation of the financial markets and by passing tax laws designed to encourage private savings. Right now, Americans have one of the lowest savings rates in the world. Americans save about 4.6% of their disposable income; the Japanese save 17.2%, the Canadians 12.1%, and the West Germans 12.9%. U.S. savings are only 16% of our gross domestic product; savings account for 31% of GDP in Japan, 23% in West Germany, and 22% in Canada.

In recent years, American consumers have been living beyond their means and cutting back on savings to buy more foreign goods than they export. These lower savings rates force American companies to pay high interest rates for scarce capital, hurting their ability to modernize plants. At the same time, the trade deficit puts more money in foreign hands, making it easier for foreigners to improve their competitive positions.

Increased private savings would help the trade deficit in the short run— since consumers would be buying fewer foreign goods on credit. In the long run it would help productivity—since increased savings would make capital less scarce and hence less expensive.

U.S. tax policy has also got to do more to encourage savings and investment. Unfortunately, the so-called Tax Reform Act of 1986 does neither. Over the next five years, corporations are going to be stuck with an increased tax bill of $120 billion. Some service industries will benefit but capital-intensive industries, which are having the hardest time with foreign competition, will be hit with $150 billion in new taxes. Worse, the tax bill will give them the old one-two punch: the elimination of investment taxes will lower demand for their products while taxes on their earnings will skyrocket.

Of course, even a policy that encourages new investment and technology is not enough. American management is going to have to improve the way it uses high technology. GM, for example, spent millions building a high-tech plant in Hamtramck, Michigan, but the robots spray-painted each other instead of cars and the company had to ship the cars to a 57-year-old plant to be repainted.

A plea for consistency in formulating public policy is always in order. Criticizing American business for its short-term outlook is a popular pastime in Washington. Corporate America has forgotten about long-term investment in the pursuit of short-term gains, the standard refrain goes.

Fair enough. But what's really needed is some consistency in Washington. There is no single solution to the problems facing American industry. The tax system will have to become more supportive of capital investment. Labor will have to make concession on work rules and costs; management is going to have to make a long-term commitment to becoming competitive. All that takes time. But Congress continues to change its mind every few years. A few years ago it gave U.S. companies investment tax credits. Then, a few years later, it took them away because investment tax credits didn't solve all the world's problems. Congress needs to give up this short-term outlook and follow its own advice to American business—adopt a long-term, consistent policy. That way, American companies can make long-term investment decisions without worrying about Congress upsetting their plans next year.

Table 70   U.S. Trade

U.S. TOTAL EXPORTS
(Domestic and Foreign Merchandise, FAS; Millions of Dollars)

	1980	1983	1984	1985	1986
WORLD	220,705	200,538	217,888	213,146	217,304
DEVELOPED COUNTRIES	131,005	122,974	135,884	134,018	141,447
Canada	35,395	38,244	46,524	47,251	45,333
Japan	20,790	21,894	23,575	22,631	26,882
Australia	4,093	3,954	4,793	5,441	5,551
New Zealand	595	620	708	727	881
South Africa	2,463	2,129	2,265	1,205	1,158
Western Europe	67,668	56,132	58,019	56,763	61,642
European Community (EC-12)	58,850	48,439	50,498	48,994	53,154
Belgium/Luxembourg	6,661	5,049	5,301	4,918	5,399
Denmark	863	649	605	706	758
France	7,485	5,961	6,037	6,096	7,216
Germany, West	10,960	8,737	9,084	9,050	10,561
Greece	922	503	456	498	430
Ireland	836	1,115	1,354	1,342	1,434
Italy	5,511	3,908	4,375	4,625	4,838
Netherlands	8,669	7,767	7,554	7,269	7,847
Portugal	910	1,214	961	695	638
Spain	3,340	2,915	2,561	2,524	2,615
United Kingdom	12,694	10,621	12,210	11,273	11,418
Non-EC Europe	8,818	7,693	7,522	7,769	8,488
Austria	448	371	375	441	464
Cyprus	70	54	74	45	54
Finland	505	413	350	438	381
Gibraltar	4	28	4	13	32
Iceland	79	53	51	38	60
Malta	26	65	23	26	24
Norway	843	813	859	666	937
Sweden	1,767	1,581	1,542	1,925	1,871
Switzerland	3,781	2,960	2,562	2,288	2,976
Turkey	540	783	1,249	1,295	1,160
Yugoslavia	756	572	432	595	528
DEVELOPING COUNTRIES	80,937	72,186	74,418	71,671	70,637
Western Hemisphere	38,718	25,725	29,683	31,019	31,077
Mexico	15,145	9,082	11,992	13,635	12,392
South America	17,377	10,520	11,050	11,022	11,950
Caribbean Basin	6,223	6,052	6,528	6,199	6,595
East Asian	14,741	16,914	17,723	16,918	18,290
Hong Kong	2,686	2,564	3,062	2,786	3,030
Korea, South	4,685	5,925	5,983	5,956	6,355
Singapore	3,033	3,759	3,675	3,476	3,380
Taiwan	4,337	4,667	5,003	4,700	5,524
Other Asia	8,955	9,013	9,074	7,611	7,809
Middle East	11,900	13,796	11,133	9,709	8,415
Africa	6,436	6,486	6,561	6,183	4,820
COMMUNIST COUNTRIES	7,643	5,088	7,217	7,092	5,127
China	3,755	2,173	3,004	3,856	3,106
USSR	1,513	2,003	3,284	2,423	1,248
Eastern Europe	2,347	888	904	792	742

Table 70   U.S. Trade (continued)

U.S. TOTAL IMPORTS
(General Imports, CIF; Millions of Dollars)

	1980	1983	1984	1985	1986
WORLD	252,929	269,878	341,177	361,626	387,081
DEVELOPED COUNTRIES	130,968	157,895	208,559	232,234	254,862
Canada	41,995	52,546	66,911	69,427	68,662
Japan	32,961	43,559	60,371	72,380	85,457
Australia	2,782	2,422	2,899	3,069	2,873
New Zealand	793	828	880	969	1,097
South Africa	3,428	2,099	2,577	2,180	2,476
Western Europe	49,009	56,442	74,921	84,209	94,297
European Community (EC-12)	39,941	47,876	63,412	71,617	79,520
Belgium/Luxembourg	2,006	2,510	3,287	3,567	4,191
Denmark	767	1,126	1,518	1,796	1,869
France	5,532	6,308	8,516	9,959	10,586
Germany, West	12,370	13,229	17,810	21,232	26,128
Greece	320	256	383	427	437
Ireland	433	582	874	942	1,046
Italy	4,676	5,819	8,504	10,381	11,312
Netherlands	2,041	3,149	4,329	4,368	4,363
Portugal	283	308	519	598	600
Spain	1,329	1,689	2,627	2,773	2,956
United Kingdom	10,184	12,900	15,044	15,573	16,033
Non-EC Europe	9,067	8,566	11,508	12,592	14,776
Austria	407	468	760	889	912
Cyprus	7	16	30	16	12
Finland	480	544	857	976	986
Gibraltar	2	2	3	1	5
Iceland	210	232	219	263	249
Malta	9	11	19	35	35
Norway	2,734	1,432	2,004	1,249	1,170
Sweden	1,705	2,549	3,426	4,339	4,637
Switzerland	2,851	2,552	3,199	3,579	5,367
Turkey	187	337	464	645	690
Yugoslavia	476	424	527	601	713
DEVELOPING COUNTRIES	119,228	108,027	126,879	123,050	124,771
Western Hemisphere	38,713	43,581	50,063	49,096	44,112
Mexico	12,774	17,019	18,267	19,392	17,558
South America	15,259	17,093	22,461	22,415	19,942
Caribbean Basin	10,904	9,557	9,491	7,388	6,710
East Asian	18,805	29,561	39,135	41,880	49,106
Hong Kong	5,026	6,825	8,899	8,994	9,474
Korea, South	4,432	7,657	10,027	10,713	13,497
Singapore	1,984	2,969	4,121	4,412	4,884
Taiwan	7,362	12,110	16,088	17,761	21,251
Middle East	18,344	7,492	8,555	6,600	8,594
Africa	30,170	13,102	12,419	10,363	8,581
COMMUNIST COUNTRIES	2,729	3,955	5,738	6,342	7,448
China	1,161	2,477	3,381	4,224	5,241
USSR	485	375	600	443	605
Eastern Europe	1,079	1,100	1,752	1,671	1,600

Table 70   U.S. Trade (continued)

U.S. TOTAL TRADE BALANCES
(Domestic and Foreign Merchandise, FAS; General Imports, CIF; Millions of Dollars)

	1980	1983	1984	1985	1986
WORLD	(32,224)	(69,341)	(123,289)	(148,480)	(169,777)
DEVELOPED COUNTRIES	320	(34,921)	(72,674)	(98,216)	(113,415)
Canada	(6,600)	(14,302)	(20,387)	(22,176)	(23,330)
Japan	(12,171)	(21,665)	(36,796)	(49,749)	(58,575)
Australia	1,311	1,532	1,894	2,372	2,679
New Zealand	(198)	(208)	(172)	(241)	(217)
South Africa	(964)	31	(312)	(975)	(1,318)
Western Europe	18,942	(309)	(16,901)	(27,446)	(32,655)
European Community (EC-12)	19,192	564	(12,915)	(22,623)	(26,366)
Belgium/Luxembourg	4,655	2,539	2,014	1,351	1,208
Denmark	96	(477)	(913)	(1,091)	(1,111)
France	1,954	(346)	(2,480)	(3,864)	(3,370)
Germany, West	(1,410)	(4,492)	(8,726)	(12,182)	(15,568)
Greece	602	247	73	70	(7)
Ireland	402	533	480	400	388
Italy	835	(1,912)	(4,129)	(5,756)	(6,473)
Netherlands	6,628	4,619	3,225	2,901	3,484
Portugal	910	906	442	97	38
Spain	2,011	1,226	(66)	(249)	(341)
United Kingdom	2,509	(2,279)	(2,835)	(4,300)	(4,614)
Non-EC Europe	(249)	(873)	(3,986)	(4,823)	(6,288)
Austria	41	(97)	(385)	(448)	(448)
Cyprus	63	38	43	29	42
Finland	25	(131)	(507)	(538)	(605)
Gibraltar	2	25	1	12	28
Iceland	(132)	(179)	(168)	(225)	(188)
Malta	17	54	5	(9)	(11)
Norway	(1,890)	(619)	(1,145)	(583)	(233)
Sweden	63	(967)	(1,884)	(2,414)	(2,766)
Switzerland	930	409	(637)	(1,291)	(2,391)
Turkey	353	447	785	649	469
Yugoslavia	279	148	(95)	(6)	(185)
DEVELOPING COUNTRIES	(38,291)	(35,841)	(52,461)	(51,379)	(54,135)
Western Hemisphere	5	(17,856)	(20,380)	(18,077)	(13,035)
Mexico	2,371	(7,937)	(6,275)	(5,757)	(5,167)
South America	2,117	(6,573)	(11,411)	(11,393)	(7,992)
Caribbean Basin	(4,681)	(3,505)	(2,963)	(1,190)	(116)
East Asian NICs	(4,064)	(12,647)	(21,412)	(24,962)	(30,817)
Hong Kong	(2,340)	(4,261)	(5,836)	(6,208)	(6,443)
Korea, South	253	(1,732)	(4,045)	(4,756)	(7,142)
Singapore	1,049	790	(446)	(937)	(1,504)
Taiwan	(3,026)	(7,443)	(11,085)	(13,061)	(15,727)
Other Asia	(4,043)	(5,175)	(7,527)	(7,368)	(6,459)
Middle East	(6,444)	6,304	2,578	3,110	(179)
Africa	(23,734)	(6,616)	(5,857)	(4,180)	(3,761)
COMMUNIST COUNTRIES	5,399	1,133	1,479	750	(2,321)
China	2,594	(304)	(377)	(369)	(2,134)
USSR	1,513	1,628	2,684	1,980	642
Eastern Europe	1,268	(212)	(848)	(879)	(859)

1984–1986 unrevised data.
1980 to 1986 exports exclude undocumented exports to Canada which totalled $10.2 billion in 1986.
Parentheses indicate negative entries.
Source: U.S. Department of Commerce

Table 71　The U.S. and Its Foreign Competitors

(numbers in thousands)

Employment status and country	1977	1978	1979	1980	1981	1982	1983	1984	1985	1986
Labor force										
United States	99,009	102,251	104,962	106,940	108,670	110,204	111,550	113,544	115,461	117,834
Canada	10,500	10,895	11,231	11,573	11,904	11,958	12,183	12,399	12,639	12,870
Australia	6,358	6,443	6,519	6,693	6,810	6,910	6,997	7,133	7,272	7,562
Japan	53,820	54,610	55,210	55,740	56,320	56,980	58,110	58,480	58,820	59,420
France	22,300	22,470	22,670	22,790	22,930	23,150	23,130	23,290	23,310	23,520
West Germany	25,870	26,000	26,250	26,520	26,650	26,710	26,740	26,680	27,100	27,300
Italy	20,510	20,570	20,850	21,120	21,320	21,410	21,590	21,670	21,800	21,970
Netherlands	4,950	5,010	5,100	5,310	5,520	5,600	5,730	5,720	5,830	—
Sweden	4,168	4,203	4,262	4,312	4,326	4,350	4,369	4,385	4,418	4,437
United Kingdom	26,050	26,260	26,350	26,520	26,590	26,740	26,780	27,120	27,300	27,310
Participation rate[1]										
United States	62.3	63.2	63.7	63.8	63.9	64.0	64.0	64.4	64.8	65.3
Canada	61.6	62.7	63.4	64.1	64.8	64.1	64.4	64.8	65.2	65.7
Australia	62.7	62.0	61.7	62.2	62.0	61.8	61.5	61.5	61.8	63.0
Japan	62.5	62.8	62.7	62.6	62.6	62.7	63.1	62.7	62.3	62.1
France	57.6	57.5	57.5	57.2	57.1	57.1	56.6	56.6	56.3	56.3
West Germany	53.4	53.3	53.3	53.2	52.9	52.7	52.5	52.6	53.2	53.5
Italy	48.2	47.8	48.0	48.2	48.3	47.7	47.5	47.3	47.2	47.5
Netherlands	49.0	48.8	49.0	50.2	51.4	51.5	52.1	51.4	52.1	—
Sweden	65.9	66.1	66.6	67.0	66.8	66.8	66.7	66.6	67.1	67.3
United Kingdom	62.7	62.8	62.6	62.5	62.2	62.3	62.1	62.4	62.6	62.6
Employed										
United States	92,017	96,048	98,824	99,303	100,397	99,526	100,834	105,005	107,150	109,597
Canada	9,651	9,987	10,395	10,708	11,006	10,644	10,734	11,000	11,311	11,634
Australia	6,000	6,038	6,111	6,284	6,416	6,415	6,300	6,490	6,670	6,952
Japan	52,720	53,370	54,040	54,600	55,060	55,620	56,550	56,870	57,260	57,750
France	21,180	21,260	21,300	21,320	21,200	21,230	21,170	20,980	20,890	21,050
West Germany	24,970	25,130	25,470	25,750	25,560	25,130	24,750	24,790	24,970	25,240
Italy	19,670	19,720	19,930	20,200	20,280	20,250	20,320	20,390	20,490	20,610
Netherlands	4,700	4,750	4,830	4,980	5,010	4,970	4,900	4,920	5,080	—
Sweden	4,093	4,109	4,174	4,226	4,218	4,213	4,218	4,249	4,293	4,319
United Kingdom	24,400	24,610	24,940	24,670	23,800	23,710	23,600	23,960	24,210	24,160
Employment-population ratio[2]										
United States	57.9	59.3	59.9	59.2	59.0	57.8	57.9	59.5	60.1	60.7
Canada	56.6	57.5	58.7	59.3	59.9	57.0	56.7	57.4	58.4	59.4
Australia	59.2	58.1	57.9	58.4	58.4	57.3	55.4	56.0	56.6	57.9
Japan	61.2	61.3	61.4	61.3	61.2	61.2	61.4	61.0	60.6	60.4
France	54.7	54.4	54.0	53.5	52.8	52.3	51.8	51.0	50.5	50.4
West Germany	51.6	51.5	51.7	51.7	50.8	49.6	48.6	48.5	49.0	49.5
Italy	46.3	45.9	45.9	46.1	45.9	45.2	44.7	44.5	44.4	44.6
Netherlands	46.5	46.3	46.4	47.0	46.6	45.7	44.6	44.2	45.4	—
Sweden	64.8	64.6	65.3	65.6	65.1	64.7	64.4	64.6	65.2	65.5
United Kingdom	58.7	58.8	59.2	58.1	55.7	55.3	54.7	55.2	55.5	55.4
Unemployed										
United States	6,991	6,202	6,137	7,637	8,273	10,678	10,717	8,539	8,312	8,237
Canada	849	908	836	865	898	1,314	1,448	1,399	1,328	1,236
Australia	358	405	408	409	394	495	697	642	602	610
Japan	1,100	1,240	1,170	1,140	1,260	1,360	1,560	1,610	1,560	1,670
France	1,120	1,210	1,370	1,470	1,730	1,920	1,960	2,310	2,420	2,470
West Germany	900	870	780	770	1,090	1,580	1,990	2,090	2,130	2,060
Italy	840	850	920	920	1,040	1,160	1,270	1,280	1,310	1,360
Netherlands	250	260	270	330	510	630	830	800	750	—
Sweden	75	94	88	86	108	137	151	136	125	118
United Kingdom	1,660	1,650	1,420	1,850	2,790	3,040	3,180	3,170	3,090	3,150
Unemployment rate										
United States	7.1	6.1	5.8	7.1	7.6	9.7	9.6	7.5	7.2	7.0
Canada	8.1	8.3	7.4	7.5	7.5	11.0	11.9	11.3	10.5	9.6
Australia	5.6	6.3	6.3	6.1	5.8	7.2	10.0	9.0	8.3	8.1
Japan	2.0	2.3	2.1	2.0	2.2	2.4	2.7	2.8	2.6	2.8
France	5.0	5.4	6.0	6.4	7.5	8.3	8.5	9.9	10.4	10.5
West Germany	3.5	3.4	3.0	2.9	4.1	5.9	7.4	7.8	7.9	7.5
Italy	4.1	4.1	4.4	4.4	4.9	5.4	5.9	5.9	6.0	6.2
Netherlands	5.1	5.2	5.3	6.2	9.2	11.3	14.5	14.0	12.9	—
Sweden	1.8	2.2	2.1	2.0	2.5	3.1	3.5	3.1	2.8	2.7
United Kingdom	6.4	6.3	5.4	7.0	10.5	11.8	11.9	11.7	11.3	11.5

[1] Labor force as a percent of the civilian working-age population.
[2] Employment as a percent of the civilian working-age population.
—Data not available.
Source: U.S. Department of Labor, Bureau of Labor Statistics.

277

Table 72 Growth Rates in Real Gross National Product, 1961–1986
(percent change)

Area and country	1961–1965 annual average	1966–1970 annual average	1971–1975 annual average	1976–1980 annual average	1982	1983	1984	1985	1986	1987[1]
Developed countries	5.2	4.8	3.7	3.2	−0.5	2.8	5.0	3.0	2.7	2.8
United States	4.6	3.0	2.2	3.4	−2.5	3.5	6.5	2.7	2.9	2.9
Canada	5.6	4.8	5.0	3.1	−4.4	3.3	4.7	4.0	3.0	3.7
Japan	6.8	11.2	4.7	5.0	3.1	3.2	5.1	4.7	2.5	3.6
European Community[2]	4.7	4.5	2.8	3.0	.3	1.3	2.3	2.2	2.6	2.3
France	5.9	5.4	4.0	3.3	1.8	.7	1.6	1.4	2.1	1.6
West Germany	4.7	4.2	2.1	3.4	−1.0	1.5	3.0	2.5	2.5	1.7
Italy	5.2	6.2	2.5	3.9	−.5	−.4	2.6	2.3	2.7	2.7
United Kingdom	3.2	2.5	2.2	1.7	1.4	3.5	1.8	3.4	2.3	3.5
Developing countries	6.3	6.7	7.0	5.5	.9	.4	3.0	3.2	4.0	3.3
Communist countries[3]	4.4	5.0	4.2	2.8	2.6	3.6	3.2	3.6	4.1	NA
U.S.S.R.	4.7	5.0	3.0	2.3	2.5	3.4	1.4	1.2	3.8	1.0
Eastern Europe	3.9	3.8	4.9	1.9	.9	1.8	3.3	1.4	2.7	2.0
China	−.2	8.3	5.5	6.1	8.3	9.1	12.0	12.0	7.5	9.5

[1]Preliminary estimates.
[2]Includes Belgium-Luxembourg, Denmark, Greece, Ireland, and the Netherlands, not shown separately.
[3]Includes North Korea and Yugoslavia, not shown separately.
Sources: Department of Commerce, International Monetary Fund, country sources, and Council of Economic Advisers.

Table 73 Productivity in Various Parts of the Economy

As you can see from this chart, the productivity record of the American economy is mixed. Some parts, such as farming, continue their rapid productivity growth, while other industries in the service sector, such as real estate, finance, and insurance, have actually gotten less productive. Productivity is measured by labor productivity and by total factor productivity, which includes the productivity of capital.

(percentage increase or decrease)

	1979–1985		1986	
	Labor productivity	Total factor productivity	Labor productivity	Total factor productivity
Business economy	1.1	0.8	1.9	1.5
Farming	7.0	6.7	10.5	10.2
Communication	3.9	1.3	4.1	−0.3
Railroads	3.5	0.7	7.6	5.4
Manufacturing	3.1	2.5	3.7	3.1
Utilities	1.8	0.9	−2.7	−3.9
Trade, retail and wholesale	1.3	1.4	3.9	3.1
Miscellaneous services	0.7	0.3	−0.2	0.1
Mining	−0.2	−0.5	9.0	2.3
Finance and insurance	−1.3	−1.0	0.5	−1.3
Real estate	−1.4	−2.0	6.0	4.4
Nonrail transportation	−1.8	−0.9	1.6	2.1

Source: American Productivity Center

278

Table 74   Productivity in America: The Best and the Worst

This chart shows the manufacturing industries, with the greatest labor productivity increases and decreases between 1979 and 1985 and in 1985.

(percentage increase or decrease)

1979–1985

Best		Worst	
Nonelectrical machinery	11.6	Tobacco	−2.3
Micellaneous manufactures	4.9	Printing	−0.8
Electrical machinery	4.6	Furniture	−0.1
Textiles	3.8	Transportation equipment	1.2
Instruments	3.6		
Rubber	3.4		

1985

Best		Worst	
Nonelectrical machinery	15.5	Leather	−10.4
Petroleum	10.7	Furniture	−3.6
Primary Metal	9.2	Printing	−2.9
Chemical	7.6	Miscellaneous manufactures	−2.7
Instruments	7.3	Food	−2.0

Source: American Productivity Center

TRADE TRIVIA

1492   Columbus's arrival in the New World in 1492 leads to the discovery of a number of plants and foods that will eventually help feed Europe: corn, sweet potatoes, peppers, allspice, plantains, pineapples, and turtle meat.

1585   Jesuit missionaries introduce deep-fried cooking (tempura) to Japan.

1608   The first usable shipment of American goods sent to Europe is a cargo of pitch, tar, soap, ashes, and glass shipped from Jamestown in 1608. Even so, Captain Christopher Newport is not upset with his modest cargo. Twice before he has carried back worthless mica with him to England, thinking it is gold.

1619   The first slave is imported to the U.S., to the Virginia colony of Jamestown, by a Dutch pirate. Eventually 10 million Africans are imported to the New World.

1630   At the first Thanksgiving dinner, British colonists discover popcorn, an old Indian staple. It is not served in a paper sack or a cardboard tub; Indians bring the popped kernels to the colonists in a deerskin sack.

1638   Honeybees are imported into the U.S. The Indians call them the "white man's flies" and they spread all over the country. Later, western pioneers believe they are indigenous to the country.

late 1700s Trading recipes: Thomas Jefferson imports french fries to America after growing fond of them while serving as ambassador to France. He also popularizes the idea of eating spaghetti and the habit of eating steak with french fries.

1930 Despite a petition signed by 1,028 economists who attack the idea of restricting trade, Congress passes the Smoot-Hawley tariff bill, raising tariffs to their highest level in history. The idea is to revive the economy by restricting imports. But other countries pass similar bills and, as world trade drops, the Depression gets much worse, causing even more unemployment.

1958 The Hula Hoop fad hits the U.S. and is quickly exported overseas. Worldwide sales eventually hit over 100 million. In England, TV stations broadcast live instructions to teach straitlaced British citizens how to get into the swing of things. The "huru hoopu," as it translates in Japan, spreads through the Land of the Rising Sun to "every yard, vacant lot and alley," according to one newspaper account. But following reports of back injuries and the death of one girl who is run over by a car while chasing her run-away "huru hoopu," Tokyo police ban the toy from the city's streets. By the end of the year, the fad fades and sales drop. Phillips Petroleum, which has sold plastic to the hoop makers, advises companies to punch holes in unsold hoops and try to pass them off as lawn showers.

1968 Worldwide trade and commerce is so important that a study by French economist Jean-Jacques Servan-Shreiber notes that the production of multinational companies around the world is exceeded only by the GNP of the U.S. and the Soviet Union.

1980 One of the few successful communist-bloc imports is Rubik's Cube. Invented by a Hungarian architectural professor, it becomes a fad in his own country before being imported to the U.S. under a licensing agreement with the Ideal Toy Company. Sales of the cube reach 10 million by 1981 with nearly twice as many counterfeit versions sold. The object is to arrange all the colors so that each side of the cube is one color, no easy task when you consider that there are 43,252,003,274,489,856,000 possible patterns.

1980s The breadbasket of the world: every American farmer produces enough to feed himself, 8 foreigners, and 45 Americans.

1986 A mounting trade deficit makes the U.S. the largest debtor in the world. Its net debt, the difference in value between foreign holdings in the U.S. and American investments abroad, reaches $107.4 billion in 1985, more than that of Brazil ($94.1 billion) or Mexico ($93.1 billion). Japan is the world's largest creditor nation with net assets of $129.8 billion. Only five years earlier, the U.S. was the world's largest creditor nation, with net assets of $140.7 billion.

Table 75   The 25 Top U.S. Exporters

Rank	Company	Export sales (in millions of dollars)	Change from 1984 (percentage)	Percentage of total sales
1.	Boeing	5,861	62	43
2.	General Electric	3,349	3	12
3.	McDonnell Douglas	2,668	25	23
4.	du Pont	2,575	−3	9
5.	United Technologies	2,157	−11	14
6.	Caterpillar Tractor	1,928	9	29
7.	Hewlett-Packard	1,853	1	28
8.	Westinghouse Electric	1,070	−5	10
9.	Philip Morris	923	0	8
10.	Weyerhaeuser	793	−9	15
11.	Textron	717	72	13
12.	Lockheed	693	−8	7
13.	Archer Daniels-Midland	663	−25	13
14.	NWA	658	1	25
15.	Allied-Signal	621	−8	7
16.	Union Carbide	602	−5	7
17.	FMC	589	30	18
18.	Raytheon	579	−3	9
19.	Dresser Industries	525	24	13
20.	Deere	524	−4	13
21.	Pittston	522	−1	42
22.	Phillips Petroleum	509	14	3
23.	Eastman Kodak	498	−6	5
24.	Northrop*	463	24	9
25.	Rockwell International	445	8	4

*Excludes foreign military sales of $510 million in 1985, $434 million in 1984.
Source: Standard & Poor's Compustat Services, Inc.

Table 76   Labor Costs Around the World

The U.S. is not the most expensive labor market in the world. Here are hourly labor costs, including benefits, around the world.

Switzerland	$14.01
West Germany	13.85
U.S.	13.29
Sweden	12.53
Italy	10.82
France	10.49
Japan	7.76
United Kingdom	7.67
Greece	4.04
South Korea	1.53

Source: Business International Corporation.

PART V
The Money Game

Chapter Eighteen
THE STOCK MARKET

HIGHLIGHTS AND TRENDS

Until October 1987, you couldn't have asked for a sweeter deal than the stock market. "Bull market" hardly seems like an adequate description for the leaps and bounds the stock market took when it roared back to life in mid-1982. Not since the market climbed out of the pits in 1932 had the Dow Jones Industrial Average doubled faster. Other, broader indexes soared as well. Records were routinely broken as, in the first three months of 1987 alone, the DJIA rose more than 400 points to rise above 2,400. By August it had cracked 2,700. But by late August the market was losing ground and on October 19 plunged an incredible 508 points, the biggest drop ever. More than $500 billion dollars in asset value was erased overnight, bringing total losses for a two-month period to more than $1 trillion.

No one can say for sure just why the market went into its wild gyrations in October that saw the biggest daily gains and losses in market history (see page 295). Our trade and budget deficit problems were long with us, and the dipping dollar at the time wasn't brand-new either. The fact that the market could do so, however, had much to do with changes in the market itself. One major change is technological. The computerization of trading has accelerated the buying and selling of stock to a mind-boggling level and made the market more sensitive to the whims and wants of the powerful portfolio managers for big institutions, such as pension, insurance, and mutual funds, as well as private investment groups and the equity traders at major banks and brokerages. Also, computers have spawned trading in so-called stock-index futures (see page 323). After the October 19 debacle, a lot of people blamed futures for helping precipitate the crash.

U.S. institutions had had some trillion and a half dollars in the stock market in 1987 that they could shift around as their fingers danced across computer-panel keys. Every day the institutions made 80% of stock trades though they controlled only about a third of the equity on the U.S. exchanges. But the computer dance became the whirl of a dancing dervish.

Daily volume on the New York Stock Exchange soared to more than 600 million shares, double the previous record. That's astounding considering that 10 years earlier 30 million would have tested the Big Board's limits.

While we wonder what the market will do next, it's instructive to look at what happened with the market from the outset of the bull market in 1982 to the jitters in late 1987. The terrific bull markets of yore were based on epic events: war and peace, depression and recovery. This time around the two big pushes behind the market drive were declining interest rates and lower inflation. Humbled and battered by more than a decade of climbing inflation, the stock market came back to health after a dose of the elixir disinflation. Waning inflation results in lower interest rates. As interest rates came down, corporate earnings growth became more important to investors.

The market also capitalized on a few lucky breaks. One was a hemorrhaging in oil prices, which seemed only just after the way the OPEC price hikes of the early 1970s knocked inflation in the U.S. into double digits and were a big factor in the market battering of 1974. The drop in oil prices—from $32 a barrel to $13 by the end of 1986—helped push long-term interest rates down to 8% by the end of 1986, from 12% a year earlier.

Moreover, the market benefited from takeover-hungry corporations, takeover-fearful companies that bought up their own stock, and the mad dash for mutual funds that created new demand. Also, the new markets in stock options and futures made stocks hotter. Finally, legions of foreign investors lusted after U.S. stocks in what has been called "globalization" or "internationalization" of the marketplace.

The Japanese, in particular, with their huge trade surpluses, invested heavily in everything American from stocks and bonds to real estate. Four Japanese brokerage firms—Nomura Securities, Daiwa Securities, Nikko Securities, and Yamaichi—came on so strong that there was talk that Wall Street might eventually go the way of the consumer electronics industry.

In London, the much-touted deregulation of its Stock Exchange, or "Big Bang" as it was dubbed, shook up that domestic market and added to the fierceness of the global competition and also the problems (see "Problems in the Global Village," below.)

The joker in the deck was the U.S. dollar. From the late 1970s to the mid-1980s, the dollar had an extraordinary upsurge compared with other currencies. To everyone's dismay, that created severe economic dislocations, including an apparent severing of the link between the growth of the money supply and the GNP. The economy was sluggish but the money supply grew like kudzu in lush tropical soil. The result wasn't hard to find. The strong dollar made U.S. goods costlier, putting American companies at a serious disadvantage, and the trade deficit ballooned. Some fallout, though, helped the market. The overseas trade surplus resulted in more U.S. stock buying by foreigners.

The market got another boost in the fall of 1985 when the U.S., Japan,

Britain, West Germany, and France agreed to bring the dollar down. Then Fed Chairman Paul A. Volcker backed the plan, which meant the Fed wouldn't raise interest rates, which, in effect, would have caused the dollar to go higher. The Dow went to 1550 by January 1986, a 250-point jump from the time of the announcement in late September.

So what happened? In 1987, the Reagan administration pushed the dollar lower. A declining dollar usually spurs the economy by making U.S. goods more competitive but it also adds to inflation as the prices of imports rise. Concern developed that the dollar sank too low. Meanwhile, the market wasn't getting the titanic boost from corporate raiders that it had in 1985 and 1986. (See the chapter "Deals and Mergers.") And by 1987, stocks were at their highest price levels compared to the value of assets since 1971.

Even so, U.S. stocks still looked good when compared to a lot of foreign stocks, especially Japanese stocks. Price-earnings multiples in Japan were around 50 times earnings versus 16 in the U.S., based on Merrill Lynch's 1987 earnings estimate for the Standard & Poor's 500 Composite Stock Index (S&P 500). Dividend yields in the U.S. in the first half of 1987 were 3% versus less than 1% in Japan.

That's one reason the U.S. stock market remained strong in the face of mediocre corporate earnings and a horrific trade debt. The Treasury Department figured Japanese investors spent more than $2.5 billion buying U.S. stock during the first three quarters of 1986, 10 times more than what they spent in 1985. Other analysts say the figure was much higher. Anyway, the potential is enormous. (If market fears faded away, some seers saw $15 billion in Japanese currency coming into U.S. stocks and their total holdings reaching $100 billion by 1991.)

But all along, there were serious problems with the size of the U.S. budget deficit and the whopping trade imbalance. Meanwhile, Wall Street firms became bloated with bright young M.B.A.'s as they grasped for more and more. Cautious money managers were scoffed at. Consumers and companies overreached. Time and again, events that might have resulted in big selloffs didn't: the insider-trading scandals, the Iranian arms deal, the Latin debt problem.

What finally happened was that everything came together: fears over the bleak U.S. trade and budget deficits, an incredibly low dollar, financial innovations that made markets more efficient but also more susceptible to change, and the electronic-market global village we've created in which what adversely affects the exchanges in London, Hong Kong, or Tokyo affect New York's exchanges and vice versa.

No one, of course, can say for sure what will happen with the market. If the U.S. goes into the next recession laden with excessive debt, the Fed may feel it has to inflate the economy to stave off depression. But if inflation isn't severe and the debt is pared down, there may be "corrections" in a market that rebounds. Whatever happens, a lot of stockholders will remember the sickening feeling they had when the market whipped wildly about like a flag in a hurricane. But then the market was never meant to be considered a sure thing. About the only thing certain about the market is what J. P. Morgan noted: "It will fluctuate."

PROBLEMS IN THE GLOBAL VILLAGE

The pundits use such expressions as "globalization" and "a one-world marketplace" when bantering about securities markets. To be sure, the global economic village is with us.

This was dramatically demonstrated in the global market meltdown in October 1987 when the incredible losses on the U.S. stock market (see above) set off similar chaos in the markets in Tokyo, London, and Hong Kong.

The volume of international trading is soaring thanks to strides in communications and technology. Traders are doing more and more business in New York, London, and Tokyo, markets that compete with one another. And more trading is done in unregulated international markets, especially in the Euroequities and Eurobonds that live only in computer memories and phone links between customers and dealers.

The speedy growth of international securities markets, like a bucket of cold water thrown on Rip van Winkle, awakened a lot of domestic stock exchanges with a start and brought about better service for both investors and companies. But the rapid changes have brought about some new wrinkles for the van Winkles in the form of ruthless competition, cultural friction, and management blowups.

The fierceness of the competition in those markets was reflected in the rapid rise to prominence of dealers such as Salomon Brothers and Goldman, Sachs in London and the Japanese banks and securities firms, such as Daiwa and Nomura Securities Company, that pushed their presence on Wall Street. In the first quarter of 1987, for instance, Nomura International took first place in the primary issuance of Eurobonds, underscoring just how strong a presence the newcomers can be.

Liberalization of exchanges, particularly in London and Tokyo, has opened up new markets to new financial instruments and to new participants, a lot of them from overseas. More than ever before, individual capital markets are bound closer together through such innovations as interest-rate and currency swaps, which reached $300 billion in 1986, estimates Credit Suisse First Boston.

The internationalization took place during a raging bull market, a time when interest rates fell and stock markets soared around the world. International capital markets rose to $301.2 billion in 1986 from $256.5 billion in 1985, or double the 1983 level, according to the Organization for Economic Co-operation and Development. International equity issues skyrocketed to $11.3 billion in 1986 from $2.3 billion a year earlier.

International bond issues in 1986 shot up to $226.4 billion from $167.7 billion in 1985, or triple the 1983 level. That was despite the falling dollar throughout the year and interest-rate-rise jitters during the tail end of the year.

Well before the global meltdown, however, warning flags went up, showing that globalization isn't without its problems too. For instance, despite the growth of both issuance and secondary trading in the bond market, the market suffered a major setback in 1986 when $17 billion in perpetual floating-rate notes weren't securely placed with investors. They wound up rebounding on the professionals, who wound up passing them around among themselves and, when the selloff started, couldn't find the bottom. Many Eurobond houses and Japanese banks, which were the largest holders of the paper, had losses on the deal.

A more direct problem stemming from liberalization of the exchanges is that the changes haven't been uniform. For instance, disputes erupted between the Japanese and the British over access to each other's markets. In the U.S., protectionist pressures may lead to retaliatory actions that could reverse the liberalization.

Moreover, banks and securities firms building overseas businesses found themselves plagued with cultural problems that spilled over into management and personnel problems. For instance, with increased competition the usual high turnover of dealers moving restlessly from one house to another in the Euromarkets quickened as salaries escalated. Some houses worried about finding enough qualified personnel to continue their expansion programs.

But it was not just lower-level employee problems. Some Europeans were rankled by Americans being brought in as head of European operations when they believed themselves to be more qualified. Salomon and Citicorp, for example, had a number of top management defections in 1986 and 1987. Then there was Merrill Lynch's dismissal of a senior executive in London for insider trading, which pointed out that the insider-trading problem of Wall Street may be even more complex in international operations than in domestic ones.

Also, the intense competition led to squeezing of profit margins. Bankers complained that much of the international capital market business was unprofitable, but they took it hoping it might lead to other business.

MARKET HIGHLIGHTS

1792   Twenty-four brokers form the first organized stock market in America under a buttonwood tree at what is now 68 Wall Street.

1793   An outdoor "curb market" is created and will last some 125 years.

1817   The name New York Stock and Exchange Board is adopted for an indoor market.

1830   The Exchange has its dullest day—31 shares traded.

1830   Outdoor trading in unlisted securities begins on Wall Street.

1867   Stock tickers are introduced.

1868   Exchange memberships are sold. Previously, each member had a reserved seat for life.

1869   Gold speculation results in "Black Friday."

1878   The first telephones are introduced at the Exchange.

1886   The Exchange has its first million-share day—1.2 million shares
       are traded.
1895   The Exchange recommends that listed or traded companies issue
       annual income statements and balance sheets to shareholders.
1908   E. S. Mendels forms the New York Curb Agency, the first departure
       from informal curb trading.
1914   The Exchange closes from July 31 to December 11 for World
       War I.
1921   Curb trading is moved indoors to 86 Trinity Place.
1929   The stock market crashes—16.4 million shares are traded.
1933   The Exchange closes to March 14 for a bank holiday.
1933   The Securities Act of 1933 seeks to provide full disclosure to inves-
       tors and prohibit securities sales fraud.
1934   The Securities Exchange Act of 1934 creates the Securities and
       Exchange Commission to oversee regulation of securities trading.
1938   William McChesney Martin, Jr., is elected the first salaried pres-
       ident of the Exchange.
1939   The Maloney Act creates the National Association of Securities
       Dealers to regulate the over-the-counter (OTC) market.
1942   A record low price of $650 is paid for a seat on the Curb market.
1953   The Curb market becomes the American Stock Exchange (Amex).
1958   Mary G. Roebling becomes the first woman governor of Amex.
1964   National Association of Securities Dealers (NASD) is born and the
       OTC market takes on its current contours. Previously, a dealer
       could never be sure the price at which a stock was offered was its
       lowest selling price.
1969   A record $350,000 is paid for an Amex seat.
1977   Lynne Greenberg is the first woman broker to work on the Amex
       floor and Ginger Ketchum becomes the first woman specialist.
1982   The Big Board has its first 100-million-share day (132.7 million
       shares traded) on August 18.
1985   The 50 billionth share is traded on Big Board.
1986   On July 7 the stock market falls nearly 62 points, the largest drop
       ever up to this time.
1987   On September 21 a seat sells for a record $1.15 million.
1987   On October 19 the stock market falls 508 points, the largest drop
       ever up to *this* time.

NASDAQ   One of the more intriguing developments in the marketplace
is what has happened with NASDAQ, the National Association of Securities Dealers Automated Quotations. Founded in 1971, NASDAQ
has no trading floor but it offered computerized listings in 1987 of more
than 5,500 issues worth more than $499.8 billion. What it has done is
make the over-the-counter market—once disdained as the Casbah of
the securities industry, the haven for insignificant, risky, or even shady
stocks—respectable.
    NASDAQ is the fastest-growing securities market and, right after the

Big Board, the second-largest in the nation. Since 1976, annual share volume has exceeded 37 billion, and dollar volume of trading in 1987 passed the $499 billion mark. In preparing to participate in the global market, the National Association of Securities Dealers and the London Stock Exchange have agreed to share quotations in a two-year pilot project.

Once victims of Big Board and Amex snobbery, NASDAQ officials contend that now hundreds of their companies could find their way onto the Big Board or the Amex but don't want to do so. NASDAQ membership has grown to more than 4,400 companies from 2,500 in the last decade. Largely due to mergers and acquisitions during that period, the membership of the New York Stock Exchange (NYSE) has grown only slightly, to 1,609, while the number of members of the Amex inched up to 863 in 1987, after several years' declines.

In the past decade, NASDAQ's trading volume has increased more than 1,600% to more than 37 billion shares a year. Daily trading volume on the NASDAQ market exceeded the NYSE's for the first time in May of 1983 and has done so on other occasions. In some quarters there has even been talk that NASDAQ will run the Big Board and Amex out of business someday.

NASDAQ's sophisticated, computerized network electronically links investors in the U.S. and abroad to brokers and dealers. The NASDAQ system receives and stores price and volume data on more than 5,000 domestic and foreign securities and transmits the data to the national and international financial services industry, the financial press, and investors.

NASDAQ gives so-called insider quotations, the highest bids and lowest asks on all its securities. And for the 600 companies listed on its National Market System, introduced in 1981, it offers information on the last sale and running volume, available within 90 seconds of the trade.

NASDAQ's appeal is obvious. For one, membership is comparatively cheap: about $5,000, or about a third of what the Amex charges and about a sixth of the Big Board's ante. Also, it doesn't have disclosure rules beyond those imposed by the SEC. Moreover, a lot of corporate chieftains are enamored of NASDAQ's market-making army compared with the single floor specialist found at the Exchange. Some companies, for instance, have hundreds of dealers making market in their stock.

Something else NASDAQ has done is make both the Amex and the Big Board more competitive. Touchy about NASDAQ's technological sophistication, the exchanges continue to apply more automation to their business.

The October 1987 market collapse, however, pointed out NASD weaknesses. Some dealers dropped out during the market fall. So NASD proposed a rule that, with certain exceptions, would suspend for 30 days a market maker who withdraws bid and asked quotations in a stock. Also, because of customer complaints about not being able to

Table 77   NASDAQ Trading Volume

Year	Share volume (millions)	Average daily volume (millions)	Dollar volume (millions)
1987	37,890	149.8	499,854
1986	28,737	113.6	378,216
1985	20,699	82.1	233,454
1984	15,159	59.9	153,454
1983	15,909	62.8	188,285
1982	8,432	33.3	84,189
1981	7,823	30.9	71,057
1980	6,692	26.5	68,669
1979	3,651	14.4	44,300
1978	2,762	11.0	36,141

Source: NASDAQ.

get through phone lines, NASD moved to increase the number of small trades executed automatically by computers, eliminating the need for a phone conversation between securities dealers in such trades. For complex reasons mainly related to blue chips and foreign-driven demand for U.S. stocks in the past few years, NASDAQ had not performed up to the level of the Standard & Poor's and Dow Jones indexes. This has been especially true of the smaller OTC stocks. And in the market collapse in the fall of 1987, these issues fell more sharply than the blue chips did.

ARBITRAGE

Arbitrageurs: What they do is really pretty simple, but trying to doing it well is something else again. It involves simultaneous purchases and sales of an asset, such as a commodity or currency, in two or more markets between which there are price discrepancies. Arbs want to profit from the price difference; in effect, the arbs lessen or eliminate that difference.

The breed got a bad name in 1986–1987 when Ivan Boesky, king of the "merger arbs," got nailed for a staggering $100 million fine in the early days of the insider-trading scandals that rocked Wall Street. But merger arbitrageurs were always considered the Mississippi riverboat gamblers of the trade. The two markets being "arbitraged" in a merger are the stock market on the one hand and the buyer's private market (offer price) on the other. The arb gambles substantial sums purchasing one stock and selling another short when a merger is in the works. (The arb may short the acquirer in a cash deal too if he expects investors to punish the stock because the company is paying a rich premium for the target.) If the merger comes off, the arb makes a profit. If the deal sours, the price of the stock the arb bought can drop sharply and the short stock can rise, producing a hefty loss.

WHO OWNS STOCK?

Not surprisingly, a profile of today's typical stockholder sounds pretty much like a Dewar's profile, perhaps minus the exotic hobby of white water chess playing. He or she lives in a metropolitan area, is mid-fortyish, is well educated, uses a broker, and had a portfolio in 1985 that was valued at about $6,200.

According to the latest Big Board survey, more than 47 million Americans own stock in publicly traded companies or mutual funds. Ownership is pretty much split between men and women. The median age for adult shareholders is 45 and 45% of them hold college degrees.

Most investors—nearly 60%—have white-collar jobs, while only about 16% are blue-collar workers. Housewives, retirees, and the unemployed make up the rest. Three quarters of them have incomes above $25,000 a year.

Portfolio sizes varied greatly, of course, but 45% of investors had portfolios valued under $5,000, while 12% have portfolios with values in excess of $50,000. The median portfolio value was about $6,200.

Nearly 65% of shareowners have IRA or Keogh accounts.

Not surprisingly, more than 60% of shareholders use brokers, and about 40% of investors are introduced to the market these days through brokers. The second most popular way of getting acquainted with the market is through employee stock purchase plans (25%).

Metropolises where more than a million shareholders live are New York, Los Angeles, Chicago, Washington, Boston, and Philadelphia. New York, with 2.5 million, has the most.

Table 78   The 20 Biggest Securities Firms in the U.S. 1986

Rank (1986)	Firm	Capital (dollars)
1	Merrill Lynch & Co., Inc.	2.65 billion
2	Salomon Brothers Inc	2.32 billion
3	Shearson Lehman Brothers Inc.*	2.25 billion
4	Dean Witter Financial Services Inc.	1.37 billion
5	Prudential Bache Securities Inc.	1.26 billion
6	Goldman, Sachs & Co.	1.20 billion
7	The E. F. Hutton Group Inc.	1.14 billion
8	First Boston, Inc.	1.04 billion
9	The Drexel Burnham Lambert Inc.	949 million
10	Bear, Stearns & Co. Inc.	810 million
11	PaineWebber Group Inc.	804 million
12	Donaldson, Lufkin & Jenrette Inc.	478 million
13	Van Kampen Merritt Inc.	471 million
14	Morgan Stanley & Co., Inc.	454 million
15	Kidder, Peabody & Co., Inc.	391 million
16	Stephens Inc.	376 million
17	Smith Barney, Harris Upham & Co., Inc.	285 million
18	Thomson McKinnon Inc.	250 million
19	Spear, Leeds & Kellogg	213 million
20	A. G. Edwards & Sons, Inc.	208 million

*Acquired the E.F.Hutton Group Inc. in 1987 for $961 million, threatening Merrill's top spot.

Table 79   Securities Industry Personnel

The 1980s bull market drew more people than ever into the U.S. securities industry. The following chart includes employees in all securities and commodities brokerages, dealerships, and related services.

Year	U.S.	New York City
1986	409,800	138,400
1985	366,900	129,300
1984	342,900	121,700
1983	329,600	117,500
1982	287,600	102,700
1981	267,000	99,600
1980	243,700	90,000

Sources: U.S. Department of Labor and New York State Department of Labor.

Table 80   The 10 Largest Public Offerings in the U.S.

Amount Raised*	Company	Date Issued
$1,580.0	Nuveen Municipal	June 17, 1987
1,456.0	Consolidated Rail	March 26, 1987
1,200.0	Duff & Phelps Selected Utilities	January 21, 1987
1,900.0	Henley Group	May 20, 1986
1,178.0	Coca-Cola Enterprises	November 21, 1986
1,100.0	MFS Multimarket Income Trust	March 5, 1987
855.0	First Australia Prime Income Fund	April 17, 1986
850.0	MFS Government Markets Income Trst	May 22, 1987
824.0	Firemans Fund	October 24, 1985
750.0	Rockefeller Center Properties	April 12, 1985

* In millions
Source: Norman G. Fosback, The Institute for Econometric Research, Ft. Lauderdale, FL (1987)

RECORD SEAT PRICE

A record $1 million was paid for a seat on the Big Board on April 23, 1987. But records in the 1987 market were as long-lived as snowflakes in the Caribbean. The very next day a seat brought $1.1 million. On September 21, 1987, a seat fetched $1.15 million. In August 1978 a seat could be had for only $50,000. The earliest price of a seat was $25. There are 1,366 seats on the Big Board. Seats on the Amex in the first quarter of 1987 were selling for about a third of the NYSE record price. The cheapest seats around— about $8,200—were on the Cincinnati Stock Exchange.

The prices of seats have always been as stable as oil prices. In 1985, for instance, Big Board prices fluctuated between a low of $310,000 in January and a high of $480,000 in December. The lowest price ever in this century was $17,000, paid in 1942.

Merrill Lynch   In April 1987, Merrill Lynch & Co., one of the nation's biggest retail brokerage houses, issued a stunning admission. The company said it had lost $275 million from mortgage-securities dealings. Within months that figure increased to a whopping $377 million, an accounting trick having accounted for the earlier number. The chastened Merrill blamed an unauthorized series of transactions, and a few heads rolled. Critics, though, put some of the blame for the loss on Merrill's rush to expand its presence in the mortgage-securities business by trading in a risky way in hopes of reaping bigger profits.

While that wasn't business as usual at Merrill, bad news was. Only weeks earlier, a key London executive who was highly successful in mergers and acquisitions was swept up in an insider-trading scandal.

The company also didn't look good selling its 25% stake in a Hong Kong brokerage house after taking five years to learn that a joint venture in non–Hong Kong issues didn't pan out. Finally, Merrill's name was bandied around in the press as former CEO Donald T. Regan was bounced from his White House job as chief of staff as a result of the Contragate scandal.

While the company couldn't be held accountable for Regan's problems at the White House, he could be blamed for some of Merrill's woes. Regan was the architect of Merrill's expansion and diversification program, which ran into runaway costs. This controversial and ambitious strategy, undertaken in the late 1970s, called for creating a full-service firm offering everything from securities brokerage and investment banking to life insurance and real estate. Soon after Regan left, corporate profits tumbled and morale tumbled too. Moreover, the return on equity, an important gauge of an investment firm's performance, fell to 9.5% from Merrill's historic target of 15%.

The only trend emerging from most of the bad news was that there had to be some tinkering with the "full financial services" approach to the businesses. Indeed, that began happening.

Creating a separate partnership for the real estate business was part of a restructuring at Merrill, the first major reshaping of the full-service concept. Moreover, the retail brokerage operation was streamlined, including stepped-up efforts to become less reliant on income from commissions, which go up and down with market swings. The firm revised its commission structure, giving high performers bigger commissions and lower percentages to lower performers. Also, the "financial consultants," as brokers were dubbed, got greater incentives to sell fee-producing services, such as mutual funds and insurance.

One area in which Merrill mostly won was in beefing up its once-second-rate investment banking unit. Merrill ranked first in the first quarter of 1987 in initial public offerings of common stock, moved into second place in 1986 as an underwriter of junk bonds, and, using its own capital to finance mergers and acquisitions, forged ahead in merchant banking.

Also, the company has done remarkably well with life insurance. Since 1981, Merrill has ranked among the top 15 life insurance companies, using brokers—ahem, "financial consultants"—who draw on the resources of 130 insurance specialists to sell the product.

Despite the company's successes, those who keep an eye cocked on the blunders expect more of them. For instance, Perrin Long, a widely respected analyst with Lipper Analytical Securities Corporation, has stated that the company should concentrate on what the company knows best—the retail brokerage business. "The more they move into capital markets, the more opportunity for problems and unpleasant surprises that will impact earnings," he says.

Indeed, the company, which traces its roots back to 1885, has changed a lot more in recent years than it probably did at any other time in its history. The famed Merrill and Lynch of the corporate title were Charles Merrill and Edmund C. Lynch. Merrill was the son of a small-town

Florida doctor who studied at Amherst and Michigan and played a summer of semipro baseball before winding up in the brokerage business. Lynch was a graduate of Johns Hopkins who was selling soda fountain equipment when he met Merrill at a New York YMCA where they were lodging.

Merrill talked Lynch into joining him in the brokerage business. The two formed a partnership in 1914 and made a powerful team. Merrill set up the business deals and Lynch hammered out ironclad contracts so that nothing went wrong with them. It was Merrill, probably more than anyone else, who held the belief that stocks should be made available to everyone and thus tapped among the American public a vast reservoir of funds that could be channeled into securities investments.

Merrill was also among those who sensed that the stock market was heading for a great crash in the late 1920s. On March 31, 1928, he wrote his customers, "Now is the time to get out of debt. Sell enough securities to lighten your obligations or pay them off entirely . . . we do advise in no uncertain terms that you take advantage of present high prices and put your own financial house in order."

Merrill heeded his own advice, which enabled Merrill Lynch to weather the Depression better than most securities firms. Meanwhile, the company grew and picked up additional partners through mergers and acquisitions. Today the company has worldwide operations with some 450 branches and 10,000 or so financial consultants.

Table 81   The 20 Greatest Market Changes in the 1980s

Financial markets have gotten awfully complex in recent years. Trading goes on around the clock as the world markets are linked by sophisticated technology. New financial instruments have been devised. And the money and volume of business have grown to staggering levels. What haven't changed are the exhilarating upswings and depressing downturns that hit the market. (They simply became more dramatic in 1987.) What hasn't changed too is the often bizarre combination of theory, psychology, fear, greed, and reaction to rumors and speculation that create those peaks and valleys.

Here is a record of the big market downturns that drew such shocked international attention in October 1987. Nobody's sure what caused them but a lot of blame was given to stock-index futures trading (see "Stock Index Futures," page 323) as well as worries about the size of the U.S. federal debt and trade deficit and dollar (see "Introduction The Economy," page 1).

Date in October 1987	Decline	Percent change
19	508.00	−22.61
26	156.83	−8.04
16	108.35	−4.60
14	95.46	−3.81
6	91.55	−3.47
22	77.42	−3.82
15	57.61	−2.39

To put these staggering changes in perspective, here's a look at the 20 biggest shifts—10 upsurges and 10 plunges—in the Dow Jones Industrial Average from 1980 to the first half of 1987 and some possible reasons why the market did what it did, according to *The Wall Street Journal*'s "Abreast of the Market" column and a Market Records report by Linda Rohr Weber of Salomon Brothers.

Table 81   The 20 Greatest Market Changes in the 1980s (continued)

Date	Change	Percentage change	Reason
UPSWINGS			
August 17, 1982	38.31	4.90	Reaction to strong bond market and fall in interest rates. Declines predicted in long- and short-term interest rates, with long-term U.S. government bonds falling perhaps to 9% to 10% from 12.5% within a year; institutions holding heavy cash reserves; prime rate reduced by $\frac{1}{2}$ point recently.
November 3, 1982	43.41	4.25	Speculation that market bears hoping for post-election turndown gave up and became buyers. Also, expectations of lower interest rates; most analysts discount Tuesday's (November 2) election results as a factor.
October 6, 1982	37.07	4.09	Interest rates seen as continuing to decline. Federal Funds rate declines to between 8.5% and 9.75% most of the day from 10.27% on previous day. Rumors that the Fed will cut the 10% discount rate. Short-term money-market instruments came due and investors looking at much lower yield, enhancing the market's image.
April 22, 1980	30.72	4.05	Tumbling Treasury bill yields, down 1%, the steepest decline on record. Some banks cut prime rate. Joseph Granville says buy. Inflation news is better. Consumer prices rise to seasonally adjusted 1.4%, less than some forecasts. Dow Jones Utility Average recovered much of its decline over past two months. Interest rates spark rally.
August 20, 1982	30.72	3.66	Interest rates decline. Focus on how revenue measures in President Reagan's just-passed $98.3 billion tax package might cut federal deficit spending and reduce interest rates.
November 30, 1982	36.43	3.62	Despite a plunge in bond prices Monday (November 29), bulls buy anyway. An economic recovery after a federally fostered decline in interest rates is expected.
August 3, 1984	36.00	3.09	Second consecutive day of record volume. Block trades set a record. Stage set for the rally by technical analysts allegedly paying more attention to supply-and-demand factors.
April 3, 1987	69.89	3.01	Strong growth in S&P earnings. Corporate earnings attract investors.
December 18, 1984	34.78	2.96	Lower interest rates abet a strong year-end rally. Two big banks lower the prime rate; President Reagan and Defense Secretary Caspar Weinberger apparently agree on bigger-than-expected defense budget cuts.
August 2, 1984	31.47	2.77	Record block trades spur Wall Street's anticipated summer rally. The bluest blue chips dominate the NYSE's trading.

Table 81   The 20 Greatest Market Changes in the 1980s (continued)

Date	Change	Percentage change	Reason
DOWNTURNS			
September 11, 1986	−86.61	−4.61	Computerized hedging and arbitrage against stock-index futures abet the decline; rising institutional concern about higher interest rates and possible inflation results in selloffs, as do falling bond prices and unexpectedly higher producer price and retail sales figures.
October 25, 1982	−36.33	−3.52	Fed fails to cut Discount rate but keeps banks from cutting prime rate so market consolidated. Institutions take profits. No economic recovery on horizon.
July 7, 1986	−61.87	−3.25	Sell recommendations from certain analysts and worries about the economy result in selloff. Also, the Supreme Court invalidates parts of Gramm-Rudman budget legislation. Sales related to arbitrage between stock-index futures and stocks.
March 17, 1980	−23.04	−2.84	Disenchantment with Carter administration's newest anti-inflation program, which had no short-term relief. Chances for longer, worse recession increase. A credit squeeze looms as Fed moves to raise interest costs. Prime rate reaches high of 18.5%. Dollar strong in Europe.
March 24, 1980	−19.71	−2.84	Rising interest rates. Money-market high yields lure capital. High margin costs and margin calls are cited as reasons why margin-account investors sell. CPI expected to be high for February. Flight to Egypt of deposed Shah of Iran increases Middle East tension.
January 8, 1986	−39.10	−2.50	Reversal in Wall Street's ideas about interest rates hits the market. Strong employment figures hit the credit market, setting off interest-rate increase. Federal okay of restrictions on junk bonds sets off worry that corporate takeovers will cool off.
March 30, 1987	−57.39	−2.46	Concern about slide of dollar and higher interest rates and inflation. Dollar seems out of control.
June 9, 1986	−45.75	−2.43	Big money managers and professionals force the market down. A lot of stock selling. Also, some arbitrage plays against stock-index futures that were below index levels.
December 1, 1980	−23.89	−2.41	Massive profit taking as Middle East heats up. Big concern over rising interest rates; major banks raise prime rate to 17.75%, creating fears of another hike in the Fed's Discount rate. Worries increase over Syria and Jordan tensions and Iran-Iraq war and another OPEC price meeting.
January 7, 1980	−23.80	−2.37	Joseph Granville, overnight, says sell while in a vulnerable short-term market position.

Table 82 Exchanges' Share of Trading

U.S. STOCK MARKETS: 1987 SHARE VOLUME IN MILLIONS OF DOLLARS

NYSE	$47,801	49.0%
NASDAQ	37,890	38.9
Regional exchanges (Boston, Cincinnati, Midwest, Pacific, and Philadelphia)	7,095	7.3
Amex	3,506	3.6
NASDAQ OTC trading in listed stocks	1,170	1.2
Total	$97,462	100.0%

U.S. STOCK MARKETS: 1987 VOLUME IN MILLIONS OF DOLLARS

NYSE	$1,873,597	69.1%
NASDAQ	499,855	18.4
Regional exchanges	245,129	9.0
Amex	52,548	1.9
NASDAQ OTC trading in listed stocks	43,489	1.6
Total	$2,714,618	100.0%

Table 83 Five-Year Comparison of U.S. Stock Exchanges

Year	Companies			Issues			Share volume (millions)		
	NYSE	Amex	NASDAQ	NYSE	Amex	NASDAQ	NYSE	Amex	NASDAQ
1987	1,609	863	4,706	2,244	1,077	5,537	47,801	3,506	37,890
1986	1,573	796	4,417	2,257	957	5,189	35,680	2,979	28,737
1985	1,540	783	4,136	2,298	940	4,784	27,511	2,101	20,699
1984	1,543	792	4,097	2,319	930	4,723	23,071	1,545	15,159
1983	1,550	822	3,901	2,325	948	4,467	21,590	2,081	15,909

WALL STREET—A BRIEF HISTORY

Wall Street, aptly enough, took its name from a stockade Dutch colonists erected in 1653 as protection against assault by Indians and the English, who apparently could be as fierce as today's SEC regulators going after insider traders. Expansion soon leveled the wall, the only trace being the famed narrow lane bearing that name.

Wall Street was a commercial hub linking the ports on the Hudson and East Rivers, where most imports entered the colony. In 1725, securities joined the furs, tobacco, spices, currencies, molasses, gunpowder, and assorted whatnots being traded there.

George Washington was inaugurated in 1789 at Wall Street's Federal Hall, only steps from offices where merchants specialized in lottery tickets, insurance, and commodities brokerage. High on Washington's new presidential agenda was footing the debt of the War of Independence. Thus, he issued $80 million in government bonds. In 1791, Alexander Hamilton, the first Secretary of the Treasury, added to the number of securities available when he established the Bank of the United States and made a public share offering.

Investors usually bought the new securities through coffee shops or newspaper ads; the local press recorded fluctuations in stock prices and trading volume. Soon clever merchants kept securities on hand and sold them over the counter in their stores (and gave a name to the over-the-counter market).

Recognizing a need, the merchants organized an auction where they sold off stocks and bonds, much like the auctioning of bales of cotton or casks of sugar. The noon auction was at 22 Wall Street, or the Stock Exchange Office as it came to be known. Securities were turned over to the auctioneers by an agent or broker for the owner of the securities. Both the broker and the auctioneer took commissions from the price the shares brought. Not surprisingly, discounting cropped up. After the auction, some astute men dealt in the same securities sold at the noon auction, but they made the prices more attractive by taking smaller commissions.

To make trading easier and to try to stave off the discounters, 24 brokers met on May 17, 1792. They signed an accord known as the Buttonwood Tree Agreement, by which they pledged to avoid public auction and set the broker's commission at ¼ of one percent. The group met for a while beneath a buttonwood tree outside 68 Wall Street, but they soon moved to the Tonine Coffee House at the corner of Wall and William Streets and then to their own quarters at 40 Wall.

At the end of the War of 1812 between America and Great Britain, trade between the two countries became dynamic. Besides its ports, New York City also had an edge in becoming the nation's economic center in that Manhattan had the greatest concentration of banks that could finance such trade and commerce. By 1817 there were a dozen banks in New York, and along Wall Street was a concentration of distinguished financial institutions. Among them were Union Bank (No. 17), the Manhattan Bank

(No. 23), the Bank of America and the Bank of New York (both at No. 29), City Bank (No. 31), National Insurance Company (No. 47) and Glove Insurance Company (No. 55).

The stock market was so strong by 1817 that brokers agreed to meet regularly at set hours. A constitution creating the New York Stock and Exchange Board was drafted and a room for the exchange was rented at 40 Wall Street. Rules and regulations were established and candidates for admission were voted upon by other members, each of whom placed a black ball or white ball in a box. Losers were blackballed. Among the new regulations: members were subject to fines of 6 to 25 cents for being absent or for not wearing their hats, and even the sale of fictitious contracts was forbidden.

During the 1820s and 1830s, trading expanded in federal securities; in state and private bonds to finance roads, bridges, and canals; in municipal borrowing for water, sewerage, and lighting systems; and in the stocks of banks and insurance companies. Daily trading soared from 100 shares in 1827 to 5,000 in 1834. In 1863, a name—the New York Stock Exchange—was finally adopted for what was to become known as "the Big Board."

Not all the brokers went indoors. Most remained on the street, offering to buy or sell shares in the newer and smaller companies being founded. Such "curbstone brokers" were among the first to offer turnpike and canal shares. The "curbstone" sobriquet was descriptive of what went on. Brokers in the street sent orders by means of hand signals to assistants who either stood or perched precariously in windows of surrounding buildings furiously giving their own signals until the trading was over.

Brokerage activity picked up after Connecticut became the first state to pass a general incorporation law, which made it possible to organize companies and float stock with minimum difficulty. The Mexican War of 1846–1848 and the California Gold Rush heated up the economy. Dozens of new banks and shipping companies were formed. In the boom year 1856, more than a million shares were traded just on the outdoor market.

The crash of 1857 temporarily decimated the brokerage business, but the short-lived depression was replaced by a spectacular Civil War boom, from which emerged a new kind of curb trading. During the war years, curb traders established more than a dozen exchanges of their own, such as the nation's busiest market of the era, the New York Gold Exchange.

During ensuing decades, increased regulation was imposed on curb traders and there was increased pressure to move indoors. A site was located on Trinity Place, on the west side of Trinity Church. The New York Curb Market, as it was then known, moved inside in 1921, coinciding with the great bull market of the 1920s. By 1929, a seat sold for a high of $254,000, up from $3,750 in 1921.

The prosperity, of course, skidded to a halt with the market crash of 1929. Nor did the Curb benefit when the economy finally picked up with the prosperity induced by World War II. In 1942, average daily volume dropped to 89,000 shares and a seat sold for $650. The Curb's business picked up with the postwar boom, and to celebrate its new prosperity, the exchange was given a new name, the American Stock Exchange.

One of the results of the higher standards imposed on the curb market was losing some stocks and brokers to the emerging over-the-counter market. The OTC market, however, remained more or less a stepchild until NASDAQ came on like gangbusters in the 1980s (See "NASDAQ," page 288) *Competition* became one of the familiar words in the securities industry.

Internationalization was the other buzzword. Street talk of the coming of a global market has seen U.S. securities exchanges seeking to link up electronically with foreign markets. The Big Board extended trading hours to attract more European business. The Tokyo Exchange began admitting foreign firms to membership and other foreign stock exchanges began loosening up their requirements so foreign firms could participate in them.

DOW JONES INDUSTRIAL AVERAGE

Charles Henry Dow, *The Wall Street Journal*'s first editor, was also the granddaddy of all those daily stock-market indexes. In 1884 he came up with the first average of U.S. stock prices. Its descendant, today's Dow Jones Industrial Average, tracks the prices of 30 leading blue-chip stocks; while it's by no means the most comprehensive stock-market indicator, it's by far the most widely followed.

Dow, the son of a Connecticut farmer, also provided the foundation for the "Dow theory," which holds that a major trend in the stock market must be confirmed by similar movements in both the Dow Jones Industrial Average and the Dow Jones Transportation Average. Unless both indexes reach new highs (or lows), the theory holds, no significant new trend is confirmed.

The Dow Jones Transportation Average used to be known as the Dow Jones Railroad Average. In 1896, when following "the rails" was crucial to the U.S. economy, the average covered 20 such stocks. In contrast, the Dow Jones Industrial Average then had only a dozen stocks, representing all other types of businesses. The number was increased to 20 stocks in 1916 and to 30 in 1928.

As with all stock-market indicators, the "Dow theory" is less than infallible, but it's still watched by so many traditionalists that a lot of people put a lot of stock by it.

BULLS AND BEARS

Just about everyone seems to know that a bull market goes up and a bear market goes down. But how did the nicknames originate? One theory holds that they reflect the way the two beasts fight. A battling bull slashes upward with his horns, while a bear slashes down with his paws. Maybe. According to a Merrill Lynch spokesperson, the earliest known reference was in 1709 in the English magazine *The Tatler*. An essayist wrote that someone who "ensures a real value upon an imaginary thing is said to sell a bear." *Bull* has been around since at least 1773 when a British stock exchange member wrote, "I know not why the jobber who contracts to buy is styled a bull except that he appears, when a loser, as surly as that animal."

STOCK

A stock is a security, a certificate proving ownership in a publicly held company. Stocks are available to the general public. They make you a part owner and let you vote in the election of directors. The types of stock are described below:

Shares of *common stock* are the majority of shares outstanding. There are two kinds, growth stocks and income stocks. Growth stocks show the ability to grow faster than the average stock. Usually they have low dividend payments to shareholders but the trade-off is the anticipated higher appreciation rate. Income stocks tend to be slower-growing than growth stocks, but they tend to pay higher dividends.

Preferred stock is like a bond in that it has a permanent, specified dividend and a definite rate of return. Also, such stock is more secure than common stock. If a company goes bankrupt or is liquidated, bond-holders get their money first, but next in the pecking order come holders of preferred stock and then holders of common stock.

Penny stocks are highly speculative stocks. Some people consider them to be stocks selling for $2 or less a share while others extend the range up to $5.

Stock grants ownership in a corporation and is represented by shares that are a claim on the company's earnings and assets. *Common stock* normally lets the shareholder vote in the election of directors and in other matters that come up at the stockholders' meetings. *Preferred stock* may not give voting rights but gives the holder prior claim to assets and earnings; dividends are paid to holders of preferred stock before they are paid to those holding common stock. A corporation can issue other classes of stock, each with a set of contractual rights.

Blue-chip stocks are considered safe stocks and are generally high-priced and low-yielding. They are stocks in well-known companies with track records of profit growth, dividend payments, and good management, products, and services—for example, General Electric and International Business Machines.

A *stock option* is the right to buy a given stock (a *call*), or to sell it (a *put*) at a specified price during a defined period of time, generally three months. Investors buy and sell options in order to speculate on stock price changes or to protect or "hedge" against the risk of such price changes.

The *margin* is the amount of his or her own capital put up by the investor to help finance a securities holding. The Federal Reserve's initial margin requirement on qualified stocks was reduced to 50% from 65% on January 3, 1974. An investor wanting to buy $5,000 worth of stocks has to put up at least $2,500 in cash or in securities having a loan value of $2,500.

STOCK INDEXES AND AVERAGES

Stock indexes and averages measure and report value changes in representative stock groupings. They can be broad-based (made up of a lot of stocks and representative of a market) or narrow-based (made up of a smaller group of stocks and meant to reflect a sector of the market or an industry). Selected indexes and averages are used as the underlying values of stock-index futures, index options, or options on index futures; they let investors hedge against getting hurt too badly from general market movement. There are a lot of averages and indexes. Among the most common are those described below:

The *Amex Major Market Index* is an average of 20 blue-chip industrial stocks and options in which high-priced stocks have more influence than low-priced stocks. The American Stock Exchange came up with this index to replicate the Dow Jones Industrial Average in measuring representative performance of the stocks of major industrial companies. (See "Dow Jones Industrial Average," page 301.) This index consists of stocks on the Big Board, 15 of which are part of the DJIA. Futures on the index are traded on the Chicago Board of Trade.

The *Amex Market Value Index* measures the collective performance of more than 800 stocks traded on the Amex, representing all major industry groups. Higher-priced stocks have more influence than lower-priced stocks. The index includes stocks, warrants, and American depository receipts. (A warrant entitles the holder to buy a certain amount of common stock at a specified price, usually higher than the market price at the time of issuance, for a period of years or to perpetuity. American depository receipts, or *ADRs*, are given to Americans instead of share certificates when they buy shares of foreign-based companies in overseas markets; they are receipts held by U.S. banks and they entitle the holder to all dividends and capital gains.) Options are listed on the Amex.

Barron's Group Stock Averages are averages of stocks in more than 30 industrial groups, adjusted for splits and large dividends since 1937. Futures and options aren't traded.

The *New York Stock Exchange Composite Stock Index* relates all Big Board stocks to a total market value as of December 31, 1965, adjusted for capitalization changes. Higher-priced stocks carry more weight than lower-priced stocks. The base value of the index is $50. Futures and futures options are traded on the NYSE's New York Futures Exchange. Index options are traded on the Big Board. Similarly, the *New York Stock Exchange Telephone Index* consists of the eight common stocks of companies that constituted AT&T before it was broken up. Index options in the Telephone Index are listed on the Big Board. Other NYSE subindexes are *Financial, Industrial, Transportation,* and *Utility.*

Standard & Poor's 500 Composite Stock Index (S&P 500) reflects alterations in the total market value of 500 stocks relative to the base period 1941–1943. Higher-priced stocks carry more value than lower-priced stocks. Most of the stocks are on the Big Board; some are on the Amex or are over-the-counter stocks. There are 400 industrials, 60 transportation and utilities stocks, and 40 financial issues. The index represents some 80% of the market value of all stocks traded on the NYSE. Index options are traded on the Chicago Board of Trade. Options are traded on the Chicago Mercantile Exchange.

The *NASDAQ-OTC Price Index* is based on the National Association of Securities Dealers Automated Quotations, (See "NASDAQ," page 288) with higher-priced stocks having more influence than lower-priced stocks. It represents all U.S. over-the-counter stocks except those traded on exchanges and those that only have one market maker. It was introduced on February 5, 1971, with a base value of 100. Futures and options aren't traded.

The *Value Line Composite Index* reflects price changes of a cross-section of stocks. The index is the equally weighted geometric average of some 1,700 Amex, Big Board, and OTC stocks tracked by the Value Line Investment Survey, an investment service that ranks hundreds of stocks for performance and safety. Options are traded on the Philadelphia Stock Exchange and futures on the Kansas City Board of Trade.

The *Wilshire 5000 Equity Index* represents the value in billions of dollars of all Amex, Big Board, and OTC stocks for which quotes are available, some 5,000 stocks, as prepared by Wilshire Associates of Santa Monica, California. Changes are measured against a base value established December 31, 1980. Options and futures aren't traded in it.

Table 84   Common Stock Prices and Yields, 1949–1987

Year	Common stock prices							Common stock yields (percent)	
	New York Stock Exchange indexes (December 31, 1965 = 50)					Dow Jones Industrial Average	S. & P. 500 (1941–1943 = 10)	Dividend-price ratio	Earnings-price ratio
	Composite	Industrial	Transpor-tation	Utility	Finance				
1949	9.02					179.48	15.23	6.59	15.48
1950	10.87					216.31	18.40	6.57	13.99
1951	13.08					257.64	22.34	6.13	11.82
1952	13.81					270.76	24.50	5.80	9.47
1953	13.67					275.97	24.73	5.80	10.26
1954	16.19					333.94	29.69	4.95	8.57
1955	21.54					442.72	40.49	4.08	7.95
1956	24.40					493.01	46.62	4.09	7.55
1957	23.67					475.71	44.38	4.35	7.89
1958	24.56					491.66	46.24	3.97	6.23
1959	30.73					632.12	57.38	3.23	5.78
1960	30.01					618.04	55.85	3.47	5.90
1961	35.37					691.55	66.27	2.98	4.62
1962	33.49					639.76	62.38	3.37	5.82
1963	37.51					714.81	69.87	3.17	5.50
1964	43.76					834.05	81.37	3.01	5.32
1965	47.39					910.88	88.17	3.00	5.59
1966	46.15	46.18	50.26	45.41	44.45	873.60	85.26	3.40	6.63
1967	50.77	51.97	53.51	45.43	49.82	879.12	91.93	3.20	5.73
1968	55.37	58.00	50.58	44.19	65.85	906.00	98.70	3.07	5.67
1969	54.67	57.44	46.96	42.80	70.49	876.72	97.84	3.24	6.08
1970	45.72	48.03	32.14	37.24	60.00	753.19	83.22	3.83	6.45
1971	54.22	57.92	44.35	39.53	70.38	884.76	98.29	3.14	5.41
1972	60.29	65.73	50.17	38.48	78.35	950.71	109.20	2.84	5.50
1973	57.42	63.08	37.74	37.69	70.12	923.88	107.43	3.06	7.12
1974	43.84	48.08	31.89	29.79	49.67	759.37	82.85	4.47	11.59
1975	45.73	50.52	31.10	31.50	47.14	802.49	86.16	4.31	9.15
1976	54.46	60.44	39.57	36.97	52.94	974.92	102.01	3.77	8.90
1977	53.69	57.86	41.09	40.92	55.25	894.63	98.20	4.62	10.79
1978	53.70	58.23	43.50	39.22	56.65	820.23	96.02	5.28	12.03
1979	58.32	64.76	47.34	38.20	61.42	844.40	103.01	5.47	13.46
1980	68.10	78.70	60.61	37.35	64.25	891.41	118.78	5.26	12.66
1981	74.02	85.44	72.61	38.91	73.52	932.92	128.05	5.20	11.96
1982	68.93	78.18	60.41	39.75	71.99	884.36	119.71	5.81	11.60
1983	92.63	107.45	89.36	47.00	95.34	1,190.34	160.41	4.40	8.03
1984	92.46	108.01	85.63	46.44	89.28	1,178.48	160.46	4.64	10.02
1985	108.09	123.79	104.11	56.75	114.21	1,328.23	186.84	4.25	8.12
1986	136.00	155.85	119.87	71.36	147.20	1,792.76	236.34	3.49	16.1
1987	138.23	167.04	118.57	67.31	114.57	193.83	247.08	3.4	15.5

Source: New York Stock Exchange

U.S. EXCHANGES

American Stock Exchange, Inc.
86 Trinity Place
New York, New York 10006

Boston Stock Exchange, Inc.
One Boston Place
Boston, Massachusetts 02108

Cincinnati Stock Exchange
205 Dixie Terminal Building
Cincinnati, Ohio 45202

Internmountain Stock Exchange
373 South Main Street
Salt Lake City, Utah 84111

Midwest Stock Exchange, Inc.
440 South LaSalle Street
Chicago, Illinois 60605

New York Stock Exchange, Inc.
11 Wall Street
New York, New York 10005

Pacific Stock Exchange, Inc.
301 Pine Street
San Francisco, California 94104
233 South Beaudry
Los Angeles, California 90012

Philadelphia Stock Exchange, Inc.
Philadelphia Stock Exchange Building
1900 Market Street
Philadelphia, Pennsylvania 19103

Spokane Stock Exchange
225 Peyton Building
Spokane, Washington 99201

Chapter Nineteen

BONDS

HIGHLIGHTS AND TRENDS

The bond industry was booming in recent years but a lot of people don't realize just how big the market was. Daily trading volume in government bonds alone was over $100 billion. "The bond market is an invisible giant and the stock market is a visible dwarf by comparison," said Byron Klapper, a senior vice president at Standard & Poor's and publisher of *CreditWeek,* a monitor of corporate and municipal bond ratings. As interest rates broke out of their past staid patterns, bond prices and yields fluctuated more wildly than those of stocks. It wasn't uncommon for a $1,000 bond to rise or fall $30 in a single day's trading, versus $1.25 just a few years ago. Like stocks, bonds respond to the major influences on the economy at large. Multibillion-dollar leveraged buyouts, plunging oil prices, a lackluster Sunbelt, revitalized industrial cities, frantic takeover activity, and new types of corporate restructuring have all had a major effect on the bond market in recent years. And like the stock market, the bond market has undergone an internationalization, with a lot of foreign buyers scrambling for attractive offerings. (See "Problems in the Global Village," page 286.) But by 1987, the bull market in bonds appeared to have died out: in the first three quarters of 1987 the market had one of its worst performances ever, due largely to the nosediving dollar. Then came a rebound after the stock market crash in October, as security conscious money managers found U.S. government-backed bonds appealing. Even so, the volatility of the market worried many. Total return for 1987, as measured by Lehman's index of government and corporate bonds, was only some 2%, quite a comedown when compared with more than 15% in 1986 and 21% in 1985.

THE MARKETPLACE

In 1987, U.S. corporations sold $225 billion worth of new issues in the domestic market, down from $232 billion in 1986. Falling interest rates in the 1980s spurred the refunding of high-coupon debt and lured new issuers, especially issuers of speculative or junk bonds. Municipal bonds picked up slowly but gathered momentum following the rush to beat anticipated tax reforms under the new federal tax act in 1986. By the end of 1987, municipal new issues totaled some $101 billion, down $46 billion from 1986, according to Securities Data Company Bond Buyer. U.S. government securities have dumped $200 billion of debt on the market annually since 1985. Indeed, the trading of U.S. government securities became the world's fastest-growing area of internationalization. Fueled by the enormous federal debt, average daily volume of such securities has skyrocketed to about $250 billion, compared with $180.4 million on the New York Stock Exchange. The market swell was abetted by deregulation of financial markets overseas and 1984 U.S. legislation permitting foreign investors to buy the securities tax-free. Japan's trade surpluses resulted in tremendous excess capital flowing into U.S. securities. All of that dampened, of course, after the market meltdown in October 1987.

TYPES OF BONDS

Bonds are basically IOUs whereby the issuer (seller) promises to pay the face value (or principal amount or par value) of the bond on a specific date, or maturity date. The issuer compensates the bondholder for the use of his or her money by paying interest, usually semiannually, at a fixed percentage rate during the term of the bond, or each year the bond is held. The interest rate is the bond's coupon. Once considered a preserve of the very rich, bonds gave rise to the term "coupon clipper" as a sobriquet for those lucky enough to live handsomely by clipping their coupons and presenting them for payment.

The following are descriptions of taxable bonds:

Convertible bonds give owners the option of exchanging their bonds for common shares in the company. The number of shares is arrived at by dividing the bond's conversion price into par ($1,000). If the conversion price is $50, that means the bond converts into 20 shares.

Debentures are the most common type of taxable bonds. Debenture holders are general creditors of the corporate bond issuer. The bonds are secured by all corporate assets not otherwise pledged. Convertible bonds are examples of debentures.

Equipment trust certificates are issued in the name of a transportation company that leases equipment (freight cars, locomotives, aircraft, barges, truck trailers) from a bank. Usually a second bank acts as the trustee for bondholders. When lease payments are made, the first bank forwards funds to the trustee bank to make interest payments and for the redemption of bonds.

First mortgage bonds are among the more desirable forms of a bond issue. These bonds are the result of a bond issuer's designating certain corporate property as collateral for the issue as a way of adding additional security to it.

Flower bonds are a nice way of sidestepping some estate taxes. They can be acquired at significant discounts below par but are acceptable at par value in payment of estate taxes if the deceased was the holder at the time of death.

GNMA (Ginnie Mae) certificates are shares in pools of mortgages backed by the Government National Mortgage Association (Ginnie Mae). As monthly mortgage payments are made, the proceeds are divided among bondholders until the mortgages are paid off. The payments include both interest and principal. Similar are certificates issued by the Federal Home Loan Mortgage Corporation (Freddie Macs) and the Federal National Mortgage Association (Fannie Maes).

Income bonds are rarely issued today and, for good reason, aren't taken seriously by investors—they only pay off if the corporation operates at a profit.

Senior and *subordinated bonds:* Companies having more than one bond issue outstanding usually designate the seniority of the issues. Subordinated bonds are second to the senior issue in terms of interest payments and redemption. They become important if a company winds up in such serious trouble that it may be forced out of business.

Sinking fund bonds are designated to retire in specific numbers each year until final maturity. Normally selected by random lot, the bonds can be redeemed at par value, at a premium over par, or at a discount below par. Redemption of the bonds, usually by a trust company or trustee bank, normally starts 5 to 10 years after the bonds are issued.

Zero-coupon bonds include corporate bonds, municipal bonds, treasury bonds, and even deposit certificates from banks or savings and loans. Instead of making periodic interest payments, issuers defer the interest until maturity. Hence, these bonds are sold deeply discounted from the face value. Because they don't actually pay interest yearly, "zeros" fall more dramatically than other bonds when interest rates rise and they rise more quickly when interest rates fall.

Municipal bonds, or "tax-free" bonds, are issued by cities, counties, states, and agencies created by such governments. There are more than 20,000 issuers that have created more than 80,000 bond issues. Such bonds are usually exempt from federal taxation and usually free of city and state taxes if the investor lives in the state where the bond is issued. The Tax Reform Act of 1986 created a new class of municipals, known as "taxable municipals," which are subject to federal taxation.

The types of municipal bonds are described below:

General obligation bonds are the largest group and are backed by the full faith and credit of the issuer, including its taxing and borrowing powers. "GO bonds," as they're known, are paid back with general revenue and borrowings.

Revenue bonds are issued to fund specific projects that will generate revenues. They are paid off with the revenues collected from the bridge or tunnel or whatever project is developed with the proceeds of the bond issue.

Industrial development bonds are issued by state and local governments anxious to lure business to their regions. Many of them are now taxable under the Tax Reform Act of 1986. The proceeds are used to raise money to construct plants, industrial parks, or whatever the governments feel they can build that can be leased to private industry. The quality of the bonds generally depends on the quality of the corporations taking advantage of the new facilities.

Redevelopment agency bonds, or "tax allocation bonds," are often used to construct commercial projects such as shopping centers. They are secured by a share of property taxes generated by the developed property.

Airport bonds come in two types. The first is for general usage, such as for construction projects. The second is issued for facilities that will be leased to an airline; in this case, the security is the leasing contract with the airline, which means the quality of the bonds depends on the financial health of the particular airline, many of which don't have enviable health records.

JUNK BONDS

While bonds picked up a head of steam in recent years, junk bonds came on like gangbusters and barely flinched even when Ivan Boesky gave the business an even more unsavory image than it already had. Not until the stock market crashed in the fall of 1987 and fears of a recession set in did the business hit tough times. Quite simply, junk bonds are risky business, "speculative-grade" bonds with ratings at or below BB + or Ba1, respectively, according to the major rating services, Standard & Poor's and Moody's Investors Service. A lot of investors expect the risk to be offset by the high yield, which may be twice as much as that of AAA corporate bonds.

The bonds caught on with pension funds, mutual funds, and other investors attracted by their consistently outperforming blue chips and their low 1.5% default rate for the decade from the mid-1970s to the mid-1980s. An unprecedented one quarter of the junk bonds issued in 1986 were connected to leveraged buyouts, as corporate raiders made them a stock in trade. The underwriting of junk bonds soared from $2 billion in 1982 to $48 billion in 1986. By 1987, junk bonds accounted for some $145 billion of the $550 billion corporate bonds outstanding.

While junk bonds come under a lot of criticism, they also have plenty of defenders. Out of the 23,000 companies in the U.S. with sales over $25 million, only some 800 are considered investment-grade. That leaves most of the others few options for funding corporate growth. A lot of them have turned to junk bonds, which has spurred growth in some quarters.

Junk bonds became big business largely because of one firm, Drexel Burnham Lambert. And that was because of senior executive vice president Michael Milken, who recognized that only a small fraction of companies issuing such bonds failed to make interest or principal payments on schedule.

So, judging by the bonds' track records, anybody with a diversified portfolio could reasonably gamble on handsome gains offset by minuscule default losses. Drexel and Milken rode the market hard until the insider-trading scandals of 1986–1987 cast uncertainty over both Drexel's and Milken's futures.

Now, however, there is an increased worry about defaults. About half of all junk bonds were issued since 1985 and a lot of them were for the extra-risky leveraged buyouts. Thus, nobody knows what's going to happen in the near future. The industry survived two big hits in 1986: Boesky's insider-trading scandal and the big steel company LTV going into bankruptcy and halting payments on bonds valued at $2.1 billion. Prices dropped with each revelation but then rebounded. Nonetheless, the default rate by 1986 had hit 3%, or double the historic level. But then came the market crash in October 1987. If the economy goes into a recession, a lot of companies in soft industries that issued junk bonds could fail. If that happens, a lot of investors obviously would be hurt; Drexel Burnham, already faced with erosion of its hegemony over the market, would go into a tailspin; and the corporate raiders would have to ease up on their leveraged-buyout mania.

RATINGS AGENTS

Rating the securities racing onto the marketplace is often devilishly complex these days—and lucrative. The nation's two major credit ratings agencies, Standard & Poor's and Moody's Investment Service, are capitalizing on the boom. Not only do they make a lot of money ($1,000 for rating the simplest government bond offering to $125,000 for a complex commercial mortgage obligation), they are becoming ever more powerful.

It's not unusual for political leaders to consult with them about the soundness of everything from a contemplated municipal bond offering to a political candidate. Good ratings are like money in the bank, and when a rating slips folks tend to take it hard. When S&P devalued the credit rating of the government of Denmark, for instance, it touched off a fierce debate in the Danish Parliament. And according to one tale, when the rater lowered the rating of a Japanese company's bonds, the chairman attempted hara-kiri.

The raters have no government mandate to do their job, nor do they have subpoena powers or any other official authority. They simply study all the information they can get and then express their opinions in the form of letter and number symbols. The rating doesn't mean the raters have performed an audit or even that they back up the authenticity of the information provided them upon which a rating is based. "A credit rating is not a recommendation to purchase, sell or hold a particular security," S&P cautions.

Indeed, frequently the raters have been slow in changing their ratings, even after a company issued bad news. Nonetheless, in 1986 a record 364 corporate and international ratings affecting $217 billion of debt were downgraded by S&P. Moody's downgraded ratings of 246 corporations, affecting $197 billion in debt, during the same year.

The scope of the business is staggering. S&P, for instance, has been assigning ratings to corporate bonds since 1923, to municipal bonds since 1940, and to commercial paper since 1969. It rates some 2,000 domestic and foreign companies; 8,000 municipal, state, national, and supranational entities; and 1,300 commercial-paper-issuing entities (banks and corporations).

Moody's, which began issuing ratings for railroad bonds in 1909, expanded to industrials and public utilities in 1913 and to municipals in 1918. Today, the rater rates 19,000 long-term debt issues in global markets, 28,000 municipals, and 2,000 commercial-paper-issuing entities.

A bond's quality is measured by the safety of both its interest and principal payments. Though Moody's and S&P's letter ratings differ somewhat, the ratings descend from AAA for the most secure to C for the least secure in S&P's grading, and from Aaa to C in Moody's.

S&P	Moody's
AAA	Aaa
AA	Aa
A	A
BBB	Baa
BB	Ba
B	B
CCC	Caa
CC	Ca
C	C

C and D ratings are given to bonds no longer paying interest. C is for income bonds and D is for all other types. An NR indicates that the bond isn't rated because the rater doesn't rate that type of bond, because the rater lacks enough information to rate it, or because the bond issuer didn't request a rating.

S&P assigns a plus (+) or a minus (−) sign to some ratings ranging from AA to CCC in order to reflect a bond's relative standing within its category.

U.S. GOVERNMENT SECURITIES

U.S. government securities are generally the safest investments around. They consist of three types of debt obligation that are used to finance various federal projects: *Treasury bills,* or "T-bills," with maturities up to a year; *Treasury notes,* which generally mature in 1 to 7 years; and *U.S. government bonds,* which mature in 7 to 25 years. They can be purchased without charge directly from Federal Reserve Banks or the Bureau of Public Debt, Securities Transactions Branch, Washington, D.C. In addition, T-bills and notes can be bought for a fee from certain brokerage houses, government securities dealers, and commercial banks. And there are a lot of federal issues to buy. Annually, the federal government creates more than $200 billion in debt. But compared to other foreign government issues, those of the U.S. have such attractive yields that international trading in U.S. government securities has become the fastest-growing international market. Spurred by the ballooning U.S. federal debt, daily volume in U.S. Treasury securities has soared to some $100 billion.

T-bills make up most of government financing and are issued in five denominations ranging from $10,000 to $1 million. The investor's return is the difference between what was paid for the bill and its face value at the time of maturity. The Treasury sells them at a discount through auctions. Weekly auctions are held for bills with three- and six-month maturities. Monthly auctions are held for the other two kinds of bills, those with nine-month and one-year maturities.

Treasury notes and bonds have longer maturities than do T-bills. Notes mature within one to seven years. Bonds have maturities longer than seven years and aren't redeemable prior to the maturity date, except when there is a "call" provision whereby the bond is redeemable by the Treasury before the maturity date. Some 20 other government agencies issue debentures and notes to finance their operations; since only a few are backed by the federal government, they generally offer higher interest rates than Treasury issues. The widest-known issuers are the Government National Mortgage Association (Ginnie Mae) and the Federal National Mortgage Association (Fannie Mae).

BOND HISTORY

Nobody seems quite sure of the origins of the term *bond,* but it could have had something to do with the practice in the Middle Ages of securing a debt by giving one's bond. Kings and governments, recognizing that taxes couldn't meet all their financial demands, sought a way of making money available to the crown. Government or "crown" bonds, similar to the government bonds we have now, appeared in England, France, and the Netherlands in the 17th century. For example, the Antwerp Bourse was a major financial center where royal bonds, city bonds, and even royally guaranteed private bonds were routinely traded. But because of the ban on usury, interest was disguised.

The first bonds in England considered to be modern were the public issue of William III in 1693. By then, Parliament was strong enough to back up the issue.

UNDERWRITERS

Low interest rates to underwriters are like honey to bears. The drop in interest rates in the late 1980s saw the big underwriters setting records. But in 1987, many of the major firms saw their underwriting volume drop, both in the U.S. and abroad, from 1986. Total volume in 1987 was $281.9 billion, down 11% from 1986's record $318.4 billion, according to IDD Information Services.

Salomon Brothers Inc managed to retain its title as king of the underwriters. First Boston and Morgan Stanley were in hot pursuit.

Underwriters basically agree to bear a risk, or a part of it, in return for a payment that ensures that the risk shouldn't be all that great. Issuing houses underwrite new issues of shares so that if the issue isn't bought by the public, the underwriter takes the remainder of the issue.

A post-1985 drop in interest rates sparked the bond impetus. A lot of companies used the proceeds from the bond offerings to repay higher-rate bonds issued several years earlier. They also issued long-term bonds with rates with which they felt more comfortable. The stock market crash on October 19 didn't affect the rankings much, except for Goldman Sachs, whose post-crash volume was badly hurt.

Table 85 Leading Underwriters 1987

Managing underwriters, with full credit given to the lead manager, are ranked by amount raised on new issues of taxable securities sold in the U.S. in 1987.

| RANK | LEAD MANAGER | TOTAL AMOUNT | COMMON STOCK | DEBT AND PREFERRED STOCK | | | |
				MORTGAGE-BACKED	ASSET-BACKED	JUNK BONDS	OTHER*
1.	Salomon Brothers	$40.8	$1.8	$17.3	$3.1	$1.2	$17.4
2.	First Boston	37.6	2.2	12.1	5.1	4.0	14.2
3.	Merill Lynch	31.8	4.1	9.6	0.2	3.4	14.5
4.	Morgan Stanley	31.8	2.2	7.1	—	4.4	18.1
5.	Goldman Sachs	29.2	3.3	8.8	1.0	2.0	14.1
6.	Drexel Burnham	21.2	2.4	4.1	0.5	11.6	2.6
7.	Shearson Lehman	20.0	2.5	5.9	1.4	0.3	9.9
8.	Kidder Peabody	10.0	1.4	4.4	0.2	0.5	3.5
9.	Prudential-Bache	5.7	1.1	2.4	—	0.1	2.1
10.	Bear Stearns	5.6	0.3	3.5	—	0.1	1.7

*Includes below-investment grade convertible debt
Source: IDD Information Services

Table 86 Bond Yields and Interest Rates, 1929–1987

(percent per annum)

Year	U.S. Treasury securities				Corporate bonds (Moody's)		High-grade municipal bonds (Standard & Poor's)	New-home mortgage yields (Federal Home Loan Bank Board)	Com-mercial paper 6-months	Prime rate charged by banks	Discount rate, Federal Reserve Bank of New York	Federal Funds rate
	Bills (new issues)		Constant maturities									
	3-month	6-month	3-year	10-year	Aaa	Baa						
1929					4.73	5.90	4.27		5.85	5.50–6.00	5.16	
1933	0.515				4.49	7.76	4.71		1.73	1.50–4.00	2.56	
1939	.023				3.01	4.96	2.76		.59	1.50	1.00	
1940	.014				2.84	4.75	2.50		.56	1.50	1.00	
1941	.103				2.77	4.33	2.10		.53	1.50	1.00	
1942	.326				2.83	4.28	2.36		.66	1.50	1.00	
1943	.373				2.73	3.91	2.06		.69	1.50	1.00	
1944	.375				2.72	3.61	1.86		.73	1.50	1.00	
1945	.375				2.62	3.29	1.67		.75	1.50	1.00	
1946	.375				2.53	3.05	1.64		.81	1.50	1.00	
1947	.594				2.61	3.24	2.01		1.03	1.50–1.75	1.00	
1948	1.040				2.82	3.47	2.40		1.44	1.75–2.00	1.34	
1949	1.102				2.66	3.42	2.21		1.49	2.00	1.50	
1950	1.218				2.62	3.24	1.98		1.45	2.07	1.59	
1951	1.552				2.86	3.41	2.00		2.16	2.56	1.75	
1952	1.766				2.96	3.52	2.19		2.33	3.00	1.75	
1953	1.931		2.47	2.85	3.20	3.74	2.72		2.52	3.17	1.99	
1954	.953		1.63	2.40	2.90	3.51	2.37		1.58	3.05	1.60	
1955	1.753		2.47	2.82	3.06	3.53	2.53		2.18	3.16	1.89	1.78
1956	2.658		3.19	3.18	3.36	3.88	2.93		3.31	3.77	2.77	2.73
1957	3.267		3.98	3.65	3.89	4.71	3.60		3.81	4.20	3.12	3.11
1958	1.839		2.84	3.32	3.79	4.73	3.56		2.46	3.83	2.15	1.57
1959	3.405	3.832	4.46	4.33	4.38	5.05	3.95		3.97	4.48	3.36	3.30
1960	2.928	3.247	3.98	4.12	4.41	5.19	3.73		3.85	4.82	3.53	3.22
1961	2.378	2.605	3.54	3.88	4.35	5.08	3.46		2.97	4.50	3.00	1.96
1962	2.778	2.908	3.47	3.95	4.33	5.02	3.18		3.26	4.50	3.00	2.68
1963	3.157	3.253	3.67	4.00	4.26	4.86	3.23	5.89	3.55	4.50	3.23	3.18
1964	3.549	3.686	4.03	4.19	4.40	4.83	3.22	5.82	3.97	4.50	3.55	3.50
1965	3.954	4.055	4.22	4.28	4.49	4.87	3.27	5.81	4.38	4.54	4.04	4.07
1966	4.881	5.082	5.23	4.92	5.13	5.67	3.82	6.25	5.55	5.63	4.50	5.11
1967	4.321	4.630	5.03	5.07	5.51	6.23	3.98	6.46	5.10	5.61	4.19	4.22
1968	5.339	5.470	5.68	5.65	6.18	6.94	4.51	6.97	5.90	6.30	5.16	5.66
1969	6.677	6.853	7.02	6.67	7.03	7.81	5.81	7.80	7.83	7.96	5.87	8.20
1970	6.458	6.562	7.29	7.35	8.04	9.11	6.51	8.45	7.71	7.91	5.95	7.18
1971	4.348	4.511	5.65	6.16	7.39	8.56	5.70	7.74	5.11	5.72	4.88	4.66
1972	4.071	4.466	5.72	6.21	7.21	8.16	5.27	7.60	4.73	5.25	4.50	4.43
1973	7.041	7.178	6.95	6.84	7.44	8.24	5.18	7.96	8.15	8.03	6.44	8.73
1974	7.886	7.926	7.82	7.56	8.57	9.50	6.09	8.92	9.84	10.81	7.83	10.50
1975	5.838	6.122	7.49	7.99	8.83	10.61	6.89	9.00	6.32	7.86	6.25	5.82
1976	4.989	5.266	6.77	7.61	8.43	9.75	6.49	9.00	5.34	6.84	5.50	5.04
1977	5.265	5.510	6.69	7.42	8.02	8.97	5.56	9.02	5.61	6.83	5.46	5.54
1978	7.221	7.572	8.29	8.41	8.73	9.49	5.90	9.56	7.99	9.06	7.46	7.93
1979	10.041	10.017	9.71	9.44	9.63	10.69	6.39	10.78	10.91	12.67	10.28	11.19
1980	11.506	11.374	11.55	11.46	11.94	13.67	8.51	12.66	12.29	15.27	11.77	13.36
1981	14.029	13.776	14.44	13.91	14.17	16.04	11.23	14.70	14.76	18.87	13.42	16.38
1982	10.686	11.084	12.92	13.00	13.79	16.11	11.57	15.14	11.89	14.86	11.02	12.26
1983	8.63	8.75	10.45	11.10	12.04	13.55	9.47	12.57	8.89	10.79	8.50	9.09
1984	9.58	9.80	11.89	12.44	12.71	14.19	10.15	12.38	10.16	12.04	8.80	10.23
1985	7.48	7.66	9.64	10.62	11.37	12.72	9.18	11.55	8.01	9.93	7.69	8.10
1986	5.98	6.03	7.06	7.68	9.02	10.39	7.38	10.17	6.39	8.33	6.33	6.81
1987:												
Jan.	5.45	5.47	6.41	7.08	8.36	9.72	6.63	9.51	5.76	7.50	5.50	6.43
Feb.	5.59	5.60	6.56	7.25	8.38	9.65	6.66	9.23	5.99	7.50	5.50	6.10
Mar.	5.56	5.56	6.58	7.25	8.36	9.61	6.71	9.14	6.10	7.50	5.50	6.13
Apr.	5.76	5.93	7.32	8.02	8.85	10.04	7.62	9.21	6.50	7.75	5.50	6.37
May	5.75	6.11	8.02	8.61	9.33	10.51	8.10	9.37	7.04	8.25–8.00	5.50	6.85
June	5.69	5.99	7.82	8.40	9.32	10.52	7.89	9.45	7.00	8.25	5.50	6.73
July	5.78	5.86	7.74	8.45	9.42	10.61	7.83	9.41	6.72	8.25	5.50	6.58
Aug.	6.00	6.14	8.03	8.76	9.67	10.80	7.90	9.38	6.81	8.25	5.50	6.73
Sept.	6.32	6.57	8.67	9.42	10.18	11.31	8.36	9.37	7.55	8.75–8.25	6.00–5.50	7.22
Oct.	6.40	6.86	8.75	9.52	10.52	11.62	8.84	9.25	7.96	9.25–8.75	6.00	7.29
Nov.	5.81	6.23	7.99	8.86	10.01	11.23	8.09	9.30	7.17	9.00–8.75	6.00	6.69
Dec.	5.80	6.36	8.13	8.99	10.11	11.29	8.07	9.15	7.49	8.75	6.00	6.77

Source: Federal Reserve Board.

Chapter Twenty
FUTURES MARKETS

In the movie *Trading Places,* the streetwise Eddie Murphy sits in the posh offices of a firm speculating in futures, about to become head of the company for the owners' devious reasons. Amidst the trappings of gentility, the owners explain how the business works. The savvy Murphy picks right up on it: "You guys is bookies!"

Gambling it is—at least for the speculators. (Producers, such as farmers, may be using the futures market to hedge their basic economic position.) The risks in such speculation are so extreme that futures aren't for the fainthearted. There are so many variables involved that playing the futures market can be a frantic roller-coaster ride that leads to big rewards—or huge losses. Futures markets are actually auctions and clearinghouses for the latest information about supply and demand for an ever-expanding list of commodities. That list now includes a hodgepodge of such items as agricultural products, metals, petroleum, foreign currencies, and domestic stock indexes. The market grew like crazy, especially in financial futures—contracts based on financial instruments such as Treasury bonds and Treasury notes whose prices fluctuate with changes in interest, as well as contracts based on stock indexes. (See "Stock Index Futures," page 323.) Nearly two thirds of a million futures contracts are now bought and sold on an average day. The volume of trade for fiscal 1985–1986 hit 213.6 million, more than double what it was in 1980.

CONTRACTS

There are two kinds of futures contracts: those that call for the physical delivery of what is traded and those that call for a cash settlement in whatever month is specified. Very few contracts actually are delivered, since few investors want to take delivery of $1 million worth of Treasury bills or 10,000 bushels of wheat. But the fact that buyers can take or make delivery of most commodities helps keep futures prices and the cash market value of the commodities in line.

MARGINS

Understanding margins is essential to knowing the futures business. The term *margins* as used in futures trading is very different from the term as used in buying securities, in which it has to do with the down payment and money borrowed from a broker to buy stocks. The futures deposit is quite simply a deposit of good-faith money that can be drawn by the brokerage house to cover trading losses. Usually margins are 5–10% of the value of a futures contract. Futures accounts are debited or credited each day for the full amount of the day's change. If the futures price moves adversely, the investor must put up more money; if the change is favorable, he can take cash out of the account.

LEVERAGE

Risk is what futures trading is all about and study after study has shown that most amateurs who enter the market get bloodied. Gains and losses are often enormous and the reason is leverage. Only a relatively small amount of money (known as the initial margin) is required to buy or sell a futures contract. The smaller the margin in relation to the value of the futures contract, the greater the leverage. For instance, a margin deposit of $1,250 could let an investor buy $25,000 worth of soybeans, or $6,000 could purchase a futures contract covering $100,000 worth of stock.

OPTIONS

The revolution in financial options started with options on individual stocks, when the Chicago Board Options Exchange created centralized exchange trading of the two most common options: a *call,* which gives the buyer the right to buy 100 shares of a stock at a particular price within a given period, and its opposite number, a *put,* which gives the buyer the right to sell the stock at the specified price. But the business exploded when trading began on overall stock indexes, thereby giving traders a single instrument that enabled them to bet, in effect, on the entire stock market. The Chicago Board Options Exchange's business soared from $448 million in 1978 to the multibillion-dollar level it has reached today. The appeal of options is that they provide limited risk with theoretically unlimited profit opportunities. For example, with a limited investment, the buyer of a call can participate fully in the movement of a stock or an entire market. The most he can lose is the initial premium he paid for the option. (He often does.)

THE PLAYERS

The players are speculators and hedgers. *Speculators* try to anticipate price changes and profit through the sale and purchase or purchase and sale of a commodity or futures contract. Speculators are going up against either other speculators, who think prices are going in an opposite direction, or hedgers, who are trying to ward off risk.

Hedging is basically an insurance, a way of trying to protect yourself against the risk of an unfavorable price change. To guarantee a known price level, hedgers buy and sell in the futures market, weeks or months in advance, something they intend to buy or sell in the cash market. Say a dentist knows he needs to buy gold in eight months, but he fears that the price of gold will go up. He is concerned also because he is quoting prices to patients based on what the price of gold is now. To hold today's price of, say, $450 an ounce for delivery in eight months, he buys a futures contract at that price. If the price rises to $465 eight months later, the dentist pays his supplier that much to get the gold, but the extra $15 an ounce will be offset by his $15-an-ounce profit when his futures contract is sold. If the price of gold had dropped, his loss would have been made up by buying cheaper gold on the cash market.

Floor traders buy and sell for their own accounts and, like specialists and market makers at stock exchanges, help provide market liquidity. If a hedger or speculator won't immediately buy or sell a certain contract, usually an independent floor trader will, in the hopes of making a small gain within minutes or even seconds, say, from a quarter-of-a-cent change in the contract price.

THE HISTORY OF FUTURES

The people frantically waving and shouting on the trading floor of a futures exchange aren't bent on driving the place into chaos. Actually, their antics are what the futures markets are all about—replacing chaos with order, a system that dates back centuries.

It evolved from a market system that goes back to ancient Greece and Rome, where marketplaces with fixed times for trading utilized bartering, currency systems, and even contracting for future delivery. The Agora of Athens started as such a marketplace and evolved into a vast, busy commercial hub as Athens became the center of political and maritime power. At the pinnacle of the Roman Empire, there were nearly 20 trading centers distributing the wealth of commodities imported from across the Empire.

Although commerce was disrupted in the Dark Ages, the fundamentals of the marketplace survived in the form of medieval fairs. Such fairs were promoted by *pieds poudres,* or "men with dusty feet," who traveled across the land. Gradually, some fairs began specializing in trade between different nations. In 1215, the Magna Carta guaranteed the right of foreign merchants to travel freely to and from English fairs. Although most trading was for cash for immediate delivery, contracting for later delivery of merchandise began.

In America, before the central grain markets were created in the mid-

19th century, it was each buyer and seller for himself and there was no method for competitive bidding. Every autumn, America's farmers hauled their harvests to cities, towns, and transportation hubs in search of buyers. The supplies of grain usually far outstripped the needs of millers. The resultant gluts drove prices abysmally low so that disgusted farmers, lacking storage facilities, often wound up dumping what they couldn't sell right in the street or in nearby rivers and lakes. In the spring, there were shortages of that same wheat and corn.

Out of this mess emerged the first central markets, the forerunners of today's futures markets. Imaginative farmers and merchants began making contracts for forward deliveries, which assured them of having a buyer or seller for their commodities. Such forwarding contracts were in effect in Chicago shortly after the city's founding in 1833. In 1848, the Chicago Board of Trade was formed and forward contracting as well as cash trades were practiced.

But while forward contracts found a buyer a seller or vice versa, they did nothing about the risk of unforeseen price changes due to crop failures, transportation problems, or economic conditions. Thus, hedging (see page 317) arose to diminish the risk.

Today, the exchanges cover a plethora of "commodities." As well as farmers and grain dealers, participants include bond dealers, mortgage bankers, multinational corporations, savings and loan associations, and individual speculators. Thanks to high-tech communications, there is a global futures market. Futures prices set through competitive bidding are instantaneously relayed around the world. A South Dakota farmer, a Hong Kong exporter, a broker in London, and a New York speculator all have access to the latest market-derived price quotations.

FUTURES EXCHANGES

Most futures exchanges are not-for-profit membership associations. Membership is restricted and belongs to individuals, although companies, partnerships, and cooperatives may be registered for certain membership privileges. Some exchanges have of late offered special membership or trading privileges. The Chicago Board of Trade, for instance, has associate members who trade in designated markets, such as financial-instrument futures.

American Stock Exchange
86 Trinity Place
New York, New York 10006
Offers include options on 135 stocks and 20 over-the-counter securities, Treasury bills, Treasury notes, two broad-based stock indexes (the Major Market Index and the Institutional Index), and three narrow-based stock indexes: in computer technology, oil, and airlines.

Amex Commodities Corporation
    86 Trinity Place
    New York, New York 10006
    A subsidiary of the Amex offering cash-settled options on gold bullion.

Chicago Board of Trade
    141 West Jackson Boulevard
    Chicago, Illinois 60604
    The world's largest futures exchange is a nonprofit association providing a marketplace that includes agricultural, financial, metals, and stock-index futures and futures options in corn, silver, soybeans, Treasury bills, and Treasury notes.

Chicago Board Options Exchange
    400 South LaSalle Street
    Chicago, Illinois 60605
    The world's largest options marketplace and the only one exclusively for options trading. In addition to puts and calls on 159 of the most widely held and active stocks, it includes options on the Standard & Poor's 100 and 500 Stock Indexes, three U.S. T-bonds, three U.S. T-notes, and six foreign currencies.

Chicago Mercantile Exchange
    30 South Wacker Drive
    Chicago, Illinois 60606
    Second to the CBT in trading volume, the CME is the world's largest facility for futures with a membership of 2,725 traders. The most active contract is Standard & Poor's 500 Stock Index futures. Other futures traded include options on currencies, three short-term interest rate T-bills, Eurodollars, cattle and hogs, lumber, and pork bellies. The three divisions of the exchange include the CME, International Monetary Market, and Index and Options Market.

Chicago Rice and Cotton Exchange
    444 West Jackson Boulevard
    Chicago, Illinois 60606
    Formerly the New Orleans Commodity Exchange, the CRCE lists rough rice futures, which are traded on the floor of the Chicago Board of Trade, and short-staple cotton futures traded on the floor of the MidAmerica Commodity Exchange.

Coffee, Sugar and Cocoa Exchange
    4 World Trade Center
    New York, New York 10048
    The world's leading marketplace for futures contracts on world and domestic sugar, coffee, and cocoa as well as options on those commodities, and the inflation-futures contract, the CIP-W, is based on the U.S. consumer price index.

Commodity Exchange
  4 World Trade Center
  New York, New York 10048
    The world's leading gold-futures exchange and the third-biggest
    commodity exchange in the U.S. Contracts traded include gold,
    silver, copper, and aluminum futures and options on gold, silver,
    and copper futures.

Kansas City Board of Trade
  4800 Main Street, Suite 303
  Kansas City, Missouri 64112
    The world's primary marketplace for futures and options in hard
    red winter wheat and the first U.S. exchange to trade futures
    based on a stock market index, the Value Line Composite Index.

MidAmerica Commodity Exchange
  444 West Jackson Boulevard
  Chicago, Illinois 60606
    An affiliate of the Chicago Board of Trade, the MidAm offers
    futures contracts on financial instruments, foreign currencies, gold,
    grain, livestock, metals, soybeans, and wheat. Many contracts are
    smaller versions of contracts traded elsewhere, with inherently
    smaller margin requirements.

Minneapolis Grain Exchange
  400 South Fourth Street
  Minneapolis, Minnesota 55415
    Offers future contracts for hard red spring wheat and white wheat
    futures and options on hard red spring wheat.

New York Cotton Exchange
  4 World Trade Center
  New York, New York 10048
    The oldest exchange in New York, it offers futures contracts on
    cotton, frozen contracted orange juice (FCOJ), and liquid propane
    gas as well as options on cotton and FCOJ futures. The Financial
    Instrument Exchange division offers futures contracts on the U.S.
    Dollar Index and European Currency Units, with trading privileges
    open to all 1,300 qualified Commodity Exchange floor traders.

New York Futures Exchange
  20 Broad Street
  New York, New York 10005
    A subsidiary of the New York Stock Exchange, NYFE contracts
    include NYSE Composite Stock Index futures and options on
    futures and Commodity Research Bureau Futures Price Index
    futures.

New York Mercantile Exchange
4 World Trade Center
New York, New York 10048
  Maintains a futures market for No. 2 heating oil, unleaded
  gasoline, light sweet crude oil, platinum, and palladium and is
  adding options on several energy contracts starting with crude oil.

New York Stock Exchange
11 Wall Street
New York, New York 10005
  The world's leading stock exchange offers stocks on more than
  1,500 companies and options on its NYSE Composite Stock Index.

Pacific Stock Exchange
301 Pine Street
San Francisco, California 94104
233 South Beaudry
Los Angeles, California 90012
  Has equity trading floors in Los Angeles and San Francisco. It
  offers some 1,300 securities and offers options on 86 stocks and
  one index, the PSE Technology Index.

Philadelphia Board of Trade
1900 Market Street
Philadelphia, Pennsylvania 19103
  The subsidiary of the Philadelphia Stock Exchange offers futures
  contracts in deutsche marks, Swiss francs, Canadian dollars,
  British pounds, Japanese yen, French francs, European Currency
  Units and the National Over-the-Counter Index and options on
  actual Eurodollars.

Philadelphia Stock Exchange
1900 Market Street
Philadelphia, Pennsylvania 19103
  The nation's oldest securities exchange offers more than 1,200
  equity securities, 87 stock options, seven foreign currency options
  and three index options (Value Line, National OTC, and
  Gold/Silver). The foreign currency options program is the largest
  of its kind, offering options on deutsche marks, Swiss francs,
  Canadian dollars, British pounds, Japanese yen, French francs,
  and the European Currency Unit.

STOCK INDEX FUTURES

For years, the hottest craps game around was stock index futures. In 1987, the average daily volume of trading in the most popular contract, the Standard & Poor's 500 stock-index futures contract, was expected to hit about $12 billion, nearly double the volume two years earlier. The October 1987 market meltdown and recession jitters, however, dampened six years of explosive growth. Also, the possibility that stock-index futures and options were accessories to the market crash didn't help their image.

A lot of folks have always considered commodity trading as gambling. After all, only 4% of all commodities traded are actually delivered. The rest are tossed around like chips in Vegas. But in 1905, Justice Oliver Wendell Holmes found a way of telling the commodities market from the casino. He noted there was an obligation to make or take delivery of the commodity, even if the delivery was moot in most cases.

Who knows what the good Justice would think about stock-index futures, which were introduced on the Chicago Mercantile Exchange in 1982. Instead of prices of bushels of wheat or piles of pork bellies, traders bet on how a group of stocks will move. The most widely used group is the S&P 500. In a terraced pit about half the size of a tennis court, more than 500 traders elbow and gouge one another as they fight for position to trade the S&P Index, which became the fastest-growing futures contract ever. There's little wonder why. To buy $1 million in stock-index futures one only had to put down $100,000, or a fifth of what one would have had to put down to buy $1 million in stock.

(The difference in margins between stocks and futures goes back to 1934 when President Roosevelt proposed raising margins on both. Ever inconsistent, Congress raised them for securities but ignored futures.)

A combination of the explosion in volume in stock and bonds markets in 1986 and 1987 and deregulation loosened the Chicago exchange's hammerlock on the most popular financial contracts. New contracts sprouted up on options exchanges and over-the-counter markets.

One result of all this is concern that the small shareholder is getting the short shrift. One study has substantiated what everybody suspected: professional traders who use stock-index options and futures have occasionally dominated the stock market, at times creating wild swings in stock prices. The pros predicted that the Dow would experience 100-point rises or slides as a result of being zapped by Chicago.

As we witnessed in 1987, that's exactly what happened and, by all accounts, greatly contributed to the market craziness that saw the DJIA plummet 508 points on October 19. Critics blamed those market gyrations on traders engaging in something called "program trading." Massive blocks of stock are traded—with the assistance of computers—as investors try to profit from the price difference between stock-index futures or options and the actual cash value of the stocks that make up the index. As a kind of insurance for their portfolios when the market drops, big institutional traders sell stock-index futures. If the index keeps falling below the contracted price, the traders profit and offset the loss in the value of the stock.

Table 87 Commodities Contracts*

1972

1.	Soybeans	Chicago Board of Trade	4,043,474
2.	Pork bellies	Chicago Mercantile Exchange	2,057,064
3.	Corn	Chicago Board of Trade	1,942,120
4.	Live cattle	Chicago Mercantile Exchange	1,370,471
5.	Soybean oil	Chicago Board of Trade	1,110,776
6.	Sugar	New York Coffee and Sugar Exchange	875,178
7.	Wheat	Chicago Board of Trade	855,813
8.	Silver	Commodity Exchange	815,168
9.	Silver	Chicago Board of Trade	813,492
10.	Soybean meal	Chicago Board of Trade	630,916
		Total, all contracts	18,332,055

1977

1.	Soybeans	Chicago Board of Trade	7,996,139
2.	Corn	Chicago Board of Trade	5,021,827
3.	Silver	Commodity Exchange	3,573,301
4.	Live cattle	Chicago Mercantile Exchange	2,639,517
5.	Soybean oil	Chicago Board of Trade	2,535,046
6.	Soybean meal	Chicago Board of Trade	2,373,453
7.	Silver	Chicago Board of Trade	2,257,059
8.	Wheat	Chicago Board of Trade	1,820,790
9.	Pork bellies	Chicago Mercantile Exchange	1,358,730
10.	Live hogs	Chicago Mercantile Exchange	1,307,712
		Total, all contracts	42,880,318

1982

1.	T-bonds	Chicago Board of Trade	16,739,695
2.	Gold	Commodity Exchange	12,289,448
3.	Soybeans	Chicago Board of Trade	9,165,520
4.	Corn	Chicago Board of Trade	7,948,257
5.	T-bills	Chicago Mercantile Exchange	6,598,848
6.	Live cattle	Chicago Mercantile Exchange	4,440,992
7.	Wheat	Chicago Board of Trade	4,031,584
8.	Live hogs	Chicago Mercantile Exchange	3,560,974
9.	Soybean oil	Chicago Board of Trade	3,049,313
10.	S&P 500	Chicago Mercantile Exchange	2,935,532
		Total, all contracts	112,400,879

1987

1.	T-bonds	Chicago Board of Trade	66,841,474
2.	Eurodollar	Chicago Mercantile Exchange	20,416,216
3.	S&P 500 Index	Chicago Mercantile Exchange	19,044,673
4.	Crude Oil	New York Mercantile	14,581,614
5.	Gold (100 oz)	Commodities Exchange	10,239,805
6.	Soybeans	Chicago Board of Trade	7,378,760
7.	Corn	Chicago Board of Trade	7,253,212
8.	Deutsche Mark	Chicago Mercantile	6,037,048
9.	Japanese Yen	Chicago Mercantile	5,358,556
10.	Swiss Franc	Chicago Mercantile	5,268,276
		Total, all contracts	184,354,496

*For information on exchanges where commodities are traded see "Futures Exchanges" above.
Source: Futures Industry Association.

Table 88   Volume of Futures Trading, 1960 through 1987
(millions of contracts traded)

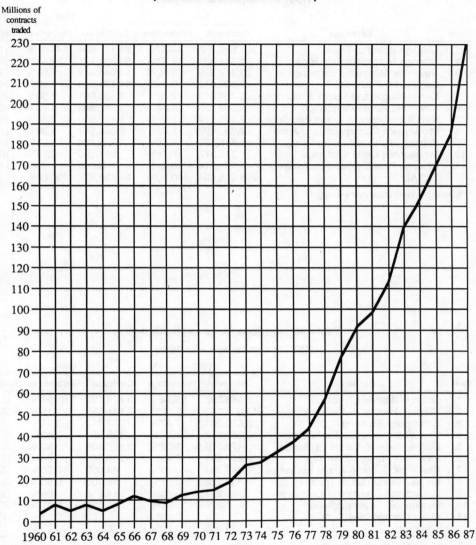

Millions of contracts traded

Source: Futures Industry Association, Inc.

Table 89 Futures Volume Highlights

(1987 in comparison with 1986)

		1987		1986		
Rank	Exchange	Contracts	Percentage	Contracts	Percentage	Rank
1.	Chicago Board of Trade	101,626,958	44.40%	81,135,634	44.01%	(1)
2.	Chicago Mercantile Exchange	71,334,072	31.17%	59,831,171	32.45%	(2)
3.	New York Mercantile Exchange	22,474,629	9.82%	14,644,413	7.94%	(3)
4.	Commodity Exchange	17,884,617	7.81%	14,174,698	7.69%	(4)
5.	Coffee, Sugar and Cocoa Exchange	5,784,383	2.53%	5,535,081	3.00%	(5)
6.	New York Futures Exchange	3,069,125	1.34%	3,182,992	1.73%	(6)
7.	New York Cotton & Citrus Exchange	2,498,014	1.09%	1,477,590	0.80%	(9)
8.	MidAmerica Commodity Exchange	2,350,692	1.03%	2,368,547	1.28%	(7)
9.	Kansas City Board of Trade	1,505,103	0.66%	1,716,686	0.93%	(8)
10.	Minneapolis Grain Exchange	317,977	0.14%	284,586	0.15%	(10)
11.	Chicago Rice & Cotton Exchange	31,114	0.01%	3,098	.00%	(11)
	TOTAL	228,876,684	100.00%	184,354,496	100.00%	

Source: Futures Industry Association.

Table 90 Options Volume Highlights

(1987 in comparison with 1986)

		1987		1986		
Rank	Exchange	Contracts	Percentage	Contracts	Percentage	Rank
1.	Chicago Board of Trade	25,466,032	55.14%	19,678,199	61.94%	(1)
2.	Chicago Mercantile Exchange	13,033,142	28.22%	8,944,353	28.15%	(2)
3.	Commodity Exchange	3,610,981	7.82%	2,353,717	7.41%	(3)
4.	New York Mercantile Exchange	3,260,642	7.06%	135,266	0.43%	(6)
5.	Coffee, Sugar & Cocoa Exchange	472,476	1.02%	260,809	0.82%	(5)
6.	New York Futures Exchange	206,631	0.45%	296,303	0.93%	(4)
7.	New York Cotton & Citrus Exchange	88,703	0.19%	64,059	0.20%	(7)
8.	Kansas City Board of Trade	33,228	0.07%	18,302	0.06%	(8)
9.	MidAmerica Commodity Exchange	12,921	0.03%	14,218	0.04%	(9)
10.	Minneapolis Grain Exchange	1,229	.00%	3,259	0.01%	(10)
11.	Amex Commodities Corp	0	0.00%	2,128	0.01%	(11)
	Total	46,185,985	100.00%	31,770,613	100.00%	

Source: Futures Industry Association.

Chapter Twenty-One
MUTUAL FUNDS

HIGHLIGHTS AND TRENDS

The 1980s may well be remembered as the decade Americans went mad over mutual funds. By the time the stock market crashed in October 1987 there were 2,300 funds and even after the crash new ones continued to be created. Mutual funds took a big hit with the market crash, however, dropping to about $800 billion in total assets from a pre-crash high of $850 billion. And if the market performs dismally, consolidation within the industry, at least among equity funds, is the likely trend. After several years of double-digit gains from stock and bond funds, gains in 1987 were minute. The average general equity fund rose only about 1.5%, while S&P's 500 index (including dividends) was up 7.2%, and fixed income funds were up only 0.62%.

Though mutual funds became familiar to many investors in the 1980s, they aren't all that new. After the end of World War II, when they had total net assets of only about $1 billion, mutual funds probably grew faster than any other major financial institution in the U.S. In the 1980s they exploded. The combined assets of mutual funds soared from $58.4 billion in 1980 to a whopping $370.6 billion at the end of 1984 to a staggering $716 billion by the end of 1986. Money-market fund assets declined slightly in 1985 but jumped to $222 billion by June 1986. The growth patterns of different types of funds largely reflected declining short-term interest rates and the bullish stock market. Bond and income funds grew mainly because investors were attracted by the relatively high returns from longer-term securities compared with those from short-term securities. Particularly hot were funds focusing on the securities of the federal government and the Government National Mortgage Association. But as go the markets, so go the funds. During the week of Black Monday (October 19, 1987), a lot of investors bailed out of mutual funds; more than $8 billion was diverted into money markets alone.

HOW FUNDS WORK

The industry is made up of investment companies that sell shares in one or more mutual funds, each of which simply consists of a pool of financial assets. Investors buy shares and get the benefits (or share the losses) of how the collective securities perform. Fund shares, which rise and fall depending upon the value of the assets, are sold publicly and are redeemable anytime. Because funds closely follow the market, investors gamble on the canniness of the fund manager to make the fund perform well. The manager determines the makeup of the fund portfolio, or assets, which can consist of stocks, bonds, gold, government securities, or whatever else falls within the fund's stated purpose. For example, bond funds are made up mostly of corporate or municipal bonds and are meant to provide regular income rather than growth. Income funds have the same goal as bond funds but include in their portfolios high-interest or dividend-paying government securities, common and preferred stock, and bonds. Equity-fund portfolios are made up primarily of common stocks and are meant to provide growth rather than dividends. Money-market mutual funds are made up of short-term market vehicles such as commercial paper, federal government securities, and bank certificates of deposit. Short-term municipal bond funds are like money-market funds but their investments are mostly tax-exempt municipal securities.

THE PLAYERS

In the 1980s, there were hundreds of funds and more popping up all the time. Sometimes it seems as if there's one for just about everybody and maybe there is. Some funds' assets, for instance, are energy company stocks; others buy only stocks in companies headquartered in a particular state, such as Ohio, or a specific country, say, Germany. Then there have been proposals for Muslim and cemetery company funds, and a junk-bond fund for nonresident aliens. Still others reflect a heightened social conscience. (See the box on page 329.) Investors can buy shares from a lot of different sources: brokerage houses, insurance agencies, financial planners, unions, and even retailers. In 1986, the department store chain K mart started offering funds at outlets in New Jersey. For years, Merrill Lynch's funds comprised the biggest group, but the most noteworthy is the maverick Fidelity Investments, now the largest family of funds and undoubtedly one of the most aggressive. (See the profile on page 330.)

TRENDS

The old saw about the past being a predictor of the future is what analysts generally cling to when talking about where mutual funds are going. As goes the market, so go most funds. Even with the tax changes knocking out a lot of IRA money that would have gone into mutual funds, the industry is expected to thrive and become more competitive over the next few years. With marketing efforts being stepped up by a lot of funds, a proliferation of specialized funds, and more retailers and others reaching out for customers, increasing numbers of individual investors are expected to open accounts. Moreover, trusts, pension funds, and other institutions are expected to continue turning to the funds, especially money-market funds, for liquidity or investments. Increased regulation, of course, can have a major impact on the industry. If banks, for instance, are allowed to sponsor and sell mutual-fund shares, competition will be hotter than ever. Money-market funds may become less enticing if reserve requirements that would reduce their yields are imposed. Nonetheless, the federal Office of Service Industries concludes that if there are no dramatic regulatory changes, "the mutual fund industry will grow at a strong rate over the next few years."

"ETHICAL" FUNDS

There are mutual funds for people who want to see their funds do good as well as do well. More than $50 billion is believed to be invested in funds with specific ethical considerations as the hallmark of their portfolios. One reason for the boom is state and city employees who say they want their pension funds invested in such a fashion. The practice isn't brand new, having become especially noticeable in the 1940s when union and government-agency fund managers wouldn't invest in companies with what they regarded as unfair labor records. Today, one of the major considerations of such funds is the elimination of apartheid in South Africa; other concerns include the environment, housing, nuclear power, and medical-care and weapons expenditures. Few funds agree, though, on precisely what is or is not "socially responsible" investing.

Probably the best known such funds were formed in the 1970s—Calvert Social Investment, Dreyfus Third Century, and Pax World. Calvert invests in stocks of companies in the businesses of protecting the environment and providing renewable energy applications while shunning weapon makers and those engaged in nuclear power or with South African holdings. Dreyfus seeks out firms with environmental concerns and enforcers of strong quality and occupational safety codes. Pax World invests in food, housing, and medical-care companies while steering clear of gambling, liquor, tobacco, and weapons companies.

Do the ethical funds pay off other than in psychic soothing? The answer is yes—at least sometimes. "Ethical" fund managers don't get off the hook just because their portfolios purport to carry extra moral weight. A survey of such funds by Lipper Analytical Securities Corporation showed in 1985 that they produced an average yield of 25.24% compared to the average fund's yield of 24.95%. "No one wants to invest in anything that's morally irresponsible," a municipal union official told *Financial World*. "But people want to make money. You won't get that many do-gooders to invest if they can't make a fair return."

Fidelity Investments   In 1946 Edward C. Johnson II, a Harvard-educated lawyer, took over management of a privately held, Boston-based mutual fund that apparently was on its last legs. One of the oldest mutual fund organizations in the nation, Fidelity had barely $3 million in assets. A cool, aloof man, Johnson—"Mister Johnson" to his employees—broke a pattern of investing in blue chips. Instead, he sought out strong stocks with the potential for good growth. The strategy paid off. Twenty years later, Fidelity had $4 billion more in assets and the company's tough relentlessness earned it the sobriquet "the Green Bay Packers of the fund league" in Adam Smith's *The Money Game*. By early 1988, Fidelity had assets of about $85 billion.

Today, Fidelity is still based in Boston and still privately held but is now run by the Mister's son, Edward C. III. More than ever, the company is known for its aggressiveness, innovativeness, and enviable track record. But after the stock market collapse in October 1987, the company faced tough challenges. The public became discouraged with mutual funds. Fidelity's sales pace was cut in half. And many customers were disappointed in the service during the market meltdown.

Fidelity has under its umbrella more than 100 portfolio funds compared with the fewer than a dozen held by most companies. Fidelity, for instance, has funds that specialize in turnaround companies, high-growth opportunities, out-of-favor issues, and over-the-counter stocks. One of the company's more controversial innovations was its sector funds, which have been compared to roulette wheels because they can be played 32 different ways. Rather than diversifying by buying stocks in different industries, Fidelity urged investors in sector funds to put all their shares in an industry they thought would do well and then switch to another industry when they thought the time was ripe.

Well before the competition, Fidelity invested heavily and smartly in advertising, technology, and a big support staff. It spent $50 million a year or so promoting its funds, more money than Anheuser-Busch has shelled out for its Bud Light TV campaign. And it had a huge service operation. Put in place a decade ago, it consisted by 1987, for example, of a sales and service force of 400 in Boston, a 650-person operation in Dallas, and a 100-person office in Salt Lake City. Even so, customers reported lengthy delays during the market panic as they tried to make changes in their holdings.

The delays were surprising because the telephone network had handled more than a call a second 24 hours a day. On the April 15, 1986, deadline for opening a tax-deductible IRA, Fidelity had a staggering 140,000 phone calls (double the usual number) and signed up an incredible 50,000 new accounts. In addition, Fidelity funds were pushed through a network of 36 discount brokerage houses as well as banks, and after having stopped dealing with unaffiliated brokers in the late 1970s, the company dealt with them again. Moreover, Fidelity continued pouring money into staff and technology to maintain its momentum. For instance, its street-level Investor Centers, where customers buy funds, trade stocks, or get money from their accounts, were supposed to be within an hour's drive of many people making $50,000 or more a year. By 1990, Fidelity expected them to be within an hour's reach of 92% of that sought-after group.

Fidelity's legions of fund managers and security analysts visited some 10,000 U.S. and overseas companies annually. Analysts were recruited fresh out of business school so that Fidelity's way of doing business was the only one they learned. They measured their results on a daily basis against how the stocks in their groups performed in the market. Within a year or so an analyst might be assigned to manage a portfolio of stocks within a certain industry, an opportunity that eluded many an analyst elsewhere for decades.

In recent years, some of the portfolio managers did very well and Fidelity went out of its way to advertise its winners. But others didn't perform as well and Fidelity didn't carve out a piece of its whopping ad budget to call attention to the mediocre to poorly performing funds. "On the average, they were average to above average," A. Michael Lipper, president of Lipper Analytical Securities, of Fidelity's overall performance, said before the stock market crashed in October 1987.

What Fidelity had was the amazing Peter Lynch and his amazing Magellan Fund. The spectacular performance of this fund, the best track record of any mutual fund over the past decade, tended to lend a magic to all of Fidelity's funds. Lynch's strategy sounded pretty simple. His 1,500-stock portfolio was largely made up of three categories: companies that were not doing very well but that potentially would do better, small profitable companies growing bigger, and undervalued companies with a wealth in assets. Magellan, however, had gotten so enormous (some $9 billion in total assets before the market crash in 1987) that it had some trouble outperforming stock market averages. But Fidelity wasn't banking on Lynch's Magellan to hit all its home runs. "We have so many funds, the odds are in our favor that we should have another doing very well," an executive noted.

Chapter Twenty-Two
INSURANCE

HIGHLIGHTS AND TRENDS

Insurance is really our "insecurity security." The market touches on just about everything from being out of work to losing everything in a flood. Dancers get their legs insured, ski resorts insure their slopes, and companies get their boards insured—when they can. No wonder. The thought of not being insured against just about every accident, stupid decision, or freak of nature can make one tremble. The cost of motor-vehicle accidents alone is some $76 billion a year. Robberies, burglaries, larcenies, and motor-vehicle thefts result in another $11 billion a year in losses. Fires consume an estimated $7.75 billion annually in property losses. The list goes on.

What it all means is that insurance is obviously big business. But it hasn't been a very good one. Property and casualty carriers had record underwriting losses in 1985, resulting in a sharp drop in the availability and affordability of some classes of liability insurance and raising a clamor for a change in the liability system. The industry, though, has had a big hand in creating its own problems. Lured by the sky-high interest rates of the first half of the decade, a lot of property and casualty insurers abandoned their traditionally conservative underwriting practices and pumped premium money into high-interest investments. The result for a while was investment earnings that more than offset the flood of red ink that hit the insurance-writing business. But don't weep for underwriters. During the 10 years from 1976 to 1985, the property and casualty insurance industry lost about $81.3 billion on underwriting but earned $119.8 billion on investment income.

Only since 1986, after being devastated from the late 1970s by ferocious competition, exorbitant civil-damage awards, plunging premiums, and other problems, has the insurance industry shown signs of perking up. Moving further into the personal-finance business, insurers have acquired several brokerage houses and developed new investment-oriented life insurance products. Also, some life and health insurers acquired hospitals and other health-care providers.

INTERNATIONALIZATION OF THE MARKETPLACE

Insurers are part of the increasing internationalization of financial services. By the beginning of 1986, 22 U.S. life insurance companies were owned by foreign-based corporations, a trend that is expected to continue. For their part, U.S. life insurance companies are making their presence felt abroad; life, health, and annuity premiums from operations abroad totaled $1.2 billion in 1985. While such income at this time is small, it is still greater than the life insurance income generated by 27 of the 50 states.

THE MONEY

Life insurance purchases in 1987 exceeded $1.5 trillion, with sales of ordinary life insurance accounting for some three quarters of that. Life insurance in force totaled $6,940 billion in 1987, up 5% from a year earlier. The average value of insurance owned by insured families was $74,600. Benefit payments, excluding health insurance, were $80 billion in 1987, up 9.6% from a year earlier. Payments to beneficiaries totaled $18.2 billion. About $27 billion was paid to life insurance policyholders and $21.3 billion to people receiving annuities, up 8.8% over 1984.

In the property and casualty segment of the business, after five years of intense competition in commercial lines, rates began to increase in mid-1984 and continued through 1987. The net value of premiums written rose to $214.0 billion in 1987 from $118.2 billion in 1984. Despite premium increases in some lines of insurance, the property and casualty insurance business sustained record underwriting losses in 1985 for the fifth consecutive year. With investment income failing for the second year in a row to offset the underwriting deficit, the industry recorded a pretax operating loss of $5.3 billion. But earnings improved dramatically in 1986. After tax credits and capital gains from the sale of assets, the industry ended 1986 with net income of $13 billion and increased this to about $14 billion in 1987.

THE PLAYERS

There are more than 5,700 insurance companies in the U.S., with assets in excess of $1.13 trillion. Some 3,500 are property and casualty insurance carriers and about 900 of them write most of the business; no one company, however, has more than 10% of the market. The biggest life insurance company in the U.S. is Prudential with assets of $91.14 billion, while the largest property and casualty insurance group is State Farm with assets of $23.78 billion.

THE PEOPLE

About 2 million people are employed by the industry and that number is growing steadily. The vast majority, some 1.3 million, are home office personnel. Life insurance carriers employ the greatest number of people, about 560,000 of the total. Health insurers employ about 170,000 and property and casualty insurers employ some 475,000. The remainder are agents, brokers, and sevice personnel.

LIFE INSURANCE

About 65% of the U.S. population is covered by life insurance. Ordinary life insurance totaling $3.3 billion represents 54% of all life insurance. Group life insurance accounts for 42% of life coverage. Annual income now payable or committed to be paid is more than $23.9 billion.

Life insurance carriers in the U.S. are divided into two types of companies: stock companies (those owned by shareholders) and mutual life insurance companies (those owned by policyholders). Like others in the insurance industry, life insurance carriers are worried about the long-term prospect of banks moving into their line of business, either by direct underwriting or by acquiring insurance companies. To hedge against what strikes many insurers as the inevitability of such competition as well as to find new markets, life insurance carriers have introduced such innovative products as variable life insurance, which gives policyholders the opportunity to earn capital gains on their insurance investment; universal life insurance, which combines the low-cost protection of term insurance with a savings portion that is invested in a tax-deferred account earning money-market interest rates; and flexible premium variable life insurance, which contains elements of both variable and the universal insurance. Life insurers have also entered the real estate market and financing.

PROPERTY AND CASUALTY INSURANCE

After cutthroat competition from 1979 to 1984, when companies fought for premiums to pump into high-yield investments, premiums started to rise and continued to rise in 1987. (Industry investments at the end of 1986 stood at $282 billion, up from $60 billion in 1972.) In 1987, the property and casualty business had a net income of about $14 billion, compared with $13 billion for the same period a year earlier.

Meanwhile, there continue to be insurance availability problems. The areas include pollution, day-care, municipal, earthquake, liquor, motor-carrier, and corporate directors' and officers' liability insurance. Some of the problems are the result of bankruptcy by some specialty insurers, especially in liquor and motor-carrier liability. Affordability problems have hit the space satellite industry and parts of the medical community, including nurse-midwives. Insurance adequacy problems have abated for many businesses, except pharmaceutical companies and businesses dealing with hazardous waste.

Aware of the problems, more than 40 states have passed tort reform measures that reduce liability exposure in the expectation of making insurance cheaper and more available for businesses, professionals, government groups, and nonprofit organizations. The insurance industry is banking that federal legislation will further ease the situation.

Table 91   The 10 Biggest Insurance Companies
(by assets, 1986)

U.S.	World
1. Prudential	1. Prudential
2. Metropolitan Life	2. Metropolitan
3. Aetna	3. Nippon Life
4. Equitable Life	4. Aetna
5. CIGNA	5. Equitable Life
6. Travelers	6. Dai-Ichi Mutual
7. New York Life	7. CIGNA
8. Teachers Insurance	8. Travelers
9. John Hancock	9. Sumitomo Life
10. State Farm Mutual	10. Prudential Corporation (U.K.)

Source: Various press accounts.

OUTLOOK

As the distinction between insurers and other segments of the financial-services industry blurs, insurers will have to continue coming up with more products. More joint ventures and acquisitions in the financial-services areas are likely. Many analysts expect that sooner or later banks will be able to engage in insurance activities and insurance companies will engage in banking activities.

INSURANCE BROKERS

There are some 500 insurance brokers in the U.S., with the top 20 companies handling more than 70% of the insurance brokered in the U.S. The total brokerage business in 1987 was estimated to be at least $6.6 billion. The two largest brokers are Marsh & McLennan, with net income in 1986 of $129.7 million on revenue of $897.6 million, and Alexander & Alexander, with net income of $41.7 million on revenues of $519 million.

Table 92   The 10 Costliest Fires in the U.S.

The San Francisco fire of 1906 was the costliest in the U.S. The estimated loss at the time was $350 million but, in 1982 dollars, that was equal to $3.5 billion.

Rank	Date	Place	Property destroyed	Estimated loss (dollars)
1.	April 18, 1906	San Francisco	28,000 buildings	350,000,000
2.	October 8–10, 1871	Chicago	17,340 buildings	175,000,000
3.	November 12, 1984	Tinker AFB, Oklahoma	Jet engine repair facility	138,000,000
4.	July 23, 1984	Romeoville, Illinois	Oil refinery	100,000,000
5.	June 6, 1982	Falls Township, Pennsylvania	Retail distribution center	100,000,000
6.	November 25, 1982	Minneapolis	Bank building	91,000,000
7.	November 9, 1872	Boston	776 buildings	75,000,000
8.	September 1, 1979	Deer Park, Texas	Tank ship	70,000,000
9.	November 28, 1981	Lynn, Massachusetts	31 buildings	70,000,000
10.	April 16, 1947	Texas City, Texas	Waterfront industrial area	67,000,000

Source: Insurance Information Institute.

Table 93   The 10 Costliest U.S. Civil Disorders

Rioting in Miami, Florida, in May 1980 resulted in the costliest insured losses on record stemming from civil disorders. Of the ten costliest, all except the one in Miami and a disturbance in New York City resulting from a massive power outage were racial riots in the 1960s.

Rank	Date	Location	Estimated loss (dollars)
1.	May 17–19, 1980	Miami	65,250,000
2.	August 11–17, 1965	Los Angeles	44,000,000
3.	July 23, 1967	Detroit	41,500,000
4.	July 13–14, 1977	New York City	28,000,000
5.	April 4–9, 1968	Washington, D.C.	24,000,000
6.	July 12, 1967	Newark	15,000,000
7.	April 6–9, 1968	Baltimore	14,000,000
8.	April 4–11, 1968	Chicago	13,000,000
9.	April 4–11, 1968	New York City	4,200,000
10.	April 4–11, 1968	Pittsburgh	2,000,000

Source: Insurance Information Institute.

HISTORY

The earliest known insurance seems to date back to Babylonian days, when ships were insured. In the fourth millenium there were "bottomry" contracts, which insured ships and didn't have to be paid back if the ships went down.

In ancient Rome, there was burial insurance in effect through burial societies that paid their members' funeral costs from monthly dues.

It wasn't until the Great Fire of London in 1666 that fire insurance became widespread. Some 14,000 buildings were destroyed and 200,000 people were left homeless. During the same century, as a result of gatherings of shippers and insurers at Edward Lloyd's coffee shop, Lloyd's of London started as an organized group of underwriters accepting maritime risks.

Insurance came to the New World in 1735 when a short-lived fire insurance company was founded. The first to succeed was the Philadelphia Contributorship, or "Hand in Hand" as it was known, which was started in 1752 by Benjamin Franklin. The first life insurance company, the Corporation for Relief of Distressed Presbyterian Ministers and of the Poor and Distressed Widows and Children of Presbyterian Ministers, was established in 1759 in Philadelphia.

Life insurance agents came into existence in 1830 when the New York Life Insurance and Trust Company was formed and began employing the first such agents. By 1869 there were so many of them that they formed their first organization.

Introduction of the automobile was swiftly followed by car insurance. The first auto liability policy was issued in 1887 to Gilbert Loomis of Westfield, Connecticut. The cost was $7.50 per $1,000 of liability.

The first group life insurance for employees was started in 1911. In 1917, life insurance for World War I servicemen was offered by the government under the War Risk Insurance Act. In 1940, legislation providing insurance for World War II service personnel was enacted by Congress, and in 1965, as a result of the Vietnam War, the insurance was provided again.

The Social Security Act was enacted in 1935. Amended at various times, the act provided benefits for survivors and dependents and for disabled workers and their dependents. It also was amended so it covered more jobs, lowered the minimum retirement age, revised contribution schedules, increased the earnings base, and in 1965, established Medicare, a health insurance program for people 65 and over.

WORKER'S COMPENSATION

Worker's compensation goes back to the 17th-century pirates, who recognized hazardous duty when they saw it.

A typical buccaneer comp schedule called for payment of 100 pieces of eight and a slave for the loss of an eye; 400 and four slaves for a left leg; 500 and four slaves for a left arm or right leg; and 600 and six slaves for a right arm. Anybody who lost a hand was out of luck. He was expected to have it replaced by a hook, which was actually considered something of an advantage because it made a good tool.

PERILS

Watch out for perils. Most property insurance policies exclude losses caused by certain perils, including rebellion, civil war, and enemy attack.

TYPES OF LIFE INSURANCE

Adjustable allows the policyholder to shift back and forth between term and whole life insurance and even to change the premium amounts paid for the policy.

Endowment insures a life for a certain period of time, such as 20 or 30 years, or to a certain age, such as 65. If the insured lives to the end of the time period, he or she receives the face amount of the policy. Essentially a savings plan as much as insurance, it gives less coverage than term or whole life insurance for the same price.

Term covers the insured for a specific time period. It requires the policyholder to pay only for the cost of protection against death. Because it usually does not build up an investment fund or have a cash value at the end of the period, premiums are lower than for whole life or endowment insurance.

Universal separates the cost of term insurance from the investment value of the policy. The cash value of the policy is set up as a fund that earns investment income, which is drawn on for the cost of term insurance. The policy is flexible in that as age and income change, a policyholder can increase or decrease premium payments and coverage or shift a portion of premiums into a savings account without penalty.

Variable lets the insured choose from among several ways of investing the value of the policy, such as common stocks or other potentially high-yielding investments. To reflect the rise or fall of the investment's performance, this insurance often comes with provisions for changes in policy cash values and death benefits.

Whole offers protection in case the insured dies and also builds up cash value. Premiums can be paid in a lump sum at the beginning of the contract, over a limited period such as 10 or 20 years, or throughout the life of the insured. This insurance typically yields a cash value that can be used as a security for borrowing or that can be taken as a cash payment at a certain age. Premiums are much higher than for term insurance.

KIDNAPPING

The 1932 kidnapping-murder of Charles A. Lindbergh, Jr., the 20-month-old son of the famous aviator, led to a new kind of insurance—kidnap and ransom insurance. Such policies reimburse ransom or extortion payments up to a certain limit, usually $1 million. Today, such policies are usually taken out by companies on key executives. Payments may now also cover rewards and other expenses, such as the interest on bank loans taken to raise the ransom. Such policies may also cover damage done by an extortionist as a means of coercion, such as contamination of a food product. The policy would cover any product recall as well as damages from the contamination.

LLOYD'S OF LONDON

Most folks contemplating sophisticated, big-time insurers think of Lloyd's of London. But Lloyd's isn't an insurance company in the usual sense but a marketplace with individual underwriting members. As a corporation, Lloyd's doesn't issue policies but sets standards for its members. Actual policies are prepared by Lloyd's Policy Signing Office but signed by individuals who will share in any losses. Worldwide, Lloyd's is organized into several hundred syndicates, each having from several to more than 500 participants. An underwriter manages each syndicate, determining which of the insurance applications brokers submit should be accepted. Americans involved with Lloyd's are primarily buyers of reinsurance, which is sharing the risk for part of the premium fee paid by the insured. Reinsurance allows insurers to take on clients whose coverage would be too great a burden for one insurer to carry.

Chapter Twenty-Three
PENSIONS

HIGHLIGHTS AND TRENDS

Remember all the talk about letting everybody stay on the job beyond age 70? It conjured up visions of vast legions crying in their beer at having to get out of the rat race as they approached their 65th birthdays. Well, maybe some folks do, but the reality is that about 70% of all employees quit work before age 65, about twice as many as in the mid-1970s.

A big reason is pensions, which, when combined with Social Security benefits, give a lot of folks an alternative to work. (In 1984, average monthly pensions for those with 30 years of service at age 65 ranged from $385 for those who had earned $15,000 a year to $886 for those who had earned $40,000. Employees with 20 years of service received $263 to $623, respectively.)

After climbing for 30 years, the number of Americans with pension coverage declined in 1985 to 43% from 45% in 1981, the Employee Benefit Research Institute reported. Moreover, the 65-and-older population is expected to double by the year 2010, thus adding to the strains on and uncertainty of Social Security (See the chapter "Social Security.") What all this means is that pension plans will increasingly be of greater importance to Americans.

THE MONEY

There is a lot of money in pensions, but the amount being placed in them is diminishing. Employee benefit assets of just the nation's 1,000 biggest pension funds for the year ended September 30, 1986, soared 24.8% to $1.339 trillion from a year earlier, according to the authoritative *Pensions & Investment Age*. Before the market crash in October 1987 they were approaching $2 trillion. Since plan contributions have been contracting and benefit payments rising, *P&I* puts most of the growth down to investment returns. In 1986, the S&P 500 returned 31.8%, for instance, and the Shearson Lehman Government/Corporate Bond Index returned 20.7%.

Of *P&I*'s top 200 funds, corporate funds showed the smallest increase—15.2%, to $445.9 billion. That reflected a downturn in contributions, but it also showed how mergers, acquisitions, and terminations of overfunded plans had thinned their ranks. Twelve company funds dropped out of the 200 while only four corporate funds moved into the ranking, leaving 108 corporate funds among the 200.

The top union funds among the 200 saw their assets jump 73% to $36 billion from $20.8 billion. The phenomenal growth reflected, in part, the fact that three new union funds joined the 200 inner circle, bringing to 10 the number of union funds among that elite group.

Assets of the 11 miscellaneous funds among the 200, such as the World Bank, United Nations, and church funds, were $94 billion, up 50.9%. The 71 public funds in the group increased to $435.9 billion, up 27.3%.

THE PLAYERS

Cashing in on the lucrative portfolio-management business is the business of those who bill themselves as investment advisers. Fifteen years ago, the breed was hard to come by. Now, of course, they're breeding like jackrabbits. The Securities and Exchange Commission calculates that at least 300 new ones go into the business every month, and that meant more than 15,000 of them for 1988. Thus, as the flow of pension dollars winds down, the competition to get those dollars is greater than ever.

Even so, the biggest—and usually those who have been around the longest—wind up managing the mostest. As of January 1, 1986, the 100 biggest money managers had total assets under their belts of about $1.5 trillion. Insurance companies and their subsidiaries had 38%, banks and trust companies and their subsidiaries 36%, and independents 26%. For instance, Wells Fargo Investment Advisors of San Francisco managed about $30 billion in 1986, while Pacific Investment Management Company of Newport Beach, California, managed $10 billion and Lehman Management Company of New York managed $9.5 billion. (For the 10 biggest investment advisers see Table 94, page 342.)

HISTORY

The nation's first pension plan was established in 1759 for widows and children of Presbyterian ministers. A century later, the first pension plan covering workers was created for retired New York City policemen. Before 1930, only about 15% of nonfarm U.S. workers were covered by pension plans. Now nearly half are covered.

TYPES OF PENSION PLANS

There are two major types of pension plans: single-employer plans, which are usually established by the employer, and multiemployer plans, which usually cover union workers and are set up by the workers and the union as a result of collective bargaining.

Defined contribution plans: The employer pays a specific amount—a percentage of salary or profits—into a pension fund. Employees may also make voluntary or mandatory contributions. The payments accumulate with investment and interest earnings in separate participant accounts.

Defined benefit plans: The benefit is determined in advance based on a benefit formula, such as payment for each year of service, or a percentage of annual salary, or average earnings over a specified number of years.

Profit-sharing plans: Employees share in an employer's profits and thus have an incentive for increased productivity. Profit-sharing plans provide supplemental income to employees and their families at death, disability, retirement, or employment termination.

401(k) cash or deferred arrangement plan: A 401(k) plan lets an employee place a portion of his or her compensation in a profit-sharing, stock bonus, or pension plan and the employee defers income tax until the money is withdrawn.

Individual retirement accounts: These were established by Congress in 1974 for workers who did not have employer-sponsored pension plans. In 1981 they were expanded to cover all U.S. workers who wanted to set aside up to $2,000 a year (the limit was $4,000 for a working couple and $2,250 for a worker with a nonworking spouse) on a tax-deferred basis. The 1986 tax law limits IRA deductions to those who aren't covered by employer-paid pension plans. All taxpayers may contribute to IRAs and have dividends and interest accumulate tax-free.

Rollovers: Individuals can roll over account balances from one IRA to another and from a qualified employer's pension plan to an IRA. To avoid tax penalties, the transfer of assets from one account to another must be done within 60 days.

Keoghs: Keogh plans are for employees of unincorporated businesses or self-employed people. The maximum that may be invested each year in such a pension plan depends on income but can be up to $30,000.

Table 94 Top Investment Manager

Top managers overall		Top equity managers		Top bond managers	
Manager	# funds using	Manager	# funds using	Manager	# funds using
J.P. Morgan	62	Alliance	34	Pacific Investment	28
Prudential	57	Capital Guardian	32	J.P. Morgan	23
Bankers Trust	52	Wells Fargo	26	Criterion	14
Aetna	45	Bankers Trust	24	Loomis, Sayles	13
TCW	44	Mellon	19	Lehman	12
		Delaware	19	MacKay-Shields	12
				Miller, Anderson & Sherrerd	12

Source: *Pension & Investment Age,* January 25, 1988.

Table 95 Top 10 Pension Funds by Assets

1. TIAA-CREF — $66.2 billion
2. California Employees' Retirement Systems — 44.0 billion
3. General Motors — 40.0 billion
4. New York State Common Retirement Fund — 38.7 billion
5. AT&T — 37.5 billion
6. New York City Retirement Systems — 33.6 billion
7. General Electric Pension Trust — 27.3 billion
8. California State Teachers' Retirement System — 23.7 billion
9. New York State Teachers' Retirement System — 23.0 billion
10. IBM Retirement Plan — 22.5 billion

Source: *Pension & Investment Age,* January 25, 1988.

Table 96 Largest union funds
($ millions)

Fund	Assets
Teamsters, Central	8,482
Western Teamsters	7,524
UMWA	4,825
Nat'l Electrical Contractors	2,770
Boilermaker Blacksmith	2,230
Bakery & Confectionery	2,000
Hospital/Health Care	1,797
Int'l Operating Engineers	1,718
Plumbers, National	1,599
Southern California UFCW	1,463
IAM Nat'l Pension Fund	1,454
Teamsters, New England	1,392
TOTAL	**37,254**

Source: *Pension & Investment Age,* January 25, 1988.

Chapter Twenty-Four
SOCIAL SECURITY

HIGHLIGHTS AND TRENDS

People keep predicting bankruptcy for the Social Security system. Seems logical, right? After all, in the mid-1970s Social Security began paying out more than it took in. (Contributions between 1973 and 1983 grew at a 12% annual rate but benefits increased at a 13% annual rate.) But what happened? Big rate increases. That will most likely be the pattern from here on in. As recently as 1963, the maximum Social Security tax was $174 a year. In the 1970s the maximum was $895 a year. Today it's more than triple that amount ($3,379.50), and while politicians seldom mention it, Social Security had a surplus of $46.9 billion at the end of 1986. The Congressional Budget Office projected a total surplus between 1987 and 1992 of $287 billion.

Most people think of Social Security as retirement insurance and that's the way we'll treat it here. But it also includes survivors insurance, disability insurance, Medicare for the aged and disabled, black lung benefits, Supplemental Security Income, unemployment compensation, and public assistance and welfare services.

Congress has also bolstered the plan by upping the eligibility requirements. By 1990, people will have to work 10 years, up from 8.5, to become eligible. Moreover, early retirement benefits are gradually decreasing, while the age at which anyone can receive full retirement benefits will rise to 67 by the year 2022. Also, high-income people on Social Security have been paying taxes on benefits since 1984.

The big problem, however, lies with today's young workers. Right now there are 3.4 employed people shelling out Social Security money to support each retiree. That will decrease to 2 workers slaving away to support one retiree. And unless someone figures out a reasonable solution, the doomsayers may not be too far off the mark. But it will be the work force that goes bankrupt trying to keep Social Security from going bankrupt. When the system started, there were few payouts. The average U.S. male industrial worker died at age 62.

HOW IS SOCIAL SECURITY FUNDED?

Social Security is a pay-as-you-go operation. The taxes collected each year are intended to cover benefits and administrative costs paid out that year and to provide a small amount as a contingency fund. The tax rate for employees and employers for 1988–1989 is 7.51% and that will go to 7.65% in 1990. The maximum taxable earnings of $39,600 will increase as well.

Self-employed people pay higher tax rates since they don't have employers to share the tax load. The self-employed tax rate of 14.10% in 1985 will increase to 15.3% by 1990.

Chapter Twenty-Five

REAL ESTATE

HIGHLIGHTS AND TRENDS

Commercial

For the past few years, the market for commercial real estate has been in its worst shape since the Depression. By 1987, office building vacancies topped 16% in downtown areas and 23% in the suburbs. The reason: oversaturation. The 1980s saw the greatest construction boom of the century. From 1981 to 1987, some 300 million square feet of office space was built each year, enough for five Manhattans. Even with the 18% interest rates of the early 1980s, money didn't stay away. Pension funds, insurance companies, banks, syndicators, and foreigners threw cash into commercial real-estate ventures as if there was no tomorrow. Wall Streeters packaged properties into real estate partnerships, investment trusts, and zero-coupon real estate bonds. "If it's flat, develop it," the saying went. Then most developers shuddered and saw what an ill-conceived boom it was. With few exceptions, office rents in cities that support skyscrapers dropped 25% to 40%. Even places once thought immune to real estate recession, such as San Francisco, Chicago, Salt Lake City, Phoenix, and Dallas, suffered. By 1987, the nation's top 15 cities had an average commercial vacancy rate of about 16%, or quadruple what it was in 1981. The rates ranged from a high of about 36% in Austin to a low of just over 9% in Boston. Even the rate in New York, which was faring relatively well at about 10%, didn't look so good when compared with the mere 2% in vacancies it had in 1981.

The reasons aren't hard to find. The oil industry's problems obviously hurt markets in the southwest, but, more to the point, sharply lower inflation hit a lot of developers hard across the nation. Many of them had continued building with the same abandon they had in the 1970s when they could bank on inflation outstripping their costs. Another factor is the new tax law, which makes it tougher to carry high-vacancy buildings. Also, a lot of those Wall Street real estate packages were based on fantasy accounting when it came to appraisals, inflation expectations, projected occupancy rates, and rent rolls. Solving the overcapacity problem will take years.

Housing

Residential real estate's prospects look robust compared with those in the commercial market. Still, whatever happened to the hot housing market that economists were predicting? Sure there are megabuck people lined up in Beverly Hills and Bel Air itching to drop $20 million for fancy digs and others willing to pay $2 million or so for houses they tear down and replace with something more to their liking. But what about the rest of Americans? The economists' scenario went like this: As mortgage rates drifted down from their 15% peak in 1981 and hit 10%, the market would go crazy. Starts would hit 2 million or so, matching or bettering starts in the 1970s. Well, the magic 10% came and sure enough there was a spurt but it petered out. The more sober 1987 estimate for housing starts was about 1.85 million and 1.8 million for 1988, neither coming close to the anticipated boom.

The major reason is that the decline in mortgage rates wasn't that dramatic. Indeed, after discounting for inflation, mortgage rates actually rose over the last few years. Also, household formations, which are what really drive housing demand, fell to about one million in 1986, down 600,000 from a year earlier. Another big problem, of course, is the cost of housing these days. In many instances, price increases offset the gains from more favorable mortgage rates. After all, the price of an average house has risen to $123,300, which is out of the reach of a lot of average Americans. But talking average costs is often talking nonsense. Trends in housing prices have always been regional. An eight-room condo in Manhattan bought for $500,000 in 1981 fetches over $1 million today, while a $600,000 hacienda bought in Houston at the same time is now worth about $200,000 less. And a $400,000 château in Mobile bought in 1981 is still worth about $400,000.

Hotels

The outlook is as bleak as it is for office buildings. Nonetheless, 80,000 new hotel rooms came on stream in 1986 while the occupancy rate fell below 65%—and that at a time when the break-even point rose to about 67%.

Shopping Centers

From 1984 to 1987, nearly as much money was spent constructing shopping centers as was spent constructing office buildings. Most of the problem properties are in the smaller strip centers along U.S. highways.

TRIVIA

• The Manhattan office market—the largest in the U.S.—consists of some 215 million square feet of space.

- With 55,000 hotel rooms, Orlando, Florida, home of Walt Disney World, ranks after only New York and Los Angeles in terms of such accommodations.
- The $250-million-a-year business of leasing furnished offices is nothing new, but lately major companies such as GTE and ITT find it cheaper to lease than to set up small branch offices for a few people. Support services include everything from telecopiers to secretaries.
- Americans spend more than $80 billion a year fixing up their properties. Painting is the leading expenditure with roofing coming next.
- Regional differences in "nice neighborhoods" makes a tremendous difference in housing prices—some $400,000. A survey by Better Homes and Gardens Real Estate Service determined that the average price of a three-bedroom home in a desirable neighborhood ranges from $475,000 in Wilton, Connecticut, down to $62,000 in Knoxville, Tennessee.

BRAINY BUILDINGS

Computers are making buildings smart. (Some of them, anyway.) The wedding of architecture and high tech has resulted in elevators that tell passengers in a soothing voice not only that they are going up or down but what the weather is like. Lights go on in offices when someone walks in and they shut off soon after the person leaves. Doors are monitored to see whether they are locked, and temperatures are monitored for the right temperateness. Lobby directories not only cross-reference companies and employees but some offer everything from calendars of sports and art events to airport maps and public-transportation guides. Some smart buildings: One Financial Plaza, Chicago; CityPalace, Hartford; Grand Financial Plaza, Los Angeles. Analysts see the market growing to $3 billion a year by 1990, when there could be more than 1,500 brainy buildings in the U.S.

THE FIRST SKYSCRAPER

The first skyscraper? Until lately, Chicago's nine-story Home Insurance Company Building in Chicago held the title. Now that's disputed. For decades, the building was considered the first of all the tall buildings held up by a skeleton of steel columns and beams rather than massive masonry walls, thus qualifying it as the first skyscraper. Now it turns out that Home Insurance was given the title by a powerful group of Chicago architects who were out to cheat Minneapolis architect Leroy S. Buffington, the patent holder on building skeletal-framed big buildings. To avoid paying royalty fees and to break the patent, the Chicago architects discredited Buffington. Instead of one of Buffington's buildings, they nominated the Home Insurance Company Building as the first innovative high building. When poor Buffington proposed a breathtaking "cloudscraper" 28 stories high, he was met with derision. Now nobody seems sure what to designate as the first skyscraper.

Table 97   Japanese Investment in U.S. Real Estate

Building	Acquirer	Estimated price (millions of dollars)
Arco Plaza, Los Angeles	Shuwa Investment Corporation	640
Hyatt Regency Waikiki Hotel, Honolulu	Azabu USA Corporation	245
ABC Building, New York	Shuwa Investment Corporation	165
Manufacturers Life of Canada, Los Angeles (50% interest)	Nomura Real Estate Development Company	120
Citicorp Center, San Francisco	Dai-Ichi Mutual Life Insurance Company	100
Essex House, New York	Nikko Hotels, Nippon Life Insurance Company, and Shimizu	100

JAPANESE REAL ESTATE INVESTMENT

Canadians remain the biggest foreign owners of U.S. real estate, but the Japanese will soon surpass them if they continue buying the way they have for the past few years. While Americans complained about sky-rocketing real estate costs, the strong yen made U.S. properties a bargain that sent Japanese scrambling into the U.S. market. The Japanese, for instance, own about a quarter of downtown Los Angeles. (Half of downtown L.A. is owned by foreigners, as well as 39% of Houston's office space, 21% of Manhattan's financial district, and 12% of Washington.) In 1986, the Japanese invested an estimated $4.1 billion in the U.S. market and a lot more in 1987. Shuwa Investment Corporation stunned the industry by alone buying $1.8 billion in real estate within 12 months.

CLOUDSCRAPERS

To hear architects these days, skyscrapers are old-fashioned. We're moving into the era of superskyscrapers as the Ramseses of our time demand colossi that will make their imprint on our megalopolises. Developer Donald Trump's plans for his Television City project call for two towers, one of which would soar 200 feet taller than the 110-story Sears Tower, currently the world's tallest skyscraper. But that's nothing. Folks at the Council on Tall Buildings and Urban Habitat at Lehigh University in Bethlehem, Pennsylvania, talk of the potential for cloud-level buildings a mile tall, or nearly four times as tall as the Sears Tower. Of course, such structures would have to cope with winds of 90 miles per hour or more, which could set them swaying like ships in a gale, creating havoc with everything that wasn't nailed down and quite literally making everybody in them seasick. Engineers are toying with braces and other alternatives to provide the necessary rigidity. Builders of New York's World Trade Center solved the sway problem by placing spongelike pads in the structure to absorb vibrations. Builders of Citicorp's New York headquarters got around it by using an 800,000-pound weight that shifts about on a high floor to counter the effects of wind.

Not everybody's into the "edifice complex." Take Norwest Corporation's new headquarters in Minneapolis. Built by Gerald D. Hines Interests and designed by Cesar Pelli, the 773-foot structure is 2½ feet shorter than the IDS Tower, the city's biggest building.

Donald Trump   To trump up attention to himself while a student at the Wharton School, Donald Trump roamed around the campus wearing maroon suits with matching shoes. Fortunately, he doesn't have to do that anymore. Today he is what he has always wanted to be—a celebrity in New York's glitzy world of the rich and powerful. He got there by putting up big real estate projects and putting his name on some of the bigger ones among them. But then, one of Trump's strengths is his blatant self-promotion. Although his Trump Organization isn't the largest of the nation's developers, it is undoubtedly the best known.

Trump capitalized on the $40 million family fortune his father Fred, a shrewd real estate builder, created by developing modest apartment complexes. With uncanny instincts for being in the right place at the right time, Donald has turned that into an estimated $1.5 billion–plus empire.

His first major development revealed his shrewdness. He converted the old Commodore Hotel into the 1,407-room Grand Hyatt Hotel. The 1975 project, undertaken in the middle of New York's fiscal crisis, included negotiations with city officials, many of whom were politically influential friends of his father. The result was a generous 40-year tax abatement for the hotel, the first awarded in Manhattan for a commercial property. When the hotel opened in 1982, the city had made a comeback and the hotel was in hot demand.

After that, he netted some $142 million when he sold condos in Trump Tower in Manhattan. He picked up another $130 million selling apartments in Trump Parc on Central Park South. Then, of course, there are the condo towers in West Palm Beach and, among other things, some 22,000 housing units in New York and New Jersey that he owns or controls. Moreover, since gaining control of three gambling establishments in Atlantic City, he has become the most powerful casino operator on the East Coast. Then, of course, there is the fortune he made as a greenmailer, garnering some $122 million in profits from his holdings in Allegis Corporation, Holiday Corporation, and Bally Manufacturing Corporation. Putting what he does into some kind of perspective, he says, "It's like a great Monopoly game."

His latest move involves 100 acres of Manhattan on the Hudson River waterfront, which he refers to in typical understatement as "the greatest piece of urban land in America—the greatest piece of land in the world!" Here he intends to erect something called Television City, a complex of apartment houses and a pair of massive office buildings, one of which will be the tallest building in the world. He envisions a TV network inhabiting one of the towers and the complex would contain 13 acres of TV studios. However, he was unsuccessful in wooing NBC and other TV companies weren't lining up to pay for Trump's vision.

The Reichmanns   The Reichmann brothers may well make up the richest family in the world, but few people outside the real estate business know who they are. Their company, Olympia & York, controls some $18 billion worth of assets in North American real estate, manufacturing, and natural resources. Along the way, Olympia & York pulled off one of the most significant Manhattan real estate transactions ever with the creation of the World Financial Center, the biggest development project in New York since Rockefeller Center. Well before the project was to be completed in 1987, the complex was 95% leased—and that at a time when most of the rest of New York's commercial real estate agents were increasingly jittery as the commercial vacancy rate approached 10%.

Paul, Albert, and Ralph Reichmann were born in Vienna, the sons of an egg exporter. With the onslaught of Nazism, the family fled first to Paris and then to Tangiers. In 1956 they moved to Toronto where they imported steel and tile. They backed into the real estate business when they sought bids for the construction of a warehouse. The bids seemed high, so they built it themselves. They built some warehouses for others, and finally branched out so that they built up a lot of Toronto itself.

In 1976, the brothers took their biggest gamble. They decided real estate in financially troubled New York City was grossly undervalued. Thus, they paid $320 million for a portfolio of eight office buildings formerly owned by the Uris family. Within a few years, the properties were worth about $2.25 billion.

Orthodox Jews, the Reichmanns strictly observe their faith. They see that construction stops on their projects at sunset on Fridays. It is even said that, in order to keep their buildings open on the Sabbath, they transfer ownership of them each Friday to a *Shabbes goy*.

SILICON VALLEY REAL ESTATE

As go computers, so go land values. At least that's the way it goes in the San Jose, California, area, known as "Silicon Valley." Once the land of microchips and honey, the valley suffered from oversupply and reduced demand in its once-lucrative real estate market. The problem, of course, was trouble in the computer industry. In its halcyon days, computer companies flocked here, turning the valley into the West Coast high-tech capital. (The Boston area remained the undisputed East Coast capital.) Silicon Valley was the driving force behind the booming Sunbelt. By 1984, two industries, electronic components (mostly semiconductor chips) and office and computing machines, provided almost half of San Jose's 294,000 manufacturing jobs. By the late 1980s, speculative research and development space made up two thirds of the more than 150 million square feet of industrial inventory. The vacancy rate was more than 30%. Rents declined and land sales fell off as much as 20% in certain locations.

POSH APARTMENTS

Manhattan now has a category of apartments called "super luxury." Take Metropolitan Tower, where one-bedroom units start around $350,000—not including stiff monthly maintenance charges. To lure the superrich, there are such amenities as a separate floor of bedrooms for bodyguards and maids ($125,000 per room), a waiting room off the parking garage for chauffeurs, a private dining club, and a communications room replete with stock quotes.

Table 98   Most Expensive Office Space
(asking rent per square foot)

Manhattan (midtown)	$75.00
Boston	49.00
Manhattan (Downtown)	48.00
Newport Beach, Cal.	45.96
Washington	45.00
Dallas	40.00
Miami	38.00
Chicago	37.00
San Francisco	34.00
Philadelphia	33.50

Source: Cushman & Wakefield, 3rd quarter, 1987.

THE RICHEST REAL ESTATE DEVELOPERS

Among those on the *Forbes* 400 list of the richest people in America, at least 47 people accumulated their fortunes in the cutthroat real estate and construction industry. Here are the wealthiest real estate developers and contractors, some of whom have also made vast fortunes outside real estate:

1. Harry Helmsley holds the title of the richest landlord with an estimated worth of well over $1 billion. His company, Helmsley-Spear, Inc., owns over $5 billion in real estate, including the Empire State Building, 50 million square feet of commercial space, 50,000 residential units, and 13,000 hotel rooms, according to *Forbes* researchers. In 1986, Helmsley and his wife, who runs a hotel chain, ran afoul of the law for avoiding sales taxes.
2. Samuel LeFrak is worth at least $950 million. He owns 87,000 apartments, most of which are in New York City, making him the nation's largest apartment owner.
3. Edward DeBartolo is to shopping malls what Thomas Edison is to the telephone. In the postwar period he profited from a new retail idea—suburban shopping malls—and today he is the largest U.S. developer and manager of shopping malls. But his $900 million fortune also includes hotels, condos, and three racetracks.
4. Alfred Taubman got his start building gas stations and then moved on to shopping centers. Now he has a controlling interest in Sotheby's, department stores, and 100 movie theaters as well as 24 million square feet of retail space. Total bankroll: about $800 million.
5. Harry Weinberg bought up vast Baltimore and Hawaiian properties. His $725 million fortune also includes securities and profits from public bus companies.
6. Donald Trump has an estimated worth of at least $700 million, according to *Forbes*. But Trump, who is not known for his modesty, claims this figure is too low. He took over his father's real estate

business and expanded it into Manhattan, built Trump Tower, and plans the world's tallest building on the west side of Manhattan. Recently, Trump has cut back developing properties in the New York market and is devoting his money to stock speculation and acquiring casino properties. (See the profile on page 349.)

7. Leonard Stern has added a real estate empire to his father's Hartz Mountain pet supply empire. Stern now owns 25 million square feet of commercial and retail space and plans housing projects for the homeless in New York City.

8. Trammell Crow owns 140 million square feet of office space, 140 million square feet of industrial space, and 12 million square feet of retail space. With over $8 billion in assets, his company, Trammell Crow Company, is the largest developer in the United States; his family fortune is over $600 million.

9. Jack Kent Cooke built and sold the Los Angeles Forum and currently owns the Chrysler Building in New York and valuable property in downtown Phoenix. His $600 million fortune also includes the Washington Redskins football team and media properties.

10. Donald Leroy Bren built his first house in 1958 and sold it to actress Jane Wyman. He expanded quickly. His billion-dollar fortune includes over 90% of the 68,000-acre Irvine Ranch, which is one sixth of Orange County.

PART VI

The Widget Makers: Industries in America

The business of America is business—and so it is, from advertising to pet food to wholesale merchants. Whenever possible, major industries are profiled according to the same format. This is the basic information you will find under each heading:

The Market: a brief summary of who buys the goods and services produced by this industry and how the industry affects the whole economy.

The Money: a summary of money made by this industry—its revenues and, where possible, profits.

The Players: a scorecard of the companies involved in this industry— how many companies are in the industry, some of the largest companies, and, where possible, what share of the market they hold.

The People: who is employed by this industry and, where possible, how much they earn.

Trends and Forecast: a brief summary of where the industry has been and where it is going through the end of this decade.

ADVERTISING

THE MARKET

Advertising has become like weather. It's everywhere—on billboards, cabs, radio, TV, magazines, and newspapers. Look up in the sky and the Goodyear Blimp might float by. If anyone can be held accountable for creating the world's first consumer-oriented economy, it's the adman.

THE MONEY AND THE PLAYERS

U.S. advertising spending topped $100 billion for the first time ever in 1986 and jumped to $109.9 billion in 1987. A lot of that was spent advertising services, real estate, and jobs as well as products. By the end of 1988, advertising spending is expected to grow to $120 billion. Worldwide spending rose to $180 billion in 1986, up 15.1% from 1985.

Large companies continue to spend a hefty share of all advertising dollars. The hundred biggest advertisers spent $27.2 billion in 1986, up from $22.5 billion in 1984.

Advertising agency billings were about $48.3 billion in 1987, up from $39.9 billion in 1985 and $23.0 billion in 1980. Agencies income also grew, from $3.7 billion in 1980 to $6.1 billion in 1985 and a projected $7 billion in 1987. In 1988 U.S. agencies are expected to have $52.8 billion in billings. Many companies are moving their advertising operations in house, but a few large advertising agencies still dominate most of the market. In 1985, the 25 largest firms took 62.2% of total agency billings. Over time, the largest advertising agencies have been increasing their share of total agency billings. The top 10 ad agencies increased their share from 11.7% in 1976 to 16% in 1986. Worldwide, the five largest mega-agencies account for 15% of all advertising billings. The top 10 advertisers, led by the nation's largest advertiser, the Procter & Gamble Company, spent $8.6 billion in 1986.

Here's how companies spend their money plugging their products:

Newspaper advertising is projected to hit $31.7 billion in 1988, up from to $27.0 billion in 1986 and $25.2 billion in 1985.

Television advertising is projected to reach $26.8 billion in 1988, up from $22.6 billion in 1986 and $20.8 billion in 1985.

Direct-mail advertising is projected to rise to $20.1 billion in 1988 after reaching $17.1 billion in 1986 and $15.5 billion in 1985.

Magazine advertising was projected to hit $5.5 billion in 1987, up from $5.2 billion in 1985.

Radio advertising is projected to grow to $8.4 billion in 1988, up from $6.9 billion in 1986 and $6.5 billion in 1985 (See the separate sections "Magazines," "Newspapers," "Radio," and "Television and Cable.")

THE PEOPLE

There were 201,500 people employed in advertising in 1986, up from 153,000 in 1980.

TRENDS AND FORECAST

In the mid-1980s, merger mania hit Madison Avenue. In 1986, for instance, 26 of the 100 largest U.S. ad agencies changed ownership. Then in 1987, the 123-year-old J. Walter Thompson was swallowed up by the British WPP Group.

Admen seemed to think merger mania would help them weather a tougher business climate on Madison Avenue. Between 1976 and 1984, the heyday of rising advertising revenues, total advertising expenditures rose by less than 10% in only one year, 1980, when they rose 9.8%. But after jumping 13.9% in the low-inflation year 1983 and 15.8% in 1984, they rose only 8.3% in 1985 and didn't return to double digit growth in 1986 and 1987.

At the same time, many big advertisers are locked in mature industries in which they don't want to raise the prices of their goods to pay for rising advertising budgets. Revenues from big spenders such as cigarette and gasoline companies are falling, and other advertisers are pressuring agencies to cut their standard 15% commission. In some cases, major advertisers are cutting out agencies altogether by buying their own media time, producing their own ads, and turning to promotions to sell their products. Overall, advertising's share of the marketing budget has dropped from 42% to 35% in the last five years, while consumer promotions such as coupons have taken a larger share, growing from 24% to 30%.

Add up all those problems and you can understand why merger mania swept Madison Avenue. As profit margins at major agencies dropped from about 16% in 1976 to well under 12% a decade later, ad agencies struggled to cut costs and add new clients. The new mega-agencies say their acquisitions will build up their market shares at a time when total advertising revenues are growing slowly. They also argue that their bigger multinational operations can better serve multinational companies, providing advertising, research, consulting, marketing, and even public relations services around the world. Maurice Saatchi, one of the two brothers who head Saatchi & Saatchi, points out that major multinational agencies increased their share of the market from 14% to over 20% in the last decade. With advertising agencies diversifying into public relations, consulting, and consumer promotions, the new mega-agencies hope to make more money outside advertising. Ogilvy & Mather, for instance, got 36% of its revenues from nonadvertising services in 1986.

Not everyone thinks bigger is better. Worried about potential conflicts of interest resulting from a single mega-agency handling their products and those of their competitors, some companies took their business to smaller agencies. Ted Bates, for example, lost about $80 million in business from Colgate-Palmolive and another $65 million from Warner-Lambert soon after its merger with Saatchi & Saatchi. Likewise, Doyle, Dane and Needham lost $100 million in accounts within weeks after merging with BBDO, forming Omnicom. Some of this business was picked up by smaller agencies who offer the advantage of specializing in certain niche markets and more personalized service.

No one expects ad revenues to pick up steam and the pressures toward diversification, acquisitions, cost cutting, and specialization are expected to continue. A banner year is expected in 1988 because of the Olympics and the elections. But the crash of 1987 will hurt ad spending if the economy slows down.

Table 99   1986 National Ad Spending by Category
(thousands of dollars)

Category	Category total	Magazine	Newspaper	Newspaper supplements	Network TV	Spot TV	Network radio	Spot radio	Outdoor	Cable TV networks
Automotive, accessories and equipment	3,754,443	597,323	734,545	20,850	921,250	1,189,521	49,547	149,973	50,995	40,439
Food and food products	3,307,079	389,463	108,663	12,083	1,445,425	933,955	62,281	280,356	10,137	64,716
Business and consumer services	2,148,935	484,424	176,161	21,217	553,458	661,012	60,766	105,097	57,397	29,403
Travel, hotels, and resorts	1,776,037	249,477	864,567	20,445	107,903	276,584	8,774	174,144	58,460	15,683
Retail	1,731,586	142,693	NC	22,758	252,626	1,106,481	81,506	57,971	52,289	15,262
Entertainment and amusements	1,686,243	25,812	18,315	1,300	591,339	960,893	5,082	18,745	36,827	27,930
Toiletries and cosmetics	1,671,306	390,692	24,522	11,997	894,926	242,345	27,922	22,746	1,525	54,631
Beer, wine, and liquor	1,413,720	225,072	77,936	12,241	547,731	250,827	24,569	177,893	62,840	34,611
Drugs and remedies	1,245,424	147,732	19,800	5,040	752,464	173,535	80,003	27,037	11,241	28,572
Confectionery, snacks, and soft drinks	1,053,038	49,316	29,892	1,891	421,180	420,742	31,196	45,327	10,342	43,152
Miscellaneous	948,518	149,483	588,979	7,020	20,806	8,147	1,191	135,772	34,080	3,040
Mail order	782,332	363,480	60,013	122,385	37,343	136,753	20,677	NA	2,401	39,280
Cigarettes, tobacco, and accessories	728,763	321,843	129,009	64,825	1,342	15,316	1,466	1,904	190,132	2,926
Apparel, footwear, and accessories	685,780	290,836	26,705	23,613	201,889	71,306	7,255	45,241	4,349	14,586
Publishing and media	662,182	175,960	241,969	21,326	14,031	125,617	6,277	34,477	36,803	5,722
Insurance and real estate	658,455	106,655	159,683	11,531	185,937	129,127	12,220	6,643	32,929	13,730
Soaps, cleansers, and polishes	630,243	50,761	6,030	1,337	386,435	158,275	9,390	NA	60	17,955
Computers, office equipment, and stationery	613,936	219,101	69,718	3,516	226,753	37,401	16,358	30,387	3,126	7,576
Household equipment and supplies	596,274	93,382	23,987	4,637	301,616	138,511	15,432	6,404	661	11,644
Sporting goods, toys, and games	476,923	75,458	7,063	1,750	145,252	223,091	1,788	5,482	327	16,712
Jewelry, optical goods, and cameras	341,867	113,358	9,253	3,743	130,851	51,133	2,323	18,445	3,142	9,619
Building materials, equipment, and fixtures	294,409	76,141	10,838	4,800	97,233	72,721	6,453	17,222	1,447	7,554
Electronic entertainment equipment and supplies	279,606	95,531	28,748	2,363	47,284	68,499	8,949	8,661	2,364	17,207
Pets, pet foods, supplies, and organizations	272,129	37,365	5,638	1,611	156,844	54,670	5,604	2,423	901	7,073
Gasoline, lubricants, and fuel	246,323	20,802	23,899	633	37,899	111,095	6,595	36,002	5,011	4,387
Household furnishings, supplies, and materials	236,165	102,967	20,180	5,785	28,032	58,100	1,367	17,861	772	1,101
Horticulture and farming	203,618	20,019	40,702	1,278	31,198	68,792	9,369	26,694	1,413	4,153
Industrial materials	137,379	47,029	59,774	169	24,272	3,684	NA	NA	773	1,678
Business propositions and employment recruitment	116,881	13,511	86,282	184	9,231	1,027	146	5,262	944	294
Freight, industrial, and agricultural development	111,649	35,599	3,923	255	27,569	35,683	5,525	NA	842	2,253
Airplanes, aviation accessories, and equipment	12,439	9,186	2,904	67	NA	99	NA	NA	56	127
Total	28,823,682	5,120,471	3,659,698	412,650	8,600,119	7,784,942	570,031	1,458,169	674,586	543,016

Notes: Categories vary among media measuring services. Totals are combined to reflect BAR/LNA categories wherever possible.
(NA) Not applicable.
(NC) Not compiled.
Sources: Newspaper from Media Records, spot radio from Radio Expenditure Reports, all other media from BAR/LNA reports.

Table 100 U.S. Advertising Expenditures, 1950 to 1987

(billions of dollars)

Year	Newspapers	Direct mail	Magazines	Business papers	Television	Radio	All other	Total
1950	2,070	803	478	251	171	605	1,322	5,700
1951	2,251	924	535	292	332	606	1,480	6,420
1952	2,464	1,024	575	365	454	624	1,634	7,140
1953	2,632	1,099	627	395	606	611	1,770	7,740
1954	2,685	1,202	629	408	809	559	1,858	8,150
1955	3,077	1,299	691	446	1,035	545	2,057	9,150
1956	3,223	1,419	758	496	1,225	567	2,222	9,910
1957	3,268	1,471	777	568	1,286	618	2,282	10,270
1958	3,176	1,589	734	525	1,387	620	2,279	10,310
1959	3,526	1,688	832	569	1,529	656	2,470	11,270
1960	3,681	1,830	909	609	1,627	693	2,611	11,960
1961	3,601	1,850	895	578	1,691	683	2,562	11,860
1962	3,659	1,933	942	597	1,897	736	2,666	12,430
1963	3,780	2,078	1,002	615	2,032	789	2,804	13,100
1964	4,120	2,184	1,074	623	2,289	846	3,014	14,150
1965	4,426	2,324	1,161	671	2,515	917	3,236	15,250
1966	4,865	2,461	1,254	712	2,823	1,010	3,505	16,630
1967	4,910	2,488	1,245	707	2,909	1,048	3,563	16,870
1968	5,232	2,612	1,283	714	3,231	1,190	3,828	18,090
1969	5,714	2,670	1,344	752	3,585	1,264	4,091	19,420
1970	5,704	2,766	1,292	740	3,596	1,308	4,144	19,550
1971	6,167	3,067	1,370	720	3,534	1,445	4,397	20,700
1972	6,938	3,420	1,440	781	4,091	1,612	4,928	23,210
1973	7,481	3,698	1,448	865	4,460	1,723	5,305	24,980
1974	7,842	4,054	1,504	900	4,854	1,837	5,629	26,620
1975	8,234	4,124	1,465	919	5,263	1,980	5,915	27,900
1976	9,618	4,786	1,789	1,035	6,721	2,330	7,021	33,300
1977	10,751	5,164	2,162	1,221	7,612	2,634	7,896	37,440
1978	12,214	5,987	2,597	1,400	8,955	3,052	9,125	43,330
1979	13,863	6,653	2,932	1,575	10,154	3,310	10,293	48,780
1980	14,794	7,596	3,149	1,674	11,424	3,702	11,211	53,550
1981	16,528	8,944	3,533	1,841	12,811	4,230	12,543	60,430
1982	17,694	10,319	3,710	1,876	14,566	4,670	13,745	66,580
1983	20,582	11,795	4,233	1,990	16,542	5,210	15,498	75,850
1984	23,522	13,800	4,932	2,270	19,670	5,817	17,809	87,820
1985	25,170	15,500	5,155	2,375	20,770	6,490	19,290	94,750
1986	26,990	17,145	5,317	2,382	23,185	6,949	20,772	102,140
1987	29,485	19,030	5,530	2,480	24,370	7,240	21,725	109,860

Source: McCann-Erickson, Inc.

Table 101 How Companies Spend Ad Dollars: U.S. Advertising Expenditures, Percentages of Total, 1950 to 1987

This chart provides a percentage breakdown of how advertisers spend their money. It shows that some media, such as television, have been increasing their share of advertising dollars while newspapers and magazines have been losing their shares of the market.

Year	Newspapers	Direct mail	Magazines	Business papers	TV	Radio	All other
1950	36.3%	14.1%	8.4%	4.4%	3.0%	10.6%	23.2%
1960	30.8	15.3	7.6	5.1	13.6	5.8	21.8
1970	29.2	14.1	6.6	3.8	18.4	6.7	21.2
1975	29.5	14.8	5.3	3.3	18.9	7.1	21.2
1980	27.6	14.2	5.9	3.1	21.3	6.9	20.9
1985	26.6	16.4	5.4	2.5	21.9	6.8	20.4
1986	26.4	16.8	5.2	2.3	22.4	6.8	20.3
1987	26.8	17.3	5.0	2.3	22.2	6.6	19.7

Source: McCann-Erickson, Inc.

359

Table 102 100 Leading National Advertisers

Rank	Company	Ad spending (thousands of dollars)
1.	Procter & Gamble Company	1,435,454
2.	Philip Morris Companies	1,364,472
3.	Sears, Roebuck and Company	1,004,708
4.	RJR Nabisco	935,036
5.	General Motors Corporation	839,000
6.	Ford Motor Company	648,500
7.	Anheuser-Busch Companies	643,522
8.	McDonald's Corporation	592,000
9.	K mart Corporation	592,000
10.	PepsiCo, Inc.	581,309
11.	General Mills	551,561
12.	Warner-Lambert Company	548,726
13.	BCI Holdings	535,852
14.	Unilever N.V.	517,746
15.	J. C. Penney Company	496,241
16.	Pillsbury Company	494,877
17.	Ralston Purina Company	478,031
18.	American Telephone and Telegraph	439,919
19.	Kraft, Inc.	437,952
20.	Chrysler Corporation	426,000
21.	Johnson & Johnson	410,672
22.	American Home Products Corporation	395,718
23.	Kellogg Company	374,142
24.	Coca-Cola Company	370,379
25.	General Electric Company	354,250
26.	Bristol-Myers Company	330,997
27.	Mars, Inc.	312,607
28.	Quaker Oats Company	309,239
29.	U.S. Government	306,094
30.	Nestlé S.A.	305,451
31.	International Business Machines Corporation	295,498
32.	Sara Lee Corporation	271,623
33.	Tandy Corporation	262,161
34.	Eastman Kodak Company	255,586

Rank	Company	Ad spending (thousands of dollars)
35.	American Cyanamid Company	248,460
36.	Colgate-Palmolive Company	237,867
37.	Sterling Drug	220,727
38.	Walt Disney Company	219,138
39.	H. J. Heinz Company	217,413
40.	Toyota Motor Corporation	208,877
41.	Honda Motor Company Ltd.	205,082
42.	Campbell Soup Company	204,233
43.	Schering-Plough Corporation	203,359
44.	Time Inc.	190,587
45.	American Express Company	190,002
46.	CBS Inc.	184,837
47.	Nissan Motor Company Ltd.	180,136
48.	Allegis Corporation	171,746
49.	Pfizer, Inc.	171,139
50.	Mobil Corporation	167,777
51.	IC Industries	165,199
52.	Goodyear Tire and Rubber Company	161,858
53.	American Brands	158,982
54.	Mazda Motor Corporation	156,846
55.	Grand Metropolitan PLC	152,919
56.	Volkswagen A.G.	152,211
57.	Revlon Group	149,225
58.	Loews Corporation	146,447
59.	S. C. Johnson & Son	144,617
60.	Texas Air Corporation	132,287
61.	Gillette Company	130,609
62.	Adolph Coors Company	129,574
63.	Stroh Brewery Company	128,690
64.	ITT Corporation	126,344
65.	American Dairy Farmers	125,832
66.	Bayer A.G.	125,720
67.	Hasbro, Inc.	125,353
68.	CPC International	121,956

Rank	Company	Ad spending (thousands of dollars)
69.	Cosmair Incorporated	120,410
70.	Dow Chemical Company	119,508
71.	E.&J. Gallo Winery	116,716
72.	American Motors Corporation	116,222
73.	Beecham Group PLC	115,877
74.	GTE Corporation	115,340
75.	Bell Atlantic Corporation	114,517
76.	AMR Corporation	112,882
77.	E. I. du Pont de Nemours and Company	112,675
78.	NYNEX Corporation	112,209
79.	Noxell Corporation	112,110
80.	Hershey Foods Corporation	111,335
81.	Wendy's International	110,001
82.	Kroger Company	108,339
83.	Delta Air Lines	104,554
84.	Greyhound Corporation	103,396
85.	US Sprint Communications Company	102,467
86.	MCA, Inc.	101,671
87.	B.A.T. Industries	100,059
88.	Zale Corporation	99,106
89.	Brown-Forman Corporation	98,921
90.	Wm. Wrigley Jr. Company	96,243
91.	Seagram Company Ltd.	94,932
92.	Xerox Corporation	92,732
93.	Warner Communications	92,150
94.	Hewlett-Packard Company	91,684
95.	Clorox Company	89,923
96.	Monsanto Company	88,660
97.	Pacific Telesis Group	87,851
98.	Federated Department Stores	85,519
99.	May Department Stores	84,853
100.	BellSouth Corporation	82,743

Source: Advertising Age.

Table 103 Advertising Spending per Capita Around the World, 1986

Australia	$150.67
Brazil	13.67
Canada	187.22
Finland	242.43
France	81.02
Germany	133.26
Italy	53.73
Japan	150.81
Spain	76.84
Sweden	130.78
Switzerland	23.04
United Kingdom	145.63
United States	424.07

Source: Starch INRA Hooper, Inc.

Table 104 Worldwide Advertising Expenditures, 1986

Country	Amount (millions of dollars)	Percentage of Total
1. United States	102,140.0	56.7
2. Japan	18,309.0	10.2
3. United Kingdom	8,222.1	4.6
4. West Germany	8,093.6	4.5
5. Canada	4,797.4	2.6
6. France	4,475.5	2.5
7. Italy	3,074.7	1.7
8. Spain	3,002.4	1.6
9. Australia	2,379.5	1.3
10. Brazil	1,958.4	1.1
11. Switzerland	1,337.5	0.7
12. Finland	1,195.4	0.7
13. Sweden	1,093.4	0.6
All other	19,931.0	11.0
Total	180,000.0	100.0

Sources: Starch INRA Hooper, Inc.

Table 105 Top 10 Market Research Companies

Companies around the world spend about $3.9 billion a year doing market research. Here are the 10 largest:

Rank	Company	Revenues (millions of dollars)	Market share (percent)	Ownership
1.	A. C. Nielsen	517	13	Dun & Bradstreet
2.	IMS International	260	7	Public
3.	SAMI/Burke	171	4	Time, Inc.
4.	AGB Research	135	3	Public (U.K.)
5.	Arbitron	122	3	Control Data
6.	Information Resources	95	2	Public
7.	GFK Nurember E.V.	70	2	Co-op (Germany)
8.	MRB Group	56	1	JWT Group
9.	Research International	50	1	Ogilvy Group
10.	Infrastat	50	1	Private
Top 10 total		1,526	39	

Source: *Advertising Age.*

Table 106 Top Five Public Relations Firms in 1986

The business of sprucing up the image of corporate America is booming. Revenues of PR firms have been growing about 20% a year. The top 50 now bring in about $534 million a year. Here are the five largest:

Firm	Net fee income (dollars)	Parent company
Hill and Knowlton	100,202,000	JWT Group
Burson-Marsteller	100,000,000	Young & Rubicam
Ogilvy & Mather PR Group	31,000,000	Ogilvy Group
Manning Selvage & Lee	21,674,000	D'Arcy Masius Benton & Bowles
Daniel J. Edelman	20,871,000	Independent

Source: *O'Dwyer's Directory of Public Relations Firms,* New York.

Table 107 The 10 Largest Advertising Agencies

Rank	Agency	Worldwide billings (in millions of dollars)	
		1986	1985
1.	Young & Rubicam	4,191.4	3,575.3
2.	Saatchi & Saatchi Compton Worldwide	3,320.0	3,033.1
3.	Ted Bates Worldwide	3,261.8	3,106.9
4.	BBDO Worldwide	3,259.0	2,894.7
5.	Ogilvy & Mather Worldwide	3,154.6	2,752.1
6.	J. Walter Thompson Co.	3,141.5	2,899.1
7.	McCann-Erickson Worldwide	2,852.7	2,454.6
8.	DDB Needham	2,557.5	2,512.9
9.	D'Arcy Masius Benton & Bowles	2,258.6	2,229.5
10.	Foote, Cone & Belding Communications	2,154.4	1,900.7

Source: *Advertising Age.* March 26, 1987. Copyright Crain Communications, Inc., 1987.

Table 108   The 10 Biggest-Spending Brand Names

Rank	Brand name	1986 Ad spending (millions of dollars)
1.	McDonald's restaurants	328.6
2.	Burger King restaurants	170.7
3.	Budweiser beer	115.8
4.	AT&T long distance lines	106.6
5.	Ford local dealers	95.5
6.	Miller Lite beer	88.1
7.	Kentucky Fried Chicken food service	83.7
8.	United Airlines passenger service	83.0
9.	Wendy's restaurants	82.4
10.	American Airlines passenger service	80.5

Source: *Marketing & Media Decisions*, "Top 200 Brands," July 1987.

J. Walter Thompson   Modern advertising all started here. Though no longer the world's biggest, JWT is the world's oldest ad agency.

Founder James Walter Thompson got his start after the Civil War when he joined the Carlton & Smith agency in New York in 1868. A decade later, when the original owner decided he'd rather sell books than advertise other people's products, Thompson bought the agency for $1,300 and even managed to come up with a new name for it.

Thompson pioneered many of the aspects of modern advertising that we now take for granted. For instance, he established magazines as a medium for advertising and was the first to recognize the importance of women's magazines. By the end of the 19th century, he'd established a virtual monopoly on magazine advertising. His agency also moved from simply selling space in newspapers and magazines to planning advertising and marketing campaigns. By 1916, the company had 177 employees and served clients that spent $3 million a year on advertising.

But Thompson made one big mistake. He decided the advertising business had peaked and sold out to a group of employees.

The new owners continued Thompson's tradition of innovation. Under Stanley Resor and Helen Landsdowne, the agency was one of earliest to rely on research, testimonial advertising, and photography. It expanded overseas and hired some of the best copywriters in the business. Radio commercials boosted revenues, helping the agency survive the Depression, and, in 1947, JWT became the first agency ever to handle a $100 million campaign.

In the 1950s and 1960s, however, the agency ignored creative changes sweeping the ad world under the influence of television. Acquiring a reputation as an old, stodgy giant, JWT slipped behind other companies, losing its rank as the world's largest ad agency.

Against that background, Don Johnston took over as CEO in 1974. He struggled to rebuild JWT's reputation and its profitability. Creativity has improved but profits haven't. Profit margins have lagged behind those in the rest of the industry, falling from 8.9% in 1978 to only 3.4% in 1986, about one third the industry average. Worse, 1986 earnings were down by one third. In 1987, the British WPP Group took over

Thompson, and Johnston left. Since then things have not gotten better: Thompson lost over $450 million in business and gained only $163 million between June and November of 1987.

SALT

Few things are as bothersome as a saltshaker that doesn't shake in damp weather. Thus, the Morton Salt Company folks knew they were onto something when they wanted to market their salt that ran free even on the lousiest days. The salt came in a nice but unexciting cylindrical blue box with a little spout. Great. But how could they let people know their salt didn't turn into a brick whenever it rained? Fortunately, they turned to the ad agency N. W. Ayer. In 1914, Morton introduced the box with the Morton Umbrella Girl whose box of salt, under her arm, is open with the salt flowing out. The slogan: "When It Rains It Pours." The moral, apparently, is that for some people you have to draw pictures.

POLITICAL BUTTONS AND PINUPS: A $3 BILLION BUSINESS

Self-promotion has come a long way. As early as 1807, the American Manufacturing Concern (now called Falcon Rule) was producing rulers, yardsticks, cribbage boards, paint stirrers, and paperweights that had companies' names printed on them. These businesses then distributed the merchandise to their customers free of charge. In 1828, Andrew Jackson became the first president to use political campaign buttons. And in 1840, a New York insurance agent noticed that his posters stayed up a lot longer if he added calendars to them.

Today, such specialty advertising is big business: about $3.1 billion in 1985, according to the Specialty Advertising Association. Some 6,000 companies manufacture or distribute specialty items—pens, cups, T-shirts, calendars, and just about any sort of gizmo that can display an advertising slogan. The most popular items are "wearables" such as T-shirts, which account for 19.3% of all sales, followed by writing instruments (16.5%) and calendars (12.1%).

SELLING BIG GOVERNMENT

Convincing someone to spend a night in Paris is one thing, selling several years in an Army barracks is another. But the federal government still tries, spending $300 million a year touting the virtues of everything from the Postal Service and the Army to the Statue of Liberty.

That makes Uncle Sam the country's 33rd-largest advertiser. The agency Young & Rubicam, for instance, has the $500 million, five-year contract to run the Army's recruiting campaign. Grey Advertising has the $35 million Statue of Liberty coin campaign and the $12 million joint services recruiting campaign. Ted Bates Worldwide receives $28.7 million to sell the U.S. Navy. J. Walter Thompson Co. has a $9.2 million Marine Corps promotion campaign and D'Arcy Masius Benton & Bowles gets $5.3 million to sell life in the Air Force.

N. W. Ayer once had the big Army contract. It pitched the joys of Army life for 40 years and was the Army's sole agency for the last 19, running a $100 million budget in recent years. In 1986, Ayer blew it when a former Ayer vice president pleaded guilty to taking kickbacks from subcontractors. The Army accused Ayer of behaving like many other defense contractors—rigging bids and padding charges, in Ayer's case to the tune of $600,000. Denying any wrongdoing, Ayer is suing the Army for breach of contract. Meanwhile, Young & Rubicam walked off with the five-year, $500 million Army contract.

FIRSTS IN ADVERTISING

3000 B.C.   The oldest surviving advertisement is a "wanted" poster for a runaway slave found in Thebes, Egypt. Until the 15th century, word of mouth, town criers, and posters advertising goods in marketplaces are the main forms of advertising.

1450   The dawn of printing also spawns a revolution in advertising. The invention of movable type allows advertisers to print flyers that can be posted in public places or put in books, pamphlets, and, later, newspapers.

1477   The first advertisement in English appears. It is for a prayer book.

1625   The first newspaper ad appears in the back of a London newspaper.

1670s   The *London Gazette* becomes the first newspaper to put out a special advertising supplement.

1704   The first regular American newspaper, the weekly *Boston News-Letter,* has the first paid ad in the colonies.

1741   The first magazine ad in America appears in Benjamin Franklin's *General Magazine.* Benjamin Franklin also improves the visual impact of early ads by using large headlines and surrounding the ads with extra white space.

1841   Volney B. Palmer starts the first ad agency in Philadelphia. He charges newspapers a 25% commission for selling advertising space to companies. By the start of the Civil War, his agents adopt the practice of holding out until right before printing deadlines, forcing publishers to lower ad rates. This allows agents to get 30% commissions.

19th century   Many firms spurn advertising because it can hurt their credit ratings. Banks believe firms that have to drum up business are confessing weak finances. The most popular products to advertise are patent medicines, a $75-million-a-year business by 1900.

1891   George Batten founds the first full-service advertising agency in New York, offering his clients such services as copy, art, production, and ad placement. Before this most agents only placed ads, but did not prepare them.

1893   The modern advertising agency system is established when the American Newspaper Publishers Association adopts a resolution giving independent advertising agencies a discount on rates and allowing no discounts on space sold directly to advertisers. This allows an ad agency to buy, say, $10,000 worth of space from a newspaper chain for $8,500, bill its client for $10,000, and pocket the difference, $1,500. The same system is now used in other media, such as radio and television.

1900   Some suggest that records for the new gramophone should include advertisements for such things as baking soda. The idea doesn't catch on.

1901   Ernest Elmo Calkins and Ralph Holden found Calkins & Holden. The company is sometimes considered the first modern ad agency because it creates advertising campaigns—rather than simply placing ads prepared by its clients—and sets up a typographical department. Doing its own graphics and layout is a revolutionary development in a period when other agencies let newspapers set and design ads as the papers see fit. Other agencies that pioneer the practice of preparing ad material are J. Walter Thompson Co., Lord & Thomas, Pettengill & Co., and N. W. Ayer. Agencies charge a 15% commission for this service in addition to the cost of materials and discounts they receive from the publications in which the ad is placed.

FIRST COMMERCIALS

Joseph Bulova, who made the famous watches bearing his name, was the first businessman to advertise on radio and TV. In 1926, the first radio spot came over Pittsburgh station KDKA when an announcer gave the time and then said, "B-U-L-O-V-A, Bulova watch time." In 1941, Bulova again made history when his company paid $9 for a 20-second TV commercial during a Dodgers baseball game.

AGRICULTURE

THE MARKET AND THE MONEY

If you want proof that success can be bad for business, consider American agriculture.

No doubt American farms are the most productive in the world. Every farm worker produces enough food for 79 other people, and that allows Americans to be some of the best-fed people in the world. In the course of a year, the average American eats about 153 pounds of meat, 256 eggs, 58 pounds of chicken, 12.1 pounds of turkey, 88.2 pounds of fresh fruit, 18 pounds of ice cream, 22.4 pounds of cheese, 4.9 pounds of butter, 64 pounds of fats and oils, 81 pounds of fresh vegetables, 121 pounds of potatoes, 169 pounds of sugar and other sweeteners, 122 pounds of wheat flour, 9.3 pounds of rice, 10.0 pounds of coffee, and 6.7 pounds of peanuts, just to name a few of the farm products sold in America. No wonder the diet industry does $10 billion worth of business every year.

All that production should add up to money in the bank, right? Wrong. The 1980s have produced a bitter harvest of rising farm foreclosures, sagging farm exports, growing farm debt, and declining profits. In 1973, farm households earned 50% *more* than the average American household; by 1984, they were earning 20% *less* than the average household. The U.S. Department of Agriculture estimates that by the end of the current farm crisis, as many as 15% of all the farms in business in 1980 may go bust. In 1986 only 68% of all farms had a positive net farm income and in 1987, the U.S. Department of Agriculture estimated that about 16% of all farms were in financial trouble. Today, despite an improvement in the farm economy, government economists rate 10% of all farms as "vulnerable" and another 12% "marginally solvent."

Farm revenues declined from $166.3 billion in 1981 to only $159.5 billion in 1986. Net income dropped from a peak of $27.4 billion in 1979 to only $12.7 billion in 1983 before recovering to $37.5 billion in 1986. Also, between 1981 and 1986, American farmers were losing their status as the breadbasket of the world as exports dropped and imports soared. By 1986, the trade surplus in agricultural goods ($5.4 billion) was only a little more than one fifth of what it was in 1981 ($26.6 billion).

THE PLAYERS

The farm crisis, which began in the 1920s, has dramatically transformed the landscape of American agriculture. In 1987, the U.S. had 2,173,410 farms on which about 1 billion acres were cultivated—only somewhat less than the amount of land cultivated in 1950 (1.2 billion acres). Today's average farm is 461 acres, more than twice the size of the 213-acre average farm in 1950. The big money needed to run a high-production, mechanized American farm has forced many small producers out of business and, over the past 50 years, polarized the industry into a few large producers and many small farms. In 1986, 72.9% of farms had sales under $50,000, yet they produced less than 15% of gross farm revenues and only 0.5% of all profits—as measured by net farm income. On the other end of the scale only 1.3% of all farms had sales over $500,000. Yet they produced 31.3% of all farm revenues and 45.9% of all net farm income. The larger farms with over half a million in farm sales also received a disproportionate share of government payments. They received 9% of all government aid while small farms with less than 50,000 in farm sales—72.9% of the total—received only 17.9%.

THE PEOPLE

Life on the farm is getting less crowded all the time. There are only 5.3 million people living on farms and 3.1 million employed on farms, down from 23 million and 9.9 million, respectively, in 1950. Some 1.26 million of the farm workers are hired hands; the rest (1.87 million) are family members. Most farm owners (85%) are male and about 94% of all farm owners are white non-Hispanics. Less than 1% of all farmland is held by either blacks or Hispanics, with other minority groups holding even smaller proportions.

TRENDS AND FORECAST

The decline of the American farm can be told with a few alarming statistics:

- Farm debt quadrupled between 1970 and 1983, when it hit $206.5 billion. In 1986 it dropped to $166.8 billion. Unofficial estimates say farm debt fell to about $158 billion by the start of 1988.
- As farms became less profitable, the value of farm assets tumbled from a peak of $1,286 billion in 1980 to only $880 billion in 1984 and a mere $691 billion in 1986. The value of farm land peaked at $823 an acre in 1982 and by February of 1987 had dropped to only $548.
- With farms in trouble, taxpayers foot the bill for increased farm aid. Despite some signs of improvement, the farm economy remains dangerously dependent on government subsidies, which have increased by leaps and bounds during the Reagan years. Over half of the farm profits (net farm income) in 1987 of about $42 billion was contributed by $22.4 billion in government subsidies.
- Critics say the billions in farm aid doesn't do much good. A 1986 General Accounting Office study found that almost two thirds of direct federal farm subsidies go to farmers with light debt and few if any financial troubles. Expensive farm programs are doing little to help farms in real trouble.
- Loan foreclosures since 1981 have added $4 billion, or about 8 million acres in farmland to the portfolios of the country's farm lenders. Of that total the Farm Credit System held 34.7% of the land, life insurance companies held 30.4% and the Farm Home Administration had 19.8%. If all the foreclosed farm land were sold, it would account for 24% of all farm land sold each year. The amount of foreclosed farm acreage would cover an area about the size of Delaware and Maryland combined.

- Banks, government agencies, insurance companies, and all other lenders lost about $11 billion from bad farm loans just between 1984 and 1986. Farm lenders could lose another $6 billion to $8 billion in 1987 and 1988, according to the U.S. Department of Agriculture. By 1989, about $20 billion or about 10% of all farm loans outstanding in the early 1980s will have been written off by lenders.
- The average farm gets only 25 cents of every dollar spent in grocery stores.
- In 1986, U.S. agriculture had an excess capacity of about 9%—meaning that there were 60 million acres of farm land producing crops that exceeded demand. For seven major crops—wheat, corn, soybeans, cotton, sorghum, barley, and oats—the level of excess capacity was a whopping 22%. About 31.1% of all wheat produced by American farmers in 1986, 782 million bushels, exceeded demand.
- Excess production made it impossible for many farmers to make a profit on their crops. For example it cost the average farmer about $2.04 to produce a bushel of wheat in 1986 but he or she could only sell it for about $1.40, producing a loss of about $75 an acre of land cultivated. Wheat farmers spent $109 an acre to plant an acre of wheat but could only sell an acre of crops for $69.
- The Farm Credit System provides farmers with inexpensive, reliable financing for new equipment and loans. It's second only to the U.S. Treasury in the amount of money it borrows on Wall Street, nearly $100 billion. But the system lost $2.7 billion in 1985 and another $1.9 billion in 1986. Meanwhile, the Farm Credit System's volume of loans that are being paid on schedule dropped from $81 billion in 1982 to only $51.2 billion at the start of 1987. Though the situation has improved since then, it's likely that Congress will approve a multi-billion bailout for the system.

Yet despite these dismal statistics, the outlook for American farmers, at least in the near future, should be brighter. A drop in oil prices during 1985 and 1986 may have saved farmers $1.8 billion in fuel and fertilizer in 1987. Speculators are also betting the worst is over. They've been buying up farm land. U.S. Department of Agriculture economists estimate that the value of farm land rose about $15 billion to $25 billion in 1987 after years of declines. In 1988, they believe the value of farm land will climb another $5 billion to $10 billion in 1988. The cost of doing business is also dropping for American farmers, thanks in part to cheaper oil and gas. The cost of producing the nation's crops fell to only $116 billion in 1987, the lowest level in 9 years. And, a strong dollar will boost farm exports. Farm exports grew in 1987 to $28 billion, reversing a recent decline in farm trade which saw exports fall from $43.8 billion in 1981 to only $26.3 billion in fiscal 1986 and the farm trade surplus plummet from only $26.6 billion in 1981 to only $5.4 billion in 1986. Put all together, these trends helped boost farm profits to about $42 billion in 1987.

THE LANDLORDS

There are some 2.3 billion acres of land in America, enough for every man, woman, and child to have just under 10 acres. About 3% of the population owns 55% of the total land and about 95% of the privately owned land in the U.S., according to a survey by the U.S. Department of Agriculture. As few as 568 corporations control, directly or indirectly, about 300 million acres or 23% of the land in the U.S. Eight oil companies have about 65 million acres.

The biggest landlord is government. The federal government owns about 34% of all land; state and local governments own 6%. Individuals and corporations control about 58%. American Indians, who once had it all, now control only 2% of the land.

Of the 1.3 billion acres of land in private hands, about 63% is agricultural or ranch land. Timber interests control another large but undetermined chunk. About 25 million acres, or only 1% of all land, is used by the nation's 47 million to 58 million home owners. Golf courses take up 1.2 million acres.

FARM EQUIPMENT

The Market and the Money

The value of farm machinery sold dropped from nearly $12 billion in 1979 to a paltry $6.3 billion in 1987. A modest improvement in the farm economy may help factory shipments grow about 3%.

The Players

The farm-equipment slump has prompted several famous manufacturers to leave the business. Wisconsin's Allis-Chalmers, New York's Sperry, and Chicago's International Harvester (now called Navistar International) all sold their farm-machinery operations to competitors. Those sales set off a trend toward consolidation and produced huge layoffs. There are only two U.S. tractor makers today, down from a dozen in 1951. At the same time, imports are grabbing more of the market, 16.8% in 1987, up from 10.6% in 1981.

The People

With output at only 50% of capacity, employment in this industry dropped from 140,000 in 1979 to only 67,100 in 1987.

The Forecast

As farm-machinery manufacturers face tough foreign competition and farmers find it hard to finance new equipment, look for continued contraction until the farm economy starts growing some profits.

Navistar International Corporation

CEO: James C. Cotting

Employees: 16,800

Assets: $1.9 billion

401 North Michigan Avenue

Chicago, Illinois 60611

312-836-2000

	1987	1986	1985	1980
Revenues (millions of dollars):	3,550	3,357	3,508	6,312
Net income (millions of dollars):	33	(2)	113	(370)
Share earnings (dollars)	.03			

What it does: The biggest maker of medium- and heavy-duty trucks in North America. The agricultural equipment operations were sold in 1985 to Tenneco, Inc., for $4.93 billion.

Navistar—once known as International Harvester—no longer makes farm products, which says a lot about the state of the farm-equipment industry.

The company's history goes back to Cyrus Hall McCormick, the son of a farmer, whiskey distiller, and unsuccessful inventor of farm equipment. But succeeding where his father failed, Cyrus invented the reaper in 1831. Farmers loved reapers and the McCormicks went on to create a vertically integrated company in the 19th century, with franchised dealers, a pioneering regional office network, and timber tracts and sawmills to produce the raw materials they needed to manufacture their machines.

In 1902, during the height of a merger mania, the McCormick family business and other major farm-equipment manufacturers merged into International Harvester, capitalized at $120 million. The firm, which controlled 85% of the market, wasn't profitable, earning only 1% on its assets. In 1906 it was reorganized with the old McCormick firm at its core and Cyrus McCormick, Jr., as its head.

Over the years, International Harvester helped transform American agriculture. Its products helped create the high-tech farm, allowing vast tracts of land to be settled and brought into production with a very small labor force. And, as the company grew and prospered, so did the McCormicks.

Like many other powerful 19th-century family dynasties, the McCormicks invested in media in order to have a voice in public opinion. During the Civil War, dynasty founder Cyrus McCormick purchased the *Chicago Times* in order to bombard readers with his unpopular pro-south views. Grandnephew Robert R. McCormick, following in this tradition of the irascible superrich newspaper publisher, gained control of the *Chicago Tribune* in 1914 and eventually radio and TV stations. Over the years, his opposition to World War I, strong attacks on the New Deal, and accusations that President Truman was soft on communism kept him in the center of controversy. Another McCormick, Anne Blaine "Nancy" Harrison, purchased the liberal *New Republic* and financed liberal movements, such as Henry Wallace's 1948 presidential bid. She sold *The New Republic* in 1974.

But in recent years, International Harvester fell on hard times. A devastating 1979 strike and a slump in the farm economy put the company in dire financial straits—revenues dropped from $8.3 billion in 1979 to only $3.6 billion in 1983. In 1985, the company sold farm operations and the name International Harvester to Tenneco, Inc., for $301 million in cash and $187 million in preferred stock.

With a new name, Navistar, the Chicago-based company has restructured its finances. Navistar hopes to be far away from the farm-equipment business that once caused it so much trouble. CEO James C. Cotting wants the company to earn half its revenues in 10 years from new businesses.

The House of Cargill   What's the biggest privately held company in the U.S.? The answer is Cargill. The name of this secretive $32-billion-a-year food and grain conglomerate is not a household word, but it is the nation's top grain exporter, largest egg producer, a major beef packer, and number-three wheat miller. A giant in soybeans, salt (it owns Leslie), cocoa and coffee trading, and corn syrup (it can produce 1.5 billion pounds of corn syrup a year), Cargill exports about 10% of the American grain that goes overseas each year. All told, you have a company with more revenues than du Pont or General Electric in 1985.

The giant grain exporter has long been closely held by the Cargill and MacMillan families. William Cargill started the company with one grain elevator after the Civil War, and rode the growing farm economy into a crop storage powerhouse. Acting as a middleman, storing and trading grain, the company had $2.2 billion in annual revenues as early as 1971.

But in the 1970s as the U.S. farm-export business took off, so did Cargill. Revenues shot up to $28.5 billion by 1981 and hit $32.5 billion in 1985, the latest years for which figures are available. The company moves grain and food around the world in its armada of 430 barges, 23 ships, 6,500 railcars and 340 grain elevators. But it's also diversified into more than 40 businesses in 50 countries, including steel mills, and it employs 46,000 people worldwide.

Most of that growth can be traced to a family policy of simply plowing profits back into the business. Since 1981, Cargill has reinvested 87% of its cash flow—only 3% of profits have been paid out in dividends.

Like the other major grain exporters—Continental, Bunge Corporation, and Louis Dreyfus—Cargill has always been privately held and has closely held its financial data. The company has been hurt by declining U.S. agricultural exports in the 1980s, but apparently not too badly. After buying a financially troubled packing company, MBPXL, which made Cargill the nation's second-largest beef packer, Cargill patiently invested millions in the troubled company until the business started turning around. That same persistence should tide the company through the current farm crisis. After all, when you're willing to sit on a multibillion-dollar industry and plow $463.5 million in profits back into capital investment in 1985 alone, there is no farm crisis. And, with a rebound in the farm trade picture, Cargill's investments should pay off.

AIRLINES

THE MARKET

Airline travel has taken off, with the number of passengers growing from 292 million on 5 million flights by major airlines in 1982 to 425 million passengers on 6.6 million commercial flights in 1986. Travelers are projected to fly 454 billion miles in 1988, making the airplane second only to the car as the most popular way to get around.

THE MONEY

The airline industry was a $55.6 billion business in 1987, up from only $36.4 billion in 1982, a bad recession year for the industry. Another $60.6 billion worth of revenues are projected to have landed in the coffers of American airlines in 1988.

But as airlines have battled each other with lower fares, more revenues haven't translated into bigger profits. Airlines lost money in 1982 and broke even in 1983. Fare wars in 1985 cut into profits and in the first quarter of 1986, fare discounting caused airlines to lose $500 million, one of the worst quarters in the industry's history. By the end of 1986, the industry had $1.3 billion in operating income but heavy interest payments produced a net loss of $235 million. In 1987, the airlines managed to avoid devastating fare discounts and the industry racked up an estimated $1.8 billion in operating income. But worries about a recession in 1988 touched off a new round of fare wars that could push the industry back into the red.

THE PLAYERS

There are some 200 commercial air carriers, operating over 4,400 planes. Only nine major carriers earned over $1 billion in revenues in 1987— Texas Air, United, American, Delta, Northwest, TWA, and Pan American. They captured 90% of the market in 1987.

While deregulation was expected to increase competition, cutthroat fare discounting has forced a wave of mergers, with only a small number of major carriers surviving in the deregulated environment. By acquiring Eastern Air Lines and People Express in 1986, Texas Air became the nation's largest carrier. Texas Air held 20% of the market, followed by United (16%), American (14%), Delta (12%), Northwest (10%), TWA (8%), and Pan American (6%), in 1986. Eight air carriers account for about 98% of the industry's operating income.

THE PEOPLE

About 435,000 people were employed by the airline industry in 1987, up from 361,000 in 1980.

DEREGULATION

Most of the industry's successes as well as many of its problems can be traced to deregulation. Only 10 years ago, a federal agency, the Civilian Aeronautics Board (CAB), regulated which airlines could fly which routes and how much they could charge for tickets. The result was a fat and happy industry, with airlines posting nice profits, union members earning hefty salaries, and consumers paying through the nose.

After removing most federal restrictions on airlines providing air-cargo service in 1977, Congress passed and President Carter signed the Airline Deregulation Act in 1978. This act gave airlines more freedom to determine what routes they could fly and phased out government control over airfares on December 31, 1982. The 1984 Civil Aeronautics Board Sunset Act transferred the remaining regulatory functions of the Civil Aeronautics Board to the Department of Transportation in 1985. The CAB, which had been the main federal regulator of the airlines industry, no longer exists.

Deregulation quickly touched off an industry-wide revolution. Several low-cost airlines, most notably People Express, entered the market, starting fare wars. Lower airfares attracted many new passengers but also put a crimp on industry profits. With increased competition and reduced profit margins, unions were forced to accept salary cuts or fewer benefits. Most analysts expect only a few major carriers to emerge from the industry-wide dogfight for larger market shares. Deregulation prompted 128 new airlines to enter the industry between 1978 and July of 1987. But many, such as People Express or Air One, went out of business or were merged with other airlines, producing a situation where major airlines control most of the major markets and traffic.

TRENDS AND FORECAST

The Federal Aviation Administration sees over 650 million passengers and 26.4 million commercial flights by 1997. Air travelers should log nearly 412 billion miles by 1988, up from only 163,000 in 1975.

Several factors are working in the industry's favor. Lower energy costs and cheaper labor contracts will help the airlines' bottom line. On the minus side, fears of a recession in 1988 have touched off a new round of fare discounts, putting more pressure on profits.

Faced with tough competition controlling labor costs is a management obsession. With pilots earning an average of $80,000 a year in 1986, companies have forced the Association of Flight Attendants and the Air Line Pilots Association to grant major concessions. These have lowered unit labor costs. At Continental, where bankruptcy proceedings let the company break the unions, unit costs were cut in half, from 40% of operating expenses in 1977 to 20% in 1984. Similarly, they dropped at Pan Am from 46.6% in 1979 to 30.3% in 1984, and at United from 45.6% in 1977 to 36.9% in 1984. In many airlines two-tier contracts were signed that paid newer employees far less than workers with seniority.

A key factor in shaping the industry's future has been mergers. As in other parts of the transportation industry (see sections below), increased competition after deregulation forced many companies to seek partners with the financial resources to ride out the fare wars or that had established routes in important markets.

Table 109 What a Mile of Air Travel Costs

Here's what a mile of air travel costs major airlines for every seat:

Carrier	1986 (cents)	1982 (cents)
American	7.77	8.19
Delta	8.78	8.03
Eastern	8.51	8.21
Northwest	7.66	7.18
Pan Am	7.39	7.82
Piedmont	9.15	8.93
TWA	7.94	8.46
United	8.27	7.64
USAir	9.53	11.07
Western	7.05	7.25

Source: Salomon Brothers.

Table 110   The World's 15 Largest Airports, 1986

Rank	City	Airport	Passengers (millions)
1.	Chicago, Illinois	O'Hare International	52
2.	Atlanta, Georgia	Hartsfield Atlanta International	45
3.	Los Angeles, California	Los Angeles International	40
4.	Dallas–Ft. Worth, Texas	Dallas–Ft. Worth International	40
5.	London	Heathrow	33
6.	Denver, Colorado	Stapleton International	33
7.	Newark, New Jersey	Newark International	29
8.	Tokyo	Tokyo International (Haneda)	27
9.	San Francisco, California	San Francisco International	27
10.	New York, New York	Kennedy International	26
11.	New York, New York	La Guardia	22
12.	Boston, Massachusetts	Logan International	21
13.	Miami, Florida	Miami International	21
14.	St. Louis, Missouri	Lambert–St. Louis International	20
15.	Frankfurt am Main	Frankfurt am Main Airport	20

Source: American Association of Airport Executives.

Texas Air Corporation
CEO: F. A. Lorenzo   333 Clay Street
Employees: 75,000   Houston, Texas 77002
Assets: $8.7 billion   713-658-9588

	1987	1986	1985	1980
Revenues (millions of dollars):	8,475	4,406	1,944	NA
Net income (millions of dollars):	(466)	73	164	
Share earnings (dollars):	—	1.67	3.59	

What it does: Subsidiaries of this holding company include Continental Airlines, New York Airlines, Texas Air Leasing Corporation for leasing aircraft, and CCS Automation Systems, which provides computer reservations, flight planning and other services.

Since deregulation, Frank Lorenzo has turned Texas Air Corporation into the country's largest airline and, in an industry filled with red ink, even managed to turn a profit of $73 million in 1986.

Lorenzo's path to power has been a simple one: relentless acquisitions and tough bargaining with unions to cut costs. Since 1980, he has snapped up Eastern Air Lines, Continental Airlines, People Express, and Frontier. He started New York Air in 1981. In 1986 alone, he bought 14% of the U.S. air travel market to boost his share to 20%.

At the same time, he straight-armed unions. In 1980, he established an industry union-busting trend by setting up New York Air as a separate subsidiary so the company wouldn't be bound by the union contracts of its small predecessor, Texas International. When Lorenzo bought Continental Airlines, he broke his labor contracts, fired two thirds of his employees, and paid those who survived about two thirds less money. Not surprisingly, airline unions helped Carl Icahn beat Lorenzo's bid for TWA.

Lorenzo has thrived by lowering fares and by reducing labor costs. But he faces some tough flying to keep his creation airborne. The union busting and rapid expansion that are the keys to Lorenzo's success could generate new problems. Lorenzo took on $3.4 billion in debt after acquiring Eastern Air Lines in early 1986. Then he promised to pay $300 million for People Express and the assets of the bankrupt airline Frontier. So, by 1987 he had $5.2 billion in long term debt. Add to that debt widespread employee discontent with Lorenzo's personnel policies and the problem of integrating new acquisitions into Texas Air. How well this upstart flies into the next decade depends on Lorenzo's ability to solve those simmering problems. The company posted a $127.7 million loss in the first half of 1987.

William P. Lear   When William P. Lear turned his attention to the business that made his name synonymous with corporate jets, he was already a wealthy inventor and businessman who had a string of patents to his credit.

In the 1920s, he had invented the first workable car radio while working in Chicago as a design engineer at Galvin Manufacturing Company, which made radio chassis. Galvin's owner, Paul Galvin, capitalized on the invention and changed the name of his company to Motorola. By 1931, Lear wasn't yet 30 years old but his radio patent royalties alone totaled $35,000.

He bought his own plane, which set off a new spate of Lear inventions. The first was an automatic navigation system using radio signals. Until then pilots navigated by keeping a lookout for landmarks and following railroad tracks. The Learoscope, as it was called, became the industry standard. Then he invented a compact, lightweight automatic pilot that could be fitted in fighter planes.

Wanting to get more return than just royalties, Lear launched Lear, Inc., in Grand Rapids, Michigan, to make aircraft instruments. During the Second World War, the company filled more than $100 million in defense contracts. The company grew after the war and Lear became very rich, but he ran into trouble with the directors of his own company when he proposed building a corporate jet. The directors vetoed the notion, saying it couldn't be done and, even if it could be built, nobody would buy the thing.

Lear promptly sold his 23% of the company and set up Lear Jet, Inc., in Wichita, Kansas. By the time the first glistening Lear Jet soared into the skies, Lear had sunk $8 million into development. His plane was an eight-passenger jet that climbed to 40,000 feet in less than 6½ minutes, about twice as fast as any other plane. By standardizing such things as headroom and interiors, he held the price to a relatively modest $649,000. Customers loved it. Sales the first year were $52 million, establishing Lear as the biggest jet aircraft maker in the world.

At age 65, Lear tried to retire but he was too restless. Soon he had set up shop to design a steam-powered car. That didn't prove feasible so he set to work on an improved corporate jet. He died in 1978 at age 76 trying to bring another of his ideas to fruition.

AMUSEMENT PARKS

THE MARKET

Here's a theme that would warm the heart of any theme park owner: about 215 million visitors poured through the turnstiles of amusement and theme parks between March and September of 1986. Attendance is expected to have grown another 4% in 1987.

THE MONEY

All those visitors added up to $2 billion in revenues for over 500 American amusement parks. In recent years the industry has been very profitable for Disney and MCA, the two largest companies. With a weaker dollar and the price of gasoline down, visits to amusement parks and revenues should continue to rise. A major problem remains liability insurance. Increased costs for liability insurance forced operators to close some operations, including the famous Coney Island roller coaster, which was closed for part of the 1986 season. While it is still a challenge to get such coverage, the industry leaders by late 1987 had fewer problems doing so.

HISTORY

The idea of amusement parks with rides, games, food, and entertainment was popularized in Europe's Renaissance festivals. The Bakken, the first continuously operating outdoor amusement park, opened in Denmark in 1583. In the late 1700s or early 1800s, a park called Jones Woods opened along the East River between 70th and 74th Streets in Manhattan. It was America's first large amusement resort and featured donkey rides, music, dancing, beer halls, bowling, gymnasium equipment, and other attractions.

In the U.S., trolley companies attracted riders by building picnic groves at the ends of lines or running trains out to the countrysides. Eventually, some of those destinations added ballrooms and mechanical rides, becoming more like today's amusement parks.

The granddaddy of today's parks is Coney Island in Brooklyn. By 1880, this beach resort was attracting visitors with not only sand and surf but also entertainment. In 1884, the first roller coaster was built by LeMarcus Thompson. In the heyday of Coney Island new subway lines gave working and middle-class patrons easy access to the park.

Realizing that the growth of suburbia and auto transportation offered new opportunities for amusement park owners, Walt Disney ushered in a whole new era of amusement parks with the opening of Disneyland in Anaheim, California in 1955. Disneyland was the first theme park, with sections of the 180-acre park such as Adventureland, Fantasyland, Fron-

Table 111 The 10 Most Popular Theme Parks

Rank	Park	Location	Attendance
1.	Walt Disney World/EPCOT Center	Orlando, Florida	22.4 million
2.	Disneyland	Anaheim, California	12.0 million
3.	Sea World of Orlando	Orlando, Florida	3.8 million
4.	Universal Studios Tour	Universal City, California	3.5 million
5.	Knott's Berry Farm	Buena Park, California	3.5 million
6.	Sea World of San Diego	San Diego, California	3.1 million
7.	Six Flags Great Adventure	Jackson, New Jersey	2.9 million
8.	Busch Gardens, The Dark Continent	Tampa, Florida	2.9 million
9.	Kings Island	Kings Island, Ohio	2.9 million
10.	Six Flags Magic Mountain	Valencia, California	2.8 million

Source: International Association of Amusement Parks and Attractions 1986.

tierland, and Tomorrowland devoted to themes. Workers dressed in costumes to carry out the themes. The Walt Disney Company continued this innovation with Walt Disney World and the EPCOT Center in Orlando, Florida.

The Walt Disney Company

CEO: M. D. Eisner

Employees: 28,000

Assets: $3 billion

P.O. Box 10099

Burbank, California 91510

818-840-1000

	1987	1986	1985	1980
Revenues (millions of dollars):	2,950	2,471	2,015	915
Net income (millions of dollars):	421	247	173	135
Share earnings (dollars):	3.05	1.82	1.29	1.04

What it does: The company is mainly engaged in family-oriented entertainment and recreation. Touchstone Pictures is now an important part of the company.

Walt Disney was probably the only man who ever brought a mouse into people's homes that no one wanted to get rid of. The Walt Disney Company's assets, however, aren't limited to Mickey Mouse and Donald Duck, movies such as *Sleeping Beauty* and *Fantasia,* and one of the longest-running television shows of all time, *The Wonderful World of Disney.* (Disney's current Sunday night show is called *The Disney Sunday Movie.*) Disney is also the world's largest and most profitable theme park operator.

Surprisingly, Walt Disney himself wasn't much of a cartoonist. But after he produced his first Mickey Mouse cartoon in 1928, his company went on to win Oscars for such pioneering films as *Fantasia.* Disney also showed his business creativity by moving into television in the 1950s, allowing his studio to prosper when other Hollywood filmmakers were only producing red ink. Disney capitalized on the growing leisure industry by building Disneyland, the world's archetypal theme park, in 1955. The company has profited by building two immensely profitable amusement parks since then.

For decades the Disney name and assets amounted to a money tree. But by the 1980s the company's money tree was wilting under years of poor management. A decade of expensive flops at the box office had left Disney with a reputation as a has-been. Corporate raiders Saul Steinberg and Irwin Jacobs were also threatening to take over the company and sell off its assets.

But in 1984, the Bass brothers purchased a 25% stake and joined with Roy Disney, Walt's nephew to bring in a new management team—Michael D. Eisner as chairman and Frank G. Wells as president and chief operating officer.

Eisner and Wells turned things around by simply using the company's old assets. For one thing, they hiked admission prices at Disney's theme parks, a move that dramatically improved profits. They also began re-releasing the company's old classics on videocassette. In 1986, the company sold 1 million cassette copies of *Sleeping Beauty* and—at $180 a set—sold out its 25,000-unit supply of six Disney classics.

Theme parks and hotels remain Disney's most profitable assets. In 1986, the parks attracted an estimated 36.4 million visitors. Money spent at Disney parks during the day and Disney hotels at night generated $403.7 million in operating income, about 70% of the company's total.

To keep the profits coming, Disney hired director George Lucas of *Star Wars* fame to design the $32 million "Star Tours" spaceship ride. Lucas also directed a $17 million 3-D movie, *Captain Eo,* with Michael Jackson. Overseas, the company is planning a French Disneyland to open in 1992 and opened a profitable Tokyo Disneyland in 1983.

Under Eisner, the studio has also produced box-office hits and successful television shows. In 1987 Disney grabbed 14% of the motion picture market, making it the second largest U.S. film studio. That was a big change from 1983, when it held only 3% of the market and ranked last among 8 big Hollywood studios.

APPAREL

THE MARKET

The jingoistic "Buy America" advertising campaign, which saw movie stars urging everyone to shell out their hard-earned money for something U.S.-made, missed the point. U.S. manufacturers, or anybody else for that matter, must have quality products made as efficiently as possible if they want to compete. The clothing industry, which has been buffeted by import tides as well as tough domestic competition for more than a decade, seems finally to be learning that. There's more concern with automation, offshore manufacturing, and turnaround time. Overall, the industry expanded by 5% in 1987, the second annual gain after a slump from mid-1984 through 1985.

The apparel market, of course, touches everyone. Take men, for instance. Each year, they buy some 12.5 million suits, 18 million bathing suits, 564 million knit shirts and sweatshirts, 31 million sweaters, and 11.6 million team sports uniforms. Not surprisingly, women buy more. For example, women buy about 254 million shirts and blouses, 32.5 million bathing suits, 105.6 million sweaters, and 152 million dresses. Then, of course, there are the billion or so articles of clothing ranging from rompers to down coats for children.

THE MONEY

More than $133 billion a year is spent for clothing. But due to intense domestic and import competition, clothing prices have increased only moderately in recent years. Some $5.2 billion worth of dresses are shipped by manufacturers each year, for example, and $3.1 billion worth of blouses and $4.1 billion worth of women's suits and coats. Annually, another $3.0 billion worth of men's suits and coats, $5.0 billion worth of work clothes for men and boys, and $2.2 billion worth of trousers are shipped. Shipments of men's skiwear alone are valued at some $41 million a year. The children's clothing market is big too: some $1.5 billion in shipments of dresses and blouses, coats and suits.

THE PLAYERS

With few exceptions, such as Levi Strauss & Co. and Crystal Brands, Inc. (maker of Izod Lacoste sportswear with its famous alligator trademark), most clothing manufacturers are small operations. The domestic apparel industry consists of some 15,000 firms utilizing about 21,000 facilities located in every state. Most of the firms produce a narrow range of products. Frequently, they are under contract to a large retailer or a larger, more diversified apparel firm. Most of the industry—60%—is found in New York, California, Pennsylvania, and New Jersey. High-fashion and tailored clothing producers are located in the mid-Atlantic cities and in California. Companies with large production runs, such as jeans concerns, are usually located in the south and southwest. Increasingly, U.S. apparel companies are opening manufacturing facilities in the Caribbean and elsewhere because of cheap labor costs. Others are contracting out to independent producers to make their products. The major designer and marketer of women's clothing Liz Claiborne, Inc., for example, has more than 80% of its merchandise made overseas.

THE PEOPLE

Apparel workers total more than 1.1 million, or about 6% of the total manufacturing work force. Most of the workers—about 80%—are women, a greater percentage than in any other manufacturing sector. More than half belong to unions, with the bulk of them represented by two unions, the International Ladies Garment Workers Union and the Amalgamated Clothing and Textile Workers Union. The average salary is about $5.35 an hour, or only about half the average $10 hourly wage paid by U.S. manufacturing overall. The low wages reflect foreign competition from big textile and apparel exporters such as Hong Kong, South Korea, the People's Republic of China, and Taiwan, nations where the hourly wage ranges from 20 cents to $1.

THE OUTLOOK

In light of spiraling imports, U.S. apparel makers are trying to take advantage of their one big advantage: their closeness to the marketplace. They are becoming more automated and shortening their lead times from fibers to shipments to retailers. Computerized reorder systems hold inventory costs down and cut delivery time. Also, they are increasingly holding down costs by setting up foreign manufacturing operations or contracting out to offshore manufacturers. Shifting demographics of the U.S. population are expected to help the market, at least for those taking advantage of opportunities. The fastest-growing segment of the population is the 35-to-54 age group, traditionally those with rising incomes and high rates of consumption.

FICKLE PREPPIES

Fickleness of style is the nightmare of the apparel trade. Look at what happened to Crystal Brands, Inc. For years, the company's Izod Lacoste sportswear had a loyal following, largely among folks who sported Izod's alligator emblem around tennis courts and golf courses. Big outlets for the line were pro shops.

In the early 1980s, the company cashed in on the "preppie" fad. Sure enough, alligators became more populous in high school cafeterias than in the Everglades. Izod Lacoste's sportswear sales mushroomed to some $425 million in 1982 from $120 million in 1979. The dazzled company beefed up staff, plants, advertising, and inventory, without noticing that the preppie fad was fading. Profit margins puckered and, by 1985, sales slipped to $276 million. The company frantically cut back everywhere and finally returned to profitability in the second quarter of 1986.

MANNEQUINS

Mannequins aren't dummies. They're clever sales promotion pieces that reflect the times. In the 1950s, Marilyn Monroe mannequins were hot. Then mannequins were shaped like Twiggy and, for a while, like Jackie O. For the 1980s, a lot are built like Joan Collins. Mannequins generally stand 5 feet 10 inches tall and are a size 6 or 8. (Male mannequins usually are a size 38 or 40.) At $700 apiece and with large clothing chains and department stores buying thousands each year, mannequins are a $1.2 billion business.

SUNGLASSES

OK, what's the "essential accessory," as *Time* magazine has called this item, that Greta Garbo, Jacqueline Onassis, and Jack Nicholson never seem to go without? The answer is sunglasses. But they aren't the only folks who walk around in the dark. The U.S. retail market accounts for more than 175 million pairs of sunglasses sold annually, making it a $1.2 billion market. Domestic production, though, only accounts for 10% of the market, with shades from Hong Kong, Korea, and Taiwan dominating among the imports. When the Sunglass Association of America established "the All-Time Sunglass Hall of Fame" in 1984, the first person inducted was General Douglas MacArthur.

Reebok When they aren't driving around in BMWs, yuppies must be running and jumping about in Reeboks. Reeboks, of course, are those graceless things that resemble nurse's shoes but aren't. They're athletic shoes and they're worth a lot of money to Reebok International Ltd. and its chairman Paul Fireman, who received a $12.1 million bonus because of the company's leaping profits in 1986. The bonus is 5% of the amount by which the company's annual pretax earnings exceed $20 million. Luckily for Mr. Fireman, pretax earnings jumped to $261.2 million in 1986 from $78.1 million in 1985. Sales were $919.4 million and $307 million, respectively.

The lion's share of Reebok profits, however, goes to Pentland Industries. This is how that came about:

A Boston businessman, Mr. Fireman was smart enough in 1979 to license the American rights to the brand name and designs of Reebok, which has been shodding British runners since 1895. He had some success in the U.S. launching the shoes but ran out of cash. In 1981, the British firm Pentland Industries bought 55% of Reebok USA for $78,000.

Where Reebok initially scored big was catching the exercise tide of aerobics, which is mostly women and men bouncing up and down in time to music. Reeboks captured 70% of the aerobic shoe business. Since then, Reebok has diversified into sports clothing, basketball shoes, and children's shoes—Weeboks.

THE TUXEDO

The tuxedo business has turned out smartly in the 1980s. In the 1960s and 1970s, the tux was well on its way to becoming a museum piece, a casualty of the convention-defying lifestyle in which a wedding party was as likely to be barefoot in the park as dressed up in church. But formality came back into vogue and sales of tuxedos have topped $100 million a year, up from $65 million in 1981. Prices range from $139 for polyester blends to $3,500 for tailored cashmere or silk numbers.

Oddly enough, this symbol of establishment elegance started out as a snub of high society. A young wag, Griswold Lorillard, scion of the tobacco fortune, raised the hackles of his social set in 1886 by showing up at the exclusive country club at Tuxedo Park, New York, wearing not just a red waistcoat but also a jacket with the tailcoat cut short, like a suit jacket. But comfort beat out convention and soon everybody copied Lorillard's style.

SHOES

Americans spend some $17 billion a year for more than 871 million pairs of shoes. Women and girls buy about two thirds of all shoes sold, the average woman buying five pairs a year. The average price of a pair of shoes is about $20, with the price of athletic shoes running about $30.

Levi Strauss How many companies can boast that they've made a success of a garment "guaranteed to shrink, wrinkle and fade"? Well, the San Francisco–based Levi Strauss & Co. can.

Levi Strauss had some tough times in the 1980s and, for a while, it looked as if this company might go the way of its guarantee. The problem was heady success making management think it could do just about anything.

The jeans craze of the 1970s had zipped up Levi Strauss's sales to dizzying levels. Arrogantly, the company diversified into hats, leather accessories, and even several lines of fashion and designer apparel. Then management ticked off the 12,000 small retailers who made up the backbone of Levi Strauss's distribution network in 1981 when the company added J.C. Penney and Sears to its outlets.

Well, a lot of those businesses never worked out and jeans sales slumped. (International sales, for instance, plunged to $601 million in 1984 from $820 million in 1982.) Hence, chief executive officer Robert Haas, the great-great-grandnephew of the company's founder, sold off or shut down many of the new lines of business, closed some 40 factories, and pared the work force from 48,000 to 36,000. Moreover, the Haas family retook control of the company in a $1.7 billion leveraged buyout to head off corporate raiders.

Today, the company's future lies in doing what it did so well in the past: making jeans and other apparel, such as shirts, slacks, and women's tops under the Levi brand.

The company was founded by Levi Strauss, an enterprising German-Jewish immigrant who landed in California with the idea of catering to gold miners' needs. Among the supplies he wanted to sell was canvas for tents. To Strauss's dismay, the tent market seemed to have been saturated. With the kind of brainstorm that separates a troubled tent maker from a true entrepreneur, Strauss decided to make his canvas into pants, which, as can be imagined, were quite durable. You can also imagine how desperate the miners were.

In 1872, Strauss's pants became even more durable after he took up Jacob Davis, a Russian-Jewish immigrant and a tailor, on his offer to buy a half share in the rights to sell his pants. Davis's genius was in putting rivets at stress points in pants to keep them from ripping. Strauss paid half Davis's $136 patent application fee for the riveting innovation as a way of buying in. Davis came to San Francisco and the company was soon churning out the products, which have changed little in more than a century. The first denim overalls were called 501 Double X, after the lot number and weight of the denim used.

When he died in 1902, the prosperous bachelor Levi Strauss left most of his estate to his nephews, Abraham, Jacob, Louis, and Sigmund Stern. Besides making jeans, they acted as wholesalers to retailers for other apparel makers, such as underwear and shirt makers. When San Francisco was leveled by the earthquake of 1906, the company continued paying its 350 employees until they could return to work and also gave its retailers no-interest loans to rebuild their businesses.

In 1927, Walter Haas, Sr., who had married into the Stern family, became head of the company, which he ran successfully through World War II, primarily as a wholesaler as well as a jeans manufacturer. It wasn't until 1948, when his sons, Walter and Peter, were running the business, that Levi Strauss gambled by moving out of wholesaling, which actually was the bulk of the business. The gamble paid off. By the late 1950s, annual sales reached about $50 million, up from some $8 million during the war years. In 1971, the company went public with the sale of 1,396,000 shares, or 13% of the stock, at $47 a share. The offering, one of the biggest ever, was sold out within a day. Today, sales are more than $2.7 billion annually.

Ralph Lauren   With his style reeking of polo players and gracious money, it's tough thinking of Ralph Lauren as a guy from the Bronx. But he grew up there apparently dreaming of something other than being a "Bronx Bomber" at nearby Yankee Stadium.

No matter, he became one of the most successful fashion designers in the business. Retail sales of his company, Polo/Ralph Lauren, are in the $1.5 billion range, and his personal wealth is estimated to exceed $300 million.

Lauren made his mark by giving people on the way up a taste of the finer clothes in life. He captured for clothing what Cary Grant captured for the motion picture screen. He caters to those with a yen for sleek sports cars, thoroughbred horses, and gracious manor houses, knowing that it's easier to dress with a touch of ready-to-wear elegance than to have to go out and buy the rest of the trappings of big wealth. One of his basic oxford-cloth shirts may cost about $70, but that's still cheaper than a Jaguar. As his brochures claim, his name has become synonymous with "originality, but always with integrity and a respect for tradition."

Today, this arbiter of American upper-middle-class taste has his name on a host of products ranging from perfume to furniture. He cultivates his elegant image by personally directing the advertising and promotion of his wares, even though most are made by independent licensees. For instance, he disdains television commercials as being too ephemeral to get his message across, preferring magazine advertising instead.

That's obviously not Bronx style, and even as a youth Ralph Lauren went his own way. The youngest of four children born to Frank and Frieda Lifschitz, he changed his name after his brother Jerry, now head of Polo's menswear design department, suggested that Lifschitz was too much of a burden to tote through life. Between them they settled on Lauren.

After dropping out of New York's City College and serving a hitch in the Army Reserve, he soon went to work as a New York regional salesman for a Boston necktie manufacturer. He made his rounds wearing tweeds and driving a British Morgan convertible. During his tenure, he designed a few ties and then went to Beau Brummell, a bigger men's furnishings company, which began making his original ties. He settled on Polo for his brand name. His early creations were four inches wide, or an inch and a half wider than traditional ties, and created the fat tie boom of the late 1960s. In 1967, his startup year, he sold $500,000 worth of ties.

The next year, with $50,000 in backing from a New York clothing manufacturer, he produced a menswear line, including wide-lapel suits and wide-collar shirts. Business boomed and, in 1971, he tried his hand at women's clothes. His first line, however, was deemed too imitative of men's clothing. Eventually, however, his subdued, elegant women's wear caught on. In 1977, his clothes reached celebrity status when Diane Keaton wore them in *Annie Hall*.

In 1972, Lauren's company hit a crisis. Though growing like crazy, the company almost went bankrupt from mismanagement. Lauren put all of his savings into the company and hired Peter Strom, who had a lot of experience in the apparel business, as his president. It was with Strom that Lauren switched from direct manufacturing almost entirely to licensing arrangements whereby the manufacturer pays for production, shipping, and certain promotional costs, a virtual risk-free deal for Lauren.

L. L. BEAN

Success just kind of sneaked up on Leon "L. L." Bean. Until age 40, he spent more time hunting and fishing than he did at the little haberdashery he ran in Freeport, Maine, with his brother, Ervin. But then in 1912 he wanted a better hunting boot and designed it himself. It had a rubber shoe bottom and a nice leather ankle section. He dubbed it the Maine Hunting Shoe. Then, from somewhere, Bean got ambition. He made some more pairs in the basement and sold them through the mail. Soon it seemed as if everybody wanted them. Bean stocked some more outdoors goods and they sold too. He sent out a catalog, describing what he had to offer. Catalog and retail store sales topped $1 million by 1937. Business was so good that in 1951 Bean, who was then 79 years old, figured the store should stay open 24 hours a day. Grandson Leon Groman took over after Bean died in 1967 and business has been better than ever.

STETSON HATS

John B. Stetson, the son of a New Jersey hatmaker, headed West in the 1850s to seek his fortune. While trekking to Pike's Peak, his party went through drastic climate changes for which none of them was properly dressed. Recalling how his father made felt at the hat shop, Stetson made proper headgear for himself and his traveling companions.

At the end of the trip, he returned East and set up a hat shop in Philadelphia. Competition was fierce and he only eked out a living until he decided to design a hat to fit the big egos as well as the heads of the cattlemen he had met out west. The result was the Boss of the Plains, as he called his hat. Lacking promotion money, he sent samples to big clothing and hat dealers in Western towns, asking them for orders. The big hat caught on big. He then turned his hand to successfully making other hat styles. Eventually, his hats were sold all over the world. In the 1950s, his company entered into licensing agreements with foreign hatmakers because it was more economical. By the 1960s, Stetsons were even licensed domestically. The company also began licensing its name for men's clothing. By the 1980s, Stetson had its name on everything from blankets to men's toiletries.

APPLIANCES

THE MARKET AND THE MONEY

Major household appliance manufacturers cooked up over $16.6 billion worth of revenues in 1987, down from $15.3 billion in 1984. That broke down to $3.4 billion worth of cooking ranges and equipment, $3.4 billion worth of refrigerators, $3.1 billion worth of laundry equipment, $2.7 billion worth of fans and housewares, $1.3 billion worth of vacuums, $203 million worth of sewing machines, and $2.5 billion worth of miscellaneous household appliances. Meanwhile, imports racked up $2.9 billion worth of sales, up from $2.1 billion in 1984.

THE PLAYERS

The top seven appliance makers in the world were Electrolux ($5.1 billion in estimated 1987 sales), General Electric ($4.4 billion), Matsushita Electric ($4.2 billion), Whirlpool ($4.0 billion), Bosch-Siemens ($2.2 billion), Philips ($2.0 billion) and Maytag ($1.6 billion), according to Goldman Sachs. Electrolux is a Swedish based company with no connection to the U.S. company of the same name. These seven companies account for over half (52%) of the 1987 $45 billion world market in appliances.

To protect their markets, domestic manufacturers have embarked on a major program of capital expenditures to modernize their plants, cut costs, benefit from economies of scale, and increase market shares. At the same time many appliance companies moved manufacturing operations of small appliances overseas to cut costs.

THE PEOPLE

The household appliance and electric housewares industry employs 127,000 people. Average hourly earnings for production workers are $10.02 and the annual payroll for the industry is $2.2 billion.

THE FORECAST

The appliance industry remains heavily dependent on certain important sectors of the economy, primarily housing starts, interest rates, and consumer spending. Lower interest rates and a pent-up demand for housing should increase the number of new homes being built, which will be good for appliance manufacturers. The 25-to-44 age group, which traditionally buys more appliances than anyone else, is also growing rapidly. But the economy is showing signs of slowing down and housing starts took a plunge at the end of 1987. With consumer spending also dropping, appliance companies may face slower sales.

General Electric Company

CEO: John F. Welch, Jr.
Employees: 359,000
Assets: $34.6 billion

3135 Easton Turnpike
Fairfield, Connecticut 06431
203-373-2211

	1987	1986	1985	1980
Revenues (millions of dollars):	39,315	36,725	29,252	24,949
Net income (millions of dollars):	2,915	2,492	2,227	1,514
Share earnings (dollars):	3.20	5.46	5.00	3.33

What it does: It makes light bulbs and GE and Hotpoint appliances; it is a defense and aerospace company that produces such things as aircraft engines, radar, and space satellites; it is a manufacturer of industrial equipment such as motors, turbines, construction equipment, and factory automation equipment; it is a builder of nuclear power plants; it is a producer of medical equipment; it is a financial services powerhouse through its ownership of Kidder, Peabody & Co., the investment banker, and the General Electric Credit Corporation; it runs General Electric Information Services Company; and, through its ownership of RCA, it runs NBC.

Thanks to Thomas Alva Edison, General Electric turned a little invention like the light bulb into an industrial empire. The company began in 1878 as Edison Electric Light Company and became General Electric in 1892. Edison left in 1894 to start a mining venture that soon went bust, but his successors made money on a list of inventions like electric elevators, the electric chair, the toaster, electric ranges, electrical equipment, electric motors, various appliances under the GE and Hotpoint label, and of course, light bulbs.

Always an influential leader in technology, GE is now becoming a test case on the direction of American manufacturing and big business. Under CEO John Welch, the company has undergone a wrenching change, keeping only the most profitable of its traditional product lines and shedding others to move into financial services and high tech. The company spent $1.1 billion to add financial services by buying Employers Reinsurance in 1984, and $600 million to buy the investment banking firm of Kidder, Peabody & Co. Its $6.4 billion acquisition of RCA in 1986 was the costliest nonoil merger ever. Meanwhile, Welch sold off $5.9 billion worth of businesses that didn't fit into his vision of GE as a high-tech and financial services powerhouse, including GE's small appliances operations and three mining and petroleum companies. Welch automated factories, moved manufacturing operations overseas, and axed over 100,000 employees, about one quarter of the work force. (The layoffs earned Welch the nickname "Neutron Jack," after the neutron bomb that leaves a factory standing but wipes out the work force.)

In 1986, core manufacturing generated only 30% of GE's earnings and Welch wants to get that share down to about 20% by 1991. But between 1982 and 1987, revenues were up 45% and operating profits climbed 61%. In 1981, when Welch took control, GE was the 10th largest company in terms of market capitalization. It is now number 3, behind IBM and Exxon, and Welch dreams of making GE number 1.

The changes have already paid dividends. A fully automated plant producing dishwashers allowed GE to increase its market share by 10 points by introducing new designs and quality. Another bright light has been General Electric Financial Services, which has been a big money-maker. The big question is whether GE can run a network like NBC, which it bought RCA to get. Also, morale at GE has been hurt by widespread shakeups and layoffs. Can employees shocked by widespread layoffs produce the kinds of innovations and products a new high-tech GE needs to survive? Making certain they do will be an even bigger deal than Welch's RCA acquisition.

Table 112 Household Appliance Data, 1978 to 1982 and 1984

Appliance	Million households						Percentage of households					
	1978	1979	1980	1981	1982	1984	1978	1979	1980	1981	1982	1984
Total households	76.6	77.5	81.6	83.1	83.8	86.3	100	100	100	100	100	100
Type appliances												
Electric appliances												
Television set (Color)	NA	NA	67.0	68.4	71.0	75.9	NA	NA	82	82	85	88
Television set (B/W)	NA	NA	41.9	39.5	38.9	37.3	NA	NA	51	48	47	43
Clothes washer (automatic)	54.0	NA	58.4	58.4	57.9	61.1	71	NA	72	70	69	71
Clothes washer (wringer)	3.4	NA	2.9	2.8	2.5	2.7	4	NA	4	3	3	3
Range (stove-top or burners)	40.7	NA	43.8	45.2	44.7	46.5	53	NA	54	54	53	54
Oven, regular or microwave	41.5	NA	48.5	48.2	49.3	54.2	54	NA	59	58	59	63
Oven, microwave	6.0	NA	11.6	14.0	17.3	29.6	8	NA	14	17	21	34
Clothes dryer	34.5	NA	38.3	37.5	37.9	39.6	45	NA	47	45	45	46
Separate freezer	27.0	NA	21.1	31.9	31.0	31.7	35	NA	38	38	37	37
Dishwasher	26.5	NA	30.4	30.5	30.3	32.5	35	NA	37	37	36	38
Humidifier	NA	NA	11.0	10.8	11.3	11.3	NA	NA	14	13	14	13
Dehumidifier	NA	NA	7.3	7.8	7.5	7.5	NA	NA	9	9	9	9
Window or ceiling fan	NA	NA	NA	NA	23.5	30.6	NA	NA	NA	NA	28	35
Whole-house cooling fan	NA	NA	NA	NA	6.5	6.7	NA	NA	NA	NA	8	8
Evaporative cooler	NA	NA	3.2	3.0	3.6	3.2	NA	NA	4	4	4	4
Gas appliances												
Range (stove-top or burners)	36.9	NA	37.5	38.2	39.0	39.0	48	NA	46	46	47	45
Oven	35.9	NA	34.2	33.0	35.0	35.9	47	NA	42	40	42	42
Clothes dryer	11.0	NA	11.8	13.1	12.2	13.7	14	NA	14	16	15	16
Outdoor gas grill	NA	NA	7.1	7.4	9.4	11.5	NA	NA	9	9	11	13
Outdoor gas light	1.3	NA	1.6	1.4	1.4	1.2	2	NA	2	2	2	1
Swimming pool heater[1]	NA	NA	0.4	0.4	0.3	0.7	NA	NA	(2)	(2)	(2)	1
Refrigerators												
One	66.0	NA	70.0	72.4	72.4	75.8	86	NA	86	87	86	88
Two or more	10.4	NA	11.5	10.5	11.1	10.3	14	NA	14	13	13	12
None	0.2	NA	0.2	0.2	0.2	0.2	(2)	NA	(2)	(2)	(2)	(2)
Air conditioning												
Central	17.6	18.7	22.2	22.4	23.3	25.7	23	24	27	27	28	30
Individual room units	25.1	23.8	24.5	26.0	25.3	25.8	33	31	30	31	30	30
None	33.8	35.0	34.9	34.7	35.1	34.9	44	45	43	42	42	40

[1]In 1984, also includes heaters for Jacuzzis and hot tubs.
[2]Less than 0.5 percent.
(NA) Not available.
Note: No data are available for 1983.
Sources: 1978 and 1979—Energy Information Administration, Form EIA-84, "Residential Energy Consumption Survey." 1980 and forward—Energy Information Administration, Form EIA-457, "Residential Energy Consumption Survey."

JACUZZIS

No, the Jacuzzi spa wasn't invented as a sybaritic place for yuppies to soak after jogging. Candido Jacuzzi came up with the tub as a form of home therapy for his son Kenny, who suffered from acute arthritis as a boy. Candido got the idea in the 1950s from whirlpool baths at a hospital where he took his son for hydrotherapy treatments. Since Candido's family made pumps and filters for industrial uses as well as swimming pools, making the Jacuzzi wasn't far afield from what their company already did. The firm then began marketing it to other arthritic sufferers through medical supply stores. Then athletes discovered the pleasure of soaking in the swirling hot tubs. It wasn't until 1968, however, that the Jacuzzi company integrated all the water pumps and jets and concealed them in the walls of a self-contained tub. Thus, the Jacuzzi could be made aesthetically appealing, and the market boomed. Richard Nixon, for instance, installed one at the White House during Watergate so he could try to soak some of his troubles away. In 1979, the Jacuzzi family sold the business to Kidde, Inc., for $70 million. (Kidde itself was acquired by Hanson Trust [U.K.] in 1987.)

HOOVER

In 1907, W. H. "Boss" Hoover was impressed when his wife's weird cousin, J. Murray Spangler, demonstrated a contraption he had invented. A janitor as well as inventor, Spangler wanted to make his job easier at the Canton, Ohio, department store where he worked. To sweep up, he made a vacuum cleaner out of an old fan motor, a soap box, a broom handle, and a pillowcase that collected the dirt.

An astute businessman and former railroad president, Hoover knew the saddlery business in which he was currently involved was doomed by the automobile. So he formed the Electric Suction Sweeper Company and, in 1908, began producing a refined model of Spangler's vacuum cleaner. The machine was originally sold in hardware stores, but then salesmen were hired and the company began advertising. The big pitch was a demonstration in the home, which almost always resulted in a sale. Following the First World War, door-to-door selling wasn't what it used to be and the company went back to selling through dealers. Hoover has been owned by Chicago Pacific since 1985.

AUTOMOBILES

THE MARKET

Every year, Americans hit the road in a big way—driving an estimated 1.65 trillion miles. That's a lot of traffic. There are 125.4 million cars and 36.6 million trucks and buses rumbling around U.S. roads, more than in any other country in the world, and they are about 36% of the world's 456.3 million motor vehicles.

In 1987, Americans bought 15.1 million new cars and trucks, below the 1986 record of 16.3 million but still the fourth highest ever. U.S. auto makers are projected to sell 7 million new cars in 1988 and 7.1 million in 1990. Foreign auto makers hope to sell 3.8 million by 1990. Nearly 16 million used cars are sold every year. About 5.3 million trucks and buses will be sold in 1988.

THE MONEY

Keeping the car on the road for those 1.65 trillion miles adds up to a big auto bill. Americans spend about $780 billion buying, renting, operating, and maintaining motor vehicles, according to the Hertz Corporation. Motor vehicle dealers sold consumers $300 billion worth of cars and trucks in 1987, up from $260.4 billion in 1985. On the factory level, U.S. auto manufacturers expect to ship nearly $120.9 billion worth of cars in 1988 (up from $119.6 billion in 1985). Truck and bus makers estimated $5.5 billion worth of shipments (up from $5.1 billion), truck trailer makers were expected to sell $3.8 billion worth (down from $3.4 billion) and the automotive parts and stamping industry was estimated to add another $97 billion worth (up from $86 billion). Some $40 billion worth of foreign cars were imported in 1987 (up from $26.6 billion) and an estimated $15.6 billion worth of auto parts and stampings were imported (up from $13.7 billion).

Those figures don't exhaust the impact of the auto industry on the U.S. economy. In the 1980s, the U.S. government has spent about $13 billion a year on highways. Each year drivers spend another $50.5 billion on auto insurance and as much as $50 billion goes to car repairs at the country's 180,000 service stations, garages, and dealerships, which employ over 360,000 people. Gas to keep the old klunker and the rest of the transportation industry going costs $95.1 billion. Tire manufacturers ship $10.7 billion worth of tires and inner tubes. And motor vehicle accidents hit the economy with a $62 billion bill.

The average owner of a large four-door sedan spends $36,800 operating his or her vehicle over its 12-year lifespan; a compact costs $28,000 over a 12-year period. The average new car made in Detroit in 1987 cost $13,602. The average used car cost about $5,200.

THE PLAYERS

Worldwide, 175 car makers produce 45 million cars, trucks and buses for a $384 billion a year industry. Here in the U.S. American auto makers are driving fewer U.S.-made cars. Detroit auto makers produced 85% of all new cars sold in the U.S. in 1970, only 74% in 1985, and were expected to sell under 70% in 1988.

The big four, General Motors, Ford, Chrysler, and American Motors, became the big three in 1986, when Chrysler agreed to acquire American Motors. In 1987, GM sold 3.73 million cars and 1.48 million trucks for a 35.3% share of all the new cars and trucks sold in the U.S. Ford sold 2.06 million cars and 1.34 million trucks for a 23.4% share of the market while Chrysler sold 1.32 million cars and 681,000 trucks for a 12% share.

In 1987, Toyota sold 6.3% of all the new cars and trucks sold in America. After that the largest foreign producers were Honda (5%), Nissan (5%), Mazda (2.4%) and Volkswagen (1.3%). By early 1990, Japanese automakers will be able to produce about 1.7 million cars in their American manufacturing plants, up from about 620,000 in 1987.

There are some 25,150 new car dealers who sell all of these vehicles.

THE PEOPLE

There were 836,000 people employed in the motor vehicle and equipment manufacturing industry in October of 1986, down from a peak of 924,000 in 1978. The average U.S. auto worker earned $19.99 an hour, compared to $13.50 in Canada, $12.89 in Germany, $8.04 in Japan, and only $1.82 in Korea.

TRENDS AND FORECASTS

Detroit's future was on the line in the early 1980s. A lot of buyers decided U.S. cars weren't worth the price and imports grabbed a growing share of the auto market. So, to fight back, Detroit went into the cost-cutting business. For example, even though sales increased by only 3% between 1980 and 1983, the three largest auto makers cut costs so dramatically that they were able to turn a $4 billion loss in 1980 into $6 billion in profits in 1983. More moderate labor pacts have saved auto companies about $6 billion; other savings came from closing 47 facilities and moving operations overseas. Cost cutting and a stronger yen cut the price advantage of $1,500 to $2,000 a car that Japan once held to only $750 to $1000 a car by the fall of 1986. With the dollar declining further, many American cars are now cheaper.

Detroit also embarked on a major quality improvement program, with Chrysler and Ford both claiming gains of 40% to 50%. Auto makers spent $1.7 billion a year in advertising how good their cars really were. And, just in case the consumer wouldn't believe Madison Avenue, auto makers sweetened the pot with low-cost auto loans. (All three auto makers have moved heavily into financial services. General Motors Acceptance Corporation, for example, is now the fourth-largest nongovernment U.S. financial institution with over 8 million customers.

But consumers still weren't convinced. U.S. Commerce Department surveys show that 13% of all American consumers won't even consider buying an American car. Other studies indicate the public doesn't think American cars have improved relative to imports. Worse, most consumers don't realize that many of Detroit's cars are now priced below Japanese cars.

As a result, even though a stronger yen has cut the sale and profits of Japanese cars, Detroit's market share has not improved and probably will not improve. As Japan's share of the U.S. market slipped, other new cars from Korea, Yugoslavia, Greece and even Mexico waited in the wings to pick up the slack. Also, "transplants" became more commonplace—U.S. plants owned by foreigners.

The foreign competition will hurt U.S. auto makers through the end of the decade. Total U.S. retail car sales are expected to grow to 10.9 million in 1990, up from a low of under 8 million in 1982, but not as high as in 1973, when 11.4 million autos were sold. Domestic car makers will continue to lose their share of the market, with the largest auto makers holding only 63.1% of the market in 1990, down from a 74% share in 1985. And, with the average new car costing about 44% of a family's income, consumers are deciding to make do with the old klunker. The average American car is now 7 years old, the oldest it's been since 1945. With the possibility of an economic downturn in 1988 or 1989, car makers are likely to see sluggish sales, forcing them to entice customers with rebates and inexpensive financing.

THE BIG THREE

General Motors Corporation
CEO: Roger B. Smith
Employees: 821,000
Assets: $79.5 billion

3044 General Motors Boulevard
Detroit, Michigan 48202
313-556-5000

	1987	1986	1985	1980
Revenues (millions of dollars):	101,782	102,814	96,371	57,729
Net income (millions of dollars):	3,550	2,945	3,999	(763)
Share earnings (dollars):	10.06	8.21	12.28	—

What it does: The nation's largest car maker; owner of Delco; a defense and aerospace giant through its subsidiary Hughes Aircraft; a major player in the data processing industry through its subsidiary Electronic Data Systems; joint owner of a robotics company; a financial services power through the General Motors Acceptance Corporation.

At GM, numbers tell the story. The largest auto maker in the world as well as the world's largest industrial corporation, GM is more powerful than many countries. In the 1980s only 24 countries have had a gross

Table 113   New Car Sales, 1972 to 1990

(thousands of vehicles)

Year	Domestic	Imports	Total
1972	9,237	1,623	10,860
1973	9,676	1,763	11,439
1974	7,454	1,413	8,867
1975	7,053	1,587	8,640
1976	8,611	1,499	10,110
1977	9,106	2,076	11,182
1978	6,312	2,000	8,312
1979	8,341	2,329	10,670
1980	6,581	2,398	8,979
1981	6,209	2,327	8,536
1982	5,757	2,223	7,980
1983	6,795	2,387	9,182
1984	7,952	2,439	10,391
1985	8,196	2,816	11,012
1986[1]	7,850	3,105	10,955
1987[2]	7,050	3,650	10,700
1988[2]	7,025	3,875	10,900
1989[2]	7,110	3,990	11,100
1990[2]	7,135	4,165	11,300

[1]Estimate.
[2]Forecast.

Sources: *Ward's Automotive Reports:* U.S. Department of Commerce: International Trade Administration (ITA), estimates and forecasts by ITA.

Table 114   American Households and Their Motor Vehicles

	Family income					
	Less than $25,000		$25,000 or more		All income categories	
	1983	1985	1983	1985	1983	1985
Fuel efficiency (miles per gallon)	14.4	15.3	15.8	16.8	15.1	16.1
Miles traveled (billions)	589	587	630	766	1,219	1,353
Households with vehicles (millions)	42.9	43.3	30.5	34.5	73.4	77.7
Vehicles (millions)	66.7	65.4	63.0	71.9	129.7	137.3
Motor fuel consumed (billion gallons)	40.8	38.2	39.8	45.7	80.5	83.9
Motor gasoline consumed (billion gallons)						
Leaded	19.2	13.5	13.2	11.0	32.4	24.5
Unleaded	20.9	24.2	25.3	33.7	46.3	57.8
Motor fuel expenditures (billion dollars)	48.1	44.8	47.3	54.3	95.4	99.1
Averages per household with vehicles						
Vehicles	1.6	1.5	2.1	2.1	1.8	1.8
Miles traveled	13,721	13,558	20,668	22,228	16,605	17,402
Motor fuel consumed (gallons)	950	883	1,305	1,326	1,097	1,079
Motor fuel expenditures (dollars)	1,121	1,035	1,552	1,575	1,300	1,274
Averages per vehicle						
Miles traveled	8,837	8,972	9,996	10,658	9,400	9,855
Motor fuel consumed (gallons)	612	585	631	636	621	611
Motor fuel expenditures (dollars)	722	685	751	755	736	722
Price of motor gasoline (dollars per gallon)						
Leaded	1.14	1.11	1.14	1.11	1.14	1.11
Unleaded	1.22	1.20	1.22	1.21	1.22	1.21

Source: Energy Information Administration, Form EIA-141 and Form EIA-429, "Residential Transportation Energy Consumption Survey."

domestic product larger than GM's sales; most countries, such as South Africa, Austria, Hungary, and Venezuela, have had a smaller GDP.

Even so, GM has acquired the reputation of a comatose giant, a symbol of what's wrong with American management and labor. The company that once supplied half the U.S. market now sells only 35%. After six years in which it spent $41.5 billion to modernize its production, GM's competitive position has actually deteriorated. In 1980 it cost GM $300 less to make a car than Ford or Chrysler. By the end of 1986, it cost GM about $300 more.

It wasn't always that way, of course. The creation of General Motors is an example of a large producer in a related industry taking advantage of new technology. William Crapo Durant ran Buick Motor and was the nation's largest carriage and wagon manufacturer when he founded GM in 1908. Over the next eight years, GM expanded by buying up Olds Motor Works, Oakland Motor Car (later Pontiac), Cadillac Motors and Chevrolet.

Durant left the company for good in 1920 and the du Ponts, who owned 28% of GM's stock, assumed financial control. Under Pierre du Pont and then Alfred P. Sloan Jr., the company also established a marketing and management formula that would make it the most successful corporation in the world. Sloan established a distinctive marketing strategy that catapulted GM past Ford Motor Company for the title of the world's largest auto producer. Ford had captured 60% of the market by producing inexpensive mass-built cars, but in the 1920s consumers wanted more than just a black box on wheels. By improving comfort, power, convenience, and style, GM captured a larger share of the market. GM also grew by making certain to differentiate the styling on each of its cars and by targeting a specific group of consumers with each car—Cadillacs for the rich, Chevrolets for the masses.

The formula was one of the most successful in the history of American industry. So, when hard times hit the auto industry in the early 1980s, many thought that GM would be the U.S. car company best positioned to survive. It was spending the most on new plants, was the furthest along in converting to small cars, and had the resources to be strongly positioned in the market when demand finally revived. While losing $763 million in 1981, the company's first loss since 1921, GM still embarked on an enormous capital spending program for new plants and equipment. GM also survived the tough times in the early 1980s with less pain than other U.S. auto makers. While American Motors lost $746 million between 1980 and 1983, Ford lost $3.26 billion between 1980 and 1982, and Chrysler lost $3.35 billion between 1979 and 1982, GM lost money only one year and actually made $533.6 million between 1980 and 1982.

This apparent strength became a real weakness, at least in the short run. Under Chairman Roger Smith the company embarked on an expensive strategy to position itself for the 21st century. GM diversified into defense, high tech, and financial services with purchases of Hughes Aircraft for $5 billion in 1985, the computer service company Electronic Data Systems (EDS) for $1 billion in cash and 11.3 million shares of GM class-E stock in 1984, and various financial services companies, and with joint ventures such as GMF Robotics in 1982. It spent billions to automate its factories and embarked on the Saturn project to build a small, fuel-efficient car. The company also diversified into financial services to help its bottom line. (As early as 1984, its finance company, General Motors Acceptance Corporation, earned $785 million, or 17% of GM's $4.5 billion net income.)

But GM was left with 1 million unsold cars in the summer of 1986, forcing it to scale back its aspirations. Smith announced in the fall of 1986 that GM would lay off 29,000 workers, close or cut back production at 11 plants, scale back capital spending, reduce spending for the Saturn project, and, overall, cut its capacity.

More cost cutting lies on the horizon. Despite lavish capital spending, it still cost GM much more to produce a car than Ford and Chrysler. The problem is that GM, unlike Ford and Chrysler, still produces most of its parts in the U.S., and ironically, some of its new high-tech factories are not working as well as hoped, with bugs in the equipment forcing the company to operate new factories at half speed.

Then, the infamous feud between EDS founder H. Ross Perot and GM chairman Smith turned into a $742 million expense. In the most expensive "get lost" message ever, GM announced in December of 1986 that it would pay three quarters of a billion dollars to buy out Perot's share in GM, which Perot acquired as part of GM's deal to buy EDS. No one liked the idea, except perhaps Smith, who was happy to get rid of his vocal critic Perot. Perot argued that the money could be better spent elsewhere, noting that $742 million could finance a new plant and maintain employment of GM workers at a time when they were facing huge cutbacks.

Still, abandoning its lavish plans is not necessarily a setback for GM. By cutting excess capacity, GM has finally realized that even the world's largest company cannot ignore a simple reality: sales of U.S. autos are not likely to reach earlier levels at any time in the near future. Adapting the company's goals and strategies to a stagnant market for American autos will eventually boost profits and lower costs.

Ford Motor Company
CEO: Donald E. Peterson
Employees: 382,274
Assets: $37.9 billion

P.O. Box 1899
Dearborn, Michigan 48121
313-322-3000

	1987	1986	1985	1980
Revenues (millions of dollars):	71,643	62,716	52,774	37,086
Net income (millions of dollars):	4,625	3,285	2,515	(1,543)
Share earnings (dollars):	9.05	12.32	13.63	—

What it does: World's second-biggest maker of cars and trucks.

Ever since Henry Ford continued producing black, stripped-down Model T's when car buyers wanted more whistles and bells, Ford has been number two in the auto industry. But in 1986, Ford earned more in profits than GM. It was the first time since 1924 that the perennial number two had beaten GM on the bottom line. Though Ford is not likely to rack up more sales than GM at any time in the near future, the company has been proving that less can be more, at least when it comes to profits. In 1987, Ford earned $1.1 billion more than GM.

Responding to hard times in the auto industry, Ford laid off 50,000 workers in the 1980s and cut the number of its assembly plants. It led the industry trend toward producing more and more cars and parts overseas. Such moves have cut operating costs by about $5 billion since 1979 and left Ford's production costs way below GM.

Meanwhile, the company moved to improve quality, which had fallen far below the high standards once set by Henry Ford, Sr. The company cites studies saying it improved quality by 50%. And, with sleek space-age design on such top-selling cars as the Ford Taurus, the company has once again emerged as an industry innovator rather than a perennial number two.

Ford's recent problems and stunning revival, however, are consistent with the company's history.

The founder of this dynasty, Henry Ford, was almost a stereotype of the inventor and mechanic who builds an industrial empire with a new product. Born on a farm, he worked as a mechanic, repairing watches, power plants, and steam tractors before working for his lifelong friend Thomas Alva Edison. But all the time he was working on the internal combustion engine, producing his first engine in 1896 and his first car in the same year. Ford's first company broke up because he concentrated on building a larger and faster car than was commercially viable. Next, he incorporated as Ford Motor Company and set about building the world's first economy car. In 1907 he cut the cost of his car to $700 from $850, and he cut it to $350 in 1916 after building Michigan's largest industrial plant in Highland Park.

This plant fulfilled Ford's dream of building a universal car. Ford Motor became the first manufacturer to produce a single model with a standardized chassis made of interchangeable parts that was produced on an assembly line. (Before this, every part was individually fitted into the car and each part and car was different.) Lowered costs allowed middle-class buyers and farmers to enter the car market for the first time. But a major labor problem erupted—there was discontent due to the monotony of the assembly line. Ford held it off by raising wages to $5 a day, about twice the pay of the highest-paid skilled workers. He also distributed about $12 million under a pioneering profit-sharing plan. These moves made him a national hero and an often-mentioned presidential contender in 1920 and 1924.

Production at the Ford plant boomed, increasing to 730,000 by 1916. There were over 7,000 dealers affiliated with the company, with at least one in every town with more than 2,000 people.

But Ford proved to be an erratic manager. In 1916 he financed a boatload of socialists and anarchists who sailed to Europe in an unsuccessful attempt to negotiate a settlement to the First World War. Then, in 1920, after blaming Jews for the failure of his Senate bid, Ford's paper, the *Dearborn Independent,* launched weekly anti-Semitic attacks, touching off boycotts of his cars.

Meanwhile, General Motors took the title of the world's largest auto maker from Ford Motor. By the beginning of the Second World War the company teetered on the brink of disaster. Ford ran the company without even the most primitive financial standards and a huge hunk of Ford Motor's more than $680 million in cash was in bank accounts bearing no interest. There was virtually no cost accounting—no one, for example, had any exact figure for how much it cost to produce a car or exactly how much money the company was making or losing. Ford's right-hand man in charge of daily operations was Harry Bennett, a former prize fighter who relied on spies and a vast army of sycophants to run the company.

The future looked no better. The company was losing $10 million a month right after World War II and the only family heir was Henry Ford II, the founder's grandson, who had been thrown out of college for cheating on a term paper.

Realizing that Henry Ford, Sr., was ruining the company, his wife and daughter-in-law and Henry Ford II ousted Bennett and his cronies. Then Henry Ford II salvaged the dynasty, bringing in strong managers such as Robert McNamara and Lee Iacocca. The company never regained its leadership of the auto industry, but he stopped the red ink. By 1950 the company turned a net profit of $265 million, and it went public in 1956. The $690 million stock sale was the largest up to that time.

Of course, the late Henry Ford II also made his mistakes, bringing out the Edsel in 1957 (a car that lost the company $250 million) and forcing out such executive stars as Lee Iacocca. The early 1980s were not only a time of industry-wide troubles but a changing of the guard at Ford.

Few have a quarrel with the company's recent management. Ford's comeback is certainly as dramatic as that of Iaccoca's revamped Chrysler Corporation. But while its strategy has dramatically improved profits, critics charge that the company is following a dangerous path. Ford produces only half its parts internally, compared to 70% for GM. By becoming increasingly reliant on foreign partners, Ford risks becoming a marketing and importing company rather than a manufacturer. Whether that gamble pays off for Ford won't be known for at least a decade. But one thing is clear: with lower operating costs and several popular cars that are sure to produce profits through 1990, the company is proving that it's possible to make money, lots of it, in a declining industry.

Chrysler Corporation
CEO: Lee Iacocca
Employees: 115,100
Assets: $14.5 billion

12000 Chrysler Drive
Detroit, Michigan 48203
313-956-5252

	1987	1986	1985	1980
Revenues (millions of dollars):	26,276	22,586	21,253	8,600
Net income (millions of dollars):	1,289	1,404	1,636	(1,709)
Share earnings (dollars)	5.90	6.31	6.25	—

What it does: Third-largest U.S. auto maker. Accounted for 10.3% of domestic registrations in 1985. Acquired Gulfstream Aerospace Corporation in August 1985 for $641.8 million.

Everyone remembers 1979 and 1980, when Chrysler lost $2.7 billion. But that wasn't the first time the company had stumbled badly. And, as Chrysler watchers wonder whether the company can continue its remarkable turnaround, it's worth remembering that the company also has a long history of turning promising products into disasters.

Chrysler was founded in the 1920s by Walter Chrysler, a tinkerer and mechanical wizard and former manufacturing vice president with GM. On his own he produced a car in 1924 that could go 50 miles an hour, an unheard-of speed for a low-priced auto. Consumers bought 32,000 of them. Chrysler became the third-largest auto maker in 1928 when it purchased Dodge.

After World War II, however, nothing went right at Chrysler. To cut costs, it simply upgraded the same model between 1942 and 1953, losing market shares. In the 1960s, when everyone wanted luxury cars, Chrysler came out with economy cars. Then, in the 1970s, when gas prices went through the roof, Chrysler built gas guzzlers few people wanted. Losses rose to over a billion dollars in 1979 and hit $1.7 billion in 1980.

But armed with guaranteed government loans and a new regime under Lee Iacocca, the company made a startling comeback. It dramatically cut costs, lowering its break-even point from 2.3 million cars to only 1.1 million, produced some new designs and best-selling cars, like its minivans, and streamlined production costs by using the same K car chassis it first used in 1981.

The question with Chrysler is simple: can it keep up the good work? Chrysler has a cost advantage over GM and Ford. It has repaid $1.2 billion in government loans and has reclaimed a big chunk of the market. Also, the company is taking care not to create new overhead expenses and to increase profits, and it has moved aggressively into financial services, with its Chrysler Financial Corporation quadrupling in size since 1983.

The same ingenuity will be needed to make its 1987 $1.5 billion deal to acquire American Motors work. The deal gives Chrysler more plants but also poses the risk that a downturn in auto sales will leave the company with too many cars sitting in showrooms. Already the company's break-even point is 1.8 million vehicles, up from the lean 1.1 million level,

Iacocca once vowed to maintain. In AMC Iacocca is also taking on another loss leader. AMC has lost a whopping $518 million during its 33-year lifetime, including $839 million since 1979 alone. On the other hand, with AMC, Chrysler gets the very popular Jeep and state-of-the-art Canadian manufacturing facilities. Keeping costs down and integrating AMC's operations into Chrysler's should help Iacocca earn his $20 million–plus salary over the next few years.

AUTO RENTAL

THE MARKET

Americans rent cars by the day, week, or month about 40 million times a year and travel about 3 billion miles in rented cars, according to the American Car Rental Association. Only 25% of this travel involves vacation or leisure rentals, with the rest coming from commercial users, large and small businesses, and corporations. Most rentals (70% to 80%) are made at airports by passengers. Rental cars normally are disposed of after only 9 to 18 months, after having traveled 18,500 miles. In contrast, the average age of a typical American passenger car is 7.7 years.

THE MONEY

All of this travel added up to a $7 billion industry in 1987. Revenues grew 370% from $936 million in 1974. Profit margins have doubled since 1985 to about 10% to 12%.

Table 115   Five Largest Car Rental Companies

Rank	Company	Number of U.S. cars	1985 revenues (millions of dollars)
1.	Hertz	140,000	925
2.	Avis	115,000	650
3.	National	105,000	575
4.	Budget	80,000	450
5.	Dollar	32,000	250

Source: *Automotive Fleet 1986 Fact Book.*

TRENDS AND FORECAST

The industry was founded in 1916, about the time that the automobile was becoming a popular form of mass transportation. But it didn't really take off until the last two decades, largely because of the growing popularity of air travel. (Most customers rent their cars from airports.) As a result, the number of rental cars grew from 364,000 in 1973 to 756,000 in 1986.

In recent years, increased revenues and changes in the tax code have touched off an industry-wide restructuring. Several years ago, huge conglomerates found it highly profitable to own rental car companies because they could depreciate the value of the fleet. But with changes in the tax code limiting those writeoffs, many of the largest car rental firms were put up for auction. UAL, Inc, for example, bought Hertz in 1985 for $587.5 million and sold it in 1987 for about $1.3 billion to Ford and Hertz officials. Avis, the second largest car rental company, went private in 1987, while Budget, the third largest, was sold in 1986 by Transamerica.

As for the future, a recession in 1988 could set off a new round of fare wars and hurt profits. But as long as air travel keeps growing by leaps and bounds, industry revenues—which depend on rentals from airports—should continue to grow.

BANKING

THE MARKET

This may come as a shock, but the banking industry doesn't exist just to loan you money when you're a little short of cash.

Traditionally, banks are in the money business. They make money by buying and selling money. Banks buy money in several ways: when they attract business deposits by providing financial services, when they attract depositors by paying interest on bank accounts, when they raise capital by selling stocks, or when they borrow money from the Federal Reserve or the money markets. Some of this money they have to keep on deposit. But most of it they sell by loaning it out at higher interest rates and by providing mortgages, short-term business loans, consumer loans, auto loans, credit cards, and a bewildering array of other types of credit. By acting as intermediaries between depositors and lenders, they not only make money but also keep the economy going, providing credit for business and consumers.

Today, however, banks sell more than money. As part of a trend towards deregulation in financial services, banks now have lots of fee services, such as corporate dividend processing, and sell investment banking services, real estate, insurance, mutual funds, and even their loans, which are packaged and sold as loan-backed securities. That fact along with tough competition in the financial services industry has been good for most consumers, allowing them to get more services and high interest rates from their banks. But it also has put banks under increased pressure as they've struggled to fight off securities firms, insurance companies, and even retailers that have entered the financial services industry.

THE MONEY AND THE PLAYERS

Commercial Banks

In 1987, the nation's 14,500 commercial banks had over 57,000 branches and held $2.2 trillion in deposits. They had an estimated $1.83 trillion loans outstanding and employed 1,580,000 people.

Most commercial banks (81.7%) are small, with assets of under $100 million. They hold 17.8% of all bank assets. On the other end of the spectrum, only 2.1% of all banks have assets over $1 billion but they hold 58.6% of all bank assets.

Savings Institutions

The country's 3,600 savings and loans have 26,017 branches and employ 499,000 people. They made $322 million worth of new mortgages. They held $789 million worth of outstanding mortgages and another $212 million in mortgage-backed securities, and they had $1.1 trillion on deposit.

AMERICA'S BANKS: JUST WHAT KIND OF BUSINESS IS THIS?

Explaining the banking system used to be a lot like writing a dictionary. You could define each part of the banking industry, saying exactly what it did, whom it served, and what it could not do. Commercial banks, for example, specialized in serving businesses, making most of their money by giving businesses short-term loans. Savings institutions took in savings from small savers and used the money to make mortgage loans.

None of these institutions sold securities, acted as investment bankers by underwriting commercial paper, peddled insurance, or sold mutual funds. There were separate industries for all that stuff, thank you. And, since no state legislator ever got elected by championing the right of big New York City banks to take over local banks, interstate banking was verboten in most parts of the country. As a result, the U.S. banking industry had thousands of banks, many of which served only one city or state. In contrast, European countries usually adopted nationwide banking systems in which a few large banks dominated the market.

This nicely defined industry, with each part serving a specific market and customers, was largely the result of one factor—government regulation. The financial services and banking industry was and is one of the most heavily regulated industries in the U.S. Despite all the hue and cry over deregulation, 10 federal agencies plus at least one agency in every one of the 50 states and over 20 self-regulatory agencies still regulate financial markets and the banking industry. The Federal Deposit Insurance Corporation, the Federal Reserve System, the Comptroller of the Currency, and the Federal Home Loan Bank Board all help regulate banks and thrifts on the federal level, making certain that a lot of paperwork must be shuffled through at least several bureaucracies before getting Uncle Sam's approval.

Of the four main regulators, the Federal Home Loan Bank Board (FHLB) regulates savings institutions and insures their deposits. The Board of Governors of the Federal Reserve System supervises bank holding companies and state banks that are members of the Federal Reserve System. The Comptroller of the Currency regulates all national banks, chartering new ones and supervising the existing ones. The Federal Deposit Insurance Corporation (FDIC) supervises all state banks that are not members of the Federal Reserve System and that are covered by the federal insurance system. It insures deposits in about 98% of all commercial banks and regulates mutual savings banks. Less than 4% of all banks are state chartered and not subject to regulation by any federal agency. These banks, however, are regulated by state agencies. (See the profiles of the Federal Reserve, the Comptroller of the Currency, the FHLB and the FDIC in the chapter "Regulation and Deregulation.")

Since 1980, however, the banking industry has been undergoing a revolution. Banks are pushing federal regulators to let them sell insurance and securities and to perform many of the functions of investment banks. Supreme Court decisions and new state laws have removed some of the barriers to interstate banking and allowed the creation of large regional banks. (Nationwide banking will come through regional agglomeration and taking over of distressed thrifts.) Though barred from many states, large New York banks are also expanding into several states, most notably Texas in 1987 and the lucrative California market after 1990.

At the same time, some deregulation in the financial services industry has forced bankers to face increased competition. Securities firms such as Merrill Lynch now broker certificates of deposit and sell lines of credit. Finance companies, especially subsidiaries of large auto makers, are stealing a large share of the auto loan market. Sears and other retailers, which were once content to sell power tools and lawn chairs, are peddling credit cards and accept deposits. And American Express touched off a pricing war with banks by directly challenging the bank's lucrative credit-card business with a revolving credit card introduced at a bargain rate.

Likewise, some strange corporate beasts, such as nonbank banks and industrial banks, have appeared on the landscape. Finance companies, mutual funds, and big retailers have set up companies that can accept federally insured deposits but are not banks as defined by law because they do not make commercial loans. To get around restrictions on interstate banking, Citicorp has set up "industrial banks" in various western states. They function like regular banks but don't violate federal laws because of a technicality that allows them to claim they don't take deposits. What they do take is "IOUs," which function like deposits and are not federally insured. The big way they've expanded is buying distressed thrifts in California, Florida, and Chicago.

All of this was a dramatic change from the good old days when bankers had a near-monopoly on low-interest deposits and borrowers had to come to them for low-rate, low-risk, loans. High-risk loans were left to finance companies, while commercial banks made their money on low-interest loans to blue-chip corporations (most corporations finance themselves through commercial paper) and wealthy individuals who had the best credit references.

Even for consumers who can't tell a nonbank bank from a bank, the 1980s have brought on remarkable changes. The most visible sign was deregulation of interest rates paid on savings accounts. In April of 1986, the last restrictions on savings deposit rates—which had been set by the regulators at 5.5%—were ended. That meant that the nation's commercial banks and thrift institutions could pay any rate they chose on millions of accounts. The Depository Institutions Deregulation and Monetary Control Act of 1980 also allowed money-market accounts, allowed mutual savings banks to make commercial, corporate, and business loans of values up to 5% of their assets, and permitted payment of interest on demand deposits (such as checking accounts). A 1982 law authorized savings and loans to make commercial loans of values up to 10% of their assets, allowed investments in nonresidential personal property, and permitted interstate and intrastate mergers of financially troubled institutions.

The brave new world of banking has been good for business by reducing the cost of borrowing and has given more affluent customers better returns on their money. Thus, it has directly helped increase investment and productivity. But the changing banking industry has been hard on smaller depositors, who face higher bank fees, and on the banks themselves, which have been losing their share of many important markets.

In the last decade many large corporate clients discovered it was cheaper to borrow funds overseas and deserted their banks to finance corporate debt in the Euronotes markets. At the same time, U.S. investment banks lured away big business borrowers and drove down loan prices by creating an astonishing array of new debt securities, which also reduced the cost of corporate borrowing and produced fat fees for the investment banks.

Faced with the loss of their bread-and-butter corporate clients, commercial banks fought to enter the investment banking business. Through European subsidiaries they began underwriting Euronotes and, as early as 1985, banks underwrote nearly $50 billion in standby credit tied to Euronotes, up from $3.3 billion in 1983.

Some of the nation's largest commercial banks, such as Citicorp, Chase Manhattan, Chemical Bank, Manufacturers Hanover, and Security Pacific, scrambled to expand their operations, hiring away top investment bankers and promoting a variety of investment banking services in full-page ads. As a result of this aggressive move into investment banking, noninterest income—a rough approximation of fees from investment banking—grew from about 24% of total income in 1979 to about 36% of total income in 1985 for the six largest New York banks.

Banks have also increasingly "securitized" loans in an attempt to improve profits. Already financial institutions are selling off securities backed by loans, mortgages, car loans, credit-card receivables, and even student loans. In 1978 only $22.5 billion worth of mortgage-backed securities were sold, but by 1985 $147.9 billion had been sold, about two thirds of the new mortgages issued that year. Banks have been selling off corporate loans, some $10 billion worth in 1986, and are pioneering other asset-backed securities. In January of 1987, RepublicBank's Delaware credit-card bank held the first public sale of $200 million in credit-card-backed notes. They were snapped up by investors.

Commercial banks have also been moving into the consumer loan market—once the preserve of finance companies and thrifts. More than half of Citibank's debt is to consumers through credit cards, credit lines, and mortgages, up from only 20% in 1980 when it, like most large New York City commercial banks, emphasized loans to major corporations. And at the same time, savings and loans have been allowed to make commercial loans of values up to 10% of their assets. Since savings institutions and commercial banks are now offering many of the same new services, the distinctions between the two have become increasingly blurred.

Besides facing competition from nonbanking companies for many of their traditional services, American banks are concerned about the growth of foreign competition, particularly from the Japanese. Japanese banks and brokerage firms were minor players in international finance a decade ago but now they routinely underwrite bond issues for companies like PepsiCo, General Motors Acceptance Corporation, General Electric, Exxon, and IBM. They hold 8.4% of the commercial loans in the U.S. Seven of the 10 largest commercial banks are Japanese; 4 of the top 10 investment bankers are Japanese. (See the table "World's Largest Investment Banks" below.) By 1995, one study suggests that the world will owe Japanese investors $1 trillion.

Table 116   World's Largest Investment Banks

Rank	Bank	Equity (billions of dollars)
1.	Nomura Securities	3.4
2.	Merrill Lynch	2.3
3.	Nikko Securities	2.1
4.	Daiwa Securities	2.0
5.	Salomon Brothers	1.7
6.	Yamaichi Securities	1.6
7.	Shearson Lehman Brothers	1.2
8.	Prudential-Bache Securities	1.0
9.	Dean Witter Financial Services	0.9
10.	Goldman, Sachs	0.9

Source: *Fortune*, October 27, 1986, citing IBCA Banking Analysis Ltd., Securities Industry Association, and company reports.

Table 117   The 25 Largest Banks in the World: Where They Come From

This chart shows that in recent years Japan has been taking over the title as the world's banker. Its banks have been aggressively cutting fees and interest rates to attract new customers from Wall Street. Flush with cash from Japan's trade surplus, Japan invested a record $68 billion overseas in the first seven months of 1986 alone. Thanks to lower interest rates, it's already captured 8.4% of the commercial loans in the U.S. Naturally, U.S. banks aren't happy about the trend. They charge that U.S. banks are saddled with heavier regulations than Japanese banks and that the Japanese have been dumping money on the U.S. market—just as they once dumped electronic goods—to gain a foothold and drive U.S. competitors out. But the strategy is working. Five of the 10 largest banks in the world are Japanese, and 13 of the top 25.

	Number of commercial banks in the top 25	
Country	1970	1987
United States	7	2
Japan	4	16
United Kingdom	3	2
West Germany	3	1
Canada	3	0
Italy	3	0

Source: *American Banker*, July 6, 1987, and July 30, 1971.

ON THE BRINK OF DISASTER?

As banks have fought to restructure the industry and capitalize on new profit-making opportunities such as investment and interstate banking, critics of the banking revolution have been wondering if the system is teetering on the brink of disaster. Their worries run something like this: Deregulation has pushed banks into all sorts of high-risk ventures. For example, new services such as trading in Euronotes in international markets are adding billions of dollars in hidden liabilities to the balance sheets of banks. Moreover, critics fear interstate banking may make it harder for smaller banks to compete, thus endangering their stability, and that larger banks that invested heavily in the now-depressed commercial real estate market or oil patch are in big financial trouble.

A few numbers seem to support the doom-and-gloom theorists of an imminent banking calamity. There were more bank failures in 1984, 79 of them, than in any year in the history of the FDIC, but in 1985 and 1986 the numbers got worse: 120 commercial banks closed in 1985, and another record was set in 1986, when 138 bit the dust. And more are on the way. Over 1,400 banks were on the agency's "problem" list (about 10% of the banks insured by the FDIC), stretching the workload of the 1,670 FDIC bank examiners to the limit. Add to that billions of dollars worth of shaky third-world debt, overburdened bank regulators, and the higher risks of competing in a deregulated marketplace, and you have set the stage for a major economic disaster, critics argue.

Certainly there are reasons for worry. At home bad farm loans have toppled some banks and overseas the third-world debt crisis looms as a major problem for U.S. banks. Following Citicorp's lead, major U.S. banks increased their reserves and wrote off some of those loans in 1987, producing the worst second-quarter losses ever. But with major lenders to the third-world saddled with at least $437 billion in debts, more write-offs are to come.

Banks are also saddled with heavy loans to the depressed commercial real estate sector—which is undergoing the worst downturn since the 1930s. Bad energy loans have also produced heavy losses, especially among Texas banks and thrifts. For example, the six largest Texas banks were faced with write-offs totaling $2.5 billion, or 3% of their total loans, in 1986. Losses on bad energy and commercial real estate loans composed a major portion of the $388 million charge for bad loans Bank of America took in the second quarter of 1986, when the bank lost $640 million.

The rising tide of bank failures has weakened major deposit insurance funds, forcing Congress to shore up the insurance system. "Outlays by the major deposit insurance funds are estimated to exceed previously planned levels by $5.8 billion in 1987 and $4 billion in 1988," Reagan's 1987 budget report admitted. Already Congress has had to bail out the Federal Savings Loan Insurance Corporation, which was virtually broke. Even the Federal Deposit Insurance Corporation is running a cash deficit of over $4 billion, up from $1.9 billion a year earlier. The deficit will not reduce the value of the FDIC's $18 billion insurance fund but will force it to replace Treasury securities with highly illiquid, depressed assets taken over from failed banks.

Yet for the moment, at least, most of these gloomy predictions miss the point. The banking industry is admittedly undergoing a shakeout, with weaker banks and thrifts going under while many other banks are emerging stronger than at any point in the last 10 years. While the number of failed banks is alarming, many are small and are hardly capable of causing major economic problems. The 120 banks that failed in 1985, for example, rep-

Table 118   The Third-World Debt Crisis
(billions of dollars)

Country	Owed to U.S. banks	Owed to other creditors
Brazil	22.4	78.6
Mexico	23.7	76.3
Argentina	8.5	40.5
Venezuela	9.1	22.9
Philippines	5.1	22.0
Nigeria	0.9	18.1
Yugoslavia	2.1	16.9
Chile	6.5	12.5
Peru	1.3	14.7
Morocco	0.9	14.1
Colombia	2.1	12.9
Ivory Coast	0.4	7.7
Ecuador	2.2	5.8
Bolivia	0.1	3.9
Uruguay	0.9	3.1

Sources: *Fortune*, Federal Reserve.

resented only 1% of all banks and just 0.1% of all bank assets. Even the huge losses endured in 1987 by U.S. banks on their third-world loans is a positive sign that they're beginning to face up to reality and strengthen their reserves. Over time, the result will improve their stability, not weaken it.

BankAmerica Corporation

CEO: A. W. Clausen   P.O. Box 37000
Employees: 73,500   San Francisco, California 94137
Assets: $99 billion   415-622-3456
Deposits: $79 billion
Loans: $65 billion

	1987	1986	1985	1980
Net income (millions of dollars):	(955)	(518)	(337)	645
Share earnings (dollars):	—	—	—	4.33

In 1980, shortly before leaving to become the head of the World Bank, A. W. Clausen, the CEO of BankAmerica, announced earnings of $645 million, a record for any American financial institution. Six years later, his successor, Samuel Armacost, announced that the bank would lose $640 million in the second quarter of 1986, one of the largest losses ever recorded in the history of U.S. banking.

In the 1970s, Clausen sowed the seeds of disaster by boosting the bank's fixed-rate mortgages, agricultural lending, construction lending, and foreign loans. At the same time he rapidly expanded, creating a large, unwieldy bureaucracy that lacked central controls and scrimped on new technology.

These tactics quadrupled the company's assets and earnings during the 1970s but caused problems when all those real estate, farm, and foreign loans began to go sour. Earnings dropped steadily between 1981 and 1984. By 1985, BankAmerica was forced into the first layoff in its 81-year history and cut its dividend for the first time in 53 years. The year ended with a $337 million loss.

But that was only the beginning. Under Clausen's hand-picked successor, Armacost, the losses mounted. Armacost compounded the bank's problems by not moving decisively to slash costs. His decision to sell BankAmerica's headquarters and cut costs came too late to stem the company's $518 million loss for 1986.

By 1986, the company's financial troubles threatened not only its bottom line but its very existence. With raiders lurking in the wings, the board of directors ousted Armacost and made the surprise decision to rehire Clausen.

Clausen's tenure as head of the World Bank from 1981 to 1986, when the World Bank floundered and found itself unable to deal with the third-world debt crisis, does not bode well for BankAmerica's future or say much for Clausen's abilities as a crisis manager. But no one expects

Clausen to lead the bank back quickly to the record profits he produced while heading BankAmerica in the 1970s. Even without its financial trouble, BankAmerica is now operating in a tough, highly competitive market for banking and financial services. But what a California franchise. For now, Clausen will be happy just cutting costs and fighting off the raiders. As a no-nonsense, autocratic manager, he may be cut out for that job. One ace in the hole he has is vice chairman Dick Rosenberg, who has a reputation as a superb retail banker. Rosenberg brought in a handpicked team to restore the retail business, which is now highly profitable.

Citicorp

CEO: John S. Reed
Employees: 88,500
Assets: $199.9 billion
Deposits: $118.1 billion
Loans: $130.2 billion

399 Park Avenue
New York, New York 10043
212-559-1000

	1987	1986	1985	1980
Net income (millions of dollars)	1,138	1,058	998	507
Share earnings (dollars):	—	7.14	7.12	4.08

In 1987, Citibank shocked the banking community with the announcement that it was setting aside $3 billion in reserves against possible losses on its third-world loans. Since the bank was one of the leaders in making foreign loans during the 1970s, it was a bitter pill to swallow, especially on the bottom line. Citibank posted a $2.5 billion loss for the second quarter, the biggest in the history of U.S. banking.

But within weeks other banks followed suit. Once again, Citibank had proved to be a leader, an innovator in the banking community. Over the years the nation's largest bank, Citibank, has established a reputation for innovation and aggressive tactics. Since its creation in 1812, Citibank has battered down regulatory barriers, stormed into new markets, and ruffled more than a few feathers in Washington and on Wall Street.

Citibank's history could double as a history of banking innovations. In the 19th century it was one of the first banks to expand overseas. In the 1910s National City Bank of New York, as it was then called, lobbied to get the 1913 Federal Reserve Act to include provisions allowing U.S. banks to establish foreign branches, and in 1914 it became the first U.S. bank to open a foreign branch. In the 1920s it got into the business of selling foreign debt to U.S. investors, even though some of its Latin American bonds were from countries that had a long history of never repaying their debts. Some things, at least, never change.

Also in the 1920s, at a time when most commercial banks dealt only with businesses, the bank was one of the first to encourage individuals to open accounts, and in 1928 it was the first to offer loans to consumers.

Many of these innovations were very controversial, putting the bank on a collision course with Congress and government regulators. During the bull market of the 1920s, National City used securities subsidiaries to act like an investment bank, underwriting stocks, selling securities, and providing loans so investors could purchase stocks and bonds. But National City came under congressional fire in the early 1930s for touting some obviously bad stocks and bonds. Sensational Senate Banking Committee hearings into the company's fraudulent investment banking practices helped pass the Glass-Steagall Act, which separated commercial banking and investment banking.

That act placed strict limits on what kinds of businesses a commercial bank could undertake. But the bank never gave up its attempt to expand and diversify. In 1968, it created Citicorp as a bank holding corporation to explore a loophole in the Bank Holding Company Act of 1956. This law restricted what kinds of businesses a bank holding company could undertake but exempted one-bank holding companies so that small banks could provide accounting, real estate sale, and other services they needed to remain profitable. Citicorp wasn't small but it was legally only one bank, even though it had hundreds of branches. That allowed it to expand into other businesses, allowing it to acquire a mortgage banking firm and a management consultancy firm. Other banks quickly followed suit. By the end of 1969, a House Banking Committee study found that 27 conglomerates had acquired or established banks and that one-bank holding companies were engaged in 20 different financial activities and 99 nonfinancial activities. The total deposits of one-bank holding companies rose to $135 billion, or about 35% of total deposits. Congress closed some of the loopholes in 1970 but nonbanking subsidiaries of banks were given the right to expand across state lines and banks were given the right to expand into areas "closely related to banking." Over the next decade, that provision helped banks break down regulatory barriers preventing them from entering other businesses. In 1983, for example, the Federal Reserve ruled that discount brokerages were "closely related to banking."

More recently, Citicorp pioneered automatic teller machines in the New York City market; moved so aggressively into investment banking that almost overnight it became the second-largest publicly owned investment banker on Wall Street; moved into information services by snapping up Quotron; and bought up banks in Texas as part of its expanding national banking system. Meanwhile, in 1986 and 1987 the bank irritated Wall Street investors by depressing earnings when it set aside huge loan reserves and increased capital.

Today, Citicorp is the nation's largest bank holding corporation and the world's second-largest bank. It does business with about 16.5 million customers, or about one in every five households in the United States.

Yet problems remain. Citibank and other major New York banks have found the move into investment banking difficult. Paying the lower salaries of commercial bankers, it has been unable to keep and attract top investment bankers. Moreover, despite its reputation as an aggressive, often arrogant commercial banker, Citibank is still considered too conservative for Wall Street, where savvy and aggressiveness are needed to pull off major deals.

Citicorp's loans to third-world countries are another problem area. At one time, about one quarter of its profits were from loans to third-world countries. But for 1987, Citicorp was expected to take a loss of about $1 billion, to increase the money set aside for bad loans. If it did, it should increase the money set aside for loan losses. Chairman John Reed's recognition that at least some of its third-world loans will not be repaid, won praise and, since Citicorp's action 50 more big banks have increased their provisions for loan losses by more than $15 billion.

Still, chairman John Reed is taking the tough steps the bank needed to stay on top, indicating that the bank has not been hurt by the change in leadership from Walter B. Wriston, who headed Citicorp for 14 years. Under Reed's leadership it seems likely that Citicorp, long an innovator, will be able to profit from a new deregulated market for financial services.

BEVERAGES: ALCOHOLIC AND NONALCOHOLIC

THE MARKET

Americans do a lot of heavy drinking. Every year the average American consumes some 24.1 gallons of beer and ale, 1.7 gallons of distilled spirits, 2.4 gallons of wine, about 44.8 gallons of soft drinks, 26 gallons a year of coffee, 27 gallons of milk, 11.2 gallons of fruit juices, and 5.2 gallons of bottled water. Some surveys indicate that soft drinks will soon replace tap water as the nation's most popular beverage for the first time in history.

THE MONEY

All of that hard drinking adds up to a tidal wave of revenues. Americans drink about $60 billion worth of alcoholic beverages each year, with about $35.7 billion spent at home and $24.2 billion spent at pubs, restaurants and other places outside the home.

Here's how U.S. beverage makers did in 1987:

Soft drink makers shipped about $20.5 billion worth of canned and bottled drinks, up from $12 billion in 1980.

About $13.0 billion worth of beer flowed out of the nation's breweries, up from $9.4 billion in 1980.

U.S. wine and brandy makers fermented a $2.9 billion river of wine, up from $2.3 billion in 1980.

And distillers shipped $3.3 billion worth of distilled liquor, down from $2.9 billion in 1980.

Another $972 million worth of beer was imported (6.7% of the market), $1.2 billion worth of wine and brandy (29.1% of the market), and $1.1 billion worth of distilled liquor (24.5% of the market). Total imports hit $3.2 billion (14.0% of the market) in 1987, up from $2.1 billion in 1980 (12.3% of the market). Only $150 million worth of soft drinks were imported.

THE PLAYERS

The beverage industry remains highly competitive, at both the production and wholesale end, yet most of the industry is dominated by a few large producers. The beer industry has grown increasingly concentrated over the years, with the top five brewers capturing 87.3% of the market, up from only 38% in 1965. The same can be said for the soft drink industry, in which the top two producers, the Coca-Cola Company and PepsiCo, control 66% of the market, up from 58.8% in 1980. The top six soft drink makers account for 87.5% of the market, up from 82.4% in 1980. The wine industry is less concentrated, with many small producers, but even so, the six largest American wineries control 52.6% of the market. In the liquor industry, the top five brands are Bacardi, Smirnoff, Seagram's 7 Crown, Canadian Mist and Popov, according to Clark Gavin Associates.

THE PEOPLE

There were about 62,000 people making alcoholic beverages in the U.S. in 1987, down from 68,700 in 1980. Another 105,000 worked in the bottled and canned soft drink industry in 1987, down from 118,000 in 1980.

TRENDS AND FORECAST

An increasingly health-conscious public and tough drunk-driving laws are expected to hold down consumption of alcoholic beverages for the next few years. Per-capita soft drink consumption, however, could hit 50 gallons per year by 1990. That should translate into increases of about 2% in revenues above inflation for the soft drink industry for the rest of the decade. The combined value of alcoholic beverages should remain virtually stagnant.

Table 119 Top 25 Imported Beers

Americans are drinking more and more imported beer. Sales of imports skyrocketed from $405 million in 1980 to $856 in 1986 and brewers of imports increased their share of the market to 6.5% from 3.9%. Here are the market shares of the 25 largest imports:

(in millions of gallons)

Rank	Brand	1986	1985	Percent change	1986 import market share	1986 total U.S. market share
1.	Heineken	81.26	78.62	3.4	29.7	1.4
2.	Corona	31.52	11.70	169.4	11.5	.6
3.	Molson	29.59	30.82	−4.0	10.8	.5
4.	Beck's	24.11	21.66	11.3	8.8	.4
5.	Moosehead	14.40	14.40	—	5.3	.3
6.	Labatt	12.15	10.80	12.5	4.4	.2
7.	St. Pauli Girl	9.60	9.90	−3.0	3.5	.2
8.	Amstel	7.65	6.50	7.7	2.8	.2
9.	Tecate	5.63	4.39	28.2	2.1	.1
10.	Dos Equis	5.16	5.40	−4.4	1.9	.1
11.	Foster's	4.38	3.37	30.0	1.6	.1
12.	Guinness	4.05	3.38	19.8	1.5	.1
13.	Old Vienna	2.95	2.84	3.9	1.1	.1
14.	Tsingtao	2.50	1.91	30.9	.9	—
15.	Sapporo	2.30	1.74	32.2	.8	—
16.	Bass	2.25	1.96	15.0	.8	—
17.	Kirin	2.22	1.70	30.6	.8	—
18.	Grolsch	2.13	2.02	5.4	.8	—
19.	Moussy	2.03	2.30	−11.7	.7	—
20.	Dab	1.60	1.60	—	.6	—
21.	Warteck	1.51	1.51	—	.6	—
22.	Carta Blanca	1.40	1.71	−18.1	.5	—
23.	Harp	1.35	.90	50.0	.5	—
24.	Kronenbourg	1.16	1.46	20.0	.4	—
25.	San Miguel	1.00	1.40	−28.6	.4	—

Source: *Modern Brewery Age* estimates, July 13, 1987.

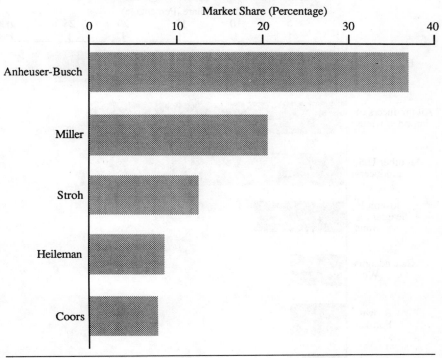

Table 120   Top Five Domestic Brewers

Market Share (Percentage)

Source: *Modern Brewery Age.*

Table 121   Top U.S. Wine Producers

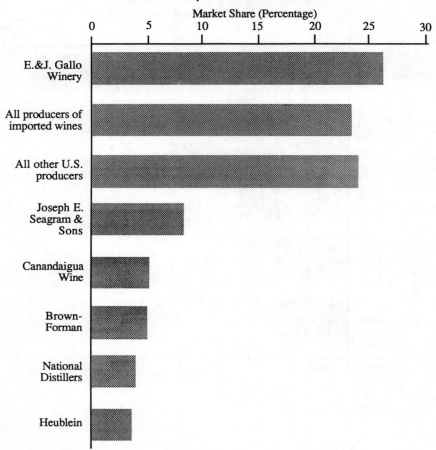

Market Share (Percentage)

Table 122 The Market for Booze

Type of distilled liquor	Market share (percentage)	
	1976	1986*
Whiskey, total	53.6	40.8
Bourbon	16.0	11.2
Canadian	11.9	12.5
Scotch	13.7	9.9
Blends	11.7	7.0
Other	0.3	0.2
Nonwhiskey, total	46.4	59.2
Vodka	17.9	20.6
Gin	9.5	8.8
Cordials	6.9	12.0
Rum	4.4	7.7
Brandy	3.9	4.8
Other	3.8	5.3

*Estimate.
Source: Clark Gavin Associates, Inc.

Table 123 Wets and Drys: The States with the Highest and Lowest Alcohol Consumption

Top five beer drinking states			Where they drink the least beer		
Rank	State	Per-capita consumption (gallons per year)	Rank	State	Per-capita consumption (gallons per year)
1.	New Hampshire	35.7	51.	Utah	13.8
1.	Nevada	35.7	49.	Oklahoma	18.1
3.	Wisconsin	32.1	49.	Arkansas	18.1
4.	Arizona	29.8	48.	Alabama	18.7
5.	Texas	29.1	47.	Kentucky	18.9
5.	Florida	29.1			

Top five wine drinking states			Where they drink the least wine		
Rank	State	Per-capita consumption (gallons per year)	Rank	State	Per-capita consumption (gallons per year)
1.	District of Columbia	6.65	51.	Mississippi	0.61
2.	Nevada	5.35	49.	Utah	0.81
3.	California	4.82	49.	Arkansas	0.81
4.	Washington	3.67	48.	West Virginia	0.82
5.	New Jersey	3.50	47.	Kentucky	0.83

Top five states for distilled liquor			Where they drink the least liquor		
Rank	State	Per-capita consumption (gallons per year)	Rank	State	Per-capita consumption (gallons per year)
1.	District of Columbia	4.93	51.	West Virginia	0.81
2.	Nevada	4.43	50.	Utah	0.89
3.	New Hampshire	4.36	49.	Iowa	1.10
4.	Alaska	2.74	48.	Arkansas	1.12
5.	Delaware	2.55	47.	Ohio	1.14

Sources: Beer Institute, Distilled Spirits Council of the United States, Wine Institute, and U.S. Department of Commerce.

Table 124 The Beverage Market

Americans drank 21.9 billion gallons of drinks in 1986 according to *Beverage World*. Here's how the market for beverages breaks down:

Type of beverage	Market share (percentage)
Soft drinks	47.9
Beer	25.8
Fruit juices and drinks	12.0
Drink mixes	5.2
Bottled water	4.7
Wines	2.6
Spirits	1.8

Source: *Beverage World*, March 1987.

Table 125 The Cost of a Drink

If a gulp of your favorite drink were exactly one ounce, this is how much it would cost:

Type of drink	Price per gulp
Spirits	$0.406
Wines	0.114
Beers	0.047
Fruit juices and drinks	0.029
Soft drinks	0.023
Drink mixes	0.011
Bottled water	0.009

Source: *Beverage World 1986/87 Databank*.

BEVERAGE TIME LINE

1855   The Miller Brewing Company is founded. A coin shortage during the Civil War sees the company mint its own Miller coins, which can be redeemed for a glass of beer.

1860   Eberhard Anheuser takes over a failing brewery. His son-in-law Adolphus Busch and Carl Conrad make the brew a success by producing a lighter beer than the beers that dominate the market. By 1901, Budweiser overtakes Pabst for the title of the best-selling beer.

1860s   Coffee becomes popular in the United States after it is issued with Army rations.

1869   Worried about teetotalers drinking wine at communion, Dr. Thomas Welch creates Welch's grape juice. His son Charles markets it as "Dr. Welch's Unfermented Wine."

1870s To market his herb tea made from wild roots and berries to tough Pennsylvania coal miners, Charles Hires calls it "root beer"—hence, "Hires Root Beer."

1885 R. S. Lazenby invents the soft drink Dr Pepper, which he calls "Dr Pepper's Phos-Ferrates."

1885 The Borden's New York Condensed Food Company (today known as Borden, Inc.) introduces the first fresh milk in bottles. Company founder Gail Borden has already introduced the first condensed milk.

1886 Coca-Cola goes on sale at Jacob's Pharmacy in Atlanta, Georgia. The headache and hangover remedy is advertised as an "esteemed Brain Tonic and Intellectual Beverage" by its inventor, John S. Pemberton. In 1891 an Atlanta pharmacist, Asa G. Candler, buys rights to the product, and in 1892 he organizes the Coca-Cola Company. The company achieves rapid growth after Candler turns Coca-Cola into a five-cent soft drink. The drink is typically dispensed from soda fountains. Only in 1899 is it bottled for the first time by Benjamin F. Thomas and Joseph B. Whitehead. For one dollar they acquire the right to bottle the drink in every state of the union, buying the syrup from Candler and reselling it to local bottlers.

1898 Many colas are appearing around the country, hoping to cash in on the popularity of Coca-Cola. One, Pepsi-Cola, is introduced by a New Bern, North Carolina, pharmacist, Caleb Bradham.

1901 Satori Kato develops instant coffee. It doesn't become popular until Nestlé introduces it as Nescafé in 1938.

1909 The tea bag and Lipton tea are introduced to America. Sir Thomas Lipton does not invent the tea bag but he is the first to market name-brand tea bags.

1916 Coke introduces its distinctive bottle, developed by Chapman S. Root of the Root Glass Company. The bottle will be synonymous with the product for the next 58 years.

1920 Prohibition creates a boom for soft drink, coffee, juice, and tea makers. Anheuser-Busch survives by selling yeast and sarsaparilla. There's also a booming market for bathtub gin. Nearly 1.4 billion gallons of hard liquor is sold illegally.

1923 Coca-Cola introduces the first "carry-home" soft drink carton, thus allowing grocers to sell larger quantities easily.

1928 Samuel and Allan Bronfman found Distiller's Company. In 1927, they bought Joseph E. Seagram & Sons. Even though it's Prohibition they ship large quantities of liquor that end up in the U.S. The family, which still owns the company, makes Seagram the world's largest producer of alcoholic beverages.

1929 C. I. Grigg invents a drink he calls "Bib-Label Lithianted Lemon-Lime Soda." In the 1930s, he comes up with a better name—7UP.

1933 The end of Prohibition hurts soft drink makers. Coke sees sales drop from 27.7 billion gallons in 1930 to only 20 million in 1933.

1933 Ernest and Julio Gallo found E.&J. Gallo Winery with $5,900. It will become the largest U.S. wine producer. The same year Lewis Rosenstiel sets up Schenley Distillers Company.
1954 Instant dry milk is introduced by Carnation.
1962 Sugar-free soft drinks become widely available with the introduction of TAB by Coke and Diet Pepsi. Some diet soft drinks were available on a limited basis in the 1950s.

SANKA

Dr. Ludwig Roselius spent years looking for a way to extract caffeine from coffee while leaving the taste intact. Finally, the head of the Cafe Haag firm in Bremen, Germany, succeeded. When Dr. Roselius brought his coffee to France, he called it Sanka, a contraction of the phrase *sans caféine,* "without caffeine."

Adolph Coors Company
CEO: W. K. Coors
Employees: 9,400
Assets: $1.3 billion

Golden, Colorado 80401
1-800-642-6116

	1987	1986	1985	1980
Revenues (millions of dollars):	1,350	NA	1,281	NA
Net income (millions of dollars):	48		53	
Share earnings (dollars):	1.32		1.52	

What it does: A major brewer.

Most companies go out of their way to avoid political and social controversies. Boycotts, after all, are bad for business and worse for marketing strategies—facts that the Coors brewery has learned in a slow and costly fashion.

Back in the 1960s, Coors beer had a cult status and demand was so great the company couldn't produce enough of it. In only a few years, without almost any advertising, it jumped from being the 16th-largest-selling beer to being the 4th. A regional brewer that only produced 200,000 barrels a year in the early 1940s, it was spewing out 13.5 million barrels in 1976.

While the company was flying high, so were the political aspirations of the company's multimillionaire brothers, William and Joseph, who ran a family brewery founded in 1873. They put up the money to found the Heritage Foundation, battled unions tooth and nail, and backed the presidential campaign of their close friend, Ronald Reagan. Joseph Coors is considered a member of Reagan's kitchen cabinet.

Meanwhile, charges of discrimination and unfair labor practices set off a series of boycotts that since the mid-1960s have pitted the company against practically every liberal constituency in the United States—feminists, unions, Chicanos, blacks, and civil-rights leaders.

In several key states, boycotts by organized labor hurt sales out of major markets. At the same time, the beer industry was undergoing a difficult restructuring, with regional brewers like Coors being forced to either go national or die. Coors's market share in California nosedived from 41% to only 14%.

Today, the next generation of Coors heirs, Jeffrey, the company's president, and Peter, the president of the brewing division, are trying to repair the mistake of their elders. They have hired public relations firms to improve the Coors image, funded minority projects, and pledged to increase minority employment. In 1987, they finally ended their feud with organized labor and the AFL-CIO agreed to call off its boycott.

But the brewery still has a long way to go to pick up the sales momentum it had in earlier years. Having bungled its opportunity to cash in on its cult status and become a major national brewery without having to spend much for advertising, the company now has to do it the hard way, with expensive national ad campaigns. Also, its attempts to diversify into such areas as manufacturing porcelain, packaging, trucking, and recycling have not produced significant profits, hardly the kind of help the brewer needs to finance its national expansion.

Coca-Cola Company

CEO: R. C. Goizueta

Employees: 28,030

Assets: $9.3 billion

310 North Avenue, N.W.
Atlanta, Georgia 30313
404-676-2121

	1987	1986	1985	1980
Revenues (millions of dollars):	7,658(n)	8,669	7,212	4,841
Net income (millions of dollars):	916	934	678	394
Share earnings (dollars):	2.43	2.42	1.72	1.06

What it does: It is the world's leading soft drink company and is involved in entertainment through Columbia Pictures. (n) restated

Coca-Cola has made some highly publicized marketing mistakes. First, Coke let its long-standing lead over Pepsi slip by failing to counter Pepsi's youth-oriented advertising. Then the company decided to change its age-old formula. What consumers wanted, some marketing genius decided, was a sweeter Coke—meaning something that tasted more like Pepsi. So in 1985, 99 years after Coke was invented, the company announced it was changing its famous formula.

Pepsi rejoiced, saying this proved it was winning the cola war, and consumers revolted. When the dust settled, Coke had to bring back the old Coke as "Coca-Cola Classic," which now outsells the new Coke by a ten-to-one margin.

But a fight over Coke's top-secret soft drink formula hasn't been the only blunder the company's made recently. Columbia Pictures, which

Coke bought for $752 million in 1983, has produced a bunch of canceled TV shows and box-office bombs, including the $17 million film *Fast Forward* that only earned $500,000 at the box office and the 1987 flop Ishtar that lost $25 million. Not surprisingly three heads of Columbia Pictures were sacked between 1982 and 1987. Its food division has produced stagnant profits and, in 1986, Wall Street never got excited about the company's initial public offering of a bottling unit. Shares were supposed to sell for $21 to $25 and raise up to $1.71 billion, the most ever raised by an initial public offering. But investors were only willing to pay $16.50 a share and the company only raised $1.18 billion, the second-largest public offering ever.

Still, the company seems to have the same luck it did when Asa G. Candler bought the rights to the formula for only $2,000. The flap over whether the new or old Coke was the real thing was probably the best free advertising any company could ever hope for. Sales soared and the combined market share of new and old Coke is larger than that of Pepsi. The booming market for videocassettes has turned the studio's old movies and TV shows into a gold mine and astute acquisitions of other entertainment properties have further helped earnings. Profits soared from $512 million in 1982 to $934 million in 1986 and Coke stock outperformed the S&P 500.

And, there was even a promising method some of Coke's worst mistakes. Since 1981, when Roberto Goizueta was appointed CEO, he's shaken up a company that looked like it was running out of steam. No longer are analysts saying it's only a matter of time before Coke slips behind Pepsi and under his direction the company has come up with a number of immensely profitable deals. For example, Coke announced in 1987, it would merge its Columbia movie and TV divisions with Tri-Star in a stock swap to create a new entertainment giant. After 31% of the shares are redistributed to Coke shareholders, the soft drink maker will get back the $1.5 billion it invested in recent years to buy entertainment properties and still own 49% of the company!

Today, Coca-Cola does business in 155 countries—you can even buy Coke at the South Pole. Long a symbol of Yankee business, it does a half-billion dollars worth of business in Latin America and $1.2 billion worth in Europe and Africa. Ever since 1899, when it sold the rights to bottle Coke throughout most of the U.S. for only $1, the company has traditionally sold syrup and let independent bottlers bring its product to the market. Today, however, as it and Pepsi scramble for every possible new market, both soft drink giants are reversing that trend. Coke, through the spun-off bottling unit, Coca-Cola Enterprises, now bottles about 38% of its product, up from only 13% a few years ago.

The Gallos   The story of Ernest and Julio Gallo is like a melodrama. Their company was founded on violent tragedy. They got embroiled in a lawsuit with a brother who accused them of cheating him out of his patrimony. Moreover, they were accused of using their company's enormous muscle in the wine industry to choke off competition and disdainfully undercut prices paid to the wine growers who depended on them for their livelihood.

Whatever their methods, they have made their E.&J. Gallo Winery in Modesto, California, the world's largest wine producer. One out of every four bottles of wine sold in the U.S. bears one of the company's brands, which include Chablis Blanc, Hearty Burgundy, Carlo Rossi, E.&J. brandy, and André champagne. The secretive Gallos don't divulge financial data, but in 1985 *Fortune* estimated that the company earned at least $50 million a year on sales of about $1 billion.

Ernest and Julio are the sons of an Italian immigrant, Joseph Gallo, who had a small vineyard. A stern taskmaster, Joseph worked his sons hard. Gallo survived Prohibition because of a government dispensation for making wine for religious and medicinal uses. In 1933, when the brothers were in their early 20s, Gallo shot his wife to death, tried to kill his sons, and then killed himself.

In the tragedy's aftermath, the brothers decided to get out of the vineyard business and make their own wine. They learned the process by reading instruction pamphlets at the public library and, when Prohibition ended, they sank $5,900 into a new winery. Early, they divided their functions by having Julio oversee the production while Ernest marketed the wine.

Over the years their operations grew, but their first major success didn't come until they introduced Thunderbird, a 60-cents-a-bottle, high-alcohol wine that became a favorite of skid row bums. Gallo made a fortune off the stuff but ever since has been trying to live down the sleazy image it gave the company. In the 1960s, it had another hit in another cheap wine, Ripple, apparently a favorite of a lot of teenagers.

The Gallos' image wasn't helped either when their younger brother, Joseph, who was 13 when their father died, charged that his brothers had cheated him. While researching their father's estate because of another feud involving the brothers, Joseph's lawyer found that his client had inherited an interest in their father's business. Joseph contended that E.&J. Gallo Winery was an outgrowth of that business, so he demanded a share.

As Gallo grew, it became the biggest grape purchaser in the region, which led to charges that the company exploited the vineyards it dealt with. The 1,500 vineyards that serviced Gallo were always on edge. The Gallos would reject a harvest out of hand or slash the price. With rare exception, the growers took it. In 1984, a grower complained to the California Department of Food and Agriculture that most of his harvest's price was cut to $275 a ton from $475. Gallo claimed the quality of the grapes wasn't high enough. Since the growers had no contract, the agency sided with the Gallos. Now the grape growers get a one-year contract from Gallo citing standards.

One reason for Gallo's success was an approach to marketing that left little to chance. Salesmen were told not only how to display merchandise, but what not to joke about (no dirty jokes) and how to cope with the various personalities of retailers.

And distributors knew that Gallo clearly didn't want them representing competitors. If a distributor didn't like it, he most likely lost Gallo's business. Because of its enormous market share, Gallo got its way. In 1976, the Federal Trade Commission said such a practice was unfair competition. For a while, Gallo had to abide by a consent order saying distributors wouldn't be punished for carrying competing brands. Then, in 1984, the FTC set aside the order, after Gallo argued that the market had become more competitive and now other wine makers had an edge.

In 1985, however, an Ohio distributor, who had handled Gallo for 40 years, sued the company for an alleged violation of antitrust laws after it canceled him because he told the Gallos he couldn't afford the size of the sales force they wanted to push their products. Without Gallo products, he argued, he often couldn't get a foot in liquor stores to sell anything. Gallo won the case, saying the company wasn't in business to open doors so competing products could enter.

That bulldozer approach keeps working. For instance, when Gallo entered the wine cooler business there were 100 brands competing. With a heavy advertising campaign and cut-rate prices that squeezed most competitors when they tried to match them, Gallo's Bartles & Jaymes brand quickly bobbed to the top.

BOOK PUBLISHING

THE MARKET

Pundits have long predicted that book lovers are an endangered species who will lose out to a semiliterate generation weaned on television and music videos. Yet, the average American buys about 6.08 books a year, up from only 2.75 per person in 1970. In 1986, book publishers earned more than $1 billion in pretax profits. A study by the Book Industry Study Group showed that since 1979 there are 8 million more Americans who regularly read books. Not everyone reads books, however: only about 20% of the public has bought a book in the last six months.

THE MONEY

Book publishing was an $11.6 billion industry in 1987, up from $6.1 billion in 1980. In 1987, a large share of the year's sales came from trade books ($2.9 billion), professional, scientific, and technical books ($2.3 billion), and college, elementary and high school texts ($3.7 billion). Religious books account for about 5% of the market. In 1988, the publishing industry expects to sell about $12.8 billion worth of books.

THE PLAYERS

There are nearly 18,000 book publishing houses in the United States and they put out nearly 55,000 different titles a year that are sold in more than 21,500 bookstores. Ease of entry into the market has allowed many small publishers to go into business: over half of the publishers have fewer than five employees, 80% have fewer than 20 employees, 94% have fewer than 100 employees.

Most books are sold and produced by a few large houses. In 1958, according to author Maxwell Lillienstein, the 50 largest trade book publishers accounted for 65% of all trade book sales, none with an overwhelmingly dominant position. But as early as 1984, five publishers had 35% of all trade book sales. The largest company overall, including textbooks, is Simon & Schuster, the publishing division of Gulf + Western, which sold about 10% of all general-interest books.

Other studies indicate that in the 1980s, the four largest publishers in each of the following segments—mass-market paperbound books, bookclub books, mail-order books, and general reference books—have controlled more than half of all sales. The top eight companies have accounted for over half the sales in textbooks, technical, scientific, and professional books, adult trade books, and juvenile books. The biggest eight religious publishers have had 49% of the market.

The same can be said of the bookstore business. There are some 21,515 bookstores in the United States (up from 8,360 in 1957 and 1977 when there were 15,188). In recent years, chains have been rapidly expanding and, by 1984, their outlets numbered 5,715, according to the *American Book Trade Directory*.

Only about 30% of all books were sold in bookstores in 1985, up from 20% in 1975; another 20% were sold through book clubs or mail order, down from 26% in 1975; U.S. libraries and institutions accounted for 9% of all sales, about the same as 1975, when they bought 8%; College store sales increased to 17% from 15% in 1975, and falling enrollments dropped the share of purchases by high schools and elementary schools to 20% in 1985, down from 26% in 1975. Imports grew to hold 7.3% of the market in 1986, up from 3.9% in 1982.

In recent years, a few large chains have increasingly dominated retail sales. By negotiating volume discounts from major publishers, chains such as Waldenbooks can heavily discount best-sellers and capture a larger share of the market. The top four companies (Waldenbooks, B. Dalton, Crown, and Barnes & Noble) now sell about 30% of all general interest books.

THE PEOPLE

There were 76,800 people employed by book publishers in 1987.

THE FORECAST

Book sales should continue to grow for several reasons. Libraries are committing more funds to book buying, consumers are likely to buy more books, as they have in recent years, and the reading-age population will have grown by over 8 million between 1986 and 1990. With declining college enrollments, however, the market for college bookstores and college textbooks will decline.

PUBLISHING GOES ON A BOOK-BUYING SPREE

Not even the book business has escaped merger mania. In the last few years companies have gone on a book-buying spree—not for new talent, but for entire publishing houses.

That has left very few independent houses. One of the biggest book buyers has been Gulf + Western. It started building a publishing empire by purchasing Simon & Schuster in 1975. It bought the fourth-largest publisher, Prentice-Hall, in 1985, and during 1986 paid more than $200 million for a dozen publishers. Simon & Schuster is now the largest publishing house.

William Morrow is part of the Hearst Corporation and Macmillan acquired Charles Scribner's Sons. Random House now also includes Alfred A. Knopf, Times Books, and Pantheon. In 1986, when $2 billion was spent on mergers and acquisitions in the book publishing industry, Doubleday & Co. was bought by Bertelsmann AG and Time Inc. swallowed

Table 126   15 Largest U.S. Book Publishers

Rank	Book operation/parent	1986 revenues (millions of dollars)	1985 revenues (millions of dollars)	Percentage change, 1985 to 1986
1.	Simon & Schuster/Gulf + Western	949.0	798.2	18.9
2.	Harcourt Brace Jovanovich, Publishers/HBJ	706.0	401.3	75.9
3.	Time	680.0	420.0	61.9
4.	Reader's Digest Books/Reader's Digest Association	675.0	550.0	22.7
5.	Bantam/Doubleday/Dell, Literary Guild/Bertelsmann	660.0	622.0	6.1
6.	McGraw-Hill Book Company/McGraw-Hill	487.7	460.2	6.0
7.	Macmillan Publishing/Macmillan	485.0	405.6	19.6
8.	Random House/Advance Publications	460.0	410.0	12.2
9.	Encyclopedia Britannica	391.0	345.0	13.3
10.	Grolier	350.6	296.1	18.4
11.	International Thomson Holdings/International Thomson Organisation	350.0	230.0	52.2
12.	Houghton Mifflin	321.3	277.5	15.8
13.	World Book Encylopedia/Berkshire Hathaway	285.5	282.9	0.8
14.	Times Mirror Book Group/Times Mirror	285.0	270.0	5.6
15.	Western Publishing	216.1	206.8	4.5
	Total	7302.2	5975.6	22.2

Source: *BP Report,* May 1987.

Table 127   Largest Bookstore Chains

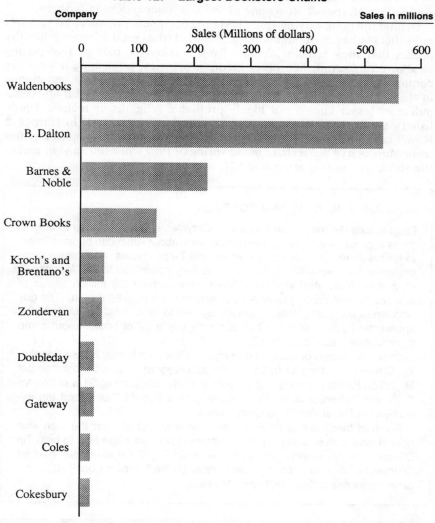

Company   Sales in millions

Sales (Millions of dollars)

Company	
Waldenbooks	
B. Dalton	
Barnes & Noble	
Crown Books	
Kroch's and Brentano's	
Zondervan	
Doubleday	
Gateway	
Coles	
Cokesbury	

Source: *BP Report,* 1987 figures.

Scott Foresman & Co. And in 1987, Rupert Murdoch's News Corporation gobbled up Harper & Row, one of the last independent publishers.

Behind the book-buying spree is simple economic pressure. To survive, publishers either must dominate their market (thus producing such healthy profits that they remain immune from a takeover bid) or risk getting swallowed up. And, like other media properties, publishing houses are commanding top dollar. For companies with expansion plans and money in the pocket, well-known independents such as McGraw-Hill and Macmillan or lesser-known but highly profitable religious or technical publishers are likely to become rich prizes in the years ahead. In Harper & Row's case, the company's board of directors could hardly resist an offer from Murdoch of $65 a share in the spring of 1987 when only a year earlier the stock was selling at around $24.

IACOCCA II, III, IV, V, AND FOREVER

Lee Iacocca did more than just revive Chrysler, he gave new life to biographies and autobiographies, even if they were about American businessmen. In recent years, publishers, like movie and TV producers, once again demonstrated that redundancy is a virtue as they scrambled to find *Iacocca II, III,* and so forth. And why not? There were already 2.6 million copies of *Iacocca* in print earning Chrysler's chairman more than $6 million. (The guy who wrote the book, William Novak, agreed to take a flat fee of $45,000, apparently figuring who the hell is gonna buy a lot of books about some cigar-smoking auto executive?)

So, in the search of *Iacocca II,* Harper & Row paid former House Speaker Tip O'Neill more than $1 million for his autobiography. David Stockman got $2 million for his memoirs and Houghton Mifflin coughed up $1.5 million for T. Boone Pickens's book. Real estate tycoon Donald Trump and top executives at Pepsi and Coke wrote books.

Some of these books have not done so well, but at least the man who helped start it all is doing just fine. William Novak got huge fees to help Tip O'Neill write his autobiography, royalties for Mobil Oil executive Herbert Schmertz's book, and money from Sydney Biddle Barrows's book about the oldest business called *Mayflower Madam.*

PAUL SAMUELSON

Professor Paul Samuelson's famed *Economics* textbook, which taught a lot of people everything they think they know about that subject, is now in its 12th edition and has sold about 4 million copies. When first published in 1948, the book wasn't loved by one and all. A reviewer for *The Annals of the American Academy of Political and Social Science,* for instance, sniffed that "it drops wisecracks at times." The newest edition is the first of Samuelson's with a collaborator, Professor William Nordhaus of Yale University.

CHEMICALS

THE MARKET AND THE MONEY

In the past this industry brought us such things as nylons, Teflon, pesticides, and worries about environmental pollution. In the future, the chemical industry is moving into biotechnology, producing a new generation of drugs, food, and chemicals. (See the "Biotechnology" part of the "Technology" section.)

Over $197.5 billion worth of chemicals were shipped by U.S. companies in 1987, making the chemical industry not only one of the nation's largest but one of its most important. Petroleum refiners ship $115.7 billion worth of products that are not included in the above figure.

The chemical industry produces industrial chemicals that make modern manufacturing possible. It manufactures and develops pharmaceuticals that have revolutionized the health-care industry, supplies the fertilizers and pesticides that have made America the breadbasket of the world, and sells household products ranging from soaps to cosmetics.

The chemical industry is made up of several important sectors. Here's a glance at each:

Petrochemicals

Shipments of petrochemicals hit $82 billion in 1987, only a 3.1% growth over 1985. This industry produces chemicals from petroleum products, which account for about 90% of all organic chemicals (i.e., chemicals made from organic materials such as petroleum). It is heavily dependent on demand for such products as rubber, synthetic fibers, fertilizers, and other products, while its profit margins are closely tied to the price of oil.

Biotechnology

The market value of products in this area is growing rapidly as basic research moves toward practical applications. In 1987, about $4.5 billion had been invested in this industry and some analysts estimate that biotech companies were spending as much as $3 billion a year in research and development. Revenues, however, remain small. According to the U.S. Commerce Department, shipment of products created by monoclonal antibodies or recombinant DNA technologies hit only $550 million in 1987, up from an estimated $60 million in 1984. (See the "Biotechnology" part of the "Technology" section.)

INDUSTRIAL CHEMICALS

Shipments of industrial chemicals inched up to $57.2 billion in 1987 from $51.6 billion in 1985. Most sales were for organic chemicals ($43.1 billion); shipments of inorganic chemicals such as alkalies, chlorine, and industrial gases totaled $14.1 billion. Shipments of industrial inorganic chemicals have declined since 1984, when the industry shipped $15.1 billion worth. Industrial chemicals are used to produce plastics, synthetic fibers, solvents, and dyes. They play a role in steel production, the manufacture of other chemicals (about two thirds of all chlorine, for example, is used to produce organic chemicals), and dozens of other industries ranging from oil recovery to medical supplies and aerospace.

Agricultural Chemicals

Hurt by a troubled farm sector, the market for agricultural chemicals continued to decline in 1987, dropping to $11.6 billion from $14.1 billion in 1984.

Rubber and Plastics

As plastics continue to replace metals, combined shipments of synthetic rubber and plastic materials increased to $30.1 billion in 1987 from $26.4 billion in 1984. Shipments of synthetic rubber, however, remained stagnant, largely because fewer autos and hence fewer tires were being manufactured.

Paints, Coatings, and Adhesives

Shipments of paints and related products hit $11.3 billion worth in 1987, up from $10.0 billion worth shipped in 1984.

Cleaning Preparations and Cosmetics

Shipments of soaps, cleaners, toilet goods, and cosmetics hit a total value of $29.7 billion in 1987, up from $27.1 billion in 1984. Sales of cosmetics, fragrances, and other toiletries accounted for over $14.0 billion of that total in 1987. Soaps and other detergents racked up $8.8 billion in sales in 1987.

The Pharmaceutical Industry

The value of shipments hit $34.0 billion in 1987, up dramatically from the $26.9 billion worth shipped in 1984. Between 1972 and 1985, shipments of pharmaceuticals grew 11% a year. That growth slowed to 7.2% in 1986 and 7.5% in 1987, but it was still much faster than inflation, which hit 4.4% in 1987. (See the section "Health Care and Services.")

Petroleum Refining

The value of shipments from petroleum refiners dropped 33.9% in 1986 to only $109.3 billion, a steep decline from $210 billion in the industry's peak year of 1981. The number of refineries also tumbled from 319 in 1980 to 219 in 1987 because higher oil prices cut demand and made it less profitable to refine products in the U.S. The collapse of prices of petroleum products improved profits in 1986, however, for refiners. Shipments grew 5.9% in 1987 to $115.7. The $115.7 billion worth of petroleum refining shipments is in addition to the $197.5 billion worth of chemicals shipped in 1987. (See the section "Oil and Natural Gas.")

The Players

The 100 largest chemical companies had sales of $126 billion and profits of $9.1 billion in 1985, according to *Chemical and Engineering News*'s annual survey of the top 100 chemical producers, while the 50 largest companies had sales of $106.6 billion and profits of $7.4 billion. Table 128 (below) lists the 10 largest companies.

TRENDS AND FORECAST

The chemical industry faced tough times in the early and mid-1980s as declining markets for many traditional products and a strong dollar hurt sales.

The industry confronted increasing foreign competition. The industry's trade surplus peaked at $14 billion in 1980 and then declined to $7.6 billion in 1986. Even with a decline in the value of the dollar in 1987, the trade surplus grew only to an estimated $9 billion in 1987.

At the same time the industry faced declining or stagnant markets for many products. High prices for oil caused many consumers to switch from petrochemicals and a stagnant U.S. industrial economy reduced the demand for many chemicals used by auto makers, the construction industry, and farmers.

Table 128   10 Largest Chemical Producers

Rank	Company	Chemical sales (millions of dollars)	Chemical sales as a percent of total company sales
1.	du Pont	11,839	43.6
2.	Dow Chemical	8,863	79.8
3.	Exxon	6,079	8.1
4.	Union Carbide	5,001	78.8
5.	Atlantic Richfield	4,915	32.8
6.	Monsanto	4,701	68.3
7.	BASF Wyandotte	3,600	100.0%
8.	Shell Oil	3,292	19.6
9.	Amoco	2,928	14.5
10.	Celanese	2,891	100.0

Source: *Chemical and Engineering News*, "Facts and Figures," June 8, 1987.

Environmental regulation further squeezed profits. Scandal over the EPA's lax enforcement of toxic waste dumps, the forced evacuation of several towns because of dioxins, and the leak of hazardous gases from a Union Carbide chemical plant in Bhopal, India, all increased the public's awareness of environmental hazards. Congress responded by tightening environmental laws and increasing the industry's cost of doing business. As early as 1984, the annual cost of controlling pollution in the chemical industry was $2.8 billion and rising. About $1.4 billion of the $8.5 billion Superfund created by Congress to clean up hazardous waste sites will come from taxes on chemical and petroleum companies, with another $2.5 billion coming from general business taxes (some of which will fall on the chemical industry). New EPA proposals to toughen environmental standards could cost the industry billions more.

The result was a painful restructuring. Chemical producers shut plants to trim excess capacity, laid off employees to improve profits, and used their cash for takeover raids in an attempt to diversify into more profitable businesses.

By 1987, however, the industry was set for a comeback. Lower oil prices dramatically improved their profit margins in the first half of 1986 and a weaker dollar was expected to improve overseas sales. Most of the less productive plants have already been closed, and if industrial demand perks up the industry could finally see some handsome profits.

E. I. du Pont de Nemours and Company

CEO: R. E. Heckert
Employees: 141,000
Assets: $26.7 billion

1007 Market Street
Wilmington, Delaware 19898
302-774-1000

	1987	1986	1985	1980
Revenues (millions of dollars):	30,468	27,148	29,483	13,652
Net income (millions of dollars):	1,786	1,538	1,118	716
Share earnings (dollars):	7.39	6.35	4.61	4.83

What it does: Du Pont runs about 90 major businesses in 50 countries and earns about one third of its revenues outside the United States. The nation's largest chemical producer, it gets about 40% of its revenues from chemicals. It also produces biomedical products, manufactures industrial and consumer products, and has over $3.4 billion a year in petroleum revenues and $1 billion a year in revenues from coal.

With a family fortune of $4.7 billion to $8.5 billion, the du Ponts are the wealthiest and most powerful dynasty in the United States. Holding 17.5% of E. I. du Pont de Nemours and Company, they are the only family to control one of the 10 largest industrial corporations. But since 1970, no family member has run the company.

Founder and French immigrant Irénée du Pont set up a gunpowder firm in the first decade of the 19th century. Thanks to government contracts and the War of 1812, business boomed. Later, the firm continued to grow because the French-trained owners made high-quality gunpowder. The du Ponts were also pioneers in setting up monopolies and controlling markets. After the Civil War they founded the Gunpowder Trade Association (later called the Gunpowder Trust) that dictated prices and kept profits high.

But with wars being scarce in the late 19th century, the family considered selling the business. But Alfred I. du Pont, T. Coleman du Pont, and Pierre S. du Pont of the family's Kentucky branch bought out the firm in 1902 for just over $12 million. By 1907, the company had already earned $47 million. But even though he kept the business in family hands, Alfred I. du Pont was forced out by T. Coleman and Pierre in 1915. Pierre, who bought out T. Coleman in 1914, then brought in his brothers, Irénée and Lammot, to run the company with him.

Early in the 20th century the company also absorbed the members of the Gunpowder Trust, becoming the nation's largest munitions manufacturer. During the First World War du Pont did a $1 billion business, producing 40% of the explosives fired by the Allies.

Armed with its wartime profits, the company made its first acquisitions outside munitions, buying a controlling interest in the ailing General Motors Corporation. With the Germans driven out of the chemical industry by the war, the du Ponts also moved into the chemical industry by buying up small, innovative companies. Since then such peacetime products as polyester, nylons, rayon, and cellophane have poured forth from du Pont almost non-stop.

Antitrust actions finally forced the family to sell its General Motors stock in the 1960s, and in 1971 the family tradition of running du Pont ended after 170 years. Of the 1,700 family members, only three were working for the company in the late 1970s even though the family controls 20% of the stock. One family member, Pete du Pont, a former Delaware governor, ran for president in 1988 as a Republican. Two others, Lammot du Pont Copeland, Jr., and Henry E. I. du Pont, managed to go bankrupt in the 1970s. However, the future of the family fortune remains brighter than that of many dynasties. The du Ponts have maintained control over their chemical company, a major feat considering the fact that many family members hardly know each other.

Meanwhile, the company has struggled with the difficulties of the chemical industry. Net income was only $1.1 billion in 1985, down from $1.4 billion in 1981. A weak market for chemical products and a strong dollar hurt its overseas sales, so du Pont trimmed its work force more than 20% to 141,000, streamlined operations, and improved productivity.

Profits are expected to rebound in the next few years and the company's traditional operations continue to churn out about $4.5 billion a year in cash flow. Using that money, the company has gone on an acquisition binge in the 1980s, spending $6.8 billion to acquire Conoco, Inc., a major oil company. With the company spending $1.1 billion a year in research, it also stands a good chance of finding more money-makers like nylon and cellophane.

W. R. Grace & Co.

CEO: J. Peter Grace
Employees: 116,900
Assets: $4.1 billion

1114 Avenue of the Americas
New York, New York 10036-7794
212-819-5500

	1987	1986	1985	1980
Revenues (millions of dollars):	4,515	6,808	7,260	6,101
Net income (millions of dollars):	142	472	147	284
Share earnings (dollars):	1.67	1.25	2.82	6.08

What it does: It is a leading producer of specialty chemicals, it distributes books, it makes specialty textiles, and it has interests in natural resources.

This is a company that turned bird droppings into a $6.8 billion business.

William Grace fled Ireland and built up the Grace shipping line from nothing by hauling guano droppings that were used as fertilizer. He also started a family tradition of using money to get political power. In 1880, he became New York's first Catholic mayor.

The company's current head, J. Peter Grace, is the third generation to run the business. When he took over the business, the company had huge holdings in agriculture, banking, and airlines in Latin America. But by 1977 the company was out of the shipping business. Believing Latin America was politically unstable, Grace sold off the company's operations there: in 1950 the company earned 66% of its sales from Latin America; by 1974, it was out of the continent.

Along the way, J. Peter Grace increased sales from $200 million to $7.3 billion in 1985 and created a huge, wobbling conglomerate. Grace has been driven by an urge to acquire, though there seems to be no rhyme or reason to his purchases. By the mid-1980s, the company operated restaurants in 35 states, owned 695 retail stores in 41 states, sold sporting goods through its Herman's Sporting Goods Retail Group, provided artificial insemination services for cows, and had holdings in oil and gas, laboratory equipment, and of course chemicals, which provide about 44% of its revenues.

Meanwhile, Grace continued the family tradition of being an expert on waste—government spending, not guano. As head of President Reagan's panel on government waste, Grace argued that there were exactly 2,478 things that could be done to save exactly $424.4 billion in government spending. Too bad all of politics isn't that precise. But no matter, Grace took his cause on the road, speaking around the country.

But while Grace claims his proposals will save the economy from being saddled with a huge government debt, Grace's critics complain that he should spend more time worrying about his company's profits. Earnings have been weak and in 1985 the largest Grace shareholder, the Flick Group of West Germany, decided to sell its 26% stake. Grace only owns 1% of the company's stock, and to fight off the prospect of an outside takeover he was forced to sell off the company's retail, restaurant, and agricultural chemicals divisions to finance a share-buying program.

That will leave the company back where it started—in the chemical business, where weak industry growth means cost cutting and streamlining.

Then there's the problem of finding a successor to Grace. He has held the top job since 1945, longer than any other chief executive at a major company. Already he's outlasted one generation of successors. Only one of his children works for the company and he is not considered likely to take over the business.

FORMICA

Formica is an example of how something takes on many uses. In 1913, Herbert A. Faber and Daniel J. O'Conor found a way to laminate insulation material for the electrical industry. They got an order to make commutator rings, replacing the mica with laminate—hence "for mica," or the Formica Company, as they called their Cincinnati-based firm.

In 1914, the young men decided to make sheet laminates. At first they had a tough time finding a supplier of resin, the key component, but eventually they did. Their first sheets of Formica laminate rolled off the press on July 4. Orders came for many uses: as parts for radios, refrigerators, and washers, and for uses in the textile industry.

It wasn't until 24 years later, when a new melamine resin entered the process, that it became possible to make the tough, durable laminate in use today. Decorative laminate became the company's major product. One of the penalties of success was the company's having to fight in court in 1978 to retain registration of the Formica trademark against charges that the name was so popular it had become the generic name for all decorative plastic laminate.

VASELINE

When in his 50s, Robert A. Chesebrough, a chemist and entrepreneur, was gravely ill with pleurisy. He promptly ordered a nurse to rub him down with Vaseline and he lived another 40 years or so. Chesebrough's faith in the product had a lot to do with the fact that he was the first person to package and promote Vaseline as a healing balm. As a young chemist, he visited oil fields and was intrigued by the paraffinlike residue called rod wax found on oil pump rods. He was told the stuff was great for putting on cuts and burns. Chesebrough distilled it and found out it did have healing properties. By 1870, he was producing quantities of what he called Vaseline Petroleum Jelly. In 1881, Standard Oil, the source of his supplies, bought the company. When the Standard Oil Trust was dissolved in 1911, Chesebrough once again had an independent company. Only in 1955 did the company merge with Pond's, a maker of skin cream.

CLUBS

Private clubs may have an old-boy image as the exclusive preserves of the elite, but it was health, not snobbery, that brought more Americans— 14 million—to clubs than ever before.

The nation's 10,000 private clubs currently employ nearly 1.5 million people, with an annual payroll of $4 billion. No exact figures for industry revenues are available, but the 4,000 clubs that belong to the Club Managers Association of America (CMAA) produced an estimated $5.3 billion in revenues in 1987, up from $5.02 billion in 1986. Surprisingly, $2.76 billion in revenues from food and beverage sales outpaced the $2.57 billion the 4,000 CMAA members took in from dues.

The cost of maintaining a country club lifestyle is going up all the time. Between 1980 and 1985, revenues for country clubs rose 39.9%, double the 19.5% rise in the CPI. But at the same time expenses were also skyrocketing, increasing 37.8%. Managing a golf course alone costs an average of $20,000 a hole, up from under $4,000 a hole in 1965.

Soaring costs are changing the country club industry. Older, exclusive clubs are in a financial bind, forcing them to either raise their rates or cut back on services. That has produced a market characterized by very expensive clubs that offer a full range of sports (tennis, swimming, and golf); some country clubs that specialize in one sport, such as golf; and superclubs, which offer just about anything. One of the first superclubs was the $44 million Sweetwater Country Club, opened in 1983 outside Houston. For $15,000 a year, it offers 27 holes of golf, pools, locker rooms, weight rooms, a basketball court, tennis courts, sports shops, a spa, card rooms, racquetball courts, a ballroom, and a vast terrain of lakes, fairways, and oak trees. Since then other clubs have spent as much as $70 million on such amenities.

COAL

THE MARKET

When you hear about the energy crisis, nobody's talking about coal.

At the current rate of production (909 million tons in 1987), the U.S. has enough coal to last 300 years. And that's after 200 years of mining 50 billion tons of coal.

Coal accounts for about 24% of the energy Americans use. Primary consumers are the electric utilities (698.6 million tons in 1987), coke plants (38.9 million tons), other industrial and transportation companies (75.3 million tons), and residences and consumers (7.7 million).

Coal is also used in coke plants as part of the production of steel, and for combustion and as a feedstock in the chemical industry, in the stone, clay, and glass industry, and in the paper and allied products industry. Another 84 million tons of coal were exported in 1987.

THE MONEY

OPEC, the oil embargoes of the 1970s, and the fall of the Shah of Iran were a boon for the coal industry. While consumers faced mounting energy bills, coal producers shipped $22.5 billion worth of coal in 1982, up from only $4.6 billion in 1972.

More recently, slumping oil prices and a rusty market for steel have put a damper on coal shipments. Shipments in 1987 hit only $21.2 billion and 1987 promises to have been no better. Part of the problem has been slumping coal prices. The cost of coal rose rapidly during the 1970s from $5 a ton in 1970 to $27 a ton in 1982, as oil prices skyrocketed. Since then the price of coal has followed oil back down, hovering around $24 a ton.

Table 129   The Largest Coal Producers

Rank	Company	Tonnage (millions of metric tons)	Percentage of U.S. total
1.	Peabody Coal Company (Newmont Mining)	62.0	7.0
2.	Consolidation Coal Company (E. I. du Pont de Nemours)	42.7	4.8
3.	Amax Coal Company (Amax)	38.3	4.3
4.	Texas Utilities (Texas Utilities)	29.8	3.4
5.	ARCO Coal Company (Atlantic Richfield)	27.3	3.1
6.	Exxon Coal USA, Inc. (Exxon)	26.2	3.0
7.	North American Coal (North American Coal)	22.4	2.5
8.	NERCO (PacifiCorp)	20.8	2.3
9.	A. T. Massey Coal Company's subsidiaries (Fluor)	19.8	2.2
10.	Sunedco Coal Company (Sun Company)	17.5	2.0

Sources: "1985 Coal Production of Leading Bituminous Organizations," *Keystone News Bulletin,* February 1986; company reports and Form 10-K's; U.S. Department of Energy.

Table 130   The Largest U.S. Coal Mines, 1985

Rank	Mine name	Type of mine	State location	1985 tonnage (millions of short tons)	Operating company
1.	Black Thunder	Surface	Wyoming	23.2	ARCO Coal
2.	Jacobs Ranch	Surface	Wyoming	13.0	Kerr-McGee
3.	Belle Ayr	Surface	Wyoming	12.8	Amax Coal Company
4.	Rosebud	Surface	Montana	12.3	Western Energy
5.	Rawhide	Surface	Wyoming	12.2	Carter Mining
6.	Eagle Butte	Surface	Wyoming	11.8	Amax Coal Company
7.	Martin Lake	Surface	Texas	11.8	Texas Utilities
8.	Cordero	Surface	Wyoming	10.1	Sunedco
9.	Monticello	Surface	Texas	9.5	Texas Utilities
10.	Caballo	Surface	Wyoming	9.0	Carter Mining

Source: *Keystone News Bulletin,* March 1985.

Table 131 U.S. Daily Per-Capita Consumption of Types of Energy in 1973, 1979, and 1986

Type of energy	Unit	1973	1979	1986	Percent change 1973–1979	Percent change 1979–1986
Petroleum products	gallons	3.4	3.5	2.8	0.7	−19.0
Natural gas (dry)	cubic feet	286	247	181	−13.6	−26.6
Coal	pounds	14.6	16.6	18.3	13.8	10.1
Hydropower electricity	kilowatt-hours	3.5	3.4	3.3	−3.2	−3.3
Nuclear power electricity	kilowatt-hours	1.1	3.1	4.7	187.7	50.7
Electricity, including hydropower and nuclear power electricity	kilowatt-hours	22.2	25.3	26.9	13.8	6.6
Motor gasoline	gallons	1.33	1.32	1.22	−0.8	−7.3
Industrial sector energy (including electric losses distributed)	thousand Btu	408	398	295	−2.5	−25.9
Total energy	thousand Btu	963	963	840	0.0	−12.8

Source: *Annual Energy Review 1986*, Energy Information Administration.

THE PEOPLE

The growing demand for coal has not translated into increased employment. Technological advances and mechanization decreased the number of coal miners from 246,000 in 1978 to only 174,000 in 1987.

TRENDS AND FORECAST

As an abundant, cheap energy source, coal has seen a resurgence in the 1970s and 1980s, growing at a compound annual rate of 17.3% between 1972 and 1982. But shipments have declined as oil and natural gas prices have continued to fall and slow growth is expected to continue through the rest of the 1980s, with coal production topping the 1-billion-ton mark in 1991.

Demand for coal in the troubled steel sector should continue to weaken and U.S. coal producers are likely to see increased competition from foreign producers, which are fighting to capture a larger share of the growing world demand. Increased environmental regulation to curb the problem of acid rain could also impose heavy regulatory and environmental costs on electric utilities and other major users of coal.

Table 132   Estimated International Recoverable Reserves of Coal, 1981[1]

(billions of short tons)

Area and country	Anthracite and bituminous coal[2]			Lignite		Total recoverable
	Recoverable	Portion surface minable	Portion coking quality	Recoverable	Portion surface minable	
North, Central, and South America						
Canada	4.18	0	1.38	2.33	2.33	6.51
United States	248.16	89.28	NA	35.25	35.25	283.41
Other	19.25	1.78	2.74	0.02	(3)	19.28
Total	271.59	91.07[4]	4.12[4]	37.60	37.58	309.20
Western Europe						
Turkey	0.20	0	0	1.90	0	2.11
United Kingdom	5.06	0	2.23	0	0	5.06
West Germany	32.98	NA	19.78	38.66	38.66	71.64
Yugoslavia	1.73	0.06	0	16.50	0	18.23
Other	3.29	0.67[4]	1.03[4]	2.24	0.07	5.53
Total	43.26	0.72[4]	23.04[4]	59.31	38.74[4]	102.58
Eastern Europe and U.S.S.R.						
Bulgaria	0.03	NA	0.02	4.00	2.65	4.03
Czechoslovakia	3.00	NA	NA	3.15	0	6.15
Hungary	0.23	0	0	4.40	0	4.63
Poland	30.00	0	6.00	13.20	13.20	43.20
U.S.S.R.	166.67	34.88	60.00	98.21	97.23	264.88
Other	0	0	0	NA	NA	NA
Total	199.93	34.88[4]	66.02[4]	122.96	113.08[4]	322.89
Africa						
Botswana	3.80	0	0	0	0	3.80
South Africa, Republic of	57.03	NA	NA	0	0	57.03
Swaziland	2.00	0	0	0	0	2.00
Other	2.43	0.55	0.15	0.11	(3)	2.54
Total	65.27	0.55[4]	0.15[4]	0.11	(3)	65.38
Middle East, Far East, and Oceania						
Australia	32.52	7.00	13.01	39.90	39.90	72.42
China	108.90	10.91	40.29	0	0	108.90
India	NA	NA	NA	1.74	1.65	1.74
Other	3.02	0.07[4]	0.69[4]	0.59	0.51	3.61
Total	144.44	17.98[4]	53.99[4]	42.23	42.06[4]	186.67
World total	724.50	145.21[4]	147.33[4]	262.22	231.47[4]	986.72

[1]The reference year for most of the reserves data in the source report is 1981.
[2]Includes subbituminous coal.
[3]Less than 5 million short tons.
[4]Not all countries in this group reported under this category.
(NA) Not available.
Note: Sum of components may not equal total due to independent rounding.
Source: Energy Information Administration, *International Energy Annual*.

COMPUTERS

THE MARKET AND THE MONEY

In recent years, while computers got faster, computer sales slowed down. Factory shipment of computer equipment by U.S. producers slumped from $49.3 billion in 1984 to only $47.9 billion in 1987. Shipments of semiconductor manufacturers, producers of the chips that make computers run, totalled $18.1 billion in 1987. Worldwide shipments of software—the programs which allow computers to run—grew 21% to $31 billion in 1987. Companies providing computer consulting and computer services had $26 billion worth of revenues in 1987.

The slowdown was particularly painful for an industry with such high expectations. Personal computers were going to remake the whole world. And there were numbers to support the hype: Retail sales of personal computers, for example, skyrocketed 60% to 70% between 1982 and 1984. Overall, factory shipments of U.S. computer equipment tripled from $6.1 billion to $20.4 billion in 1980 and then more than doubled again by 1984, hitting $49.2 billion. And along the way, manufacturers added a lot of infrastructure in hopes of duplicating growth rates that were only possible when the business was just starting out.

But in many ways the slump was inevitable. Corporations were on a cost-cutting binge for several years and, by the mid-1980s, budgets for computers, data processing, and information were large enough to attract the attention of fat cutters. Many companies decided they could get along just fine with what they already had; other consumers sat on the sidelines, waiting for the dizzying advance of technology and the release of new models to slow down.

The mass market for personal computers, meanwhile, failed to materialize, largely because computer makers forgot that they had to convince customers that the new technology was worth the price. Few households were jumping at the chance to spend $2,000 or $3,000 on a machine to balance their checkbooks.

But by 1987, there were signs that the computer slump was over. Academia got serious about computers and some universities even insisted that students buy them. And when some people, mostly professionals, used them at work, they wanted a computer at home for work they did there. Lower prices also helped renew demand for computers, and factory shipments by U.S. producers are projected to hit $52.6 billion in 1988. Here's how that money will be spent:

Supercomputers

These machines are the biggest and fastest on the market—capable of doing some 2 billion operations per second. For that supercomputing speed, companies also pay a superprice, about $5 million to $20 million a computer. U.S. manufacturers sold 65 units worldwide, worth about $660 million, in 1987.

Mainframes

These huge systems got their name because the cabinet holding the processor and memory is the most expensive part of the system. In recent years mainframes, which sell for under $1 million to over $10 million, have faced increased competition from smaller, increasingly powerful computers. As a result, they only hold about 19% of the computer market, down from 36% five years ago. Sales, accordingly, have remained stagnant: $10 billion worth of mainframes were shipped by U.S. producers in 1987, up only 5% from 1986. IBM remains the largest producer of mainframes, and the six largest U.S. companies produced about three quarters of all mainframes sold.

Medium-scale Computers or Minicomputers

These machines, which sell for $15,000 to $1 million, have in recent years become faster, smaller, and more powerful than ever before. Despite predictions that they would be squeezed out by increasingly less expensive and more powerful computers on the top end of the market and increasingly powerful personal computers (known as supermicrocomputers) on the low end of the market, about $17.4 billion worth of midrange computers were sold in 1987. Two big firms, IBM and Digital Equipment Corporation, account for about 40% of all sales.

Microsystems or Personal Computers

These small computers, which sell for as little as $100 and as much as $15,000, revolutionized the computer market. Thanks to PCs, computers are no longer huge machines that take up whole floors of specially designed, air-conditioned buildings. Only a few years after Apple introduced the first mass-produced personal computer, sales grew over 70% in 1982 and 1983, with 1984 showing another 60% jump. Soon, everyone would have a computer in their homes, the industry predicted.

Soon never quite arrived. Most people discovered that they didn't need a computer to do their taxes. And business cut back spending for personal computers. Factory shipment of personal computers remained stagnant in 1985 and 1986 at $6 billion, while 1986 retail sales grew only 9% to $14.6 billion.

Still, the slump of 1985 and 1986 seems to be over. Sales in 1987 hit 4 million units. Business bought about 60% of the $7 billion spent on PCs. In 1988, retail outlets expect to sell $18 billion worth of PCs and hope to see the market grow to $23 billion in 1992. Shipment from the factory should total about $8 billion in 1988. The growth was helped by inexpensive models that have dropped the price of a fully equipped computer to the price of a fancy typewriter, and by increased capital spending.

Thankfully, the industry has also abandoned the idea that a technological revolution will sell itself. Some of the most successful retailers learned that direct sales calls on customers, which were the key to IBM's success in selling mainframes in the 1960s, are also the best way to sell personal computers. Direct sales calls allow the salesperson to tailor computer systems to the needs of business customers (60% of all sales) and to convince the customers that all this high-tech babble about bytes, RAM, and smart cards can actually add up to improved productivity and profits.

Software

Software is the computer program, the language or instructions that tells the equipment (the hardware) what to do. Since many people still don't understand how to get the most out of their computer hardware, it's not surprising that software has been the fastest-growing part of the computer industry. Worldwide revenues grew 50% in 1983 and 1984 and have grown 25% to 30% a year since then, despite the problem of software piracy, which allows users to copy programs worth hundreds of dollars for as little as $1—the cost of a new disk. Software sales hit $31 billion in 1987 and will top $38 billion in 1988.

Software sales for PCs hit $4 billion in 1987 and are expected to hit $11.5 billion in 1991. That growth has produced one software billionaire, William Gates, the cofounder of Microsoft. (See the profile below.)

Semiconductors

A slump in computer equipment sales and tough foreign competition have put U.S. makers of computer chips on the brink of disaster. The value of factory shipments by U.S. chip makers dropped to $16 billion in 1986 from $17.8 billion in 1984 and produced heavy losses throughout the industry. Intel, the world's third-largest chip maker, lost $183 million in 1986, while the five largest chip makers lost $110.3 million. Only Motorola, the largest chip maker, made money, $194 million on nearly $5.9 billion in sales. But in 1987, shipments rebounded to $18.1 billion and are expected to reach $20.3 billion in 1988.

In the long run, increased demand for computer chips in everything from autos to watches is expected to improve sales. The weaker dollar has improved the industry's competitive position, and an agreement between U.S. and Japan may prevent Japanese companies from dumping computer chips on the world market at prices below what it costs to produce them to increase their sales. To bolster profits, U.S. chip makers are manufacturing specialized chips for the defense industry and other uses.

THE PLAYERS

Tables 133 to 136 (below) list some of the largest data processing companies, software producers, and personal computer makers.

Table 133   The 15 Largest Data Processing Companies

Rank	Company	Data processing revenues (billions of dollars)
1.	International Business Machines Corporation	48,554.0
2.	Digital Equipment Corporation	7,029.4
3.	Sperry Corporation	4,755.1
4.	Burroughs Corporation	4,685.3
5.	NCR Corporation	3,885.5
6.	Control Data Corporation	3,679.7
7.	Hewlett-Packard Company	3,675.0
8.	Wang Laboratories	2,428.3
9.	Xerox Corporation	1,959.0
10.	Honeywell Inc.	1,951.9
11.	Apple Computer, Inc.	1,753.8
12.	American Telephone & Telegraph Company	1,500.0
13.	TRW Inc.	1,450.0
14.	Tandy Corporation	1,200.0
15.	Data General Corporation	1,199.0

Source: *Datamation,* June 15, 1986.

Table 134   The Most Popular Software Programs

		Market Share	
Rank	Program/Manufacturer	Percentage of unit sales	Percentage of dollar sales
1.	1-2-3/Lotus	11	16
2.	dBASE III/Ashton-Tate	8	15
3.	WordPerfect/WordPerfect	7	9
4.	AppleWorks/Apple	9	8
5.	Microsoft Word/Microsoft	5	6
6.	Microsoft Excel/Microsoft	3	4
7.	pfs:First Choice/Software Publishing	5	3
8.	Microsoft Works/Microsoft	4	3
9.	Print Shop/Brøderbund	3	1
10.	Omnis III/Blyth Software	0.5	1

Table 135   The Largest Personal Computer Companies

		Market share (percentage)	
Rank	Company	1986	1985
1.	IBM	29.8	40.5
2.	Apple	9.2	10.3
3.	COMPAQ	6.6	5.2
4.	Zenith	3.5	2.4
5.	Tandy	6.6	4.6
6.	Commodore	1.9	3.8
7.	Others, primarily clone makers	42.4	33.2

Source: Dataquest.

Table 136 Top 10 Worldwide Semiconductor Manufacturers

Manufacturer	1986 Rank	1985 Rank	1986 sales (millions of dollars)	1985 sales (millions of dollars)
NEC	1	1	2,638	1,984
Hitachi	2	4	2,305	1,671
Toshiba	3	5	2,261	1,468
Motorola	4	2	2,025	1,830
Texas Instruments	5	3	1,820	1,742
Philips/Signetics	6	6	1,356	1,068
Fujitsu	7	7	1,310	1,020
Matsushita	8	10	1,233	906
Mitsubishi	9	11	1,177	642
Intel	10	8	991	1,020

Source: *Dataquest*, January 1987.

THE PEOPLE

The computer revolution was supposed to do more than just put a computer in every home—it was also supposed to put food on the table, replacing jobs in declining smokestack industries. So far that promise has been largely unfulfilled. Total employment in the semiconductor industry dropped from 192,000 in 1984 to 181,000 in 1987. The number of people employed in the computer equipment industry tumbled from 374,000 in 1984 to only 332,000 in 1987.

Ironically, overseas production, one of the big reasons behind the slump in employment, is increasing sales and bringing the dream of a low-priced computer in every home closer to reality. Many of these clones are produced in Asia with cheaper labor. To compete, American manufacturers have moved manufacturing operations overseas, which has lowered costs and increased sales but also cut employment.

International Business Machines Corporation
CEO: John F. Akers
Employees: 403,508
Assets: $15.3 billion

Old Orchard Road
Armonk, New York 10504
914-765-1900

	1987	1986	1985	1980
Revenues (millions of dollars):	54,217	51,250	50,056	26,213
Net income (millions of dollars):	5,258	4,789	6,555	3,562
Share earnings (dollars):	8.72	7.81	10.67	6.10

What it does: The 4th-largest industrial company in the United States, the largest electronics company in the United States, the world's largest computer maker. This company makes typewriters, personal computers, telecommunications equipment, and mainframes, in which it holds about half of the market. In 1985 it was the nation's 15th-largest military contractor and the 7th-largest contractor for military research and development.

Unlike most creators of high-tech companies, the man behind the rise of International Business Machines (IBM) was a salesman, not a techie or engineer. Thomas Watson was hired in 1914 to run the Computing-Tabulating-Recording Company, the producer of the electrical punch-card computing system developed for the 1890 census. Watson, who arrived with a reputation as a super salesman, revamped the company (which changed its name to IBM in 1924) with daily pep talks to his salesmen, songs like "Hail to IBM," and a rigorous dress code—dark suits and white shirts.

The emphasis on sales set the pattern for IBM's growth. It dominated the market for time clocks and punch-card tabulators in the 1920s and the electric typewriter market in the 1930s and 1940s. Never known for its technical innovation, the company made its push into computers after others had already started, but it quickly bowled over the competition with an expert sales force that carefully tailored its products to consumer needs and with adept marketing. By the late 1960s the company held 80% of the world market.

The decade between 1975 and 1985 saw revenues more than triple; profits soared from $1.9 billion to $4.7 billion. Though competitors introduced the first minicomputer and personal computer, IBM came roaring back into the personal computer market as soon as it was apparent there was money to be made, capturing over half the market.

But problems loom. Smaller companies such as Digital Equipment Corporation cut into the market for large mainframes by convincing customers they could get along with minicomputers. Cheaper and often more sophisticated PCs, on the other end of the market, cut IBM's PC sales. And, as computer buyers increasingly wanted computer systems that would allow them to link together—network—their mainframes, midrange computers and even PC's into one system, IBM's various computers became less, not more compatible with each other.

These troubles hit home in a big way in 1986: profits, already down in 1985, plummeted and IBM has been struggling ever since to regain its blue-chip image. To compete with smaller, nimbler competitors, IBM has streamlined management and announced a raft of new products. It spent $17 billion revamping its plants and cut product development time by a year. The company wants to cut costs by $2.25 billion. Though maintaining its long-standing policy of no layoffs, attrition helped shrink its payroll by 15,000. IBM has increased its role in developing new software, shifted 11,000 employees to sales, began working on software that would link all of its machines and planned a more aggressive marketing strategy. These changes represent a return to Watson's strategy of salesmanship and attention to the consumer.

So far, however, there has been no dramatic turnaround. The quarter ending September 30th, 1987 ended five straight quarters when profits declined. But that quarter showed only a modest increase in profits and despite the company's struggle to retain its edge, there is no sign that big blue will return to the decades of double digit growth that made it a blue chip stock.

Digital Equipment Corporation
CEO: K. H. Olsen
Employees: 114,000
Assets: $8.4 billion

146 Main Street
Maynard, Massachusetts
617-897-5111

	1987	1986	1985	1980
Revenues (millions of dollars):	9,389	7,590	6,686	2,368
Net income (millions of dollars):	1,137	617	447	160
Share earnings (dollars):	8.53	4.81	3.71	2.73

What it does: A major designer and maker of computers, related equipment, and software supplies.

In 1987, sales at Digital Equipment Corporation (DEC) grew 23% to over $9.3 billion. And that was just an average year: over the last 20 years, Ken Olsen's computer company has been growing at an annual rate of 20% to 30% a year. But no one was crying at DEC. Thanks to that success, DEC has emerged with the reputation as the only computer company to ever successfully challenge IBM.

The key to DEC's success is Olsen's emphasis on new products. While 40% of IBM's products are less than two years old, 85% of DEC's are. By creating the minicomputer, DEC played a major role in reducing the size of mainframes and laying the groundwork for the personal computer revolution.

Olsen grew up in a religious Connecticut family, whose fundamentalist values he keeps as a regular churchgoer and fund-raiser. In high school he acquired a reputation for technical wizardry by repairing radios. In the late 1940s at MIT, he worked on the university's first computer—which was nicknamed "the expensive typewriter."

When IBM won the contract to produce MIT's SAGE computer, Olsen was assigned to the liaison team. He hated Big Blue's regimented corporate bureaucracy, but it wasn't until 1957 that he carried out his vow that he could do better than IBM. He founded DEC with the idea of producing a minicomputer.

Reducing the size of computers and making them more accessible to many businesses was a profitable idea. Revenues hit $10 million by 1964 and $1.4 billion by 1978. But, as for many high-tech corporations, the hard part was learning how to manage this growth. And Olsen was not a promising candidate to make the transition from engineer to manager. His only management experience had been running a Sunday school.

Still, twice he's successfully overhauled the company's management structure. In 1964, when the company had outgrown its anarchic beginning, he introduced a management structure that gave a senior official responsibility for a whole product line. That system encouraged entrepreneurial and technological development, the key to the company's early success, while managing to introduce more control over product creation, development, and sales. Then, in 1983, when the company had to impose a more centralized management structure to make certain its products were compatible with each other, Olsen centralized development of new products.

At first this seemed to be a disaster. The company failed in its introduction of a line of PCs, earnings slumped temporarily because of an accounting error, and some top people left, disgruntled with the new, more disciplined corporate culture. Yet soon, introducing its new VAX computers, DEC jumped ahead of the competition, capturing an ever-larger share of the market from IBM. And, in 1988, DEC took a major step to integrate PC's into its systems. It announced a joint plan with Apple Computer to develop communications and software programs to make Apple's computers compatible with DEC's popular VAX minicomputer. That move will help DEC do battle with IBM in the growing networking market. If DEC wins the battle, Olsen will soon have a personal fortune even larger than the $490 million he was worth in 1987.

Apple Computer, Inc.
CEO: John Sculley
Employees: —
Assets: $1.6 billion

20525 Mariani Avenue
Cupertino, California 95014
408-973-3840

	1987	1986	1985	1980
Revenues (millions of dollars):	3,041	1,902	1,918	117
Net income (millions of dollars):	280	154	61	12
Share earnings (dollars):	2.11	2.3	.99	.24

What it does: A leading maker of personal computers. Its Apple II's are sold mainly to schools and homes. Its Macintosh is aimed at the office market.

When John Sculley wrested control of Apple Computer, Inc., in 1985 from cofounder Steven P. Jobs, he must have thought he had just stuck his head in a blender. A slowdown in economic growth saw a slowdown in businesses buying big computers. There were 400 or so companies making or marketing personal computers, which seemed like 399 too many. Consumers were confused and starting to wonder whether they needed computers after all. The result was a slump that hit just about everyone and Apple worse than most.

Sculley put Apple through the wringer. He reorganized the company, including laying off about 20% of the work force and shutting down domestic and overseas operations. The Lisa computer, which never caught on, was abandoned. He beefed up the Macintosh for business use and succeeded in getting software companies to write better business software packages for the machine. He also effectively got rid of Apple cofounders Steve Jobs and Steve Wozniak.

What Sculley probably did best was sell the Mac door to door. The former president of PepsiCo had made his mark in marketing. Thus, when the company verged on introducing the new enhanced Macintosh computer, he marched into the headquarters of corporations such as General Electric and du Pont to huckster the machine personally. One of his selling points was that the PC was easy to use. The upshot was that Apple doubled the shipments of its Mac in 1986 at a time when the entire computer industry saw an increase of 9%. Apple was back in business in a big way.

Ironically, what Sculley did was prove that Jobs was on the right track. Jobs had marketed the Apple, the Apple II Plus, and the Macintosh as easy-to-use alternatives to IBM PCs and their clones. With his friend Wozniak, Jobs founded Apple in 1975 with the capital he got from selling his Volkswagen microbus. He managed to turn that into a $300 million fortune.

Jobs was one of the first people to realize the microprocessor's potential for putting low-cost computing power into the hands of individuals. Unlike other computer pioneers, Jobs thought consumers would find personal computers more appealing if sold in a "user-friendly" consumer package instead of an industrial-style steel box.

Thus, he humanized his computers. The packaging plus the name Apple set Jobs's first computer apart from the cold, impersonal world usually associated with the computer industry. The strategy worked. Besides selling his Apple to a much wider audience than techies, Jobs kept coming up with add-ons for the Apple. Soon hosts of people adapted his PC to thousands of different uses. As a result, the subsequent Apple II Plus had more software made for it than any other computer.

Stories about Jobs's own interests also set him apart from the mainstream of corporate America. He dabbled with such esoterica as meditation, vegetarianism, and communal and primal therapy.

Meanwhile, the company grew like crazy, but Jobs wasn't either much of a businessman or much of an administrator. Production schedules ran way behind and a couple of major products flopped, such as the Lisa and the Apple III, which were designed to attract business users. Eventually, he brought Sculley into the operation. In time, the top officers were at each others' throats over what the company needed. Cofounder Wozniak left the company in disgust and Jobs was kicked upstairs and then left. The most obvious reason for Sculley's winning the day was that, in 1985, Apple posted its first loss. By 1987, the company was on firm footing once again and business was booming.

Microsoft Corporation

CEO: William H. Gates
Employees: 2000
Assets: NA

16011 Northeast 36th Way, Box 97017
Redmond, Washington 98073-9717
206-882-8080

	1987	1986	1985	1984
Revenues (millions of dollars):	345.9	198.0	61.0	117.0
Net income (millions of dollars):	71.9	39.3	24.1	15.8
Share earnings (dollars):	1.30	1.56	1.04	.69

What it does: Develops and markets systems and applications for microsoftware. Its MS-DOS operating system is used by IBM and IBM-compatible microprocessors. A new operating system, OS/2, is for IBM's newest PCs.

When the computer industry shook out the technical wizards who lacked the savvy to run the companies they founded, William H. Gates III stood apart. The chairman of Microsoft Corporation, one of the biggest software companies in the business, not only remained in control but took the company to ever-new heights. In 1987, at age 31, he became a billionaire as a result of the company's stock doing so well.

One of Gates's biggest successes came in 1987 when he convinced a reluctant International Business Machines, already a star customer, to use a newly developed piece of software called Windows in its personal computers. With IBM as a customer, sales were guaranteed to be in the millions of dollars.

With his big glasses and messy, mousy hair, the boyish-looking Gates was a stereotype of the computer nerd who launched a company when he was only 19 years old. In 1975, he dropped out of Harvard and teamed up with another computer junkie, Paul Allen, who ever since has taken a back seat to Gates in the business. They cofounded Microsoft to sell a version of the BASIC computer language they had written while in high school in Seattle.

The third person involved in Microsoft's rise, Kazuhiko Nishi, was another young computer junkie. Fast-talking, excitable, and flamboyant, he learned everything he could about computers and started a newsletter about them after dropping out of Tokyo's prestigious Waseda University. In 1978, Nishi flew to the U.S. to talk to Gates about becoming Microsoft's Far East agent. They struck a partnership arrangement. At the time, Microsoft sold software that let people write programs for personal computers. Both Nishi and Gates wanted to help companies design PCs and supply their software.

When he returned to Japan, the brash Nishi persuaded a manager at the big NEC Corporation to meet Gates and Allen. The result was NEC's gambling on letting Nishi and his American friends play a major role in the design of a new PC. The resultant P8100 was a success and helped make PCs hot in Japan. Also, Gates and Nishi soon became famous in Japan by giving dozens of press interviews on the future of technology. Microsoft benefited by Japanese companies' buying software and design services.

The deals Nishi struck grew bigger. For instance, an accidental meeting with the president of Kyocera Corporation, a major industrial ceramics firm, resulted in the company's backing a laptop computer, which Nishi had thought up. Gates and Nishi made the machine and lined up distributors on three continents. Their biggest coup came in 1980 when IBM chose Microsoft MS-DOS operating system software for a prototype PC. The IBM contract was worth gold, immediately making Microsoft one of the most important companies in the software business.

As Microsoft became more successful, relations between Gates and Nishi deteriorated. Gates put more organizational structures in place, including the use of seasoned managers. Those managers couldn't stand Nishi's cowboy way of doing business. His unorthodox approach was what was needed for a little company out to make its mark, but it proved expensive and wasteful for a big company. Eventually, Gates and Nishi's partnership dissolved.

CONSTRUCTION

THE MARKET AND THE MONEY

The real estate market is in the doldrums and the long-awaited housing boom never gets off the drawing boards of industry forecasters. Even so, about $397 billion worth of new construction was put up in 1987 and the industry is expected to grow another 0.2% in 1988, according to forecasts and estimates by the International Trade Administration. That would appear to be a dramatic improvement over 1982 when $247 billion was spent and 1977 when $188 billion was spent on new construction.

Unfortunately, a lot of that growth can be accounted for by inflation. But even if we adjust for inflation and express the value of new construction in constant 1982 dollars, about $344 billion was spent on new construction in 1987, $246.6 billion in 1982, and $295.9 billion in 1977.

Overall, new construction in 1987 equaled 8.9% of the GNP, up from 7.7% in 1982 but well below the postwar peak of 11.9% in 1966.

Table 137 (below) shows how, adjusted for inflation and expressed in 1982 dollars, the country spends its construction dollars.

THE PLAYERS

The construction industry remains one of the few major industries that is dominated by small businesses. Only about 5% of all construction firms have receipts of more than $2.5 million a year and there are more than 1.28 million self-employed workers in the construction industry, indicating that there were many small proprietors or working partners. The typical U.S. construction firm in 1982, the most recent data available, has only nine employees and annual receipts of $688,077.

In contrast, the nation's largest construction firms, such as Bechtel, are multinationals that do a large proportion of their business overseas. Overall, the top 250 international contractors did $73.9 billion worth of business outside the U.S. in 1986, with U.S. contractors capturing about 31% or $22.6 billion. That represents a big drop from 1980 when the 250 largest firms did $108.9 billion worth of business and U.S. companies captured 41% of those revenues. The five largest contractors are as shown in Table 138 (below).

Table 137 Value of New Construction in Constant 1982 Dollars
(billions of dollars)

	1977	1982	1987*	1988**
Total new construction	295.9	246.6	344.0	344.5
Residential	148.3	84.7	171.9	174.2
Single-family	100.2	41.5	97.5	99.5
Multifamily	16.2	15.5	22.4	20.2
Home improvement	32.0	27.7	52.0	54.6
Private nonresidential	87.0	108.1	106.1	102.5
Manufacturing facilities	12.2	17.3	10.5	11.0
Offices	8.4	23.0	20.5	17.4
Hotels and Motels	1.5	4.1	6.0	5.4
Other commercial	15.1	14.2	22.5	22.0
Religious	1.7	1.5	2.3	2.3
Educational	1.1	1.5	2.7	2.8
Hospital and institutional	5.2	5.9	5.1	5.4
Miscellaneous buildings	1.9	1.7	2.6	2.6
Telephone and Telegraph	6.3	7.1	7.5	7.8
Railroads	2.0	2.6	2.5	2.4
Electric utilities	17.1	18.3	14.9	14.2
Gas utilities	3.8	5.5	4.9	5.0
Petroleum pipelines	1.8	0.4	0.3	0.3
Farm structures	7.0	3.7	1.7	1.6
Miscellaneous structures	2.0	1.3	2.1	2.1
Public works	60.5	53.8	66.0	67.8
Housing and redevelopment	1.5	1.7	1.4	1.4
Federal industrial	1.3	1.6	1.4	1.5
Educational	8.7	5.9	7.4	7.8
Hospital	2.8	2.0	1.8	1.9
Other public buildings	5.8	5.8	9.7	10.1
Highways	16.6	16.3	19.6	20.2
Military facilities	2.2	2.2	3.5	3.4
Conservation and development	5.8	5.0	4.8	4.4
Sewer systems	8.0	5.5	8.5	9.1
Water supplies	2.7	2.9	3.3	3.5
Miscellaneous public structures	5.3	4.9	4.7	4.7

*Estimated
**Projected.
Sources: U.S. Department of Commerce, Bureau of the Census, and International Trade Administration (ITA). Estimates and forecasts by ITA.

Table 138 Construction Contracts

Rank	Company/location	1986 contracts (in millions of dollars)
1.	Bouygues/Clamart, France	7,450.0
2.	Shimizu Construction Company Ltd./Tokyo	7,129.4
3.	Bechtel Group, Inc./San Francisco	7,079.0
4.	M.W. Kellogg Company/Houston	6,945.0
5.	Taisei Corporation/Tokyo	6,865.0

Sources: *International Construction Week, Engineering News-Record.*

THE PEOPLE

There were some 5.1 million people employed in the construction industry in 1987, about 5% of all workers. About 1.28 million self-employed people worked in the construction industry as proprietors or working partners. Another 12.5 million workers are employed in industries that are dependent on construction as a major market for their products and services.

Unions now represent only 22% of all construction workers, down from at least 75% 15 years ago. That low representation has kept down wages, which rose only 1% in 1986 and only 3.3% a year between 1981 and 1985, according to Cahners Economics. In contrast, construction wages grew at an annual rate of about 6.6% a year in the 1970s.

DESIGN

Designing America's new construction produced $45.6 billion worth of billings for U.S. design, architectural, and engineering firms in 1987, down from $46.1 billion in 1986. Billings are expected to rise to $46.2 billion in 1988 according to International Trade Administration projections.

Small firms have also dominated the design, architectural, and engineering industry. More than half of the 96,859 architectural and engineering establishments surveyed in 1982, in the most recent census of service industries, didn't have a payroll—meaning they were individual proprietorships. But the remaining 45,341 establishments had over 96% of the industry's receipts. And the 500 largest architectural and engineering firms chalked up $13 billion worth of revenues in 1987. Twenty-six of these companies had billings of over $100 million. The top five architectural and engineering firms according to *Engineering News-Record* were: (1) Morrison-Knudsen Engineers, Inc., of San Francisco, California, (2) CRS Sirrine, Inc., of Houston, Texas, (3) Sargent & Lundy of Chicago, Illinois, (4) Gibbs & Hill, Inc., of New York, New York, and (5) CH2M Hill, Inc., of Corvallis, Oregon.

Architectural and engineering companies earned about 80% of their income from engineering services, 17% from architectural services, and 3% from surveying.

Architectural, design, and engineering firms employed 697,400 people who earned an average of $12.66 an hour.

Table 139   Home Construction

In 1986, home builders obtained permits to construct 1.8 million housing units valued at $97.1 billion. The breakdown by region:

Region	Units	Value in billions of dollars
South	678,796	32.9
West	504,543	30.5
Midwest	291,580	16.4
Northeast	286,574	17.3

Source: *The Wall Street Journal*, March 26, 1987.

HOUSING

There are now about 100 million places to live in the United States. If you want to buy all of them, it will cost you about $5 trillion dollars. Or, if you have more modest ambitions, the value of the average single-family house is now $65,000. That's good news if you bought a house in the Great Depression, when the average price was $2,938, and watched the market go up, but bad news if you want to buy one today. The average new American house sold for $111,800 in 1986, up from $76,400 in 1980.

Rising prices have made buying that dream house a nightmare for many people. The percentage of housing units that are owner-occupied rose from 44.9% in 1910 to 64.4% in 1980 but by 1987 had dropped to 57.3%. As a result, about 32.4% of all residences are rented. But even rents are no bargain. The average rent hit $315 a month in 1987, a 31% increase over 1980.

The vast majority of Americans (67%) live in what the government describes in unhomey language as "single-unit housing"—meaning homes where only one family lives. Another 12.4% live in housing complexes of two to four units and 16.2% live in apartment buildings of five or more units. Mobile homes house 4.4% of the population.

Table 140   The Biggest Home Builders Aren't So Big

In the housing industry, big isn't so big. The average U.S. home is built by a contractor that builds fewer than 25 a year, and the nation's largest home builder, Trammell Crow Company, produced only 14,545 housing units in 1986, less than 1% of the 1.81 million housing starts that year. There are more than 93,000 home builders and the 100 largest home builders provided only 16% of the market. Here's how *Builder* magazine ranks the builders:

Rank	Company	1986 housing production	Gross revenue (millions of dollars)
1.	Trammell Crow Company—residential	14,545	1,100
2.	Cardinal Industries	10,090	611
3.	Pulte Home Corporation	9,200	837
4.	U.S. Home Corporation	8,494	767
5.	Oxford Development Corporation	8,475	625
6.	Ryan Homes	7,951	631
7.	Lincoln Property Company	7,266	2,383
8.	The Ryland Group	6,556	677
9.	Jim Walter Corporation	6,403	319
10.	Nash Phillips-Copus	6,157	496

Source: *Builder*, May 1987.

CONSTRUCTION TRIVIA

Cement dates back to the Roman period, when builders mixed ash from volcanoes with lime. The mixture would harden when mixed with water. An Englishman, Joseph Aspdin, invented a better-quality cement in 1824 known as "portland cement" because it looked like rocks from the Isle of Portland when it hardened. Reinforced cement, which revolutionized modern building, dates from 1845, when the Frenchman J. L. Lambot built boats out of it.

The world's tallest office building is the Sears Tower in Chicago. Its 110 stories rise 1,454 feet into the air. Nearly 16,700 people work in the building, which was completed in 1974 and has 16,000 windows. But the Tower's total area is only 4.4 million square feet, only a little more than half the area of the twin towers of the World Trade Center in New York City. The taller of the two World Trade Center towers rises 1,362 feet; both towers together have 8,740,000 square feet, making them *the world's largest office buildings* in terms of rentable space.

The invention of the elevator can be traced to the construction industry. In the 1850s, contractor Elisha Graves Otis, building a bedstead factory in Yonkers, New York, developed a plan for hoisting platforms to move materials and therefore speed construction. He called his invention (later the basis of the Otis Elevator Company) an "elevator."

The largest U.S. hotel is the Hilton Hotel in Las Vegas with 3,174 bedrooms, 125,000 square feet of convention space, and a 10-acre rooftop recreation deck. *The tallest U.S. hotel* is the 748-foot Detroit Plaza Hotel.

The world's tallest apartment building exclusively for residential housing is the Lake Point Tower in Chicago, standing 70 stories and 645 feet high.

The contractor that built most of the largest projects over the years is undoubtedly the Army Corps of Engineers. In 1776, troops under George Washington built two forts on Dorchester Heights, Boston, giving them a commanding position above Boston Harbor. Realizing that similar construction projects might be needed in the future, Washington created the Army Corps of Engineers. Since then it has undertaken some of the world's largest construction jobs, such as flood control projects in the Mississippi River Valley.

The largest private house in the world is the 250-room Biltmore House that was constructed for the Vanderbilts in the 1880s on 119,000 acres of land. The house and 12,000-acre estate, currently owned by Vanderbilt heirs George and William, is valued at $55 million.

The biggest building to be demolished, a kind of reverse construction record, was the 21-story, 600-room Traymore Hotel in Atlantic City in 1972.

PUBLIC HOUSING, FROM CONSTRUCTION TO DEMOLITION

Public housing started out in the 1930s as a way of providing temporary shelter to poor families. The temporary shelter, however, soon became permanent. By 1970, the heyday of the public housing program, the federal government had 126,800 units of public housing under construction.

Recently, budget cutbacks and the Reagan administration's emphasis on providing rent vouchers have nearly eliminated the federal government's role in providing new public housing. Under current programs, families are given subsidies for the rental of private housing. Even though rent subsidies cost the government nearly $12.9 billion in 1987 and will cost an estimated $13.4 billion in 1988, the Reagan administration argues it's cheaper than building new public housing.

Meanwhile, many public housing projects have begun to fall apart. Governments, unable to afford badly needed repairs and prevented by law from raising the rents, abandoned some projects. Others have been condemned as unsafe. In St. Louis, things got so bad at the infamous Pruitt-Igoe project that the city simply blew the place up.

As a result, the federal government has been demolishing more public housing than it builds. In 1978, for example, the federal government built 68,509 more units of public housing than it demolished. But by 1983, it demolished 6,651 more units than were built. There was another deficit in 1984 and in 1985, the most recent year for which figures are available, only a tiny surplus of 1,426 units of public housing was produced.

COSMETICS, SOAPS, AND CLEANING PREPARATIONS

THE MARKET AND THE MONEY

Keeping America clean and beautiful, at home and at the factory, put about $29.7 billion into the coffers of American companies in 1987, up from $27.9 billion in 1985.

Soaps and detergent manufacturers, for example, cleaned up with $8.8 billion worth of factory shipments in 1987.

The so-called polish and sanitation goods industry—makers of polishes, household bleaches, toilet bowl cleaners, scouring powders, and stuff like Windex—wiped up about $4.3 billion in factory shipments.

Even prettier factory sales come from the cosmetics, fragrance, and toiletries industry: American manufacturers are projected to have shipped about $14.0 billion worth of cosmetics, fragrances, and toiletries in 1987. Retail sales were much higher, at least $20 billion.

Unlike most industries, this industry has cleaned up foreign competitors. Imports control only about 2% of the market. Even in the cosmetics and toiletries sector, in which French perfumes have had a long-standing romance with American consumers, only $431 million worth of imports hit the market in 1987.

THE PEOPLE

About 124,000 people are employed in this industry, about the same as in 1984.

The Procter & Gamble Company

CEO: John G. Smale
Employees: 73,200
Assets: $13.7 billion

P.O. Box 599
Cincinnati, OH 45201
Phone: 513-983-1100

	1987	1986	1985	1980
Revenues (millions of dollars):	17,000	15,439	13,552	10,772
Net income (millions of dollars):	327	709	635	640
Share earnings (dollars):	1.87	4.20	3.80	3.87

What it does: Sell a wide variety of soaps, foods, over-the-counter drugs, and toiletries, including Tide, Crest, Ivory soap, peanut butter, mouthwash, Spic and Span cleaner, Crisco shortening, Pampers disposable diapers, Charmin toilet paper, Folger's coffee, Pringle's potato chips, Pepto-Bismol, Vicks, acne products, Head and Shoulders shampoo, drugs, and vitamins.

It all started with lard. William Procter and James Gamble used lard to make soap and candles in 1837. They got a big boost from contracts to supply soap and candles to the Union Army during the Civil War. Another boost came in 1878 when the company introduced a new kind of white soap called Ivory. (Later a mistake in its factory produced a batch of soap that floated, which was an immediate hit with consumers. Soon all Ivory soap was made according to the new formula.) Crisco shortening, Tide, Duncan Hines, Charmin, Pampers, and thousands of other products eventually followed.

Massive advertising expenditures ($1.4 billion in 1986), a reputation for quality backed by years of research (the company's top-selling Tide took 20 years to develop), and a willingness to buy into a market with timely acquisitions made the company the nation's largest supplier of household products.

But in the late 1970s P&G stumbled. Its share of the lucrative disposable diapers market slipped from 69% in 1978 to only 47% in 1985. The toothpaste wars cut P&G's lead from 19 percentage points in 1979 to only 1.5

points in 1985. The company seemed to have neglected its primary money-makers, and when it flexed its marketing muscle to fight back, the costs were astronomical. About $1 billion was spent advertising its two new versions of Pampers alone. But the costly campaigns helped the company return to the top of the heap, regaining its lead in toothpaste and disposable diapers.

At the same time, the company spent $2 billion to buy such companies as Richardson-Vicks, Inc., to become almost overnight one of the nation's largest over-the-counter drug makers. The move into the pharmaceuticals market, which has been growing faster than P&G's other mature, slow-growth markets, should also help the company's growth.

Revlon, Charles Revson, and Ronald Perelman   Charles Revson founded Revlon in 1932 with $300 and over the years built it up with a nearly infallible eye for marketing, packaging, and advertising. He even managed to stand out in an industry known for strong, autocratic entrepreneurs. A megalomaniac who did everything by instinct rather than research, Revson terrorized his employees, phoning executives at two in the morning about insignificant details of a new advertising campaign. He lavishly endowed charities and hospitals and probably spent more on underwear than most of his employees earned in a year, yet he was known to throw a fit if he caught an employee discarding pencil stubs. But no matter—for years the company battled Avon for the top of the cosmetics market.

Things turned ugly after Revson's death in 1975. The new CEO, Michel Bergerac, gave the company some needed financial controls, but earnings slid as competitors raced ahead. Estée Lauder took over the top end of the cosmetics market while low-priced brands such as Maybelline and Cover Girl took over the lower end of the market. Bergerac's diversification into drugs, medical equipment, and other products never quite worked out. By 1985 Revlon was number three in the cosmetic industry and slipping.

That's when, an upstart, Ronald Perelman, entered the scene. Perelman grew up rich but determined. Armed with an M.B.A. from Wharton and experience in running his family's metal fabricating business, he started with a $2 million investment in Cohen-Hatfield Industries, a small jewelry distributor, bought MacAndrews & Forbes Group, licorice extract and chocolate maker, and used it as a vehicle for ever larger takeovers: Technicolor, and then Pantry Pride in 1985. Using the profits from selling off Pantry Pride's assets and $700 million in junk bonds, he financed his $1.8 billion takeover of Revlon in late 1985.

Perelman created his empire with a simple strategy: buy undervalued assets with cash and junk bonds, sell off assets to reduce debts, and keep the core businesses as cash cows, producing more income for even larger takeovers. Even when he didn't capture his price, Perelman made money. In 1986, for example, he made a $4.1 billion bid for Gillette but the deal fell through when the Ivan Boesky insider-trading scandal made it difficult to obtain financing—so Perelman had to settle for a $43 million profit.

By 1987, Perelman, then only 44, was worth $300 million. He promises to use the same wizardry he's used as a corporate raider to put a prettier face on Revlon's earnings. His method is a lot like Revson's: great advertising and exciting new products.

Perelman's confusing financial empire releases no separate figures on Revlon's cosmetics earnings. But cosmetics profits may have risen 20% in 1986 and more were expected in 1987. Already, Perelman claims he has accomplished his goal and is planning more corporate raids, hoping to turn more ugly ducklings into attractive investments.

Max Factor   Max Factor brought a little bit of Hollywood to the average American woman. His cosmetics were originally created for motion picture stars, and his success led to other women wanting to look like them. Factor was more than willing to oblige.

Quite literally, Max Factor worked with makeup most of his life. At 13, he dropped out of school and became a makeup apprentice with a traveling opera company in Eastern Europe. He displayed an early aptitude for working with the creams and rouges and other secrets of the trade and in time was appointed a makeup man with Russia's Royal Ballet.

In 1904, he emigrated to the U.S. with his wife and three children, setting up a wig-and-makeup concession at the St. Louis World's Fair. Eventually, he opened a cosmetics shop in Los Angeles, where he and his children made the products that were sold. As the film industry established itself in L.A., business picked up. In 1914, when Henry B. Walthall became the first actor in filmdom to wear makeup, Max Factor was the man who had done the job on him and his reputation, if not Walthall's, was assured.

He made a fortune doing the faces of Hollywood stars and was working for every studio. The demands of film with its harsh lights and screen magnification led Factor to create a new greasepaint that didn't leave actors and actresses with a caked look the way traditional makeup did. His makeup looked realistic on film. Factor also developed several other cosmetics, including a pancake makeup that could be used when films were made in color.

Factor got caught up in the glitter of Tinsel Town. He opened a huge, white, neoclassical cosmetics factory, which was as gaudily glorious as anything a movie mogul could have created. Colored floodlights bathed the entrance on opening day and legions of film stars, such as Claudette Colbert and Jean Harlow, dedicated various rooms. The glitz factor naturally helped Factor. By 1930, his products were sold in more than 80 countries. After he died in 1938, his sons ran the company until they sold it for $480 million to Norton Simon.

ELIZABETH ARDEN

Florence Nightingale Graham moved to New York from Toronto in 1908 and didn't become a nurse but a cosmetician. Two years later, she changed her name to Elizabeth Arden and opened her own business. She appropriated Elizabeth from a friend and Arden from a poem. By 1914, she was on her way to becoming a multimillionaire. The key to her success was two products she and a chemist, A. F. Swanson, developed: Ardena Skin Tonic and Amoretta. In all, she developed more than 300 cosmetics. When she died in 1966 at age 75, she was a successful thoroughbred horse breeder.

CREDIT CARDS

THE MARKET AND THE MONEY

For nearly 106 million Americans, plastic credit is a way of life—so much so that they don't just have just one card, but an average of 6.9 each. That's 731 million credit cards held by American consumers.

All those cards let consumers rack up $152.6 billion in outstanding bills on credit cards in 1986, up from a mere $83.2 billion in 1982. Visa cards alone are used for about 5,340 charges every minute during the busy Christmas buying season. Thanks largely to plastic, consumer installment credit stands at a record 19.4% of disposable income. And, it seems, the better educated you are, the more you love going into debt: college graduates put an average of $391 on their credit cards every month, people with some college education charge $159, high school graduates rack up $83, and those with some high school charge $51 a month, according to the Federal Reserve and *American Demographics* magazine. Nearly half of all consumers (49%) pay off their credit-card balance each month. Another 34% pay off part of the balance and 16% say whether they pay varies from month to month, according to an *American Banker* survey.

THE PLAYERS

Nearly 2,000 companies issue credit cards, but the top three easily outdistance their rivals. In American wallets and purses are some 93 million Visa cards, up from 66.1 million in 1982; 72.4 million MasterCards, up from 53.4 million in 1982; and 16.3 million American Express Cards, up from 11.1 million in 1982. Consumers charged $75.2 billion on their Visa cards in 1985, up 96% from 1982; $55.5 billion on the MasterCard, up 80% from 1982; and $55.5 billion worth of bills on American Express, up 79% from 1982. Citibank is the top bank issuing credit cards, with 9 million cards. Sears's new Discover card has already found its way into 8 million pockets. But plastic credit isn't without risk. Credit-card companies wrote off $3 billion in bad credit-card debt in 1986.

American Express Company
CEO: James D. Robinson III
Employees: 78,747
Assets: $106 billion

American Express Tower
World Financial Center
New York, New York 10285-4805
212-640-2000

	1987	1986	1985	1980
Revenues (millions of dollars):	16,141	14,652	11,850	5,505
Net income (millions of dollars):	533	1,110	810	376
Share earnings (dollars):	1.20	2.46	1.78	1.32

What it does: Second-largest financial services company in America. Best known for traveler's checks and credit cards, this diversified financial services company is also an investment banker, retail stockbroker, and owner of the Trade Development Bank, IDS Financial Services, First Data Resources, and Shearson Lehman Brothers.

In the 1980s American Express has become the most successful company in capitalizing on the promise of providing diversified financial services. American Express holds the distinction of being the first service company—financial or otherwise—to earn more than $1 billion in profits.

Many companies had been busy creating diversified financial services by putting banking, consumer lending, credit, brokerage, insurance, real estate sale, mortgages, and other financial services under one roof. The idea was great but in practice few companies figured out how to integrate all of these new businesses into one profitable company. Real estate brokers didn't sell enough mortgages, executives used to running a securities firm or a retail outlet didn't know how to handle insurance salespeople or real estate brokers. The result for many companies was predictable: poor profits.

Not so at American Express. After paying $915 million in 1981 for the nation's most profitable national retail brokerage, Shearson Loeb Rhodes, it bought the major Swiss bank, Trade Development Bank, for $520 million in 1983, Investors Diversified Services now (IDS Financial Services), for $727 million in 1983, and the investment bankers Lehman Brothers Kuhn Loeb for $380 million in 1984. Then in 1987 it snapped up the problem ridden E. F. Hutton Group for $961 million. The result was record profits of $1.1 billion in 1986, on sales of $14.65 billion, making American Express the largest service company in the U.S.

The architect behind those numbers is James D. Robinson III, CEO of American Express. Scion of a well-connected Atlanta banking family, Robinson was only 40 when he took over American Express in 1977. Today, he is known for his clout and his salesmanship on Capitol Hill.

Wall Street is also impressed with Robinson and how American Express became one of the few companies to thrive under financial deregulation. But part of that success could be traced into the company's history. American Express actually got its start pushing for another kind of deregulation. Founder Henry Wells fought the government's postal monopoly successfully in 1845 when he started delivering mail between New York and Buffalo for only 6 cents a letter, compared to 25 cents for the government. The U.S. Post Office soon dropped its rates, however, and regained its lost customers.

Wells, though, stayed in the express mail business, forming American Express with his two main competitors in 1850. Its traveler's checks appeared in 1891. Later, American Express capitalized on its traveler's check experience and reputation to become the largest credit-card company.

The company's recent move into financial services hasn't always been smooth. A foray into insurance with Fireman's Fund produced not only lots of red ink but an SEC investigation. When the cable boom didn't turn out as profitable as expected, the company sold off its share of the Warner Amex Company, a joint venture with Warner Communications. In 1987 the company wrote off $870 million to boost loss reserves for bad Latin American debt.

American Express broke tradition in 1987 to bring out the Optima credit card. The Optima card allows American Express customers the luxury of charging goods and services to a revolving line of credit. (Holders of regular American Express credit cards have to pay off amounts owed at the end of each month.) Low interest rate charges made the card an immediate success. But it exposed the company to the possibility of a credit-card war and the risk of assuming large amounts of consumer credit.

DEFENSE AND AEROSPACE

THE MARKET AND THE MONEY

Fortress America costs taxpayers a fortune. Nearly 1.6 trillion Defense Department dollars were pumped into the economy during the first six years of the Reagan administration, the biggest peacetime defense buildup in U.S. history.

As Defense Department spending took off, growing from $134 billion in 1980 to more than $282 billion in 1987, profits for the aerospace industry also went into the stratosphere. The nation's top defense contractor, General Dynamics, for example, saw profits from its military aerospace contracts shoot up from 6.9% of total sales in 1980 to 10.3% in 1984; General Electric, the second-largest contractor, meanwhile, improved from 10.5% to 13.7%. According to the U.S. Navy, profits for Defense Department contractors are 15% to 20% higher than profits earned on private civilian work.

But after 1984, the Pentagon came under fire for $400 hammers, $7,300 coffeepots, and a $2 trillion national debt. The good old days of guns on credit ended. Congress did nothing about budget deficits but it did cut defense spending and forced the Defense Department to get more bang for its buck. New rules increased competitive bidding, forced defense contractors to pay for any cost overruns, and required companies to pick up a greater share of the costs of weapon development.

The result was a slowdown for defense contractors and the aerospace industry. In 1985, revenues of nine large aerospace and defense contractors increased 16% over 1984, but profits leveled off, dropping 1%. In 1986 revenues also increased, 12%, to over $79 billion, but profits took a nosedive, falling 41%, to only $1.7 billion. The ninth-largest contractor, United Technologies, for instance, reported net income of $73 million, down from $313 million in 1985.

Sales and profits will be no better over the next few years. Thanks to arms programs that have already received funding, the Defense Department will spend $81 billion for new military hardware in fiscal 1988, one of the highest totals in peacetime history. But after that, the defense budget for the rest of the 1980s will be lucky to keep up with inflation, barring, of course, a major foreign policy crisis. As a result, many defense contractors will have to retrench, cutting employees and shutting down plants.

While Congress cut military budgets and the Defense Department started paying attention to costs, the industry was hit with a slowdown in the commercial aircraft market. Shipments of large transports grew 10% in 1986, and sales of helicopters stayed about the same. But the market for smaller aircraft worsened for the eighth year in a row, producing the worst sales of light aircraft on record. As a result of the slowdown in civilian sales, the aerospace industry depends on military contracts. Table 141 (below) shows how shipments in the airplane industry have broken down for the last few years.

Table 141   U.S. Aircraft Shipments, 1970 to 1988
(value in millions of dollars)

					Civil							
	Aircraft total		Total		Large transports		General aviation[1]		Helicopters		Military total	
Year	Units	Value	Units	Value	Units	Value	Units	Value	Units	Value	Units	Value
1970	11,632	7,511	8,098	3,544	311	3,158	7,292	337	495	49	3,534	3,967
1971	11,161	6,593	8,142	2,971	223	2,580	7,466	322	453	69	3,019	3,622
1972	13,072	6,220	10,542	3,417	199	2,787	9,774	558	569	72	2,530	2,803
1973	16,539	8,176	14,688	4,814	274	3,873	13,646	828	768	113	1,851	3,362
1974	17,192	8,595	15,292	5,270	317	4,207	14,166	909	809	154	1,900	3,325
1975	16,918	9,355	15,179	5,305	285	4,006	14,056	1,033	838	266	1,739	4,050
1976	17,865	9,001	16,489	4,705	217	3,155	15,451	1,226	821	324	1,376	4,296
1977	19,392	9,092	18,047	4,512	159	2,672	16,904	1,488	984	352	1,345	4,580
1978	19,881	10,179	18,885	6,460	241	4,308	17,811	1,781	833	371	996	3,719
1979	19,302	15,028	18,465	10,598	376	8,030	17,048	2,165	1,041	403	837	4,430
1980	14,660	18,845	13,613	12,953	383	9,793	11,877	2,486	1,353	674	1,047	5,892
1981	11,860	20,157	10,798	13,287	388	9,731	9,457	2,920	953	636	1,062	6,870
1982	6,248	19,266	5,089	8,619	236	6,254	4,266	2,000	587	365	1,159	10,647
1983	4,407	25,232	3,354	10,232	262	8,493	2,691	1,470	401	269	1,053	15,000
1984	3,931	25,754	2,995	8,354	188	6,343	2,431	1,681	376	330	936	17,400
1985	3,597	28,446	2,678	11,311	273	9,375	2,029	1,431	376	505	919	17,135
1986[2]	3,266	34,119	2,154	12,670	329	11,120	1,495	1,262	330	288	1,112	21,449
1987[3]	2,835	35,640	1,785	13,540	355	11,900	1,160	1,320	270	320	1,050	21,100
1988[3]	2,990	36,120	1,980	14,820	380	13,000	1,270	1,420	330	400	1,010	21,300

[1]Excludes off-the-shelf military aircraft.
[2]Estimated.
[3]Forecast.
Sources: U.S. Department of Commerce: International Trade Administration; general aviation: General Aviation Manufacturers Association.

Aerospace industry sales of such things as aircraft, engines, parts, missiles, and space vehicles hit a record $102.9 billion in 1987, way up from $58.5 billion in 1980 and $21.1 billion in 1972. Sales should hit $110.4 billion in 1988.

In recent years, the military has expanded its share of total aircraft shipments from 36% in 1979 to 59% in 1987. However as military spending slows, sales of civilian aircraft will assume a larger role. In 1988, it's projected that $36.1 billion worth of planes will be sold, with about $21.3 billion worth of sales coming from the military.

GUNS, BUTTER, AND THE ECONOMY

Remember the 1960s when President Johnson decided we could afford guns and butter—a war on poverty and a war on communism in Southeast Asia? For a while, fueled by huge federal spending, the economy went into overdrive. But in the end the public got neither guns nor butter. Soon we were stuck with the economic counterpart to the famous domino theory: massive government spending soon produced inflation and reallocated money from the private sector to the public. That worked against productivity and investment. The economy had a hangover from all the free-flowing government money that lasted through most of the 1970s and early 1980s.

Up to then, few people had doubted the economic benefits of military spending. After all, the U.S. spent 11% of its GNP on defense in 1955, far more than it did at the height of the Reagan defense buildup in 1984, when defense ate up only 6.4% of the GNP, or even at the height of the Vietnam War, when 9.6% of GNP went for guns. And in the 1950s and 1960s, the economy seemed to be doing just fine. Government expenditures for defense created jobs and produced all sorts of great spin-offs— like Tang, high-powered computer chips, jet engines, and graphite tennis rackets—that vastly improved life on the home front.

Headaches produced by lavish spending for guns and butter in the 1960s and early 1970s, however, produced a more skeptical view of military spending. Already, some economists returned to the traditional view— once expressed by 18th-century economist Adam Smith—that military spending diverts money from the private sector and more productive uses.

Noting that about one third to one half of all the nation's scientific talent since the beginning of the Cold War has gone into military-related research, critics of defense spending argue that government support for defense research and development channels money away from the private sector and research that would improve productivity and produce profitable consumer products. While Americans build tanks and missiles, the Japanese and Germans build Sonys and cameras. We get higher taxes. They get a bigger share of the world market for consumer goods.

Of course, declining productivity and the inability of American companies to compete on the world market aren't just the fault of military spending. But in recent years it has become more apparent that guns don't always produce butter. The President's Commission on Industrial Competitiveness, for example, found in 1985 that the Pentagon's research is now so exotic that it has few commercial applications. According to government estimates, military research eats up 27% of all research and development (R&D) in the U.S., in contrast to only 4% in Germany and 1% in Japan. (Private estimates put the figure at 35% to 40% of all R&D). The result, according to economists Mary Kaldor, Margaret Sharp, and William Walker, is that countries with low military budgets have done well on the world market while countries such as the U.S. and the United Kingdom with higher expenditures as a percentage of GNP do poorly.

Linked with worries about the U.S.'s ability to compete on world markets and spend money to develop new technologies is declining political support for defense spending. Faced with the choice of cutting social or defense programs, traditional pork-barrel politics that justify defense spending have come under attack. A 1985 study by Employment Research Associates in Michigan found that only 25% of all congressional districts, located in only 15 states, collect more from defense spending than they spend in taxes for defense.

The Pentagon counters that the nation needs a certain level of defense spending to maintain an infrastructure—the factories and skills—in case of war or national emergency. Otherwise, it is impossible to mobilize quickly and efficiently for war, as the U.S. learned at the beginning of World War II. And a 1985 study by Chase Econometrics indicates that there is still some life in the argument that military spending helps the economy—at least in the immediate vicinity of the spending. Chase found that 6 of the 10 fastest growing local economies in the U.S. were in areas that received high levels of defense spending.

SECRECY AND THE BOTTOM LINE

Say you want to find how much a defense contractor gets from the government and what kinds of contracts the company has. A reasonable request, most investors would assume. After all, such information provides the key to projecting a company's future earnings and profitability. So you check government publications and company reports to find out what new missiles and gizmos are under development. Right?

Wrong. Many multibillion-dollar Defense Department contracts are not listed in SEC filings. About $22 billion worth of programs in the proposed budget for 1988 are "black programs," according to the Center for Defense Information. Very little information, financial or technical, is released about these top-secret programs—such as research on stealth missiles and bombers.

The idea, of course, is to keep the Russians from using company reports to figure out top-secret weapons systems. But the same secrecy forces Wall Street analysts to work in the dark to project companies' future earnings or, in some cases, to turn into spies, seeking classified information so they can decide which aerospace stocks to buy or sell.

For example, in the third quarter of 1986, Northrop reported that a large, classified government contract forced the company to write off $90 million and reduce future projections of profit margins. No further elaboration was made by the company.

Seeking to piece together the puzzle, some analysts pointed out that Northrop had been the prime contractor for the $50 billion job of building an advanced technology bomber. Did Northrop run into problems with the contract? Maybe. Maybe not. In early 1988, reports were circulating that Northrop had actually won a $2 billion dollar contract to start production of the Stealth bomber.

Faced with such secrecy, Wall Street grumbles that investors who finance America's defense companies know less about their cash flow than the average Russian spy. They say that keeping financial details from investors may actually hurt national security by making it more difficult for defense companies to raise capital on Wall Street.

COSTS, CORRUPTION, AND NATIONAL DEFENSE

Defense contractors have been spending a lot of time defending what they do with taxpayers' money.

No wonder. Besides the usual scandals about billion-dollar defense systems that don't work and $4 computer chips that anyone but the Pentagon could buy for 40 cents, the mid-1980s saw a raft of corruption and cost-overrun cases. Consider:

- Litton, the nation's 19th-largest Defense Department contractor, pleaded guilty to 325 counts of defrauding the government with at least $6.3 million in overcharges. Litton agreed to repay $15 million.
- A House Government Operations Committee report asserted that lax management had allowed contractors to overprice subcontracts. The cost: $1.3 billion in 1984 alone.
- A *New York Times* survey of government audits of NASA and the space shuttle found that at least $3.5 billion was wasted through abuses and mismanagement. The shuttle, which blew up in 1986 because of design flaws, was projected to cost $675 million when first proposed but it ended up costing $1.47 billion and was nowhere near as productive as NASA planners had first envisioned. Instead of a 65,000-pound payload, it could only carry 53,000 pounds; instead of the 60 planned fights a year, it could only manage 22. As a result, the cost per launch soared from a planned $28 million to $279 million. The cost per payload pound soared from $270 to $5,264.
- Government investigators found that kickbacks from subcontractors— which do $50 billion worth of Defense Department business—were widespread. Employees from such major companies as Hughes Aircraft Company, the Northrop Corporation, Hughes Helicopters, the Raytheon Company, and Teledyne were convicted for taking kickbacks from subcontractors.

- Dozens of Defense Department and military personnel involved in buying military supplies were arrested for taking bribes or stealing parts in a wide-ranging FBI probe.
- At one point in 1986, 45 of the top 100 Defense Department contractors were under investigation, according to the Inspector General's office.

The problems go beyond a few abuses. What's at fault is the way the military does business.

Many of the worst problems can be traced to the Pentagon. Government regulations and red tape, for example, add billions to Defense Department bills. Remember those $4 computer chips that should cost 40 cents? The problem wasn't a greedy defense contractor but the Pentagon's demand for extra testing and paperwork.

Every day, the military signs 52,000 contracts—the Air Force alone entered into 5 million contracts in 1985. Unfortunately, most of those contracts are wrapped up in mountains of red tape.

Military procurement remains one of the most complex systems known to man—which may explain why a lot of expensive weapons systems never work. Defense firms typically face over 44,000 specifications for a weapons system. The instructions on procurement run 32 volumes and take up six feet of shelf space. One Pentagon study found that regulations accounted for one third of procurement costs.

An example of how Pentagon red tape costs money is a simple comparison between how the private and public sectors carry out a contract. McDonnell Douglas, for example, found that specifications for a military aircraft were set out in over 24,000 documents, insuring that the project was quickly snarled in lots of red tape and costly paperwork. In contrast, a $2 billion McDonnell Douglas contract to supply Delta Air Lines with passenger aircraft produced only 10 documents. Freeing defense contractors from costly red tape might do more than just cut costs. It could improve the quality of weapons.

Also, military planners encourage waste by adding lots of whistles and gizmos to design specs. As a result, weapons systems get so complicated they can only be operated and serviced by highly trained personnel. And contractors are constantly forced into costly delays by military planners who suddenly decide a weapon system suddenly needs to do something it was never intended to do.

Even worse is the cozy relationship between the military and private sector that has grown up over the years. As late as the early 1980s, most military contracts were still awarded without competitive bidding on a cost-plus basis—meaning that the contractor was assured of making a profit no matter how high costs rose. Pentagon bureaucrats also had little incentive to rock the boat. Many officers and officials counted on retiring from their military jobs to cushy high-paying jobs with defense contractors.

Since then, the Pentagon has tried to improve the way it does business. Under strict new procurement policies, companies now bear a portion of the initial research and design costs on many big projects. More importantly, many R&D contracts are on a fixed-price basis, rather than cost-plus. Such costs can total billions of dollars. Competitive bidding has increased and contracts have been changed to make companies responsible for cost overruns.

More competition in the long run will help control costs, but in the short run it is forcing military contractors to assume new risks. For example, two groups of contractors competing for the contract to make the Air Force's advanced tactical fighter are getting $691 million apiece for research and development, but are forced to sink about $500 million or $1 billion of their own money into the project. The winner will get a $40 billion contract to build 750 planes. Competitive pressures to keep costs and profits low will probably mean that real profits might not come until the turn of the century, when the plane is sold to foreign governments. But that's how the free market operates.

THE BUSINESS OF FLYING BUSINESS

Corporate airplanes are often a symbol of management waste, a perennial target of shareholder discontent. Yet according to the annual survey of business aviation by Aviation Data Service, 328 of the 500 largest industrial corporations own their own plane. Over 63,000 U.S. business and corporate airplanes fly about 11.4 million hours a year, according to the National Business Aircraft Association.

Actually, many of the complaints about corporate jets are misplaced. Most of the large business fleets of aircraft and helicopters are owned by oil, aerospace, and defense companies. They use these planes to demonstrate the planes they sell or to reach far-flung oil fields. Helicopters are often used to reach oil rigs at sea.

But even if many large companies need planes for business, not enough of them have been buying new planes. The industry is in its worst recession ever. General aviation manufacturers, which produce small fixed-wing aircraft for business, regional airlines services, and recreation, shipped 17,811 planes in 1978 valued at $1.78 billion, but in 1987, only 1,160 planes valued at only $1.32 billion were delivered. A survey by the National Business Aircraft Association indicates that the number of business airplanes sold dropped from 4,078 in 1979 to only 915 in 1984. Sales of corporate jets, according to Drexel Burnham Lambert, declined from a peak of 389 in 1981 to only about 95 in 1986.

Obviously, that has hurt the companies that make most of the planes American businesses and corporations use. Some of the largest—Beech Aircraft, a subsidiary of Raytheon Company; Cessna, bought by General Dynamics in 1985; and Piper Aircraft, a subsidiary of Lear Siegler—have all seen huge drops in sales.

One important factor behind the decline of sales of business aircraft is the ruined oil economy. Many oil companies sold off their planes, glutting the market and cutting demands for new aircraft. Another factor is cor-

Table 142   The Largest Corporate Fleets

Rank	Company	Number of aircraft 1986	1985
1.	Chevron	39	46
2.	Allied-Signal	29	46
3.	United Technologies	29	31
4.	Tenneco	27	28
5.	du Pont	24	24
6.	Mobil	23	25
7.	Rockwell International	22	20
8.	Exxon	19	18
9.	Occidental Petroleum	15	20
10.	General Motors	13	15

Source: Aviation Data Service Inc. (Av Data, Wichita), May 1987.

porate cost cutting. Also, the industry is facing a liability crisis, with the cost of insurance adding $70,000 to the cost of every plane, up from the $2,111 in insurance premiums plane makers were paying as late as 1972. With sales showing no signs of improving in the near future, business plane makers could be in for more turbulent weather.

General Dynamics Corporation
CEO: Stanley C. Pace
Employees: 106,000
Assets: $4.9 billion

7733 Forsythe Boulevard
St. Louis, Missouri 63105
314-889-8200

	1987	1986	1985	1980
Revenues (millions of dollars):	9,344	8,892	7,952	4,056
Net income (millions of dollars):	437	(53)	383	195
Share earnings (dollars):	10.26	—	9.05	3.58

What it does: The nation's largest defense contractor.

General Dynamics, which gets nearly 90% of its revenues from government contracts, provides the Defense Department with such major weapons systems such as the F-16 fighter, the M-1 tank, the Tomahawk cruise missile, and the Trident submarine, as well as some bad publicity for the Pentagon.

The head of its Electric Boat Division had to flee the country to avoid federal prosecution on kickback charges. The company was suspended twice in 1985 from bidding on government contracts. Four current and former executives were indicted for overcharges connected with the Sergeant York antiaircraft gun. Some of the more notorious charges included allegations that the company got the Pentagon to pay for its corporate barbershop, dog-kennel fees, and country-club dues.

None of the allegations were proven and the Justice Department eventually dropped all charges. That confirmed the company's contention that the indictments shouldn't have been filed to begin with. But by that time the damage to the company's reputation had been done.

To clean up its image, General Dynamics hired Stanley Pace—an executive known for his honesty and integrity. Pace hired an ad agency to clean up the firm's image and put through tough new management rules. The scandals haven't ruined the company's defense business, but profits did tumble after three record years and the company posted losses of $52.5 million on revenues of $8.89 billion in 1986.

The company's feuds with the Pentagon even involved the Crown family, which controls the company and owns 21.4% of its stock. In 1986, the government attempted to revoke the security clearance of Lester Crown, who now runs the family's business, because of his involvement in a bribery scandal in the 1970s.

Starting with a small sand and gravel company, Lester's father Henry used a heavy dose of loans to build up a billion-dollar Crown family fortune. He sold his Material Service Corporation to General Dynamics in 1966 and then he bought his way back in, taking control of General Dynamics. Now that Henry is sick and no longer active in day-to-day business, Lester oversees a family empire valued at about $2.1 billion. Its holdings include a 21.4% stake in General Dynamics, 10.5% of Chicago Pacific, 4% of Hilton Hotels, 1% of Transworld, 14% of the New York Yankees, real estate, and holdings in other public companies.

Lockheed Corporation
CEO: Lawrence O. Kitchen
Employees: 97,000
Assets: $6.2 billion

4500 Park Granada Boulevard
Calabasas, California 91399
818-712-2000

	1987	1986	1985	1980
Revenues (millions of dollars):	11,321	10,273	9,535	5,396
Net income (millions of dollars):	421	408	401	28
Share earnings (dollars):	6.64	6.18	6.10	0.51

What it does: Primarily engaged in the research, design, and production of military aircraft, missiles, space systems, and electronic systems.

Here is a company with a knack for getting into trouble and surviving. Lockheed was founded in 1916 by Allan and Malcolm Loughead, who later changed their names to Lockheed and Jack Northrop who later founded another famous defense contractor that bears his name. The company went bankrupt in 1931 but under new owners began producing military planes. In the 1960s Lockheed became the nation's number-one defense contractor.

At this point, the company lost some key defense contracts and fell behind in the production of new planes. In 1971, Lockheed escaped bankruptcy by only one vote, when Congress approved a $250 million bailout. Such a narrow escape from disaster would have prompted most companies to behave themselves for a while. Instead, Lockheed used some of its new cash to bribe foreign officials, including a former prime minister of Japan and Prince Bernhard of the Netherlands.

More recently, profits returned, but the controversies haven't gone away. A few years ago, the company got into hot water by somehow managing to lose 1,400 top-secret documents relating to the stealth program, a research project intended to produce planes that cannot be detected by radar. Then, the company got its usual bad publicity when Representative John Dingell cited internal Air Force findings that Lockheed's 50-plane contract for C-5B transport planes was overpriced by about $1 billion. After negotiations, the company agreed in 1987 to give up $350 billion on the Air Force's option to buy 21 planes. Still, profits in 1986 were up 2% to $408 million on revenues of $10,273 billion.

McDonnell Douglas Corporation

CEO: Sanford N. McDonnell
Employees: 109,164
Assets: $8.3 billion

P.O. Box 516
St. Louis, Missouri 63166
314-232-0232

	1987	1986	1985	1980
Revenues (millions of dollars):	13,146	12,831	11,666	6,198
Net income (millions of dollars):	313	277	346	145
Share earnings (dollars):	7.75	6.86	8.60	3.65

What it does: The leading manufacturer in fighter aircraft for the military.

In the early 1980s, James Worsham, the president of the Douglas division of McDonnell Douglas Corporation, literally bet the company on a deal. He signed a contract with American Airlines that would allow American to return $400 million worth of narrow-body MD-80s within 30 days if it didn't like them.

The gamble was particularly risky, for in the 1970s and early 1980s, McDonnell Douglas Corporation's commercial airline manufacturing business had lost money, reflecting the aerospace giant's lost dominance in the jet airplane business. Sales of commercial jets dropped from 300 in 1968 to only 50 in 1982.

American decided to keep the planes and, in 1986, McDonnell Douglas's jet operations actually made money. It shipped an estimated 95 jets, nearly twice as many as it had four years earlier.

The company got its name in 1967 when two large family-owned companies, McDonnell and Douglas, merged. Douglas had been created by Donald Wills Douglas in 1920 and got off the ground with its famous DC series in the 1930s. But the company lost control of the new jet plane market to Boeing in the late 1950s and was losing money by the time it was taken over the James S. McDonnell. He created McDonnell in 1939 and built it up with fighter sales. McDonnell's nephew Sanford played a major role in convincing the company's board to put up the money for the risk MD-80s. Sanford is now chairman.

Boeing
CEO: Frank A. Shrontz   P.O. Box 3707
Employees: 140,000   Seattle, WA 98124
Assets: $11 billion   206-655-2121

	1987	1986	1985	1980
Revenues (millions of dollars):	15,355	16,341	13,636	8,131
Net income (millions of dollars):	480	665	566	505
Share earnings (dollars):	3.10	4.28	3.75	5.25

What it does: Leading manufacturer of commercial and military aircraft. In the six-year period from 1980 to the end of 1985, the company got 63% of its revenues and 42.3% of its profits from selling commercial aircraft, 23% of its revenues and 43.2% of its profits from selling military aircraft, and 9% of its revenues and 13% of its profits from selling missiles and space vehicles.

Boeing is one of the few American airplane makers constantly able to make money selling commercial aircraft. Since introducing the 707, the first commercially successful jetliner, Boeing has set the industry standard for jetliners. More than half of the 10,000 jetliners outside the Soviet Union were made by Boeing. And its military aircraft are no less famous: the company built the famous flying fortress, the B-17, as well as the famous B-52 and the Minuteman missile.

It all started in 1916 when pilot William Edward Boeing got tired of waiting six months to get spare parts for his aircraft. So he set up a factory near downtown Seattle. Today the company is the city's largest employer.

Despite Boeing's successes in pioneering commercial jetliners, the company hasn't always flown smoothly. In the late 1960s, the airline industry didn't go for Boeing's 747 jumbo jet, and in the 1970s when Congress cut funding for the SST (supersonic transport) plane, the company was forced to cut its work force from 105,000 to only 38,000.

Though recovered from that debacle and producing record profits in recent years, Boeing faces new risks with its 7J7 plane. Designed to dramatically improve fuel efficiency, the plane could be less of a bargain if oil prices remain low. Moreover, a cash-poor airline industry is less willing to replace its aging fleet. Finally, recognizing the problems with the program, Boeing announced in 1988 that it was delaying work on the 7J7. That caused some anxiety at Boeing's corporate headquarters because the 7J7 was slated to be Boeing's big money maker in the late 1990s.

At the same time, the company has been trying to expand its defense contracting. It lost a bidding war to GM in 1985 for Hughes Aircraft, but with a cash hoard of some $3.6 billion, the company is likely to acquire a major defense contractor. The strategy of expanding its defense operations when the Pentagon is cutting spending has its risks. But experience at competing in the cost-competitive commercial airplane market will give Boeing a head start in an increasingly cost-conscious defense industry. Boeing still held 55% of the commercial jet aircraft market in 1987 and its latest versions of the 737 and 747 are a smash hit, racking up an unprecedented $16 billion in advance orders.

THE ARMS TRADE

Coup d'états, invasions, guerrilla wars, buying communist arms and selling them to anticommunist guerrillas, shoring up an embattled despot—it's all part of the arms trade, a risky but lucrative profession. Self-styled "merchants of death" do $30 billion a year in legitimate business and billions more in the black market arms trade.

Arms dealers aren't too particular about ideology, only the ability to pay. Many arms dealers have no qualms about arming dictators on the right, religious fanatics like Khomeini, or guerrilla armies on the left. Sometimes arms dealers work on their own, subverting the foreign policy of their own country by selling stolen parts and arms to enemy nations. Sometimes they act as proxies for the CIA or the KGB.

Since sales often take place in a shadowy world of offshore dummy corporations and Swiss bank accounts, most arms dealers don't have to worry about adverse publicity. Disclosure of secret U.S. arms sales to Iran was a rarity that put several arms dealers on the cover of *Time* magazine and in the witness stand at 1987 congressional hearings.

But even before the Iran arms scandal brought the industry a lot of unwanted publicity, all was not right in the international arms trade. Around the world the war business is booming. Worldwide military expenditures hit $900 billion in 1985 and have been growing 3.5% a year faster than inflation. But the Reagan administration has put severe limitations on selling arms to some old and very large customers, such as Iran and South Africa. Restrictions on sales of certain high-tech weapons, lower oil prices, and the cash-strapped third world have also cost arms traders billions in sales. As a result, the international arms trade dropped from $52.6 billion in 1982 to $43.2 billion in 1985, the most recent figures available from the U.S. Arms Control and Disarmament Agency.

Between 1981 and 1985, the Soviet Union was the world's largest arms dealer, supplying $55.7 billion in arms, while the U.S. was a close second with $49.2 billion and 26% of the world arms market. The tables below show where the guns went and who supplied them.

Table 143 World Arms Transfers, 1981 to 1985

(billions of dollars)

		Who bought the arms						
	Total arms transfers	Middle East	Europe	Africa	East Asia	Latin America	South Asia, Oceania	North America (excluding Central America)
Soviet Union	55.7	18.4	8.6	13.8	4.9	4.2	5.8	0
Warsaw Pact Countries*	13.1	4.4	4.5	2.8	0.3	0.8	0.3	0
Other communist countries	9.4	7.1	0.05	1.5	0.3	0.1	0.4	0.001
United States	49.2	15.1	16.1	1.4	9.8	1.3	3.7	1.8
NATO	44.7	22.4	4.1	6.5	2.1	5.2	2.3	2.1
Other noncommunist countries	16.0	8.6	1.9	1.6	1.5	1.9	0.3	0.2
Total	188.1	76.0	35.3	27.5	18.9	13.5	12.7	4.1

*Excludes the Soviet Union.
Source: U.S. Arms Control and Disarmament Agency, *World Military Expenditures and Arms Transfers, 1986.*

Table 144 World Military Expenditures, 1984

Country	Military spending (billions of dollars)	Rank in spending	Number of soldiers (millions)	Rank in number of soldiers
Soviet Union	260	1	4.5	1
United States	237	2	2.2	3
United Kingdom	25.4	3	0.34	20
China	24.0	4	4.1	2
West Germany	22.8	5	0.49	13
France	22.4	6	0.57	11
Saudi Arabia	22.2	7	0.095	49
Iraq	14.6	8	0.79	7
Poland	13.4	9	0.43	17
Japan	12.7	10	0.24	27
Iran	11.4	11	0.335	21
East Germany	10.7	12	0.24	28
Italy	10.1	13	0.508	12
Czechoslavakia	7.6	14	0.213	29
Canada	7.6	15	0.082	52
Israel	7.2	16	0.205	31
India	7.1	17	1.4	4
Romania	5.4	18	0.244	26
North Korea	5.2	19	0.78	8
Egypt	5.1	20	0.47	15

Source: U.S. Arms Control and Disarmament Agency, *World Military Expenditures and Arms Transfers, 1986.*

Table 145 Top Defense Department Contractors

| Company | Major Products | Prime contract awards | | |
		Thousands of dollars	Percent of total	Cumulative percent of total
Total defense contracts		145,742,058	100.00	100.00
Total, 100 companies and their subsidiaries		98,621,062	67.67	67.67
1. General Dynamics Corporation	F-16 Falcon fighter aircraft. Nuclear submarines. Tomahawk, Sparrow, Stinger, and RIM-66 standard missile systems. M-1 tank. MK-15 close-in weapon system.	8,012,975	5.50	5.50
2. General Electric Company	F-100, T-700, J-85, J-79, and TF-34 turbofan and turbojet engines. Nuclear reactors for submarines. Underwater sound equipment. Transmission components for M-2 infantry fighting vehicles. RDT&E for missile and space systems and electronic and communications equipment.	6,847,079	4.70	10.20
3. McDonnell Douglas Corporation	F-18 Hornet, F-15 Eagle, AH-64 Apache, KC-10 Extender, and AV-8 Harrier aircraft. Tomahawk and Harpoon missile systems. RDT&E for aircraft, missile, and space systems and electronics and communication equipment.	6,586,311	4.52	14.72
4. Rockwell International Corporation	B-1 bomber. MX, Hellfire, and Minuteman missile systems. Space vehicles. Various electronics and communication equipment.	5,589,681	3.84	18.55
5. General Motors Corporation	Maverick, Phoenix, and TOW missile systems. T-56 aircraft engines. Guided missile systems for F-14 and F-18 fighter aircraft. Fire control equipment for M-1 tank. Components MK-48 torpedo.	5,069,296	3.48	22.03
6. Lockheed Corporation	C-5 Galaxy, C-130 Hercules, and P-3 Orion aircraft. RDT&E for missile and space systems, electronics and communication equipment, and weapons. Space vehicles.	4,896,318	3.36	25.39
7. Raytheon Company	Patriot, Sparrow, Hawk, Maverick, and RIM-66 standard missile systems. RDT&E electronics and communication equipment.	4,051,573	2.78	28.17
8. The Boeing Company, Inc.	Electronic countermeasures and aircraft accessories for B-1 bomber. Miscellaneous equipment, management services, etc., for H-46 Sea Knight, B-52 Stratofortress, C-135 Stratolifter, E-3A, and A-6 Intruder aircraft. CH-47 Chinook helicopter. MX missile. Miscellaneous electronics and communication equipment.	3,556,026	2.44	30.61
9. United Technologies Corporation	F-100, J-52, and TF-30 aircraft engines. UH-60 Blackhawk, CH-53 Sea Stallion, and SH-60 Seahawk helicopters. Space vehicle components.	3,527,014	2.42	33.03
10. Grumman Corporation	F-14 Tomcat, E-2 Hawkeye, EA-6B Prowler, A-6 Intruder, and C-2 Greyhound aircraft. RDT&E for aircraft and electronics and communication equipment.	2,967,495	2.04	35.06
11. Martin Marietta Corporation	Pershing, Hellfire and SICBM missile systems. A-64 Apache aircraft. Guided missile launchers. RDT&E for MX and Titan missile systems and space transportation systems.	2,935,397	2.01	37.08

(RDT&E) Research, development, technology, and equipment.
Source: U.S. Department of Defense.

Table 146   The Burden of Military Spending Around the World

This chart shows the relative burden of military spending around the world. The far left column shows military expenditures (ME) as a percentage of gross national product (GNP). The chart also breaks down countries by GNP per capita. The breakdown shows that Ethiopia, for example, spends between 5% and 9.99% of its GNP on its military even though it is very poor, with a GNP of under $200 per capita. It is safe to assume that Ethiopian military spending is a greater burden on its people than military spending in the U.S. and other more affluent countries.

ME/GNP* (percentage)	GNP per capita (1983 dollars)					
	Under $200	$200–499	$500–999	$1,000–2,999	$3,000–9,999	$10,000 and over
10% and over	Cambodia† Laos		Yemen (Aden) Egypt Yemen (Sanaa)	Iraq Korea, North Syria Jordan Nicaragua Mongolia†	Oman Israel Saudia Arabia Libya Soviet Union	Qatar
5–9.99%	Ethiopia	Cape Verde† China Vietnam† Zambia Somalia	Angola Lesotho Zimbabwe El Salvador	Lebanon† Peru Taiwan	Bulgaria Greece Iran Germany, East	United Arab Emirates United States
2–4.99%	Burma Burkina Faso Equatorial Guinea† Guinea-Bissau† Mali	Pakistan Afghanistan† Mauritania† Mozambique† India Burundi Kenya Tanzania Guinea† Senegal Madagascar Indonesia Benin Togo Liberia Rwanda† Sudan	Morocco Guyana Honduras Thailand Botswana† Bolivia	Cuba Korea, South Turkey Albania† South Africa Chile Malaysia Argentina Yugoslavia Portugal Tunisia Uruguay Algeria Congo Suriname Panama	Czechoslovakia Poland Singapore United Kingdom Romania France Hungary Bahrain Netherlands Belgium Australia Italy Trinidad and Tobago Spain Gabon	Kuwait Germany, West Sweden Norway Denmark Canada Switzerland
1–1.99%	Bangladesh Malawi Chad Nepal	Central African Republic† Haiti Sri Lanka Sao Tome and Principe† Zaire Uganda	Cameroon Papua New Guinea Nigeria Swaziland Ivory Coast Philippines	Guatemala Paraguay Ecuador Colombia Fiji Dominican Republic Costa Rica	New Zealand Ireland Venezuela Cyprus Austria	Finland
Under 1%		Niger Sierra Leone The Gambia†		Brazil Jamaica Mexico Mauritius	Barbados Malta Ghana	Japan Luxembourg Iceland

*Countries are listed within blocks in descending order of the percentage of their GNP they spend on the military.
†Reliable 1984 data not available; ranking based on rough estimates.
Source: U.S. Arms Control and Disarmament Agency, *World Military Expenditures and Arms Transfers, 1986.*

EDUCATION

THE MARKET AND THE MONEY

Knowledge may be power, but getting it costs money. About $307.6 billion will have been spent for education in America's schools during the 1987–1988 school year, up from $288.4 billion in 1986–1987 and $247.2 billion in 1984–1985. Over $328 billion is projected to be spent in the 1988–89 school year. That money goes to educate some 58 million students in American schools and colleges. In 1987, students receive nearly 1 million bachelor's degrees, 294,000 master's degrees, 78,000 first professional degrees, and 34,000 doctorates.

Thanks in part to all that money, today's Americans are better educated than ever before.

Almost one fifth of the population (19.4%) has graduated from college, up from only 11.0% in 1970. Only 26.1% of the population has not graduated from high school, compared to 76.5% in 1940. And the median education of Americans is 12.6 years, up from 8.6 in 1940.

Education, of course, doesn't end with graduation. The American Society for Training and Development estimates companies spend a hefty $30 billion a year on formal courses and training programs for their employees. Another $180 billion, they estimate, is spent annually for unstructured on the job training and supervision.

BUYING AN EDUCATION

In recent years, the costs of higher education have gone through the roof, with tuition increasing 3.2 times for public schools and 3.7 times for private schools between 1970 and 1986. In 1987 the average cost of sending a student to a four-year college jumped 8.2%—twice as fast as inflation—to an average of $5,793, with the cost of a private school hitting $10,199. And the cost of sending a son or daughter to a more prestigious private university was even higher, hitting $17,990 at Bennington, the nation's most expensive school; $17,100 at Harvard; $17,020 at Yale; and $16,835 at Stanford. Tuition between 1970 and 1987 increased about 7.8% a year, and about 9.8% between 1980 and 1987, twice as fast as the 4.9% annual inflation rate for the 1980s.

A lot of these increases were forced on college officials to make up for expenses that were deferred during the 1970s. With double-digit inflation, faculty salaries lost 20% of their purchasing power and new construction and debt service were deferred. Now the bills are coming due. Faculty costs are once again going up, and colleges are forced to pay for long-overdue construction and maintenance.

These rising costs have hit families and students hard. Students unable to pay the $70,000 it now costs to get an Ivy League education have turned away from private schools to state schools.

Yet many parents continue to pay the price. With a tight marketplace, many parents and students are working harder than ever for the prestigious sheepskin from one of the nation's top schools. Despite increasing costs, applications were up 11% to 6,887 for the 803 positions at the Harvard Graduate School of Business Administration.

To pay, students increasingly turned to the bank. The number of students borrowing money to pay for college has more than tripled from 991,000 borrowing an average of $1,311 in 1975 to 1984, when 3.4 million borrowing an average of $2,326 in 1984. Thus, a generation graduates from school with heavy debts. In 1985, the median debt for college graduates of public schools was $8,000; the average private school student shouldered $10,000 in debt. By 1990, the average debt could rise to $14,000.

Those debts are small compared to the debts of graduates of professional schools: the typical graduates of some law schools will have to repay $25,000 in loans and many medical students are starting practices $35,000 or more in the hole. The typical M.B.A. steps into the business with a $15,000 debt. That's one reason why $6.8 billion in student loans are in default.

THE M.B.A. BUSINESS

A tighter job market and increasing skepticism about the value of a liberal arts degree have combined to produce an explosion in business education, especially M.B.A.'s.

As recently as 1960, only 4,643 M.B.A.'s (Masters of Business Administration degrees) were granted. But by 1970, the number of M.B.A.'s jumped 21,599, then to 54,000 in 1981, and hit 71,000 in 1986. And more are on the way, with another 200,000 students studying for M.B.A.'s.

Students are fighting for places in the country's top B-schools. And why not? Average starting salaries at the country's top-rated Harvard Graduate School of Business Administration, where only 13% of the applicants are accepted, is $50,225. Salaries at the second-place Stanford University Graduate School of Business, where only 10% of the applicants are accepted, are slightly more, at $50,725. And in many cases an M.B.A. is a ticket to advancement. Harvard boasts that its graduates make up about one fifth of the top three officers of *Fortune* 500 companies and that over 3,500 Harvard alumni head U.S. corporations. However, even though an MBA may now be the passkey to top corporate jobs, the 1987 stock market crash will produce a tougher job market. (Salaries calculated by NYU Business School.)

ACADEMIA AND CORPORATE AMERICA

University research and the prospects of improving American technology are going hand and hand as corporations increasingly fund academic research. Corporate donations to colleges and universities are up dramatically in recent years, hitting $1.57 billion in 1985, about 25% of the total voluntary gifts made. It was the first time ever that corporate donations surpassed alumni gifts.

If the past is any yardstick, corporate gifts to universities are a good investment. At Stanford, for example, a close working relationship between academia and business in the 1930s helped produce the legendary Silicon Valley. (See the profile of the area in the ''Electronics'' section.) More recently, cash-strapped universities and businesses needing new technology have entered into new partnerships, breaking down the anti-business climate that infected many universities during the 1960s. In the 1980s, Harvard Medical School, for instance, teamed up with du Pont for genetic research; Carnegie-Mellon University is cooperating with Westinghouse in robotics; the Massachusetts Institute of Technology is working with Exxon on combustion research and with such firms at ITT and General Motors at its Polymer Processing Laboratory. Stanford continues to work with corporate sponsors in microelectronics and biotechnology. Monsanto has a 10-year, $52 million pact with Washington University.

Despite fears among some critics that universities are sacrificing their independence, the alliance between industry and academia could work wonders for both. Faced with declining government spending for research, universities have watched their laboratories age and deteriorate. Corporate spending allows them to improve their facilities and hire new researchers. At the same time, business, faced with foreign competition, needs new technology to increase productivity and profits.

Funding for research and development at universities has grown dramatically, hitting $4.1 billion in 1985, up from $2.8 billion in 1975. Nationwide funding has also grown, hitting $123 billion in 1985, up from around $60 billion in the early 1970s. Industry and government each spend about half. But these outlays don't match what was spent in the early 1960s, when the economy was much healthier. After adjusting for inflation, funding for research and development remained virtually stagnant between 1967 and 1977. And, as a percentage of the GNP, it actually declined between 1964, when it was 3%, and 1985, when it was 2.7%. Much more needs to be done before the country can regain its edge in technology and productivity. (See the chapter ''Trade, Productivity, and Staying Ahead.'')

EDUCATION ON THE JOB

Formal employee training on the job is now a $30 billion industry, with government spending another $5 billion for training programs and business kicking in about $180 billion for informal training, according to a survey by Anthony Patrick Carnevale, the chief economist at the American Society for Training and Development. Similarly, a 1986 survey by *Training* magazine estimates that 38.8 million employees received 1.2 billion hours of formal employer-sponsored training at a total cost of $29 billion in 1987. What American business gets for this money will probably make the difference between improved productivity in the workplace and declining competitiveness in the international market.

American employers have discovered that they need better-educated employees to run highly automated factories or high-tech offices, yet many employees enter the job market unable to adapt to an increasingly complex workplace. A 1986 study by the U.S. Department of Commerce found that some 17 million Americans, or about 13% of all adults, were illiterate. Earlier studies found that 14% of the population can't fill out a check properly and nearly 33% can't do simple math. Jonathan Kozol, author of *Illiterate America,* estimates that illiteracy costs the economy $20 billion a year.

For many businesses, the costs of poorly educated employees are easy to see. In auto companies, supervisors quickly discovered that employees could not understand and operate some of the new robots and automated machinery. To remedy the problem, car makers are spending millions to upgrade the educational skills of their employees. Under a 1984 contract with the United Auto Workers, GM agreed to spend $200 million in basic skills programs; Ford is spending another $120 million.

But in many cases, the costs of illiteracy and poor education are more difficult to detect. No one knows how many employees work slowly or are unable to get the most out of their office machinery because of educational handicaps. But one visible sign of the problem is the fact that the service economy has seen virtually no improvement in productivity even though companies have spent tens of billions of dollars on new computers and telecommunications equipment in the past decade.

In other cases, the problem of improving productivity isn't so much teaching people basic educational skills as teaching them how to adapt to a new markets and technology. Training systems will have to teach managers how to administer high-tech workplaces, how to use more cost-efficient management techniques, and how to get employees to improve the quality of their products. Education and training aimed at getting the most out of America's human resources will, in the long run, probably improve productivity more than new technology.

COLLEGE AS BANKER

The knowledge business these days is huge and costs more and more all the time. As a result, colleges and universities are scrambling around like bankers and commodities brokers, as they come up with innovative ways to help people finance whopping education costs.

Our institutions of higher learning, of course, are used to offering scholarships and work programs to needy students. But spiraling costs and reduced federal financing have made financing college a tougher proposition. A $2,500 loan in the 1960s or 1970s stretched pretty far. Today, it can keep a kid for a handful of weeks at Sarah Lawrence or Harvard, where room, board, and tuition top $17,000 a year.

The upshot is that few families can afford to pay for college out of current income and not that many can afford to plan ahead. Today, a lot of colleges find that up to one third of their operating funds start as loans to parents and students. Up to half of the nation's 10 million undergraduates are in debt when they leave school.

Here are some of the ways some institutions of higher learning are trying to help parents cope with the financial hardship of educating their offspring:

- Schools such as Duquesne University and Canisius College are treating education like a futures market. By depositing money now for their small children, parents are guaranteed that their children's tuition will be prepaid. The younger the child, the less money that must be plunked down. The school invests the money until the child is ready to enter the college. (Unfortunately, the deposit doesn't guarantee the child getting accepted by the school, which is a whole other problem.) In cases in which the student is rejected, parents get their initial investment back.
- To safeguard parents against cost increases while their son or daughter moves from freshman to senior, dozens of schools, such as Columbia University and the University of Southern California, offer prepayment plans. Families cough up four years' tuition when the child enters and they are protected against cost increases. Some colleges will even lend parents the money.
- In response to the agricultural doldrums, Minnesota's state universities let children of distressed farm families go to school on a part-time basis for free. The free tuition covers six credit hours a semester.
- To make student loans easier to come by, such schools as the University of Rochester have struck deals with local banks to get favorable rates for their students. To do so, the schools accept part of the risk if the student defaults.
- Schools such as Yale have established loan programs with their own money. The University of California at Berkeley offers several kinds of loans, including an interest-free loan for needy students.

Table 147   Who Got Training on the Job, 1987

Job category	Projected number of individuals trained (in millions)	Mean number of hours delivered	Total hours of training delivered (in millions)
Middle managers	3.13	36.6	114.6
Professionals	5.91	35.8	211.4
Executives	0.94	36.3	34.0
Salespeople	3.26	42.6	138.8
First-line supervisors	4.10	33.3	136.4
Senior managers	1.36	33.6	45.5
Production workers	8.66	29.1	252.1
Customer service people	5.86	26.8	157.0
Administrative employees	2.25	21.8	49.1
Office/clerical employees	3.37	16.9	56.9
Total	38.82		1,195.8

Source: *Training,* October 1987, The Magazine of Human Resources Development. Copyright 1987. Lakewood Publications Inc.

Table 148   The Growth of University Executive Education
(United States and Canada)

Retraining programs for American managers are now big business, largely because American companies are scrambling to adjust to rapidly changing marketplaces and new management strategies. In 1985, some 14,600 executives were sent off to management programs, up 4,600 in only three years, according to Bricker Executive Education Service. A dozen executive programs at Harvard already bring in $7.2 million a year and Duke is building a $14 million executive education center. Here's how the field has grown:

	1985	1982	1962
Academic institutions offering executive training	70	59	39
General management programs	139	93	39
Participants	10,200	6,900	1,500
Functional management programs	77	76	9
Participants	4,400	3,100	400

Table 149　Spending on Education Around the World

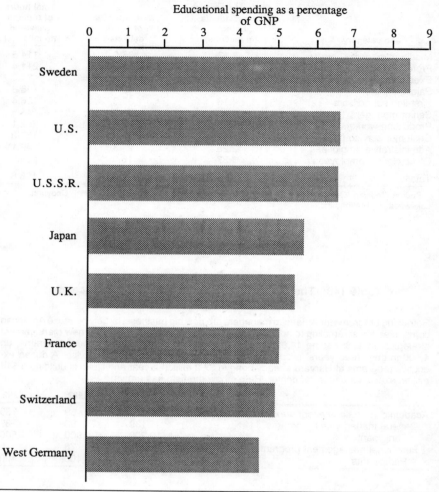

Educational spending as a percentage of GNP

Source: UNESCO.

Table 150 The Richest Schools in the U.S.

The Texas economy may be in trouble, but not the University of Texas. In 1985 its endowment surpassed Harvard's for the first time on record, making it the richest school in the U.S.

School	Endowment (millions of dollars)	
	1985	1984
University of Texas	2,927.2	2,273.3
Harvard	2,694.8	2,486.3
Princeton	1,519.2	1,287.9
Yale	1,308.7	1,060.7
Stanford	1,083.9	944.0
Columbia	978.6	855.2
MIT	770.2	645.6
University of California	716.8	716.8
University of Chicago	640.8	517.1

Source: *The Chronicle of Higher Education.*

Table 151 Schools That Spent the Most on Research

School	Amount spent (millions of dollars)
Johns Hopkins	388.6
MIT	243.0
University of Wisconsin—Madison	208.4
Cornell	203.2
Stanford	199.2
University of Minnesota	173.3
University of Washington	164.0
University of Michigan	163.7
University of California—Berkeley	149.9

Source: National Science Foundation.

Table 152 The Education of America

	Percentage not high school graduates		Percentage with four years of high school or more		Median years completed
	Total	With fewer than 5 years of school	Total	Percentage who have attended college four years or more	
Persons 25 years old and over:					
1940	75.5	13.7	24.5	4.6	8.6
1950	65.7	11.1	34.3	6.2	9.3
1960	58.9	8.3	41.1	7.7	10.5
1970	44.8	5.3	55.2	11.0	12.2
1980	31.4	3.4	68.6	17.0	12.5
1983	27.9	3.0	72.1	18.8	12.6
1984	26.7	2.8	73.3	19.1	12.6
1985	26.1	2.7	73.9	19.4	12.6

Source: U.S. Bureau of the Census.

483

Table 153   Starting Salaries for M.B.A.'s from Top B-Schools

School	1975	1980	1985
Harvard	$18,000	$31,000	$50,225*
Stanford	18,500	32,000	50,725
Wharton	16,900	27,000	48,348
Columbia	17,000	26,500	47,369
Chicago	NA	NA	46,000*
NYU	15,500	25,000	46,099
Northwestern	15,600	24,600	48,550*
Dartmouth	17,100	27,900	49,100
Virginia	17,200	26,300	46,011

Estimated by NYU. NA = Not Available
Sources: Various schools.

Table 154   What an Education Means for a Family's Income

Educational level of the family's chief wage earner	Median income
Elementary school	$11,309
Fewer than 8 years of school	10,124
8 years of School	12,270
High school	20,934
1–3 years of high school	15,171
4 years of high school	23,134
College	33,250
1–3 years of college	27,337
4 years or more	39,506
Median income of all households	22,618

Source: U.S. Bureau of Census, *Current Population Reports*, P-60, No 154.

Table 155   Dollars for Diplomas: Starting Salaries for Graduates

	Bachelor's degree			Master's degree		
	1980	1984	1987	1980	1984	1987
Accounting	$15,516	$19,524	$21,744	$18,204	$23,193	$25,956
Business, general	14,616	18,660	20,412	21,540	28,500	28,656
Chemistry	17,508	21,072	25,572	20,256	26,736	27,996
Mathematics	17,700	23,400	25,944	20,220	28,764	27,948
Humanities	12,888	17,724	20,256	15,708	18,732	22,644
Social sciences	12,864	17,424	21,876	15,576	19,776	21,996
Computer science	18,696	24,552	26,364	22,296	30,060	33,804

Source: College Placement Council, Inc., *The CPC Salary Survey: A Study of Beginning Offers*, July 1987.

484

Table 156   Business Support of Education

In recent years voluntary corporate support for education has grown dramatically, exceeding support from foundations, religious organizations, and all other groups. In 1985, for the first time ever, contributions from business slightly exceeded the $1.46 billion in contributions given by alumni.

(millions of dollars)

	1970	1975	1980	1981	1982	1983	1984	1985	1986
Estimated voluntary contributions for colleges and universities, total	1,780	2,160	3,800	4,230	4,850	5,160	5,500	6,315	7,400
Business contributions	269	357	696	778	976	1,112	1,271	1,574	1,702
Percentage of total	15.1%	16.5%	18.3%	18.4%	20.1%	21.6%	23.1%	25%	22.9%

Source: Council for Financial Aid to Education, *Voluntary Support of Education,* annual.

ELECTRONICS

THE MARKET

What steel and heavy industry were to the 19th-century American economy, electronics is to the 21st century. Auto companies, appliance manufacturers, machine tool makers, and companies in a host of other mature manufacturing industries are all hoping that high-tech electronics will allow them to improve designs and survive a tough battle with foreign competitors.

But it would be wrong to see the market for electronics products only in terms of the distant future. Despite the industry's futuristic image, companies involved in the design, development, manufacture, assembly, application, or servicing of electronic equipment, systems, or components already form one of the nation's largest industries. By producing products as varied as industrial robots for the factory, miniature electronic circuits for silicon chips, electronic mail for business, lasers for Star Wars, and television sets for the living room, the industry is now the largest manufacturing employer in the U.S. One out of every nine manufacturing jobs is in electronics, the American Electronics Association reports. Overall, 4% of all jobs are in electronics or in an industry that would not exist without electronics. Employment in the electronics industry is three times that of automotive manufacturing and nine times that of the basic steel industry.

THE MONEY

The ever-expanding range of electronics products has translated into one of the world's fastest-growing industries. The U.S. electronics industry has grown from a $200 million industry in 1927 to $198.9 billion in 1985 and $209.7 billion in 1986, according to the Electronic Industries Association (EIA). By the end of the 1980s, the EIA forecasts, electronics is expected to rival the automobile, steel, and chemical industries in sales volume.

Factory sales of U.S. electronics makers broke down as follows:

- U.S. factory sales of computers and industrial electronics: $66.0 billion in 1986, down from $67.9 billion in 1985.
- Communications equipment and systems: $63.1 billion in 1986, up from $56.0 billion in 1985.
- Electronic components: $37.4 billion in 1986, up from $36.8 billion in 1985.
- Other related products and services (computer software, the electronic contents of other industries such as vehicles and aircraft, and the value of related service industries): $36.8 billion in 1986, up from $32.5 billion in 1985.
- And consumer electronics: $6.5 billion in 1986, up from $5.7 billion in factory sales by U.S. manufacturers in 1985, according to the EIA. (See the "Consumer Electronics" part of this section, the "Computers" section, and the "Robots and Office Automation," "Lasers," and "Telecommunications" parts of the "Technology" section.)

These figures, which are based on factory shipments from U.S. companies, do not include imports, which are very important in some parts of the industry, such as consumer electronics. Like most other manufacturing industries, the electronics industry has been hurt by a strong dollar and a growing appetite for cheaper foreign goods. Exports grew in 1986 to $33.5 billion, up from $31 billion in 1985 and $23.5 billion in 1981. But imports rose much faster, from $19.7 billion in 1981 to $43.4 billion in 1985 and $50.3 billion in 1986. As a result, the positive trade balance of $3.9 billion in electronic products in 1981 became a trade deficit of $16.9 billion in 1986.

THE PLAYERS AND THE PEOPLE

About 1.77 million people are employed in the electronics industry. Although many parts of this highly competitive industry are dominated by small firms, a few large firms capture a large part of the sales. Table 157 (below) lists the country's 20 largest electronics companies.

TRENDS AND FORECAST

There's little doubt that the demand for electronics will grow dramatically over the next few years, as it has in the past. But it is questionable how much of this growth will benefit U.S. companies. In the last decade, the U.S., long the leader in electronics and high technology, has faced in-

Table 157 Top 20 Electronics Companies

Rank	Company	Electronics sales (millions of dollars)	Total company revenue (millions of dollars)
1.	IBM	50,056.0	50,056.0
2.	AT&T Technologies	17,641.9	34,909.5
3.	General Motors	9,503.8	96,371.6
4.	General Electric	7,590.0	28,285.0
5.	Xerox	7,545.0	8,732.1
6.	Digital Equipment	7,029.4	7,029.4
7.	ITT	7,010.0	11,871.0
8.	Honeywell	6,624.6	6,624.6
9.	Hewlett-Packard	6,571.0	6,571.0
10.	Motorola	5,443.0	5,443.0
11.	Burroughs	5,037.7	5,037.7
12.	Sperry	5,000.0	5,717.6
13.	Texas Instruments	4,924.5	4,924.5
14.	RCA	4,851.0	8,972.1
15.	NCR	3,952.0	4,317.2
16.	Raytheon	3,794.0	6,408.5
17.	Control Data	3,679.7	3,679.7
18.	Rockwell	3,591.0	11,741.4
19.	TRW	3,344.5	5,917.2
20.	North American Philips	3,279.0	4,395.2

Source: *Electronic Business,* July 15, 1986.

creasing competition from foreign producers. The U.S. now imports more than it exports of communications products (in which there was a $1.6 billion trade deficit in 1986), consumer electronics (a $15.6 billion deficit), electron tubes (a $48 million deficit), electronic parts (a $3.5 billion deficit), and solid-state products (a $1.1 billion deficit).

Only in industrial electronic products did the U.S. export more than it imported. But the $3.8 billion trade surplus in industrial electronic products in 1986 represented a sharp drop from 1981, when the surplus stood at $10.5 billion. The U.S. Commerce Department estimates that imports held 16% of the market in electrical and electronic equipment in 1984, up from only 7.6% in 1972. Most sectors of the electronics industry are expected to continue to lose their market shares to foreign producers. Overall the U.S. had a $16.9 billion dollar trade deficit in electronics, down from a surplus of $6.7 billion in 1980.

Behind the wave of imports are several factors. A strong dollar and lower overseas labor costs allowed foreign competitors to undercut U.S. rivals. Unlike some U.S. high-tech companies that made important technological breakthroughs and then stumbled when it came to bringing their products to the market, Japanese and other foreign producers have proved to be remarkably adept at adapting basic U.S. technology, cutting production costs, and, most importantly, finding consumer applications for high-tech breakthroughs. Moreover, at least in the 1970s, Japan and West Germany spent more of their GNP on nondefense research and devel-

Table 158   Top 10 Electronics Employers

Rank	State	Employees, June 1986
1.	California	588,000
2.	New York	210,000
3.	Massachusetts	206,000
4.	Texas	151,000
5.	New Jersey	113,000
6.	Florida	103,000
7.	Illinois	93,000
8.	Pennsylvania	88,000
9.	Minnesota	70,000
10.	Arizona	60,000

Source: American Electronics Association.

opment than the U.S. With 65% of U.S. research and development money going to defense, both Japan and Germany far outstrip the U.S. in civilian applications of high technology and electronics. As a result, U.S. companies face the dismal prospect that, unless this trend is reversed, they may fall behind in basic research and technological development.

Increased foreign competition has prompted American companies to change the way they do business. To cut costs, many manufacturers have moved their operations overseas, allowing foreign producers to make the products and then putting their names on the goods. Critics say "outsourcing" leaves U.S. companies without the technological and production skills they need to compete in the future and a strong dollar should slow the movement of electronics jobs overseas. But it's also clear that outsourcing lets U.S. companies cut costs and concentrate on marketing and product development. The trend also allows the U.S. to respond more quickly to changes in the market (an important factor in a highly volatile industry like electronics) than they would if they manufactured all of their own parts and products.

SILICON VALLEY

In Palo Alto, California, there's a garage known as "the birthplace of modern electronics." There, Lee De Forest perfected the vacuum tube, which was the basis of radio transmission and the beginnings of modern media. But that's not the only famous garage near Silicon Valley and the Bay Area of San Francisco. For some reason, this area has been to modern electronics what the Tigris-Euphrates Valley was to early civilization.

Consider: In the early 1900s, amateur radio hams in the Bay region began experimenting with ham radios, much like the Silicon Valley computer whizzes who built the first personal computers and video games in the 1970s. One, Ralph Heintz, established the first wireless communication from an airplane to the ground and went on to found Heintz & Kaufman, a pioneer in the field of aircraft radio. Another was Charles Litton, who eventually founded Litton Industries. An Oakland company named Magnavox produced the first public address system. Sigurd and Russell Varian and William Hansens invented the klystron that was the basis of modern radar systems and William Hewlett and David Packard founded their company in another Palo Alto garage.

A key factor in the development of Silicon Valley as a high-tech paradise was the presence of Stanford University, just as MIT brought early computer wizards such as Ken Olsen of Digital Equipment Corporation and An Wang of Wang Laboratories to the Boston area.

In 1925, Fred Terman, son of the man who developed the IQ test, took charge of a radio communications laboratory in Stanford. Like many early Silicon Valley companies, it started in less than perfect quarters—an attic. But Terman's influence was to shape the direction of the area's technology for the next 40 years. Many of his students, such as William Hewlett and David Packard, founded major electronics companies, and he talked Stanford University into giving the Varians use of the physics lab during the final stages of their research into radar. In the next 30 years, that minor investment brought the university $2 million in royalties.

But Terman did more than inspire a generation of talented researchers. Noticing that many firms moved out of the region and that many of his most talented students were forced to move east to find jobs, Terman worked with the University to create the Stanford Industrial Park on land left to it by Leland Stanford, the railroad tycoon. Stanford's bequest prohibited the university from selling the land, so developing the fields as an industrial park was about the only way the university could make money on it. Early tenants were Varian Associates and Hewlett-Packard.

At this point, in the early 1950s a critical mass began to form between the university's research facilities and Silicon Valley's new high-tech entrepreneurs. As the region's reputation grew, national companies, such as Lockheed, Sylvania, Admiral, Kaiser, and General Precision moved into the area. And as the first generation of companies grew into industrial giants, young scientists left them to form new, innovative companies.

Success, of course, has its price. Picturesque orchards gave way to suburban sprawl and traffic jams. Many of the older, once-entrepreneurial companies have developed the hierarchical formal management culture of eastern companies they once ridiculed.

And in recent years, troubles in the semiconductor industry have endangered the area's economy. About 17,500 jobs were lost as electronics companies moved their manufacturing operations overseas. About 35% of the research and factory space in Silicon Valley is vacant, the country's highest industrial vacancy rate. Despite the losses, unemployment is only 5.5%, and the presence of Stanford and many other major electronics companies promises that the area will continue to produce wizards such as David Packard and Steven Jobs.

H. Ross Perot and Electronic Data Systems   Back in 1962, H. Ross Perot had a good idea. He knew that the computer market was growing— after all, he'd just sold his yearly quota of IBM computers in only 19 days. The problem was that few people knew what to do with these new machines. What they needed, he reasoned, was a company that would design computer systems, help companies set them up, and tell them how to use them. Thus, Electronic Data Systems (EDS) was born.

By the mid-1980s, when his Electronic Data Systems was acquired by General Motors for $1 billion in cash and 11.3 million shares of GM class-E stock, it was the second-largest company in the $30-billion-a-year computer services industry. Perot is now the third-wealthiest man in America, richer than David Rockefeller or even another high-tech computer wizard, David Packard. And, along the way, he's managed to become just as famous, or controversial, depending on your viewpoint.

In the foreign policy arena, Perot first got headlines for his long-standing concern for American prisoners of war in Vietnam. In 1969, he tried to deliver 26 tons of food to American prisoners of war in Hanoi. The communist government refused to let the Texas billionaire in. Then, in 1979, he dispatched a team to rescue EDS executives being held in Teheran during the hostage crisis. The episode became the basis of the TV mini-series and a best-selling book *On Wings of Eagles*. Later, he was involved in the plan to provide a $1 million ransom for U.S. hostages in Lebanon. The plan, which called for Drug Enforcement Administration agents to pay the money, was never carried out. Closer to home, Perot helped push tough drug laws and an educational reform package through the Texas legislature.

Perot's business dealings have been no less visible. After selling out his share of EDS to General Motors, he was given a seat on the board. Soon he was telling the company just how to sell autos. His comments about GM's bloated bureaucracy, top-heavy management, abysmal quality control, and poor performance rang true but were not appreciated by GM's top management. Eventually, they decided to buy him out for $742 million, a move that left people wondering how the company could afford to buy out a Texas billionaire when it was in the middle of its worst layoffs ever.

Hewlett-Packard Company

CEO: David Packard   3000 Hanover Street
Employees: 84,000   Palo Alto, California 94304
Assets: $6.3 billion   415-857-1501

	1987	1986	1985	1980
Revenues (millions of dollars):	8,090	7,102	6,505	3,099
Net income (millions of dollars):	644	516	489	269
Share earnings (dollars):	2.50	2.02	1.91	1.12

What it does: It is the largest maker of electronic test and measurement equipment and a leading maker of minicomputers.

David Packard and William Hewlett founded this electronics and computer giant in a Palo Alto garage with an investment of $538 each. Their Stanford University professor, Fred Terman, remembers he could always tell how business was going by where their car was parked. If it was parked in their garage, orders were down; if the car was parked in the driveway, business was booming.

And boom it did, after they invented the audio oscillator to measure sound waves. Walt Disney put in their first big order because he needed the equipment to create the elaborate sound system for the film *Fantasia*.

Since then, the founders and the company have prospered as the country's largest manufacturer of electronic test and measurement instruments, a leading minicomputer maker, the nation's ninth-largest electronics manufacturer, and a leading manufacturer of computer peripherals. David Packard, who provided the business savvy, has become one of the most visible prophets of Silicon Valley and a Republican party power broker. He was appointed Deputy Secretary of Defense under President Nixon, was chairman of the United States–Japan Advisory Commission under President Reagan, and subsequently headed the President's Blue Ribbon Commission on Defense Management. His 17% stake in the company is worth about $2 billion, while William Hewlett's 8.5% stake is worth about $1 billion.

CONSUMER ELECTRONICS

The Market

The typical American home is becoming a sophisticated media center, thanks to consumer electronics. Currently there are 485 million radios in the U.S. and 201 million televisions reaching 98% of all households. VCRs can be found in half of all homes (up from 20% in 1984), color TV in 92% home computers in 17%, audio systems in 88%, telephone answering machines in 15%, cordless telephones in 16%, and projection TVs in 3%. In 1986, Americans bought 41.1 million radios, 4.8 million audio systems, 296 million blank videocassettes, 29.7 million blank audio cassettes, 13.5 million VCRs, 36.3 million units of portable audio tape equipment, 18.2 million color TVs, 4.9 million telephone answering machines, 4.0 million black-and-white TVs and 3.8 million personal computers, 12.4 million microwave ovens, 4.4 million cordless phones and 24.1 million phones with cords, according to the Electronic Industries Association.

The Money

Retail sales of consumer electronics amounted to $40 billion in 1986, up slightly from $34 billion in 1984. Factory shipments (from domestic and foreign producers) totaled $28.7 billion in 1986, up from $23.4 billion in 1984. That figure included $328 million in 1986 (down from $419 million in 1984) for black-and-white TVs; $6.02 billion (up from $5.53 billion in

1984) for color TVs; $5.26 billion (up from $3.5 billion in 1984) for VCRs; $1.37 billion (up from $976 million in 1984) for audio systems; $1.36 billion (up from $913 million in 1984) for separate stereo components; $408 million (down from $661 in 1984) for home radios; $2.8 billion (down from $2.48 billion in 1984) for audio systems for cars; $1.39 billion (up from $1.19 billion in 1984) for portable audio tape equipment; $1.48 billion (up from $931 million in 1984) for blank videocassettes; $304 million (up slightly from $275 million in 1984) for blank audio cassettes; and another $7.37 billion (down from $5.68 billion in 1984) for personal computer software, programmable video games, video game cartridges, telephones, telephone answering devices, and videodiscs.

Overall, the consumer electronics market has quadrupled since 1974. Prices, however, have remained low. While the consumer price index for all items has increased from a baseline of 100 in 1967 to 328, the cost of a television on the index has actually declined to 83.1 and sound equipment stands only at 102.8.

The Players

Imports dominate the markets. TVs, audio cassette recorders, VCRs, portable and table radios, and automobile tape players are a few of the products that are mostly or exclusively imported. Imports, for example, account for 60% of all radio and television sets sold in the U.S. U.S. imports are 13 times greater than exports, hitting $15.7 billion in 1985 (up from $6.7 billion in 1981). Meanwhile, exports increased from $544 million in 1981 to only $1.2 billion in 1986. That discrepancy has produced a rising trade deficit, which hit $14.6 billion in 1986, up from $6.2 billion in 1981.

FOOD

THE MARKET

Americans ate up an estimated $513 billion worth of food and beverages at home and at restaurants in 1987. Most of that money, about $329 billion, was spent at home. Table 159 (below) shows how they spent those food dollars.

TRENDS AND FORECAST

America's food business, from agriculture to processing plants to the supermarket, was once the most successful in the world. Thanks to its efficiency, Americans only spend about 12% of their income on food, less

Table 159   The Food Industry

(factory shipments by U.S. producers in millions of dollars)

	1972	1982	1987[1]
Total	115,051	280,530	321,792
Meat products	31,477	67,604	69,711
Meat packing plants	23,003	44,854	42,467
Sausage and prepared meats	4,632	12,278	14,234
Poultry dressing plants	3,254	9,045	11,019
Poultry and egg processing	588	1,427	1,991
Dairy products	16,312	38,772	44,041
Creamery butter	808	1,687	1,722
Cheese, natural and processed	3,195	10,763	11,960
Condensed and evaporated milk	1,668	4,731	5,798
Ice cream and frozen desserts	1,245	2,855	3,784
Fluid milk	9,396	18,736	20,777
Preserved fruits and vegetables	11,480	29,874	37,297
Canned specialties	1,877	4,141	5,237
Canned fruits and vegetables	4,044	9,283	10,739
Dried fruits and vegetables	607	1,745	1,696
Sauces and salad dressings	1,167	4,269	5,750
Frozen fruits and vegetables	1,849	5,375	6,327
Frozen specialties	1,936	5,061	7,548
Grain mill products	12,163	31,386	37,182
Flour and grain mill products	2,380	4,933	5,554
Cereal breakfast foods	1,126	4,132	6,975
Rice milling	681	1,934	1,673
Blended and prepared flours	705	1,419	1,738
Wet corn milling	832	3,268	4,470
Dog, cat, other pet food	1,402	4,402	5,664
Prepared animal feed	5,037	11,298	11,108
Bakery products	7,896	17,808	21,989
Bread, other bakery goods	6,132	13,143	14,750
Cookies and crackers	1,764	4,665	7,239
Sugar and confections	6,622	15,575	18,221
Cane sugar, except refining	407	1,114	1,249
Cane sugar refining	1,743	3,040	2,790
Beet sugar	880	1,516	1,908
Confectionery products	2,473	6,773	8,431
Chocolate and cocoa products	736	2,217	2,771
Chewing gum	383	915	1,072
Fats and oils	6,901	16,753	18,669
Cottonseed oil mills	459	933	940
Soybean oil mills	3,357	8,604	9,208
Vegetable oil mills	252	557	605
Animal/marine fats and oils	765	1,753	1,944
Shortening and cooking oils	2,068	4,906	5,972
Beverages	13,869	38,802	47,302
Malt beverages	4,054	11,183	13,142
Malt	226	662	608
Wine, brandy, brandy spirits	865	2,786	2,967
Distilled and blended liquors	1,798	3,126	3,669
Soft drinks, carbonated water	5,454	16,808	21,751
Flavorings, extracts, syrups	1,472	4,237	5,165

493

Table 159   The Food Industry (Continued)

(factory shipments by U.S. producers in millions of dollars)

	1972	1982	1987[1]
Miscellaneous foods	8,335	23,959	27,380
Canned fish and seafood	810	1,849	745
Fresh or frozen fish/seafood	1,084	4,009	4,230
Roasted coffee	2,329	5,827	7,124
Manufactured ice	116	230	245
Pasta products	348	1,065	1,232
Food preparations, not elsewhere classified	3,648	10,979	13,804

Sources: U.S. Department of Commerce: Bureau of Census, and International Trade Administration (ITA). Printed in *U.S. Industrial Outlook 1987—Food.*
[1]Estimated.

than anywhere in the world. In third-world countries, families spend as much as 62% of their budgets on food. (See also the "Agriculture," "Beverages," and "Restaurants" sections.)

But in recent years, the food business has been undergoing a tumultuous reorganization. Since 1979, nearly 1 million jobs have been lost on American farms or in businesses dependent on agriculture for their prosperity, such as agricultural equipment makers and rural stores. Food processing plants, most of which are also located in rural areas, have also lost 130,000 jobs since 1979. At the same time, the number of people employed selling food in the nation's grocery stores has grown by 400,000 since 1979, when 2.02 million were employed.

And, throughout the 1980s, food companies have been eating up their competitors or disgorging food divisions at a record-breaking pace. Nearly 50 major food mergers have taken place in the last few years, producing some of the biggest deals of the 1980s. R. J. Reynolds, for example, paid $4.9 billion for Nabisco, while Philip Morris paid $5.6 billion for General Foods in 1985. And 1986 saw Beatrice Companies arrange for a $6.2 billion leveraged buyout while Dart & Kraft reorganized its operations and spun off its four nonfood divisions as Premark International. (See the profile of Kraft below.)

These megadeals reflected the interest tobacco companies have in diversifying out of their core businesses and the fact that it's simpler to increase your market share in a mature market, such as food, by buying a new company. At the same time, domestic producers are continuing to fight to cut costs by selling off unprofitable operations so they can finance the expensive advertising campaigns needed to promote new products.

One new problem facing the American food industry has been fighting off increased foreign competition. Already overseas farmers are undercutting the prices of many American farmers, and the Japanese have managed to capture over 9% of the dried soup market in just the last few years. Agricultural exports and exports of processed food have dropped while imports have skyrocketed. Foreign investors have also poured nearly $11.2 billion worth of investments into the U.S. food industry, more than into any other manufacturing business except chemicals. American food producers can also expect to face increased foreign competition. Many countries that once needed American farm products to feed their populations are now food exporters.

POPCORN POPPING PROFITS

If you're an average American, you will eat about 46 quarts of popcorn this year, according to the Popcorn Institute. And if you wonder why anyone would start a trade association to represent popcorn makers, remember, this is a big business. The Popcorn Institute represents popcorn makers that produce 685 million pounds of popcorn a year—about 85% the total U.S. production. Annual sales of popcorn easily top $1 billion.

Popcorn has always been big at the movies, where theater owners count on getting an extra buck worth of profit at the concession stand from every ticket buyer. But it wasn't until the 1970s that popcorn sales really took off at the retail level. Pillsbury played a major role by introducing popcorn that could be popped in a microwave oven. That sent sales of microwave popcorn up from virtually nothing to $196 million in 1986. And a promotion by Beatrice/Hunt-Wesson Foods for its Orville Redenbacher's line of popcorn helped increase sales. That promotion spent more than 10 times in advertising what the industry used to spend in an entire year. The result: sales of unpopped popcorn rose as much as 16% a year and the amount of unpopped popcorn sold at retail stores rose from 171 million pounds in 1979 to over 271 million recently, according to Selling Areas–Marketing, Inc.

Table 160   The 10 Largest Bakers

The 40 largest bakers account for more than half of all wholesale bakery sales, according to *Bakery Production and Marketing* magazine's annual ranking of the largest wholesale bakers. Sales of baked goods hit $30.6 billion in 1985 and $32.7 billion in 1986. Cookies and crackers accounted for 28% of the market in 1986, followed by white bread and rolls (28%), variety bread and rolls (19%), sweet goods (17%), and donuts (8%), according to *Bakery Production and Marketing* magazine. Here are the 10 largest bakers:

Rank	Company	1985 revenues (millions of dollars)	Plants	Employees
1.	Nabisco Brands USA	$1,734	12	9,500
2.	Continental Banking Company	1,600	53	22,400
3.	Campbell Taggart, Inc.	1,044	59	19,000
4.	Keebler Company	988	10	8,943
5.	Interstate Bakeries Corporation	704	27	11,200
6.	Flowers Industries, Inc.	557	30	10,000
7.	Sunshine Biscuits, Inc.	490	8	5,000
8.	American Bakeries Company	461	17	6,600
9.	Entenmann's Inc.	450	4	3,734
10.	Kitchens of Sara Lee	405	3	1,550

Source: *Bakery Production and Marketing* magazine, June 6, 1986.

THE BAGEL WARS

In recent years, Lender's, the nation's largest bagel baker, and Sara Lee have squared off over the $400-million- to $500-million-a-year bagel market. Americans already eat about 8 million bagels a day, but about four out of every five Americans have not yet tried one. Lender's and Sara Lee want to change all that and make bagels a national food, as popular in Peoria as they are in New York.

The first shot in the bagel wars was fired in August of 1985, when Sara Lee introduced its frozen bagel line, challenging Lender's, which holds about 34% of the market. Sara Lee soon had 6% of the market.

Lender's responded by opening the world's largest bagel plant in the middle of Illinois, calling its plant the "Bagel Capital of the World." The Mattoon, Illinois, plant can turn out 1 million bagels a day and will be able to produce 2 million by 1988. Kraft, which owns Lender's, invested $10 million in automated bagel lines, an 80-foot-tall, 250-foot-long bagel freezer, and a 70-yard-long bagel oven.

Although 57% of all bagels are still sold fresh, the bagel market never went national because fresh bagels go stale within about 12 hours. Frozen bagels allow bakers to go national and millions of dollars in advertising have helped sales of bagels to jump 30%. Lender's, which already produces 3 million bagels a day, had to rush to complete the Illinois plant to meet the new demand.

While Sara Lee and Lender's battle for control of the bagel market, no one agrees on how bagels originated. One story has it that a Polish baker gave one to the King of Poland in 1683 after he defeated Turkish invaders. Another version says they were invented around 1610 by poor Polish Jews who considered the white roll a delicacy. The name comes from the German word *boug* meaning "ring."

PIZZA FACTS

Pizza now has a major share of the U.S. food market. Consider a few facts about this $15-billion-a-year industry:
- Americans eat about 75 acres of pizza every day—and that's a big pizza pie.
- The average American eats seven pizzas a year.
- All of this is produced by the 45,000 pizzerias in the U.S. They represent about 10.8% of all restaurants, more than the 8.5% of restaurants specializing in hamburgers.
- Pizza chains have captured about 55% to 60% of the $15 billion national pizza market.

Table 161 The Five Largest Pizza Companies

Rank	Company	Number of restaurants
1.	Pizza Hut	5,120
2.	Domino's	3,140
3.	Little Caesar	900
4.	Pizza Inn	736
5.	Godfather's	671

Source: National Association of Pizza Operators.

CANNED FOOD

Canned food was first developed for Napoleon's army. (See "Firsts in Food" below.) Today it is one of the country's most popular ways of preserving foods. There are about 1,700 canning plants in the U.S., Puerto Rico, and the Virgin Islands, producing some 1,400 different canned food items. Each year, more than 1 billion cases of canned food are packed in 37 billion metal and glass containers. The average American eats about 150 pounds of canned food a year, about 11% of the food we eat each year.

GRILLING FOR DOLLARS

You may think that barbecues are fun but, for the Barbecue Industry Association, this is serious business. An estimated 180 million Americans enjoy barbecued foods every year, generating $6 billion in sales of briquets, grills, charcoal, lighter products, tools, and groceries.

The competition is heating up. As sales of barbecue sauce have grown 33% over the last three years, major food companies, Kraft, General Foods, and others, have beefed up their ad campaigns. Kraft, for example, spends about $10 million a year to capture a larger share of the $350 million market for barbecue sauce. That has bowled over Heinz (a mere $4.5 million on advertising barbecue sauce) and Hunts ($3.8 million), giving Kraft about half the market.

Kraft, Inc.

CEO: John M. Richman

Employees: 51,000

Assets: $9.3 billion

1 Kraft Court

Glenview, Illinois 60025

319-998-2000

	1987	1986	1985	1980
Revenues (millions of dollars):	9,876	8,742	7,920	NA
Net income (millions of dollars):	489	413	466	
Share earnings (dollars):	3.60	2.93	3.22	

What it does: Producer and marketer of processed and dairy foods. Also produces household products and nonconsumer products. Food products account for 71% of sales and 70% of profits.

While Wall Street was still on a binge of mergers and acquisitions, Kraft discovered that there was more profit to be made in sticking to its own basic industry, food.

Six years after buying up Dart Industries in 1980 and becoming Dart & Kraft, the company decided it was time to get back to basics. On October 28, 1986, the company officially split up. Its nonfood operations became Premark International while Kraft returned to its core business, with almost all of its $9.5 billion in sales from food. Kraft retained a 25% stake in Premark, which markets such products as Tupperware and West Bend appliances.

Spinning off its nonfood operations had already become an industry trend by the time Kraft got around to doing it. In 1985, food giants like General Mills sold off its toy, clothing, and other businesses, Ralston Purina Company spun off some restaurants, and Beatrice Companies sold Avis.

The new company is already in better shape than the pre-1980 Kraft. Return on equity hit an estimated 23% in 1987, up from 15% in the late 1970s, and profit margins grew from 3% to over 5% in the same period, according to Value Line estimates.

The company goes back to 1903, when James Kraft began wholesaling cheese. After a merger with Phenix Cheese in 1928, the new company, Kraft-Phenix, accounted for 40% of the cheese consumption in the U.S. The company was bought in 1930 by National Dairy Products Corporation, founded by Thomas McInnerney. In 1969, the company adopted the name Kraftco and in 1976 became simply Kraft Inc. By that time the company was most famous for its ersatz products, such as Miracle Whip and Velveeta. But today the company also produces such natural foods as Philadelphia Brand cream cheese, Frusen Glädjé ice cream, and Celestial Seasonings Herb Teas, as well as Duracell batteries. A major force in the food service and food products industries, Kraft got 89% of its sales and 96% of profits from food in 1986.

FIRSTS IN FOOD

1808   The first canned food is developed for Napoleon's army.
1819   Ezra Daggett and Thomas Kensett set up the first canning operation in the U.S. William Underwood founds one of the nation's oldest canning companies in 1822, the William Underwood Company. His grandson pioneers the use of heat sterilization and the scientific use of bacteriology to make food canning safer.
1892   Henry Heinz gets the idea of making his company's slogan "57 Varieties" when he sees an advertisement for "21 Shoe Styles." The Heinz company already has more than 60 varieties—Henry just likes the sound of the number 57.
1894   Milton Hershey markets his Hershey's Milk Chocolate bar.
1897   Dr. John Dorrance develops a way of taking the water out of soup without hurting the flavor. Dorrance is a nephew of Joseph Camp-

bell's partner and Campbell's Condensed Soup markets the product. Unlike earlier soups, which had been sold in bulky cans, Campbell's Soup is much lighter and more convenient for grocers and consumers.

1904   An ice cream stand runs out of dishes so a nearby Syrian-American pastry maker, Ernest Hamwi, makes pastries in the shape of cornucopias. It is the origin of the ice cream cone.

1914   Morton Salt adds magnesium carbonate to its salt, which allows the salt to pour in wet weather—hence the famous slogan, "When It Rains It Pours."

1912   The National Biscuit Company (now Nabisco) markets Oreo cookies. Since then it's sold more than 100 billion Oreos, enough to stretch to the moon and back twice.

1913   Stuck with a lot of extra peanuts, Philip Lance starts roasting them and making peanut butter, which had been invented in 1890. To demonstrate how good his product is, he smears it on bread and gives it to customers—hence the first commercial peanut butter sandwich.

1914   Eskimos, the experts on all things frozen, play a role in the development of frozen food. Clarence Birdseye, while visiting Labrador, notices that the Eskimos frozen food resists spoilage. He develops the first quick freezing technique in 1924 and in 1930 his Bird's Eye Frosted Foods hit the market.

1923   A peanut butter sandwich and a chocolate bar get mushed together in H. B. Reese's lunch bag. The Reese's Peanut Butter Cup is born.

1925   The Jolly Green Giant is introduced on vegetable cans, but at this time he is portrayed as a dwarf. A decade later a new variety of peas called "green giants" is introduced, so the dwarf becomes both a giant and "jolly."

1927   Mrs. Daniel Gerber tells her husband she's tired of straining vegetables by hand for their young daughter. Dan Gerber and his father, who are already in the canning business, solve the problem by introducing the first nationally distributed strained baby food, Gerber.

1930   The Continental Baking Company introduces the first sliced bread under its Wonder Bread label. The same year, the company introduces Hostess Twinkies.

1936   Robert Hunsicker manufactures dog food by hand in his basement. It is the beginning of Alpo.

1937   Sylvan Goldman of Oklahoma City invents the shopping cart so his customers can buy more.

1949   Charles Lubin develops Sara Lee Original Cheese Cake. He is the first to market bakery products in supermarkets. In the 1950s he sells his goods in the aluminum foil that they were baked in, thus creating a popular marketing technique.

1954   C. A. Swanson & Sons introduces the TV dinner. Today sales of complete frozen dinners top $1 billion a year.

POTATO CHIPS

A disgruntled diner and a disgusted Indian inadvertently teamed up in 1853 to create what have become America's top snack food—potato chips. The setting was the gracious Moon's Lake Hotel in Saratoga Springs, New York. The Indian was a chef, George Crum. The diner's name was lost and is probably best forgotten. Anyway, the patron ordered french fries but kept snottily sending them back to the kitchen, saying they were too thick. The peeved Crum finally sliced them wafer-thin and boiled them to a crisp. The diner was finally delighted, and so were a lot of other folks who tried what became a specialty at the hotel and then spread far and wide.

FOREST AND PAPER PRODUCTS

THE MARKET

Trees are some of man's best friends. Just look at the industries that depend on them: logging, paper, sawmills, construction, publishing, furniture, and the container industry are some of the primary consumers. As a result, the forest and paper products industry is heavily dependent on the state of the economy and consumer spending. (The joke in Oregon, a state that is heavily dependent on lumber, is, "When the economy gets the sniffles, Oregon gets pneumonia.") A weak economy and lower consumer spending, for instance, cut housing starts, which lowers the demand for wood; cut advertising dollars, which lowers the publishing demand for paper; and hurt the demand for consumer goods, which cuts demand for paper used to package various products.

THE MONEY

The first American business was a sawmill, established in Jamestown in 1608, and one of the first American exports, shipped to England that same year, was lumber. In 1987, the wood products industry cut down $44.7 billion worth of wood products. The industry's 1987 revenues included $6.4 billion from plywood and particleboard, $16.7 billion from saw mills, and $7.3 billion from logging camps and log contractors.

Paper and allied products added another $106.7 in 1987, up from $98 billion in 1985. Shipments in 1988 are expected to have grown about 2.6% faster than inflation, according to International Trade Administration forecasts.

Table 162 The Wood Products and Paper Industry

Here's how the International Trade Administration estimates the revenues of various sectors of this industry. U.S. manufacturers produced paper products in 1986 that had a surface area of 283.6 billion square miles!

	1986 shipments (millions of dollars)	1986 employment
Total wood products	40,751	444,300
Logging camps and log contractors	7,587	85,600
Sawmills and planing mills	13,631	143,000
Hardwood dimension and flooring	1,440	25,600
Millwork	7,340	75,100
Wood pallets and skids	1,408	22,800
Hardwood plywood	1,305	19,000
Softwood plywood	4,070	40,000
Particleboard	1,120	7,000
Wood preserving	1,670	11,300
Structural wood members, not elsewhere classified	1,180	14,900
Total paper and allied products	107,567	622,300
Pulp mills	4,491	17,000
Paper and board	40,370	190,000
Corrugated and solid fiber boxes	13,335	102,000
Folding paperboard boxes	4,466	45,500
Setup paperboard boxes	531	9,700
Sanitary food containers	2,982	22,600
Fiber cans, drums, and similar products	1,615	13,400
Bags, except textile bags	5,954	50,800
Sanitary paper products	10,965	39,500
Paper coating and glazing	6,632	42,600
Envelopes	8,697	26,300
Die-cut paper and board	2,270	17,500
Pressed and molded pulp goods	1,939	3,200
Stationery products	238	13,500
Converted paper, not elsewhere classified	3,082	28,700

Source: International Trade Administration.

Table 163   The Largest Lumber Producers of North America

Rank	Company Number of mills Headquarters	Hardwood and softwood lumber production (in millions of board feet)	
		1985	1984
1.	Weyerhaeuser Company 30 mills Tacoma, Washington	2,609.0	2,989.0
2.	Louisiana-Pacific Corporation 64 mills Portland, Oregon	1,997.0	2,012.0
3.	Champion International Corporation 30 mills Stamford, Connecticut	1,837.4	1,840.5
4.	Georgia-Pacific Corporation 37 mills Atlanta, Georgia	1,684.0	1,650.0
5.	Canadian Forest Products Ltd. 14 mills Vancouver, British Columbia	1,301.8	1,223.3
6.	British Columbia Forest Products Ltd. 10 mills Vancouver, British Columbia	1,195.7	1,123.0
7.	West Fraser Mills Ltd. 6 mills Quesnel, British Columbia	1,047.9	965.6
8.	MacMillan Bloedel Ltd. 11 mills Vancouver, British Columbia	979.0	845.0
9.	Weldwood of Canada Ltd. 7 mills Vancouver, British Columbia	912.0	796.0
10.	Boise Cascade Corporation 17 mills Boise, Idaho	802.0	801.2

Source: *Forest Industries*, July 1986.

Weyerhaeuser Company
CEO: G. H. Weyerhaeuser
Employees: 35,000
Assets: $7 billion

Corporate Headquarters Building
Tacoma, Washington 98477
206-924-2345

	1987	1986	1985	1980
Revenues (millions of dollars):	6,989	5,652	5,206	4,536
Net income (millions of dollars):	446	277	200	321
Share earnings (dollars):	3.18	1.91	1.32	2.47

What it does: The biggest company in wood products in terms of net sales. A major producer of pulp, paperboard, and corrugated containers.

Frederick Weyerhaeuser arrived in America in 1852 from Germany. By the time he died in 1914, his Weyerhaeuser Timber Company owned about 2 million acres of forest. Today, the company's far-flung operations involve just about every aspect of the wood products industry: its sawmills produce lumber, paper mills produce wood pulp and papers, packaging operations produce containers and packages. Its real estate and financial services operations could even sell some of the company's millions of acres of timber land.

But hard times have forced the family-controlled giant to change its ways. An industry-wide slump caused earnings to drop. The Canadians dumped lumber on the U.S. market at cheaper prices. Other companies slashed labor costs by obtaining hefty givebacks from unions or, when that failed, shutting unionized plants and opening nonunion ones. In response, under CEO George Weyerhaeuser—the third generation of the family to run the company—the company cut labor costs and slashed its payroll from 42,800 in 1981 to 35,000 in 1987.

Already the bitter medicine is paying dividends for the sick company. Earnings jumped 38% in 1986 on a 9% increase in sales. With the industry finally showing signs of reviving and the Canadian government imposing a 15% export tax on Canadian lumber exported to the U.S. rather than risk a U.S. duty on such lumber, Weyerhaeuser should harvest some even larger profits.

CHRISTMAS TREES

Christmas trees first appeared about 400 years ago in Germany and by the 19th century the custom had spread through most of northern Europe. In America, it's safe to say that today's $600 million Christmas tree business was an outgrowth of the American Revolution: Hessian mercenaries fighting on the side of the British brought the German custom to the U.S. By 1851, demand was so great that Mark Carr hauled two ox sleds of Christmas trees from upstate New York to the streets of New York City, where he set up the first Christmas tree retail lot. Today, Americans buy over 32 million natural Christmas trees, according to the National Christmas Tree Association. About 100,000 people are employed full- or part-time in the Christmas tree industry. Sales top $600 million a year.

FRANCHISES

THE MARKET

If the American commercial landscape looks redundant, it is. Since 1960, franchises have become one of the most popular ways of marketing goods and services. Already one third of all retail dollars are spent at franchise operations. Nine out of 10 people over the age of 12 eat regularly in fast-food franchises. Every night of the year more than 300,000 people stay in Holiday Inns, a franchise operation.

THE MONEY

Franchise sales will hit $632.4 billion in 1988, up from about $591.3 billion in 1987. In 1987 franchises owned by larger competitors sold $76.3 billion worth of goods and services and $515 billion was sold by independent franchise owners. Sales can also be broken down another way. In 1987, nearly $421 billion (71%) of these sales came from product and trade name franchisers, such as gas stations, soft drink bottlers, and auto dealerships, which have independent sales relationships with the suppliers. The rest, about $151 billion in 1986, were earned by franchise operations known as business format franchisers. In those operations, which include McDonald's, the franchise operators not only use a product, trade name or service, but also use the company's marketing strategy, its business format, its manuals for quality control and operations, and, at times, even its architectural design for the outlet.

Retail franchise sales, which include the $50-billion-a-year fast-food franchise business, dominate the franchise business, accounting for $515 billion in 1987. That was about 87% of all franchise sales and 33% of all retail sales in the U.S.

THE PLAYERS

There are over 450,000 franchise establishments in the U.S.

THE PEOPLE

About 7.3 million people will earn a living from franchises in 1988.

TRENDS AND FORECAST

The first franchise operations were started by the I. M. Singer Company in 1851 to sell sewing machines. In 1898, General Motors used franchises to enhance its marketing, and, soon afterward, the idea spread to other auto makers, soft drink producers, gasoline service stations, and a variety of other businesses. Franchising really took off when Ray Kroc turned McDonald's into the largest fast-food restaurant. (See the profile of

Table 164   Sales by Franchises
(billions of dollars)

Year	Total	Company-owned	Franchise-owned
1972	143.9	16.8	127.1
1975	185.8	24.7	161.1
1980	334.4	48.5	285.9
1981	364.4	55.1	314.2
1982	376.4	35.1	321.3
1983	422.8	59.1	363.7
1984	492.1	63.6	428.5
1985	543.0	68.3	474.7
1986	556.2	70.0	486.2
1987*	591.2	76.3	515.0
1988**	632.4	81.3	550.8

*Estimated.
**Forecast.
Source: U.S. Department of Commerce, International Trade Administration.

McDonald's in the "Restaurant" section.) Franchise operations often offer owners a competitive advantage with nationwide and local advertising that increases product identification, direction and management help in daily operations, and a well-established reputation for reliability and quality. As a result, franchise sales now equal about 20% of the GNP and may grow to as much as half of all retail sales by the year 2000.

FUNERALS

Americans now spend $10 billion to $12 billion a year on funerals and about $2,750 for the average funeral at the country's 22,000 funeral homes. About 14% of all Americans who died were cremated in 1986, up from 10% five years earlier. Industry analysts expect that figure to grow to as much as 30% by 2000.

Most funeral home companies continue to be small, family-run operations. Service Corporation International (SCI) of Houston, Texas, is, however, a notable exception. Aided by a public offering in 1969, SCI began buying funeral homes from retiring owners and today is the country's largest owner and operator of funeral homes. It has 320 funeral homes, 80 cemeteries, 40 florists, and even a casket company for the closest thing to full service in the funeral industry.

SCI is also a pioneer in what might be called death insurance. In 1978, the company began promoting its Guardian Plan, an insurance plan that pays for a funeral even if costs go up or a customer dies before all the premiums are paid. Sales of such plans grew from $8 million to $108 million in the fiscal year that ended April 30, 1986. SCI's profits hit $48.9 million in 1986 on $331 million in sales.

GAMBLING

THE MARKET AND THE MONEY

All of the talk about speculation on Wall Street and merger mania pales in comparison to a much older form of speculation—gambling. Americans now bet over $190 billion a year, according to *Gaming and Wagering Business* magazine. Lottery wagers hit $12 billion in 1986, up 10% in a year, and estimates of illegal betting on sports range from $20 billion to $70 billion. As early as 1981, the National Football League produced a study saying $50 billion a year was bet on pro football. Other estimates say $600 million was bet on the 1987 Super Bowl alone, with Las Vegas bookies handling $75 million.

The big winners are those taking the bets. The total gaming win (wagers less payouts for winning bets) for owners of various types of gambling operations hit $18.8 billion in 1984, the most recent year for which a breakdown was available, according to *Gaming & Wagering Business* magazine. That meant casino operators took in $5.1 billion (27% of the total profits), lotteries $4.1 billion (22%), horse racing operators $2.4 billion (13%), operators of charitable games and bingo $1.4 billion (7%), jai alai and dog racing operators $0.6 billion (3%), and illegal gambling bookies and operators $5.2 billion (28%), according to *Gaming & Wagering Business* magazine.

THE PLAYERS

In legal gambling, the biggest operators are state and local governments. They pull in $12 billion a year from lotteries and casinos. In 1986 some 56 million customers walked into casinos and lost an estimated $5.8 billion.

TRENDS AND FORECAST

There was a time when gambling was the closest thing to a no-risk business. That is, of course, if you were the one taking the bets.

Take slot machines. Operators pay about $5,000 for each machine. You don't need someone to operate a slot machine. You just line the machines up against a wall and bettors pump money into them. At popular casinos, a $5,000 machine will earn over $100,000 a year. Each year bettors lose over $3 billion at the slots, more money than they drop at the tables.

The odds are also very good if you run the tables. Typically the odds are rigged in favor of the house by a small margin. In roulette the odds are about 5.3% in the house's favor, 1.5% in baccarat, and 1.4% in craps. For slots, the house advantage is a hefty 11%. But odds are even worse than they seem. These odds are for each bet and very few bettors go all the way to Atlantic City or Las Vegas to place one bet. If the house advantage is 5.3% at roulette and if you bet five times in a row, you'll lose on the average, 5.3% on each bet, or 23.8% of your original investment after five bets. As a result, bettors at most Atlantic City casinos post heavy losses, dropping about 16% of their money in craps and black-jack, 25% in roulette, and 15% in baccarat.

But in recent years, the money-making machine has not produced the same old profits. The big problem is increased competition and ever-growing costs. At the Las Vegas gambling tables, success lured other operators into the market. Legalized gambling in Atlantic City cut into the profits in Vegas and overbuilding in Atlantic City has reduced profits there. New federal rules that require casinos to report all cash transactions over $10,000 are also cutting into the betting of high rollers, who want to keep their cash flow hidden from the IRS.

The result: a 1986 study of Las Vegas casinos by the *Las Vegas Review-Journal* showed that about one third of all Las Vegas casinos were in the red and at least two casinos were in Chapter 11 or had just gotten out of it.

Table 165   The Billion-Dollar Lottery

States earned a record $12.22 billion on lottery sales in 1986, up 20% from the year before. Six states sold more than $1 billion in tickets:

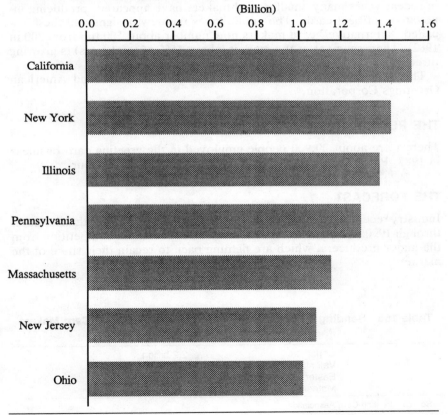

Source: *Gaming & Wagering Business.*

GREETING CARDS

THE MARKET

Americans buy 7 billion greeting cards a year, sending 2.2 billion on Christmas and another 850 million on Valentine's Day, according to the Greeting Card Association. And don't forget the 1.6 billion birthday cards sent each year.

THE MONEY

All of those cards added up to about $2.1 billion worth of factory shipments in 1987. Another $2.3 billion worth of cards will be manufactured in 1988.

THE PLAYERS

Three major companies hold about 80% of the greeting card market. But in recent years many smaller card makers have appeared, producing innovative, offbeat cards. The public loves the new designs and these so-called "alternative" card makers now number about 500 (up from 200 in 1982). Their segment of the market (about 15% of total sales) is growing three times faster than the industry as a whole.

The two largest card makers remain Hallmark Cards and American Greetings Corporation.

THE PEOPLE

There were about 20,900 people employed in the greeting card business in 1987. Production workers earn an average of $9.97 an hour.

THE FORECAST

Industry receipts are expected to grow 2% to 3% a year faster than inflation through 1990. Alternative card makers can expect more competition from the major producers, which are fighting back to regain their share of the market.

Table 166   Sending a Card: The Most Popular Holidays for Card Makers

Holiday	Number of cards sent
Christmas	2.2 billion
Valentine's Day	850 million
Easter	185 million
Mother's Day	145 million

Source: Greeting Card Association.

> **HALLMARK**
>
> More than 20 million copies of Hallmark's "Thinking of You" card have been sold.

HEALTH CARE AND SERVICES

THE MARKET AND THE MONEY

Health care costs continue to hit feverish levels. Total costs of health care and services will hit $544 billion in 1988, up from $499 billion in 1987. Way back there in 1972, they were only $93.9 billion.

Such bills can put companies in intensive care. U.S. companies now spend about $91 billion providing health insurance to 130 million workers and family members, up from $25.5 billion a little more than a decade earlier. *Fortune* 500 firms now pay an average of $100 million a year for

Table 167   The Cost of Health Care

Here's how the country spends its health care dollars:

(billions of dollars)

	1972	1980	1987	1988
Total expenditures	93.9	248.1	498.9	544.0
Health services and supplies	87.4	236.2	481.6	525.6
Personal health care	80.5	219.7	441.2	481.8
Hospital health care	35.2	101.6	193.5	211.1
Physicians' services	17.2	46.8	102.1	111.4
Dentists' services	5.6	15.4	32.7	35.5
Other professional services	1.8	5.7	16.2	18.3
Drugs and medical sundries*	9.3	18.8	32.7	35.5
Eyeglasses and appliances	2.3	5.1	8.8	9.5
Nursing homes care	6.5	20.4	42.0	46.0
Other health services	2.6	6.0	13.1	14.5
Program administration and net cost of insurance	4.8	9.2	25.9	28.0
Government public health programs	2.1	7.3	14.5	15.8
Research and construction of medical facilities	6.6	11.9	17.3	18.4
Research**	2.4	5.4	9.0	9.8
Construction	4.2	6.5	8.3	8.6

*Does not include drugs or sundries dispensed from hospitals or doctors' offices. Those costs are listed under the costs for hospitals or physicians' services.

**Research costs of drug companies and other manufacturers of equipment and supplies are included in the expenditure class in which the product falls.

Sources: Bureau of Data Management and Strategy of the Health Care Financing Administration; U.S. Department of Commerce. Estimates for 1986 by the Department of Commerce and International Trade Administration (ITA). Forecasts for 1987 by the Department of Commerce and ITA.

health insurance, almost double the $55 million they paid only five years ago. In 1987, private health care plans, which cover 190 million Americans, spent $155 billion to cover health care costs of the people they insure. These insurance costs were up $14 billion in only one year.

In the 1950s, patients picked up about two thirds of their medical bills. But by the mid-1980s, federal, state, and local governments paid 40% of all personal health care expenditures; private health insurance picked up 32%, and patients paid only 28%.

To stop the hemorrhaging, both the public and private sector have demanded that the entire health care system undergo radical surgery, and some reforms have been made. By putting a cap on Medicare payments for specific illnesses and operations in 1983, the federal government helped hold down costs. Caps on government payments for health care have cut the use of expensive equipment and treatments—with the side effect of putting a damper on the medical equipment market. Companies adopted stricter insurance policies, forcing their workers to pay part of the costs, and turned to HMOs—health maintenance organizations—to cut hospital costs. In recent years, *Fortune* 500 companies have shifted $6 billion worth of medical bills back on their employees.

Still, health care costs raced ahead of inflation, rising 11.3% a year between 1980 and 1985, when there was talk that the corner had been turned on health care costs. (In 1984, then-Secretary of Health and Human Services Margaret Heckler had the temerity to suggest that the Reagan administration had "broken the back" of health care inflation.) In 1987, health care costs jumped 9%, more than twice the inflation rate.

Worse, health care costs are eating up an even bigger share of the GNP. About 5.9% of the GNP went to health care in 1965; by 1980 it was 9.1%, according to the Department of Health and Human Services. In 1987, a record 11.2% of the GNP was leeched off by the health care industry.

For individuals those costs can be staggering. About 38.7% of the population spends more than $1,500 a year on health care and, with the average hospital stay costing $369 a day, 16.8% of the public spent more than $5,000 a year, according to the Department of Health and Human Services. Such costs are particularly hard on the elderly. About 1.5 million Americans in the country's 19,100 nursing homes spend an average of $22,000 a year. Private insurers cover only about 2% of the $42 billion spent on nursing home care in 1987.

THE PLAYERS

There are some 520,000 doctors in the country. Their average earnings are about $110,000 after paying such expenses as nurses' wages, rents, and malpractice insurance. About 16,800 new doctors graduate from the nation's medical schools each year. Money spent on physicians' services topped $100 billion for the first time in 1987, and will hit $111 billion in 1988.

TRENDS AND FORECAST

The health care industry is undergoing a major transformation in the way it spends money and provides services. Here are the winners and losers:

HMOs

Capitalizing on a cost-conscious market, HMOs have grown dramatically. In December of 1986 there were 593 HMOs that provide health care to over 25 million Americans, about 10.4% of the population. HMOs typically provide all a patient's health care for a fixed fee. By the start of 1988, over 30 million Americans, about 12% of the population, was enrolled. That has given them an incentive to cut costs but many doctors have attacked the HMOs for skimping on services. There is little controversy over their popularity, however. The number of people enrolled in HMOs has more than tripled since 1980. The largest HMO, Kaiser Permanente, is still not-for-profit, but many other HMOs have given up their nonprofit status and gone to Wall Street to raise capital. Currently investor-owned companies serve about 22% of the people enrolled in HMOs. Of the top five HMOs, only the fourth- and fifth-ranked HMOs are investor-owned. (See Table 168 below.)

Hospitals

Hospitals are the hardest hit by cost cutting. At the high-water mark of health care inflation in 1982, hospitals racked up 42% of the nation's health care bill. Today, the nation's 6,800 hospitals face a sicker financial climate. Hospitals are stuck with 1.3 million beds, many more than they need. Occupancy rates fell from 75% in 1980 to around 65% in 1985. They could drop below 60% by 1990. Hospital admissions have fallen because of Medicare restrictions. In 1988 Americans will spend $211 billion on hospital care, up front $193 billion in 1987 and $156.2 billion in 1984.

The Hospital Corporation of America, the largest hospital management chain in the U.S., is already showing the effects. Profits dropped 4% in 1985 and 38% in 1986. In 1987, it sold 104 of its less profitable acute care hospitals, emphasizing psychiatric care, which is less susceptible to spending cuts. Even so, more and more hospitals are privately owned. There are about 1,360 investor owned hospitals with 162,000 beds.

Table 168   Largest HMO Chains

Rank	Company	Number of people enrolled
1.	Kaiser Foundation Health Plans	4,903,767
2.	Maxicare Health Plans Inc.	2,170,638
3.	Health Insurance Plan of Greater New York	960,940
4.	CIGNA Health Plan	946,702
5.	United HealthCare Corp.	917,909

Inter Study, as of December 1986.

Table 169　The Largest Hospital Management Chains, 1986

Rank	Company	Beds	Number of units
1.	Hospital Corporation of America*	64,700	428
2.	American Medical International	19,764	123
3.	Humana, Inc.	17,288	85
4.	National Medical Enterprises	5,292	43

*Sold units to Health Trust in last quarter of 1987.
Source: Modern Healthcare, June 5, 1987.

Medical and Dental Equipment

For manufacturers of medical and dental equipment and supplies, a cost-cutting environment was a mixed blessing. The U.S. market for medical and dental equipment and supplies rose from $14.1 billion in 1982 to an estimated $20.8 billion in 1987 and will hit $22.5 billion in 1988. To reduce costs, hospitals and doctors have pushed for better deals. Also, companies face more price competition in many traditional products. At the same time, however, cost-saving products, which allow patients to avoid spending additional time in hospitals, show strong sales. The home diagnostic kit market, for example, could grow to $875 million a year by 1990, more than double the 1986 level.

Pharmaceuticals

A brighter spot in the health care industry is pharmaceuticals. Drug stocks have soared. Helped by a weaker dollar, pharmaceutical shipments rose from nearly $26.8 billion in 1984 to $34 billion in 1987.

The industry's shipments jumped 7.6% not up to the banner days of the 1970s, when drug sales shot up more than 15% a year. Profit margins continue to be squeezed by high research and development costs, the threat of litigation, heavy government regulation, and, most importantly, competition from cheaper generic drugs.

Table 170　The Largest Drug Makers, 1985

Rank	Company	Sales (billions of dollars)
1.	Merck	2.8
2.	American Home Products	2.5
3.	Hoechst	2.4
4.	Ciba-Geigy	2.3
5.	Bayer	2.3
6.	Pfizer	2.0
7.	Warner-Lambert	1.9
8.	Abbott	1.9
9.	Eli Lilly	1.8
10.	Bristol-Myers	1.8

Source: Robert Flemming & Co.

Table 171 The Largest Investor-Owned Nursing Homes

As the country gets older and older, privately owned nursing home companies become increasingly attractive investments. Here are the five largest:

Rank	Company	Beds	Units
1.	Beverly Enterprises	127,349	1,178
2.	Hillhaven Corporation	48,378	387
3.	ARA Living Centers	29,735	265
4.	National Heritage	23,001	201
5.	Manor Care Inc.	18,105	138

Source: *Modern Healthcare,* June 5, 1987.

Table 172 The Price of an Organ: Average Costs of Organ Transplants

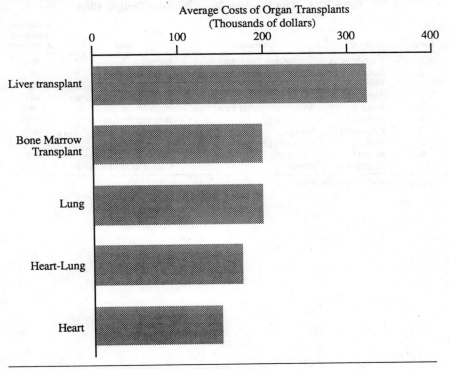

Average Costs of Organ Transplants
(Thousands of dollars)

Sources: Equitable Life Assurance Society, Hewitt Associates.

Table 173   The Body Shop: Plastic Surgery Costs, 1988

Want a perfect nose? A tucked tummy? Or tired of those wrinkles? Well, take a look at some of the average prices for plastic surgery. Financing a new face-lift can add a few more worry lines.

Operation	Cost
Eye lift	$1,000–4,000
Face lift	2,000–10,000
Ear reduction	1,000–3,500
Nose job	1,500–6,000
Breast enlargement	1,800–4,000
Tummy tuck	2,000–6,000
Breast lift	2,000–7,000

Source: American Society of Plastic and Reconstructive Surgeons.

Table 174   The World's Most Popular Drugs, 1986

Rank	Drug	Company	Use	Revenues (millions of dollars)
1.	Tagamet	SmithKline Beckman	Ulcers	890
2.	Zantac	Glaxo	Ulcers	727
3.	Feldene	Pfizer	Arthritis	467
4.	Tenormin	ICI	High blood pressure	420
5.	Inderal	American Home Products	High blood pressure	405
6.	Voltaren	Ciba-Geigy	Arthritis	402
7.	Naprosyn	Syntex	Arthritis	400
8.	Valium	Hoffman-La Roche	Anxiety	400
9.	Amoxil	Beecham	Infection	390
10.	Aldomet	Merck	High blood pressure	370

Source: Robert Flemming & Co.

FAT PROFITS FOR THE DIET INDUSTRY

When Americans set out to lose weight, their wallets usually get lighter faster than they do. Each year, Americans chow down about $513 billion of food and beverages. Then they go out and spend another $10 billion trying to win the battle of the bulge with such things as diet food, health club memberships, diet drugs, fat farms, and weight loss classes. Diet pills and diet powders bring in at least $350 million. Another $800 million goes for frozen diet dinners. Routinely, strange diet books based on eating all the watermelon or pizza you want become best-sellers. Market research shows that 60% of all American women are on a diet at some point during the year.

What comes of all this? Certainly not thinner people. About the only things hotter at the food counter than dietary products is high-calorie food. The average American eats 150 pounds of caloric sweeteners (such as corn syrup and sugar) every year, up 20 pounds in only a decade. Makers of high-calorie ice creams such as Häagen-Dazs and Frusen Glädjé have increased their sales, as have cookie makers. The average American is six pounds heavier than he or she was in the 1960s. About 20% of all women between 25 and 34 are overweight, more than ever before. Makers of large-size clothing are now doing an $8 billion business.

No matter. Obviously, it's the thought that counts in the diet industry. And thoughts of a new thinner self have pushed some companies into large profits.

Take Weight Watchers. It was founded in 1963 by a 214-pound housewife named Jean Nidetch. By organizing weekly meetings at which people talked about their food binges the way alcoholics discuss uncontrollable drinking binges, she discovered a way to shed pounds and add heft to her pocketbook. Today, more than 25 million Americans have attended Weight Watchers meetings and 700,000 people are currently enrolled. Taken over by H. J. Heinz Company in 1978, the $400 million diet empire now includes a magazine with a circulation of 900,000, diet books, seminars, and diet frozen dinners.

PSYCHIC INCOME

A few numbers tell a lot about the nation's state of mind: About 5 million people now visit psychiatrists, up from only a half-million 30 years ago. One in five Americans has had some type of mental health treatment, compared to about one in eight in 1960. And the stigma of seeing a psychiatrist is vanishing. Years ago, visiting a psychiatrist could damage a person's reputation or, as it did with Senator Thomas Eagleton in 1972, cost him a vice-presidential nomination.

But as psychotherapy has become more acceptable, business, insurers, and governments face mounting psychiatric bills. Seeing a shrink can cost $50 to $125 a session and many patients spend over $3,000 a year. No estimates of the costs of psychotherapy are available. It's believed they are growing 10% to 20% a year, much faster than any other part of the nation's health care costs.

Take phobias for example, the nation's number-two mental health problem after alcoholism. An estimated 13 million Americans have phobias such as a fear of flying, fear of heights, or one of the most common phobias, the fear of leaving the house—agoraphobia. Fear of flying alone is believed to cost the airlines about $1.5 billion a year.

Psychologist Robert L. DuPont has already turned treating those fears into a $1.2 million business. He has six centers that treat 2,000 patients for phobias in Virginia, Maryland, and Washington, D.C.

Nor is Dr. DuPont's success an isolated case. Today there are some 50 centers and 250 specialists that treat phobias, up from only 2 centers a dozen years ago.

BUSINESS AND AIDS

AIDS is already a major epidemic. By 1987 some 32,000 cases of AIDS had been reported in the U.S., with about half of those victims already dead. As many as 50,000 to 125,000 people show signs of infection and another 1,500,000 people may carry the disease but show no symptoms, according to the Centers for Disease Control. With no cure in sight, as many as 100,000 people may be infected by 1991 and as many as 10 million more may carry the virus without showing any symptoms.

AIDS poses major economic and ethical problems for American business. Productivity lost because of illness and premature deaths caused by AIDS could cost U.S. industry as much as $55 billion by 1991. Insurance companies face rising claims for medical care, while businesses wonder where they will find the money to treat employees with AIDS. The disease has already infected the blood supply and a misplaced fear of catching AIDS while donating blood has hurt efforts to replenish it. Before a 1987 ruling by the Supreme Court prohibiting discrimination against persons with AIDS, widespread public hysteria about the disease often led employers simply to dismiss AIDS patients, provoking an ethical and legal crisis for many companies.

With some drugs showing promise for prolonging the life of AIDS patients but no cure in sight, treating and caring for AIDS patients promises to be a billion-dollar industry. Today, the cost of treating an AIDS patient from the time he or she is diagnosed to the time of death is about $150,000. By 1991 the health care costs for AIDS will be as much as $16 billion a year. Insurance officials estimate that costs to their industry alone will be about $10 billion by that time.

So far, insurance claims for AIDS have been modest. Lincoln National Life Insurance Company has paid out $10 million on 250 policies, Transamerica has spent $6.2 million on 68 life insurance policies, and Northwestern Mutual Life Insurance Company has paid out $6.5 million on 87 life insurance policies, according to an informal 1987 survey by *The New York Times*.

But worried life insurance companies are testing people over the age of 16 for AIDS and placing restrictions on policies. The result is a legal battle between insurers and gay-rights activists. In court suits against insurance companies, they claim insurance companies are discriminating against gays and using sexual orientation as a criterion for underwriting insurance. If insurers lose that battle they could face a $10 billion tab to pay for AIDS patients.

ASPIRIN

When the U.S. government sold off properties after the First World War that had been seized from enemy aliens, it created a bonanza for some companies. For instance, the booty included stock in the Friedrich Bayer & Co., of New York, which had a plant that made a lot of drugs and a little-known product called Aspirin. Sterling Drug, Inc., seeing Aspirin as an analgesic it needed for its own product line, bid $5.3 million for the Bayer Company. Bringing its own marketing expertise to bear, Sterling turned *aspirin* into a household word.

GILLETTE

Young King Gillette was always casting around to invent a disposable something so that people would have to keep buying the thing. In 1895, annoyed one day that his straight razor was so dull it was unusable, he had a eureka—a razor with disposable blades.

But one person's good idea hits another's crazy bone. For years his pals joshed him about the silly thing he was trying to invent. Worse, toolmakers smirked and told him to forget it when asked for help in solving problems to get a blade holder to work. Finally, he badgered an MIT instructor, William E. Nickerson, into collaborating with him.

In 1903, the first year the Gillette safety razor hit the market, a grand total of 51 were sold at $5 apiece. But by 1906, production soared to 300,000 razors and 500,000 blades. Business really took off during the First World War when the U.S. military, concerned about battlefield sanitary conditions, ordered 3.5 million razors and 36 million blades. When the soldiers returned home, Gillette's business continued to boom thanks to a generation of young men who had gotten used to the razors.

Table 175   Disabilities in America

About 37.4 million Americans, about 24% of everyone over the age of 15, have difficulty performing one or more basic physical activities. About 13.5 million people (7.5%) have a severe disability. A partial breakdown:

19.2 million people have difficulty walking a quarter mile.
7.9 million are unable to walk a quarter mile.
18.2 million have difficulty lifting a weight equivalent to a full bag of groceries.
7.8 million are unable to lift the same weight.
18.2 million people have trouble climbing a flight of stairs without stopping to rest.
5 million can't climb a flight of stairs.
12.3 million people have trouble reading newsprint even with glasses or contact lenses.
7.7 million have hearing troubles.
481,000 can't hear a normal conversation.
2.5 million have a problem making their speech understood.

Source: U.S. Census Bureau.

HOTEL AND LODGING

THE MARKET

Sometimes it's a wonder that you can catch anyone at home. Sixty-three percent of all U.S. residents take one or more trips for business or pleasure at least 100 miles from home every year. Each day about 11 million Americans travel at least 100 miles from home on a trip requiring an overnight stay. Another 25.4 million visitors came to the U.S. in 1986. All of that travel adds up to 250 million guests in the course of the year, more than the U.S. population.

Typically, lodgers break down like this: 40% are business travelers, 25% are on vacation, 5.5% are on government business, 25% are attending a conference, and 4.5% have other reasons for their stays, according to the American Hotel and Motel Association. The average hotel stay is 3.5 days for pleasure and 1.3 days for business. The more than 21 million visitors to the U.S. are another source of revenue. The average foreign visitor stayed 9.4 nights in a hotel or motel. (See the section "Travel.")

THE MONEY

The lodging industry generated some $45.3 billion in revenue in 1987 (up from $17.7 billion in 1977 and $38.9 billion in 1984); it pays over $12.2 billion a year in wages and salaries and $4.1 billion in federal taxes.

Part of this money came from the $90 billion a year (up from $61 billion in 1984) that American business spends on travel and entertainment. Doing business on the go, after all, is not cheap. It costs an average of $152.84 a day for an executive to work out of town. The average room rate for a hotel or motel alone is $61.95.

In recent years, dramatic growth in the number of rooms available, however, cut into the industry's profits. Despite a 3.6% rise in the average room rate, occupancy rates dropped 3.5% in 1986 as the number of hotel and motel rooms outpaced demand. With occupancy rates at 64.7%, hotels suffered a $56-a-room pretax loss, compared to a profit of $505 in 1984, according to a study by Laventhol & Horwath. But in 1988 the occupancy rate is expected to improve to 67% and revenues should hit $47.5 billion.

THE PLAYERS

There are 45,000 lodging establishments in the U.S., with some 2.6 million rooms, according to the American Hotel and Motel Association. About 66% of the rooms were occupied each night in 1987, versus 64.9% in 1986 and down from 67.9% in 1984. The number of rooms has been growing by 60,000 to 85,000 a year since 1983. About $32 billion has been spent in the last decade on hotel construction, $7.2 billion in 1986 alone.

Most hotels have fewer than 75 rooms; they account for 51.2% of all hotels and 17.4% of all available rooms. Hotels larger than 600 rooms

Table 176   Top Five Companies in the Lodging Industry

Rank	Company	Number of properties	Number of rooms
1.	Holiday Corporation	1,907	357,614
2.	The Sheraton Corporation	508	142,000
3.	Ramada Inns, Inc.	575	138,000
4.	Hilton Hotels Corp.	271	97,535
5.	Quality International, Inc.	801	95,393

Source: *1987 Hotels & Restaurants International;* a Cahners publication.

represent only 1% of the total number of properties but rent 16.8% of the available rooms.

THE PEOPLE

The lodging industry employs 1.4 million people and pays over $12.2 billion a year in wages and salaries. The lodging industry created over 50,000 jobs in 1987.

TRENDS AND FORECAST

The outlook for the lodging industry in the near future is mixed. On the plus side, low prices for gas and air travel are always good news for the lodging industry. Demographically, rapid growth in number of middle-aged and retired Americans augurs well for the industry since these age groups have more money and time to spend on travel. And a weakened dollar should also help spur domestic travel.

But even though overall long-term prospects are positive, the industry faces a number of problems. Overbuilding, as noted above, has cut into profits, and high vacancy rates continue to cause problems for hotel owners. At the same time, stagnant corporate profits are forcing many companies to look for ways to cut their travel and entertainment budgets. Yet as the oversupply of hotel rooms decreases, profits should pick up.

Marriott Corporation
CEO: J. W. Marriott, Jr.
Employees: 194,600
Assets: $4.6 billion

1 Marriott Drive
Washington, D.C. 20058
301-897-9000

	1987	1986	1985	1980
Revenues (millions of dollars):	6,522	5,267	4,242	1,719
Net income (millions of dollars):	223	192	167	72
Share earnings (dollars):	1.67	1.40	1.24	.52

What it does: Operates hotels and has extensive food service and restaurant operations.

The company started in 1927 as a root beer and taco stand. Founder J. Willard Marriott, Sr., who worked as a waiter at his first stand, eventually expanded into providing bag lunches for Eastern Air Lines and the U.S. Navy. The first Marriott hotel didn't go up until 1957; today, there are about 142 Marriott hotels and resorts around the world. In addition, the Marriott empire, which raked in $6.5 billion in revenues in 1987, includes 1,700 restaurants, 90 flight kitchens providing food to airlines, 1,400 food service contracts, and 17 luxury resorts.

The architect of much of that expansion is the founder's son, J. W. "Bill" Marriott, Jr. He clocks some 200,000 miles a year, overseeing his own divisions and making certain they provide top services. He also tends to the business of power in a big way: he is active in the grass-roots political arm of the U.S. Chamber of Commerce, he is the director of the Business-Industry Political Action Committee, and, as chairman of Citizen's Choice, he has enrolled 75,000 people to campaign for a smaller federal government.

Unlike his father, who financed the company's expansion from revenues, the younger Marriott has borrowed heavily to finance the company's rapid expansion. He's also committed to spending more than $3 billion over the rest of the decade to develop more hotels and life-care centers for senior citizens. One of his biggest gambles was a 50-story, 1,876-room hotel that opened in the heart of New York's Times Square. With a $400 million price tag, the hotel was the costliest ever built in the U.S. In an overbuilt hotel market, it will be a while before these and other investments pay off.

Still, the bottom line supports the company's expansion strategy. Revenues grew from $890.4 million in 1976 to $3.5 billion in 1984 and $6.5 billion in 1987, while net income grew from $30.8 million in 1976 to $135.3 million in 1984 and $223 million in 1987.

LAW

THE MARKET AND THE MONEY

The U.S. is one of the most litigious nations ever created, spending more money ($70.6 billion in 1987) on legal bills and employing more lawyers (618,000) than any other major country. About half of these legal fees are spent by business, with individuals picking up the rest of the tab. The legal services industry employs about 1 million people.

Going to court was never cheap, but since the early 1970s the bill for legal services has exploded. Americans spent only $10.9 billion on legal services in 1972, but in 1988 they should spend $78.5 billion.

The number of cases and suits brought by American lawyers is also skyrocketing. There are no detailed statistics on the number of cases filed in all of the nation's courts, but in U.S. District Courts the number of tort cases filed grew from 25,691 in 1975 to 41,593 in 1985 while the number of personal injury cases filed grew from 21,221 to 37,560. The number of personal injury cases caused by product liability increased from 9,677 to 12,507 between 1984 and 1985. The number of cases involving contract disputes increased from 22,905 in 1975 to 102,642 in 1985; bankruptcy cases increased from 395 to 6,331 and civil rights cases, including employment rights cases, increased from 10,392 to 19,553 in the same period, according to the annual report of the Administrative Office of the U.S. Courts. Overall, the number of civil cases filed in U.S. District Courts more than tripled, growing from 87,300 in 1975 to 273,670 in 1985.

With more cases than ever before filed in U.S. courts, it's not surprising that the number of jury awards in liability and malpractice cases has skyrocketed. The number of tort cases filed in federal court increased 62% in the last decade while product liability cases increased 370%. At the same time the number of jury awards in liability and malpractice cases tripled and the number of million-dollar verdicts in medical malpractice cases rose from 20 in 1980 to 71 in 1984. The growth in mergers and acquisitions and personal bankruptcies has also helped hike legal fees.

About $15 billion to $20 billion is spent each year to litigate or settle claims made in personal injury cases, a study by the C. V. Starr Center for Applied Economics at New York University says. That bill could rise to $38 billion a year by 1990.

Another growth sector of the legal industry has been prepaid legal plans. Currently some 15 million Americans are covered by prepaid plans, which charge annual fees for providing such services as telephone consultation, letter writing, documents review, and general legal advice.

On an individual level, the legal services business provides some hefty salaries. The average lawyer's household makes $121,913 a year, an American Bar Association study says, and has a net worth of $500,000. One in nine lawyers is a millionaire.

THE PLAYERS

In 1986 the number of lawyers dropped for the second straight year, to 618,000. That same year 1,034,000 were employed in legal services. About 18% of all attorneys are women, but with women accounting for nearly 40% of all first-year law students, women will be making a larger impact on the industry.

According to the American Bar Foundation there is about one lawyer for every 310 Americans. Most of these lawyers (64%) practice in small firms with 2 to 3 lawyers, 29% practice in 4-to-10-lawyer firms, and 7% are employed in large firms with 10 or more lawyers. The median age of a lawyer is only 38, down from 45 to 46 in 1970.

An Altman & Weil survey of law-firm economics breaks down how lawyers spend the money they receive for legal services: about 15.2% of all receipts is spent on support staff, 13.3% on miscellaneous expenses, 7.3% on occupancy, 3.3% on paralegals, 3.2% on equipment, and 1.6% on reference materials. The rest, 56.1% of all receipts, becomes lawyers' incomes.

TRENDS AND FORECAST

The number of students in law school increased dramatically in the late 1970s and early 1980s, peaking in 1982, when a record 127,828 students were enrolled. Since then, however, the number of law students has declined, to 124,092 in 1985, largely because an oversupply of young lawyers cut salaries and job opportunities. Yet there is little doubt that the legal services field will continue to grow as it has in the past. Clinics and government programs serve many poor people who were once unable to afford legal services. And with the price for many simple legal services falling or remaining stable, more people will turn to lawyers. Coupled with the fact that more businesses require high-priced legal services to navigate their way through complex government regulations, product liability suits, mergers, financing, and overseas trade, the industry should continue to see rapid growth.

NOTHING'S SACRED

More and more members of the clergy and religious groups are getting sued these days. Some 2,000 or so cases are pending nationwide and some $100 million was awarded in a recent 18-month period to those suing the religious, according to one estimate. The most serious cases involve child abuse, paternity, and embezzlement. "At one time, churches were protected by charitable immunity, but that's not the case anymore," the Reverend Dean Kelley of the National Council of Churches told The New York Times.

Table 177 10 Biggest Law Firms

Rank	Law firm	Number of lawyers
1.	Baker & McKenzie	946
2.	Jones, Day, Reavis & Pogue	828
3.	Skadden, Arps, Slate, Meagher & Flom	818
4.	Finley, Kumble, Wagner, Underberg, Manley, Myerson & Casey	597
5.	Hyatt Legal Services	636
6.	Morgan, Lewis & Bockius	584
7.	Gibson, Dunn & Crutcher	579
8.	Sidley & Austin	563
9.	Shearman & Sterling	506
10.	Pillsbury, Madison & Sutro	477

Source: *National Law Journal.*

Table 178 10 Biggest Corporate Legal Departments

Rank	Company	Number of lawyers
1.	AT&T	434
2.	Exxon	414
3.	General Electric	293
4.	Sears, Roebuck	269
5.	Chevron	235
6.	Mobil	227
7.	Prudential	210
8.	Citicorp	203
9.	IBM	189
10.	Amoco	188

Source: *National Law Journal.*

Table 179 Where the Lawyers Are: States with the Most and Least Lawyers per Capita

Rank	State	Number of lawyers per 1,000 residents
1.	Washington, D.C.	40
2.	New York	3.57
3.	Alaska	3.37
7.	Illinois	2.84
8.	California	2.74
22.	Texas	2.12
33.	Pennsylvania	1.92
49.	South Carolina	1.34
50.	West Virginia	1.32
51.	North Carolina	1.27

Source: *Legal Times,* September 23, 1985.

LEASING

"Don't buy, lease" is becoming the motto of American business. About 8 out of every 10 companies lease equipment. In 1988, American businesses are expected to lease $90.6 billion worth of equipment. That's a dramatic change from 1978, when Americans leased $22.3 billion worth of equipment.

Leasing plays a major role in a company's decision to acquire new equipment. It finances 45% of all capital expenditure for aircraft, 35% for railway equipment, 31% for motor vehicles, 23% for ships and boats, and 15% for computers, and plays a major role in the acquisition of agricultural and production machinery and medical equipment.

In 1985, about 26% of the money spent on leasing went for computers, 11.8% for telecommunications equipment, 10.5% for aircraft, 6.9% for trucks and trailers, 6.2% for industrial equipment, 5% for manufacturing equipment, 4.2% for project equipment, 2.8% for medical equipment, 2.4% for construction equipment, 1.7% for agricultural equipment, and 1.7% for railroad equipment, according to a survey by the American Association of Equipment Lessors.

Why lease? Executives give the following reasons, according to a poll by Lieberman Research, Inc.: 38% because it improves their cash flow, 28% because of tax benefits, 17% for better asset management, 17% because it is convenient, and 7% for accounting or balance-sheet reasons. Others add that leasing allows a company to acquire equipment without having to make major cash outlays and gives a company more flexibility, allowing it to trade in computers and other high-tech equipment as more advanced models hit the market. Many companies like the fact that leasing allows them to finance 100% of the cost of new equipment.

But while leasing continues to be attractive to many companies, the changed tax code is likely to put a damper on the kind of growth the industry saw in the early 1980s. While the industry grew at an annual rate of 19.7% between 1978 and 1985, it grew only 8% between 1985 and 1986 and is expected to grow 10.2% in 1988.

MACHINE TOOLS

THE MARKET

The machine tool industry is small, accounting for only about 10 cents of every $100 in goods and services produced in the U.S., according to the National Machine Tool Builders' Association. But its products play a key role in the economy. Machine tools are used in factories around the world to cut, form, or shape the metal used in a variety of products, ranging from power plants to household appliances. The major consumers of machine tools are companies in such metalworking industries as aerospace, the auto industry, weapons manufacturing, machinery production, and toolmaking, to name a few.

THE MONEY

Decline in the U.S. manufacturing sector coupled with increased foreign competition means hard times for the machine tool industry. The value of shipments totaled only $2.1 billion in 1987, down dramatically from its peak of 5.6 billion in 1979. This decline, of course, hurts the industry's profits, with machine tool companies showing a -0.5% net operating profit in 1985, according to the U.S. Department of Commerce.

THE PLAYERS

The most recent survey of the industry (1982) indicates that there are 1,290 machine tool companies, most of which employ fewer than 50 people. Several hundred small companies have gone out of business since 1982 and those remaining face fierce competition from foreign producers, which now hold about 50% of the market, up from 23% in 1980, according to the National Machine Tool Builders' Association.

THE PEOPLE

There were some 64,300 people employed in the machine tool industry in 1987, down from a peak of 81,600 in 1980, according to the U.S. Department of Labor. Average weekly earnings were around $450 a week.

TRENDS AND FORECAST

No immediate turnaround is seen for the machine tool industry. The industry is threatened by a shift to plastic and the decline of several big customers of machine tools, such as the steel industry. Although several hundred small companies have already gone out of business, more mergers or bankruptcies are expected. Still, a weaker dollar will keep imports from grabbing a larger market share, and some U.S. producers are more efficient. The survivors, Daniel R. D. Senso of Standard & Poor's believes, will be companies offering sophisticated machine tool systems that include integrated software.

MAGAZINES

THE MARKET AND THE MONEY

The periodicals industry had revenues of over $17.1 billion in 1987, of which $8.2 billion came from advertising. Consumer magazines received $5.5 billion in advertising, and business publications took in $2.5 billion.

There are more than 11,590 different magazines in the U.S. 1987, most of which have very small circulations. The nation's 1,859 consumer magazines sell 324 million copies per month and produce about 62% of the industry's revenues. Business and professional magazines produce 30%; farm periodicals earn 2%. Comic books are a $125-million- to $150-million-a-year business, with companies such as Marvel selling 7.2 million a month. Another $118 million worth of magazines were imported in 1987. Revenues for the periodicals industry should hit $18.2 billion in 1988.

THE PLAYERS

There are some 3,200 magazine companies in the U.S. but only 4 account for 22% of the money earned by the magazine industry. The largest magazines are listed in Table 180 (below).

Table 180   20 Largest Magazines, 1986

Rank	Magazine	Average paid circulation per issue (in thousands)	Rank	Magazine	Average paid circulation per issue (in thousands)
1.	Reader's Digest	17,300	11.	Ladies' Home Journal	5,121
2.	TV Guide	16,874	12.	Time	4,832
3.	Modern Maturity	13,597	13.	National Enquirer	4,504
4.	NRTA/AARP News Bulletins	13,170	14.	Guideposts	4,281
5.	National Geographic	10,691	15.	Playboy	3,901
6.	Better Homes and Gardens	8,012	16.	Redbook	3,891
7.	Family Circle	6,554	17.	The Star	3,560
8.	Woman's Day	5,631	18.	Newsweek	3,053
9.	McCall's	5,275	19.	Cosmopolitan	2,935
10.	Good Housekeeping	5,142	20.	Sports Illustrated	2,875

Source: Magazine Publishers Association.

Table 181   Top Five Magazine Advertisers
(millions of dollars)

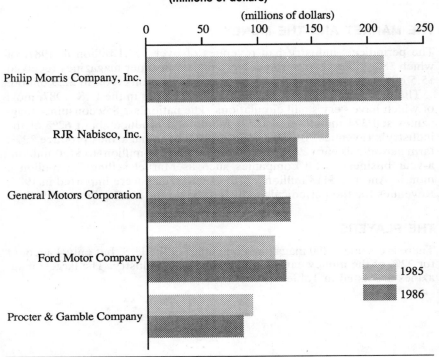

Source: *Leading National Advertisers Special Report,* September 24, 1987.

Table 182   Top Magazine Advertising Industries

Rank	Industry	Expenditures
1.	Automotive	$597.3 million
2.	Business and consumer services	489.4 million
3.	Toiletries and cosmetics	390.4 million
4.	Food	389.5 million
5.	Mail order	357.0 million
	Total	$5.12 billion

Source: Magazine Publishers Association.

Table 183 Top Business Magazines, Ranked by Revenues

Magazine	Advertising pages		Revenues	
	1985	1986	1985	1986
Business Week	4,214.48	3,893.17	$169,099,552	$166,617,226
Forbes	3,711.32	3,418.62	115,725,641	114,040,935
Fortune	3,272.88	2,907.92	115,743,456	110,060,022
Inc.	1,149.95	1,029.39	32,067,595	31,283,881
Industry Week	1,077.25	1,148.32	15,790,504	17,923,094
The Economist	2,512.10	2,411.72	13,484,012	14,013,040
Venture	903.38	850.41	11,516,100	12,394,586
American Way	1,485.04	1,315.32	11,401,815	9,587,493
Black Enterprise	789.00	799.39	9,625,266	NA
Nation's Business	416.38	399.58	10,004,111	9,736,841
Dun's Business Month	611.65	502.83	8,978,133	7,694,124
Financial World	604.27	751.31	4,440,702	6,831,208
Harvard Business Review	410.94	402.98	3,455,250	3,769,537
Savvy	396.36	398.48	3,520,081	3,686,378
High Technology	346.72	229.89	4,815,625	3,357,265
Total	21,901.72	20,459.33	$529,667,843	$510,995,630

(NA) Not available.

The Annenbergs and Triangle Publications The founder of the Annenberg media dynasty was Moses Annenberg, a German-Jewish immigrant who got into the newspaper business during the bloody circulation wars in Chicago. (At that time, rival newspapers hired armed thugs to make certain their papers got distributed and their competitors' didn't.) Annenberg thrived. In 1920, he founded the *Daily Racing Form* and later he founded the Nationwide News Service, a telephone and telegraph wire service with a monopoly on horse racing information. It served bookies in 39 states and was a veritable gold mine, giving Annenberg America's highest income in the 1930s, about $6 million a year. By the late 1930s the Annenberg empire also included newspapers in Philadelphia and Miami.

But in the late 1930s President Roosevelt, angry with Annenberg-owned newspapers' attacks on the New Deal, unleashed a massive IRS investigation. Moses was convicted of $9.6 million in income tax evasion, the largest conviction until the 1980s, and sent to prison.

When Moses died in 1942, his only son Walter was suddenly forced to take over the family business at age 32. His problem was trying to salvage the family finances and at the same time clear its reputation, tarnished by his father's income tax evasion conviction and published reports linking his father to organized crime.

Walter solved the family's financial problems once and for all in 1952, when he brought out *TV Guide,* which in 1974 became the first magazine ever to sell more than 1 billion copies in a year. The family's reputation also improved, thanks to beefed-up editorial quality at *The Philadelphia Inquirer,* lavish political contributions to the Republican party, and huge charitable contributions, including the creation of the Annenberg School of Communications at the University of Pennsylvania.

Today, Walter is a close friend and confidant of President Reagan, and he served as ambassador to England under President Nixon. The family has sold off its 19 TV and radio stations and such newspapers as *The Philadelphia Inquirer,* but the holdings of Triangle Publications are worth over $2 billion. Walter's 20% share of the company plus his other assets makes him worth over $650 million. The Annenberg media empire still includes *TV Guide,* the world's most popular magazine, *Seventeen, Daily Racing Form,* and *Good Food.*

Time Inc.

CEO: J. R. Munro

Employees: 19,000

Assets: $4.3 billion

Time & Life Building
Rockefeller Center
New York, New York 10020
212-586-1212

	1987	1986	1985	1980
Revenues (millions of dollars):	4,193	3,762	3,404	2,882
Net income (millions of dollars):	250	376	200	141
Share earnings (dollars):	4.18	5.95	3.15	2.51

What it does: The nation's leading publisher of magazines, including *Time, Fortune, Sports Illustrated,* and *People.* A major book publisher. Owns the nation's second-largest cable TV operation and the biggest cable TV programmer, Home Box Office.

Henry Luce might be called the father of modern magazine journalism. His *Time* magazine is the largest weekly newsmagazine. But the company is also one of the nation's largest book publishers, the owner of the Book-of-the-Month Club, the operator of America's second largest cable TV operation and the owner of HBO, and the publisher of *Sports Illustrated, Fortune, Money,* and *People.*

This $3.76 billion company started in 1923 with $86,000. Luce, who was born in China and educated at Yale, founded *Time* with his classmate Briton Hadden. Its punchy prose style quickly boosted circulation. In 1930, Luce started *Fortune,* a pioneer in business journalism. In 1936, he bought an unprofitable humor magazine, *Life,* and transformed it into the standard for photojournalism for the next 40 years.

Luce came under fire over the years for keeping strict editorial control over his magazines, and his magazines developed a reputation as freespending operations. *Life,* for example, once fitted out a DC-8 as a flying editorial office for 40 staff members in 1965. As the plane flew from London to New York, staffers processed photographs, researched facts, and wrote copy for a special 21-page color spread on Winston Churchill. And, in 1983, on the company's 60th birthday 1,700 *Time* employees partied on the Queen Elizabeth II.

But those free-spending days are long gone at *Time* and elsewhere in the publishing world. Time blew $25 million on the magazine *Picture* and dropped another $47 million on its badly conceived *TV-Cable Week*. As earnings slumped, raiders appeared. Under Chairman J. Richard Munro and President Nicholas J. Nicholas Jr., *Time* responded with hundreds of layoffs, sold its corporate headquarters for $118 million and bought back 10 million shares of stock. All of that helped *Time* adjust to the slow growth of magazine revenues, and profits were up a whopping 88% in 1986, to $376.3 million in net income on $3.8 billion worth of revenues. But in 1987, profits tapered off to $250 million.

S. I. Newhouse, Jr.   After S. I. Newhouse, Jr., bought *The New Yorker* in 1985, the talk of the town was that he would shake things up at the prestigious magazine. Well, that wasn't idle gossip. Newhouse first installed Steven T. Florio as publisher, and Florio promptly and unceremoniously dumped most of the circulation and ad salespeople. And, after a delicate waiting period, Newhouse replaced legendary editor William Shawn with Robert A. Gottlieb, former editor-in-chief of Alfred A. Knopf, Inc.

Such behavior struck a lot of people as high-handed when it came to the venerable magazine, which in its 60 years had become a benchmark for literary excellence. But what a lot of people didn't realize—and Newhouse very much did—was that *The New Yorker* had been showing its age. There were even people audacious enough to wonder whether *The New Yorker* hadn't simply run its course. Circulation was static. Ad pages had plummeted. The magazine was only holding its revenue growth by driving up ad prices, which made advertisers mad.

That Newhouse moved quickly to solve the problems wasn't unusual. Close attention to the bottom line has always been his company's successful guiding principle.

Newhouse's Advance Publications, Inc., is the largest privately held communications conglomerate in the nation. As chairman, he oversees all the magazine and book operations, which include Condé Nast Publications and Random House. Some 25 newspapers and several cable TV systems are under the direction of Newhouse's brother, Donald, who is president of Advance.

When people describe S. I., they inevitably use terms such as "a workaholic" and "a modest man who is private to the point of self-effacement" and say that "in business, he's a highly intelligent professional who hires good people and delegates to them."

Actually, those phrases echo the descriptions of his father, who started the Newhouse empire in 1922 by buying a Staten Island newspaper when he was only 16 years old. Like his father, Newhouse is at his desk by 5 A.M., but he is, if anything, even more active than his father was.

Newhouse began making his mark in 1960 when he begged his father to buy Condé Nast. His father did and told him to "go in and learn what makes it work." Joining as a member of *Glamour*'s merchandise and promotion department, he swiftly learned as much as he could and wound up beefing up circulation.

After that, he ran from one success to another. For instance, he launched the health and fitness magazine *Self* in 1979 before anybody else in the business recognized the potential for such a publication. Also in 1979, he acquired *GQ—Gentleman's Quarterly*. The magazine's circulation has since topped 700,000, up from 180,000, and ad pages have jumped above 2,000 from 800. Four years later, Advance gobbled up *Gourmet,* and ad pages went up there too.

Newhouse showed his ingenuity again in 1983 when the 80-year-old *House & Garden* underwent a metamorphosis from a home improvement magazine to an architectural magazine that competes with *Architectural Digest*. Ad revenues doubled just between 1983 and 1985.

Newhouse's only flop to date has been his attempt at reviving the high-society magazine *Vanity Fair*. When he acquired *The New Yorker,* pundits said it was a graceful way to distract everyone while Newhouse killed off the expensive loser. But hold on. In its first two years, Advance dumped an estimated $30 million into *Vanity Fair* and went through several editors, but in 1985 ad pages began going up and in 1986 circulation almost doubled from the 1984 level, to 400,000. Newhouse hasn't shown any signs of pulling the plug, and some analysts have said even *Vanity Fair* might become a winner.

"Si's philosophy is get it done," notes one of his employees. "That's what happens."

MINING

THE MARKET

"Without minerals, modern society wouldn't exist," notes Simon D. Strauss, one of the nation's leading mining and metals authorities. Indeed, one only has to glance around and see that derivatives of minerals are used just about everywhere: food and clothing, highways and housing, office complexes and computers. Raw materials production accounts for only 1% of the GNP, but materials derived from minerals make up 9% of the GNP.

Smelters, refiners, and other processors of intermediate goods such as aluminum, cinder blocks, fertilizers, and steel consume minerals directly. Some 90 metals and nonmetallic minerals are produced, including such high-value metals as gold and silver and nonmetallics such as gravel and sand, which are only profitable when produced in vast quantities.

THE MONEY

Mining has been in the doldrums for years. Nonfuel mineral production in 1987 was estimated to be about $25.1 billion, up from the $23.3 billion it had been each year since 1984. Indeed, since 1974, after 30 years of rapid growth, the market has slowed for most minerals and, in a few cases, actually declined. Overproduction in many cases has led to excessive inventory buildup and prices have weakened. On a constant-dollar basis, the value of mineral production has declined annually by about 4.4% since 1979. In current dollars, production value increased in 1978–1979 and peaked in 1981. That was followed by a sharp decline in 1982 and a moderate recovery in 1983–1984. There was greater price volatility in metals than in nonmetals: the value of metals increased 16% in 1987 after dropping 6% in 1985, while the value of nonmetals increased only 2% in 1983 and dropped only 3% in 1984.

U.S. production was little affected by the 1986 runup in prices of precious metals caused by turmoil in South Africa. The value of nonmetallic mineral production, however, has risen every year but three since 1961. One exception was a 14% decline in 1982. In 1985 and 1986, it rose 2% and 4%, respectively.

THE PLAYERS

Six U.S. companies ranked among the world's 20 largest mining companies in 1985: Fluor Corporation, Irvine, California; Aluminum Company of America (Alcoa), Pittsburgh, Pennsylvania; Kaiser Aluminum and Chemical Corporation, Oakland, California; Rosario Resources Corporation, Greenwich, Connecticut; AMAX, Inc., Greenwich, Connecticut; and ASARCO, Inc., Jersey City, N.J.

THE PEOPLE

Employment declined in the 1980s, reflecting increased automation. Nonmetallic mining employment was 106,800 in 1987, down 1.6 percent from 1986. Production workers numbered 81,500, down 1.5% for the period. Metals employment, however, increased 2.9% in 1987 to 42,300 while the number of production workers rose 4.6% to 31,900. Part of that overall decline was due to mine closings in 1986. Strikes closed three zinc mines, a U.S. Steel strike shut down the biggest iron ore producer, and LTV Corporation's bankruptcy resulted in the forced closing of Reserve Mining, a big iron ore producer 50% owned by LTV.

TRENDS AND FORECAST

U.S. mineral production is expected to grow modestly in 1988 and may exceed $30 billion in 1992. Production, of course, depends upon prices. A significant increase in metals prices would see a production increase, providing the higher demand wasn't met by more economical imports and reduced exports. But any price increase over the next few years is expected to be modest.

THE DIAMOND CARTEL

Why does the diamond market seldom get soft? The answer is the Central Selling Organization, which is an amazing marketing system. CSO is controlled by the prominent South African diamond mining firm DeBeers, which, with its affiliates, accounts for about 50% of the world's gem and industrial diamond production.

Competitive selling would undercut the price of diamonds, wrecking gems' lure as a long-term investment. To make sure that doesn't happen, CSO buys 50% of the diamonds that DeBeers and its affiliates don't produce and thus acts as a cartel.

Even so, recessions occasionally hit diamonds too. The price of a top-quality one-carat flawless polished diamond rose to about $65,000 in 1980 and then plummeted to about $19,000 in 1982. The U.S. Justice Department takes a dim view of the monopolistic CSO practices, but so far the U.S. hasn't been successful with any of the legal proceedings it has brought to bear, since neither CSO nor DeBeers has offices in the U.S.

GOLD

The U.S. surpassed Canada in 1986 to become the world's third-largest gold producer, after South Africa and the Soviet Union, according to the Gold Institute.

The institute's annual report, *World Mine Production of Gold, 1985–1989,* estimates that production by South Africa and the Soviet Union will be 54.5% by 1989, down from 58.4% in 1986 and 66.3% in 1984. Total world production in 1986 was 50.8 million ounces, up from 48.6 million ounces in 1985 and 46.2 million ounces in 1984.

Meanwhile, the U.S. produced about 3.5 million ounces in 1986, up considerably from 2.4 million ounces a year earlier. One reason for the increase: the U.S. Mint sold about 1.8 million ounces of gold for the minting of eagle coins.

TWO BITS

Ever wonder why *two bits* means a quarter? Since there were no American coins in colonial days, Spanish milled dollars or "pieces of eight" were popular coins in circulation. They were often cut into pieces, or "bits," to make change. *Two bits* referred to a quarter's worth of silver.

GOLD COINS

The U.S. stopped issuing gold coins when the nation went off the gold standard in 1933 during the Great Depression. Up to then, the government had issued 75 million eagle pieces ($10), 88 million double eagles ($20), 20 million quarter eagles ($2½), and 19½ million $1 pieces. Also, there were only a few $4 ("Stella") gold pieces minted in 1879 and 1880, and they are the rarest U.S. coins today.

There were also commemorative coins issued to celebrate the Louisiana Purchase Exposition (1903), the Lewis and Clark Expedition (1904–1905), the Panama-Pacific Exposition (1915), the McKinley Memorial (1916–1917), the Grant Memorial (1922), and the Philadelphia Sesquicentennial (1926). Today, a set of the Panama-Pacific coins, consisting of two $50 gold coins, a $2½ gold coin, a $1 gold coin, and a 50-cent silver coin, all in uncirculated condition, is worth about $25,000.

A high-relief double eagle $20 gold piece designed by Augustus Saint-Gaudens and dated 1907 was considered the most beautiful gold coin ever made. President Theodore Roosevelt approved the design because he wanted U.S. coins to be art objects, but only 20 of the coins were struck because pragmatic bankers were afraid they wouldn't stack neatly. One of these coins sold in 1975 for $225,000—a world record for a single coin.

INDUSTRIAL DIAMONDS

Until the middle of the 19th century, diamonds weren't much good for anything but admiring, lusting after, hoarding, and putting in jewelry. Unsuitable diamonds were thrown away.

Then in 1862, the not-so-hot diamonds became industrial diamonds when the first diamond drill was built to bore into rock cores. Today, diamonds are used as grit in cutting and polishing, in glass cutters, in saw blades for cutting stone, and in dies for high-speed drawing of fine wire.

In 1955, General Electric produced synthetic diamonds that became fierce rivals of natural diamonds. Today, synthetics account for about 80% of all industrial diamonds by weight.

THE ONLY DIAMOND MINE IN THE U.S.

Apparently, the only active diamond mine in the U.S. is located near Murfreesboro, Arkansas. It is a tourist attraction.

BIRTHSTONES

Month	Stone
January	Garnet
February	Amethyst
March	Aquamarine or bloodstone
April	Diamond
May	Emerald
June	Pearl or alexandrite
July	Ruby or star ruby
August	Peridot or sardonyx
September	Sapphire or star sapphire
October	Opal or tourmaline
November	Topaz
December	Turquoise or zircon

GOLD DISCOVERED

Gold was discovered in California on January 24, 1848, by James W. Marshall at Sutter's Mill, starting the famed Gold Rush. By 1849, 80,000 prospectors had moved there. The Alaskan Gold Rush of 1898 brought more than 30,000 people to the territory.

Cecil Rhodes   In 1870, when he was 17 years old, Cecil John Rhodes, the British imperialist and diamond magnate, went to Africa from England to join his brother Herbert on a cotton plantation. The next year, the brothers staked a claim in the newly opened Kimberley diamond fields, where Cecil was to make most of his fortune.

He returned to England in 1873 to attend Oxford, but Africa was in his blood, and his repeated trips there delayed his taking a degree until 1881. One of those trips inspired him to dream of British domination of Africa, "from the Cape to Cairo," as he spoke of it.

Meanwhile, his power within the diamond industry grew ever greater and, in 1880, he started the DeBeers Mining Company, which at the time was the second-largest diamond producer. The next year, the year he received his Oxford degree, he entered the Parliament of Cape Colony, a seat he was to hold until his death in 1902.

Largely at his instigation, Great Britain, in 1885, established a protectorate over Bechuanaland. Three years later, the conniving Rhodes had the Matabele ruler give him mining concessions in Matabeleland and Mashonaland. Through the British South Africa Company, he soon established complete control over the region. He also established a monopoly of Kimberley diamond production by the creation of DeBeers Consolidated Mines.

In 1890, Rhodes became prime minister and actually attempted to become a dictator. He limited African voting by disenfranchising illiterate people. He also became involved in an aborted plot to overthrow the government and he was forced to resign as prime minister in 1896. The following year, the British House of Commons found him guilty of grave breaches of duty as prime minister and administrator of the British South Africa Company.

After that, he spent his time primarily developing the country that was named Rhodesia in his honor. When he died, he left most of his huge fortune to public service, including the establishment of Rhodes scholarships at Oxford for students from British colonies, the U.S., and Germany.

Table 184   Mining

Foreign producers supply many of the most important minerals needed by U.S. industry.

Mineral	Percentage imported 1986	Major sources	Uses
Columbium	100	Brazil, Canada, Thailand, Nigeria	Steel making, aerospace
Graphite	100	Mexico, China, Brazil, Malagasy Republic	Metallurgical processes
Manganese	100	South Africa, France, Brazil, Gabon	Steel making
Mica (sheet)	100	India, Belgium, France, Japan	Electronic and electrical equipment
Strontium	100	Mexico, Spain	TV picture tubes, pyrotechnics
Platinum group	98	South Africa, U.K., U.S.S.R.	Catalytic converters for autos
Bauxite and alumina	97	Australia, Guinea, Jamaica, Suriname	Aluminum
Cobalt	92	Zaire, Zambia, Canada, Norway	Aerospace alloys
Diamonds (industrial)	92	South Africa, U.K., Belgium, Ireland	Machinery for grinding and cutting
Tantalum	91	Thailand, Brazil, Australia, Malaysia	Electronic components
Fluorspar	88	Mexico, South Africa, China, Italy	Metallurgical and chemical industries
Chromium	82	South Africa, Zimbabwe, Turkey, Yugoslavia	Stainless steel
Nickel	78	Canada, Australia, Norway, Botswana	Stainless steel and other alloys
Potash	78	Canada, Israel, East Germany, U.S.S.R.	Fertilizer
Tin	77	Thailand, Brazil, Indonesia, Bolivia	Cans, electrical construction
Zinc	74	Canada, Mexico, Peru, Australia	Construction and transportation materials
Cadmium	69	Canada, Australia, Mexico, West Germany	Plating and coating of metals
Silver	69	Canada, Mexico, U.K., Peru	Photography, electrical components
Barite	66	China, Morocco, India, Chile	Oil drilling fluids

Source: Bureau of Mines.

MOTORCYCLES

THE MARKET

Motorcycles, once a mode of transportation associated with Hell's Angels and California state troopers, are now a big and quite respectable business. More than 7.7 million motorcycles, scooters, and ATVs (all-terrain vehicles) are in use in America, according to the Motorcycle Industry Council. About 6 million Americans own motorcycles, another 38.9 million people ride them, and motorcycles are ridden about 15.57 billion miles a year.

THE MONEY

The industry generated an estimated $7.2 billion in consumer sales, service, and state taxes and licensing in the U.S. in 1985, according to the Motorcycle Industry Council. About $2.79 billion of that total, 38.7%, came from retail sales of new motorcycles, scooters, and ATVs. Those retail sales were down from 1984, when $2.83 billion worth of motorcycles were sold, but up from 1981 ($2.16 billion) and 1970 ($1.03 billion).

THE PLAYERS

Over the past few decades, imports have captured most of the U.S. market in motorcycles. The four leading imports, Honda (58.5% of all new motorcycle sales), Yamaha (15.7%), Kawasaki (10.4%), and Suzuki (10.0%), hold 94.6% of the market. Harley-Davidson, the fifth-largest manufacturer with a 4.1% share of the market, is the only large U.S. producer remaining. There are some 12,845 retail outlets selling motorcycles and related products.

THE PEOPLE

With most motorcycles produced overseas, few Americans are employed in the manufacture of this product. Retail outlets employ 62,555 people with an estimated payroll of $777 million.

THE FORECAST

The boom the industry saw in the 1960s and 1970s is over, and sales slumped 13% in the first half of 1987. An agreement by several major Japanese producers to stop production of all terrain vehicles because of safety concerns will further hurt the industry. A number of dealers are expected to go out of business or diversify into new areas of business. Harley-Davidson, America's only major producer, was once on the verge of bankruptcy, but it has made major progress in cutting costs, improving quality, and attracting new customers. The company is profitable and growing. Still, foreign producers such as Honda will continue to expand their market shares and there is little chance that Harley or any other American producer will regain a major share of the U.S. motorcycle market.

HONDA MOTORCYCLES

It took a Japanese to make motorcycles socially acceptable in America. Until the 1960s, the popular image of a guy on a motorcycle was a thug who was out to terrorize nice little towns. (We didn't know Malcolm Forbes was a motorcyclist then.) Aware of the problem, Soichiro Honda, head of Honda Motor Company, softened up Americans with a clever ad campaign when he introduced his motorcycles to the U.S. market in 1962. The national ad campaign, designed by Grey Advertising of Los Angeles, centered on the slogan, "You Meet the Nicest People on a Honda." The models in the ads looked more like Pat Boone than Hell's Angels. Within six years, the company sold a million motorcycles in the U.S. By the early 1970s, the company had run most U.S. competitors off the road, capturing almost half of the U.S. market. (And in 1975, Honda introduced its first family car, the Civic, and has been a major thorn in U.S. car makers' sides ever since.)

MOVIES, VIDEOCASSETTES, AND MOVIE THEATERS

THE MARKET

Nearly 120 million Americans go to the movies each year: 37% see a movie at least once a month, 47% see at least one movie every 1 to 6 months; and 16% see at least one movie every 6 to 12 months, according to the Motion Picture Association of America. The average American attends the movies about 4.7 times a year.

With competition from TV, cable, and VCRs, ticket sales are down in movie theaters around the country. Only 1.083 billion tickets to movie theaters were sold in 1987, up from 1.056 billion in 1985 but well below the high of 1.2 billion in 1984. Worse, current ticket sales are about the same as in 1960, when the population was much smaller.

But if the movie business isn't boffo at the box office, it's booming at home. The number of videocassettes rented grew from only 108 million in 1981 to 1.2 billion rentals in 1985, according to Paul Kagan Associates. The number of prerecorded videocassettes sold to stores for rental or sales to customers should hit 130 million in 1988, up from 75 million in 1986 and up from only 53 million in 1985, according to the Electronic Industries Association.

Increased demand for more movies on cable and video led to a record number of new movies in 1987. Film makers started 578 motion pictures in 1987 and distributed 511 films, way up from the 174 to 250 films that were started each year between 1973 and 1983. Hollywood studios started 155 pictures in 1987, while independents set the cameras rolling on 423 films.

THE MONEY

Americans and Canadians spent about $4.25 billion on movie tickets in 1987, with theatergoers paying an average of $3.92 a ticket. Motion picture theaters earn over $1 billion from popcorn and soda sales at the concession stands, which produce as much as 75 cents worth of profit for every ticket sold. Incidentally, theaters get about 60% of the box-office receipts, with the rest of the money going to the studios, producers, and distributors.

Once upon a time, movie makers made their money by renting films to movie theater owners. But VCRs and cable TV are changing all that. Between 1980 and 1986 about 85% of the new revenues were produced by pay TV and home video. Purchases of movies by pay TV operators such as HBO skyrocketed from $150 million in 1980 to $550 million in 1987 while sales of videocassettes grew to $2.8 billion, surpassing the money movie studios made by renting their films to motion picture theaters.

As a result, Hollywood and independent film makers find themselves increasingly dependent on home video and new sources of revenue. In 1980 the movie industry received 76% of its revenues from renting films to movie theaters. Only 5% of its revenues came from pay TV and a paltry 1% came from videocassettes. But by 1987, 39% of its revenues came from cassettes an 8% came from pay TV. Rentals to theaters produced only 42%, with the rest coming from TV networks and TV syndication (7%) and miscellaneous other sources (4%).

Filmmakers get no money from the rental of videocassettes, but sales of videocassettes are an important source of income. (See below for VCR sales.) Without revenues from selling movies on videocassettes, some studios would have lost money in recent years.

The videocassette market is likely to get more important in the future, with video sales and rentals topping $7.5 billion in 1987. In 1987, Hollywood shipped 110 million prerecorded videocassettes worth $2.8 billion at wholesale in 1987, according to the Electronic Industries Association. That surpassed the amount moviemakers earned delivering films to theaters. The EIA estimates that 130 million prerecorded videocassettes worth $2.99 billion will be sold in 1988.

But the most popular way of seeing a movie on the VCR is rental. There are over 20,000 outlets that rent video cassettes. Paul Kagan Associates estimates that the number of tapes rented grew from 108 million to $1.2 billion in 1985 while the dollar value of video rentals grew from $351 million to $2.9 billion. Video Marketing estimates that rentals hit $4.7 billion in 1987, up 16% from 1986. It estimates that the $7.5 billion earned by rentals and sales produced $3 billion in revenues for Hollywood studios and other suppliers of videos. The number of households with VCRs hit 52% in January of 1988 and should reach 60% by the end of 1988.

About 7.5 million "adult" or pornographic videocassettes were sold in 1986, according to *Adult Video News*. Sales topped $300 million.

Foreign film markets are also an important source of revenue, with producers earning 40 to 50 cents of every dollar from renting films to foreign theaters. Without those overseas markets or income from auxiliary sources such as videocassettes, only 2 out of every 10 films would break even. For example, *Police Academy 4* made only $14 million in domestic rentals to theaters, just enough money to cover the $14 million the film cost. But it produced $51.8 million in overseas revenues, bringing Warner Brothers a handsome profit. Even so, 6 out of 10 films lose money.

THE PLAYERS

Even though it costs American producers millions to produce the average film, 578 pictures went into production and 511 were released in the U.S. in 1987, the highest total in a decade. These films are shown on 20,612 screens (2,148 of which are drive-ins) in the U.S. and Canada. About 10% of those films released each year will produce 45% of all box-office revenues. Each of the four largest movie theater chains—United Artists Theater Circuit, Cineplex Odeon, American Multi-Cinema and General Cinema—has over 1,000 screens in North America. While the number of drive-ins fell 23.3% in the early 1980s, the number of indoor screens, spurred by a trend toward multiplexes, increased 22% between 1980 and 1985.

Despite all that's been said about the rise of independent film production, the major studios still capture most of the market. Table 185 (below)

Table 185   Shares of the Film Exhibition Market, 1970 to 1986

Year	Columbia	Twentieth Century Fox	MGM/UA	Paramount	Universal	Warner Bros..	Disney	Orion	Tri-Star
1970	14%	19%	9%	12%	12%	5%	9%	3%	—
1975	13	14	11	11	25	9	6	5	—
1980	14	16	7	16	20	14	4	2	—
1981	13	13	9	15	14	18	3	1	—
1982	10	14	11	14	30	10	4	3	—
1983	14	21	10	14	13	17	3	4	—
1984	16	10	7	21	8	19	4	5	5%
1985	10	11	9	10	16	18	3	5	10
1986	9	8	4	22	9	12	10	7	7
1987	4	9	4	20	8	13	14	10	5

Source: *Variety*, January 14, 1987.

lists the top film studios and what shares they have held of the film exhibition market.

Like the rest of the media and entertainment business, the movies have continued a trend toward increased concentration. Gulf + Western and Coca-Cola were corporate pioneers in the film industry, buying major studios. (See the box "Media Concentration," below.)

The major studios are also under increased pressure from TV networks to reduce production costs for TV shows and movies. Already, some studios use fewer action shots, since it costs money to blow up buildings and cars or stage expensive chase scenes.

Recently, major film studios or their parent companies have been buying up theaters. MCA, Cannon, Gulf + Western, and Tri-Star have all bought shares in theater chains. These purchases broke down the long-standing legal barrier between movie producers and theater owners that had been established to increase competition. But the Justice Department hasn't complained and the studios may ask the courts to rescind consent decrees from the late 1940s that barred them from theater ownership.

Owning theaters should be good for revenues. Major studios are assured showcases for films, particularly weaker movies that might not get shown by independent theaters. At the same time, the move toward major studios owning theaters could hurt smaller producers and make it harder for them to get their films into the marketplace.

Still, independent producers remain an important part of the market. In 1986, for example, two independently produced films, *Platoon* and *A Room with a View,* each got eight nominations for Oscars and earned huge profits. *Platoon,* which cost $6 million, grossed $69 million.

Around the world, American filmmakers still control the market. American films are distributed in more than 100 countries and American television films and programs are shown in more than 90 international markets. That fact allows the film industry to make a $1.2 billion positive contribution to the U.S. balance of payments each year.

The last several years have been good ones for Hollywood, as the home video, cable and other markets demanded more movies and programming. But the days of wine and roses are coming to an end. A wave of layoffs swept the Hollywood TV production community in the wake of the October 1987 crash, leaving 1,000 people without a job, and the home video market is slowing down after years of spectacular growth. Sales of pre-recorded videocassettes are projected to grow just 8% in 1988 and are not expected to return to double digit growth in the near future. At the same time, the stocks of movie makers who went public in 1986 and 1987 have taken a beating. Steep fourth quarter losses in 1987 by such studios as MGM/UA, Cannon and New World Pictures also point to tougher financial times. That will produce a real western style shootout, with weaker production companies falling by the wayside.

THE PEOPLE

About 101,000 people are employed in movie theaters, down from 114,800 in 1982 and 126,700 in 1972.

Table 186 Box-Office Revenues

Year	Box-office revenues (millions of dollars)	Theater employment
1972	1,583	126,700
1975	2,115	131,200
1980	2,749	123,900
1981	2,960	122,000
1982	3,445	114,800
1983	3,697	109,500
1984	4,030	108,100
1985	3,749	107,800
1986	3,833	106,000
1987	4,250	103,800

Source: *Variety*.

Paramount When Frank Mancuso took over as head of Paramount, the timing was hardly auspicious.

The previous chairman, Barry Diller, left in 1984 after clashing with Martin Davis, chairman and CEO of the parent corporation, Gulf + Western; he headed up Marvin Davis's Twentieth Century Fox Film Corporation. A short while later, Paramount president Michael Eisner left to head The Walt Disney Company.

When Mancuso was plucked from Paramount's marketing division to run the studio, people weren't sure whether to congratulate him or offer their condolences. For one, Mancuso didn't have any direct production experience. For another, the Diller-Eisner team had chalked up some of Tinsel Town's biggest movie hits, such as *Raiders of the Lost Ark*, *Star Trek II*, and *Beverly Hills Cop*. They'd done more than OK with Paramount TV productions too: *Family Ties* and *Cheers* for starters. Moreover, the inventory they left behind contained a lot of junk, including the unmemorable *Explorers* and *King David*.

For a while, it looked as if things would never get better. In a scramble to acquire movies, Mancuso's Paramount acquired bombs such as *Silver Bullet* and *D.A.R.Y.L.* Two Christmas releases, *Young Sherlock Holmes* and *Clue*, never met expectations. By the end of 1984, it looked like the end of Paramount. In 1985, Paramount had anemic U.S. box-office receipts.

But if anything, Mancuso proved steadfast. He had joined Paramount in 1962 as a distribution man in Buffalo. After a brief assignment to L.A., he spent the rest of his career in marketing in New York. Back on the West Coast, he began putting his marketing sophistication to work. One example was *Top Gun,* one of the hottest movies of the 1980s. At a cost of $17.5 million, *Top Gun* grossed some $400 million.

The script for *Top Gun* came in under Mancuso's predecessors, who weren't keen on it, and it looked as if it would go nowhere. But a copy was slipped to Mancuso, who not only liked it but became an advocate for it. When the movie was made, he built up word-of-mouth enthusiasm by holding sneak previews across the country. He also oversaw a clever TV ad campaign for the film.

While proving himself a forceful advocate, Mancuso also surprised movieland by what he did with the film *The Two Jakes,* a sequel to *Chinatown.* In theory, the film was a hot property; in reality it was a mess. Producer Robert Evans and writer-director Robert Towne didn't appear to agree on anything. Paramount had sunk some $2 million into the venture when Mancuso thought better of it. Stepping out of his collegial, negotiating management style, he pulled the plug. Even though Evans fought hard to have the film reinstated, Mancuso held his ground.

Under the new regime, Paramount also brought John Hughes, writer-producer of *The Breakfast Club,* from Universal; Hughes has since made such money-makers as *Pretty in Pink* and *Ferris Bueller's Day Off.* The studio also struck a new, long-term agreement that keeps superstar Eddie Murphy and his production company at Paramount. Also, the producer of the top-rated TV show *Family Ties,* Gary David Goldberg, renewed his contract with Paramount. One lesson Mancuso's marketing background obviously taught him was to go with winners, and it is still paying off with such blockbusters as *Crocodile Dundee* and *The Untouchables.*

Table 187 Videocassette Rentals

Year	Units rented (in millions)	Average price (dollars per unit)	Total rentals (millions of dollars)
1981	108.0	3.25	351.0
1982	199.5	3.00	598.5
1983	378.0	2.80	1,058.4
1984	705.6	2.60	1,834.6
1985	1,237.7	2.35	2,908.5

Sources: Paul Kagan Associates, Inc.; *The VCR Letter,* May 30, 1987.

Table 188   Tape Rentals by Program Type

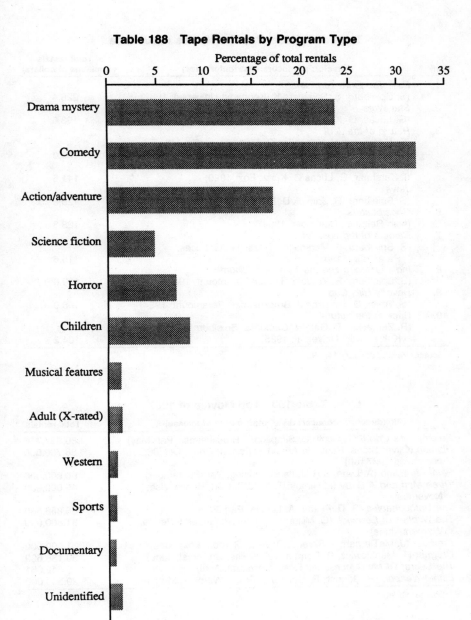

Percentage of total rentals

Source: A. C. Nielsen Company.

Table 189 Most Popular Movies of All Time

Rank	Title (Director; producers; distributor; year)	Total rentals (millions of dollars)
1.	E. T. The Extra-Terrestrial (S. Spielberg; S. Spielberg/K. Kennedy; Universal; 1982)	228.4
2.	Star Wars (G. Lucas, G. Kurtz; Fox; 1977)	193.5
3.	Return of the Jedi (R. Marquand; H. Kazanjian/G. Lucas/Lucasfilm Ltd.; Fox; 1983)	168.0
4.	The Empire Strikes Back (I. Kershner; G. Lucas/G. Kurtz; Fox; 1980)	141.6
5.	Jaws (S. Spielberg; R. Zanuck/D. Brown; Universal; 1975)	129.5
6.	Ghostbusters (Ivan Reitman; Columbia; 1984)	128.3
7.	Raiders of the Lost Ark (S. Spielberg; F. Marshall/H. Kazanjian/G. Lucas; Paramount; 1981)	115.6
8.	Indiana Jones and the Temple of Doom (S. Spielberg; R. Watts/G. Lucas; Paramount; 1984)	109.0
9.	Beverly Hills Cop (M. Brest; D. Simpson/J. Bruckheimer; Paramount; 1984)	108.0
10.	Back to the Future (R. Zemeckis; B. Gale/N. Canton/S. Spielberg/F. Marshall/ K. Kennedy; Universal; 1985)	104.2

Source: *Variety*, January 14, 1987.

Table 190 Top Movies of 1987

Title (director; producer; distributor; month of release)	Total rentals
Beverly Hills Cop II (T. Scott; D. Simpson/J. Bruckheimer; Par; May)	$80,857,776
Platoon (Oliver Stone; Hemdale Arnold Kopelson; Orion; Oct '86, continuing 1987 run)	66,700,000
Fatal Attraction (A. Lyne; S.R. Jaffe/S. Lansing; Par; September)	60,000,000
Three Men and A Baby (L. Nimoy; T. Field/R. Cort; Buena Visa; November)	45,000,000
The Untouchables (B. DePalma; A. Linson; Par; June)	36,866,530
The Witches of Eastwick (G. Miller; N. Canton/P. Guber/J. Peters; Warners; June)	31,800,000
Predator (J. McTiernan; J. Silver/J. Davis/L. Gordon; Fox; June)	31,000,000
Dragnet (T. Mankiewicz; D. Permut/R.K. Weiss; Universal; June)	30,138,699
The Secret Of My Success (H. Ross; Universal; April)	29,542,081
Lethal Weapon (R. Donner; R. Donner/J. Silver; Warners; March)	29,500,000

Source: *Variety*.

Table 191   Largest Theater Circuits

Rank	Company Headquarters	Screens	Locations	Number of drive-in screens
1.	United Artists Theater Circuit East Meadow, New York	2,048	485	38
2.	Cineplex Odeon Toronto	1,664	492	48
3.	American Multi-Cinema Kansas City	1,528	277	8
4.	General Cinema Chestnut Hill, Massachusetts	1,358	332	0
5.	Carmike Columbus, Georgia	669	220	0

Source: *Variety*, January 20, 1988.

Hollywood's Most Successful Director   After directing or producing 5 of the 10 most popular movies ever made, Steven Spielberg is Hollywood's most successful filmmaker. He has directed or produced 21 hits that have grossed over $1 billion, including *Jaws* and one of the world's most popular movies ever, *E. T.*, which has taken in $228.4 million at the box office.

Critics often turn up their noses at Spielberg's sugarcoated films, damning his reliance on special effects and cute but harmless characters. His success, however, has turned Spielberg into a one-man conglomerate. His entrepreneurial talents first came to light as a child in Arizona where he charged other kids 35 cents to see rented movies and his own eight-millimeter movies. Now he runs his own production company, Amblin Entertainment, and is involved in dozens of film projects, television programs, and licensing deals. With his name nearly as well known as Walt Disney's, Spielberg is the closest thing in Hollywood to an old-time movie mogul. He is so powerful that studios usually pick up the costs of his film projects, making most of his productions and Amblin risk-free operations. The company's facilities, located near Universal Studios, were even paid for by Universal, which has first rights to Spielberg's movies.

With his track record, four major studios have asked him to head up their operations. But for now, Spielberg likes things the way they are. One recent production, *An American Tail,* cost $8 million and grossed $41.4 million between November of 1986 and February of 1987.

NEWSPAPERS

THE MARKET

Besides having an important political and social role by conveying news about domestic and international issues, newspapers constitute one of the largest advertising markets in the U.S. About 63 million daily newspapers are circulated in the U.S. each day and more than 108 million American adults read a daily paper at least once a week. Weekly papers reach another 50 million people.

THE MONEY

Newspapers continue to lead all other media in advertising volume. Advertising revenues hit $29.2 billion in 1987. That was $5 billion more dollars than was spent on their nearest competitor, television. Ads account for 80% of all newspaper revenues.

THE PLAYERS

There are 1,657 daily newspapers in the U.S., which reach about 62.5 million people. Sunday newspapers now number 809, reaching 61.5 million people, and weekly newspapers total 7,600, reaching 47.6 million people.

Control of the news continues to be held in a very small number of hands. The top 25 companies own 565 newspapers reaching 37.9 million people every day, or about 58.6% of all the people who read newspapers. Only 156 companies own more than one newspaper but these chains own 1,186 newspapers, about 71% of all daily newspapers, and control 77% of daily newspaper circulation.

THE PEOPLE

There were about 420,000 people employed in the newspaper industry in 1987, up from 419,900 in 1980 and 248,500 in 1947.

TRENDS AND FORECAST

Total newspaper circulation grew rapidly between 1904 and 1954, from 50.5 million to 136.4 million. But faced with increasing competition from television and other media, daily newspaper circulation stagnated and has remained virtually constant since 1970. (See also Table 100, the chart on advertising revenues by medium, in the section "Advertising" for the growth of newspaper ad revenues.)

Table 192   Newspapers in the U.S.

	Daily Newspapers					
	Morning and Evening		Sunday		Weekly Newspapers	
Year	Number	Circulation (thousands)	Number	Circulation (thousands)	Number	Circulation (thousands)
1946	1,763	50,927	497	43,665	NA	NA
1960	1,763	58,882	563	47,699	8,174	20,974
1970	1,748	62,108	586	49,216	7,612	27,857
1980	1,745	62,201	735	54,672	7,954	42,348
1985	1,674	62,723	797	58,817	7,704	48,988
1986	1,657	62,489	809	61,515	7,711	50,098
1987	NA	NA	NA	NA	7,600	47,593

(NA) Not available.
Source: American Newspaper Publishers Association, *Facts About Newspapers: 1987. Editor & Publisher.*

Stagnant circulation and increased competition from TV produced an industry-wide shakeout in the 1960s and 1970s. In many cities, many papers closed or merged with other papers, often leaving one paper, such as *The Washington Post,* holding a near-monopoly over the newspaper market of a major city. Even the survivors struggled to attract new readers with special lifestyle or suburban sections. To reduce costs, publishers went on the offensive with unions, demanding changes in work rules and less expensive union contracts while spending millions to install electronic printing and production technology. Capital expenditures rose to $1 billion for the first time ever in 1985, from $805 million in 1982, according to *Presstime.* That dramatically lowered labor costs from 37% of total expenditures in 1975 to only 30% by 1983.

But after decades of struggle, lowered costs and rising advertising expenditures have made newspapers increasingly profitable—a fact that outside investors soon noticed. The value of newspaper properties has skyrocketed in recent years. Newspaper chains continue to buy more newspapers and the number of papers owned by chains increased by 17% in 1985 alone. Lured by record prices for newspapers and media properties, several independent newspaper families sold their holdings.

By 1987, a slowdown in advertising revenues lowered the value of many media properties, especially independent TV stations. But high-tech production, cost cutting, and innovative marketing during the last decade have put newspapers in a better position to weather the slowdown in ad revenues than many of the free-spending media companies, such as CBS, which are struggling to adapt to a new age of austerity. Though the industry continues to face strong competition from television, cable, and other media, profit margins are remaining high.

Table 193 The 20 Largest Newspaper Companies*

Rank	Company	Circulation (in thousands)	Number of dailies
1.	Gannett	5,827	92
2.	Knight-Ridder	3,831	33
3.	Newhouse Newspapers	3,034	27
4.	Times Mirror	2,714	9
5.	Tribune	2,641	9
6.	Dow Jones	2,514	23
7.	New York Times	1,744	26
8.	Scripps-Howard	1,640	23
9.	Hearst Newspapers	1,582	15
10.	Thomson Newspapers	1,539	99
11.	News America Publishing	1,257	3
12.	Cox Enterprises	1,250	20
13.	Capital Cities/ABC	937	9
14.	Freedom Newspapers	923	30
15.	Ingersoll Newspapers	869	34
16.	Washington Post	803	2
17.	Central Newspapers	295	7
18.	Chronicle Publishing	755	7
19.	Donrey Media Group	751	57
20.	Copley Newspapers	745	12
	Total:	37,885	565

Source: Facts About Newspapers 1987. Morton Research, Lynch, Jones & Ryan; Audit Bureau of Circulation.
*Average for six months ended Sept. 30, 1986.

Table 194 10 Largest Daily Newspapers

Rank	Newspaper	Circulation in thousands of copies as of September 30, 1987
1.	The Wall Street Journal	1,962
2.	New York Daily News	1,615
3.	USA Today	1,324
4.	Los Angeles Times	1,113
5.	The New York Times	1,023
6.	Chicago Tribune	765
7.	The Washington Post	716
8.	New York Post	690
9.	The Detroit News	686
10.	Detroit Free Press	649

Source: Audit Bureau of Circulation.

The Washington Post Company
CEO: Katharine Graham   1150 15th Street, N.W.
Employees: NA   Washington, D.C. 20071
Assets: NA   202-334-6600

	1987	1986	1985	1980
Revenues (millions of dollars):	1,315	1,200	1,079	660
Net income (millions of dollars):	186	100	114	34
Share earnings (dollars):	14.52	7.80	8.66	2.44

What it does: Publisher of *The Washington Post* and *Newsweek* magazine. Operates television stations and is a major cable TV operator.

In the late 1960s and 1970s *The Washington Post* was alternately lambasted and heralded for its hard-hitting coverage of the Vietnam War, U.S. foreign policy, and of course the Watergate scandal. But controversy is nothing new at *The Washington Post*. Founded in 1877, it prospered as a sensationalist daily but declined in the 1920s. Copper magnate and financier Eugene Meyer purchased the paper in 1933 and began its rehabilitation by improving editorial quality. When Meyer became president of the World Bank in 1946, he handed the paper over to his daughter, Katharine, and her husband, Philip Graham.

During the next 15 years, Philip built up the paper and the family's media holdings, acquiring *Newsweek* and television stations. He also used the paper to become a well-known liberal Washington insider, pushing the political career of Lyndon Johnson and acting as a close political confidant of the Kennedys. After his suicide in 1963 many people wrongfully thought his shy and retiring wife, Katharine, would be unable to manage the paper. As publisher of the *Post,* she hired the Washington bureau chief of *Newsweek,* Ben Bradlee, as editor, kept the paper well managed, and continued to expand the family's media holdings. Bradlee, for his part, expanded the paper's coverage, introduced more critical reporting of the Washington scene, and gained a national reputation.

Since breaking the Watergate story, the *Post* has battled *The New York Times* for the title of the nation's best, or at least most influential, newspaper. The *Post* is now the nation's 8th-largest daily and The Washington Post Company is the 16th-largest newspaper company in the U.S.

Since 1979, Katharine Graham's son, Donald E. Graham, has served as publisher. Under Donald's management, the paper has emphasized local news and become more sedate, a fact that itself has produced a controversy over whether the paper is as hard-hitting as it should be.

The company, which also owns *Newsweek,* four TV stations, and a cable network, saw profits drop 12% in 1986 to $100 million on revenues of $1.2 billion, largely because of financial problems at *Newsweek*. In 1987, profits rose to $186 million, through the sale of assets. But with the *Post* enjoying a virtual monopoly in Washington, D.C.—reaching

76% of the households in the nation's capital—the paper can easily finance an ever-expanding Graham media empire. Katharine Graham controls a majority of the voting stock and the Graham family holdings were worth $662 million in the summer of 1987.

News Ltd.

CEO: K. Rupert Murdoch
Employees: NA
Assets: NA

2 Holt Street
Sydney, Australia 2010
011-612-288-3000

	1986	1985	1984	1980
Revenues (millions of dollars):	NA	1,640	1,610	NA
Net income (millions of dollars):		64	83	
Share earnings (dollars):	.62	.48	.61	

What it does: This Australian company with major operations in the U.S. and the United Kingdom primarily produces newspapers, magazines, theatrical films, and TV programming.

Rupert Murdoch has undoubtedly replaced William Randolph Hearst as the media mogul everyone loves to hate. Liberals fume at his habit of injecting a right-wing slant in the editorials and news of his papers. Wall Street wonders about his habit of borrowing every cent he can get his hands on. And, with banner headlines, innuendo, and half-naked girls, he has singlehandedly revived the fine art of yellow journalism. No one, right, left, or center, has ever accused him of good taste.

But, as with Hearst, no one can deny the size or power of his ever-growing media empire. Murdoch owns 49% of his Australian News Ltd., giving him control of Twentieth Century Fox Film Corporation; Fox Broadcasting Company (which owns 6 television stations and reaches 22% of U.S. television homes); one of Australia's most popular commercial networks, the 41-station 10 Network; the Sky Channel, an English-language television program service seen by 5 million households in 14 Western European countries; 21 U.S. trade and consumer magazines, including *New York* magazine; about 30% of the newspaper circulation in Britain; 4 daily newspapers, and 8 weeklies that reach 1.95 million readers every day; the book publisher, Harper & Row; and, of course, his Australian newspaper empire of 8 dailies and 26 nondailies that reaches 1.14 million readers a day, including *The Sunday Mail,* his first paper. That list doesn't include his airline, oil, or real estate holdings. Overall, the Murdoch empire reaches one quarter of all English-speaking people in the world.

Murdoch has set his sights on ever bigger fish. In 1985, Murdoch announced plans to start a fourth television network, the Fox Broadcasting Company. The idea was hardly new. Over the years, several other billionaires and media powers, such as former Metromedia owner John W. Kluge and Gulf + Western, have dreamed of capturing a share of the lucrative network TV market. But so far, the idea of a fourth network has remained the business equivalent of the Holy Grail—a romantic dream promising great riches and offering almost certain failure.

Murdoch's planning for a fourth network began, when he bought half of Twentieth Century Fox from Marvin Davis and six Metromedia stations from John Kluge, who had dreamed of starting a fourth network for nearly 20 years. That $2.6 billion investment created the Fox Broadcasting Company, which overnight could reach 22% of all households. Building from that base, Murdoch planned to offer some original programming, such as *The Late Show Starring Joan Rivers*. But, as in most of his operations, he planned a cut-rate network and kept costs low by avoiding the temptation to offer complete prime-time programming. Later, as the network produced more revenues, it would add more programming.

Murdoch may have the deep pockets to sustain the $50 million a year in losses it will take to get a fourth network off the ground, but even his huge media empire may not be able to succeed where others have failed. First, the huge debts he's piled up in recent years could unhinge his dreams. Most of his cash flow comes from Britain; a drop in the pound or a recession in ad revenues could make it impossible for him to generate enough cash flow to finance the $2.6 billion in debt his new network cost. His attempt to program Joan Rivers opposite Johnny Carson on late-night television was a bomb. Though he's right that there is a market for programming for independent stations and cable operators, he will have to come up with shows people want to watch—always the bugaboo in television.

The Hearsts   The Hearst empire began in silver and ended up in newsprint, where it mined even greater riches.

George Hearst founded the family fortune with gold and silver mines. Though he suffered a few serious financial setbacks, he was remarkably successful in finding new mining properties, including three of the west's most profitable mines, the Ontario Mine of Utah, the Homestake in South Dakota, and the Anaconda in Montana.

Later, to fulfill his political ambitions, he purchased the San Francisco *Examiner* and served in the U.S. Senate. It was his son, William Randolph, however, who created the Hearst media dynasty. William got his first editorial experience running the *Harvard Lampoon*. When he was tossed out of Harvard, he went to work at Joseph Pulitzer's *New York World*. There he learned yellow journalism, which was Pulitzer's specialty, not the kind of investigative or thoughtful efforts that now win Pulitzer Prizes.

The lesson that sex, violence, and sensationalism sell papers was one that Hearst soon applied to his father's *Examiner*. Circulation took off and Hearst rapidly expanded his empire, using a formula that became his trademark—a mixture of crusading journalism, sensationalism, and, at times, outright lies. His papers, for instance, fabricated some of the stories that helped lead to the Spanish-American War and gained a reputation for yellow journalism that has tarnished the Hearst papers ever since.

But it would be wrong to view the Hearst legacy as simply one of sensationalism. Hearst was one of the first publishers to understand the importance of creating a media conglomerate to cut costs and increase circulation. He profited from the fact that new printing and telecommunications technologies made it possible to create mass-market newspapers. And he boosted salaries and editorial spending as a way of increasing circulation. By 1935 he had 90 newspapers, as well as such magazines as *Good Housekeeping, Cosmopolitan,* and *Harper's Bazaar.*

Like his father, Hearst had political ambitions, and his newspaper empire helped him win two terms in the House of Representatives. But he failed in presidential campaigns and after 1917, when he began his love affair with actress Marion Davies, he passed his time spending money. He spent millions buying art and millions more on promoting Davies's acting career, with little success. By the mid-1930s his free-spending ways had brought his empire to the brink of financial ruin and he was forced to give up daily control of his papers. Though the empire survived, many of his papers continued to lose money. By the late 1970s, the Hearst empire only published 10 papers.

Today the family runs a far-flung and highly profitable media conglomerate. It is a powerhouse in book publishing with Arbor House, Avon, William Morrow & Co., and various trade publications. It is the 24th-largest electronic media company, with 6 VHF TV stations, interests in cable networks, 4 AM radio stations, and 3 FM radio stations. It is the 12th-largest newspaper publishing empire, with 15 dailies including the San Francisco *Examiner,* the *Los Angeles Herald Examiner,* and the *Houston Chronicle.* It has 13 magazines including *Cosmopolitan, Good Housekeeping, Popular Mechanics, Town & Country, Redbook, Sports Afield,* and *Esquire,* which it bought for $40 million, just to name a few. A hundred years after William Randolph Hearst took over his father's San Francisco *Examiner* in 1887, the company had somewhere between $2 billion and $3 billion in estimated revenues. (It doesn't put out financial statements.)

In the 1980s, the Hearst empire has been growing at a breathtaking pace. Since 1979, Frank A. Bennack, the company president, has spent $1.5 billion on acquisitions. That growth has helped the family trust grow to an estimated $2 billion.

Yet while the empire is growing, the family is taking a smaller role in its affairs. Although about 15 Hearst family members work at the privately owned company or serve on its board of directors, only one is responsible for line operations—William Randolph Hearst III, the publisher of the San Francisco *Examiner.*

The Times Mirror Company
CEO: Robert F. Erburu
Employees: 30,600
Assets: $2.9 billion

Times Mirror Square
Los Angeles, California 90053
213-972-3700

	1987	1986	1985	1980
Revenues (millions of dollars):	3,154	2,920	2,947	1,857
Net income (millions of dollars):	266	408	237	139
Share earnings (dollars):	2.06	3.16(n)	3.49	2.04

What it does: Major newspaper publisher with cable TV, broadcast TV, book publishing, information services, and magazine holdings. (n) adjusted for stocksplit.

The Chandlers   The crown jewel of the Chandler media empire is the *Los Angeles Times,* the fourth-largest newspaper in the U.S., which produces about 30% of the company's revenues. The Chandler family media empire also includes the nation's eighth-largest cable television business with some 825,000 subscribers, four network television stations, 272,000 acres of timberland, and such popular magazines as *Outdoor Life, Popular Science,* and *Golf.*

Since World War II, heavy spending on editorial has made the *Los Angeles Times* and other Times Mirror newspapers some of the best in the country. But quality and an evenhanded editorial stance are relatively new phenomena. In earlier years, the *Los Angeles Times* had a reputation as an unabashed apologist for California's elite, a paper that hewed to one political line and ignored or ridiculed all others.

General Harrison Gray Otis bought the paper in the 1880s and ran it with Harry Chandler, who married his daughter. They refused to let unions into the paper (only for a brief period in the late 1960s was the *Los Angeles Times* a union paper) and spent decades attacking such ideas as the eight-hour day. In politics, the paper either ridiculed or refused to cover liberal politicians it didn't like, gaining a reputation for censoring ideas of which it disapproved. Its unabashed editorial support for Richard Nixon virtually created his career.

But the idea that a paper's news stories ought to support the publisher's voting habits changed dramatically under the stewardship of Otis Chandler. He took over the paper in 1960, beefed up editorial, and gave its writers new independence.

Over the years, the Chandlers and the current outside managers have followed one consistent strategy: invest for the long haul. Currently the company is pushing hard to enter the New York market with the prize winning Long Island paper, *Newsday.* The paper is losing $10 million a year, but has already dramatically improved circulation. If successful, the expansion could position the company in one of the nation's largest markets. But as in many of its previous expansion plans, the company's heavy spending has crimped profits and hurt the price of its stock.

OIL AND NATURAL GAS

THE MARKET

The U.S. is the largest market for energy products in the world. Even though we have less than 5% of the world's population we use 25% of the energy produced each year.

Nearly two thirds (65%) of the energy we use each year comes from oil and natural gas, down from 77% in 1973. Oil is our most popular energy source (43.1% of the energy consumed). Cheap oil has made petroleum a more attractive energy source and in 1986 energy consumption of oil increased by 3%, the first increase in eight years.

Since 1958 natural gas has been the second most popular source of energy in the U.S. But in 1986, natural gas slipped behind coal to become the third most popular source of energy, with 22.3% of the market, compared to 23.4% for coal. Hydroelectric power supplies 4.7% of our energy needs; nuclear power provides about 6%.

In America, each man, woman, and child consumes 2.8 gallons of oil and more than 181 cubic feet of natural gas a day. Every day the average American uses 1.22 gallons of motor oil.

The U.S. used 31.89 quadrillion Btu of petroleum and 16.53 quadrillion Btu of natural gas in 1986. A quadrillion Btu provides the same energy as 45 million short tons of coal, 60 million short tons of oven-dried hardwood, 170 million barrels of crude oil, and 29 days' worth of petroleum imports and is enough energy to power all the cars in America for 27 days.

Nearly all of our natural gas consumption comes from domestic producers, which supplied 17.2 trillion cubic feet of gas in 1985 and 1986, the equivalent of about 8.4 million barrels of oil a day. However, the U.S. imported about $14.4 million barrels of crude oil a day in 1987, while it produced only 8.3 million barrels a day, the lowest level in 11 years. Proven reserves of crude oil in the U.S. fell from 36.3 billion barrels in 1972 to only 26.9 billion barrels in 1986. Reserves of natural gas fell from 266 trillion cubic feet in 1972 to 191 trillion cubic feet in 1986.

Motorists are the biggest users of oil, buying 7,258,000 gallons of gasoline a day and a total of 8.5 million gallons of motor fuel.

In 1986, overall, transportation used 63.1% of all the petroleum products used in the U.S., 24.6% went to industry, residential and commercial users used about 8.3%, and electric utilities used 4%.

For natural gas, however, the picture is quite different. In 1986, the leading consumer was industry (38.6%), followed by residential users (27.5%), electrical utilities (16.2%), commercial users (14.7%), and transportation (3%).

THE MONEY

All the energy used by American consumers adds up to a lot of dollars. In 1984, the most recent year for which figures are available, the U.S.

spent $437.9 billion on energy, most of which, $224.7 billion, was spent on petroleum products. Another $77.1 billion was spent by consumers on natural gas.

Because of its importance as an energy source, the petroleum industry sends an enormous amount of money cascading through the economy. Revenues can be broken down into various sectors:

U.S. producers shipped only $40.05 billion worth of crude oil in 1986, only about half of the $78.88 billion worth shipped in 1985 and way below the peak of $99.4 billion worth in 1981.

Natural gas also took a dive, to only $31.31 billion worth, down from a peak of $48.49 billion worth in 1984.

About $24.18 billion worth of crude oil and $13.46 billion worth of petroleum products were imported in 1986, a huge drop from the $61.90 billion worth of crude oil and $12.54 billion worth of petroleum products that were imported in 1980.

U.S. petroleum refiners shipped $115.7 billion worth of refined petroleum in 1987, down from $194.1 billion worth in 1982. About $12.7 billion worth of refined petroleum was imported in 1986. Petroleum refiners expect to ship $146.2 billion worth in 1987, according to International Trade Administration estimates.

On a retail level, the 15 major oil companies have nearly 150,000 gas stations; about $86.6 billion was spent at American gas stations in 1986, down from $101.2 billion in 1985.

A dramatic drop in the money oil companies spend on exploration and capital has hurt the oil equipment industry. Shipments of oil machinery dropped to only $1.5 billion worth in 1987, down from $10.1 billion worth in 1981. The International Trade Administration expects a slight recovery for 1988, to $1.6 billion worth.

Gas utilities has some $63.3 billion dollars worth of sales in 1985.

THE PLAYERS

During the oil boom of the early 1980s there were nearly 20,000 independent oil companies. Since then, well over a quarter of them have gone out of business. Not surprisingly, the top oil companies play a major role in U.S. production, with the largest 6 accounting for about one third of U.S. oil production and the largest 20 oil companies controlling about three fifths of all U.S. oil production. (See Table 195, the chart of largest oil and gas companies, below.)

In recent years, foreign oil producers have become less important in the U.S. market. Oil imports dropped from a peak of 46.5% of the market in 1977 to 27.8% in 1985. In 1986, however, cheap foreign oil increased its market share to about one third of all U.S. consumption (32.8%). Though the Organization of Petroleum Exporting Countries (OPEC) controls about two thirds of the world's oil reserves, it has been unable to control world oil prices the way it did in the 1970s. OPEC countries accounted for 72.3% of all U.S. imports and 33.6% of the U.S. consumption of oil in 1977, but a world oil glut cut OPEC's market share to

Table 195   Big Oil

Rank	Company	Fiscal year ended	Net sales (dollars)
1.	Exxon Corporation	December 31, 1986	74,987,000
2.	Mobil Corporation	December 31, 1986	48,706,000
3.	National Intergroup, Inc.	March 31, 1987	45,413,000
4.	Texaco, Inc.	December 31, 1986	31,613,000
5.	E. I. du Pont de Nemours and Company	December 31, 1986	27,148,000
6.	Chevron Corporation	December 31, 1986	26,245,000
7.	Amoco Corporation	December 31, 1986	18,281,000
8.	Shell Oil Company	December 31, 1986	18,222,000
9.	Occidental Petroleum Corporation	December 31, 1986	15,344,143
10.	Atlantic Richfield Company	December 31, 1986	14,993,000

Source: Company reports.

only 42.5% of all net imports and only 11.6% of U.S. consumption in 1985. However, cheap oil, which has driven U.S. producers out of the market, is allowing OPEC to regain some of its market. In 1986 OPEC increased its share of imports to 52.5% and its share of total U.S. consumption to 17.1%.

Oil imports from Arab members of OPEC have also dropped dramatically from 3.1 million barrels a day in 1977 to only 470 million barrels a day in 1985. That drop cut their market share in the U.S. from a peak of 38.2% of all imports and 16% of all U.S. consumption in 1979 to only 11% of all imports and 3% of U.S. consumption in 1985. However, imports from Arab OPEC nations rebounded to 1.14 million barrels a day in 1986 and their market share increased to 21.7% of all imports and 3.7% of U.S. consumption.

THE PEOPLE

About 1.7 million people were employed in the petroleum and natural gas industry in 1986, according to the U.S. Department of Labor.

TRENDS AND FORECAST

In 1986 the bottom fell out of the oil market, with the price dropping below $10 a barrel briefly in April of 1986, less than a third of the November 1985 price of $31. After years of seeing gas do nothing but go up, consumers were overjoyed. Yet not everyone was applauding. Plunging oil prices touched off a national debate over the effects of cheap oil, making it clear that cheap oil is a mixed blessing.

On the plus side, a drop in oil prices cuts inflation, encourages lower interest rates, means big savings for consumers on their gas and heating bills, cuts costs in such industries as chemicals, refining, and airlines, and saves farmers money—at a time when they badly need some help. Lower prices for gas also boost the travel and tourism industries and, at least in the short run, reduce the trade deficit. But cheap oil hurts energy-producing states and makes it harder to promote energy conservation. It cripples U.S. attempts to increase domestic production and increases imports, which make the country more vulnerable to a new oil embargo or troubles in the Persian Gulf. Also hurt are banks that hold billions of dollars in loans to energy companies and oil-producing countries such as Mexico. Lower oil prices will squelch the coal industry's recovery since the price of coal drops whenever the price of oil does. And, in the long run, lower oil prices could hurt the trade deficit since some oil-producing countries will be able to afford fewer American exports.

That the oil and natural gas industry plays such a major role in the health of the economy comes as no surprise to anyone who lived through the oil crisis of the 1970s. Following the first oil embargo, from mid-October 1973 to mid-March 1974, nearly 20,000 gas service stations, about 10% of the total, were shut down. In just one year, a jump in world oil prices cost the U.S. economy about $60 billion in lost production. Rising oil prices also helped fuel the inflationary fires of the 1970s, which eventually forced the Federal Reserve to adopt a tight-money policy that sent the economy spinning to the worst recession since the 1930s. And rising imports of oil hurt the U.S. trade balance. The U.S. had a negative trade balance in petroleum of $4.6 billion in 1972 before the embargo and a trade deficit of $79.3 billion in 1980.

The energy crisis forced a major reevaluation of U.S. energy policy. Congress deregulated large parts of the nation's natural gas reserves. The federal government tightened fuel standards for cars in an attempt to reduce gas consumption, and funding was provided for alternative energy sources such as synthetic fuels and solar energy. And a separate cabinet-level agency was created, the U.S. Department of Energy. Under the Reagan administration, the federal government also moved to open up government-owned lands for oil and natural gas production.

A more important factor in changing consumption and production was the role of private markets. As long as oil was cheap, industry and consumers bought petroleum-based products. While the GNP, adjusted for inflation, grew only 8.9% between 1929 and 1940 and total energy consumption actually declined 0.7%, the use of petroleum grew 39.8%. Between 1929 and 1973, petroleum use grew 6.58 times, outracing the GNP, which grew 3.98 times, and overall energy consumption, which grew 3.13 times, according to the U.S. Department of Energy.

In the 1970s and early 1980s this picture changed. Between 1970 and 1984, use of petroleum as energy grew only 14.6%, while the GNP, adjusted for inflation, grew 52.6% and total energy use grew 9.4%, according to the U.S. Department of Energy.

U.S. production also responded to market pressures. A barrel of Saudi light went for $1.35 in 1970, rose to $2.10 in 1973, and then, under pressure from the Arab oil embargo, skyrocketed to $9.60 in 1974. The same scenario was repeated a few years later, when the Iranian embargo sent the price of Saudi light up from $13.34 in 1979 to $26.00 in 1980 and $34.00

in 1982. That meant the price of Saudi light grew 1,974.1% between 1970 and 1984, while the price of a barrel of U.S. oil at wellhead rose 713.8%, according to the Energy Information Administration. These price hikes meant U.S. reserves that had been unprofitable in pre–oil embargo days were once again good investments.

The total number of oil and gas wells drilled grew from 37,602 in 1973 to 82,101 in 1982, a record. Crude oil production grew slowly from 2.9 billion barrels in 1976 to 3.17 billion in 1983, while imports fell more than half from 2.41 billion in 1977 to only 1.17 billion in 1985. These were the boom years for the oil and natural gas industry—the value of production at wellhead grew from $17.7 billion in 1973 to $138.2 billion in 1981.

But once again the market broke. Prices for a barrel of oil dropped to $28 in 1984, as low as $10 in 1986, and then stabilized at $17 to $19 in the beginning of 1987. That sent the oil industry into turmoil. Wells drilled with the expectation that oil would sell for $30 and $40 a barrel now were unprofitable. Domestic oil and natural gas exploration dropped dramatically. The number of wells dropped to an estimated 39,423 in 1986 and only 37,508 in 1987, half the level in 1984 and the lowest since 1974. In contrast, 88,101 wells were completed in 1981, a record. There were only 920 active rigs in 1987, compared to 3,970 in 1981, according to Hughes Tool Company. Only 3,957 wildcat wells were expected to be drilled in 1987, a 48% drop in only a year, according to *Oil and Gas Journal.*

Oil companies cut their drilling and exploration expenses dramatically, as much as one third to two thirds in 1986 alone. That has wreaked havoc on the oil equipment and oil services industry. Expenditures for drilling and equipping wells fell from $43.2 billion in 1981 to only $11.8 billion in 1986 and only $10.9 billion in 1987, according to *Oil and Gas Journal.* Twelve major U.S.-based equipment and oil service companies posted losses of $1 billion in 1985. By 1986 the Hunt brothers Penrol Drilling Corporation, the largest owner of offshore rigs worldwide, went into bankruptcy. Analysts expect five or six of the largest oil service companies to go bust by 1990.

These grim statistics indicate that the nation's ability to respond to another oil embargo or crisis will be crippled. The U.S. imports about one third of its crude now but, with price drops and cuts in domestic production, the future of energy self-sufficiency looks bleak. By the year 2000, the U.S. will consume 17.4 million barrels of oil a day but only produce 7.7 million, according to projections by the Energy Information Administration. The U.S. will have to import 9.7 million barrels a day, 55% of all U.S. consumption.

Some industry watchers, such as Charles J. DiBona, president of the American Petroleum Institute, believe that increased reliance on foreign oil could leave the U.S. faced with an economic shock as great as that experienced during the embargoes of the 1970s: "We're falling into the same trap of vulnerability," DiBona warns.

Savings in recent years from a drop in the price of energy have reduced concerns about an energy crisis in the near future. Yet it's worth remembering that world consumption of oil stands at nearly 20 billion barrels a year, about 5 billion more than is being found. Annual oil discoveries are only 40% of what they were in the 1950s and 1960s, when 35 billion barrels of oil were found yearly. That means OPEC will be producing 56% of the world's oil in 2000, up from 37% today, according to Energy Information Administration projections. As a result OPEC may eventually be able to reassert its lost economic and political clout.

Another energy crisis would, of course, solve problems in the oil patch. But in the short run, the industry is likely to face more of the same. Industry restructuring—reflected in the trend toward limited partnerships and mergers—should continue. Production and exploration expenditures should fall. Oil service and equipment companies will face more tough times. But gas stations should find that cheaper gas attracts more customers.

In the natural gas industry, the story is very much the same. A surplus of natural gas should last until 1989 to 1990 and moderate price increases.

Table 196   Value of U.S. Fossil Fuel Production, 1949 to 1986

(billions of dollars)

Year	Crude oil Current	Crude oil Constant	Natural gas (marketed production) Current	Natural gas (marketed production) Constant	Bituminous coal, subbituminous coal, and lignite Current	Bituminous coal, subbituminous coal, and lignite Constant	Anthracite Current	Anthracite Constant	Total Current	Total Constant
1949	4.68	19.91	0.33	1.40	2.14	9.11	0.38	1.62	7.53	32.04
1950	4.95	20.71	0.44	1.84	2.50	10.46	0.41	1.72	8.30	34.73
1951	5.69	22.67	0.52	2.07	2.63	10.48	0.42	1.67	9.26	36.89
1952	5.79	22.71	0.64	2.51	2.29	8.98	0.39	1.53	9.11	35.73
1953	6.32	24.40	0.76	2.93	2.25	8.69	0.31	1.20	9.64	37.22
1954	6.44	24.49	0.87	3.31	1.77	6.73	0.25	0.95	9.33	35.48
1955	6.88	25.29	0.94	3.46	2.09	7.68	0.21	0.77	10.12	37.20
1956	7.30	25.98	1.11	3.95	2.41	8.58	0.24	0.85	11.06	39.36
1957	8.09	27.80	1.17	4.02	2.50	8.59	0.23	0.79	11.99	41.20
1958	7.37	24.81	1.32	4.44	1.99	6.70	0.19	0.64	10.87	36.59
1959	7.47	24.57	1.57	5.16	1.97	6.48	0.18	0.59	11.19	36.80
1960	7.42	24.01	1.79	5.79	1.95	6.31	0.15	0.49	11.31	36.60
1961	7.58	24.29	1.99	6.38	1.85	5.93	0.14	0.45	11.56	37.05
1962	7.76	24.33	2.22	6.96	1.89	5.92	0.13	0.41	12.00	37.62
1963	7.96	24.57	2.36	7.28	2.01	6.20	0.16	0.49	12.49	38.54
1964	8.03	24.41	2.33	7.08	2.17	6.60	0.15	0.46	12.68	38.55
1965	8.15	24.11	2.57	7.60	2.27	6.72	0.13	0.38	13.12	38.81
1966	8.72	24.91	2.75	7.86	2.42	6.91	0.10	0.29	13.99	39.97
1967	9.39	26.16	2.91	8.11	2.55	7.10	0.10	0.28	14.95	41.65
1968	9.79	25.97	3.09	8.20	2.55	6.76	0.10	0.27	15.53	41.20
1969	10.42	26.18	3.52	8.84	2.80	7.04	0.10	0.25	16.84	42.31
1970	11.19	26.64	3.73	8.88	3.77	8.98	0.11	0.26	18.80	44.76
1971	11.71	26.37	4.05	9.12	3.90	8.78	0.11	0.25	19.77	44.52
1972	11.71	25.18	4.28	9.20	4.56	9.81	0.09	0.19	20.64	44.38
1973	13.07	26.40	4.98	10.06	5.05	10.20	0.09	0.18	23.19	46.84
1974	22.00	40.74	6.48	12.00	9.50	17.59	0.15	0.28	38.13	70.61
1975	23.45	39.54	9.05	15.26	12.47	21.03	0.20	0.34	45.17	76.17
1976	24.37	38.62	11.57	18.34	13.19	20.90	0.21	0.33	49.34	78.19
1977	25.79	38.32	15.82	23.51	13.70	20.36	0.20	0.30	55.51	82.49
1978	28.60	39.61	18.18	25.18	14.49	20.07	0.18	0.25	61.45	85.11
1979	39.45	50.19	24.16	30.74	18.36	23.36	0.20	0.25	82.17	104.54
1980	67.93	79.26	32.09	37.44	20.20	23.57	0.26	0.30	120.48	140.57
1981	99.40	105.74	39.51	42.03	21.51	22.88	0.24	0.26	160.66	170.91
1982	90.03	90.03	45.56	45.56	22.62	22.62	0.23	0.23	158.44	158.44
1983	83.05	79.93	43.57	41.93	20.11	19.36	0.21	0.20	146.94	141.42
1984	84.10	77.94	48.49	44.94	22.75	21.08	0.20	0.19	155.54	144.15
1985	78.88	70.74	43.17	38.72	22.06	19.78	0.22	0.20	144.33	129.44
1986	40.05	35.01	31.31	27.37	21.67	18.94	0.17	0.15	93.20	81.47

Source: Energy Information Administration.

Table 197 International Consumption of Petroleum Products, 1960–1984

(millions of barrels per day)

Year	Organization for Economic Co-operation and Development (OECD)[1]											Brazil	China	Mexico	U.S.S.R.	Total world	Noncommunist world
	Australia	Canada	France	West Germany	Italy	Japan	Spain	United Kingdom	United States	Other OECD	Total						
1960	0.22	0.84	0.56	0.63	0.44	0.66	0.10	0.94	9.80	1.28	15.47	0.27	0.17	0.30	2.38	21.34	18.32
1961	0.23	0.87	0.63	0.79	0.54	0.82	0.12	1.04	9.98	1.45	16.46	0.28	0.17	0.29	2.57	23.00	19.57
1962	0.25	0.92	0.73	1.00	0.67	0.93	0.12	1.12	10.40	1.62	17.74	0.31	0.14	0.30	2.87	24.89	21.20
1963	0.29	0.99	0.86	1.17	0.77	1.21	0.12	1.27	10.74	1.85	19.26	0.34	0.17	0.31	3.15	26.92	22.90
1964	0.32	1.05	0.98	1.36	0.90	1.48	0.20	1.36	11.02	2.30	20.70	0.35	0.20	0.33	3.58	29.08	24.76
1965	0.35	1.14	1.09	1.61	0.98	1.74	0.23	1.49	11.51	2.30	22.44	0.33	0.23	0.34	3.61	31.14	26.45
1966	0.37	1.21	1.19	1.80	1.08	1.98	0.31	1.58	12.08	2.61	24.20	0.38	0.30	0.36	3.87	33.56	28.53
1967	0.41	1.25	1.34	1.86	1.19	2.14	0.36	1.64	12.56	2.72	25.48	0.38	0.28	0.39	4.22	35.59	30.08
1968	0.45	1.34	1.46	1.99	1.40	2.66	0.46	1.82	13.39	3.08	28.05	0.46	0.31	0.41	4.48	38.96	32.96
1969	0.49	1.42	1.66	2.33	1.69	3.25	0.49	1.98	14.14	3.49	30.94	0.48	0.44	0.45	4.87	42.89	36.37
1970	0.51	1.49	1.89	2.43	1.84	3.85	0.56	2.09	14.70	3.88	33.23	0.51	0.62	0.50	5.30	46.38	39.08
1971	0.54	1.53	2.05	2.61	1.93	4.18	0.60	2.09	15.21	3.95	34.71	0.56	0.79	0.52	6.65	50.00	41.05
1972	0.54	1.62	2.24	2.76	2.07	4.36	0.67	2.24	16.37	4.29	37.15	0.65	0.91	0.56	6.10	52.42	43.80
1973	0.59	1.71	2.42	2.92	2.15	5.07	0.74	2.30	17.31	4.38	39.58	0.77	1.12	0.61	6.57	56.39	46.92
1974	0.62	1.74	2.26	2.61	2.09	4.96	0.78	2.14	16.65	4.23	38.08	0.83	1.38	0.67	7.01	55.91	45.69
1975	0.60	1.69	2.14	2.52	1.94	4.50	0.84	1.87	16.32	4.11	36.53	0.87	1.58	0.74	7.47	55.48	44.47
1976	0.62	1.74	2.28	2.71	1.99	4.77	0.98	1.86	17.46	4.40	38.81	0.97	1.68	0.80	7.65	58.74	47.32
1977	0.66	1.75	2.24	2.84	1.91	5.23	0.93	1.88	18.43	4.43	40.29	1.01	1.83	0.84	8.18	61.63	49.36
1978	0.61	1.74	2.17	3.05	1.95	5.14	0.95	1.85	18.85	4.47	40.76	1.06	1.81	0.99	8.47	63.30	50.52
1979	0.61	1.86	2.39	3.07	2.01	5.48	0.98	1.93	18.51	4.72	41.57	1.18	1.85	1.10	8.58	65.17	51.99
1980	0.59	1.95	2.26	2.71	1.93	4.96	0.99	1.73	17.06	4.47	38.64	1.16	1.83	1.27	8.75	62.99	49.69
1981	0.58	1.84	2.02	2.45	1.87	4.85	0.94	1.59	16.06	4.11	36.31	1.10	1.68	1.40	8.90	60.99	47.86
1982	0.66	1.62	1.94	2.32	1.78	4.55	1.01	1.59	15.30	3.88	34.64	1.08	1.66	1.48	8.82	59.45	46.42
1983	0.63	1.49	1.91	2.29	1.73	4.37	1.02	1.52	15.23	3.70	33.90	1.01	1.72	1.43	8.90	58.76	45.66
1984	0.68	1.50	1.86	2.30	1.64	4.58	0.92	1.82	15.73	3.64	34.66	1.07	1.72	1.48	8.65	59.70	46.73

[1] "Other OECD" includes the United States territories of Puerto Rico, Virgin Islands, and Guam.

Note: Sum of components may not equal total due to independent rounding.

Sources: United States: 1960 through 1976—Bureau of Mines, Mineral Industry Surveys, *Petroleum Statement, Annual*. 1977 through 1980—Energy Information Administration, Energy Data Reports, *Petroleum Statement, Annual*. 1981 and forward—Energy Information Administration, *Petroleum Supply Annual*. U.S.S.R.: 1960 through 1976—U.S.S.R. Central Statistical Office, *Narodnoye Khozyaystvo SSSR (National Economy U.S.S.R.)*, and *Vneshnyaya Torgvliya SSSR (Foreign Trade of the U.S.S.R.)*, annual issues. 1977 through 1979—U.S.S.R. Central Statistical Office, *Narodnoye Khozyaystvo SSSR (National Economy U.S.S.R.)*, annual issues; U.S.S.R. trade as imports reported by their trading partners in official trades statistics of the respective countries. 1980 and forward—Energy Information Administration, *International Energy Annual*. China: 1960 through 1979—Central Intelligence Agency, unpublished data. 1980 and forward—Energy Information Administration, *International Energy Annual*. All other countries: 1960 through 1969—Bureau of Mines, *International Petroleum Annual*, 1969. 1970 through 1978—Energy Information Administration, *International Petroleum Annual*, 1978. 1979 and forward—Energy Information Administration, *International Energy Annual*.

562

Table 198 Estimated International Crude Oil and Natural Gas Proved Reserves, End of Year 1976 and 1986

Area and country	Crude oil (billions of barrels) 1976	Crude oil (billions of barrels) 1986	Natural gas (trillions of cubic feet) 1976	Natural gas (trillions of cubic feet) 1986
North America				
Canada	6.2	6.9	56	100
Mexico	7.0	54.7	12	77
United States	30.9	24.6	216	185
Total	44.1	86.1	284	362
Central and South America				
Argentina	2.3	2.3	7	23
Bolivia	0.2	0.1	5	5
Brazil	0.8	2.3	1	3
Chile	0.2	0.3	2	4
Colombia	0.8	1.3	5	4
Ecuador	1.7	1.7	12	4
Peru	0.7	0.5	2	1
Trinidad and Tobago	0.5	0.6	3	10
Venezuela	15.3	25.0	41	59
Other	(²)	(²)	(³)	(³)
Total	22.6	34.1	78	114
Western Europe				
Denmark	0.3	0.4	1	3
Italy	0.3	0.7	7	8
Netherlands	0.1	0.2	62	70
Norway	5.7	10.5	19	103
United Kingdom	16.8	9.0	30	33
West Germany	0.3	0.3	8	7
Other	1.1	0.8	16	5
Total	24.6	21.9	141	230
Eastern Europe and U.S.S.R.				
U.S.S.R.	78.1	59.0	918	1,550
Other(⁴)	3.4	1.9	12	16
Total	81.5	60.9	930	1,566
Middle East				
Bahrain	0.3	0.1	3	7
Iran	63.0	48.8	330	450
Iraq	34.0	47.1	27	28
Kuwait¹	70.6	94.5	34	41
Oman	5.8	4.0	2	8
Qatar	5.7	3.2	28	152
Saudi Arabia¹	113.2	169.2	66	130
Syria	2.2	1.4	1	4
United Arab Emirates	31.2	33.1	23	105
Other	(²)	0.5	(³)	1
Total	325.9	401.9	513	925
Africa				
Algeria	6.8	8.8	126	106
Angola	1.2	1.1	2	2
Cameroon	0.0	0.5	0	4
Congo	0.3	0.7	0	3
Egypt	2.0	3.6	3	9
Gabon	2.1	0.6	3	1
Libya	25.5	21.3	26	21
Nigeria	19.5	16.0	44	47
Tunisia	2.7	1.8	7	3
Other	0.5	0.6	(³)	7
Total	60.6	55.2	209	201
Far East and Oceania				
Australia	1.4	1.7	32	19
Bangladesh	0.0	0.0	8	13
Brunei	1.6	1.4	8	7
China	20.0	18.4	25	30
India	3.0	4.2	4	18
Indonesia	10.5	8.3	24	49
Malaysia	2.4	2.8	15	49
New Zealand	0.2	0.2	6	6
Pakistan	0.1	0.1	16	19
Thailand	(²)	0.1	1	7
Other	0.2	0.3	6	12
Total	39.4	37.4	145	229
World total	598.7	697.4	2,300	3,626

¹Includes one-half of the Partitioned Zone (formerly called Neutral Zone).
²Less than 0.05 billion barrels.
³Less than 0.5 trillion cubic feet.
⁴Includes also Cuba, Mongolia, North Korea, and Vietnam.

Note: Sum of components may not equal total due to independent rounding.

Note: All reserve figures except those for the U.S.S.R. and natural gas reserves in Canada are proved reserves recoverable with present technology and prices. U.S.S.R. figures are "explored reserves," which include proved, probable, and some possible. The Canadian natural gas figure includes proved and some probable. The latest Energy Information Administration data for the United States are for December 31, 1985.

Sources: United States: 1976—[See Table 41.] World total: Derived by Energy Information Administration. All other data: 1976—Oil and Gas Journal, December 27, 1976. Petroleum Publishing Company, Tulsa, Oklahoma. 1986—Oil and Gas Journal, December 22/29, 1986. Penn Well Publishing Company, Tulsa, Oklahoma. The Energy Information Administration does not necessarily subscribe to the Oil and Gas Journal data but reproduces them as a matter of convenience.

Table 199   Where We Get Our Energy

(in quadrillion Btu)

Year	Petroleum	Percentage of total	Natural gas	Percentage of total	Coal	Percentage of total	Nuclear	Percentage of total	Hydroelectric	Percentage of total	Total*
1973	34.840	46.9	22.512	30.3	12.970	17.5	910	1.2	3.056	4.1	74.288
1980	34.202	45.0	20,390	26.8	15,420	20.3	2.739	3.6	3,120	4.2	75.955
1984	31.004	42.1	18,510	24.5	17,070	23.3	3.546	4.8	3,720	5.3	74,060
1986	31,890	43.1	16,530	22.4	17,320	23.4	4,480	6.1	3,500	4.7	73,930

Source: Energy Information Administration.
*Total includes other sources not listed separately.

Table 200   Who Uses Energy: Energy Consumption by End Use Sector

(in quadrillion Btu)

Year	Residential and commercial	Percentage of total	Industrial	Percentage of total	Transportation	Percentage of total
1973	24.15	32.5	31.54	42.5	18.60	25.0
1980	25.66	33.8	30.61	40.3	19.69	25.9
1984	26.41	35.6	27.77	37.5	19.88	26.8
1986	26.13	36.2	27.39	36.6	20.36	27.2

Source: Energy Information Administration.

Texaco, Inc.

CEO: James W. Kinnear
Employees: 51,000
Assets: $34.9 billion

2000 Westchester Avenue
White Plains, New York 10650
914-253-4000

	1987	1986	1985	1980
Revenues (millions of dollars):	35,300	32,591	47,514	52,485
Net income (millions of dollars):	(440)	725	1,233	2,643
Share earnings (dollars):	—	3.01	5.11	9.79

What it does: The parent company, Texaco, Inc., and two other subsidiaries are in Chapter 11 to avoid paying a $9.1 billion damage award to Pennzoil. The company eventually reached a $3 billion settlement with Pennzoil. It gets about half of its operating profits from overseas oil sales and half from sales in the U.S.

In 1984, Texaco offered to buy Getty Oil, even though Pennzoil thought it already had an agreement to purchase Getty. The final Texaco bid was $29 more than the $100-a-share bid Pennzoil had agreed to pay, but breaking a contract at the last moment for a higher price is risky business, even if you are the 3rd-largest oil company and Pennzoil is the 36th-largest. Lawyers for the Getty family (see the profile on page 122) were worried enough to insist that Texaco indemnify the family for any subsequent lawsuits. But Texaco contended that no legal contract with Pennzoil had existed, and decided to go ahead with the deal, agreeing to protect the Gettys from any damages. The disastrous result was Texaco agreeing to pay Pennzoil $3 billion after losing the dispute in court.

The Getty deal wasn't the first time Texaco had moved quickly to get a rich price. It was founded by Joseph Cullinan, a former Standard

Oil employee who started the Texas Fuel Company in 1902 with the backing of the New York financier Arnold Schlaet. By 1904 Texaco produced 5% of the country's oil. In the 1930s Texaco joined with Standard Oil of California to develop the rich Saudi oil fields. That fabulous find made it one of the world's most profitable oil companies.

But the company's arrogance eventually caught up with it. Its reputation was tarnished during the early 1940s when its president, Torkild Rieber, allowed the company to sell oil to Nazi Germany and let Nazi agents work out of the company's headquarters. The scandal cost Rieber his job.

Later, the company made another major blunder when it failed to plan for the future and develop new oil reserves outside the Middle East. As a result the company's gas sales dropped from first to fourth in the 1970s when its U.S. oil fields began to dry up.

In the 1980s, what some viewed as a rebirth of Texaco's arrogance in the Getty takeover resulted in Pennzoil's $15 billion lawsuit. Texaco didn't take the suit very seriously at first, but a jury in Pennzoil's home state of Texas did, awarding Pennzoil $10.5 billion in damages, plus interest. A Texas appeals court reduced that to $9.1 billion, but upheld the original judgment. The Supreme Court blocked the company's attempt to move the case out of Texas into New York so it wouldn't have to post a $12 billion bond while the case was on appeal. When Texaco tried to settle, offering Pennzoil $2 billion, Pennzoil refused—and Texaco declared bankruptcy.

Going into Chapter 11 let the company avoid putting up a $12 billion bond while it appealed the case. But eventually Texaco settled for $3 billion and is expected to emerge from bankruptcy proceedings in the spring of 1988. However, that doesn't end the company's troubles. The company lost about $4.9 billion in 1987 because of the impact of the Pennzoil debacle and a company restructuring. The Department of Energy is trying to get Texaco to pay $2.1 billion in claims for overcharging customers from 1973 to 1981 when price controls were in effect. Worse, the IRS is seeking about $6.5 billion in back taxes. Texaco says both claims are way out of line, but as company executives struggle to get the company on its feet, raiders like Carl Icahn—who held $300 million worth of Texaco stock in early 1988—are threatening to take a run at the company.

ENERGY TIME LINE: THE OIL, GAS, COAL AND NUCLEAR POWER INDUSTRIES

400,000 to 360,000 B.C. *Homo erectus,* the first erect hominid, uses fire to cook meat.

A.D. 347 The Chinese bore 800 feet into the ground in search of oil and gas.

615 The Japanese drill wells for natural gas.

700s   Windmills can be found in the Arab world.

900   The Chinese pipe gas through bamboo and use it for lighting.

Middle Ages   Sicilians gather oil off the coast for use as fuel. Other Europeans use oil as medicine and fuel but its use is limited by their crude methods of producing oil. Typically, medieval Europeans gather oil by skimming it off ponds.

1577   Origin of the word *gas* can be traced back to the laboratory of Baptist Van Helmont of Brussels. While this alchemist is heating some unidentified material, a small explosion occurs. He calls it *gas*.

1700   Around this time, several steam engines are invented. In 1707 a Frenchman, Denis Papin, describes a steam engine he's created and builds the first steamboat. Thomas Savery patents a steam engine in 1698, and in 1705 Thomas Newcomen and Savery invent the Newcomen steam engine. The Newcomen engine plays an important role in the Industrial Revolution.

1700s   But through most of the early Industrial Revolution water and the waterwheel provide most of the power. Overshot waterwheels, similar to those used in 18th-century Europe, date from the 4th or 5th century A.D. in the Roman Empire.

1783   James Watt invents a steam engine that dramatically improves the efficiency and power of the Newcomen steam engine. In 1881 his name, "Watt," became an international unit of power.

1792   William Murdock of Scotland lights his house with gas produced from coal.

1800   The first modern electric battery is invented by an Italian, Alessandro Volta. His name became the basis of the word *volt,* a measurement of electricity.

1812   The first gas company is created in London.

1816   The first gas company in the U.S. is created in Baltimore after Rembrandt Peale gives a public demonstration of gas lighting. The first street lamps are lit in 1817. By 1852 gas lights outnumber oil lamps in New York City and by 1859 over 300 U.S. cities are lit by gas.

1818   F. De Larderel builds the world's first geothermal plant in Tuscany, Italy, when he uses heat rising out of the ground to process boric acid.

1820   Natural gas is discovered near Pittsburgh, Pennsylvania, during drilling for salt water. The gas is accidentally ignited and the saltworks plant burns down.

1838   The first practical electric motor is invented by an American, Thomas Davenport, who uses it to power a drill.

1840   Gas meters appear, allowing companies to charge customers based on the amount of gas they use. Before this invention gas companies charged a flat fee.

1850   Oil and natural gas producers still obtain these products from coal or by skimming them off ponds and streams. The meager production became inadequate as whale oil used to light homes became less abundant.

1859   The first oil well is dug in Titusville, Pennsylvania, by Edwin Drake. He is hired by a Yale professor, Benjamin Silliman, and a group of businessmen who have created the Pennsylvania Rock Oil Company. At a depth of 69½ feet Drake hits oil, touching off an oil boom in Pennsylvania. Silliman's company eventually becomes Seneca Oil Company. In contrast to the 69½ feet Drake drills to hit oil, the average well in 1987 is 4,711 feet deep.

1860   There are 206 gas companies. They produce 4 billion cubic feet of gas which is sold for $11 million, according to the 1862 U.S. census report.

1861   The first oil refinery is set up in the oil region of Pennsylvania.

1865   The first railroad tank car is invented.

1878   A Frenchman, Mouchot, produces a small solar power plant that is strong enough to operate a steam engine.

1878   Pennsylvania passes a law to preserve petroleum production, perhaps the first conservation legislation ever.

1878   Thomas Edison patents his electric lamp.

1879   The first oil pipeline is created, running 110 miles through the Allegheny Mountains to Williamsport, Pennsylvania. A shorter, 5-mile pipeline had been laid in 1865 between Pithole City and the Oil Creek Railroad. Today, there are some 227,000 million miles of pipelines for oil and refined production.

1881   The first electric power station is built in England. It is powered by natural gas and most of its electricity is used to light lamps in Godalming, Surrey.

1884   The first steam turbine is built by an Englishman, Sir Charles Algernon Parsons.

1886   The German ship *Gluckauf* is the first tanker designed to transport oil.

1887   The first electric heating system is patented in the U.S. by Dr. W. Leigh.

1900   Natural gas has been found in 17 states, with Pennsylvania ranking as the leading producer. But the value of total production is only $23.7 million.

1900s   At the beginning of the century, kerosene is the main product of U.S. oil refiners and gas is considered a waste product. As the auto creates more demand for gas, refiners search for a way of producing more gas during the refining process. This problem is solved in 1913 by the development of the thermal cracking process by Dr. William Burton and Dr. Robert Humphreys.

1911   The Supreme Court dissolves Standard Oil, the world's largest oil monopoly, into 34 competing companies.

1912   One century after the first gas company is founded, there are 2,090 natural gas companies.

1914   Thomas Edison invents the first alkaline storage battery.

1918   Natural gas is discovered in Potter County, Texas. This is part of the world's largest producing gas reserve, the Panhandle Field, which covers 1.6 million acres.

1920   The production of cheap cars by Henry Ford dramatically increases the number of cars on the road to 9 million from only a half-million in 1910 and fuels the demand for gas that is key to the development of the oil industry. But powering cars isn't the only way that the auto industry creates demand for oil: eventually petroleum asphalt is used to pave roads.

1921   The gas industry serves 49 million people and supplies gas to 7 million gas stoves and 1.5 million gas water heaters.

1930s   The creation of the Tennessee Valley Authority and other electrification programs during the Roosevelt administration increases the use of electricity and energy.

1938   The Natural Gas Act is passed, beginning federal regulation of the gas industry. The law gives the Federal Power Commission authority to regulate transportation and sale of natural gas.

1946   Demand for oil and natural gas continues to skyrocket. For the first time, petroleum supplies more of the nation's energy than coal.

1953   The world's first nuclear power plant goes into operation in the U.S.

1960   The Organization of Petroleum Exporting Countries (OPEC) is formed. Iran, Iraq, Saudi Arabia, Kuwait, and Qatar, the original members, are later joined by Venezuela, Indonesia, Libya, Abu Dhabi, Algeria, Nigeria, Ecuador, and Gabon. With oil selling for $1.80 a barrel, the organization has little power. But four years later the organization begins the first of many moves that will increase its power: in November of 1964, OPEC negotiates a larger share of oil-company profits. However, in 1967, an OPEC boycott following the Six-Day War fails to catch on and the price of oil remains at $1.80, and in 1969 the discovery of oil in Alaska the North Sea seems to indicate that OPEC's power will wane. In fact, the opposite occurs. After threatening to nationalize their oil fields, OPEC nations negotiate an ever-larger share of profits from the major oil companies, and in 1971, for the first time, the organization agrees on a price increase. Following the Yom Kippur War in 1973, OPEC doubles its price to $5.12 a barrel, and by 1981 the price hits $35.00 a barrel. But a growing worldwide oil glut forces price cuts and OPEC has lost its market share in recent years.

1963   The first breeder reactor starts working in the U.S.

1965   An electrical blackout in the northeast leaves 30 million Americans in seven states over an 80,000-square-mile area without power.

1972   Cheap oil and gas has created an economy heavily dependent on oil and gas as energy sources. About 75% of all energy needs are taken care of by oil and natural gas, up from 57.8% in 1950.

1973–1974   America's dangerous dependence on foreign oil becomes apparent when OPEC embargoes shipments of oil to the U.S.

1977   The Department of Energy Organization Act creates the Federal Energy Regulatory Commission, which replaces the Federal Power Commission. This independent regulatory commission has power over the transmission of natural gas, sales of natural gas drilled before 1977, interstate pipelines, interstate sale of electricity, interconnection rates and charges among electric utilities, stock issues of electric utilities, and oil pipelines.

1979   The Iran oil embargo touches off a new wave of shortages and price hikes. Spot market prices rise from less than $3 a barrel in 1973 to more than $40 in 1980. This causes many oil and natural gas companies to make plans as if oil prices will continue rising. When oil prices begin to fall in 1981, a wave of bankruptcies and heavy losses follows.

1980   When oil prices hit the skids, the prices for stocks of oil companies drop to absurdly low levels—making the companies attractive to takeover attempts. These companies' assets are worth two and sometimes three times as much as the stock. Since many believe that oil prices will eventually recover, buying these low-priced stocks is much like buying oil at $5 a barrel. In 1981, the sale of Conoco to du Pont touches off a major industry-wide restructuring. Several large companies, such as Marathon Oil, Gulf Oil, and Getty Oil, are also sold. Other companies, such as Atlantic Richfield and Phillips Petroleum, leverage their balance sheets or make other moves to fend off raiders. The trend puts more money in individual stockholders' pockets but reduces money available for exploration and development, making the U.S. potentially more dependent on OPEC in the 1990s.

1983   The first sun-powered industrial complex is put into operation in Lyons, France.

1985   OPEC sees its share of U.S. consumption of oil fall to only 11.6%, down from 33.6% in 1977.

1986   As oil prices drop momentarily below $10 a barrel, oil rig counts fall to the lowest level since 1940. Bad loans made to energy producers during the boom period of 1979 to 1981 cause major banks in Texas and the southwest to post record losses. By the end of the year, an OPEC production agreement stabilizes prices at around $18 a barrel.

Exxon Corporation

CEO: Lawrence G. Rawl   1251 Avenue of the Americas
Employees: 102,000   New York, New York 10020
Assets: $69.5 billion   212-333-1000

	1987	1986	1985	1980
Revenues (millions of dollars):	84,120	76,555	92,869	110,191
Net income (millions of dollars):	4,840	5,360	4,870	5,350
Share earnings (dollars):	3.43	7.42	6.46	6.15

What it does: The world's biggest petroleum company.

The late 1980s has been a period of restructuring for Exxon Corporation, the world's biggest oil company.

Long described as a jumbo elephant, Exxon is now a trimmer elephant. Faced with a 50% drop in crude oil prices, the behemoth cut its work force to 102,000 from 182,000. Capital and exploration spending was down 40% in 1986 from 1985. The oil refining operation was cut 1.5 million barrels a day.

Moreover, the company shed its nuclear and Reliance Electric Company subsidiaries to an investment group that included Prudential-Bache Securities and Citicorp Capital Investors. And the company in 1986 also sold the Exxon headquarters in midtown Manhattan for $610 million; the building, which will continue to serve as the company's headquarters, was jointly owned by Exxon and the Rockefeller Group.

The company also slowed down its acquisition strategy. The last big acquisition was in 1985, when Exxon picked up 49% of Hunt Oil Company's interest in a production-sharing deal with the Yemen Arab Republic, including the huge Alif oil field.

But don't feel sorry for the giant just because oil hit a downturn. The slimming down was applauded on Wall Street as necessary for a highly profitable company to stay that way. The nation's second-largest corporation (after General Motors) still managed to have enormous profits in 1987, $4.84 billion on revenues of $84.12 billion, not bad by any measure.

Today, Exxon and its divisions and affiliated companies operate in the U.S. and more than 80 countries. The main business remains energy, involving exploration for and production of crude oil and natural gas, manufacturing of petroleum products, and sale and transportation of crude oil, natural gas, and petroleum products. The company also explores for mines and sells coal.

Exxon Chemical Company is a major maker and marketer of petrochemicals. Exxon also explores for and mines minerals other than coal. Moreover, the company conducts extensive research programs supporting its businesses and provides capital to new innovative ventures, some of which aren't related to its lines of business.

Historically, Exxon is an offshoot of the Standard Oil Company. The company was incorporated in New Jersey in 1892 as the Standard Oil Company of New Jersey as a result of a court order to dissolve John D. Rockefeller's monopolistic Standard Oil Trust (See the profile of the Rockefellers on page 117.) Before long, however, the trust was back in business under a different name, Standard Oil Company. In 1911, the Supreme Court, operating under the Sherman Antitrust Law, then broke Standard Oil into 34 oil companies.

On its own, Standard Oil of New Jersey set itself up as a holding company and grew through a dizzying series of mergers and acquisitions involving U.S. companies and companies all over the world. In 1928, for instance, the company acquired shares in Creole Petroleum Company of Venezuela. In 1932, the company bought stock in Standard Oil of Indiana. By the mid-1940s, the company had acquired ownership of oceangoing tankers, and soon it had pipeline activities and interests in synthetic rubber, chemicals, coal, minerals, and power generation—all of which made it very big indeed.

Marvin Davis By the time Marvin Davis graduated from Syracuse University in 1947, his father Jack was interested in oil. An English immigrant and former boxer, the elder Davis packed his beefy, six-foot-four-inch son off to set up an office in Denver to look for black gold.

Look he did. Davis the younger traipsed around the Rocky Mountains, drilling one dry hole after another. A wildcatter, he went after highly speculative wells in uncharted regions, figuring if you drill enough you've got to make a strike sooner or later. He also proved good at raising other people's money for his explorations. By the 1960s, he was head of Davis Oil Company and had made several discoveries in Wyoming.

When oil prices skyrocketed in the late 1970s, Davis found himself courted by legions of celebrities, including Gerald R. Ford and Henry A. Kissinger, who wanted to invest in his wells. Davis's business boomed and he turned his little oil company into TCF Holdings, with interests in real estate, banking, and energy worth $1 billion or so.

Along the way, Davis earned himself a reputation as a tough, demanding deal maker and proved himself a master at timing. For instance, he stoked up a bidding for his oil properties and then sold about a third of them to Hiram Walker Resources Ltd. for $630 million. Then he sold 80% of his real estate company's interests in four new office buildings in Denver to Prudential Insurance Company for $500 million. A short while later, the price of oil sank and the office building market nosedived.

That was about the time Davis got interested in show biz. He said he wanted "fun investments" and decided to take over Twentieth Century Fox Film Corporation. What could be more fun than running a movie studio?

For help with the takeover, he turned to the commodities trader Marc Rich, with whom he had been involved in some big gas and oil deals. (Rich subsequently became a fugitive from justice and Davis got into hot water himself over some of the deals he had made with Rich.) They didn't have much trouble with Fox, which was a mess. Senior managers were at each other's throats, and an attempted leveraged buyout had just flopped. Davis actually managed to look like a white knight. He bid $720 million for the company (but he only put up $55 million). And he promised to keep the management in place.

So much for promises. Within weeks, Fox chairman Dennis C. Stanfill resigned, charging that Davis interfered with his running of the company, and he filed a $40 million breach-of-contract suit against Davis. Other executives quit or were fired. Davis then began shifting Fox's assets to his holding company. To pay his huge debt, he sold off Fox's music publishing, the Coca-Cola bottling operation, and various real estate holdings, as well as theaters in Australia and New Zealand. All told, he took some $500 million from Fox. Nonstudio revenue disappeared.

In the interim, Davis was bitten by the show biz bug. He hit the celebrity circuit, making a mad round of parties and gatherings. He paid $22 million for Kenny Rogers's Beverly Hills mansion and had his own star-studded parties.

Unfortunately, there's more to making movies than playing like a movie mogul. Davis waded into Fox's business, hiring his 26-year-old son, John, as a producer and giving him a seat on the board. And he applied his oil well theory to movie-making: if you make enough, you're bound to have a hit.

He didn't hit any celluloid gushers but managed to make a lot of losers. Fox was bathed in red ink and, by 1985, Davis sold his Fox interests (except for some real estate) to media mogul Rupert Murdoch for $575 million. But Davis still did OK. Even after paying off his whopping debt, he was believed to have made at least $350 million from the Fox deal.

The show biz bug apparently is still with Davis. In 1986, he tried to take over CBS Inc. but was rebuffed. Industry watchers are just wondering what area of show business he will try to cozy up to next.

BP America

CEO: Robert B. Horton
Employees: 42,000
Assets: $15.9 billion

200 Public Square
Cleveland, Ohio 44114
216-586-4141

	1986	1985	1984	1980
Revenues (millions of dollars):	9,219	13,002	12,251	11,023
Net income (millions of dollars):	(345)	308	1,488	1,811
Share earnings (dollars):	—	1.31	6.14	7.37

What it does: A unit of British Petroleum.

The history of the Standard Oil Company is the story of how a once-mighty company is dwarfed once by the courts, resurges, and then is dwarfed again, but this time by management stupidity.

In 1863, John D. Rockefeller (see the profile on page 117) and three partners established a 10-barrel-a-day oil refinery in Cleveland, which already had a thriving oil industry. Their Standard Oil Company of Ohio was capitalized at $1 million. By strict economies, mergers, and agreements with competitors, by building up large cash reserves, and by ruthlessly crushing weaker opponents, Rockefeller soon controlled 90% of the oil refining industry.

By 1882, Rockefeller's diverse holdings were tied together into the Standard Oil Trust, which virtually ran the industry. The power of Rockefeller's monopoly was enhanced by rebate agreements he forced on railroads and his control of pipeline distribution. In 1892, court action forced the trust to dissolve, but Rockefeller soon set up the Standard Oil Company of New Jersey. A holding company with capitalization of $110 million, the new company was merely the old trust.

In 1911, the year Rockefeller retired with his fabulous fortune, the U.S. Supreme Court under antitrust provisions ordered Standard Oil to be broken down into 34 companies. Some of the corporations that emerged from the pieces became Exxon, Chevron, and Amoco. Of the newly formed independents, Standard was left the smallest, with one refinery, a marketing region limited to Ohio, and no crude oil or pipelines. Standard had been knocked out of the big leagues.

Over the years, the company moved into chemicals, coal, and plastics while continuing refining and regional marketing of oil. In 1970, Standard gambled big, a move that resulted in its being catapulted back into the big time.

Standard exchanged a special stock interest equal to about 25% of the company to acquire the big Alaska holdings of British Petroleum (BP), including Prudhoe Bay, which was believed to contain large oil reserves. In 1977, Standard began pumping Alaskan crude oil through 800 miles of pipeline, a project that had set the company back $15 billion. The gamble was worth it. Standard became one of the nation's biggest companies and one of the largest holders of U.S. oil reserves.

Knowing the Prudhoe Bay oil wouldn't last forever, Standard unwisely diversified by buying the big copper producer, Kennecott Corporation, for $1.77 billion in 1981. Kennecott rewarded Standard by posting whopping losses in ensuing years. Then Standard shelled out $1.7 billion to drill another Alaskan well that came up dry. All told, Standard has spent more than $5 billion on oil exploration and leases in the 1980s and has had little to show for it.

As a result of the Alaskan holdings agreement with BP, Standard became 50% owned by BP in 1978. Eventually, that grew to 55%. BP sat back and watched Standard's diversification and exploration misadventures until crude oil prices tumbled. Early in 1986, BP waded in and sacked Standard's two top executives and put in its own man, Robert B. Horton, as chairman and chief executive. In 1987, BP offered Standard shareholders $7.4 billion for the rest of the company. Thus, Standard, after starting off with a boom and ending up with a bust, became merely the unit of a bigger oil company.

PACKAGING AND CONTAINERS

THE MARKET

Providing the containers and packaging for most of the products consumed in the U.S. is a monumental task. Each year, Americans buy some 109 billion metal cans (including 37 billion beer cans, 41 billion soft drink cans and 27 billion food cans), 42 billion glass containers, 18.7 billion plastic bottles, 2.4 billion pounds of plastic used as refuse bags and film, 2.4 billion aerosol containers, 2.1 billion plastic food containers, and 81.1 billion metal and plastic tops and closures for containers. No wonder the garbage can fills so quickly.

THE MONEY

Producing a wide variety of packaging and containers adds tens of billions of dollars to the economy. American manufacturers produced $12 billion worth of metal cans in 1987, $5.3 billion worth of glass containers, $1.9 billion worth of plastic bottles, $6.5 billion worth of all types of bags, except for textile bags, $4.8 billion worth of folding paperboard boxes, $14.5 million worth of corrugated and solid fiber boxes, paperboard boxes, and $3.2 billion worth of sanitary food containers.

PACKAGING FIRSTS

1795   Nicolas Appert discovers a method of preserving food in airtight glass jars covered with five layers of cork. The process, which is still used, is called appertization.

1810   Peter Durand takes out a patent on a process using tin cans to preserve food. Bryan Donkin and John Hall produces the first food in tin cans in 1813.

1830s   While working at his father's store, Francis Wolle is faced with tedium of making handmade paper bags. So he invents a machine that can manufacture paper bags, which he patents in 1852. In 1883, Charles Stillwell invents a machine to make grocery bags with a flat bottom.

1840   No one has yet invented the can opener so labels commonly instruct consumers to "cut round on the top near to the outer edge with a chisel and hammer." When the first can opener makes its appearance is something of a mystery, one of those subjects that seems to have eluded academic study. The first wall-mounted can opener does not appear until 1927. It is marketed by the Central States Manufacturing Company of St. Louis.

1896   Colgate Company, founded as a soap shop 90 years earlier by William Colgate, introduces the first toothpaste in a tube.

1908   Small paper cups, later called Dixie cups, appear.

1947 R. J. Reynolds markets Reynolds Wrap. The rolls of aluminum foil
     radically change household food storage and cooking.
1952 Dow Chemical markets a plastic film, Saran Wrap.
1960 The aluminum can for soft drinks is introduced, replacing glass
     containers, which have dominated the market.
1963 The flip-top for aluminum cans is introduced by Alcoa, doing away
     with the need to use a can opener or "the church key."
1971 Dow Chemical introduces its Ziploc plastic bags.

PETS

THE MARKET

About 52.8% of all American households have a pet, with 38.7% of all
households owning a dog and 29.4% owning a cat. About 25% to 30% of
the 51.6 million dogs owned by pet lovers in America are purebred but
only 7% of the 56.2 million cats have pedigrees. There are some 340 million
to 500 million tropical fish around and 27 million caged birds are owned
by Americans. Pet owners buy 9.4 billion pounds worth of pet food and
pay 115 million visits to veterinarians every year.

THE MONEY

Americans spend about $3.9 billion a year on veterinarian care ($2.6 billion
for dog care and $1.3 billion for cat care) and another $5.3 billion on pet
food ($3.3 billion for dog food and $2 billion worth of cat food). Pet store
sales of fish total about $219 million a year.

   The average dog owner spends about 6% of his or her grocery bill on
dog food and the average cat owner spends about $1,000 a year on the
pet.

   One of the fastest growing areas is gourmet pet food. About $1.5 billion.
worth of gourmet dog food and $207 million worth of gourmet cat food
were sold in 1986.

THE PLAYERS

Some 20,959 veterinarians get most of their business from treating small
pets (as opposed to farm animals). About 10,000 pet shops dot the land,
along with 11,000 pet grooming shops, 7,000 kennels, 300 pet cemeteries,
and 19,000 dog food vendors. The pet food business, like the human food
business, is highly concentrated, with the largest seven companies controlling over 76% of the market. And, as you'll see from the chart in this
section listing the seven largest pet food producers, many of the top pet

food companies, such as Nestlé and H. J. Heinz, are also among the top food companies.

TRENDS AND FORECAST

Although Americans spend four times more feeding pets than babies, the pet food industry has only been growing 2% to 3% a year. As dog ownership has declined, from 41% of all households in 1981 to 38.7% in 1986, consumption of dog food has also declined, from 7.2 billion pounds in 1985 to 7 billion in 1986. But because more and more households own cats, the market for cat food has been growing at an annual rate of 8% a year, according to Business Trend Analysts. Since pet ownership is peaking and perhaps reaching a saturation point, sales of dog food should grow only about 2% a year and annual growth of cat food should grow 5% a year through 1991.

Table 201　The Largest Pet Food Producers

(total 1986 market: $5.62 billion, up 3.6%)

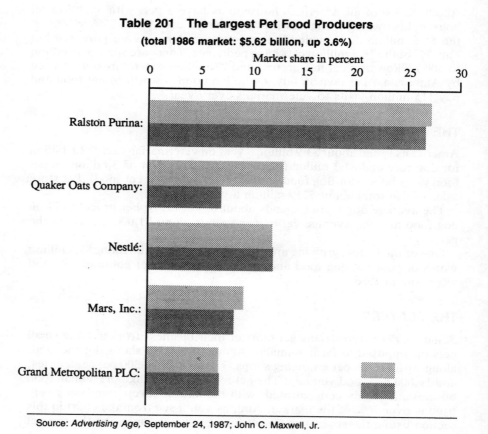

Source: *Advertising Age,* September 24, 1987; John C. Maxwell, Jr.

PET PAMPERING

Dogs that pig out on gourmet food and find they no longer fit into their designer outfits can work it off at the doggie spa. No kidding.

The posh people palaces Neiman-Marcus and Harrod's as well as upscale pet food stores now stock fancy English doggie biscuits that sell for $6.50 for a 10-ounce bag. Dogwear, Inc., of New York City makes designer outfits, including a satin blouse with a red sash and a black skirt. Then there's Charmaine's Doggery in Los Angeles where, for $50 a session, doggies get a diet plan and a workout program, including treadmills and whirlpool baths. And once Fifi's presentable again, you can have her portrait painted for $150 to $2,000 at Countryhouse Studios, Annville, Pennsylvania.

PHOTOGRAPHY

THE MARKET AND THE MONEY

There are so many shutterbugs around it sometimes seems as if every man, woman, and child has two cameras. Indeed, saturation is a problem in the photography business.

The big picture reveals an industry that sold over $15.8 billion worth of equipment and supplies in 1987. But a closer look reveals that American companies saw their factory shipments drop $16 billion in 1984 while sales of imports grew from 2.9 billion in 1984 to $4 billion in 1987. That decline can be blamed on a saturated consumer market for traditional photographic equipment and supplies, increased foreign competition, and new types of leisure activities, such as use of VCRs, that have cut into sales of photographic equipment.

To improve profits, photography companies are pushing new products, such as photocopiers, micrographics equipment, and laser printers.

THE PLAYERS

Kodak, which virtually created the consumer photography industry, dominates the industry. With $13.3 billion in sales and $1.2 billion in profits in 1987, it sold a whopping four fifths of all color film in the U.S. (See the profile below.) Far behind is number two, Polaroid, with $1.6 billion in sales and $103.5 million in profits. Imports, however, have captured a major share of the market, 20% of the market for photographic equipment supplies and a higher percentage in certain parts of the industry, such as 35-millimeter cameras, in which they have a virtual monopoly.

THE PEOPLE

About 98,000 American workers find employment in the photographic equipment or supply industry. That is a dramatic cutback from the 119,000 employees working in the industry as recently as 1982. With companies continuing to cut costs and fighting to maintain profits in a stagnant market, further cutbacks are expected.

TRENDS AND FORECAST

This is a mature industry with few prospects for growth in its traditional products. Even with a weaker dollar, U.S. producers will lose business and the overall market will remain flat.

Eastman Kodak Company
CEO: Colby H. Chandler
Employees: 121,450
Assets: $6.4 billion

343 State Street
Rochester, New York 14650
716-724-4000

	1987	1986	1985	1980
Revenues (millions of dollars):	13,305	11,550	10,631	9,734
Net income (millions of dollars):	1.178	374	332	1,153
Share earnings (dollars):	3.52	1.66	1.46	4.77

What it does: World's largest producer of photographic supplies. Also manufactures chemical products.

For the first time in years, the bottom line at Kodak made a very pretty picture in 1986. Earnings at the largest U.S. photography company increased 14% in 1986 to roughly $374 million on sales of $11.5 billion. In 1987, they grew to $1.2 billion on sales of $13.3 billion.

But a new picture of financial health at Kodak came after five years of slumping profits. Only a few years ago, it looked as if Kodak had lost touch with its innovative past. Kodak staked its future on the disc camera, while the Japanese came out with improved, low-priced 35-millimeter cameras that took much better pictures. So consumers bought Japanese. Kodak's film monopolized the market until Japanese film makers brought out faster-speed film. Again consumers bought Japanese. Kodak's market share fell from nearly 100% to 82% in only 15 years. And consumers were complaining about the quality of Kodak's photo finishing. Many customers stopped paying 20% more to get Kodak to develop their pictures. Photo finishing sales fell to only $60 million in 1986 from $200 million five years earlier.

Turning things around wasn't easy. The company abandoned its guaranteed lifetime employment policy, cutting 25,000 jobs and thinning management ranks by 25%. It fought off Fuji Photo Film Company in the film market and beat back competition from one-hour minilabs that cut into the demand for its photographic paper. But there still is a long way to go.

But competition seems to be revitalizing the company. Increased emphasis on product development led to the introduction of 100 new products in 1986, the most ever. The company is also hard at work on systems to produce instant photographic images electronically, a process that one day might replace conventional photography. In early 1985, Kodak spent $5.1 billion in cash to buy Sterling Drug Inc., making it a big player in the $110 billion a year worldwide pharmaceutical market.

Kodak is also aggressively expanding into new areas. With its plastics and chemical business bringing in $2 billion a year, the company started a drug company from scratch and moved into the batteries industry with a lithium battery that lasts twice as long as most batteries. It became one of the three top U.S. makers of floppy magnetic disks for computers.

Those new products would continue the company's tradition of technological innovation, started by its founder, George Eastman. Irritated by the size and weight of early photography equipment, he worked to make photography simpler, cheaper, and more accessible to the average American. In 1884, he introduced the world to a new product—film on rolls. In 1888, he followed up that success with the world's first light portable camera. The $25 camera came with 100 exposures' worth of film. After the pictures were taken, the customer mailed in $10 and the camera to Kodak. By 1900, Kodak brought out the Brownie camera, which cost only a dollar, and the first 15-cent rolls of film. These created a mass consumer photography market and Kodak's fortune. Today, Kodak will have to show the same creativity George did.

PRINTING

THE MARKET AND THE MONEY

The printing and publishing industry in the U.S. produces most of the books, magazines, greeting cards, advertising flyers, and business forms we use, all of which adds up to a $129.3 billion industry. Businesses that specialize in printing books do a $3.2 billion business; commercial printers (including letterpress, lithographic, and gravure printers) add $41.6 billion; typesetters do a $1.7 billion business; platemakers $2.8 billion; and shipments of business forms add $6.8 billion. (See the "Newspapers," "Book Publishing," "Magazines," and "Greeting Cards" sections.)

THE PLAYERS

The printing and publishing industry is a highly competitive business, characterized by many small shops and rapidly changing technologies. There are about 53,000 printing and publishing establishments, employing 1.8 million people in 1988.

In the last 20 years, the industry has undergone a technological revolution. Today, computerized typesetting, laser printing, electronic graphics and page layouts, new inks, microprocessor-controlled printing processes and automated binding, and many other new techniques are allowing U.S. printers to increase their output dramatically. These technological advances are expected to continue, as capital expenditure in the graphic arts industry and publishing industry run over $5 billion a year.

THE PEOPLE

Rapid technological advances have increased productivity and output while allowing employers to cut payroll costs. The number of production workers in the industry has, for example, declined as a percentage of total employment from 61% in 1965 to 55% in 1985. Currently, 1.4 million people work in the printing and publishing industry with an annual payroll of $30 billion.

RADIO

THE MARKET

Radio reaches 99% of all households and there are some 507 million radios in use, according to the Radio Advertising Bureau, including 127 million car radios. Every day radio reaches 80% of all Americans, and during the course of a week 95.2% of the population listens to radio. The average American over the age of 12 spends about one eighth of his or her day, or 3 hours and 6 minutes, listening to the radio. In the average hour, listeners hear 12.7 commercials lasting a total of 10 minutes and 6 seconds on AM radio and 11.9 commercials totaling 9 minutes and 17 seconds on FM.

THE MONEY

Radio advertising topped $7 billion in 1986 and grew to $7.3 billion in 1987, more than double the $3.55 billion of revenues in 1980.

THE PLAYERS

There are 8,807 commercial radio stations in the U.S., of which 4,863 operate on the AM band and 3,944 are commercial FM stations. In addition, there are 1,263 noncommercial FM stations, bringing the total number of radio stations, commercial and noncommercial, to 10,070.

THE PEOPLE

There are currently 116,400 people employed in radio, up from 94,427 in 1980 and 64,939 in 1970.

TRENDS AND FORECAST

With rising ad revenues, radio properties were hot in 1986. Some $2.5 billion to $3 billion worth of radio stations changed hands, twice the dollar amount of 1985 and up dramatically from the $339 million worth of stations sold in 1980, according to the FCC. The outlook remains positive. Radio advertising is expected to grow in the late 1980s faster than the economy but not quite as fast as the double-digit growth seen in the first half of the decade.

Table 202 Most Popular Types of Programming on Radio, 1987–1988

How AM and FM stations program by format: There are 4,863 commercial AM stations and 3,944 commercial FM stations licensed by the Federal Communications Commission operating in the United States (as of December 31, 1986); 1,263 noncommercial stations can also be found, primarily on the FM dial.

A programming format usually defines the kind of audience attracted to a particular radio station. The following formats are in use:

(percent of AM and FM stations in the top 100 markets programming each format)

Format	AM	FM	Total AM/FM
Adult contemporary	19.5	20.4	20.0
Country	16.8	15.0	15.9
Rock/CHR	4.1	19.4	11.8
Album-oriented rock (AOR)	0.7	13.4	7.1
MOR/nostalgia	13.1	1.5	7.3
Easy listening	1.5	10.5	6.0
Religious	8.0	3.1	5.5
News/talk	12.0	0.9	6.5
Black/R&B	5.1	2.2	3.7
Urban contemporary	1.9	4.4	3.2
Golden oldies	5.2	1.1	3.2
Spanish	4.4	0.8	2.6
Classical	1.2	2.1	1.7
All news	3.4	0.0	1.7
Soft contemporary	1.4	4.1	2.8
Variety	1.3	0.4	1.0

Source: *Radio Facts 1987–1988,* Radio Advertising Bureau.

Table 203   Radio Advertising Revenues
(in millions of dollars)

Year	Network	National spot	Local/retail	Total
1987e	370.9	1,298.3	5,615.9	7,285.1
1986	380.0	1,332.6	5,313.1	7,025.7
1985	328.7	1,319.4	4,915.0	6,563.1
1984	288.0	1,184.4	4,412.0	5,884.4
1983	253.5	1,022.8	3,739.0	5,015.3
1982	217.5	909.4	3,365.0	4,491.9
1981	195.9	854.3	3,007.0	4,057.2
1980	157.9	746.2	2,642.9	3,547.0
1979	138.5	637.3	2,396.6	3,172.4
1978	126.4	589.7	2,179.2	2,895.3
1977	118.1	521.3	1,873.1	2,512.5
1976	92.2	494.6	1,639.3	2,226.1
1975	72.7	416.3	1,403.3	1,892.3
1974	60.3	386.8	1,308.8	1,755.9
1973	59.4	382.3	1,205.4	1,647.1
1972	65.0	384.3	1,098.4	1,547.7
1971	55.1	378.0	954.6	1,387.7
1970	48.8	355.3	852.7	1,256.8
1969	50.9	349.6	799.9	1,200.4
1968	54.7	342.2	733.4	1,130.4
1967	58.2	298.3	641.2	997.6
1966	57.4	292.6	607.6	957.7
1965	54.3	261.3	553.0	868.7
1964	54.0	244.1	504.2	802.3
1963	51.5	231.0	465.0	747.6
1962	44.9	218.2	434.2	697.3
1961	47.7	205.6	397.7	651.0
1960	44.9	208.0	401.6	654.5
1955	64.1	120.4	272.0	456.5
1950	131.5	118.8	203.2	453.4
1945	134.0	76.7	99.8	310.5
1940	73.8	37.1	44.8	155.7
1935	39.7	13.8	26.1	79.6

All expenditures in actual dollars for that year.
Sources: Federal Communications Commission 1935 through 1980. Radio Advertising Bureau compilations 1981 to present from: Ernst & Whinney—network; Radio Expenditure Reports—national spot, projected to estimated total from previous trends of RER's share of total FCC billings 1978–1980; Radio Advertising Bureau's Local Business Barometer—local/retail.
eestimate

RAILROADS

THE MARKET

Railroads are, at the same time, the nation's most popular way of moving freight and one of America's least popular way to travel.

Americans ride 12 billion passenger miles on railroads each year. That's only about 0.66% of the 1.812 billion passenger miles American travelers rack up each year. That makes railroads the least common way of taking a trip, behind private autos, domestic airways, and even buses. The nation's largest passenger railroad, Amtrak, carries 20.9 million passengers and takes in $610.9 million in revenues.

But railroads are still the largest mover of freight in the U.S., handling 37.2% of all freight tonnage (See Table 204, "Who Moved America's Goods," below.) In 1987, railroads are expected to have moved 930 billion ton-miles worth of freight—a common measure of freight referring to the movement of one ton of goods (2,000 pounds) for one mile. Put in another way, America's largest railroad lines (Class 1 carriers with revenues of over $88.5 million, which account for over 90% of the freight handled by the industry) shipped 19.3 million carloads in 1985, or about 1.3 billion tons worth of goods over the nation's 161,000 miles of track. Coal (536.7 million tons), farm products (124.6 million tons), nonmetallic minerals (not including fuels, 107.2 million tons), and chemicals and allied products (106.1 million tons) accounted for the most freight tonnage. Coal (5,669 million carloads), farm products (1,467 million carloads), chemical and allied products (1,288 million carloads), and food and kindred products (1,201 million carloads) filled up the most train cars among Class 1 carriers.

THE MONEY

While railroads moved more freight, they earned less money than trucking companies. Trucks picked up $217.1 billion in revenues in 1987 and a projected $217.1 billion in 1988, while railroads only earned $26.5 billion in 1987 and a forecast $27 billion in 1988. Coal remained the railroad industry's biggest earner, producing 23.3% of gross revenues. Farm products (6.9% of gross revenues), chemical and allied products (11.8%), transportation equipment (11.0%), food and kindred products (8.0%), and pulp, paper, and allied products (5.8%) are also big revenue producers.

Table 204 Who Moved America's Goods
(percentage of freight moved by weight)

Year	Railroads	Motor vehicles	Inland waterways	Oil pipelines	Domestic airlines
1986*	35.9	25.5	15.1	23.2	0.28
1984	37.2	24.1	15.9	22.6	0.26
1980	37.5	22.3	16.4	23.6	0.20
1970	39.7	21.3	16.5	22.3	0.17
1960	44.1	21.7	16.7	17.4	0.07
1950	56.2	16.3	15.4	12.1	—
1940	61.3	10.0	17.7	9.5	—

Source: Transportation Policy Associates, Washington, D.C., *Transportation in America*, March 1986.
*Estimate

THE PLAYERS

There are about 500 railroad companies, but in this capital-intensive industry there are only a few major players. Only 17 railroads had revenues of $88.5 million or more and they handled over 90% of the industry's freight. The top seven lines generated about 80% of the industry's total revenues. A decade earlier, the top five rail companies picked up 40% of the industry's revenues, indicating how several major mergers have increased industry concentration since deregulation.

THE PEOPLE

Even with featherbedding, there were only 270,000 railroad workers earning an average of $14.30 an hour in the railroad industry in 1986. That was far fewer than the 526,000 employees in 1972 or the industry's peak employment of over 2 million in 1920, when railroad workers earned $3.75 an hour.

TRENDS AND FORECAST

A few figures show the decline of American railroads:

- Railroads operate about 161,000 miles of track today. In 1960, they operated 217,552 miles, down from a peak of 254,251 in 1916.
- Class 1 railroads carried 1,312.1 million tons of goods in 1985, down from 1970 (1,484 million tons), 1951 (1,477 million tons), and 1943 (1,421 million tons). But during this same period, railroad companies' share of total freight shipped fell from 72.5% of all freight in 1943 to 56.8% in 1951, 39.8% in 1970, and 37.2% today.
- Amtrak carries about 20.9 million passengers a year, far fewer than the 706.5 million passengers who rode the rails in 1947 and the 1.2 billion passengers who took a train trip in 1920.

Still, it would be wrong to see the future of railroads as a simple reflection of the past, with the industry continuing to decline. Railroads have held their share of transportation revenues since deregulation in 1980 and are working hard to improve long-term profitability.

Several major mergers, successful efforts to cut labor costs, and deregulation have all helped the railroads. The Railroad Revitalization and Regulatory Reform Act of 1976 was the first piece of transportation deregulation. It allowed railroads some limited rate-setting authority. Following deregulation of the airlines in 1978 and the trucking industry in 1980, Congress passed and President Carter signed into law more substantial legislation, the Staggers Rail Act of 1980. This act introduced price competition and limited the Interstate Commerce Commission's jurisdiction over rates to those rates where a railroad dominated a market.

The act was a major shot in the arm for the ailing industry. After it eased the rules on mergers, several major mergers took place and the industry-wide restructuring helped reduce costs and increase efficiency. Letting railroads have more freedom over rates helped them compete more effectively with trucking, and in 1983 the Interstate Commerce Commission ended a half-century-long ban that prevented airlines from acquiring trucking companies.

Productivity has also soared, up 380% since 1955, and unit labor costs have fallen 36% in the last decade. Even so, labor costs still eat up nearly half of operating revenues. And the average cost of a railroad worker is $40,972, a whopping 53% higher than the $26,799 earned by the average trucker in wages and benefits, according to the Association of American Railroads.

All of this adds up to modest growth, reviving an industry that was once thought to be dying. Freight tonnage is supposed to grow only slightly, at an annual rate of 1.8% through 1992, according to the U.S. Commerce Department. But lower fuel costs, mergers that improve the utilization of equipment, and cheaper labor costs will all help the industry reduce costs and hold its share of the country's transportation dollars. The big uncertainty is the economy, since railroad revenues are closely tied to the health of construction, agriculture, steel, autos, chemicals, and especially coal, which accounts for about 40% of its tonnage, according to Commerce Department estimates. (See the section "Mining.")

RECORDS

THE MARKET

Sales of records are stuck in the same old groove, producing a stagnant market for prerecorded music. Critics blame everything from the aging of America to the lack of interesting new popular music. Whatever, the industry shipped 726.2 million records and tapes in 1978 but, by 1982, that number had dropped to 577.7 million. Even by 1987, when sales recovered to an estimated 663.3 million records, tapes, and compact discs, sales were below the 1978 peak. In 1986, the last year for which a detailed breakdown of sales is available, 22% fewer singles were sold than in 1985 and the number of long-playing (LP) and extended-play (EP) records dropped from 167 million in 1985 to 125.2 million. Only increases in sales of cassettes and compact discs made up the difference. At the same time, the industry has become more dependent on a few big hits. In recent years only megahits by artists such as Michael Jackson and Bruce Springsteen produced the sales and profits the industry needed to stay above water.

THE MONEY

Rising album prices and increased revenues from cassettes and compact discs have propped up the industry's revenues, but only barely. Industry revenues more than doubled between 1973 and 1978, when they hit $4.1 billion. But then weak sales dropped revenues to only $3.6 billion in 1982. Since then sales have recovered, hitting $4.5 billion in 1986 and $4.67 billion in 1987. But record manufacturers should ship $5.5 billion worth of records in 1988. Worldwide sales grew 15% to $14 billion in 1986.

Thirty years ago, everyone was saying rock was just another fad. Well, rock music now holds 33% of the market, followed by pop/easy listening (20%), country (10%), black dance music (9%), shows/soundtracks (4%), gospel (4%), classical (4%), jazz (3%), children's music (3%), and other recordings (10%), according to the Recording Industry Association of America.

TRENDS AND FORECAST

Demographics and technology are both ganging up on this industry. An older public means there are fewer young people to buy records. And, in the last decade, technological changes have hurt sales. Cassette machines let consumers tape albums at home, hurting sales of records. Record and tape piracy, counterfeiting, and bootlegging have also been made easy by these newer technologies. Consumers tape enough music to fill up 564 million albums a year, costing the record industry as much as $1.5 billion in sales. To recoup some of those losses, the industry has been pushing, unsuccessfully, to add a tax to blank cassette tapes. But not everyone shares this dim view of home taping. Many critics say home taping in-

Table 205   Record Industry Manufacturers' Unit Shipments

(millions; net after returns)

	1973	1974	1975	1976	1977	1978	1979	1980	1981	1982	1983	1984	1985	1986	Percentage change, 1985 to 1986
Singles	228.0	204.0	164.0	190.0	190.0	190.0	195.5	164.3	154.7	137.2	124.8	131.5	120.7	93.9	−22
LPs/EPs	280.0	276.0	257.0	273.0	344.0	341.3	318.3	322.8	295.2	243.9	209.6	204.6	167.0	125.2	−25
CDs	—	—	—	—	—	—	—	—	—	—	.8	5.8	22.6	53.0	+134
Cassettes	15.0	15.3	16.2	21.8	36.9	61.3	82.8	110.2	137.0	182.3	236.8	332.0	339.1	344.5	+2
8-tracks	91.0	96.7	94.6	106.1	127.3	133.6	104.7	86.4	48.5	14.3	6.0	5.9	3.5	1.7	−51
Totals	614.0	592.0	531.8	590.9	698.2	726.2	701.1	683.7	635.4	577.7	578.0	679.8	653.0	618.3	−5

Record Industry Manufacturers' Dollar Value of Shipments

(millions of dollars, at suggested list price)

	1973	1974	1975	1976	1977	1978	1979	1980	1981	1982	1983	1984	1985	1986	Percentage change, 1985 to 1986
Singles	190.0	194.0	211.5	245.1	245.1	260.3	275.4	269.3	256.4	283.0	269.3	298.7	281.0	228.1	−19
LPs/EPs	1,246.0	1,356.0	1,485.0	1,663.0	2,195.1	2,473.3	2,136.0	2,290.3	2,341.7	1,925.1	1,689.0	1,548.8	1,280.5	983.0	−23
CDs	—	—	—	—	—	—	—	—	—	—	17.2	103.3	389.5	930.1	+139
Cassettes	76.0	87.2	98.8	145.7	249.6	449.8	604.6	776.4	1,062.8	1,384.5	1,810.9	2,383.9	2,411.5	2,499.5	+4
8-tracks	489.0	549.2	583.0	678.2	811.0	948.0	669.4	526.4	309.0	49.0	27.9	35.7	25.3	10.5	−58
Totals	2,001.0	2,186.4	2,378.3	2,732.0	3,500.8	4,131.4	3,685.4	3,862.4	3,969.9	3,641.6	3,814.3	4,370.4	4,387.8	4,651.1	+6

Source: Recording Industry Association of America Market Research Committee.

creases the public's interest in music and, in the long run, does not harm sales.

Another problem is music that follows the same old formulas. The industry is stumbling in the area of developing new talent. With sales falling, the recording industry is not taking any chances with new talent. Since 1978, the number of new-album releases has dropped almost 50% and seems likely to stay low. Skimping on long-term investments always bodes badly for the future of any industry.

Warner Communications, Inc.

CEO: Steven Ross
Employees: 11,660
Assets: $3.22 billion

75 Rockefeller Plaza
New York, New York 10019
212-484-8000

	1987	1986	1985	1980
Revenues (millions of dollars):	3,403	2,848	2,235	2,059
Net income (millions of dollars):	328	186	195	137
Share earnings (dollars):	2.04	1.26	1.44	1.10

What it does: An entertainment and communications conglomerate with major record, film, book, and cable TV interests.

Warner Communications, Inc.'s history doesn't make much sense. (Maybe it does to chairman Steven Ross and a few old-timers in high-level executive offices.) A successor to something called Kinney Services, Inc., it used to be in the funeral parlor, parking lot, and crematory businesses. Today, Warner is in the communications and entertainment business and publishes *Mad* magazine.

Under Ross, Warner became a huge show biz conglomerate in the 1970s when the company went on an acquisition binge. Ross picked up cable television systems, a recording studio, a toy company, and a theme park. Ross was making deals everywhere. He sold 50% of the company's cable operations to American Express for $175 million, then turned around and bought Samuel Goldwyn Studios for $35 million.

In 1982, he dumped the toy company and bought Popular Library from CBS. In 1983, he exchanged Warner's interest in The Movie Channel and $40 million to acquire 40.5% interest in Showtime/The Movie Channel, a joint venture with Viacom International (Viacom later bought out Warner). In 1984, he acquired a 42.5% interest in BHC, Inc., an independent TV broadcasting system. And he took the company into the video game business.

All the while, Warner obviously was getting bigger and more powerful as an entertainment conglomerate. Warner became the second-largest record company, after CBS, with the likes of its Atlantic Records; became a big book publisher with Warner Books; enhanced its reputation as a major film producer with Warner Bros.; and became a big factor in television through its broadcasting, cable, and programming interests.

Not that Warner digested everything well. One acquisition, Atari, for instance, rode to prosperity on its video games, such as Pac-Man, and at one point provided more than 60% of Warner's profits. Kids tired of the games, though, and Warner took a bloodbath, losing $1 billion between 1983 and 1984 on Atari and other holdings.

But Ross proved his dexterity under fire by embarking on a crash turnaround program and within three years managed to do just that by selling off Atari and other assets and cutting costs wherever he could. By 1987, the company was earning $328 million on revenues of $3.4 billion.

While brushing up against the stars he dealt with, Ross began living like one: shuttling to his East Hampton estate in the company helicopter, taking breaks at the lavish Warner villa in Acapulco, being trailed by a company-paid bodyguard, escorting beautiful stars, hanging out with the likes of Clint Eastwood.

And Ross paid himself well. In fact, his latest compensation package, which critics claim was railroaded through in 1987 by Ross's rubber-stamp, in-house board members, set him up to become one of the highest paid chief executives in the nation.

The contract has a platinum parachute of about $90 million if Warner is taken over at a certain share price. If that doesn't happen, there is the possibility he will make $142.6 million between 1987 and 1996. If Warner's stock price and the company's profits should rise a modest 10% a year compounded annually, which is hardly unreasonable, Ross will get an average of $14 million a year in salary and bonuses. Not bad for a guy whose company once was in the funeral parlor business.

MAKING MUSIC PAY

Retail sales of music instruments hit $3 billion in 1987 while at the factory level U.S. music makers sold $646 million worth of instruments in 1987. But there are discordant notes being sounded from the Far East. American manufacturers, who held 86% of the markets as late as 1980, when they shipped $1.02 billion worth of musical instruments, now only hold 47% of the market. And the $730 million worth of imports—about 53% of the market—aren't just cheap electronic music makers. Imports of grand pianos, for example, increased 17% in 1986 to $70 million, with Japan accounting for 55% and South Korea supplying 29%. It all translates into a stagnant industry, with U.S. companies battling foreign music makers. A mere 11,000 people are employed in this industry.

Bruce Springsteen   His songs tell of working-class woes, but his popularity has made Bruce Springsteen one of the wealthiest men in rock and roll. [Though his finances remain a closely guarded secret, *Forbes* estimates that Bruce's $56 million in income in 1986 and 1987 make him the biggest-paid rock musician.] His *Live/1975–85* album, released in 1986, earned him millions of dollars. He'd also already sold 38 million albums, including 18 million *Born in the U.S.A.* albums sold that earned Springsteen at least $25 million in the bank. He probably earned $50 million from the $90 million in ticket sales during his 15-month "Born in the U.S.A." tour and $8 million in souvenirs from the tour. Millions more come in from song royalties, which have already made him one of the 10 best-paid songwriters in history.

Still, CBS doesn't mind all the money it pays him in royalties. Bruce and a few other top artists have produced boss profits for CBS Inc. For example, CBS record profits dropped from $92.8 million in 1978 to $51 million in 1979, modestly recovered to $72.3 million in 1980, and dropped again in 1981 to $58.9 million and in 1982 to $22.2 million. This forced CBS to close manufacturing plants and sales branches, lay off staff, and tighten control on marketing and artist development expenditures. But the music video fad and an improved economy picked up sales. In 1983, fueled by Michael Jackson's *Thriller* album, CBS profits soared to $109.4 million. In 1984, on the basis of continuing sales of *Thriller* and Bruce Springsteen's *Born in the U.S.A.,* CBS record profits jumped to a record $123.5 million. But in 1985, without those big hits, record profits fell back to $87.2 million.

In 1986, faced with stagnant TV ad revenues and slumping ratings, CBS found that records were the key to its profitability. Profits were up dramatically in the first half of 1986, largely because of the hit soundtrack from the movie *Top Gun* and releases from Billy Joel, Barbra Streisand, and the Rolling Stones. Then, at the end of the year and in early 1987, record sales of Bruce's live album kept profits up. "Records bailed them out," said Robert Ladd, media analyst for E. F. Hutton & Co.

But despite the profits produced by the record division, CBS's Chairman Laurence Tisch sold the division to Sony for about $2 billion in 1987. With CBS, the world's largest record company, in the hands of the Japanese, that left only two American companies, Warner Communications and MCA's record unit, with a significant presence in the worldwide record market. In 1986, the German-based company Bertelsmann AG bought RCA, and other major labels such as PolyGram and Capital are owned by Europeans.

Table 206　Top-paid Entertainers

Forbes estimates entertainment's biggest earners. Perspective: median compensation of 800 leading corporate executives in 1986 was $706,000.

Rank	Star/age/occupation	Gross income (millions of dollars)		Two-year total
		1986	1987	
1.	William H. Cosby, Jr./actor, comedian, author	27	57	84
2.	Sylvester Stallone/actor, writer	53	21	74
3.	Bruce Springsteen/rock singer	29	27	56
4.	Charles M. Schulz/cartoonist (Peanuts)	25	30	55
5.	Eddie Murphy/comedian, actor	23	27	50
6.	Steven Spielberg/movie producer, director	27	23	50
7.	Madonna (Louise Ciccone)/rock singer	21	26	47
8.	Whitney Houston/pop singer	20	24	44
9.	Michael Jackson/pop singer	12	31	43
10.	Johnny Carson/TV host, producer	20	20	40
11.	U2/rock group (4 members)	8	29	37
12.	ZZ Top/rock group (3 members)	26	5	31
13.	Jim Davis/cartoonist (Garfield)	15	16	31
14.	Bon Jovi/rock group (5 members)	10	19	29
15.	Arnold Schwarzenegger/actor	8	18	26
16.	Kenny Rogers/country singer	10	16	26
17.	Van Halen/rock group (4 members)	22	3	25
18.	Wayne Newton/pop singer	12	12	24
19.	Neil Diamond/pop singer	13	11	24
20.	Prince (Rogers Nelson)/rock singer	15	8	23

Source: *Forbes.*

RESTAURANTS

THE MARKET

As one wit once put it, "eating out" is America's favorite cuisine. Americans eat out 3.7 times a week, for a total of 45 billion meals in restaurants and school and work cafeterias each year. About 42.5% of our food dollar goes to restaurants, up from 1955, when the average American spent about 25.4 cents of every food dollar eating out, and 1980, when 36 cents of every food dollar was spent away from home.

During a two-week period, about 8 out of 10 adults will eat out at least once. The average check is $3.41.

The most popular meal for eating out may surprise you. It is dinner, which accounts for 39% of the meals eaten away from home. Lunch is a close second with 38%, breakfast 9%, and snacks 15%, according to a survey commissioned by the National Restaurant Association.

THE MONEY

The food service industry earned between $189 billion and $206 billion in 1987, according to various estimates. That included, in part, $71.2 billion from full-service restaurants, $55.8 billion from fast-food restaurants, $12.3 billion in hotels and motels, $5.9 billion from food sold in recreational facilities, $8.1 billion in retail outlets, $8.8 billion in bars and taverns, $4.2 billion in schools, $7.9 billion in hospitals, $4.1 billion in nursing homes, $6.7 billion in business and industry, $5.1 billion in colleges, $1.0 billion in the military, and $4.3 billion from vending machines, according to the National Restaurant Association.

Adjusted for inflation, the 400 largest companies in the restaurant industry grew at a frenetic pace during the 1960s and 1970s—10.4% a year between 1964 and 1969, 8% between 1970 and 1974, 5.5% between 1975 and 1979, and 3.2% between 1980 and 1984, according to the magazine *Restaurants & Institutions*. But after a slump in the middle of 1984, food service revenues grew only 1.7% in 1985 and only 1.4% in 1986.

THE PLAYERS

There are about 258,000 restaurants in the U.S. Most of the money (51%) is earned by the 400 largest food service companies, which account for $94.3 billion, according to *Restaurants & Institutions*. The top 100 food service companies capture 26.9% of all revenues. Leading the pack is McDonald's, which opened its 9,000th unit in Sydney, Australia, in February of 1986, and since then has been opening a new restaurant every 17 hours. The second-largest company in the restaurant business is Pillsbury, which owns Burger King, a chain that opens a new restaurant every day.

Despite Burger King's and McDonald's heroic efforts to put a fast-food restaurant on every block, the number of restaurants has dropped since 1972, when there were 274,000 eateries.

THE PEOPLE

Some 8 million people are employed in the food service industry, earning $53 billion in wages and benefits, according to the National Restaurant Association. About two thirds of these workers are women; one quarter are teenagers.

TRENDS AND FORECAST

After years of rapid expansion, growth in the food service industry has slowed down since 1984. In 1987 sales are expected to have increased 6.4%, or 2.4% when adjusted for inflation, to $197.5 billion, according to National Restaurant Association estimates.

Over the next decade, several demographic trends favor the restaurant business: More working parents and single-parent households, for example, mean more people will be eating out. An increasingly older population is cause for some concern since older people spend less of their food budget eating out (only 33% for those 55 to 64 compared to 43% for those under 25 and 39% for those 25 to 34 years old.) But older Americans are eating out more than ever before, so an increasingly healthy and mobile older population may not hurt the industry's long-term outlook. The Tax Reform Act of 1986, which reduced to 80% the deductions for entertainment and business meals, hasn't yet done any significant damage to the industry.

Industry problems include tougher drunk-driving laws that will continue to hurt liquor sales and a decline in the teenage population that will drive up wages and costs. The industry also remains heavily dependent on the growth of discretionary income among consumers. With consumer debt at record levels, consumer spending is not likely to grow as fast as it did during the 1960s or 1970s. Still, the long-term outlook remains bright as Americans spend more and more of their food budget away from home. Look at some of the findings of the *Restaurants and Institutions* Annual Report:

RESTAURANT TRIVIA

- The fast-food industry is facing new attitudes toward diet. Hamburgers, which took a 51% bite out of fast-food sales in 1979, have slipped to 49%. Steaks account for 19% of fast-food sales, compared to 21% in 1979. The winners were chicken, which grew from 9% to 10%, and health food and pizza, which grew from 8% in 1979 to 12% today.
- Steakhouses do an $8.8-billion-a-year business.
- Cafeterias do a $3-billion-a-year business.
- Americans eat $7.2 billion worth of pizza a year outside their homes.
- Mexican fast food adds up to a lot of pesos—$2.4 billion in annual sales.
- Chicken consumption is 279 million pounds. Restaurants specializing in chicken do a $7.6 billion business annually.
- The Super Bowl is also a lucrative food market. Interstate United sold $1.2 million worth of food and beverages during the 1984 Super Bowl.
- The average cost of an airline meal hit $5 in 1985 as airlines spent $1.4 billion on food. In 1975 the average meal cost $2.41. Still, food accounted for only 3.1% of the airlines' operating cost, down from 1975, when it accounted for 3.4% of costs.

McDonald's Corporation
CEO: F. L. Turner
Employees: 127,000
Assets: $6 billion

McDonald's Plaza
2111 Enco Drive
Oak Brook, Illinois 60521
312-575-3000

	1987	1986	1985	1980
Revenues (millions of dollars):	4,893	4,144	3,695	2,184
Net income (millions of dollars):	596	480	433	221
Share earnings (dollars):	3.14	3.73	3.33	1.63

What it does: The major force in the fast-food industry. At the beginning of 1987, there were some 7,300 units in the U.S. and 2,200 in other nations.

Seeing the exploding growth of suburbia and the growing interest in fast food, a 52-year-old entrepreneur named Ray Kroc struck a deal in 1954 with the two McDonald brothers to franchise their San Bernardino, California, burger stand. Kroc's first McDonald's opened in 1955 in Des Plaines, Illinois. By 1958, a sign appeared over its golden arches: "100 million hamburgers served." Kroc bought out the McDonalds in 1961 for a paltry $2.7 million and achieved systemwide sales of $1 billion by 1972. Shortly after his death in 1984, the company celebrated its 30th anniversary by selling its 50 billionth burger. The company was the first food service company to become part of the prestigious Dow Jones Industrial Average.

In recent years, McDonald's has worked overtime to keep the 18 million customers who visit the chain every day all around the world. When Americans lost some of their ardor for beef, the company started selling Chicken McNuggets and, in 1986, started testing McPizza and salads. The company relies on a $550 million advertising budget to beat Burger King, Wendy's and other competitors in the burger wars. As the country has become saturated with fast-food chains, McDonald's has aggressively expanded overseas, with more than 530 restaurants in Japan alone. Revenues topped $4 billion in 1986, up 13% from 1985, and net income of $480 million soared up 11% from a year earlier. The figures are whoppers when one remembers the entire food service industry only grew 1.4% in 1986.

Table 207   Top 10 Restaurant Markets

Rank	Metropolitan area	Sales (in billions of dollars)
1.	New York	3.01
2.	Los Angeles–Long Beach	2.97
3.	Boston-Lawrence-Salem-Lowell-Brockton	1.83
4.	Chicago	1.71
5.	San Francisco	1.20
6.	Washington	1.19
7.	Philadelphia	1.17
8.	Detroit	1.12
9.	Anaheim–Santa Ana	1.02
10.	Houston	.98

Source: *Restaurant Business.*

Table 208   Top Five Restaurant Chains

Rank	Organization Headquarters	1986 sales (millions of dollars)	Number of units, 1986
1.	McDonald's Corporation Oak Brook, Illinois	12,400	9,410
2.	Burger King (Pillsbury) Miami, Florida	5,000	5,024
3.	Kentucky Fried Chicken (PepsiCo.) Louisville, Kentucky	3,500	6,575
4.	Wendy's Dublin, Ohio	2,747	3,727
5.	Pizza Hut (PepsiCo.) Wichita, Kansas	2,503	5,646

Source: © 1987 *Restaurants & Institutions,* a Cahners publication.

Table 209   Five Largest Independent Restaurants

Rank	Restaurant City Owner	Sales (millions of dollars)	Opened	Seats	People served per year
1.	Hilltop Steak House Saugus, Massachusetts Frank Giuffrida	26.9	1951	1,300	2,350,000
2.	Tavern on the Green New York, New York Warner LeRoy	24.9	1934	1,200	710,000
3.	Phillips Harborplace Baltimore, Maryland Brice and Shirley Phillips	15.0	1980	700	540,000
4.	Anthony's Pier 4 Boston, Massachusetts Anthony Athanas and family	13.6	1963	370	600,000
5.	Smith & Wollensky New York, New York Alan Stillman	13.6	1977	400	300,000

Source: © 1987 *Restaurants & Institutions,* a Cahners publication.

594

RETAIL

THE MARKET AND THE MONEY

Retail sales hit $1.58 trillion in 1987 and should grow to $1.6 trillion in 1988. Department store sales are projected to total $161 billion in 1988 while apparel and accessory stores will rack up $93 billion in sales. Eating and drinking establishments should ring up sales of $172 billion according to the U.S. Dept. of Commerce.

About one third of all retail establishments are small, with no paid employees; about 43% have fewer than 10 employees. Larger stores, with more than $500,000 in annual sales, earn more than three quarters of all retail sales. The largest 50 retailers control about one fifth of the market and stores with 10 or more branches account for 95% of all department store sales, 56% of all drug store sales, half of all shoe sales, one quarter of the revenues of eating places, and 57% of all grocery store sales.

THE PEOPLE

The retail trade employed about 18.5 million people in 1987, up from 11.8 million in 1972. About 18% of all nonagricultural workers earn their paychecks in the retail industry.

Wal-Mart Stores, Inc.
CEO: David S. Glass
Employees: 185,000
Assets: $4.9 billion

P.O. Box 116
Bentonville, Arkansas 72712
501-273-4000

	1987	1986	1985	1980
Revenues (millions of dollars):	11,909	8,451	6,401	1,643
Net income (millions of dollars):	450	327	271	55
Share earnings (dollars):	.80	.58	.48	.11

What it does: A discount retailer, operating some 860 department stores in 22 states.

When seen rattling around the dirt roads of Bentonville, Arkansas, in his old Ford pickup truck with his hunting dog, it's kinda hard to believe that unassuming Sam Moore Walton can scrape together more than a few bucks to buy shotgun shells down at Wal-Mart, the big discount store on the other side of town.

But, heck, "Mr. Sam," as he's known to folks around Bentonville, could buy out the whole darn store if he wanted. Fortunately for him, he doesn't have to. He is the major stock holder in the company which owns that Wal-Mart and 860 or so others in 22 states in the midwest and the Sunbelt. According to *Forbes* magazine that makes him the richest man in the country, with, oh, say, about $6 billion in stock.

Ever since *Forbes* came out with Mr. Sam's little secret in 1985, life

Table 210   How the Country Spent Its Retail Dollars
(billions of dollars)

Kind of business	1970 sales	1980 sales	1985 sales	1986 sales
Retail trade total	368.4	959.6	1,379.9	1,454.4
Durable goods stores, total	109.2	299.0	514.2	568.0
Automotive dealers	62.6	164.4	312.8	335.8
Building materials, garden supply, hardware and mobile homes dealers	17.6	50.7	74.1	88.0
Building materials, supply stores	11.2	35.0	53.8	65.6
Hardware stores	3.2	8.3	11.1	10.7
Furniture, home furnishings, and equipment	17.7	44.1	68.1	78.5
Furniture, home furnishings stores	10.6	26.3	36.9	41.8
Household appliance, radio, TV dealers	6.0	13.9	26.2	41.8
Nondurable goods stores, total	259.2	660.6	859.7	886.4
Apparel and accessory stores	20.2	48.1	69.7	80.8
Men's, boys' clothing and furnishings stores	4.4	7.6	8.3	9.6
Women's clothing and specialty stores, furriers	7.7	18.5	29.1	33.9
Family clothing stores	3.8	11.0	18.3	18.6
Shoe stores	3.6	8.4	10.9	14.9
Drug and proprietary stores	13.8	30.7	46.0	49.3
Eating and drinking places	31.1	89.9	131.0	144.9
Food stores	88.7	219.5	282.2	296.0
Gasoline service stations	29.2	93.8	100.8	86.6
General merchandise stores	52.0	113.9	159.5	155.9
Department stores	40.2	93.9	150.6	
Variety stores	6.6	7.9	8.9	8.5
Liquor stores	8.3	16.9	17.8	19.8
Nonstore retailers	NA	22.8	27.0	26.7
Mail-order houses	NA	4.4	4.6	3.3

Source: U.S. Department of Commerce.

has gotten more complicated for him. He used to sneak off and do some bird hunting whenever the mood struck. Now, he sneaks around whenever he gets wind that yet another reporter is in this town of 9,900 or so citizens to bird-dog him until he answers questions such as, "What's it like to be filthy rich?" and "How did you make so much money?"

The answer to the first question is easy. Though a lot of folks might find it hard to believe, money doesn't mean a heck of a lot to Mr. Sam. A folksy guy, he always lived modestly. He doesn't know what all the fuss is about, because, as he says, "It's only paper money." (His shrunk by $2 billion in the market meltdown of October 1987.)

As for the second question: Mr. Sam is the personification of the American work ethic. He spotted an opportunity, worked hard, was a square shooter with his employees and customers, and kept plowing his profits back into the business to make it better and bigger.

After graduating from the University of Missouri in 1940, he got a job with J. C. Penney at $85 a month. When war broke out, he spent three years as an Army intelligence officer. When he left the service in 1945, he borrowed $25,000 and opened a five-and-dime in Newport, Arkansas. When the landlord refused to renew his lease several years later, he packed up and moved to Bentonville. (One reason he picked the little town was because of the good hunting around there.)

In 1962, he got the notion that small-town people would appreciate a discount general store with friendly folks selling quality merchandise. He liked people so much that he believed his salespeople—"associates," as he called his employees—should like people a lot too and treat customers real well. He opened his first store and his instincts paid off. He opened another and then another and then . . .

In 1970, Wal-Mart went public. The company joined the Big Board two years later when sales were $72 million and there were 41 stores. Employees got stock options after working a year for the company, and Mr. Sam always encouraged his associates to put whatever money they could into the company. As a result, there are an awful lot of millionaires walking around Bentonville today thanks to a landlord who once made Mr. Sam go to another town.

HOME SHOPPING

The folks who are bent on turning the U.S. into a nation of couch potatoes moved a step closer with the introduction of home shopping. Now you don't have to stir off the sofa to order up anything from a fur coat to a power mower. Just flick on the TV, watch one of the shopping shows on cable until you find something you lust after, and phone in your order.

The business might have passed the $2 billion mark in 1987, Paul Kagan, the cable analyst, stated. Even if it came close, that's remarkable considering that sales in 1986 were about $450 million, up from almost zilch a year earlier.

For years, various companies played around with home shopping, many of the efforts resembling late-night schlock commercials that sold old Eddie Fisher albums or knives with Japanese names that turned carrots into gold. Maybe it was just an idea that had to wait its time, because even a lot of the shows being aired resemble bargain-basement fire sales.

Nonetheless, the impressive numbers being rung up on the cash register set a lot of respectable companies thinking that home shopping might revolutionize retailing as well as make people a little lazier. Sears, Roebuck and Company, for instance, linked up with QVC Network, Inc. to sell Sears products on a home shopping program that reaches millions of viewers.

And there's nothing schlocky about Wall Street's reaction to the business. Home Shopping Network, Inc., a pioneer in the field, was the hottest new issue of 1986. The stock was offered at $18 a share on May 13 and soared to $42 on the first day of trading. Within weeks, it passed $120 and split three for one. That meant owners Lowell W. Paxson and Roy M. Speer had combined holdings of about $600 million. But in 1987 stocks of home shopping companies dropped, and the industry faced a shakeout.

TUPPERWARE

In 1950, Earl Tupper had a problem. Five years earlier, Earl had developed the first airtight plastic containers, which he called Tupperware. But sales weren't so hot. Then he had an idea. Maybe Tupperware could be sold at parties women gave in their homes in exchange for a little gift. Four years later, sales hit $9 million as an army of 9,000 women held Tupperware parties. Rexall Drugs bought his company in 1958.

TIFFANY

Charles Tiffany came to New York in 1837 with the idea of opening a store that was a far cry from his dad's general store in Plainfield, Connecticut. He opened a jewelry store. Soon, he and a partner had a growing reputation for the quality of the English and Italian jewelry they sold. When the European diamond market became depressed in 1848, they began making their own jewelry. Their designs, such as the Tiffany ring setting—a diamond mounted in raised prongs—became much sought after, making Tiffany & Co. the biggest jewelry firm in the U.S. After Charles's death in 1902, his son Louis Comfort Tiffany, who died in 1933, began making the iridescent glass used in jewelry and vases, among other things that bear his name.

LENOX CHINA

That the U.S. makes fine china owes a lot to Walter Lenox. Until 1894, when he started making porcelain dinnerware modeled after that made by the Irish company Belleek Pottery, all fine china was imported. His company came to prominence when Tiffany's placed a large order about 10 years later. But not everybody's happy for everybody who gets Lenox. When Nancy Reagan gave the company a $209,508 order for White House dinnerware, she was widely criticized for her extravagance.

FULLER BRUSH

The work world didn't start out promising for the young Canadian Alf Fuller. By the time he was 18, he had been fired as a ticket taker after taking a break by joyriding in a car and crashing, fired as a stable hand for forgetting to take care of a horse, and fired as a messenger—a job his brother gave him—after losing a package. In 1905, figuring the only way he couldn't get fired was working for himself, he started selling brushes door to door. Surprising everybody, he was successful. The next year, he began making the brushes he sold. By 1910, he had 25 salesmen pounding on people's doors to sell Fuller brushes. In 1943, the year Alf retired, his company's sales were $10 million.

PARKER PEN

When George S. Parker was teaching telegraphy in Janesville, Wisconsin, he sold pens to his students. As the salesman, he felt an obligation to fix the pens when they went on the fritz, which they constantly did. While tinkering, he concluded he could make a better pen. By 1890, he had patented his first pen and, with a partner, W. F. Palmer, launched the Parker Pen Company.

During the First World War, Parker's Trench Pen was the favorite of American soldiers on the front; they could make their own ink by disolving a pill of black pigment in water in the pen's cap. Sales rose after the war, declined for a bit during the Depression, and then rose again when the company introduced the Parker Vacuumatic, which more than doubled the capacity of similar-sized pens. Parker toured the world, creating an international network of distributors. In 1939, the Parker 51 fountain pen with its classic design was introduced and became a best-seller and the model for fountain pens ever since.

FOOD

The Market and the Money

In 1987 Americans spent about $308 billion on food at all types of retail outlets and about $290 billion of the total sold in the country's 154,000 grocery stores and supermarkets. But most of those sales, (72%), took place in the country's 30,505 supermarkets, according to *Progressive Grocer*. Large chains with 11 or more supermarkets or grocery stores also controlled a large part of the market. These chains rang up $171.5 billion worth of total $308 billion in retail food sales. In 1988 all retail outlets and grocery stores are expected to sell $323 billion worth of food, with grocery stores and supermarkets selling about $306 billion of that total. Chains should sell about $178 billion worth of goods. The average customer spent $16.33 every time he or she visited a supermarket, up from $14.33 in 1981, according to the Food Marketing Institute.

Consumers are finding more items on supermarket shelves and buying more nonfood items in supermarkets and groceries. The average supermarket carries 17,459 different items, up from 12,000 in 1983. About 5,100 new products make their way onto supermarket shelves each year. And nonfood items account for 25% of all supermarket sales, up from 6% to 8% in the 1960s. Americans now buy nearly half of their magazines and one third of their nonprescription drugs in supermarkets.

The Players

The average supermarket has $206,543 in sales per week, or about $8.43 of sales per week for every square foot in the store. Profits in this business are still determined by volume, with the average supermarket earning 1.19 cents of profit for every dollar of sales.

Just as supermarkets (stores with more than $2 million in average sales) capture a large proportion of industry sales (71.8%), large chain operators (those companies with 11 or more establishments) also hold a large share of the market, about 55%.

The People

The food retailing industry employs about 2.9 million people, up from 2.48 million in 1982.

Trends and Forecast

The outlook continues to be favorable for food retailers. Increased use of computers, less expensive labor contracts, and a trend toward large superstores or superwarehouses have also reduced costs for many operators. However, a slow growing population and a trend towards eating out will slow the industry's growth and hurt profits.

COUPONS

U.S. manufacturers issue about 179.8 billion coupons a year. But only a relatively small proportion, about 6.49 billion, are actually redeemed, for an approximate value of $2.24 billion, according to the Food Marketing Institute.

Table 211   Five Largest Supermarket Chains

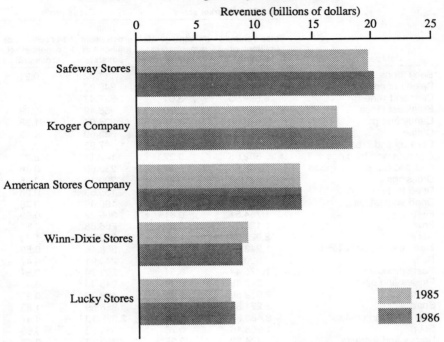

Revenues (billions of dollars)

Table 212 The Supermarket Market: Sales by Category

Category name	Supermarket sales		Gross profit	
	1986 sales volume (millions of dollars)	Percentage of supermarket sales	1986 gross profit (millions of dollars)	Percentage of supermarket gross profit
Baby foods	1,193.76	0.54	111.32	0.21
Baking needs	4,015.76	1.83	848.60	1.62
Beer and wine	6,599.99	3.01	1,527.43	2.92
Breakfast foods	4,829.66	2.20	936.49	1.79
Candy and gum	2,610.88	1.19	824.04	1.58
Coffee	3,968.60	1.81	583.80	1.12
Cookies and crackers	4,609.27	2.10	1,107.98	2.12
Desserts and toppings	582.65	0.27	142.11	0.27
Diet and low-calorie foods	905.66	0.41	239.96	0.46
Dressings	1,431.38	0.65	290.19	0.56
Dried fruits	458.66	0.21	135.50	0.26
Dried vegetables	713.53	0.33	186.49	0.36
Fish	1,784.51	0.81	360.22	0.69
Fruit	1,128.57	0.51	266.68	0.51
Juice	2,929.66	1.33	623.38	1.19
Meat and specialty foods	1,243.80	0.57	308.46	0.59
Nuts	830.60	0.38	244.91	0.47
Pasta products	1,175.44	0.54	299.26	0.57
Pickles and olives	849.45	0.39	245.46	0.47
Sauces	2,079.60	0.95	498.36	0.95
Snacks	3,271.88	1.49	956.59	1.83
Soft drinks and mixes	8,483.84	3.87	2,339.13	4.47
Soup	1,668.16	0.76	356.53	0.68
Spices and extracts	774.22	0.35	269.77	0.52
Spreads	1,059.36	0.48	226.52	0.43
Syrups	445.36	0.20	102.17	0.20
Tea	735.81	0.34	168.05	0.32
Vegetables	2,476.51	1.13	602.23	1.15
Total grocery edibles	62,856.57	28.63	14,199.40	27.16
Household supplies	7,780.22	3.54	1,715.40	3.28
Paper, plastic, film, and foil	8,305.00	3.78	1,473.58	2.82
Pet foods	4,485.72	2.04	955.67	1.83
Tobacco products	7,749.95	3.53	1,067.58	2.04
Total grocery nonedibles	28,320.89	12.90	5,212.23	9.97
Bakery foods	7,585.89	3.46	1,555.11	2.98
Dairy products	20,665.49	9.41	4,724.65	9.04
Deli	5,163.25	2.35	1,432.78	2.74
Frozen foods	13,903.28	6.33	3,811.14	7.29
Ice cream	2,283.61	1.04	698.78	1.34
Meat	36,994.74	16.85	7,509.92	14.37
Produce	19,449.63	8.86	6,301.68	12.06
Total perishables	106,045.89	48.32	26,034.06	49.80
General merchandise	9,827.37	4.48	3,488.72	6.67
Health and beauty aids	8,679.67	3.95	2,222.00	4.25
Unclassified	3,769.61	1.72	1,115.80	2.15
Total supermarket	219,500.00	100.00	52,272.21	100.00

Source: *Progressive Grocer,* July 1987.

ANIMAL CRACKERS

A couple of bakeries tried selling animal cookies, but what they lacked was National Biscuit Company's clever marketing when it launched Barnum Animals in 1902. Kids loved the little packages decorated with circus animals and they thought the little string on top of the box was a great handle. (Actually, the handle was just a piece of luck for the company, which had put the string there so the boxes could be hung on Christmas trees.)

OREO COOKIES

Nobody's sure how Oreo cookies got their name. And National Biscuit Company, which introduced them in 1912, isn't sure how they became the runaway best-selling cookie in the world. They came to market with two other cookies, Mother Goose Biscuits and Veronese Biscuits, from which the company apparently expected great things. But people were really waiting for Oreos. Today, about 5 billion Oreos are eaten each year by Americans alone.

HERSHEY

In 1884, Milton Hershey talked a banker into giving him a $700 loan to launch his candy business in Lancaster, Pennsylvania. When the note fell due, Hershey not only couldn't pay, but he wanted to borrow $1,000 more to buy equipment. To press his case, he invited the banker to his "factory," which turned out to be a shabby little place where his "employees"—his mom and his Aunt Mattie—sat wrapping caramels. In defiance of his profession, the banker gave him the loan. A little while later, Hershey received enough money for candy he had shipped to England to pay off his debts and his business expanded like mad.

Hershey started making chocolate in 1892, after he saw a demonstration by German chocolate makers at the Chicago Exposition. When the exposition ended, he bought the demonstration equipment, hired some professional chocolate makers, and, convinced that chocolate was the way to go, sold off his caramel business in 1900 for $1 million. His strategy was to concentrate on one product, mass-produce it, and price it so everyone could afford it. Needless to say, it worked.

SHOPPING MALLS

The Market

There are approximately 24,700 shopping centers in the U.S., covering nearly 3.4 billion square feet of leasable space, up from only 100 shopping

Table 213   The Largest Shopping Malls in the U.S.

Rank	Center Location	Owner	Total gross leasable space (thousands of square feet)
1.	Del Amo Fashion Center Torrance, California	Carson-Madrona Company The Torrance Company	2,650
2.	Lakewood Center Mall Lakewood, California	Macerich Company	2,400
3.	Woodfield Shaumburg, Illinois	Woodfield-Taubman Company The Homart Development Company	2,300
4.	Randal Park Mall North Randall, Ohio	The Edward J. DeBartolo Corporation	2,097
5.	South Coast Plaza and Town Center Costa Mesa, California	C. J. Segerstrom and Sons	1,800

Source: *Shopping Center Development Handbook, 2nd Edition,* Executive Group of the Commercial and Retail Development Council of the Urban Land Institute.

Table 214   The Largest Shopping Center Developers-Owners

	Company	GLA Developed/ Acquired	Last Year's Rank
1.	The Edward J. DeBartolo Corp. *Youngstown, OH*	12,191,467	21
2.	Philips Int'l/The Realco Group *Great Neck, NY*	12,109,337	5
3.	Melvin Simon & Associates *Indianapolis, IN*	11,560,997	8
4.	Trammell Crow Company *Dallas, TX*	11,483,132	11
5.	J.W. O'Connor & Co., Inc. *New York, NY*	11,331,000	4
6.	Southmark Commercial Mgmt. *Dallas, TX*	9,731,573	2
7.	Kravco Company *King of Prussia, PA*	9,647,685	36
8.	Schostak Bros. & Co., Inc. *Southfield, MI*	9,590,000	15
9.	HSW Investments, Inc. *Fort Lauderdale, FL*	9,355,000	13
10.	Concord Assets Group *Boca Raton, FL*	9,054,412	3

Source: *National Mall Monitor,* January–February 1988 edition.

centers in 1950. In 1985 alone, construction on over 2,171 shopping centers was started, a record. Half of all retail sales are made in shopping centers, up from 42% in 1982 and 25% in 1974, according to the Urban Land Institute.

The Money

Retail sales at American shopping centers have climbed to over $500 billion, according to the International Council of Shopping Centers, up from $273 billion in 1978. Since few owners or managing companies of shopping centers are publicly held, there are no figures on profitability.

The People

Nearly 6.8 million people are employed in shopping centers.

THE WORLD'S LARGEST SHOPPING MALL

The title of the world's largest shopping mall belongs to the West Edmonton Mall, located in the unlikely setting of Edmonton, Canada. The 110-acre mall has over 800 shops, several dozen restaurants, 34 theaters, an 18-hole miniature golf course, a 10-acre water park for swimming and sunning, two dozen amusement rides, and a 360-room hotel. And if that isn't enough to attract visitors, there are also monkeys, tigers, and four submarines that prowl a 438-foot-long lake infested with real sharks. Believe it or not, it's all indoors under one roof.

The developers, the four Ghermezian brothers—Raphael, Eskandar, Nader, and Bahman—have spent over $650 million to build the mall, even though they admit Edmonton's 500,000 population is too small to support the project. So why did they build it?

The project was conceived in the late 1970s during the oil boom when Edmonton's economy and population were booming. After coming to Canada in the 1950s from Iran, the Ghermezians had bought some 15,000 acres of underdeveloped Edmonton land for under $200 an acre. By the early 1980s that same land was selling for $40,000 an acre. But as the mall was being built, the oil economy went bust and now it's an open question whether the mall can survive. Normally, a mall this size would need to be in a city five times Edmonton's population. The Ghermezians scoff at that criticism, arguing that they had always meant the tourist trade to support the mall. The mall's amusement park will attract tourists, but how many of them will be willing to brave the 40-degree-below temperatures of Edmonton in the winter for a vacation shopping spree remains to be seen.

STEEL

THE MARKET

Once the mighty symbol of American manufacturing, steel is now the symbol of its decline. As manufacturers replace steel with products such as plastic, consumption of steel continues to fall. In 1988, the U.S. economy is expected to consume only 90 million tons of steel, down from the 98.9 million consumed in 1984 and far less than the average of 107 million tons of steel consumed in the U.S. during the 1970s. With imports cutting into the market, U.S. steel makers are expected to produce only 83.5 million tons of steel, way down from 127 million tons in 1977. (See also the "Mining" section for information on closely related markets.)

THE MONEY

As you might imagine, a rusty steel market has corroded steel mill revenues. American steel makers are expected to ship only $40.1 billion worth of steel in 1987, some $7.9 billion less than 1984 and way below the 1981 record of $62.8 billion.

Imports, on the other hand, have grabbed a hefty share of the U.S. market: the value of imports hit $8.1 billion in 1986, down from a record $10.1 billion in 1984, but up from $8.8 billion in 1982 and $2.7 billion in 1972.

Although sales recovered from the 1982 slump, steel makers aren't forging any profits. In 1986, six large steel makers lost a whopping $5.7 billion, with the nation's largest steel maker, USX Corporation, losing $1.8 billion. However analysts believe that the six companies turned a profit of about $1 billion in 1987 and could make $1.2 billion in 1988.

THE PLAYERS

In 1976, domestic steel producers produced 128 million tons of raw steel and controlled about 86% of the market; in 1988, they are expected to have produced only 83 million tons and control only about 78% of the market.

Even so, big steel remains big. The country's six largest producers account for 58.8% of the domestic steel market (down from 65.9% in 1984). USX, the nation's largest steel maker, held 11.2% of the market at the end of the second quarter in 1987 (down from 17.1% in 1984); the next-biggest, LTV, held 14.2% (down from 17.1% in 1984); Bethlehem Steel held 12.9% (up from 12.6% in 1984); Armco had 7.0% (up from 6.2%); Inland captured 6.8% (down from 7% in 1984); and National Intergroup held 6.7% (up from 5.9%).

THE PEOPLE

There were 237,000 employees in the steel industry in 1987, down from 308,000 in 1984 and 543,000 in 1972. Wages and benefits for production workers averaged about $22 an hour.

TRENDS AND FORECAST

In case you haven't heard, the steel industry was in bad shape for most of the 1980s. Consider a few facts:

- Many U.S. steel companies are producing more red ink than steel. Between 1982 and 1986, the six largest steel makers lost $12 billion. In April 1985, Wheeling-Pittsburgh went into bankruptcy, and in 1986, LTV, the second-largest steel maker, followed.
- Since 1972, some 700 steel plants and related facilities have been closed, cutting total capacity by 22%. Most cuts came between 1982 and 1984, when steel capacity was reduced by 20 million tons, or about 14%, the U.S. Commerce Department says.
- The steel industry had the capacity to turn out 127.9 million tons at the start of 1986 but operated at only two-thirds capacity. In 1987, after closing 450 plants since 1980, the industry was operating at only 80% capacity.
- Competing with high-tech foreign producers, the domestic steel industry badly needed to modernize its plants. But in 1986 the steel industry spent only 780 million on capital, down from 1984's $1.2 billion and way less than the $2.4 billion spent in 1981 before a recession hit the steel market. After the bankruptcy of Wheeling-Pittsburgh Steel Corporation in 1985 and LTV's bankruptcy in 1986, investors may not be willing to cough up the capital needed to save the industry.
- Demand for steel in certain key sectors of the economy, such as the auto industry, will continue to drop. Domestic auto makers continue to lose ground to foreign producers and the cars they do make use less steel.
- It cost steel makers an estimated $3.2 billion to shut plants between 1983 and 1988, or about $75,000 per laid-off worker. That severely limits the amount of capital they can spend on modernizing existing plants.
- Steel operations that haven't slipped into bankruptcy face tough competition from companies that are operating out of Chapter 11. Analysts estimate that the companies in bankruptcy (24% of the market) have negotiated savings in labor, energy, and raw materials that save them as much as $50 a ton. Those cost advantages will hurt companies such as Bethlehem that face heavy debt loads.

Yet the steel industry may finally be ready to forge some profits. After losing $12 billion between 1982 and 1986, the six largest producers made money in 1987, and 1988 profits may grow about 20% to $1.2 billion.

Capacity has been cut by 27% since 1982, according to the U.S. Commerce Department, and the industry has spent $8 billion to upgrade its plants. Productivity grew 15% a year between 1982 and 1985, and a weaker dollar has increased the industry's competitiveness. In 1987 it cost U.S. steel makers 29% less to make a ton of steel than it did in 1982. As a result, U.S. steel was actually cheaper to produce than Japanese steel. While Japanese production costs soared 24% to $508 a ton, U.S. steel makers could forge a ton of steel for only $431. U.S. companies hope that this advantage will allow them to recapture 4 million tons of production from foreign producers.

But long-term problems remain; with consumption still dropping, U.S. producers will have to shut down more plants and reduce their capacity. Low cost mini mills have done the best, increasing their share of the market from 5% in 1970 to 20% in 1985. Profits, then, continue to depend on how well the industry can reduce excess capacity, cut costs and modernize its plants.

USX Corporation

CEO: David M. Roderick   600 Grant Street
Employees: 69,424   Pittsburgh, Pennsylvania 15230
Assets: $16.6 billion   412-433-1121

	1987	1986	1985	1980
Revenues (millions of dollars):	14,836	14,900	20,879	12,492
Net income (millions of dollars):	206	(1,833)	598	504
Share earnings (dollars):	.54	—	1.94	5.77

What it does: Still the nation's largest steel maker, the company now has extensive holdings in energy, oil, chemicals, real estate, and transportation. Steel now provides less than one third of its revenues and energy provides over half.

After it lost $1.5 billion in 1982 and 1983, some analysts said 1986 was supposed to be the year when things finally got better at USX Corporation, once known as U.S. Steel Corporation. The company had earned a $598 million profit in 1985 and analysts said the steel industry was out of the intensive care ward. Instead, the country's largest steel maker was hit with new problems. A $3 billion deal for Texas Oil was completed in February of 1986, just as oil prices took a plunge. A July reorganization of the company dropped *Steel* from the company's name. In August, the United Steelworkers of America went on strike. In the fall, with no settlement in sight, corporate raider and Australian financier Robert Holmes à Court and later Carl Icahn bought up large chunks of the company's stock. Ichan made an $8 billion bid to take control of the company in October, but his bid failed. By the end of 1986, thanks to non-recurring charges, losses totaled a whopping $1.833 billion on revenues of only $14.9 billion—down 29% in only a year. In 1987, revenues declined to $14.8 billion, but the company managed to eke out a $206 million profit.

The problems facing USX today were unthinkable in the 1960s. The company was set up by J. P. Morgan in 1901 but traces its lineage back to steel and coke operations created after the Civil War by Andrew Carnegie. This frugal Scotsman trounced his competitors with a simple strategy of massive capital spending to improve productivity, a tough stance at the bargaining table that produced some of the bloodiest strikes in the nation's history, and a penchant for expanding production during depressions, thus lowering prices and forcing competitors out of business. Carnegie finally sold his steel company for nearly $500 million to J. P. Morgan in 1901. Morgan added several other companies and created U.S. Steel, a company that controlled 65% of the steel market in 1902.

Although the company's share of the market had dropped to 40% by 1930, U.S. Steel remained a powerhouse until the late 1970s. By then, the company had forgotten Carnegie's tradition of spending money to improve plant productivity; the newest plant was built in 1953. Absurd as it seems, many of its other mills dated back to the 19th century. No wonder the company was hard hit by the drastic downturn in the steel industry and increased foreign competition.

Chairman David M. Roderick has spent most of the 1980s pushing the company through a painful period of retrenchment. Roderick closed more than 150 plants and facilities, cut steel-making capacity by 24%, sold $3 billion in assets, and laid off more than 50,000 employees, two thirds of the company's white- and blue-collar workers. Even so, steel operations took a $978 million loss between 1980 and 1985.

At the same time, the company has moved in new directions, struggling to find new products and industries that can help it survive into the 21st century as one of the nation's largest corporations. The company shelled out $5.9 billion in 1982 for Marathon Oil Company and $3 billion for Texas Oil and Gas Corporation in 1986. Its aptly named U.S. Diversified Group unit, which was up for sale in early 1988, is involved in such businesses as real estate and transportation. As early as 1985, steel provided only about one third of the company's revenues, down from 73% in 1976. USX had only 11.2% of the market in the second quarter of 1987, a shadow of its glory days, when it held well over half of the market.

With its energy businesses accounting a large share of revenues, it was hardly any surprise when the company changed its name in 1986 to USX Corporation, replacing the word *Steel* in its name with an *X*. The insider-trading scandal on Wall Street may have saved USX from Carl Icahn and the raiders. With all the problems facing the company, management may wish it was so lucky. But in 1987, there were hints that the company was finally making its long-awaited revival. For the year, USX earned a $206 million profit, and despite losses in the fourth quarter, its profits per ton of steel doubled from $18 in the third quarter to $36 in the fourth. Quotas on foreign steel, a weaker dollar, and increased spending for capital goods also allowed the company to increase prices and profits. However, its energy holdings continued to drag down earnings.

Table 215 Big Steel

Rank	Company	1986 Corporate sales (thousands of dollars)	1986 Net income (thousands of dollars)
1.	USX Corporation	14,938,000	−1,833,000
2.	LTV Corporation	7,271,400	−3,251,600
3.	Bethlehem Steel Corporation	4,332,900	−152,700
4.	Inland Steel Industries, Inc.	3,173,242	19,264
5.	Armco, Inc.	2,640,500	−472,000
6.	National Steel Corporation	2,127,767	−59,898

Source: Company reports.

TECHNOLOGY

BIOTECHNOLOGY

Biotechnology offers the possibility of altering and manipulating the building blocks of life through molecular and cellular manipulation, enzyme technology, microbial technology, genetic engineering, and bioprocess engineering. Potential applications range from pesticides and more productive plants and animals in agriculture to new drugs in the health field, biodegradable plastics in the chemical industry, metal-leaching organisms that would aid in the metal recovery industry, biosensors in the factory, and vitamin supplements in the food industry, just to name a few. No doubt biotechnology will eventually touch off a revolution in the farm, factory, and health-care fields, just as the development of the chemical industry did in the earlier decades of the 20th century.

Some 300 firms are now involved in the field, providing goods and services, including about 215 large firms that have expanded into the field with in-house operations or through joint ventures. So far these firms derive a significant share of their revenues, about $300 million, from research and development contracts. The U.S. Department of Commerce believes that shipments of products based on technologies using monoclonal antibodies or recombinant DNA hit $550 million in 1987, way up from $60 million in 1984. AIDS testing using monoclonal antibodies produced $75 million to $100 million in revenues in 1987. Another $4.5 billion has been invested in this field.

Market value of biotechnology could rise to $1.5 billion by 1990, according to U.S. Commerce Department analysts. Yet, as with most emerging technologies, many new companies may not survive the transition from research to the actual development and marketing of products. And many research investments may not pay off in the near future. As a result, investments in this industry remain risky, holding a potential for high returns and big losses.

INFORMATION

The Market

Imagine pressing a button and having instant access to some of the nation's largest libraries. Press another button and you have news that hasn't even hit the newsstand. If the idea interests you then you'll probably understand all the hype about computer databases and the videotext industry. In recent years, database companies promised companies and consumers that they could obtain information easily and quickly through their computers, accessing breaking news on mergers as well as databases on industry performances and old newspaper articles on Hollywood stars. In 1987, there were about 700,000 subscribers to databases and about 100,000 subscribers to telebanking services.

The Money

So far, however, computer databases, some of which were used to research this book, are only a small but growing industry—a $1.6 billion industry in 1985, according to SRI International. The most popular databases among consumers were those providing securities and commodities quotes, bringing in $560 million. After that, professional databases (providing legal, medical, and other information) brought in $213 million, followed by scientific and technical databases ($91 million); abstract, bibliography, and other text databases ($76 million); nonbusiness consumer databases ($48 million); and other numeric databases, which include databases providing credit and other financial information ($623 million).

The Players

Some 1,400 companies are trying to position themselves as major players in the electronic information market. But eight large companies garner almost all of the industry's receipts.

DATABASE MOGULS

CompuServe has the largest number of subscribers of any database service—250,000. Owned by H&R Block, it brought in $109.9 million in revenues in 1986 by providing such services as news, information, shopping, mail, and financial data. Other large consumer-oriented services include Qube Cable Network (owned by Warner Communications and American Express), which provides polling services, viewer conferencing, games, and some information, and The Source (owned by Reader's Digest), with revenues of $14 million. Probably the biggest gamble in the videotext industry has been taken by IBM and Sears. Since 1984, they've invested $250 million on the Trintex network that provides shopping, banking, electronic mail, information, and educational services.

Trends and Forecast

No doubt the computer database and electronic information industry will one day take its place with book publishing as a major industry. Already computerized information services have been a boon to Wall Street and companies that need ready information on the market, credit ratings, etc. Database companies positioned to capitalize on that part of the industry will continue to do well: business subscribers to videotext services have been growing at a rate of 50% per year.

But all the hype about future sales and a new age of information has not impressed the general public. Many full-text databases for newspapers charge well over $100 an hour for time spent on-line. Since most databases have only a limited history, tracking information back only to 1980 or 1979, many researchers find that a computer has not replaced a good librarian. Similarly, the average consumer has found little reason to pay $100 an hour or more to access newspaper articles. The number of consumer subscribers to videotext services will hit 780,000 in 1985.

Such problems have also hurt companies in the field. New companies face the startup costs of putting large amounts of information on-line. Some media companies such as CBS and The New York Times Company entered the field but found it was difficult to recoup their huge investments. When profits did not live up to their expectations, they dropped out. The remaining companies have settled into profitable niches, with the largest ones catering to businesses and brokerage houses that need instant information and are willing to pay heavily for it.

Some analysts have taken a rosy view of the industry's future, arguing that electronic databases will produce revenues of $12 billion to $18 billion by 1992. There is little doubt that electronic information has already revolutionized the way Wall Street does business, allowing brokers access to news and markets around the world. But a mass audience will only be found after on-line charges drop drastically. A more reasonable estimate comes from SRI. It projects that the field will grow at only 10% to 15% a year through 1990.

LASERS

The Market

Once considered a high-tech curiosity, the stuff of a Buck Rogers serial rather than a business with practical applications, lasers are transforming dozens of industries. Current applications of lasers range from shooting down missiles to scanning prices in supermarkets, from the shaping of corneas to repairing detached retinas. Lasers can be used on credit cards to produce holograms that may dramatically cut credit-card fraud, in laser light shows, in laser printing and desktop publishing, in missile guidance, in neurosurgery to remove brain tumors, in satellite communications, in satellite tracking, in sighting military targets, in the treatment of skin ailments, and in videodisc and compact audio disc players.

The Money

Only 27 years after the first laser was developed in 1960, dozens of practical applications for laser technology added up to a $562.4 million worldwide commercial market for lasers in 1987, up from $474 million in 1985, according to Laser Report. Sales for military applications hit about $70 million in 1987. In 1985, the most popular industrial use of lasers was to process materials ($127 million), followed by medicine ($83.7 million), research and development ($117.1 million), and printing ($34.2 million), according to *Laser Report*.

The Players

Some 80 companies make lasers but only about 10% of these companies earn more than $10 million a year. The largest is Spectra-Physics, Inc.

Trends and Forecast

With some of the industry's sales and technological development tied to military spending, the future of Star Wars and the U.S. defense buildup will play an important role in the industry's future. Another major uncertainty is how well companies manage to find practical applications for technological breakthroughs. Sales grew only 6% in 1986 after growing 20% to 30% a year between 1980 and 1985. Nonetheless, *Marketing Research Report* believes sales will grow 26% a year through 1991.

ROBOTS AND OFFICE AUTOMATION

The Market

Faced with tough competition, American manufacturing and service companies are rushing to automate their workplaces. By adding robots in factories and high-tech phone systems, professional workstations, microcomputers, and word processors to the office, managers hope to cut costs and dramatically improve productivity, allowing them to compete with cheaper offshore labor.

The Money

The office automation market (which includes such products as word processors, office telephone equipment, key systems, dictation equipment, electronic typewriters, computers, copiers, and calculators for the office) hit $17.9 billion in 1984 and is expected to increase to $52.9 billion in 1988, according to the International Data Corporation. In industry, the U.S. automation market (which includes robotics and computer-based and programmable controllers of industrial equipment) is now worth about $25 billion by some estimates. (Not included in those figures is the tiny but growing market for home robots, which may be cute but, as yet, can't perform even simple household chores. Some 10,000 to 12,000 of these robots were sold for $20 million in 1984. Manufacturers of home robots predict this industry will hit $1 billion to $2 billion in sales by the end of this decade.)

The largest portion of the industrial automation market is the $7 billion industry of producing control and processing equipment. Much smaller is the robotics industry. About 6,748 robots worth $483.2 million were shipped in 1985 by American producers; foreign producers sold another 4,313 worth $126 million in 1985 to American business. But sales dropped in 1986, with U.S. suppliers selling only 5,713 units worth $363.8, and industry projections indicate that sales may have fallen another 30% in 1987. Currently, there are 16,000 robots in American factories, about one third as many robots as in Japanese factories. The Robotic Industries Association estimates that nearly a quarter of a million industrial robots will be in use in the U.S. by 1995. Another important area of growth is the computer-aided design, manufacture, and engineering (CAD/CAM, CAE) industry, which hit $4 billion in 1986, up from $765 million in 1981. CAD/CAM involves technology that uses computers to design and manufacture products; CAE involves tools that design and simulate the performance of integrated circuits and systems.

Trends and Forecast

Most analysts and U.S. government statisticians see a bright future for the office and industrial automation industry, as illustrated by some of the projections cited above. But, as with all high-tech industries, a bit of skepticism is in order. The history of technology is filled with optimistic projections followed by disappointing results. Despite the need to automate the workplace, actual sales remain heavily dependent on the ability of American companies to finance new equipment. For example, faced with sluggish auto sales, General Motors decided in 1986 to cancel $80 million worth of contracts for robots, forcing GMF Robotics Corporation (owned equally by General Motors and Japan's Fanuc Ltd.) to lay off 200 employees (about 28% of its work force) and delay plans for an automated factory where robots would produce robots. As a result, sales plummeted in 1986 and 1987, illustrating how rosy predictions are heavily dependent upon the state of the economy and American industry.

TELECOMMUNICATIONS

THE MARKET

Judging by the numbers, a lot of people never get off the phone. There are about 200 million phones in the U.S. and about 86 million individual customers who use over 124 million access lines. Some 92.5% of all homes have a telephone, with each customer paying an average of $727 per year for each access line. For their money, Americans make 1,241,994,488 calls in an average day or about 453.3 billion calls a year—about 900 calls a year or 2.5 calls a day for each person. Businesses make about 20% of all long distance calls within the U.S. and about 63% of all calls are made during regular business hours. To provide those services, phone companies have $207.3 billion worth of equipment and spend $20 billion a year on new construction and equipment, creating a large market for telecommunications equipment. Phone companies have about $1,826 worth of plant and equipment invested in each access line.

THE MONEY

Telephone companies had $127 billion worth of revenues in 1987. Total phone revenues should hit $138 billion in 1988.

THE PLAYERS

There are 1,426 telephone companies in the U.S. but only a few dominate the market. The 24 former Bell System companies (22 of which were made into independent companies by the AT&T divestiture) had $61.2 billion in revenues (78.1% of all revenues) compared to $16.6 billion (21.2%) in revenues for the 653 largest independent companies and only $561 million (0.7%) in revenues for the smallest 749 independent phone companies, according to the United States Telephone Association. The market dominance can also be found in the long-distance market, where, despite tough competition from U.S. Sprint and MCI, AT&T has kept about four fifths of the market. Only two other companies, MCI and U.S. Sprint, have more than 1% of the long-distance market.

THE PEOPLE

Some 725,000 people are employed by phone companies, most of whom (525,000) work in the companies that once made up the Bell System. These employees earn an annual payroll of $21.4 billion, or about $29,576 per employee, with Bell workers getting slightly more, about $32,163. Phone companies have about $275,832 invested in plant and equipment for every employee.

TRENDS AND FORECAST

Like several other industries—most notably power utilities and rail-roads—phone companies traditionally operated in markets characterized by very little competition and a great deal of government regulation. The theory behind this state of affairs was simple: Phone companies were considered a kind of natural monopoly that should be regulated rather than dismantled. Since the cost of setting up a phone company was so high and the benefits of having two competing phone companies so small, government trustbusters made little effort to dismantle the powerful Bell System. Instead, large phone companies were heavily regulated.

The result was AT&T, not only the largest company in the world but one of the best phone systems in the world. But in the 1960s and 1970s technological and political changes touched off a sweeping restructuring of the phone industry. New technology made it economically feasible for companies to set up their own telecommunications systems outside AT&T, making the idea of a "natural monopoly" in the telecommunications in-dustry less attractive. Prodded by court rulings, a sluggish FCC began allowing private long-distance systems in the late 1960s.

At that time, AT&T was coming under increasing attack from antitrust lawyers at the Justice Department. In 1956, AT&T settled a 1949 Justice Department antitrust suit by agreeing to limit its business to common-carrier communications services and to government contracts. The com-pany also agreed to manufacture only those products needed by the Bell System and to make its rich store of patents available to anyone without charge.

But the 1956 settlement didn't end AT&T's antitrust problems. In 1974, the Justice Department filed a new antitrust suit charging AT&T, Western Electric, and Bell Laboratories with a conspiracy to monopolize the in-dustry. The suit languished during the mid-1970s, but in 1982 the Justice Department and AT&T announced a new consent decree. Under its terms AT&T divested itself in 1984 of 22 local operating companies. These companies are broken into seven holding companies, the so-called Baby Bells. AT&T was also released from the 1956 decree that restricted the businesses it could enter.

For several years after the AT&T breakup, the Baby Bells thrived while their former parent company struggled. The Baby Bells jacked up local rates an average of 40% a year and used their cash to enter new businesses. Southwestern Bell, for example, spent $1.2 billion to buy Metromedia's cellular telephone operations, and others have even expanded overseas.

But the Baby Bells suffered a setback in their fight for further dereg-ulation when the courts held in September 1987 that they could not move into long distance or phone manufacturing. Then in December the FCC ordered the Baby Bells to cut $1 billion off the access fees they charge to let long distance companies complete their calls to local customers. Long distance companies such as AT&T pay half their $50 billion in revenues to the Baby Bells in access charges, but the Baby Bells had wanted to cut access charges by only $210 million.

As a result, the Baby Bells face a tougher financial climate. State regulators are less likely to let them jack up local phone rates while the courts and congress are unlikely to let them enter a number of new businesses. Nonetheless, the lobbying fight goes on, as Baby Bells argue they should be given more freedom to set up data bases over phone lines and even enter the cable TV industry. (See 10 largest utility companies on pp 667 for financial data on some Baby Bells.)

The FCC issued a number of decisions that dramatically changed the nature of the industry. Between 1968 and 1982, the FCC helped break the phone monopoly by allowing other companies to sell devices that connect with AT&T networks and by permitting consumers to buy their own telephones. In 1980 it increased competition by allowing independent companies to resell AT&T services, and in 1982 it allowed smaller, non-monopoly companies to change services or rates without regulatory approval. It has reduced the regulatory burden of entering new markets, such as cellular mobile phones, by holding lotteries instead of lengthy hearings. By shifting costs from long distance to local usage, the commission moved toward market pricing of long-distance services, which had traditionally been set higher than necessary in order to subsidize local service. (That subsidy amounted to about $11 billion in higher long-distance rates a year, or about 40% of long-distance revenues, before divestiture.)

But not all of those decisions increased competition. Many new companies entered the industry when FCC mandated discounts on local network connection fees, allowing companies to buy access from local companies at lower prices than AT&T and retail it at a profit. But these discounts are ending, putting some companies out of business and limiting the price edge of surviving companies, such as MCI. Both U.S. Sprint and MCI posted large losses in the final quarters of 1986, and some analysts look for an industry shakeout. According to this line of thinking, a few large companies will survive—such as MCI with its backing from IBM—while smaller companies will be forced to consolidate or find a profitable niche.

Yet despite an industry-wide restructuring that is expected to cut jobs and force many smaller long-distance companies out of business, the outlook is generally bright for industry revenues. U.S. Commerce Department analysts expect revenues of the telephone and telegraph service industries to grow at an annual rate of 3 to 5% through 1992.

American Telephone and Telegraph Company

CEO: James E. Olson
Employees: 302,000
Assets: $37.9 billion

550 Madison Avenue
New York, New York 10022
Phone: 212-605-5500

	1987	1986	1985	1980
Revenues (millions of dollars):	33,598	34,087	34,417	NA
Net income (millions of dollars):	2,044	139	1,557	
Share earnings (dollars):	1.88	.05	1.37	

What it does: It provides long-distance services and sells and manufactures telecommunications equipment.

In the decades after Alexander Graham Bell patented the phone in 1876, his company wrote the book on how to be a successful monopoly.

Graham took little interest in managing the Bell Telephone Company and the bankers who financed the company soon took control. One of their first problems was fighting off the hundreds of legal challenges to Bell's patents. Western Union, for example, had bought rights to another phone created by Elisha Gray (Gray had the misfortune of filing his patent for a phone only two hours after Bell did) and hired Thomas Edison to build a better phone system. But it agreed to stay out of the phone business in exchange for 20% of Bell's phone rental receipts.

Winning those legal battles gave the company time to grow larger and stronger under the protection of Bell's patents. By the time the company's patents expired in 1893, the company was large enough to quash the independent phone companies by cutting rates and refusing to connect them to the Bell System. In 1899 the company was reorganized as American Telephone and Telegraph, with AT&T running the long-distance business and acting as a holding company for local phone companies. The company merged with Western Union in 1910 but, under growing attack for its power, AT&T was forced to get out of the telegraph business and submit to increased government regulation.

The company's economic clout was also aided by its leadership in technology. AT&T bought up a large interest in Western Electric in 1881, and in the 20th century Western Electric and Bell labs were to develop such products as television transmission, the silicon solar cell, the transistor lasers, and satellite communications. That technological innovation made the company a power in the defense and space industry, supplying equipment for the Pentagon and NASA.

By 1979 the company had $113 billion in assets, was the nation's largest employer with over a million workers, and churned out some $45.3 billion in sales. Its monopoly on phone service had grown from 50% in 1910 to 80%. But in the early 1980s it was becoming apparent that the days of the world's largest monopoly were numbered. Support for various proposals to deregulate the phone industry was growing in Congress. The company was in court with the Justice Department and William McGowan's MCI over antitrust violations.

Finally, in 1982, as a 1974 Justice Department antitrust suit was finally moving toward trial, AT&T cut a deal that allowed it to retain the competitive business of long-distance service and equipment manufacturing while spinning off its 22 operating phone companies that are now grouped into seven regional holding companies of about equal size.

Analysts claimed that the company—with its reputation as a lumbering, slow-footed giant—would lose sales in the telecommunications equipment market and as much as 40% of its long-distance service by 1990 to upstarts like MCI. The bright spot was that AT&T could enter the growing computer and office automation field, expand international sales, and enlarge its base in the telecommunications equipment field, while shedding local phone service (some three quarters of its assets), which might be less profitable in a deregulated environment.

Things didn't work out that way. With an advertising budget 8 to 10 times larger than rivals such as Sprint and MCI, AT&T held onto most of the long-distance market it was supposed to lose.

But the company never picked up the computer business it was supposed to gain from deregulation. AT&T lost $0.5 billion in 1985 and another $1.25 billion in 1986 on its computer operations. Computer losses in 1987 could add another $0.75 billion in red ink.

And competing in a deregulated environment has not been easy. The company has ordered massive layoffs of employees, who had once considered their jobs lifetime sinecures. Deregulation of the phone industry has also given foreign companies, especially Japanese companies, a growing share of the U.S. market. Local phone companies, which were once required to do business with AT&T, can now shop for the best price.

By 1987, there were promising signs that Chairman James E. Olson's management had led the company through the trauma of divestitures. Losses were slashed in the computer operations by 70%, $1 billion was cut out of back-office expenses and the company held its status as the world's largest supplier of telecommunications equipment, with 30% of the world market. The results boosted earnings to over $2 billion.

MCI Communications   MCI started in 1968 with just three employees, at a time when AT&T served the telecommunications needs of most of the country. But by breaking Ma Bell's monopoly on long-distance service in a landmark antitrust case, William G. McGowan, chairman and chief executive officer of MCI Communications Corporation, forever changed the industry. He won a $17 billion settlement with AT&T (later reduced to a paltry $133 million) and helped create political support for a plan to deregulate the telecommunications industry.

That victory translated into tremendous growth for his fledgling empire. MCI also entered into a partnership with IBM (which gave Big Blue 16% of MCI stock) that could give it $400 million in reserves to draw upon. But for McGowan and his new backer IBM the tough part may very well be competing and surviving in a deregulated marketplace. AT&T is 12 times larger and has been able to outspend MCI eight to one in long-distance advertising. Through rate cuts AT&T countered MCI's price advantage and confounded early predictions that AT&T would lose much of the long-distance market. Going head to head with a colossus like Ma Bell has also forced MCI to cut costs, sell its paging and cellular phone unit, and cut back on marketing its electronic mail system. Losses totaled $431.5 million in 1986 on revenues of $3,592 million. MCI's charismatic chairman gave up control of day-to-day operations following a heart transplant, but has since returned to direct long-term strategy.

ITT Corporation
CEO: Rand V. Araskog
Employees: 123,000
Assets: $35.8 billion

320 Park Avenue
New York, New York 10022
212-752-6000

	1987	1986	1985	1981
Revenues (millions of dollars):	19,500	17,437	14,663	NA
Net income (millions of dollars):	1,020	540	294	
Share earnings (dollars):	6.76	3.23	1.89	

What it does: In December 1986, the company combined its telecommunications operations with those of Compagnie Générale d'Electricité, forming a joint venture, Alcatel N.V., based in the Netherlands. ITT holds 37%.

ITT was founded in 1920 by sugar broker Sosthenes Behn and took off in 1925 when an antitrust suit forced AT&T to sell off its overseas manufacturing operations. After buying that business, the company succeeded in becoming for the whole world what AT&T was to the U.S. ITT controlled major phone systems in Europe and Latin America and produced much of the phone equipment used around the world.

But in the 1960s, fearing takeovers and regulation by foreign governments, ITT under Harold Geneen expanded out of its core telecommunications business. Geneen wanted to make the company a diversified conglomerate and, by the late 1970s, it was the largest baking company in the U.S., the second-largest hotel chain, a book publisher, and an insurance company, as well as a power in the telecommunications industry overseas.

The company had also added to its reputation for intrigue, which started when ITT had helped rearm Nazi Germany. More recently, ITT channeled secret funds to overthrow Chile's President Allende, who had pledged to nationalize the company's phone operation in the 1970s, and made illegal contributions to President Nixon.

But Geneen's conglomerate was never very profitable. What was lacking was a way of melding all the different businesses into a profitable company. Profits were a paltry $382 million on sales of $22 billion in 1979.

So, under CEO Rand V. Araskog, the company began a campaign to trim down and shape up its balance sheet. Araskog sold off $4 billion worth of companies like C&C Cola and Continental Baking. But ITT was still in such different businesses as financial services, defense electronics, semiconductors, insurance, automotive supplies, pump making, and telecommunications. Sales in 1985 dropped to $20 billion but profits were only $294 million.

The company also stumbled badly in its attempt to revitalize its core telecommunications operation. Araskog had dreamed of making the company a technological powerhouse, but ITT had ignored the U.S. telecommunications and information market for too long. Its personal computer never made a dent in the U.S. market, and after spending $1 billion to develop its System 12 switching technology, problems forced the company to give up trying to adapt it to the American market. Realizing the company couldn't capitalize on the promise of a growing telecommunications market, ITT decided to sell a major stake in its European telecommunications and equipment operation to Compagnie Générale d'Electricité of France, ending its reign as Europe's largest supplier of equipment.

Today, ITT's largest business is insurance. ITT Financial Corporation produces only 7% of sales but 30% of earnings. The company may find its future as a financial powerhouse rather than a telecommunications giant.

Table 216   Top 20 Telephone Companies

Rank	Company	Access lines (thousands)	Revenues (millions of dollars)
1.	Bell Atlantic Corporation*	15,508	9,921
2.	BellSouth Corporation*	15,045	11,444
3.	Ameritech*	14,755	8,500
4.	NYNEX Corporation*	13,962	10,394
5.	Pacific Telesis Group*	12,068	8,548
6.	Southwestern Bell Corporation*	11,772	7,118
7.	U S WEST, Inc.*	11,332	7,569
8.	GTE Corporation	11,127	8,780
9.	United Telecommunications, Inc.	3,381	2,220
10.	Contel Corp.	2,280	1,835
11.	Southern New England Telephone Company*	1,711	1,359
12.	Centel Corporation	1,354	833
13.	ALLTEL Corporation	953	545
14.	Cincinnati Bell, Inc.	726	478
15.	Puerto Rico Telephone Company	639	406
16.	Rochester Telephone Corporation	478	400
17.	Century Telephone Enterprises, Inc.	227	146
18.	Pacific Telecom, Inc.	225	196
19.	Telephone and Data Systems, Inc.	206	128
20.	Lincoln Telephone and Telegraph Company	202	139

*Formerly part of AT&T.
Source: *Phone Facts 1987,* United States Telephone Association.

Table 217   Average Daily Calls and Toll Messages

(Bells and independents)

Local calls	1,161,352,890
Toll messages	102,183,979
Local calls per average access line	9.89
Toll messages per average access line	0.871

Source: *Telephone Statistics: 1987,* United States Telephone Association.

TELEVISION AND CABLE

THE MARKET

Of all American households, 95.3% own a television, up from 9% in 1950 and 87% in 1960. There are 84.9 million television sets in the U.S., 77.7 million of which are color. The average household watches television 7 hours and 5 minutes a day. In 1987, for the first time ever, cable reached half of all TV viewers, about 43.4 million.

THE MONEY

Overall, television advertising is expected to hit $26.8 billion in 1988, thanks to the presidential election and the Olympics, which always boost ad revenues. In 1985 and 1986, TV ad growth has slowed, falling below double-digit rates of increase for the first time in a decade. Network advertising actually dropped 2.8% in 1985, in the face of increased competition from cable and independent television. In 1987 network television ad revenue grew only 4% to 8.9 billion, while local spot advertising grew only 6% (down from 12.4% in 1985 and 14% in 1986), aggravating the financial problems of independent television stations that depend on local spot revenues. Cable operators earned some $11.2 billion in 1987.

If you wanted to buy all the cable systems in the U.S. it would cost you about $67 billion, while it would cost $38 billion to buy all the nation's TV stations, according to an estimate by *Broadcasting*.

The four largest owners of TV stations are Capital Cities/ABC, with eight stations (which reached 24.4% of television market), NBC/GE, with seven stations (21.0%), CBS, four stations (19.5%), and 20th Century Fox, seven stations (19.3%), according to *Broadcasting*.

TRENDS AND FORECAST

The mid-1980s saw major changes in the television business. An advertising slump cut network revenues already hurt by increased competition from cable, independent television, and the threat of a fourth network. The government did not stop outside buyers from taking over networks, allowing Laurence Tisch to take over CBS, Capital Cities to take over ABC, and General Electric to take over NBC's parent, RCA.

Most of the turmoil in network TV can be traced to the fact that this is a mature industry with a stagnant or declining viewing audience. Over half the population now owns a VCR, a fact that poses several problems for the networks. The home video industry does not compete with networks for ad dollars but it could hurt audience levels. Many viewers are simply renting their own movies, finding this a great way to avoid being subjected to network programming. Other viewers are zapping the ads— that is, they are recording programs and then fast-forwarding past the ads to avoid the unpleasant experience of having a soap commercial interrupt their favorite movie or show.

Cable poses another problem. About half of all TV homes now subscribe to cable. Cable advertising revenues were over $1.3 billion in 1987 and could rise to $2 billion by the end of the decade, according to the Cable-television Advertising Bureau.

Independent TV, meaning television stations that are not affiliated with any of the three networks, has also increased its share of the market and ad revenues. The number of independent stations skyrocketed from 112 in 1980 to 308 in 1988. These stations which thrive on sports, reruns of popular shows, movies and kids shows, cut into the audience reached by network affiliates. In one year alone, independents grew from a 14 share (or percentage) of the television audience in prime time in October 1986 to a 17 share in October 1987, while the networks' share of the audience fell by four percentage points. Some of these stations got into financial trouble in 1986 and 1987 when ad revenues slowed, forcing several systems into bankruptcy.

Also facing the networks is the ever-present threat from a fourth network. In 1985 and 1986, Rupert Murdoch bought Twentieth Century Fox, a film studio, and six independent TV stations owned by Metromedia. His Fox Broadcasting Company has signed up 93 affiliates and now offers five hours of prime-time programming a week.

This competition has hurt the networks' share of the prime-time audience. To preserve profits in an era of stagnant revenues, all of the networks have been slashing costs. Jobs have been cut, even in news divisions that were once immune to budget squeezes, and the networks are going after programming costs, which account for about two thirds of all costs, or about $4 billion.

Network TV remains an industry whose profitability is driven by hits, not cost cutting. NBC came out of one of the worst periods in network revenues by simply airing a slew of hit shows, which of course boosts ad rates.

Networks can't own more than a certain number of shows and are totally barred from syndicating television shows. However, the companies that produce and distribute television shows also find that hits produce fat profits. But network television remains the easiest way for many advertisers to reach mass audiences and is unlikely to disappear. King World harvests more than $100 million a year for its *Wheel of Fortune,* which costs less than $4 million a year to produce. Viacom Enterprises is expected to gross a half-billion dollars on *The Cosby Show* in the first syndicated-rerun cycle, which will begin in 1988. That is more than double the previous record, which was set by Twentieth Century Fox's *M*A*S*H.*

Table 218 Time Spent Viewing Per TV Home—Per Day

(annual averages)*

1951	4 hours 43 minutes	1970	5 hours 54 minutes
1952	4 hours 48 minutes	1971	6 hours 1 minute
1953	4 hours 44 minutes	1972	6 hours 7 minutes
1954	4 hours 42 minutes	1973	6 hours 16 minutes
		1974	6 hours 14 minutes
1955	4 hours 49 minutes	1975	6 hours 12 minutes
1956	4 hours 58 minutes	1976	6 hours 12 minutes
1957	5 hours 4 minutes	1977	6 hours 14 minutes
1958	5 hours 11 minutes	1978	6 hours 13 minutes
1959	5 hours 1 minute	1979	6 hours 26 minutes
1960	5 hours 4 minutes	1980	6 hours 34 minutes
1961	5 hours 8 minutes	1981	6 hours 43 minutes
1962	5 hours 5 minutes	1982	6 hours 49 minutes
1963	5 hours 7 minutes	1983	6 hours 55 minutes
1964	5 hours 20 minutes	1984	7 hours 8 minutes
1965	5 hours 31 minutes	1985	7 hours 7 minutes
1966	5 hours 30 minutes	1986	7 hours 10 minutes
1967	5 hours 37 minutes	1987	7 hours 5 minutes
1968	5 hours 44 minutes		
1969	5 hours 48 minutes		

*September to August.
Source: Nielsen Media Research.

Table 219 Television Advertising Trends and Projections

(in millions of dollars)

	Network			Spot			Local			National syndication		
Year	Millions of dollars	Percent change	Percent TV	Millions of dollars	Percent change	Percent TV	Millions of dollars	Percent change	Percent TV	Millions of dollars	Percent change	Percent TV
1960	820	5.7	50.4	527	8.4	32.4	280	4.9	17.2	—	—	—
1961	887	8.2	52.5	548	4.0	32.4	256	−8.6	15.1	—	—	—
1962	976	10.0	51.4	629	14.8	33.2	292	14.1	15.4	—	—	—
1963	1,025	5.0	50.4	698	11.0	34.4	309	5.8	15.2	—	—	—
1964	1,132	10.4	49.5	806	15.5	35.2	351	13.6	15.3	—	—	—
1965	1,237	9.3	49.2	892	10.7	35.5	386	10.0	15.3	—	—	—
1966	1,393	12.6	49.3	988	10.8	35.0	442	14.5	15.7	—	—	—
1967	1,455	4.5	50.0	988	0.0	34.0	466	5.4	16.0	—	—	—
1968	1,523	4.7	47.1	1,131	14.5	35.0	577	23.8	17.9	—	—	—
1969	1,678	10.2	46.8	1,253	10.8	35.0	654	13.3	18.2	—	—	—
1970	1,658	−1.2	46.1	1,234	−1.5	34.3	704	7.6	19.6	—	—	—
1971	1,593	−3.9	45.1	1,145	−7.2	32.4	796	13.1	22.5	—	—	—
1972	1,804	13.2	44.1	1,318	15.1	32.2	969	21.7	23.7	—	—	—
1973	1,968	9.1	44.1	1,377	4.5	30.9	1,115	15.1	25.0	—	—	—
1974	2,145	9.0	44.2	1,495	8.6	30.8	1,211	8.6	25.0	—	—	—
1975	2,306	7.5	43.9	1,623	8.6	30.8	1,334	10.2	25.3	—	—	—
1976	2,857	23.9	42.6	2,154	32.7	32.0	1,710	28.2	25.4	—	—	—
1977	3,460	21.1	45.4	2,204	2.3	29.0	1,948	13.9	25.6	—	—	—
1978	3,975	14.9	44.4	2,607	18.3	29.1	2,373	21.8	26.5	—	—	—
1979	4,599	15.7	45.3	2,873	10.2	28.3	2,682	13.0	26.4	—	—	—
1980	5,130	11.5	45.0	3,269	13.8	28.6	2,967	10.6	26.0	50	—	0.4
1981	5,575	8.7	43.7	3,746	14.6	29.3	3,368	13.5	26.4	75	50.0	0.6
1982	6,210	11.4	42.9	4,364	16.5	30.1	3,765	11.8	26.0	150	100.0	1.0
1983	7,017	13.0	42.5	4,827	10.6	29.3	4,345	15.4	26.4	300	100.0	1.8
1984	8,526	21.5	43.8	5,488	13.7	28.1	5,084	17.0	26.1	400	33.3	2.1
1985	8,285	−2.8	40.4	6,004	9.4	29.2	5,714	12.4	27.8	530	32.5	2.6
1986	8,570	3.0	38.5	6,570	9.0	29.5	6,514	14.0	29.3	610	13.0	2.7
1987e	8,914	4.0	38.1	6,835	4.0	29.2	6,905	6.0	29.5	760	25.0	3.2
1990	10,843	—	33.8	9,603	—	29.9	10,572	—	32.9	1,090	—	3.4
1995	15,042	—	28.9	15,542	—	29.8	19,591	—	37.6	1,941	—	3.7

Sources: GNP, U.S. Department of Commerce, 1960–1985. Ad volume, McCann-Erickson, 1960–1987. TV ad volume, McCann-Erickson, 1960–1985. All other figures are Television Bureau estimates.
 e estimate

Table 220   Top TV Programs

The most-watched individual network programs, ranked by average audience estimates:

M*A*S*H	February 1983	60.2%
Dallas	November 1980	53.3
Roots, Part VIII	January 1977	51.1
Super Bowl XVI	January 1982	49.1
Super Bowl XVII	January 1983	48.6
Super Bowl XX	January 1986	48.3
Gone with the Wind*	November 1976	47.5
Super Bowl XII	January 1978	47.2
Super Bowl XIII	January 1979	47.1

*Shown as Part I and Part II on different nights, each night ranking seventh.
Source: Nielsen Media Research.

Table 221   Cable Ad Revenue: 1980 to 1987

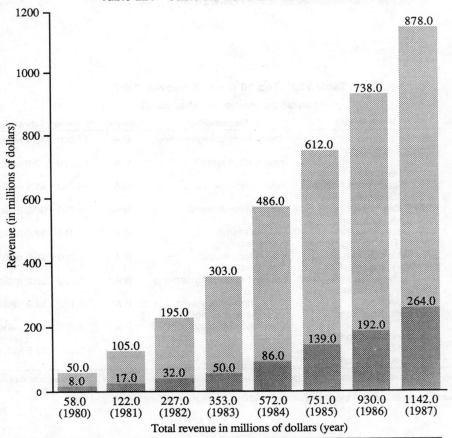

Source: Revenue estimates from Paul Kagan Associates, Inc., published in Cable TV Advertising, April 30, 1987.

Table 222   Top 10 Multiple-System Cable Operators

(as of September 30, 1987)

Rank	Operator	Basic Subscribers
1.	Tele-Communications, Inc. (TCI)	4,609,406
2.	American Television and Communications (ATC) (Time Inc.)	3,590,000
3.	Continental Cablevision	1,497,000
4.	Storer Cable Communications	1,418,000
5.	Cox Cable Communications, Inc.	1,406,900
6.	Warner Cable	1,368,600
7.	Comcast Cable Communications	1,281,400
8.	United Cable TV	1,122,300
9.	Newhouse Broadcasting Corporation	1,032,400
10.	Viacom Enterprises	1,013,300

Source: Paul Kagan Associates, Inc., *Cable TV Investor,* Nov. 17, 1987.

Table 223   Top 10 Cable Networks, 1987

(ranked by number of subscribers)

Rank	Video service	Programming	Category[1]	Systems	Subscribers
1.	ESPN Bristol, Connecticut	Sports events/programming	B/A	17,000	43.7 million
2.	WTBS Atlanta, Georgia	Independent station	B/A	11,870	42.0 million
3.	CNN (Cable News Network) Atlanta, Georgia	News/special features	B/A	10,790	41.1 million
4.	USA Cable Network New York, New York	Sports/entertainment	B/A	9,200	39.0 million
5.	CBN Cable Network Virginia Beach, Virginia	Religious/family programming	B/A	7,710	37.0 million
6.	MTV (Music Television) New York, New York	Videos/rock music programming	B/A	4,710	35.8 million
7.	The Nashville Network (TNN) Nashville, Tennessee	Country music programming	B/A	5,200	35.0 million
8.	Nickelodeon New York, New York	Programming for young people and all ages	B/A	5,150	34.2 million
9.	Lifetime New York, New York	Information/entertainment	B/A	3,400	33.2 million
10.	Nick at Nite New York, New York	Variety	B/A	3,860	31.5 million

[1]B/A—basic/advertising; small fee to operator; usually no additional fee to subscriber; service accepts national cable advertising.

Source: National Cable Television Association, *National Cable* Network Directory, August 1987.

NBC When Robert C. Wright took over NBC, late-night talk-show host David Letterman joked that the former head of GE's plastics division and small appliance operations would push for a miniseries about the development of the toaster oven.

The joke says a lot about what's happening at the networks. Since GE took over RCA, and with it NBC, Wright is the first manager from the appliance and financial services company to take over NBC. Wright did head a cable company for several years but, unlike his predecessor Grant Tinker, Wright has little in his background to prepare him for the difficulties of running a major network. How Wright handles the company will be a test case of network management in an age when all three networks have fallen under the control of outside corporations.

Already, Wright's hands-on style indicates that he is using traditional management techniques to improve company profits. Even though NBC was on top of ratings, Wright started his tenure in 1986 by cutting 150 jobs and circulating memos asking department heads to cut 5% of their budgets. Then he had the temerity to suggest that all employees contribute to a political action committee, angering the news division and producing a flap that was played out on the front pages of *The New York Times*.

But Wright has been popular on Wall Street, often named as the leading candidate to succeed Jack Welch as the head of GE. In 1987, NBC remained on top of the prime-time ratings. Operating profits hit a record $400 million in 1986, up from $48 million five years earlier.

CBS Inc.
CEO: Laurence Tisch   51 West 52nd Street
Employees: — 7,000   New York, New York 10019
Assets: —   212-975-4321

	1987	1986(n)	1985	1980
Revenues (millions of dollars):	2,762	2,808	—	N/A
Net income (millions of dollars):	452	325	—	—
Share earnings (dollars):	17.74	15.42		

What it does: A major broadcaster. (n) restated

Son of a wealthy cigar manufacturer, William Paley first discovered radio as a way of selling his father's cigars. In 1927, with dad's money, he founded his own radio network, the Independent Broadcasting Corporation, which in 1928 became the Columbia Broadcasting System.

By the end of the 1930s CBS had 114 affiliated stations and $30 million in revenue, a twentyfold increase in only 10 years. Though CBS was dwarfed by NBC in the 1930s, Paley built up the radio network with innovative programming and news. Paley's talent for programming also helped CBS when commercial television finally got off the ground in the late 1940s. Paley hired top NBC radio stars like Jack Benny, George Burns, Gracie Allen, Edgar Bergen, and Red Skelton after NBC decided it didn't want to match CBS's salaries, in part because NBC believed radio stars couldn't make the transition to TV. With these personalities in its lineup, CBS quickly became the biggest network, winning the ratings war. (By the end of 1985, CBS was first 25 of the previous 29 years and six straight years until 1986, when NBC moved ahead.) Paley's stable of top CBS radio journalists—Edward R. Murrow, Howard K. Smith, and others—also adjusted well to the new medium, establishing CBS news as the standard of network journalism.

Paley's management style set the tone for CBS. A broadcaster with a deft touch for programming and a man with exquisite personal taste, Paley put CBS on top of the ratings battle with a mix of hard news and middlebrow programming. Somehow *The Beverly Hillbillies* and the award-winning program *60 Minutes* existed on the same channel.

CBS made Paley a rich man, worth an estimated $320 million today, and the head of a multinational media conglomerate, with revenues of $4.75 billion in 1986. CBS was not only a powerhouse in television and radio, but also one in the record industry, publishing, magazines, etc. Yet the former cigarmaker remained in many ways the classic entrepreneur, unwilling to relinquish control over his creation. Six replacements were groomed for the job and then axed. "Paley rears his presidents as disposable lighters," said media securities analyst Anthony Hoffman after another heir apparent was fired in 1980.

The company also stumbled badly in many of its acquisitions. It lost $30 million on its cable network, for instance, and another $30 million on movie ventures. A symptom of its poor handling of acquisitions was the New York Yankees. The Bronx Bombers were in first place when CBS bought them in 1964, last place when they were sold.

The failure to put together a new management team and CBS's inability to diversify left it unable to compete in the new tighter market for network advertising in the mid-1980s. Then president Thomas Wyman managed to get the board to remove Paley and name himself as chairman, but Wyman soon came under fire for his management policies. First CBS assumed a heavy debt load to fight off a takeover bid by Ted Turner and then the company fired hundreds of employees to cut costs and pay off the debts. Laurence Tisch's Loews Corp. was also buying stock. Wyman put Tisch on the board and Tisch said he had no plans to take over the company. But after acquiring a 25% stake, Tisch promptly threw out Wyman in the fall of 1986 and became chairman himself. Since then, Tisch has ruthlessly cut costs, sold off unprofitable properties such as the publishing unit, and profitable ones, such as the recording division, and slashed corporate perks. When Tisch sold the CBS record division to Sony for about $2 billion in 1987, the company was back where it was decades ago—simply a broadcasting company. But with a $3 billion cash horde, Tisch could be ready to embark on a new round of acquisitions. (See the profile of the Tisch brothers on page 120.)

For now, CBS is sitting at number two in the ratings and prospects for an immediate turnaround appear dim. The gilt-edged perks of the Paley era—the limos, the first-class travel, the executive dinning rooms, and more—are all taboo. "Everyone always looked to CBS as the standard bearer of the broadcasting industry," says Robert Smith, dean of Temple University's School of Communications and Theater. "Now they're looking at the company to see the way all the broadcasters may go in a new era." So far, what's happening at CBS indicates that no one network will dominate the tube, setting the standards for news and entertainment the way CBS did under Paley.

TOBACCO

THE MARKET

Increased concerns about health, rising prices, and fewer younger smokers have caused consumption of tobacco products to fall dramatically in the last decade. The percentage of adults who smoke has dropped from 55% to below 30%. The number of cigarettes smoked per capita dropped to only 3,200 in 1987, down from 4,092 in 1976, while per-capita cigar consumption fell from 75 in 1976 to 42 in 1984 and per-capita consumption of smoking tobacco dropped from .75 pounds to only .36 pounds. But analysts expect consumption to drop at a slower rate in the next few years and stabilize some time after that. Remaining smokers are also expressing a growing fondness for stronger cigarettes. Brands with over 15 milligrams of tar or more capture 48% of the market, up from 40% in 1980. Americans smoked about 573 billion cigarettes in 1987. That same year, cigar consumption fell under 3 billion for the first time in recent history, only one third of the peak reached in 1964. Americans in 1987 smoked 22.6 million pounds of smoking tobacco, only one third of the 1970 peak. About 70% of all smoking tobacco was used by pipe smokers; the other 30% was used by people who roll their own cigarettes.

THE MONEY

The tobacco industry shipped about $18.1 billion worth of products in 1987, up from $14.3 billion in 1984 and $4.2 billion in 1972. Most of those revenues came from cigarettes, which accounted for $16.6 billion. Cigar makers continued their decline, getting only $253 million, while makers of chewing and smoking tobacco sold $977 million worth of products, up from $875 million in 1984.

THE PLAYERS

Many small farmers depend on the tobacco industry for their livelihood, but most of the industry sales are captured by the largest cigarette producers. The largest, Philip Morris, held about 37% of the market in 1986, followed by R. J. Reynolds (32%), Brown & Williamson (11.5%), Loew's (8.1%), and American Brands (7.2%).

THE PEOPLE

About 45,000 people find employment in the cigarettes, cigar, chewing tobacco, and smoking tobacco industry, down from 49,700 in 1982 and 54,900 in 1972.

TRENDS AND FORECAST

Faced with declining per-capita consumption and slow growth in industry sales, many larger producers have diversified into new fields. R. J. Reynolds, which now gets about three fifths of its revenues from nontobacco sources, spent $5 billion to acquire Nabisco in 1985, while Philip Morris paid $5.6 billion for General Foods. To grab a bigger share of a shrinking pie, tobacco companies have also experimented with pricing and marketing gimmicks to attract new customers.

Overall, the threat of liability suits and declining consumption continues to hang over the industry. Cigar makers will undoubtedly continue their decline, while growing health concern about snuff could derail growth in that industry. Faced with these prospects, it's likely that tobacco companies will continue to view their operations as a way of raising money to expand into other industries, as the leading firms have already done. The only bright spot has been exports, which hit nearly $1.5 billion in 1986, up from nearly $1.1 billion in 1980.

TOYS

THE MARKET

Toys are for kids and, of course, the adults who buy them. Currently, prospective buyers are parents, relatives, and grandparents of the 51.3 million children under 15 in the U.S. About 30% of all households have one child under the age of 12.

THE MONEY

On the retail level toy business was a $12 billion industry in 1985, up 8% from 1984, and up from 1981, when $9.2 billion worth of toys were sold.

Those sales broke down as follows: 31.6% of retail toy sales revenues were from dolls and action figures, 11.6% were from games and puzzles, 10.1% were from preschool and infant toys, 9.5% were from activity toys (which include musical instruments and books), 9% were from toy vehicles, 8.6% were from riding toys, 7.6% were from stuffed animals, 4.2% were from arts and crafts, and 7.8% were from other toys.

Big money in this industry comes in the form of a hit, such as Monopoly (over 100 million sold in the last 50 years) or the Cabbage Patch Kids, which earned Coleco $600 million in 1985 alone and helped the company earn a record $82.6 million in profits. In contrast, Coleco took a $118.6 million charge against earnings in 1984 because of poor sales from its Adam computer, and without a hit in 1986, the toy company lost money. But in recent years, the industry has faced problems. Factory shipments of U.S. toy makers were only $2.8 billion in 1987, down from $3.8 billion in 1984.

THE PLAYERS

Americans buy their toys at discount stores (35%), toy stores (16%), variety stores (8%), department stores (6%), Sears, Ward's, or Penney's (5%), and catalog showrooms (3%). About 32% of these stores are located in shopping centers; 16% are downtown stores and 26% are neighborhood stores. In 1984, the top three toy store chains were Toys "R" Us ($1.65 billion in sales), Child World ($450 million in sales), and Kay Bee ($325 million in sales), according to *Discount Store News*.

THE PEOPLE

Employment in the toy, doll, and game industry declined to 30,700 in 1987, down from 39,900 in 1984 and 71,700 in 1972. Wages also remain low, about $5.88 an hour, compared to $9.53 for all manufacturing workers.

POOL TABLES

When he moved from Switzerland to Cincinnati, John Brunswick was sorely disappointed by the quality of the town's bumpy billiard tables. A professional cabinetmaker, he set about making a professional pool table. In 1845, he showed his flawless table to pool hall owners, who immediately placed orders for ones just like it. Brunswick cranked them out for the next 20 years and then merged with two rivals to form the Brunswick Corporation. The company got into the bowling business in the 1880s when big pool halls began putting in bowling alleys. Brunswick started making bowling balls and pins.

MONOPOLY

If George Parker's parents had had it their way, Monopoly would still only be a market most companies dream about. Young George had a flair for making up board games. When only 16, he created a game called Banking and managed to make and sell 500 of them around Christmastime. His parents apparently found such a pursuit trivial and, for some reason, steered him toward journalism. A respiratory illness, however, forced him to give up his job reporting for a Boston newspaper. He fell back on his old passion for making games. With his brother Charles, he formed Parker Brothers (brother Edward joined two years later) and went on to make such games as Monopoly and Clue.

Lionel Trains For a while, Joshua Lionel Cowen was stuck. Around the turn of the century, he had invented a tiny electric motor and got it to rotate a fan. The electric fan had worked like a charm, but it didn't give a breeze. Then he recalled carving toy locomotives as a child. His tiny battery-powered motor, he thought, could power little trains.

He was right, of course, which he learned after designing a little railroad car and a 30-foot circle of brass track. Initially, he saw the train as a way to attract attention to other merchandise in store windows. But the first store he sold it to asked for six more the next day. A customer had bought the first. Taking a hint, Lionel took his invention to novelty shops, where it sold right away.

As more and more homes got electricity, more people bought the little trains. Business really picked up in 1903 when he issued a catalog of items, such as different kinds of cars and a little suspension bridge, which set a lot of boys and men salivating. Lionel patented a track design, the Lionel Standard, which became the standard for rival companies as well.

During the First World War, Lionel had to get out of the toy business temporarily in order to make equipment for the armed forces. When peace returned, Lionel smoothly went back to trains. The Depression hit the company hard, and luckily salvation came with the introduction of the Mickey Mouse handcar, the hottest-selling toy in 1934. A miniature Mickey and Minnie Mouse stood on a little car on either side of a handbar. Their rubber legs moved up and down as the handbar seesawed between them.

The Second World War saw the company once again making military equipment. Inadvertently, Lionel wound up one of the biggest chicken and egg producers in the nation. This came about because Lionel researchers determined that day-old egg whites bound paint to the bowls of compasses the company was making better than anything else. Eggs were in short supply, so the company set up its own chicken and egg operation.

Back in the train business after the war, Lionel grudgingly shifted the style of trains the company made to diesel from steam. His belief in authenticity overruled his preference for steam engines. The first Lionel diesel, the Santa Fe F-3, turned out to be the best-selling engine ever. And more than kids and hobbyists turned to the little trains. The trains were put to work carrying radioactive material in military and cancer research laboratories. They even hauled hamburgers from kitchen to customer in some luncheonettes.

In the late 1950s, the company ran into trouble because of a marketing decision. Big discount retail stores were opening, driving Lionel's long-time customers, the small hobby shops, out of business. Instead of capitalizing on the greater volume of business the discounters offered, Lionel remained loyal to the little guys. Competitors capitalized by going with the big discounters and Lionel lost market share. The company also failed to recognize competition from model planes and slot cars that were siphoning off sales. Also, when television began consuming so much consumer time, interest in hobbies fell off. From a peak of $32.9 million in 1953, sales plunged to $14.4 million in 1958. Cowen sold his holdings and retired.

Things went from bad to worse. The company tried to diversify into everything from fishing tackle to cameras and microwave equipment. Rising costs saw the company move manufacturing operations to Japan and quality deteriorated. The once-hefty catalog shrank to a puny eight pages. Finally, Lionel went belly-up.

In 1969, General Mills bought the remaining equipment and designs for trains from the Lionel Corporation and began paying Lionel royalties for the use of the name. In 1970, under General Mills, a new Lionel catalog was issued and advertising was pitched at young fathers who had grown up with the trains in the 1940s. The tactic worked. Every year, little girls as well as little boys are introduced to the joys of Lionel trains.

TRAVEL

THE MARKET

Americans like to get around. Each year, they make a mind-boggling 1.1 billion trips longer than 100 miles and spend over 5.7 billion nights away from home. That makes the travel industry (which includes 30 interrelated businesses from lodging establishments to airlines, restaurants to cruise lines, as well as car-rental firms, travel agents, and tour operators) the third-largest retail service industry in America. (Many of these subcategories of the travel business are discussed in separate sections. See the

"Airlines," "Amusement Parks," "Auto Rental," "Hotels and Lodging," "Restaurants," and "Railroads" sections.)

THE MONEY

Americans spent about $292 billion on travel in 1987 and are expected to have spent another $317 billion in 1988.

In 1985, when $257 billion was spent while traveling, Americans spent $50 billion on public transportation (which grew at an annual rate of 9.9% between 1980 and 1985), $40 billion on auto transportation (a 1.9% annual rate of growth), $46 billion on lodging (a 12.1% annual rate of growth), $76 billion on food (a 9.5% annual rate of growth), $26 billion on amusement and recreation (an 11.5% annual rate of growth), and $19 billion on incidentals (a 7.9% annual rate of growth). The tourism and travel industry also generated $25 billion in federal, state, and local taxes.

Americans spent $100 billion on vacations in 1986 and spent another $85 billion to $90 billion on business travel.

Each year, about one fifth of all Americans take a business trip or visit a convention. That totals 185 million business trips in 1985, up 14% from 1984. Business spends 41% of its travel and entertainment budget on air travel, 22% on lodging, 17% on meals, 14% on entertainment, and 6% on auto rentals, according to the American Express Travel Management Services.

A weaker dollar also put more money into the coffers of the travel industry. The number of overseas visitors to the U.S. hit 28 million in 1987. In 1986 overseas visitors spent $14.1 billion. In contrast, Americans spent $24.4 billion abroad, producing a $10.3 billion deficit that accounted for 7% of the country's trade deficit, according to the U.S. Commerce Department.

THE PLAYERS

The travel service industry includes U.S. airlines, intercity bus companies, Amtrak, automobile services, commercial lodging places, campgrounds and trailer parks, eating and drinking places, amusement and recreation facilities, automobile rental, taxicab companies, travel agents, and general merchandise and miscellaneous retail stores that provide services for people away from home.

THE PEOPLE

Nearly 5.5 million people are directly employed in the industry, which pays $51 billion in wages and salaries and is the top employer in 13 states. It is the first-, second-, or third-largest employer in 41 states. Directly or indirectly, the travel industry employs about 1 of every 15 working Americans.

TRENDS AND FORECAST

An increasingly older America means that more retirees will be traveling. Smaller families could mean more discretionary income and a weaker dollar will force more people to travel in the U.S. Even so, the industry still faces problems with traffic congestion, a glut of hotel rooms, excess airline capacity, and alternatives to business and leisure travel (such as the dramatic growth of local parks, amusement facilities, VCRs, and improved telecommunication, such as videoconferencing) that could cut into revenues for business and pleasure travel.

In general, the industry's rapid growth of 12.7% a year between 1972 and 1982 will not be repeated in the near future.

TRAVEL TRIVIA

- When planning vacations, Americans in 1986 chose to go to cities rather than the beach for the first time in history. About 31% planned to visit a city, 30% were going to the shore, 18% visited a small town or rural area, 8% headed for the mountains, 7% went to the lake, and 7% visited a state or national park.
- Forty-one foreign visitors arrive in the U.S. every minute. Foreign visitors spend $22,000 a minute and generate $291 worth of local taxes, $851 in state taxes, and $1,392 in federal taxes every minute. Fifty-five foreign tourists arriving in the U.S. create one job.
- Foreign tourists are keen on sampling American cuisine. Collectively they consume 4,400 pounds of hamburger every hour.
- About 11% of all jobs created in 1984 were in the travel and tourism industry.
- Twelve cents of every dollar spent on tourism goes to taxes.
- Back to nature is now a big business. There are 13,000 campgrounds in the U.S. The 8,000 private campgrounds in the U.S. took in about $2 billion in 1985 and retailers sold about $775 million worth of camping equipment, excluding clothing and footwear.
- If foreign tourism dropped 1%, 28,000 jobs and $95 million worth of taxes would be lost.
- California has over 512,000 people employed in the travel and tourism industry, more than any other state.
- State governments go all out to attract tourists. States spent $189 million on tourist promotion in the 1984–1985 fiscal year, with Illinois heading the list at $14.4 million. California spends $5.8 million a year to advertise its sights, up from nothing in 1984. Even Iowa, with the lowest advertising budget of any state, spends $1.4 million. Illinois says its campaign to attract tourists created 2,200 jobs and $30.8 billion in tax revenues.
- Travelers annually spend the most money in these states: California ($29 billion), Florida ($17.6 billion), New York ($15.6 billion), Texas

Table 224 The Largest Convention Cities

Metropolitan area	Number of convention delegates, 1986
1. New York, New York	4,519,000
2. Chicago, Illinois	2,030,000
3. Dallas, Texas	1,967,000
4. Atlanta, Georgia	1,575,000
5. Las Vegas, Nevada	1,519,421
6. Washington, D.C.	1,143,840
7. San Francisco, California	1,066,000
8. Houston, Texas	1,054,673
9. Los Angeles, California	965,031
10. Anaheim, California	925,532
11. New Orleans, Louisiana	830,000
12. St Louis, Missouri	792,100
13. Orlando, Florida	680,611
14. Columbus, Ohio	558,786
15. Detroit, Michigan	531,991
16. San Diego, California	522,049
17. Denver, Colorado	507,463
18. Phoenix, Arizona	488,000
19. Boston, Massachusetts	440,000
20. Seattle, Washington	425,672
21. Oklahoma City, Oklahoma	400,000
21. Atlantic City, New Jersey	400,000
23. Louisville, Kentucky	386,000
24. Kansas City, Missouri	380,000
25. Philadelphia, Pennsylvania	365,000

Copyright © by CMP Publications, 600 Community Drive Manhasset, New York 11030.
Source: *Business Travel News* August 24, 1987.

Table 225 Travel Services

Year	Expenditures*** (billions of dollars)	Employment (millions)	Travel price index (1982 = 100)
1972	60	2.70	36.5
1977	117	4.17	55.7
1978	130	4.40	60.3
1979	144	4.45	69.5
1980	175	4.62	84.0
1981	192	4.72	94.8
1982	198	4.24	100.0
1983	209	4.30	104.0
1984	235	4.77	107.9
1985	255	5.01	113.1
1986	271	5.24	112.6
1987*	292	5.46	118.2
1988**	317	5.70	123.5

*Estimated.
**Forecast.
***Includes both U.S. and foreign visitor expenditures on travel in America.
Sources: U.S. Travel Data Center and U.S. Travel and Tourism Administration.

($14.9 billion), and New Jersey ($11.4 billion), according to the Travel Industry Association of America.

- About 228 million visitors annually travel to U.S. Forest Service recreational sites. The Forest Service offers 114,664 developed family camp and picnic sites, 320 swimming developments, 1,106 boating sites, and 307 winter-sports sites. All of these facilities could accommodate 1.67 million people. About 15.2 million hunters use Forest Service lands, as do 15.6 million fishermen.

TRUCKING

THE MARKET

In the transportation industry, trucks haul less freight than railroads but make far more money than any form of transportation.

Trucks haul 77% of the dollar value of all freight carried in America and 37% of the total freight tonnage, according to the American Trucking Associations. The industry's 5.3 million trucks log over 138 billion miles, carrying 2 billion tons of freight.

Without the trucking industry, a lot of products would have a tough time reaching factories and retail outlets. About 85% of all furniture, fixtures, and appliances are carried to market by trucks. Nearly 80% of all the food, rubber products, and plastic goods are moved by trucks, as well as 70% of all lumber, wood products, steel, sheet metal, cable, wire pipes, rods, and other semifinished metal products. Moreover, about two thirds of all U.S. communities rely on trucks exclusively for freight transportation.

THE MONEY

The revenues in this growing market added up to an estimated $217 billion in 1987, up from $205.3 billion in 1985. Revenues may hit $221.2 billion in 1988.

Profit margins for the whole industry are not available, but truckers regulated by the Interstate Commerce Commission earned $1.4 billion in profits on $50.7 billion in revenues in 1986. Two UPS companies were the two largest trucking companies, with $7.4 billion in combined revenues. The third largest, Yellow Freight Systems, had $1.6 billion in revenues.

THE PLAYERS

There are some 260,000 trucking firms in the U.S., as well as many other firms operating trucks as part of their business. Deregulation made it easier for smaller firms to enter the industry but the increased competition has put a crimp on profits. Profit margins for trucking companies regulated by the ICC dropped from 2.92% in 1978, before deregulation, to only 0.77% in 1982. Even in 1986, the best year since deregulation, profit margins only hit 2.78%. Meanwhile 3,467 trucking companies went bankrupt between 1980 and mid-1987.

THE PEOPLE

The trucking industry employs or contributes to the employment of some 7.4 million people as drivers, deliverymen, managers, warehouse workers, office support staff, truck dealers, highway construction personnel, and workers in truck manufacturing plants, according to the American Trucking Associations.

TRENDS AND FORECAST

In the 1970s, like the rest of the transportation industry, trucking was heavily regulated. Under the 1935 Motor Carrier Act, which was passed at the urging of the railroad companies, trucks were brought under the jurisdiction of the Interstate Commerce Commission. By the mid 1970s the ICC had the power to certify truckers and regulate the services they provided, their rates, and mergers and acquisitions.

The Motor Carrier Act of 1980 removed many of these regulations, allowing truckers increased freedom to set rates and making it easier to enter the trucking business. More than 19,000 new firms entered the industry in the first two years alone after the act became effective. Many new firms were low-cost, nonunion companies that helped lower freight rates, giving consumers a break but causing hard times for many firms with expensive Teamster contracts. As in most other segments of the transportation industry, deregulation led to mergers and a few larger companies getting a larger market share in some parts of the freight business. For example, the 10 largest companies in what is called the less-than-truckload segment of the industry now have 60% of the market, up from under 40% in 1978.

The effects of deregulation and increased competition are likely to continue for some time, with new bankruptcies and pressure on unionized firms likely to continue.

The Teamsters The dubious distinction of being the most corrupt union falls to the Teamsters. Though one of the nation's most politically powerful unions with 1.7 million members, the union has been crippled by the fact that every one of its presidents between 1951 and 1981 was indicted and convicted for crimes committed while in office. The current president of the Teamsters, Jackie Presser, has been indicted for bilking the union out of more than $700,000 by putting organized crime figures on the union payroll for no-show jobs.

The union traces its origins back to the Team Drivers International Union, founded in 1898, and the Teamsters National Union, founded in 1902 when some Chicago members of the Team Drivers rebelled against union leadership. Samuel Gompers patched up their differences and the International Brotherhood of Teamsters was born in 1903. The first president, Cornelius Shea, was indicted and acquitted for extorting money from company owners, creating a climate of scandal that has dogged the union ever since.

The union's biggest advances occurred in the 1930s, when it engaged in a long and bloody organizing campaign. During that drive Jimmy Hoffa, a tough-talking charismatic son of a coal miner, rose in the ranks by organizing several successful strikes. Hoffa, a Trotskyite in the 1930s, combined an infectious enthusiasm for unions with a penchant for violence. Truck owners were also not shy about using violence either. Hoffa's first contact with organized crime was with local mobsters who were hired by management to stop the union. After several meetings with Hoffa the mob agreed to remain neutral in future union-management disputes.

The union's real strength, however, was not violence but its ability to deliver higher wages and benefits. Industry working conditions and wages were abominable as late as the 1940s and the Teamster leadership held the respect of most members simply because of its ability to deliver the bacon, which largely remains true today.

But by the 1950s it was apparent that the union had strong connections with organized crime. Investigations of union corruption by the Kefauver Committee, the Kennedys, and later investigators uncovered a number of alarming problems. Union racketeers, for example, bilked the pension fund out of hundreds of millions of dollars, making it difficult for many former truckers to collect their pensions. The Teamster pension fund was so misused it became known as "the bank for the mob" because of its long-standing practice of loaning money to mob-backed enterprises. It has been said that Teamster money built Las Vegas as well as poured millions into nearly bankrupt businesses whose only qualification for a loan was making a kickback to trustees of the pension fund. The Teamster Pension Fund for the Central States was so badly run that the Labor Department imposed a trusteeship over it in the late 1970s.

Equally profitable was providing insurance for the teamsters. Allen Dorfman, a former schoolteacher with no experience in insurance, used his organized crime ties to set up an insurance company that earned $10 million a year in premiums by providing the Teamsters with insurance. Others set up businesses that charged exorbitant fees for managing health and welfare insurance funds. In one case, a mobster, Louis Ostrer, managed to eat up 75% of the $5.1 million in insurance premiums Teamsters union locals collected. One Teamsters local in New Jersey is currently under federal receivership to prevent a mob-dominated leadership from running the union's finances. Hoffa himself was sent to prison and was eventually assassinated by organized crime figures when he attempted to return to union leadership.

Still, corruption doesn't seem to hurt the union's political power. Because of Hoffa's feud with the Kennedys, the Teamsters became the only union to embrace the Republican Party. That won them favors from President Nixon and later President Reagan. President Reagan, who appointed Presser to his transition team in 1980 and the inauguration committee in 1984, came under strong attack from his own President's Commission on Organized Crime for associating with a union leader with reported organized crime ties.

The leadership's preoccupation with scams has, however, weakened the Teamsters' economic clout. The union has been losing members since deregulation. Tainted by charges of corruption, it has been unable to win new members. At the same time, deregulation forced many union trucking companies out of business because of competition from low-cost nonunion haulers. That has forced the union to temper its wage demands and makes the leadership more vulnerable to union dissidents who would like to clean house. Until that happens there is little chance the union will attract new members and unionize an increasingly non-union industry.

UTILITIES: ELECTRICAL

THE MARKET

Although only 8% of all homes had electricity in 1907 and less than half as late as 1924, 98.8% of all homes had electricity by 1956. Today, utilities serve about 101.5 million customers, virtually the whole population. The average customer pays $1,489 a year for electricity, with the average residential customer paying $663 and the average commercial customer paying $4,177 a year.

The nation's 89.7 million residential customers consume 34.4% of the nation's electricity. The 10.7 million commercial customers eat up 26.3% and the 708,000 industrial customers consume 36%. Electrical utilities produce most of their electricity (55.8%) from coal. Nuclear power (16.6%), hydroelectric power (11.7%), natural gas (10.0%), and oil (5.5%) produce the rest of our electricity.

THE MONEY

Electrical utilities earned $149.8 billion in 1985, most of which was earned by investor-owned electrical utilities. These companies earned $125.5 billion in operating revenues in 1985, up 4.5% from 1984, according to the Edison Electric Institute, and $18.5 billion in net income, down 5.8% from 1984.

THE PLAYERS

Privately owned utilities produce about three quarters of our electricity. There are 2,009 privately owned electric power plants with a capacity to produce 514.9 million kilowatts, compared to 1,466 publicly owned plants that have the ability to produce 157.6 million kilowatts.

TRENDS AND FORECAST

The outlook for electrical utilities is bright. Several factors should boost earnings. First, the industry should have more cash now that construction expenditures are slowing down. The industry spent heavily in the late 1970s and early 1980s on new plants. Dramatic cost overruns for nuclear plants hurt earnings in many cases and forced at least one system to default on bonds issued to finance construction costs, but by 1987 most of those plants were completed or written off. Generally speaking, electrical utilities should have more cash and better earning prospects between now and 1990 than they've had for nearly a decade. At the same time the cost of fuels, such as coal, used to produce electricity are expected to continue to fall.

But some problems remain. Some utilities with new nuclear plants may not be allowed rate increases that will allow them to recover the costs of these plants. As the nuclear plants of the 1960s grow old and need to be replaced, utilities could face astronomical shutdown costs because of the cost of entombing nuclear wastes. And new regulations to control acid rain could force many utilities using coal-fired generating plants to make costly capital improvements.

Table 226 Utilities at a Glance

This chart summarizes the state of the electrical utility industry, showing generating capacity, fuel used, sales, customers, revenues, balance sheets, and other basic data.

	Total electric utility industry		Increase	
	1985	1984	Amount	Percent
Generating capacity (kW in thousands)				
Installed name plate at beginning of year	672,462	658,182	14,280	2.2
Balance at December 31	688,733	672,462	16,271	2.4
Electric power supply (kW in thousands)				
Capability at time of summer peak load (contiguous U.S.)	621,597	604,240	17,357	2.9
Noncoincident summer peak load (contiguous U.S.)	460,503	451,150	9,353	2.1
Capacity margin (contiguous U.S.)	25.9%	25.3%		
Generation (kWh in millions)				
Hydro	281,149	321,150	(40,001)	(12.5)
Conventional steam	1,803,323	1,765,608	37,715	2.1
Nuclear steam	383,691	327,634	56,057	17.1
Internal combustion	1,662	1,901	(239)	(12.6)
Total generation	2,469,841**	2,416,304**	53,537	2.2
Purchases from industrial sources	25,137	17,746†	7,391	41.6
Imports from Canada and Mexico	45,901	42,219	3,682	8.7
Total energy input†	2,540,879**	2,476,269*††	64,610	2.6
Fuel				
Average cost of fuel per net kWh	2.27¢	2.41¢	(0.14)¢	(5.8)
Pounds of coal per net kWh generated	0.990	0.990	0.000	0.0
Average Btu per net kWh generated	10,426	10,385†	41	0.4
Energy (Btus in quadrillions)				
Annual production of energy	64.73ᵖ	65.85†	(1.12)	(1.7)
Total energy supply and disposition	78.06ᵖ	77.91†	0.15	0.2
Energy sales (kWh in millions)				
Residential	797,010ᵖ	782,608†	14,402	1.8
Commercial	608,480ᵖ	578,083†	30,397	5.3
Industrial	821,990ᵖ	835,486†	(13,496)	(1.6)
Street and highway lighting	13,954ᵖ	14,205†	(251)	(1.8)
Other	73,572ᵖ	70,203†	3,369	4.8
Total sales to ultimate customers	2,315,006ᵖ	2,280,585†	34,421	1.5
Exports to Canada and Mexico	4,965	2,558	2,407	94.1
Energy accounted for but not sold	11,167ᵖ	13,807†	(2,640)	(19.1)
Lost and unaccounted for	209,741ᵖ	(179,319)†	(30,422)	17.0
Total disposition of energy†	2,540,879ᵖ	2,476,269†	64,610	2.6
kWh used per customer (average for year)				
Residential	8,959ᵖ	8,978†	(19)	(0.2)
Commercial	57,369ᵖ	55,205†	2,164	3.9
Total ultimate customer	23,005ᵖ	23,152†	(147)	(0.6)
Customers at year end (thousands)				
Residential	89,741ᵖ	87,939†	1,802	2.0
Commercial	10,726ᵖ	10,565†	161	1.5
Industrial	708ᵖ	526†	182	34.6
Street and highway lighting	141ᵖ	140†	1	0.7
Other	203ᵖ	201†	2	1.0
Total ultimate customers	101,519ᵖ	99,371†	2,148	2.2
Revenues (millions of dollars)				
Residential	58,973ᵖ	56,116†	2,857	5.1
Commercial	44,237ᵖ	41,254†	2,983	7.2
Industrial	41,445ᵖ	40,796†	649	1.6
Street and highway lighting	1,425ᵖ	1,376†	49	3.6
Other	3,757ᵖ	3,551†	206	5.8
Total revenues from ultimate customers	149,836ᵖ	143,093†	6,743	4.7
Exports to Canada and Mexico	25	22	3	13.6
Total revenues from sales of energy	149,861ᵖ	143,114†	6,747	4.7
Average annual revenue per customer:				
Residential	662.88ᵖ	643.75†	19.13	3.0
Commercial	4,170.74ᵖ	3,939.57†	231.17	5.9
Total ultimate customers	1,488.97ᵖ	1,452.62†	36.35	2.5
Average revenue per kWh:				
Residential	7.40¢ᵖ	7.17¢†	0.23¢	3.2
Commercial	7.27¢ᵖ	7.14¢†	0.13¢	1.8
Total ultimate customer	6.47¢ᵖ	6.27¢†	0.20¢	3.2
Economics and other				
Miles of overhead electric line, 22 kV and above	607,052	601,261†	5,791	1.0
Employees of investor-owned electric utilities	524,503	516,100	8,403	1.6
Plant ratio—kWh generated/kW of capacity‡	3,629	3,632	(3)	NA

Note: Total may not equal sum of components due to independent rounding.
*Represents reclassification in ownership between industrial and electric utility plants and rerating of turbines within the electric utility industry.
**Total includes generation by wind (1984—6.5 kWh in millions; 1985—5.8 kWh in millions) and generation by solar (1984—5.2 kWh in millions; 1985—10.6 kWh in millions).
†Excludes industrial for own use.
‡On basis of installed name plate capacity.
ᵖPreliminary.
†Revised.
( ) Denotes negative figure.
NA Not applicable.
kW kilowatt.
kWh kilowatt-hour.
kV kilovolt.

Table 226 Utilities at a Glance (continued)

Financial (millions of dollars)	Investor-owned electric utilities		Increase	
	1985	1984	Amount	Percent
Combined balance sheets: assets				
Utility plant:				
Electric	317,392	277,374	40,018	14.4
Other	18,954	18,219	735	4.0
Total utility plant	336,345	295,592	40,753	13.8
Accumulated provision for depreciation and amortization	92,567	84,306	8,261	9.8
Net utility plant	243,778	211,285	32,493	15.4
Nuclear fuel	13,979	11,587	2,392	20.6
Accumulated provision for amortization of nuclear fuel assemblies	5,461	4,219	1,242	29.4
Net nuclear fuel	8,518	7,368	1,150	15.6
Construction work in progress	84,092	95,491	(11,399)	(11.9)
Net total utility plant	336,389	314,145	22,244	7.1
Other property and investment	9,557	9,359	198	2.1
Total current and accrued assets	40,427	37,823	2,604	6.9
Total deferred debits	16,194	18,065	(1,871)	(10.4)
Total assets	402,567	379,392	23,175	6.1
Capitalization and liabilities				
Capitalization:				
Common capital stock	51,556	47,842	3,714	7.8
Other paid-in capital excluding retained earnings	34,036	33,886	150	0.4
Retained earnings	43,902	40,423	3,479	8.6
Total common capital stock equity	129,495	122,151	7,344	6.0
Preferred stock	30,614	29,882	732	2.4
Total long-term debt	148,944	141,693	7,251	5.1
Total capitalization	309,052	293,727	15,325	5.2
Total other noncurrent liabilities	3,278	NA	NA	NA
Total current and accrued liabilities	38,718	36,851	1,867	5.1
Total deferred credits and operating reserves	21,509	22,232	(723)	(3.3)
Contributions in aid of construction	156	145	11	7.6
Deferred income taxes	29,853	26,438	3,415	12.9
Total liabilities	402,567	379,392	23,175	6.1
Combined income statements:				
Operating revenues—electric department	125,547	120,090	5,457	4.5
Operating expenses including maintenance	70,300	68,161	2,139	3.1
Depreciation, depletion, and amortization	10,302	9,249	1,053	11.4
Taxes	20,748	19,883	865	4.4
Total operating expenses	101,350	97,294	4,056	4.2
Operating income	24,197	22,796	1,401	6.1
Other income (nonoperating), net	7,445	7,290	155	2.1
Other departments	1,333	1,378	(45)	(3.3)
Income before interest charges (gross income)	32,976	31,465	1,511	4.8
Total interest charges	12,794	11,771	1,023	8.7
Income before extraordinary items	20,183	19,694	489	2.5
Extraordinary items	(1,659)	(22)	1,637	N/A
Net income	18,525	19,672	(1,147)	(5.8)
Preferred dividend charges	2,877	2,828	49	1.7
Available for common stock	15,647	16,844	(1,197)	7.1
Common dividends	11,817	11,077	740	6.7
Net income After dividends	3,830	5,767	(1,937)	(33.6)
Electric utility financing:				
Long-term debt	12,517	10,173[r]	2,344	23.0
Preferred stock	655	888	(233)	(26.2)
Common stock	1,650	930	720	77.4
Total capital	14,822	11,992[r]	2,830	23.6
Construction expenditures:				
Production	21,372	23,939	(2,567)	(10.7)
Transmission	1,863	2,250	(387)	(17.2)
Distribution	6,590	5,899	691	11.7
Other	3,468	3,197	271	8.5
Total	33,294	35,285	(1,991)	(5.6)

Note: Total may not equal sum of components due to independent rounding.
[r]Revised.
( ) Denotes negative figure.
NA Not applicable.
Source: Edison Electric Institute.

Table 227   Highest and Lowest Utilities Bills in the U.S.

10 LOWEST AND HIGHEST TYPICAL MONTHLY RESIDENTIAL BILLS FOR 500 KILOWATT-HOURS FOR PRIVATELY OWNED UTILITIES SERVING COMMUNITIES OF 50,000 OR MORE, JANUARY 1, 1986

Utility	Lowest bill (dollars)	Utility	Highest bill (dollars)
Lakeview Light and Power Company (Washington)	17.75	Consolidated Edison Company of New York (New York)	71.25
Washington Water Power Company (Washington)	19.88	Long Island Lighting Company (New York)	64.34
Idaho Power Company (Idaho)	20.91	San Diego Gas and Electric Company (California)	59.98
Portland General Electric Company (Oregon)	24.12	Philadelphia Electric Company (Pennsylvania)	59.75
Louisiana Power and Light Company (Louisiana)	25.07	United Illuminating Company (Connecticut)	58.47
Puget Sound Power and Light Company (Washington)	26.03	Jersey Central Power and Light Company (New Jersey)	56.86
Pacific Power and Light Company (Oregon)	26.61	Northern Indiana Public Service Company (Indiana)	55.64
Montana Power Company (Montana)	27.08	Atlantic City Electric Company (New Jersey)	54.45
Minnesota Power and Light Company (Minnesota)	27.28	Public Service Electric and Gas Company (New Jersey)	54.12
Northern States Power Company (North Dakota)	29.36	Eastern Edison Company (Massachusetts)	53.08

10 LOWEST AND HIGHEST TYPICAL MONTHLY RESIDENTIAL BILLS FOR 500 KILOWATT-HOURS FOR PUBLICLY OWNED UTILITIES SERVING COMMUNITIES OF 50,000 OR MORE, JANUARY 1, 1986

Utility	Lowest bill (dollars)	Utility	Highest bill (dollars)
Seattle City of (Washington)	9.92	Norwalk Third Taxing District (Connecticut)	48.64
Provo City of (Utah)	15.29	Garland City of (Texas)	46.72
Palo Alto City of (California)	17.50	Riverside Utilities Department (California)	46.62
Eugene City of (Oregon)	18.06	Salt River Project (Arizona)	43.81
Tacoma City of (Washington)	19.20	Anaheim City of (California)	43.56
Austin City of (Texas)	20.59	Tallahassee City of (Florida)	43.37
Snohomish County Public Utility District No. 1 (Washington)	22.85		

Note: Bills shown are for the winter period.
Source: Energy Information Administration Form EIA-213, "Typical Net Monthly Bills."

Table 228 Energy Expenditure Estimates, 1970, 1975, and 1980 to 1984

(billions of dollars)

Energy source	1970	1975	1980	1981	1982	1983	1984
Coal							
Coking coal	1.2	3.7	3.7	3.8	2.7	2.1	2.5
Steam coal	3.4	9.4	18.9	22.4	23.7	24.9	26.6
Total	4.6	13.0	22.6	26.2	26.4	27.1	29.0
Natural gas	10.9	20.0	51.1	60.6	68.2	72.0	77.1
Petroleum products							
Asphalt and road oil	0.7	1.9	3.5	4.2	3.5	3.9	4.5
Aviation gasoline	0.3	0.4	0.9	0.9	0.8	0.8	0.7
Distillate fuel oil	6.3	15.7	40.8	48.2	44.1	40.4	43.0
Jet fuel	1.4	4.2	13.9	15.6	15.0	14.0	15.1
Kerosene	0.6	0.9	2.3	2.2	2.3	2.0	1.9
Liquefied petroleum gases	2.4	5.2	10.9	11.9	12.9	14.1	14.3
Lubricants	1.6	2.3	5.0	5.9	5.2	5.3	5.9
Motor gasoline	31.6	59.4	124.4	138.1	130.3	118.1	114.4
Residual fuel oil	2.0	10.4	21.6	22.7	17.6	14.1	14.4
Other petroleum products[1]	1.1	3.2	15.8	16.9	12.0	10.8	10.5
Total	48.2	103.7	239.2	266.6	243.7	223.4	224.7
Nuclear fuel, wood, and waste electricity generation	[2]	0.5	1.2	1.4	1.7	1.8	2.4
Imports of coal coke	[2]	0.2	0.1	[2]	[2]	[2]	[2]
Exports of coal coke[3]	0.1	0.1	0.1	0.1	0.1	[2]	0.1
Total primary energy	63.7	137.3	314.0	354.8	339.9	324.3	333.2
Electric utility fuel[3]	4.3	16.4	37.4	43.3	41.3	41.3	43.4
Electricity purchased by end users[4]	23.5	50.9	98.5	116.5	127.4	134.7	148.1
Total energy[5]	82.8	171.8	375.1	428.0	426.0	417.7	437.9

[1]Includes pentanes plus petrochemical feedstocks, special naphthas, petroleum coke, still gas, wax, and miscellaneous products.
[2]Less than $0.05 billion.
[3]In determining total energy expenditures, this is a negative quantity.
[4]These are sales. In determining total energy expenditures, this is a positive quantity.
[5]There are no direct fuel costs for hydroelectric, geothermal, centralized solar, or wind energy. Wood and other biomass fuels are not included, except those consumed at the electric utilities.
Note: Sum of components may not equal total due to independent rounding.
Source: Energy Information Administration, *State Energy Price and Expenditure Report 1984*.

Table 229　Top Five Nations in Nuclear Energy

Country	Number of plants	Capacity (megawatts)
U.S.	126	116,939
France	63	63,068
Soviet Union	73	61,938
Japan	51	40,484
West Germany	26	27,580

Source: *Nuclear World News,* August 1987.

Table 230　Net Generation of Electricity by the Electric Utility Industry by Energy Source, 1949–1986

(billions of kilowatt-hours)

Year	Coal	Petroleum	Natural gas	Nuclear power	Hydroelectric power	Geothermal and other	Total
1949	135	29	37	0	90	—	291
1950	155	34	45	0	96	—	329
1951	185	29	57	0	100	—	371
1952	195	30	68	0	105	—	399
1953	219	38	80	0	105	—	443
1954	239	32	94	0	107	—	472
1955	301	37	95	0	113	—	547
1956	339	36	104	0	122	—	601
1957	346	40	114	—	130	—	632
1958	344	40	120	—	140	—	645
1959	378	47	147	—	138	—	710
1960	403	48	158	1	146	—	756
1961	422	49	169	2	152	—	794
1962	450	49	184	2	169	—	855
1963	494	52	202	3	166	—	917
1964	526	57	220	3	177	—	984
1965	571	65	222	4	194	—	1,055
1966	613	79	251	6	195	1	1,144
1967	630	89	265	8	222	1	1,214
1968	685	104	304	13	222	1	1,329
1969	706	138	333	14	250	1	1,442
1970	704	184	373	22	248	1	1,532
1971	713	220	374	38	266	1	1,613
1972	771	274	376	54	273	2	1,750
1973	848	314	341	83	272	2	1,861
1974	828	301	320	114	301	3	1,867
1975	853	289	300	173	300	3	1,918
1976	944	320	295	191	284	4	2,038
1977	985	358	306	251	220	4	2,124
1978	976	365	305	276	280	3	2,206
1979	1,075	304	329	255	280	4	2,247
1980	1,162	246	346	251	276	6	2,286
1981	1,203	206	346	273	261	6	2,295
1982	1,192	147	305	283	309	5	2,241
1983	1,259	144	274	294	332	6	2,310
1984	1,342	120	297	328	321	9	2,416
1985	1,402	100	292	384	281	11	2,470
1986	1,388	137	248	414	291	12	2,489

Source: Energy Information Administration, *Annual Energy Review.*

Table 231   International Primary Energy Production by Source, 1975–1986

(quadrillions of Btu)

Year	Crude oil[1] and natural gas plant liquids	Natural gas[2]	Coal	Hydroelectric power[3]	Nuclear power[3]	Total[4]
1975	117.22	43.90	66.17	15.03	3.85	246.18
1976	127.09	45.68	68.01	15.07	4.52	260.38
1977	132.10	46.88	69.17	15.51	5.42	269.08
1978	132.79	48.24	70.33	16.74	6.45	274.54
1979	138.52	51.57	74.52	17.64	6.73	288.97
1980	133.00	52.75	75.68	18.16	7.50	287.10
1981	125.24	54.16	75.82	18.42	8.54	282.19
1982	119.51	53.66	78.96	18.86	9.35	280.33
1983	119.04	53.97	78.97	19.76	10.67	282.42
1984	122.18	58.61	82.91	20.26	12.82	296.78
1985	119.96	60.28	85.83	20.78	14.89	301.73
1986	126.12	62.63	88.22	20.73	16.40	314.09

[1]Includes lease condensate.
[2]Dry production.
[3]Net generation, i.e., gross generation less plant use.
[4]Total excludes wood, waste, geothermal, wind, photovoltaic, and solar thermal energy.
Note: Sum of components may not equal total due to independent rounding.
Source: Energy Information Administration, *International Energy Annual.*

VIDEO GAMES, JUKEBOXES, AND PINBALL MACHINES

THE MARKET

Imagine an industry where people put money in a slot and you collect it. That's the coin-operated amusement industry, a world of video games, arcades, pinball machines, jukeboxes, and pool tables.

THE MONEY

Coin-operated games take quarters, nickels, and dimes, but the coin-operated game and music industry isn't small change. Total revenues stood at $4 billion, and that was a $4.9 billion drop from 1982, the height of the video game fad, when Americans pumped $8.9 billion worth of change into games, according to a survey by *Play Meter.*

**Table 232   Average Weekly Gross Slot-Machine Collections
by Type of Machine**

Type of machine	1986	1984	1981
Pool tables	$61	$60	$ 67
Nonvideo arcade games	55	59	36
Electronic dart games	44	57	—
Video games	57	53	140
Counter games	—	52	37
Kiddie rides	33	50	—
Pinball games	51	41	66
Phonographs	55	40	66
Shuffleboards	—	30	31
Foosballs	—	26	28

Source: *Play Meter,* November 1986.

THE PLAYERS

The coin-operated game industry is made up of 4,500 operators who own 1,450,000 games that are played at 350,000 locations. That may confirm your suspicions that video games are everywhere, but actually the number of coin-operated games and outlets has declined. In 1983, there were 11,000 operators who had 1,876,389 coin-operated games at 417,267 locations. While the number of operators and games has declined, however, the average revenues have increased from $546,000 to about $889,000 in 1986, according to *Play Meter*.

TRENDS AND FORECAST

The industry faced a few hard years in 1983, 1984, and 1985, when revenues dropped by more than half. In 1987, the industry expected to have seen its first year since 1982 when the number of operators or revenues didn't decline. But even though the remaining operators are healthier than ever, the survivors are looking into expanding into other areas such as coin-operated food and beverage machines, pay phones, or cigarette machines as a way of hedging their bets. And although the worst is over, tough drinking laws are hurting revenues at taverns, and coin-operated games are still a favorite scapegoat of local governments, which have long viewed pinball machines and video games as a breeding ground for juvenile delinquents. That has translated into high taxes that threaten profit margins. Video games, it seems, have grown from a youthful fad into a mature industry with stagnant revenues.

WHOLESALE TRADE

THE MARKET

"I can get it for you wholesale" is no meaningless refrain. There are over 321,000 wholesaling firms acting as middlemen and -women between suppliers and a variety of government agencies, professionals, and retail outlets that buy their products. Few consumers ever see these wholesale merchants, but they perform a vital economic function by grading and sorting products into smaller lots, by extending credit to retailers, by providing marketing and promotional help, by establishing markets for manufactured products, and by distributing a wide variety of goods, from motor vehicles and auto parts to wheat, groceries, chemicals, paper, beer, and gasoline.

THE MONEY

Wholesale merchants racked up an estimated $1,42 billion in sales in 1987, with durable goods contributing $660 billion in sales and nondurable goods hitting $760 billion. A forecast by the International Trade Administration estimates that wholesale trade will grow 2% to $1,448 billion in sales in 1988.

THE PLAYERS

Though the wholesale industry is composed mostly of small, highly competitive firms, a few larger firms garner most of the sales. In the *1982 Census of Wholesale Trade,* which contains the most recent available figures, only 1.6% of all wholesale establishments had annual sales of $25 million or more. But these large firms accounted for nearly half (46%) of all wholesale sales. On the other end of the scale, 88.7% of all wholesalers had less then $5 million in annual sales; collectively, these smaller firms racked up only 26.7% of all wholesale sales.

THE PEOPLE

Employment in this industry hit 6 million in 1988, up from 5.3 million in 1982 and 4.1 million in 1972.

Table 233   The Wholesale Market

(millions of dollars)

Kind of business	Sales			
	1975	1980	1985	1986
Wholesale merchants, total	561,637	1,124,646	1,374,752	1,381,311
Durable goods, total	231,692	483,079	630,312	664,108
Motor vehicles, auto parts, and supplies	39,681	83,142	132,391	145,216
Furniture and home furnishings	8,265	16,276	24,210	26,337
Lumber and other construction materials	17,261	36,390	46,193	51,435
Sporting, recreational, photographic, hobby goods, toys, and supplies	NA	NA	16,282	NA
Metals minerals, except petroleum	NA	63,436	60,933	57,347
Electrical goods	22,747	48,889	88,753	92,350
Hardware, plumbing, heating equipment, and supplies	15,200	29,109	41,263	43,618
Machinery, equipment, and supplies	69,153	140,680	165,820	169,216
Miscellaneous durable goods	NA	NA	54,467	60,508
Nondurable goods, total	329,945	641,567	744,440	717,203
Paper and paper products	11,215	22,608	36,798	40,521
Drugs, drug proprietaries, and druggist sundries	8,750	13,802	25,095	27,576
Apparel, piece goods, and notions	NA	NA	40,701	NA
Groceries and related products	95,754	155,372	217,085	234,748
Farm-product raw materials	83,264	125,433	93,252	79,195
Chemicals and allied products	NA	NA	24,716	NA
Beer, wine, and distilled alcoholic beverages	19,370	31,911	39,358	40,262
Miscellaneous nondurable goods	43,651	77,501	104,008	109,170

(NA) Not available.
Source: Bureau of the Census, U.S. Department of Commerce.

PART VII

The Heavy Hitters: America's Biggest Companies

THE 50 LARGEST INDUSTRIAL COMPANIES*
(Revenues and Net Income in Millions of Dollars;
Share Earnings in Dollars)

1. **General Motors Corporation (GM)**
   CEO: Roger B. Smith   3044 General Motors Boulevard
   Employees: 821,000 (a)   Detroit, Michigan 48202
   Assets: $79.5 billion (a)   313-556-5000

	1987	1986	1985	1980
Revenues:	101,782	102,814	96,371	57,729
Net income:	3,550	2,945	3,999	(763)
Share earnings:	10.06	8.21	12.28	—

What it does: This giant accounts for over half of all the cars assembled in the U.S. In 1984, it acquired Electronic Data Systems Corporation, a major computer services company.

2. **Exxon Corporation (XON)**
   CEO: Lawrence G. Rawl   1251 Avenue of the Americas
   Employees: 102,000 (a)   New York, New York 10020
   Assets: $69.5 billion (a)   212-333-1000

	1987	1986	1985	1980
Revenues:	84,120	76,555	92,869	110,191
Net income:	4,840	5,360	4,870	5,350
Share earnings:	3.43	7.42	6.46	6.15

What it does: A giant energy company.

*Based on the *Fortune* 500 ranking.
(a) For period ending December 31, 1986.
(b) For period ending June 30, 1987.
(c) For period ending September 30, 1987.

3. **Ford Motor Company (F)**
   CEO: Donald F. Petersen   P.O. Box 1899
   Employees: 382,274 (a)   Dearborn, Michigan 48121
   Assets: $37.9 billion (a)   313-322-3000

	1987	1986	1985	1980
Revenues:	71,643	62,716	52,366	37,086
Net income:	4,625	3,285	2,515	(1,543)
Share earnings:	9.05	12.32	9.09	—

What it does: World's second biggest maker of cars and trucks.

4. **International Business Machines Corporation (IBM)**
   CEO: John F. Akers   Old Orchard Road
   Employees: 403,508 (a)   Armonk, New York 10504
   Assets: $15.3 billion (a)   914-765-1900

	1987	1986	1985	1980
Revenues:	54,217	51,250	50,056	26,213
Net income:	5,258	4,789	6,555	3,562
Share earnings:	8.72	7.81	10.67	6.10

What it does: World's biggest maker of computers and information processing equipment and systems.

5. **Mobil Corporation (MOB)**
   CEO: Allen E. Murray   150 East 42nd Street
   Employees: 127,400 (b)   New York, New York 10017
   Assets: $39.4 billion (b)   212-883-4242

	1987	1986	1985	1980
Revenues:	56,446	49,865	60,609	62,726
Net income:	1,264	1,407	1,040	2,813
Share earnings:	3.08	3.45	2.55	6.62

What it does: A major international oil company. In 1984, it acquired Superior Oil for $5.7 billion.

6. **General Electric Company (GE)**
   CEO: John F. Welch, Jr.   3135 Easton Turnpike
   Employees: 359,000 (a)   Fairfield, Connecticut 06431
   Assets: $34.6 billion (a)   203-373-2211

(a) For period ending December 31, 1986.
(b) For period ending June 30, 1987.
(c) For period ending September 30, 1987.

	1987	1986	1985	1980
Revenues:	39,315	36,725	29,252	24,949
Net income:	2,915	2,492	2,227	1,514
Share earnings:	3.20	5.46	5.00	3.33

What it does: It is a diversified maker of high-technology electrical and related products. In June 1986, it acquired RCA Corporation, a major communications and entertainment company.

7. American Telephone and Telegraph Company (T)

CEO: James E. Olson   550 Madison Avenue
Employees: 302,000 (b)   New York, New York 10022
Assets: $37.9 billion (b)   212-605-5500

	1987	1986	1985	1980
Revenues:	33,598	34,087	34,417	NA
Net income:	2,044	139	1,557	
Share earnings:	1.88	.05	1.37	

What it does: It offers long-distance services and sales and manufacturing of telephone equipment. In 1985, sales of service provided 49% of revenues.

8. Texaco, Inc. (TX)

CEO: James W. Kinnear   2000 Westchester Avenue
Employees: 51,000 (b)   White Plains, New York 10650
Assets: $34.9 billion (a)   914-253-4000

	1987	1986	1985	1980
Revenues:	35,300	32,591	47,514	52,485
Net income:	(440)	725	1,233	2,643
Share earnings:	—	3.01	5.11	9.79

What it does: On April 12, 1987, the company filed for Chapter 11 under the federal bankruptcy code, thus making Pennzoil an unsecured creditor in its $10.5 billion damage award against this major petroleum company. In December 1987, Pennzoil agreed to settle for $3 billion.

9. E. I. du Pont de Nemours and Company (DD)

CEO: Richard E. Heckert   1007 Market Street
Employees: 141,000 (a)   Wilmington, Delaware 19898
Assets: $26.7 billion (a)   302-774-1000

	1987	1986	1985	1980
Revenues:	30,468	27,148	29,483	13,652
Net income:	1,786	1,538	1,118	716
Share earnings:	7.39	6.35	4.61	4.83

What it does: Nation's biggest chemical maker with interests in various chemicals, plastics, man-made fibers, health care, and industrial products. Owns Conoco, which has large oil, gas, and coal reserves.

(a) For period ending December 31, 1986.
(b) For period ending June 30, 1987.
(c) For period ending September 30, 1987.

10. Chevron Corporation (CHV)

CEO: George M. Keller

Employees: 51,095 (a)

Assets: $35.1 billion (a)

225 Bush Street

San Francisco, California 94104

415-894-7700

	1987	1986	1985	1980
Revenues:	29,100	24,351	41,742	41,553
Net income:	1,007	715	1,547	2,401
Share earnings:	2.94	2.09	4.52	7.02

What it does: Multinational integrated oil company. In 1985, U.S. exploration and production accounted for 58% of operating profits, foreign 27%. Acquired Gulf Oil Corporation (1984) for $13.3 billion.

11. Chrysler Corporation (C)

CEO: Lee Iacocca

Employees: 115,000 (c)

Assets: $14.5 billion (c)

12000 Chrysler Drive

Highland Park, Michigan 48203

313-956-5252

	1987	1986	1985	1980
Revenues:	26,276	22,586	22,586	8,600
Net income:	1,289	1,404	1,389	(1,709)
Share earnings:	5.90	6.31	6.25	—

What it does: Third-largest U.S. auto maker. Accounted for 10.3% of domestic registrations in 1985. Acquired Gulfstream Aerospace Corporation in August 1985 for $641.8 million.

12. Philip Morris Companies, Inc. (MO)

CEO: Hamish Maxwell

Employees: 111,000 (a)

Assets: 17.6 billion (a)

120 Park Avenue

New York, New York 10017

212-880-5000

	1987	1986	1985	1980
Revenues:	27,695	25,409	15,964	9,650
Net income:	1,842	1,478	1,255	549
Share earnings:	7.75	6.20	5.24	2.20

What it does: The largest cigarette company in the U.S. Holds important positions in the food and brewing industries.

13. Amoco Corporation (AN)

CEO: Richard M. Morrow

Employees: 46,775 (a)

Assets: $23.7 billion (a)

200 East Randolph Drive

Chicago, Illinois 60601

312-856-6111

(a) For period ending December 31, 1986.

(b) For period ending June 30, 1987.

(c) For period ending September 30, 1987.

	1987	1986	1985	1980
Revenues:	22,391	18,281	26,922	26,133
Net income:	1,360	747	1,953	1,915
Share earnings:	5.31	2.91	7.42	6.54

What it does: Multinational and domestic integrated petroleum company. In 1985, U.S. petroleum exploration and development accounted for 42% of profits, foreign 37%.

14. RJR Nabisco, Inc. (RJR)

CEO: F. Ross Johnson
Employees: 120,000 (c)
Assets: $15.9 billion (c)

300 Galleria Parkway
Atlanta, Georgia 30339
404-852-3000

	1987	1986	1985	1980
Revenues:	15,766	16,998	13,533	NA
Net income:	1,209	1,064	1,001	
Share earnings:	4.70	3.83	3.60	

What it does: Nabisco entered into a $4.9 billion merger with R. J. Reynolds in 1985 forming one of the world's biggest consumer products companies, with major packaged food holdings and the second-largest cigarette company.

15. Shell Oil Company (SUO)

CEO: John F. Bookout
Employees: 32,641 (b)
Assets: $26.2 billion (b)

1 Shell Plaza
Houston, Texas 77002
713-241-6161

	1987	1986	1985	1980
Revenues:	20,852	17,353	20,477	19,959
Net income:	1,230	883	1,650	1,542
Share earnings:	NA	NA	NA	NA

What it does: Merged in June 1985 with SPNV Holdings, Inc., a subsidiary of Royal Dutch/Shell Group.

16. Boeing (BA)

CEO: Frank A. Shrontz
Employees: 140,000 (a)
Assets: $11 billion (a)

P.O. Box 3707
Seattle, Washington 98124
206-655-2121

	1987	1986	1985	1980
Revenues:	15,355	16,341	13,636	8,131
Net income:	480	665	566	505
Share earnings:	3.10	4.28	3.75	5.25

What it does: Leading manufacturer of aircraft—commercial (49% of profits in 1985) and military (41%).

(a) For period ending December 31, 1986.
(b) For period ending June 30, 1987.
(c) For period ending September 30, 1987.

17. **United Technologies Corporation (UTX)**
    CEO: Robert F. Daniell   755 Main Street
    Employees: 192,000 (a)   Hartford, Connecticut 06101
    Assets: $11.3 billion (a)   203-728-7000

	1987	1986	1985	1980
Revenues:	17,170	15,669	14,991	12,324
Income from	591	48	636	393
continuing				
operations:				
Share earnings:	4.52	.07	4.76	3.64

What it does: A major maker of commercial and military aircraft engines, helicopters, flight systems products, escalators, elevators, and other products.

18. **Procter & Gamble (PG)**
    CEO: John G. Smale   P.O. Box 599
    Employees: 73,200 (c)   Cincinnati, Ohio 45201
    Assets: $13.7 billion (c)   513-983-1100

	1987	1986	1985	1980
Revenues:	17,000	15,439	13,552	10,772
Net income:	1,870	709	635	640
Share earnings:	3.27	4.20	3.80	3.87

What it does: A major maker of household, pharmaceutical, personal care, food, and beverage products.

19. **Occidental Petroleum Corporation (OXY)**
    CEO: Armand Hammer   10889 Wilshire Boulevard
    Employees: 42,353 (b)   Los Angeles, California 90024
    Assets: $17.5 billion (b)   213-879-1700

	1987	1986	1985	1980
Revenues:	17,096	15,344	14,534	12,476
Net income:	240	181	696	711
Share earnings:	1.06	.72	2.21	8.82

What it does: A diversified energy company.

20. **Atlantic Richfield Company (ARC)**
    CEO: Lodwrick M. Cook   515 South Flower Street
    Employees: 31,300 (a)   Los Angeles, California 90071
    Assets: $21.6 billion (a)   213-486-3511

	1987	1986	1985	1980
Revenues:	16,829	14,993	22,492	22,915
Net income:	340	615	333	1,592
Share earnings:	6.68	3.38	1.55	6.40

What it does: The largest integrated domestic oil company.

(a) For period ending December 31, 1986.
(b) For period ending June 30, 1987.
(c) For period ending September 30, 1987.

21. **Tenneco, Inc. (TBT)**
    CEO: Robert Blakley   P.O. Box 2511
    Employees: 107,000 (c)   Houston, Texas 77252
    Assets: $27.7 billion (a)   713-757-2131

	1987	1986	1985	1980
Revenues:	14,790	14,529	15,244	12,620
Net income:	(132)	(29)	(1)	713
Share earnings:	—	—	—	5.84

What it does: A diversified company engaged in oil and natural gas pipeline operations, shipbuilding, manufacture of farm equipment, agriculture, land development, and other activities.

22. **USX Corporation (USX)**
    CEO: David M. Roderick   600 Grant Street
    Employees: 69,424 (c)   Pittsburgh, Pennsylvania 15230
    Assets: $16.6 billion (c)   412-433-1121

	1987	1986	1985	1980
Revenues:	14,836	14,900	20,879	12,492
Net income:	206	(1,833)	598	504
Share earnings:	.54	—	1.94	5.77

What it does: Formerly U.S. Steel, it is the nation's biggest steel maker. It changed its name in July 1986.

23. **McDonnell Douglas Corporation (MD)**
    CEO: Sanford N. McDonnell   P.O. Box 516
    Employees: 109,164 (c)   St. Louis, Missouri 63166
    Assets: $8.3 billion (c)   314-232-0232

	1987	1986	1985	1980
Revenues:	13,146	12,831	11,666	6,198
Net income:	313	277	346	145
Share earnings:	7.75	6.86	8.60	3.65

What it does: The leading manufacturer of fighter aircraft for the military.

24. **Rockwell International Corporation (ROK)**
    CEO: Robert Anderson   600 Grant Street
    Employees: 121,194 (a)   Pittsburgh, Pennsylvania 15219
    Assets: $7.7 billion (a)   412-565-2000

	1987 (n)	1986	1985	1980
Revenues:	12,123	12,296	11,388	6,907
Net income:	635	611	595	280
Share earnings:	2.27	4.12	4.00	1.88

What it does: A diversified company that is a leading maker of military aircraft. It makes electronics, space systems and rocket engines, automotive components, and other products. (n) restated. Year ends September 30.

(a) For period ending December 31, 1986.
(b) For period ending June 30, 1987.
(c) For period ending September 30, 1987.

25. Allied-Signal, Inc. (ALD)

CEO: Edward L. Hennessy, Jr.
Employees: 114,000 (b)
Assets: $10.8 billion (b)

Columbia Road and Park Avenue
Morristown, New Jersey 07960
201-455-2000

	1987	1986	1985	1980
Revenues:	11,116	9,988	8,183	5,300
Net income:	656	605	(279)	288
Share earnings:	3.90	3.26	—	5.43

What it does: A diversified company providing a broad range of products and services to the auto, electronics, and aerospace industries.

26. Eastman Kodak Company (EK)

CEO: Colby H. Chandler
Employees: 121,450 (c)
Assets: $6.4 billion (c)

343 State Street
Rochester, New York 14650
716-724-4000

	1987	1986	1985	1980
Revenues:	13,305	11,550	10,631	9,734
Net income:	1,178	374	332	1,153
Share earnings:	3.52	1.66	1.46	4.77

What it does: World's largest producer of photographic supplies. It also manufactures chemical products. Imaging accounted for 78% of sales, chemical products 22% in 1985.

27. Dow Chemical Company (DOW)

CEO: Frank P. Popoff
Employees: 51,000 (a)
Assets: $12.2 billion (a)

Willard H. Dow Center
Midland, Michigan 48674
517-636-1000

	1987	1986	1985	1980
Revenues:	13,377	11,113	10,500	10,272
Net income:	1,245	732	58	805
Share earnings:	6.50	3.87	.31	4.42

What it does: Second-largest diversified chemical company. Basic chemicals and plastics were 58% of sales in 1985; special chemicals for industry were 24%.

28. Westinghouse Electric Corporation (WX)

CEO: John C. Marous, Jr.
Employees: 111,000 (b)
Assets: $8.7 billion (b)

Westinghouse Building
Pittsburgh, Pennsylvania 15222
412-244-2000

(a) For period ending December 31, 1986.
(b) For period ending June 30, 1987.
(c) For period ending September 30, 1987.

	1987	1986	1985	1980
Revenues:	10,679	10,731	10,700	8,514
Net income:	739	671	605	403
Share earnings:	5.12	4.42	3.52	2.36

What it does: It is the nation's second-largest maker of electrical equipment and it has holdings in radio and TV broadcasting, financial services, and franchise bottling and distribution.

29. The Goodyear Tire and Rubber Company (GYR)

CEO: Robert E. Mercer

Employees: 115,000 (a)

Assets: $8.6 billion (a)

1144 East Market Street

Akron, Ohio 44316

216-796-2121

	1987	1986	1985	1980
Revenues:	9,000	9,224	8,492	8,498
Net income:	771	124	412	207
Share earnings:	12.73	1.16	3.84	3.18

What it does: Leader in the original equipment and replacement tire market in the U.S.

30. Lockheed Corporation (LK)

CEO: Lawrence O. Kitchen

Employees: 97,000 (c)

Assets: $6.2 billion (c)

4500 Park Granada Boulevard

Calabasas, California 91399

818-712-2000

	1987	1986	1985	1980
Revenues:	11,321	10,273	9,535	5,396
Net income:	421	408	401	28
Share earnings:	6.64	6.18	6.10	.51

What it does: Primarily engaged in the research, design, and production of military aircraft, missiles, space systems, and electronic systems.

31. Phillips Petroleum Company (P)

CEO: C. J. Silas

Employees: 21,000 (a)

Assets: $12.3 billion (a)

Phillips Building

Bartlesville, Oklahoma 74004

918-661-6600

	1987	1986	1985	1980
Revenues:	10,917	9,786	15,636	13,773
Net income:	35	228	418	1,070
Share earnings:	.06	.89	1.44	7.01

What it does: A large integrated oil company.

(a) For period ending December 31, 1986.

(b) For period ending June 30, 1987.

(c) For period ending September 30, 1987.

32. Xerox Corporation (XRX)

CEO: David T. Kearns
Employees: 100,367 (a)
Assets: $10.6 billion (a)

P.O. Box 1600
Stanford, Connecticut 06904
203-329-8700

	1987	1986	1985	1980
Revenues:	10,320*	19,335*	11,761	8,037
Net income:	578	465	475	565
Share earnings:	5.35	4.28	3.47	6.55

*Excludes financial services revenue.
What it does: The leading U.S. producer of copying and duplicating machines.

33. Sun Company, Inc. (SUN)

CEO: Robert McClements, Jr.
Employees: 23,645 (a)
Assets: $11.7 billion (a)

100 Matsonford Road
Radnor, Pennsylvania 19087
215-293-6000

	1987	1986	1985	1980
Revenues:	9,820	10,047	14,435	13,242
Net income:	348	385	527	723
Share earnings:	3.21	3.54	4.72	5.92

What it does: A major domestic integrated oil company.

34. PepsiCo, Inc. (PEP)

CEO: D. Wayne Calloway
Employees: 214,000 (c)
Assets: $8 billion (c)

700 Anderson Hill Road
Purchase, New York 10577
914-253-2000

	1987	1986	1985	1980
Revenues:	11,485	9,109	7,653	4,956
Net income from continuing operations:	595	463	420	234
Share earnings:	2.30	1.77	1.50	.86

What it does: The second-largest producer of soft drinks.

35. BP America (—)

CEO: Robert B. Horton
Employees: 42,100 (c)
Assets: $15.9 billion (c)

200 Public Square
Cleveland, Ohio 44114
216-586-4141

(a) For period ending December 31, 1986.
(b) For period ending June 30, 1987.
(c) For period ending September 30, 1987.

	1987	1986	1985	1980
Revenues:	14,611	9,219	13,002	11,023
Net income:	564	(345)	308	1,811
Share earnings:	NA	—	1.31	7.37

What it does: A major oil company. Formerly Standard Oil, it became a subsidiary of British Petroleum Company in May 1987.

36. General Dynamics Corporation (GD)

CEO: Stanley C. Pace
Employees: 106,000 (a)
Assets: $4.9 billion (a)

7733 Forsythe Boulevard
St. Louis, Missouri 63105
314-889-8200

	1987	1986	1985	1980
Revenues:	9,344	8,892	7,291	4,056
Net income:	437	(53)	383	195
Share earnings:	10.26	—	9.05	3.58

What it does: A leading defense contractor with strong positions in aircraft, submarines, tanks, missiles, and gun systems.

37. Kraft, Inc. (KRA)

CEO: John M. Richman
Employees: 51,000 (c)
Assets: $9.3 billion (c)

1 Kraft Court
Glenview, Illinois 60025
312-998-2000

	1987	1986	1985	1980
Revenues:	9,876	8,742	7,920	NA
Net income:	489	413	466	
Share earnings:	3.60	2.93	3.22	

What it does: Producer and marketer of processed and dairy foods. It spun off its nonfood products holdings as Premark International in October 1986.

38. The Coca-Cola Company (KO)

CEO: Roberto C. Goizueta
Employees: 28,030 (c)
Assets: $9.3 billion (c)

P.O. Drawer 1734
Atlanta, Georgia 30301
404-676-2121

	1987	1986	1985	1980
Revenues:	7,658	6,977 (n)	7,212	4,841
Income from continuing operations:	916	934	678	394
Share earnings:	2.43	2.42	1.72	1.06

What it does: The world's leading soft drink company. Also holds major position in fruit juices, including Minute Maid, and is a growing presence in the entertainment industry through Columbia Pictures. (n) restated

(a) For period ending December 31, 1986.
(b) For period ending June 30, 1987.
(c) For period ending September 30, 1987.

39. Minnesota Mining and Manufacturing Company (MMM)

CEO: Allen Jacobson
Employees: 82,006 (b)
Assets: $7.9 billion (c)

3M Center
St. Paul, Minnesota 55144-1000
612-733-1110

	1987	1986	1985	1980
Revenues:	9,429	8,602	7,846	6,079
Net income:	918	779	664	678
Share earnings:	4.02	3.40	2.89	2.85

What it does: A highly diversified maker of industrial, commercial, health care, and consumer products.

40. Sara Lee Corporation (SLE)

CEO: John H. Bryan, Jr.
Employees: 92,400 (c)
Assets: $1.9 billion (c)

Three First National Plaza
Chicago, Illinois 60604
312-726-2600

	1987	1986	1985	1980
Revenues:	9,404	8,707	8,117	NA
Net income:	266	228	206	
Share earnings:	2.34	1.99	1.80	

What it does: A diversified producer of processed food and other consumer products, including apparel and vacuum cleaners.

41. ITT Corporation (ITT)

CEO: Rand V. Araskog
Employees: 123,000 (c)
Assets: $35.8 billion (c)

320 Park Avenue
New York, New York 10022
212-752-6000

	1987	1986	1985	1980
Revenues:	19,500	17,437	14,663	NA
Net income:	1,020	540	294	
Share earnings:	6.76	3.23	1.89	

What it does: In December 1986, the company combined its telecommunications operations with those of Compagnie Générale d'Electricité, forming a joint venture, Alcatel N.V., based in the Netherlands. ITT holds 37%.

42. Union Carbide Corporation (UK)

CEO: Robert D. Kennedy
Employees: 50,290 (b)
Assets: $7.6 billion (a)

39 Old Ridgebury Road
Danbury, Connecticut 06817
203-794-2000

(a) For period ending December 31, 1986.
(b) For period ending June 30, 1987.
(c) For period ending September 30, 1987.

	1987	1986	1985	1980
Revenues:	6,914	6,343	6,390	NA
Net income:	232	496	(581)	
Share earnings:	1.76	4.78	—	

What it does: A leading producer of plastics, petrochemicals, industrial gases, specialty chemicals, and carbon products.

43. Anheuser-Busch Companies, Inc. (BUD)

CEO: A. A. Busch III

Employees: 39,800 (a)

Assets: $5.8 billion (a)

One Busch Place
St. Louis, Missouri 63118
314-577-2000

	1987	1986	1985	1980
Revenues:	8,258	7,677	7,683	3,822
Net income:	615	518	444	172
Share earnings:	2.04	1.69	NA	NA

What it does: Major brewer with holdings in food production and theme parks; also owns the St. Louis Cardinals baseball team.

44. Digital Equipment Corporation (DEC)

CEO: K. H. Olsen

Employees: 114,000 (c)

Assets: $8.4 billion (c)

146 Main Street
Maynard, Massachusetts 01754
617-897-5111

	1987 (n)	1986	1985	1980
Revenues:	9,389	7,590	6,686	2,368
Net income:	1,137	617	447	160
Share earnings:	8.53	4.81	3.71	2.73

(n) For fiscal year ended September 30.

What it does: A major designer and maker of computers, related equipment, and software supplies.

45. Unocal Corporation (UCL)

CEO: Fred L. Hartley

Employees: 17,000 (c)

Assets: $9.8 billion (b)

P.O. Box 7600
Los Angeles, California 90051
213-977-7600

	1987	1986	1985	1980
Revenues:	9,393	8,353	NA	NA
Net income:	181	175		
Share earnings:	1.56	1.51		

What it does: Primarily a domestic integrated oil company.

(a) For period ending December 31, 1986.
(b) For period ending June 30, 1987.
(c) For period ending September 30, 1987.

46. Unisys (UIS)

CEO: W. M. Blumenthal
Employees: 93,000 (b)
Assets: $9.3 billion (b)

Unisys Plaza
Detroit, Michigan 48232
313-972-7000

	1987	1986	1985	1980
Revenues:	9,712	7,432	5,038	2,857
Net income:	578	(43)	248	82
Share earnings:	3.15	—	5.46	1.99

What it does: Formerly Burroughs Corporation, this is the world's second-biggest data processing company. The acquisition of Sperry Corporation in 1986 makes it a leading maker of computer systems.

47. Caterpillar, Inc. (CAT)

CEO: G. A. Schaefer
Employees: 54,173 (b)
Assets: $3.7 billion (b)

100 Northeast Adams Street
Peoria, Illinois 61629
309-675-1000

	1987	1986	1985	1980
Revenues:	8,180	7,321	6,725	8,598
Net income:	319	76	198	565
Share earnings:	3.20	1.77	2.02	6.53

What it does: The biggest manufacturer of earth-moving and construction equipment. Also makes diesel and natural gas engines and turbines.

48. Raytheon Company (RTN)

CEO: T. L. Phillips
Employees: 73,200 (b)
Assets: $3.9 billion (b)

141 Spring Street
Lexington, Massachusetts 02173
617-862-6600

	1987	1986	1985	1980
Revenues:	7,659	7,308	6,409	5,002
Net income:	445	393	376	282
Share earnings:	6.12	5.10	4.60	3.32

What it does: Diverse manufacturer of electronic equipment and components.

49. The LTV Corporation (LTV)

CEO: Raymond A. Hay
Employees: 48,300 (a)
Assets: $5.5 billion (a)

P.O. Box 655003
Dallas, Texas 75265-5003
214-979-7711

(a) For period ending December 31, 1986.
(b) For period ending June 30, 1987.
(c) For period ending September 30, 1987.

	1987	1986	1985	1980
Revenues:	7,581	7,271	8,199	5,330
Net income:	503	(3,252)	(723)	127
Share earnings:	4.24	—	—	2.71

What it does: This steel company filed for protection under Chapter 11 of the federal bankruptcy code on July 17, 1986. It was unable to meet more than $2 billion in debt service and pension obligations due through 1988.

50. Georgia-Pacific Corporation (GP)
CEO: T. Marshall Hahn, Jr.
Employees: 40,000 (c)
Assets: $5.1 billion (a)

P.O. Box 105605
Atlanta, Georgia 30303

	1987	1986	1985	1980
Revenues:	8,603	7,223	6,716	NA
Net income:	458	296	187	
Share earnings:	4.23	2.64	1.61	

What it does: Maker and distributor of a wide range of building and pulp and paper products.

THE 10 LARGEST SAVINGS INSTITUTIONS*
(Net Income in Millions of Dollars; Share Earnings in Dollars)

1. Financial Corporation of America (FIN)
CEO: William J. Popejoy
Employees: 6,160 (c)
Assets: $33.4 billion (c)

18401 Von Karman Avenue
Irvine, California 92715
714-553-6900

	1987	1986	1985	1980
Net income:	(468)	95	53	13
Share earnings:	—	2.18	1.01	.73

2. Great Western Financial Corporation (GWF)
CEO: James F. Montgomery
Employees: 12,000 (c)
Assets: $27.6 billion (a)

8484 Wilshire Boulevard
Beverly Hills, California 90211
213-852-3411

	1987	1986	1985	1980
Net income:	210	301	202	39
Share earnings:	1.67	6.28	4.45	1.30

*Based on the *Fortune* 500 ranking.
(a) For period ending December 31, 1986.
(b) For period ending June 30, 1987.
(c) For period ending September 30, 1987.

3. **H. F. Ahmanson and Company (AHM)**

CEO: Richard H. Deihl
Employees: 9,200 (c)
Assets: $27.5 billion (c)

3731 Wilshire Boulevard
Los Angeles, California 90010
213-487-4277

	1987	1986	1985	1980
Net income:	200	303	221	54
Share earnings:	2.03	3.22	2.63	2.34

4. **CalFed, Inc. (CAL)**

CEO: George P. Rutland
Employees: 7,000 (b)
Assets: $23.1 billion (c)

5670 Wilshire Boulevard
Los Angeles, California 90036
213-932-4321

	1987	1986	1985	1980
Net income:	167	164	135	NA
Share earnings:	6.67	7.03	6.02	

5. **Meritor Financial Group (MTOR)**

CEO: Frederick S. Hammer
Employees: 5,725 (c)
Assets: $19.6 billion (c)

1212 Market Street
Philadelphia, Pennsylvania 19107
215-636-6000

	1987	1986	1985	1980
Net income:	(396)	23	65	NA
Share earnings:	—	.65	1.84	

6. **GlenFed (GLN)**

CEO: Norman M. Coulson
Employees: 6,446 (c)
Assets: $19.5 billion (c)

P.O. Box 1709
Glendale, California 91209
818-500-2000

	1987 (n)	1986	1985	1980
Net income:	148	88	56	NA
Share earnings:	6.81	4.11	2.64	

(n) For fiscal year ended June 30.

7. **Great American First Savings Bank (GTA)**

CEO: Gordon C. Luce
Employees: 4,000 (c)
Assets: $14.3 billion (c)

600 B Street
San Diego, California 92183
619-231-1885

	1987	1986	1985	1980
Net income:	87	94	43	NA
Share earnings:	367	4.18	2.29	

(a) For period ending December 31, 1986.
(b) For period ending June 30, 1987.
(c) For period ending September 30, 1987.

8. Golden West Financial Corporation (GDW)
CEO: Herbert M. Sandler   1901 Harrison Street
Employees: 2,000 (b)   Oakland, California 94612
Assets: $13.2 billion (b)   415-446-6000

	1987	1986	1985	1980
Net income:	151	184	160	38
Share earnings:	4.84	5.89	5.14	.37

9. Gibraltar Financial Corporation of California (GFC)
CEO: Herbert J. Young   9111 Wilshire Boulevard
Employees: 2,545 (b)   Beverly Hills, California 90213
Assets: $14.6 billion (b)   213-278-8720

	1987	1986	1985	1980
Net income:	(131)	49	39	(5.3)
Share earnings:	—	2.66	2.34	—

10. Home Federal Savings and Loan Association (HFD)
CEO: Kim Fletcher   707 Broadway
Employees: 3,600 (a)   San Diego, California 92101
Assets: $13.3 (c)   619-699-8000

	1987	1986	1985	1980
Net income:	100	103	73	NA
Share earnings:	4.69	4.87	3.53	

THE 10 LARGEST UTILITIES*
(Revenues and Net Income in Millions of Dollars; Share Earnings in Dollars)

1. GTE Corporation (GTE)
CEO: Theodore F. Brophy   One Stamford Forum
Employees: 160,000 (a)   Stamford, Connecticut 06904
Assets: $27.4 billion (a)   203-965-2000

	1987	1986	1985	1980
Revenues:	15,421	15,112	14,372	9,529
Net income:	1,118	1,153	(198)	447
Share earnings:	3.29	3.53	—	1.96

What it does: One of the nation's biggest telephone systems.

*Based on the *Fortune* 500 ranking.
(a) For period ending December 31, 1986.
(b) For period ending June 30, 1987.
(c) For period ending September 30, 1987.

2. BellSouth Corporation (BLS)

CEO: John L. Clendenin
Employees: 99,000 (c)
Assets: $26.2 billion (a)

1115 Peachtree Street, N.E.
Atlanta, Georgia 30375
404-420-8600

	1987	1986	1985	1980
Revenues:	12,269	11,444	10,664	NA
Net income:	1,664	1,589	1,418	
Share earnings:	3.46	3.38	3.13	

What it does: The largest telephone holding company in the U.S.

3. NYNEX Corporation (NYN)

CEO: Delbert C. Staley
Employees: 95,200 (c)
Assets: $22.4 billion (c)

335 Madison Avenue
New York, New York 10017
212-370-7400

	1987	1986	1985	1980
Revenues:	12,084	11,342	10,314	NA
Net income:	1,276	1,215	1,095	
Share earnings:	6.26	6.01	5.43	

What it does: A communications and local exchange telephone company.

4. Bell Atlantic Corporation (BEL)

CEO: Thomas E. Bolger
Employees: 81,000 (c)
Assets: $21.2 billion (c)

1600 Market Street
Philadelphia, Pennsylvania 19103
215-963-6000

	1987	1986	1985	1980
Revenues:	10,298	9,920	9,084	NA
Net income:	1,240	1,167	1,092	
Share earnings:	6.24	5.85	5.47	

What it does: A major telephone company.

5. Pacific Gas and Electric Company (PACGE)

CEO: Richard A. Clarke
Employees: 29,200 (a)
Assets: $21.2 billion (a)

77 Beale Street
San Francisco, California 94106
415-781-4211

	1987	1986	1985	1980
Revenues:	7,185	7,817	8,431	5,259
Net income:	597	1,081	1,030	524
Share earnings:	1.53	2.60	2.65	3.60

What it does: A major utility.

(a) For period ending December 31, 1986.
(b) For period ending June 30, 1987.
(c) For period ending September 30, 1987.

6. **Pacific Telesis Group (PAC)**
   CEO: Donald E. Guinn
   Employees: 73,000 (c)
   Assets: $21 billion (c)

   140 New Montgomery Street
   San Francisco, California 94105
   415-882-8000

	1987	1986	1985	1980
Revenues:	8,131	8,977	8,499	NA
Net income:	850	1,079	829	
Share earnings:	2.21	2.51	2.27	

What it does: A spinoff from AT&T in 1984 and one of the biggest telephone holding companies in the U.S.

7. **Southwestern Bell Corporation (SBC)**
   CEO: Zane E. Barnes
   Employees: 67,450 (c)
   Assets: $21.3 billion (c)

   One Bell Center
   St. Louis, Missouri 63101
   314-235-9800

	1987	1986	1985	1980
Revenues:	8,002	7,902	7,925	NA
Net income:	1,047	1,022	996	
Share earnings:	3.48	3.42	3.33	

What it does: An AT&T spinoff in 1984 and one of the largest telephone holding companies in the U.S.

8. **U S WEST, Inc. (USW)**
   CEO: Jack A. MacAllister
   Employees: 68,496 (c)
   Assets: $19.1 billion (c)

   7800 East Orchard Road
   Englewood, Colorado 80111
   303-793-6500

	1987	1986	1985	1980
Revenues:	8,445	8,308	7,813	NA
Net income:	1,005	924	926	
Share earnings:	5.31	4.86	4.84	

What it does: A major telephone holding company in the U.S.

9. **Ameritech (AIT)**
   CEO: William L. Weiss
   Employees: 78,480 (c)
   Assets: $18.7 billion (c)

   30 South Wacker Drive
   Chicago, Illinois 60606
   312-750-5000

	1987	1986	1985	1980
Revenues:	9,536	9,362	9,021	NA
Net income:	1,188	1,138	1,077	
Share earnings:	8.47	7.87	7.35	

What it does: One of the telephone holding companies spun off from AT&T in 1984.

(a) For period ending December 31, 1986.
(b) For period ending June 30, 1987.
(c) For period ending September 30, 1987.

10. **The Southern Company (SOCO)**
CEO: Edward L. Addison
Employees: 31,700 (a)
Assets: $18.1 billion (a)

64 Perimeter Center East
Atlanta, Georgia 30346
404-393-0650

	1987	1986	1985	1980
Revenues:	7,010	6,847	6,814	3,670
Net income:	554	883	829	344
Share earnings:	1.92	3.17	3.20	2.23

What it does: A major coal-based utility serving much of the southeastern U.S.

THE 10 LARGEST TRANSPORTATION COMPANIES*
(Revenues and Net Income in Millions of Dollars; Share Earnings in Dollars)

1. **Allegis Corporation (AEG)**
CEO: Frank A. Olson
Employees: 64,000 (c)
Assets: $8.7 billion (a)

P.O. Box 66100
Chicago, Illinois 60666
312-952-4000

	1987	1986	1985	1980
Revenues:	8,292	9,196	6,383	5,041
Net income:	335	12	(49)	(21)
Share earnings:	6.02	.25	—	—

What it does: Its subsidiaries include United Airlines, Inc., and Westin Hotel Company.

2. **United Parcel Service of America, Inc. (—)**
CEO: G. C. Lamb
Employees: 168,200 (a)
Assets: $4.8 billion (a)

51 Weaver Street
Greenwich, Connecticut 06836
203-622-6000

	1986	1985	1984	1980
Revenues:	8,619	7,686	6,832	NA
Net income:	668	568	476	
Share earnings:	3.96	3.36	2.82	

What it does: The subsidiaries of this holding company deliver small packages and parcels throughout the U.S., West Germany, and parts of Canada.

3. **Burlington Northern, Inc. (BNI)**
CEO: Richard M. Bressler
Employees: 44,200 (a)
Assets: $10.6 billion (a)

999 Third Avenue
Seattle, Washington 98104
206-467-3838

*Based on the *Fortune* 500 ranking.
(a) For period ending December 31, 1986.
(b) For period ending June 30, 1987.
(c) For period ending September 30, 1987.

	1987	1986	1985	1980
Revenues:	6,620	9,914	8,651	3,954
Net income:	367	(860)	685	223
Share earnings:	4.93	—	8.03	3.78

What it does: A major railroad and natural resources company. In 1986, profits were penalized by a $1.9 billion pretax writedown of its oil and gas and rail properties and a $121 million reserve for claims under a coal rate dispute.

4. Union Pacific Corporation (UNP)

CEO: Drew Lewis
Employees: 36,574 (c)
Assets: $10.6 billion (c)

345 Park Avenue
New York, New York 10154
212-418-7800

	1987	1986	1985	1980
Revenues:	5,943	6,688	7,908	NA
Net income:	583	(460)	501	
Share earnings:	5.10	—	4.18	

What it does: A holding company with subsidiaries operating rail transportation, real estate, mining, and oil and gas exploration, development, and production.

5. CSX Corporation (CSX)

CEO: Hays T. Watkins
Employees: 54,500 (b)
Assets: $13.2 billion (b)

P.O. Box C-32222
Richmond, Virginia 23261
804-782-1400

	1987	1986	1985	1980
Revenues:	8,043	6,345	7,288	4,841
Net income:	432	418	(118)	281
Share earnings:	2.78	2.73	—	2.85

What it does: Has rail, barge, container shipping, and trucking units as well as energy and real estate holdings.

6. AMR Corporation (AMR)

CEO: Robert L. Crandall
Employees: 63,000 (c)
Assets: $8.4 billion (c)

P.O. Box 619616
DFW Airport, Texas 75261-9616
817-355-1234

	1987	1986	1985	1980
Revenues:	7,197	6,018	6,131	3,821
Net income:	198	279	346	(76)
Share earnings:	328	4.63	5.94	—

What it does: Holding company for American Airlines and has subsidiaries engaged in the transportation of passengers and freight and ground handling.

(a) For period ending December 31, 1986.
(b) For period ending June 30, 1987.
(c) For period ending September 30, 1987.

7. Sante Fe Southern Pacific Corporation (SFX)

CEO: Robert D. Krebs
Employees: 50,000 (c)
Assets: $11.7 billion (c)

224 South Michigan Avenue
Chicago, Illinois 60604
312-786-6000

	1987	1986	1985	1980
Revenues:	5,448	5,631	6,282	NA
Net income:	373	(268)	460	
Share earnings:	2.37	—	2.62	

What it does: A transportation-based conglomerate with railroad, pipeline, trucking, real estate, petroleum, and minerals holdings.

8. Delta Air Lines, Inc. (DL)

CEO: Ronald W. Allen
Employees: 51,546 (c)
Assets: $1.2 billion (c)

Hartsfield Atlanta International Airport
Atlanta, Georgia 30320
404-765-2600

	1987	1986	1985	1980
Revenues:	5,318	4,460	4,865	2,957
Net income:	264	47	259	93
Share earnings:	5.90	1.18	6.50	2.34

What it does: Historically, one of the nation's most profitable airlines. Expanded in December 1986 with the acquisition of Western Air Lines for about $785 million.

9. Texas Air Corporation (TEX)

CEO: F. A. Lorenzo
Employees: 75,000 (b)
Assets: $8.7 billion (b)

333 Clay Street
Houston, Texas 77002
713-658-9588

	1987	1986	1985	1980
Revenues:	8,475	4,406	1,944	NA
Net income:	(466)	73	164	
Share earnings:		1.67	3.59	

What it does: Subsidiaries of this holding company include Eastern Air Lines, Continental Airlines, and SystemOne, a travel agency and computerized reservation service.

10. Norfolk Southern Corporation (NSC)

CEO: Arnold B. McKinnon
Employees: 36,000 (c)
Assets: $9.7 billion (b)

One Commercial Place
Norfolk, Virginia 23510-2191
804-629-2600

	1987	1986	1985	1980
Revenues:	4,128	4,076	3,825	NA
Net income:	172	519	500	
Share earnings:	.91	2.74	2.65	

What it does: A transportation services concern with both rail and trucking operations.

(a) For period ending December 31, 1986.

(b) For period ending June 30, 1987.

(c) For period ending September 30, 1987.

THE 10 LARGEST RETAILING COMPANIES*
(Revenues and Net Income in Millions of Dollars;
Share Earnings in Dollars)

1. Sears, Roebuck and Company (S)
CEO: Edward A. Brennan
Employees: 465,500 (a)
Assets: $65.9 billion (a)

Sears Tower
Chicago, Illinois 60684
312-875-2500

	1987	1986	1985	1980
Revenues:	48,439	44,282	40,715	25,161
Net income:	1,649	1,351	1,303	610
Share earnings:	4.35	3.62	3.53	1.93

What it does: A diversified merchandise, insurance, and financial services company.

2. K mart Corporation (KM)
CEO: Joseph E. Antonini
Employees: 320,000 (a)
Assets: $10.6 billion (b)

3100 West Big Beaver Road
Troy, Michigan 48084
313-643-1000

	1987	1986	1985	1980
Revenues:	23,182	23,812	22,035	14,118
Net income from continuing operations:	570	570	472	252
Share earnings:	2.84	2.84	2.42	1.34

What it does: The nation's second-largest merchandise retailer.

3. The Kroger Company (KR)
CEO: Lyle Everingham
Employees: 170,000 (a)
Assets: $4.1 billion (b)

1014 Vine Street
Cincinnati, Ohio 45202
513-762-4000

	1987	1986	1985	1980
Revenues:	17,600	7,123	15,967	NA
Net income from continuing operations:	183	55	159	
Share earnings:	2.20	.60	1.81	

What it does: Operates some 1,300 supermarkets and more than 700 convenience stores.

*Based on the *Fortune* 500 ranking.
(a) For period ending December 31, 1986.
(b) For period ending June 30, 1987.
(c) For period ending September 30, 1987.

4. J. C. Penney Company, Inc. (JCP)

CEO: William R. Howell
Employees: 176,000 (a)
Assets: $10.5 billion (b)

1301 Avenue of the Americas
New York, New York 10019
212-957-4321

	1987 (n)	1986	1985	1980
Revenues:	15,332	14,740	13,747	10,823
Net income:	608	530	386	283
Share earnings:	4.11	3.19	5.31	4.04

What it does: One of the nation's biggest retailers of family apparel, home furnishings, and leisure lines. (n) Year ends January 30, net for 1986 restated.

5. American Stores Company (ASC)

CEO: Lennie S. Skaggs
Employees: 120,000 (c)
Assets: $3.6 billion (c)

P.O. Box 27447
Salt Lake City, Utah 84127
801-539-0112

	1987	1986	1985	1980
Revenues:	14,148	14,021	13,890	6,420
Net income:	164	145	397	52
Share earnings:	4.45	3.79	4.11	1.37

What it does: A leading supermarket and drug store operator.

6. Wal-Mart Stores, Inc. (WMT)

CEO: Sam M. Walton
Employees: 185,000 (c)
Assets: $4.9 billion (c)

P.O. Box 116
Bentonville, Arkansas 72712
501-273-4000

	1988 (n)	1987	1986	1985	1980
Revenues:	15,959	11,909	8,451	6,401	1,643
Net income:	628	450	327	271	55
Share earnings:	1.11	.80	.58	.48	.11

(n) For fiscal year ended January 31, 1988.

What it does: A discount retailer mainly operating some 860 discount department stores in 22 states.

7. The Southland Corporation (—) (SLC)

CEO: Jere W. Thompson
Employees: 67,200 (a)
Assets: $3.4 billion (a)

P.O. Box 719
Dallas, Texas 75221
214-828-7011

(a) For period ending December 31, 1986.
(b) For period ending June 30, 1987.
(c) For period ending September 30, 1987.

	1986	1985	1984	1980
Revenues:	8,619	8,622	8,040	NA
Net income:	200	212	160	
Share earnings:	3.96	4.41	3.41	

What it does: Operates the largest convenience store chain in the world. Went private in 1987.

8. Federated Department Stores, Inc. (FDS)

CEO: Howard Goldfeder
Employees: 133,000 (c)
Assets: $5.6 billion (c)

7 West Seventh Street
Cincinnati, Ohio 45202
513-579-7000

	1987	1986	1985	1980
Revenues:	11,007	10,512	9,978	3,601
Net income:	307	288	281	277
Share earnings:	3.28	2.97	2.94	2.86

What it does: Operates department stores, mass merchandising operations, supermarkets, and specialty stores.

9. The May Department Stores Company (MA)

CEO: David C. Farrell
Employees: 151,000 (b)
Assets: $3.3 billion (b)

611 Olive Street
St. Louis, Missouri 63101
314-342-6300

	1987	1986	1985	1980
Revenues:	10,582	10,376	9,542	5,054
Net income:	427	381	347	167
Share earnings:	2.76	2.44	2.20	1.23

What it does: Acquired Associated Dry Goods in 1986, which doubled this major department store's presence.

10. Dayton Hudson Corporation (DH)

CEO: Kenneth A. Macke
Employees: 140,000 (b)
Assets: $5.4 billion (b)

777 Nicollet Mall
Minneapolis, Minnesota 55402
612-370-6948

	1987	1986	1985	1980
Revenues:	10,113	9,359	8,255	3,777
Net income:	216	255	280	126
Share earnings:	2.21	2.62	2.89	1.33

What it does: A diversified retailer operating over 500 stores.

(a) For period ending December 31, 1986.
(b) For period ending June 30, 1987.
(c) For period ending September 30, 1987.

THE 10 LARGEST COMMERCIAL BANKS*
(Net Income in Millions of Dollars; Share Earnings in Dollars)

1. **Citicorp (CCI)**
   CEO: John S. Reed
   Employees: 88,500 (c)
   Assets: $199.9 billion (c)
   Deposits: $118.1 billion (c)
   Loans: $130.2 billion (c)

   399 Park Avenue
   New York, New York 10043
   212-559-1000

	1987	1986	1985	1980
Net income:	(1,138)	1,058	998	507
Share earnings:	—	7.14	7.12	4.08

2. **BankAmerica Corporation (BAC)**
   CEO: A. W. Clausen
   Employees: 73,500 (a)
   Assets: $99 billion (c)
   Deposits: $79 billion (c)
   Loans: $65 billion (c)

   P.O. Box 37000
   San Francisco, California 94137
   415-622-3456

	1987	1986	1985	1980
Net income:	(955)	(518)	(337)	645
Share earnings:	—	—	—	4.33

3. **The Chase Manhattan Corporation (CMB)**
   CEO: Willard C. Butcher
   Employees: 45,500 (c)
   Assets: $100 billion (c)
   Deposits: $67 billion (c)
   Loans: $70 billion (c)

   One Chase Manhattan Plaza
   New York, New York 10081
   212-522-2028

	1987	1986	1985	1980
Net income:	(895)	585	565	365
Share earnings:	—	6.63	6.39	10.47

4. **J. P. Morgan & Co., Incorporated (JMP)**
   CEO: Lewis T. Preston
   Employees: 15,500 (c)
   Assets: $78 billion (c)
   Deposits: $46.5 billion (c)
   Loans: $31.8 billion (c)

   23 Wall Street
   New York, New York 10015
   212-483-2323

	1987	1986	1985	1980
Net income:	83	873	705	337
Share earnings:	.39	4.74	3.91	2.06

*Based on the *Fortune* 500 ranking.

(a) For period ending December 31, 1986.

(b) For period ending June 30, 1987.

(c) For period ending September 30, 1987.

5. **Manufacturers Hanover Corporation (MHC)**
   CEO: John F. McGillicuddy
   Employees: 29,320 (c)
   Assets: $75.3 billion (c)
   Deposits: $46.3 billion (c)
   Loans: $53.4 billion (c)

   270 Park Avenue
   New York, New York 10017
   212-286-6000

	1987	1986	1985	1980
Net income	(1,140)	377	407	229
Share earnings:	—	7.99	8.38	6.87

6. **Security Pacific Corporation (SPC)**
   CEO: Richard J. Flamson
   Employees: 43,400 (b)
   Assets: $74.3 billion (c)
   Deposits: $44.8 billion (c)
   Loans: $51.5 billion (c)

   333 South Hope Street
   Los Angeles, California 90071
   213-613-6211

	1987	1986	1985	1980
Net income:	16	460	391	NA
Share earnings:	.01	4.28	3.85	

7. **Chemical New York Corporation (CHL)**
   CEO: Walter V. Shipley
   Employees: 29,077 (b)
   Assets: $78.0 billion (c)
   Deposits: $52.2 billion (c)
   Loans: $50.1 billion (c)

   277 Park Avenue
   New York, New York 10172
   212-310-6161

	1987	1986	1985	1980
Net income:	(854)	402	390	NA
Share earnings:	—	7.57	7.33	

8. **Bankers Trust New York Corporation (BT)**
   CEO: Charles Sanford
   Employees: 11,800 (c)
   Assets: $56.8 billion (c)
   Deposits: $30.4 billion (c)
   Loans: $26.3 billion (c)

   280 Park Avenue
   New York, New York 10017
   212-250-2500

	1987	1986	1985	1980
Net income:	285	428	371	181
Share earnings:	.02	6.01	5.39	7.21

(a) For period ending December 31, 1986.

(b) For period ending June 30, 1987.

(c) For period ending September 30, 1987.

9. First Interstate Bancorp
CEO: Joseph J. Pinola
Employees: 35,000 (c)
Assets: $50.5 billion (c)
Deposits: $36.7 billion (c)
Loans: $33 billion (c)

P.O. Box 54068
Los Angeles, California 90054
213-614-3001

	1987	1986	1985	1980
Net income:	(556)	338	313	233
Share earnings:	—	7.19	6.84	5.91

10. Wells Fargo and Company (WFC)
CEO: Carl E. Reichardt, Jr.
Employees: 20,200 (c)
Assets: $45 billion (c)
Deposits: $32 billion (c)
Loans: $36 billion (c)

420 Montgomery Street
San Francisco, California 94163
415-781-2235

	1987	1986	1985	1980
Net income:	51	274	190	122
Share earnings:	.52	5.03	4.15	2.66

THE 10 LARGEST FINANCIAL COMPANIES*
(Revenues and Net Income in Millions of Dollars; Share Earnings in Dollars)

1. Federal National Mortgage Association (FNM)
CEO: David O. Maxwell
Employees: 2,410 (c)
Assets: $99.6 billion (c)

3900 Wisconsin Avenue, N.W.
Washington, D.C. 20016
202-537-7000

	1987	1986	1985	1980
Revenues:	10,078	10,540	10,342	5,013
Net income:	362	183	37	115
Share earnings:	4.66	2.49	.52	2.42

What it does: The nation's biggest mortgage lender is a government-sponsored, publicly held company.

2. American Express Company (AExp)
CEO: James D. Robinson III
Employees: 78,747 (a)
Assets: $106 billion (b)

American Express Tower
World Financial Center
New York, New York 10285-4805
212-640-2000

*Based on the *Fortune* 500 ranking.
(a) For period ending December 31, 1986.
(b) For period ending June 30, 1987.
(c) For period ending September 30, 1987.

	1987	1986	1985	1980
Revenues:	16,141	14,652	11,850	5,505
Net income:	533	1,110	810	376
Share earnings:	1.20	2.46	1.78	1.32

What it does: A major travel-related services company with international banking, investment and insurance services.

3. Salomon Inc (SB)

CEO: J. H. Gutfreund   1221 Avenue of the Americas
Employees: 8,338 (d)   New York, New York 10020
Assets: $78.4 billion (d)   212-764-3700

	1987	1986	1985	1980
Revenues:	6,033	6,789	5,701	NA
Net income:	142	516	557	
Share earnings:	.86	3.45	3.78	

What it does: This holding company's Salomon Brothers is an international investment banker and market-making firm. Its Philipp Brothers is an international marketer of industrial raw materials and its Phibro Energy is a global trader of crude oil and refiner.

4. Aetna Life and Casualty Company (AET)

CEO: James T. Lynn   151 Farmington Avenue
Employees: 41,000 (c)   Hartford, Connecticut 06156
Assets: $73 billion (c)   203-273-0123

	1987	1986	1985	1980
Revenues:	22,100	20,482	18,612	13,436
Net income:	921	1,043	376	428
Share earnings:	7.48	9.12	3.32	5.75

What it does: Nation's biggest investor-owned insurance company with a major presence in life, health, and property-casualty insurance.

5. Merrill Lynch & Co., Inc. (MER)

CEO: William A. Schreyer   165 Broadway
Employees: 47,000 (a)   New York, New York 10080
Assets: $53 billion (b)   212-637-7455

	1987	1986	1985	1980
Revenues:	10,868	9,606	7,117	3,022
Net income:	391	469	224	203
Share earnings:	3.58	4.44	2.24	2.77

What it does: One of the biggest firms in the securities industry and a major presence in the insurance industry.

(a) For period ending December 31, 1986.
(b) For period ending June 30, 1987.
(c) For period ending September 30, 1987.
(d) For period ending October 31, 1987.

6. CIGNA Corporation (CI)

CEO: Robert D. Kilpatrick
Employees: 50,056 (b)
Assets: $51.9 billion (b)

One Logan Square
Philadelphia, Pennsylvania 19103
215-523-4000

	1987	1986	1985	1980
Revenues:	16,909	17,064	16,196	NA
Net income:	728	817	(732)	
Share earnings:	8.64	9.92	—	

What it does: One of the nation's largest insurance-based financial services organizations. A leader in property-casualty, life, and health insurance, annuities, and financial services fields.

7. First Boston, Inc. (FBC)

CEO: Peter Buchanan
Employees: 5,400 (c)
Assets: $42.7 billion (c)

Park Avenue Plaza
New York, New York 10055
212-909-2000

	1987	1986	1985	1980
Revenues:	1,322	1,309	888	214
Net income:	109	181	130	34
Share earnings:	3.12	5.14	4.29	1.42

What it does: Holding company for First Boston Corporation, a leading securities underwriter and dealer.

8. The Travelers Corporation (TIC)

CEO: Edward H. Budd
Employees: 31,000 (c)
Assets: $49.5 billion (c)

One Tower Square
Hartford, Connecticut 06183
203-277-0111

	1987	1986	1985	1980
Revenues:	17,500	16,047	14,547	8,790
Net income:	374	546	375	366
Share earnings:	4.10	5.52	4.18	4.32

What it does: One of the nation's biggest stock insurance companies, it embraces all phases of life and property-casualty insurance.

9. Morgan Stanley Group, Inc. (MS)

CEO: S. P. Gilbert
Employees: 6,500 (b)
Assets: $35 billion (b)

1251 Avenue of the Americas
New York, New York 10020
212-703-4000

(a) For period ending December 31, 1986.
(b) For period ending June 30, 1987.
(c) For period ending September 30, 1987.
(d) For period ending October 31, 1987.

	1987	1986	1985	1980
Revenues:	3,147	2,463	1,795	NA
Net income:	231	201	106	
Share earnings:	8.99	8.42	5.32	

What it does: The company's Morgan Stanley & Co. subsidiary is a leading investment banking firm.

10. Bear Stearns Companies (BSC)

CEO: Alan C. Greenberg
Employees: 5,915 (b)
Assets: $29.7 billion (b)

55 Water Street
New York, New York 10041
212-952-5000

	1987 (n)	1986	1985	1980
Revenues:	1,774	1,409	NA	NA
Net income:	173	131		
Share earnings:	2.02	1.55		

(n) For fiscal year ended April 30, 1987.

What it does: Holding company for Bear, Stearns & Co., a leading investment banking and brokerage house.

(a) For period ending December 31, 1986.
(b) For period ending June 30, 1987.
(c) For period ending September 30, 1987.
(d) For period ending October 31, 1987.

TABLES

682

INDEX